Fortress Dark and Stern

Fortress Dark and Stern

The Soviet Home Front during
World War II

WENDY Z. GOLDMAN AND DONALD FILTZER

OXFORD
UNIVERSITY PRESS

Oxford University Press is a department of the University of Oxford. It furthers
the University's objective of excellence in research, scholarship, and education
by publishing worldwide. Oxford is a registered trade mark of Oxford University
Press in the UK and certain other countries.

Published in the United States of America by Oxford University Press
198 Madison Avenue, New York, NY 10016, United States of America.

Library of Congress Cataloging-in-Publication Data
Names: Goldman, Wendy Z., author. | Filtzer, Donald A., author.
Title: Fortress dark and stern : the Soviet home front during World War II /
Wendy Z. Goldman and Donald Filtzer.
Other titles: Soviet home front during World War II
Description: New York, NY : Oxford University Press, [2021] |
Includes bibliographical references and index.
Identifiers: LCCN 2020037848 (print) | LCCN 2020037849 (ebook) |
ISBN 9780190618414 (hardcover) | ISBN 9780190618438 (epub) |
ISBN 9780190092672
Subjects: LCSH: Soviet Union—History—1939–1945. |
World War, 1939–1945—Soviet Union. |
World War, 1939-1945—Evacuation of civilians—Soviet Union. |
Soviets (People)—Evacuation and relocation, 1942–1945. |
Soviet Union—History—German occupation, 1941–1944. |
War and society—Soviet Union—History. | Soviet Union—Social conditions—1917–1945.
Classification: LCC DK273 .G585 2021 (print) | LCC DK273 (ebook) | DDC 940.53/47—dc23
LC record available at https://lccn.loc.gov/2020037848
LC ebook record available at https://lccn.loc.gov/2020037849

DOI: 10.1093/oso/9780190618414.001.0001

1 3 5 7 9 8 6 4 2

Printed by Sheridan Books, Inc., United States of America

To all those who fought against fascism on the home front and the battlefield, in the forests, camps, and ghettos, and to our fathers, Lawrence Goldman and David Filtzer, soldiers both.

We dedicate this book and these many years of research to you.

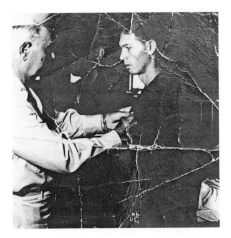

Lawrence Goldman, Private First Class, receiving the Purple Heart after his transport ship was kamikazied in the Pacific

David Filtzer, army surgeon, who treated ex-prisoners in the liberated Nazi concentration camps

Contents

Acknowledgments

We are grateful to all the many individuals and institutions who helped make this book possible. During the years this book was in the making we received joint and individual research support from the American Council of Learned Societies, the Department of History of Carnegie Mellon University, the National Endowment for the Humanities, and the Wellcome Trust (grant number WT087202MA). We owe a great debt to the archivists and staff in Russia, and Nina Ivanovna Abdulaeva, head of Reading Room 1 at GARF (State Archive of the Russian Federation) in particular, who assisted us in various projects over many years. We also thank the librarians at the Sechenov Central Scientific Medical Library, Moscow, and Sue Collins, Senior Librarian, and Barry Schles, Circulation Associate, at Hunt Library at CMU. Their knowledge and professionalism were indispensable to the successful completion of our research. We are grateful to Ed Serotta, Director of the Centropa Archive, and Michal Friedman for bringing the rich holdings of this repository of oral histories and photographs to our attention.

Many valued colleagues shared their advice, knowledge, research materials, and findings with us, including Natalie Belsky, Fran Bernstein, Chris Burton, Mark Harrison, Donna Harsch, Dan Healey, Naum Kats, Catriona Kelly, Martin Kragh, Rebecca Manley, Alexis Peri, Brandon Schechter, Charles Shaw, Peter Solomon, Carmine Storella, Ronald Suny, and Lynne Viola. Sergei Karpenko, Aleksei Kilichenkov, and Igor Kurukin spent many hours discussing various aspects of the war and provided unique insights into the Russian perspective. Michael David and Dennis Brown were always on hand to answer questions on medicine and health. The anonymous readers for Oxford University Press devoted much time to comment extensively and productively on an earlier version of the manuscript. Tanya Buckingham, Creative Director of the University of Wisconsin Cartography Laboratory, and Austin J. Novak did an excellent job preparing the frontline maps. Susan Ferber, history editor at Oxford University Press, worked closely on all these many pages to create a better book. Karen Anderson, as she has done on several of our books, and working under extremely difficult conditions, did a superb job copy editing our manuscript. All their efforts are warmly appreciated.

We benefited greatly from the comments and discussions when presenting papers and early drafts of the book's chapters at various seminars, symposia, lectures, and conferences. An abbreviated list includes the Association for Slavic, East European, and Eurasian Studies (ASEEES); the European Social Sciences History conference; Department of History, University of Arizona; Carlow University; the E. P. Thompson Lecture at the University of Pittsburgh; Elihu Rose Lectures in Modern Military History, Jordan Center, New York University; Japanese Society for the Study of Russian History, Aoyama Gakuin University, Tokyo; International Cultural Studies Program, East-West Center, University of Hawaii, Manoa; National Research University Higher School of Economics, Moscow; Charles University, Prague; Heinrich-Heine Universität, Düsseldorf; University of Southern Alabama; University of Michigan Russian Studies Workshop; Central European University, Budapest; workshop, "Russian and Soviet Healthcare in Comparative Perspective," University College Dublin; German Historical Institute, London; Institute of History, Polish Academy of Sciences, Warsaw; Russian and Soviet Cultural and Social History Seminar, University of Oxford; colloquium, "Medicine and Public Health in the USSR and the Eastern Bloc, 1945–1991," Paris. Thanks to Indiana University Press for permission to republish some material from the chapter, "Not by Bread Alone: Food, Workers, and the State," in Wendy Z. Goldman and Donald Filtzer, eds., *Hunger and War: Food Provisioning in the Soviet Union during World War II* (Bloomington: Indiana University Press, 2015), pp. 44–97.

We owe a special debt of gratitude to our partners, Natasha Kurashova, who provided invaluable help with translation issues and daily insights into the social and historical context of our research, and Marcus Rediker, whose enthusiasm for and insight into the many aspects of politics, writing, and organization provided immeasurable help. Needless to say, without the steady interest, critical commentary, and loving support of these two people, the book would have been much diminished.

Terms and Abbreviations

alimentarnaia distrofiia	nutritional dystrophy, Soviet medical term for starvation disease
cadre workers	workers, usually, but not necessarily, skilled, with long experience working in industry or in their particular enterprise
Chief Administration	a subdivision of a People's Commissariat; in Russian *glavnoe upravlenie*, abbreviated to *glavk* (plural, *glavki*)
Commissariat	*see* People's Commissariat
district committee	executive organ of district-level bodies of Communist Party, trade union, or other organization; in Russian, *raionnyi komitet* or *raikom*
evakopunkt (plural, *evakopunkty*)	evacuation center; in Russian, *evakuatsionnyi punkt*
Executive Committee	ruling committee of government (as opposed to Communist Party) bodies; in Russian, *ispolnitel'nyi komitet* or *ispolkom*
frontovik	frontline soldier
FZO	Factory Training School (shkola fabrichno-zavodskogo obucheniia) under the Chief Administration of Labor Reserves, a three- or six-month training school for "mass" trades
GKO	State Committee for Defense (Gosudarstvennyi komitet oborony)
Gosplan	State Planning Commission (Gosudarstvennaia planovaia komissiia)
Gulag	Chief Administration of Camps, more generally used as the name for the system of NKVD labor camps
GUTR	Chief Administration of Labor Reserves (Glavnoe upravlenie trudovykh rezervov)
ITR	engineering and technical personnel/specialists (*inzhenerno-tekhnicheskie rabotniki*)
kolkhoz	collective farm; in Russian, *kollektivnoe khoziaistvo*
kolkhoznik (plural, *kolkhozniki*)	collective farmer or collective farm member
Komsomol	Communist Youth League, formally known as the All-Union Leninist Communist Union of Youth

Labor Army	composed of Soviet citizens, mainly of German ancestry, subject to deportation and internal exile and placed under the control of the NKVD during the war; also included other groups subject to suspicion and some peasants mobilized from Central Asia; in Russian, *Trudovaia armiia*
militia	police (*militsiia*) – the regular police force, as distinct from the secret police
NKVD	People's Commissariat of Internal Affairs (Narodnyi komissariat vnutrennikh del), in charge of the system of labor camps (Gulag) and police (militia)
opolchenie	home front militia
orgnabor	organized recruitment of workers
ORS (plural, ORSy)	Department of Workers' Provisioning (Otdel rabochego snabzheniia)
OSMCh	Special Construction and Erection Units (Osobye stroitel'no-montazhnye chasti)
Osoaviakhim	Society for the Promotion of Defense, Aviation and Chemical Construction (Obshchestvo sodeistviia oborone, aviatsionnomu i khimicheskomu stroitel'stvu), Soviet civil defense organization
Osobstroi	Administration of Special Construction of the NKVD of the USSR (Upravlenie osobogo stroitel'stva NKVD SSSR)
People's Commissariat	ministry (e.g., of Internal Affairs, of the Iron and Steel Industry, etc.); after the war the title was officially changed to Ministry
Procuracy	Public Prosecutor's Office
Procurator	Public Prosecutor
prodovol'stvennye normy	ration allowances, or list of items to which different groups were entitled
province	largest territorial subdivision of a republic; in Russian, *oblast'* (plural, *oblasti*)
provincial committee	executive organ of province-level bodies of Communist Party, trade union, or other organization; in Russian, *oblastnoi komitet*, or *obkom*
RSFSR	Russian Soviet Federative Socialist Republic (Rossiiskaia Sovetskaia Federativnaia Sotsialisticheskaia Respublika)
RU	Trade School (remeslennoe uchilishche) under the Chief Administration of Labor Reserves, a two-year training school in skilled trades
SE	Soviet (Council) for Evacuation (Sovet po evakuatsii)

soviet	council; in Russian, *sovet*
sovkhoz	state farm (literally "soviet farm" – *sovetskoe khoziaistvo*)
Sovnarkom	Soviet (Council) of People's Commissars, equivalent to the cabinet of the Soviet government
SSSR	Union of Soviet Socialist Republics (Soiuz Sovetskikh Sotsialisticheskikh Respublik)
State Sanitary Inspectorate	subdivision of the People's Commissariat of Public Health; in Russian, Gosudarstvennaia sanitarnaia inspektsiia), abbreviated to Gossaninspektsiia or GSI
SU RSFSR	Statistical Administration of the RSFSR (Statisticheskoe upravlenie RSFSR)
territory	administrative subdivision of a republic, equivalent to a province; in Russian, *krai* (plural, *kraiia*)
TsK	Central Committee (Tsentral'nyi Komitet)
TsSU	Central Statistical Administration (Tsentral'noe statisticheskoe upravlenie)
VKP(b)	Communist Party of the Soviet Union (Vsesoiuznaia Komunisticheskaia partiia (bol'shevikov))
voenkomat (plural, *voenkomaty*)	draft board (*voennyi komissariat*)
VTsSPS	All-Union Central Council of Trade Unions (Vsesoiuznyi tsentral'nyi sovet professional'nykh soiuzov)
zemlianki	earthen dugouts
ZhU	trade school (zheleznodorozhnoe uchilishche) to train skilled workers for the railways; equivalent to an RU

Units of Measurement

Soviet documents use metric measurements. For distances and area we have converted these to United States units (miles, acres) with the original metric figures in parentheses. For weights and volume, in particular in our discussions of food and the rationing system, we have retained metric units. The Soviet wartime rationing system was hierarchically tiered, based on increments of 100 grams of bread per day. Other food allowances were in multiples of 100 grams per month. Daily milk allowances for small children followed this same pattern. The logic of the system, as well as deviations from it, are clearer if the units remain metric.

Basic conversions are as follows:

100 grams = 3.53 ounces;
1 kilogram (1,000 grams) = 2.2046 pounds;
1 liter = 2.113 US pints (1.76 Imperial pints).

List of Major Wartime Commissariats

Glavnoe upravlenie trudovykh rezervov	Chief Administration of Labor Reserves
Narodnyi komissariat aviatsionnoi promyshlennosti (Narkomaviaprom)	People's Commissariat of the Aviation Industry
Narodnyi komissariat avtomobil'noi promyshlennosti	People's Commissariat of the Motor Vehicle Industry
Narodnyi komissariat boepripasov	People's Commissariat of Ammunition
Narodnyi kommissariat chernoi metallurgii (Narkomchermet)	People's Commissariat of the Iron and Steel Industry
Narodnyi komissariat elektropromyshlennosti (Narkomelektroprom)	People's Commissariat of the Electrical Industry
Narodnyi komissariat elektrostantsii	People's Commissariat of Electric Power Stations
Narodnyi komissariat gosudarstvennogo kontrolia	People's Commissariat of State Control
Narodnyi komissariat gosudarstvennoi bezopasnosti (NKGB)	People's Commissariat of State Security
Narodnyi komissariat iustitsii (Narkomiust)	People's Commissariat of Justice
Narodnyi komissariat khimicheskoi promyshlennosti	People's Commissariat of the Chemical Industry
Narodnyi komissariat legkoi promyshlennosti (Narkomlegprom)	People's Commissariat of Light Industry
Narodnyi komissariat lesnoi promyshlennosti (Narkomles)	People's Commissariat of the Timber Industry

Narodnyi komissariat mashinostroeniia (Narkommash)	People's Commissariat of the Machine-Building Industry
Narodnyi komissariat miasnoi i molochnoi promyshlennosti	People's Commissariat of the Meat and Dairy Industry
Narodnyi komissariat minometnogo vooruzheniia	People's Commissariat of Mortar Armaments
Narodnyi komissariat morskogo flota	People's Commissariat of the Maritime Fleet
Narodnyi komissariat neftianoi promyshlennosti	People's Commissariat of the Oil Industry
Narodnyi komissariat oboronnoi promyshlennosti	People's Commissariat of the Defense Industry
Narodnyi komissariat oborony	People's Commissariat of Defense
Narodnyi komissariat pishchevoi promyshlennosti	People's Commissariat of the Food Industry
Narodnyi komissariat po stroitel'stvu (Narkomstroi)	People's Commissariat of Construction
Narodnyi komissariat po stroitel'stvu predpriiatii tiazheloi industrii (Narkomtiazhstroi)	People's Commissariat of Construction of Heavy Industry Enterprises
Narodnyi komissariat po stroitel'stvu voennykh and voenno-morskikh predpriiatii	People's Commissariat of Construction of Military and Naval Enterprises
Narodnyi komissariat promyshlennosti stroitel'nykh materialov	People's Commissariat of the Construction Materials Industry
Narodnyi komissariat putei soobshcheniia (NKPS)	People's Commissariat of Railways
Narodnyi komissariat rechnogo flota	People's Commissariat of the River Fleet
Narodnyi komissariat rezinovoi promyshlennosti	People's Commissariat of the Rubber Industry
Narodnyi komissariat rybnoi promyshlennosti	People's Commissariat of the Fishing Industry

Narodnyi komissariat sel'skokhoziaistvennogo mashinostroeniia (Narkomsel'mash)	People's Commissariat of Agricultural Machine-Building
Narodnyi komissariat srednego mashinostroennogo (Narkomsredmash)	People's Commissariat of Medium Machine-Building
Narodnyi komissariat stankostroeniia SSSR	People's Commissariat of Machine Tools of the USSR
Narodnyi komissariat sudostroitel'noi promyshlennosti	People's Commissariat of the Shipbuilding Industry
Narodnyi komissariat sviazi (Narkomsviaz)	People's Commissariat of Communications
Narodnyi komissariat tankovoi promyshlennosti (Narkomtankprom)	People's Commissariat of the Tank Industry
Narodnyi komissariat tekstil'noi promyshlennosti	People's Commissariat of the Textile Industry
Narodnyi komissariat tiazhelogo mashinostroeniia (Narkomtiazhmash)	People's Commissariat of Heavy Machine-Building
Narodnyi komissariat torgovli SSSR (Narkomtorg)	People's Commissariat of Trade of the USSR
Narodnyi komissariat transportnogo mashinostroeniia	People's Commissariat of Transport Machine-Building
Narodnyi komissariat tselliuloznoi i bumazhnoi promyshlennosti	People's Commissariat of the Cellulose and Paper Industry
Narodnyi komissariat tsvetnoi metallurgii (Narkomtsvetmet)	People's Commissariat of Nonferrous Metals
Narodnyi komissariat ugol'noi promyshlennosti (Narkomugol')	People's Commissariat of the Coal Industry
Narodnyi komissariat vnutrennikh del (NKVD)	People's Commissariat of Internal Affairs

Narodnyi komissariat vodnogo transporta	People's Commissariat of Water Transport
Narodnyi komissariat voenno-morskogo flota	People's Commissariat of the Navy
Narodnyi komissariat vooruzheniia	People's Commissariat of Armaments
Narodnyi komissariat zagotovok	People's Commissariat of Procurements
Narodnyi komissariat zdravookhraneniia (Narkomzdrav)	People's Commissariat of Public Health
Narodnyi komissariat zemledeliia (Narkomzem)	People's Commissariat of Agriculture
Narodnyi komissariat zernovykh i zhivotnovodcheskikh sovkhozov SSSR	People's Commissariat of Grain and Livestock State Farms

Cities Whose Wartime Names
Have Changed

Modern name in parentheses

Chkalov (Orenburg)
Gor'kii (Nizhnii Novgorod)
Kalinin (Tver')
Kuibyshev (Samara)
Leningrad (St. Petersburg)
Molotov (Perm')
Molotovsk (Severodvinsk, Arkhangel'sk province)
Ordzhonikidze (Vladikavkaz)
Stalingrad (Volgograd)
Stalino (Donetsk)
Stalinsk (Novokuznetsk)
Sverdlovsk (Ekaterinburg)
Voroshilovgrad (Lugansk)

Fortress Dark and Stern

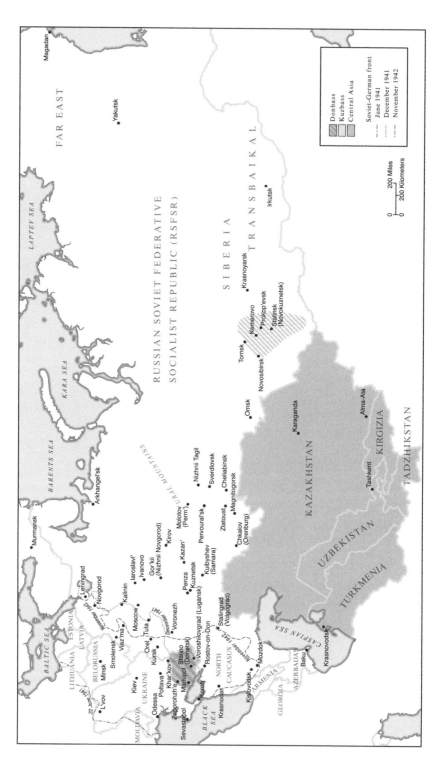

The Soviet Union, 1941–1945, front lines, June 1941–November 1942

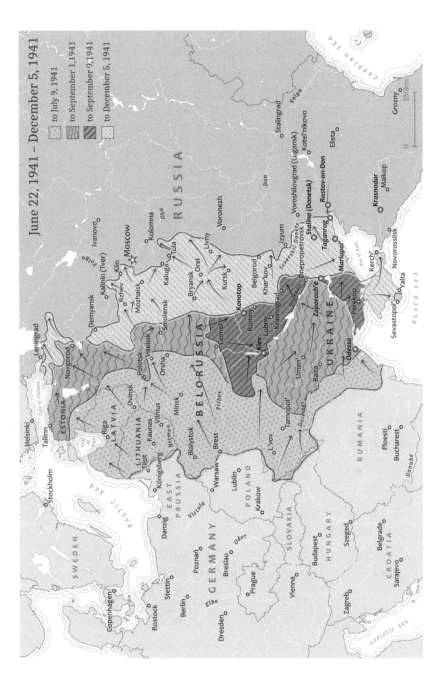

June 22, 1941 – December 5, 1941

	to July 9, 1941
	to September 1, 1941
	to September 9, 1941
	to December 5, 1941

RUSSIA

UKRAINE

BELORUSSIA

ESTONIA

LATVIA

LITHUANIA

EAST PRUSSIA

POLAND

GERMANY

SLOVAKIA

HUNGARY

RUMANIA

CROATIA

SWEDEN

BALTIC SEA

BLACK SEA

CASPIAN SEA

ADRIATIC SEA

Sea of Azov

Gulf of Finland

Gulf of Riga

0   250km

Front lines, June 22, 1941–December 5, 1941

Front lines, December 5, 1941–May 5, 1942

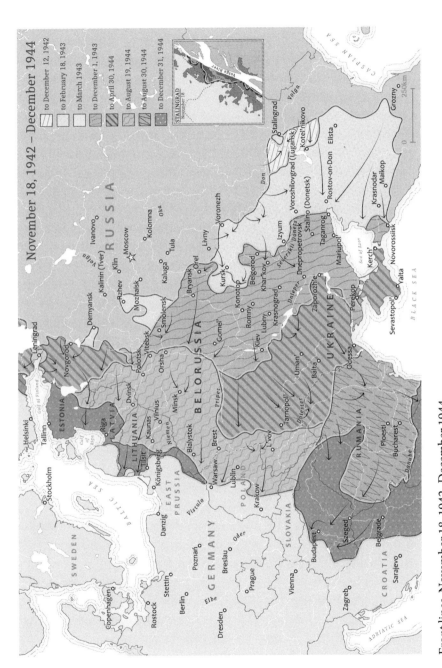

November 18, 1942 – December 1944

to December 12, 1942
to February 18, 1943
to March 1943
to December 1, 1943
to April 30, 1944
to August 19, 1944
to August 30, 1944
to December 31, 1944

Front lines, November 18, 1942–December 1944

Introduction

Total War

The story of war is typically a tale of heroic men in battle. Yet this book tells an equally epic tale—that of the workers, peasants, women, teenagers, and older citizens who made up the Soviet home front during World War II. Indeed, the Allied victory over the Nazis was built on the efforts on the Soviet home front population to arm and equip the Red Army.[1]

When the Germans invaded the Soviet Union in the early morning hours of June 22, 1941, the country adopted a policy of total war in which every precious resource, especially labor, was mobilized for production for the front. The human cost of total war was heavy. Raissa Smelaya was only fifteen when she went to work at a foundry polishing shells after being evacuated from Kiev:

> We worked in two shifts: the first shift from 7 a.m. to 7 p.m. and the second shift from 7 p.m. to 7 a.m. I received a worker's card for one kilo of bread. The bread was heavy and sticky and one kilo wasn't that much. My mother and Hanne received cards of non-manual workers for 300 grams of bread. They were nurse attendants in hospital. Workers at the plant got a bowl of soup and cereal at the canteen. I took soup home in a jar. My mother added some water to it and had it with Aunt Hanne. I was growing up and didn't have enough food. We didn't have any clothes to exchange for food. We were on the edge of survival throughout the three years in evacuation. I had dystrophy. Once I found potato peels in a pile of garbage. I brought them home. My mother washed and boiled them and we ate them.[2]

During the war years, the state assumed the height of its massive mobilizing power. It evacuated the industrial base from west to east, along with millions of people. It subjected civilians to a compulsory labor draft and placed all workers under military discipline. And it centralized all food, channeling it to the population through a strict rationing system. This book, the first broad, archivally based history of the home front, explores the relationship of state and society from invasion to liberation, from evacuation to reconstruction.[3] Focusing on the cities and industrial towns, it shows how the state mobilized people from every republic for "total war" and highlights the responses of ordinary citizens at a time of grave crisis. State policy and popular response were indeed inextricably intertwined. The efforts of individuals would have lacked any collective power without the mobilizing initiative of the state. And none of the state's vast mobilizing initiatives would have been possible without the efforts of ordinary people. Workers dismantled the factories, mines, and great iron and steel complexes, loaded the machinery into boxcars, and traveled east with their disassembled factories in vast convoys. Their living and working conditions, especially in the eastern towns, were grim. Millions of mobilized peasants, vocational students, and urban residents worked far from home, lived in barracks, and ate in canteens. Meyer Goldstein, a Red Army officer, remembered his family's experience:

> Many people could not survive evacuation to the east. My mother's sister Ita was in evacuation together with her in Yangiyul, and there she died from cold and starvation. . . . For women, evacuation was extremely hard to bear. They worked for themselves, for their brothers, for their husbands, and devoted everything to the soldiers. They did not eat enough or sleep enough. . . . Golda, my mother's youngest sister, had the best education. Before the war she was an active Komsomol member. . . . In evacuation she ended up in Sverdlovsk, caught cold and died there.[4]

Factories ceased to produce consumer goods and building materials for civilian use. The military and the defense factories appropriated the greatest share of fuel sources. People lived and labored in unheated, and often unlit, quarters. Municipal water pumping stations occasionally shut down for lack of fuel, shutting off the water supply to public baths, apartment buildings, and houses. Even bakeries, the heart of a ration system based on bread, were forced at times to close, halting the production and distribution of the daily bread ration, the main and sometimes only source of food.[5] Military historians widely acknowledge the critical role of the home front in the Red Army's ability ultimately to "contain and then drive back" the Germans. In the words of one, "no other population was asked to make this level of sacrifice." Despite "staggering losses" of equipment in 1941–1942, for example, workers managed at great cost to replenish the stock by the end of 1942.[6] In the slogan of the time, front and rear became "a single and undivided fighting camp." This was no mere catchphrase. German air raids and bombardment created mass casualties in cities as far east as Gor'kii. Ordinary people, like soldiers, were forbidden to evade a mobilization order, leave their jobs, or be late or absent without permission. They had no choice about where they would be deployed. The armaments that workers produced went directly to the front where their family members were often fighting. A young woman in the eastern town of Molotov wrote to a friend at the front about a fellow worker:

> At 6:00 in the morning, they rise from their cots and, wrapped up in their fathers' cotton padded jackets, they hurry off—in hard frost, and in fearsome snowstorms, knee-deep in snow, in rain, and autumn mud—to a distant factory in order to stand at the most complicated machines. Looking at him, it is difficult to believe that he is fourteen or fifteen years old. He stands on two boxes in order to reach the machine's spindle. He applies his whole body to the handle in order to switch over the speed. If you could only see how he works! It is as if he merges his whole being with the machine and overtakes it. He grows tired, very tired. But does anyone see him crying? He cannot work more slowly because his father and brother are smashing the enemy with his shells. This is not heroics, this is just normal, everyday life in our rear.[7]

The output of every sector, including metals, fuel, transport, food, and consumer goods, was either converted or diverted to defense.[8] The country had begun preparing for total war in the 1930s, when the state restricted consumption and adopted increasingly strict labor legislation.[9] Soviet citizens, closely following the rise of fascism, understood well that war was likely.

As the international situation steadily worsened, Maksim Litvinov, Commissar of Foreign Affairs, made repeated offers of "collective security" to France and Britain, proposing a united front against German aggression. Neither Britain nor France was eager to repeat the horrors of World War I and, assuming Adolf Hitler's aims to be limited, they spurned the Soviet offers in favor of a policy of appeasement. As Hitler marched east, Joseph Stalin became increasingly fearful of being "pulled into a premature war without reliable allies."[10] In August 1939, he responded to an offer by Hitler and signed a ten-year nonaggression pact, known as the Molotov–Ribbentrop Pact. According to a secret provision, Germany would occupy western and central Poland, and the Soviet Union would take over eastern Poland and the Baltic states. Stalin believed the Pact would buy his country time and help to create a buffer zone if Hitler did attack. In his view, he had turned the tables on the Western powers, who secretly hoped that Hitler would march east and destroy Bolshevism.[11] Yet Stalin was wrong. With the invasion of Poland, the British and French abandoned the policy of appeasement and declared war on Germany.

The Pact proved short-lived. Unbeknownst to Stalin, Hitler informed his top commanders in July 1940 that he planned to attack the Soviet Union in the spring of 1941. In December he signed the Barbarossa order detailing plans for the invasion.[12] In March 1941, he summoned 250 officers to Berlin where he lectured them on the special nature of the coming war.[13] Heinrich Himmler as Reichsführer-SS was assigned special tasks in the conquered areas, and would use Einsatzgruppen (task forces) of security police, which would eventually murder millions of civilians, including almost two million Soviet Jews. A jurisdictional order issued on May 13 explained that Soviet political officers, Communist Party officials, Jewish POWs and civilians, gypsies, and partisans were to be handed over to the SS or Einsatzgruppen. The so-called Commissar Order on June 6 sanctioned the immediate shooting of all Communist Party members and officials.[14]

The Nazis envisioned the Soviet Union as a rich source of food, raw materials, and labor for the new Reich.[15] The aim was to destroy Bolshevism, eliminate the Soviet state, and establish a German empire in the east.[16] The experience of World War I convinced Hitler that Germany could not wage a successful war unless both the army and the cities could be provisioned with food.[17] To this end, Herbert Backe, a fierce proponent of eastern conquest, devised his Hunger Plan, which proposed the mass murder of Slavs and Jews and the elimination of all "useless eaters."[18] A May 1941 memo declared: "1. The war can only continue to be waged if the entire Wehrmacht is fed from Russia during the third year of the war. 2. As a result, x million people will doubtlessly starve." The "x" was yet unknown. Nazi Party leaders such as Himmler and Hermann Göring soon began to quote a figure of "20 to 30 million." The cities, in particular, were expected to die out.[19] The Wehrmacht, which later tried to dissociate itself from the ensuing mass murder and genocide, readily accepted the plan.[20] According to the Hunger Plan, the Slavs would no longer pose an "ecological obstacle to the proper cultivation" of the east. Fourteen million Soviet peasants would be used as slaves, a tiny number integrated into German society, and the remaining seventy million deported to the Soviet Arctic where they would eventually die of overwork.[21] The High

Command of the armed forces gave officers the right to decide on the spot whether any civilian who was accused of criminal action should be shot, as well as instructions for collective reprisals against villages and cities. A guideline issued to the 3.6 million soldiers on the eastern front called for "ruthless and energetic measures against Bolshevik agitators, guerrillas, saboteurs, Jews, and total elimination of all active and passive resistance." In essence, these were instructions for mass murder, not war.[22]

On June 22, 1941, with no warning, Germany launched Operation Barbarossa with the mightiest military force ever concentrated in a single theater of war. The invasion consisted of a three-pronged attack: north toward Leningrad, due east toward Smolensk and Moscow, and south toward Kiev. The German blitzkrieg, with its signature elements—heavy bombing, rapid tank advance, and infantry—overran the border. Although Soviet citizens understood the invasion as part of a larger struggle against fascism, neither they nor state leaders and military officers fully grasped the barbarity of Nazi aims. In the months that followed, the Red Army fell back in disarray, the front lines collapsed, and millions of soldiers were killed, encircled, and taken prisoner. By the end of 1941, the Germans had occupied Belorussia, the Baltic states, Crimea, and almost all of Ukraine; they surrounded Leningrad in what would become the longest siege in modern history; and they reached the outskirts of Moscow.

Later, in his speech to the 20th Party Congress in 1956, Nikita Khrushchev blamed Stalin for this initial military disaster. He charged Stalin with decimating the officer corps in the purges of 1937–1939, foolishly trusting the Pact, encouraging the false belief that war would be fought offensively beyond Soviet borders, ignoring intelligence that an attack was imminent, dismissing strategies for orderly retreat, and failing to prepare the country properly for war.[23] While historians still debate these charges and the reasons for the debacle, all agree that Soviet forces on the eve of the invasion were poorly situated, trained, and equipped, and that the consequent losses were devastating to the army, the economy, and the Soviet people.[24]

In contrast to the state's initial failures on the military front, it managed to act decisively and, by and large, effectively on the home front. Khrushchev's damning critique of the lack of military preparation did not extend *ipso facto* to domestic policy, a finding which calls for a reevaluation of the state's overall wartime record. The state moved rapidly to activate the existing commissariats, soviets, and party, Komsomol, and union organizations to build a vast mobilizing machine connecting the localities to Moscow.

Work on Stalin's wartime leadership has focused on the State Committee for Defense (GKO), the newly created emergency body holding full military, economic, and political power, but much less attention has been paid to the wartime organizations that developed and implemented the GKO's decrees. This book brings the state back into the social history of the home front, not as a vague synonym for power, but as a group of concrete, functioning organizations. The Commissariat of Trade, for example, was repurposed to develop and administer a new ration system. Local soviets took responsibility for assembling people for labor mobilization, while the industrial commissariats organized the evacuation of their respective enterprises. The NKVD, too, assumed a new wartime role: deporting hundreds of thousands of people in national groups suspected of disloyalty or collaboration, deploying prisoners on vast military construction projects, and organizing deportees into a new body known unofficially as "the Labor Army." Alongside existing state bodies, the Party and Soviet of People's Commissars created formidable new groups that wielded unprecedented powers. Within two days of the invasion, they established the Soviet for Evacuation (SE), which by fall 1942 had organized the transport of more than 2,400 industrial enterprises, almost 8 million animals, and up to 25 million people.[25] Its success, in inverse proportion to the losses on the battlefield, was largely responsible for the country's rebuilding of the defense industry in the east. A similar pattern of emergency response followed to mobilize labor. Eight days after the invasion, the state created the Committee to Distribute the Labor Force (the Komitet), which would assume vast powers to assess employment in every province and republic, meet industry's demands for labor, and oversee the transfer of newly mobilized people to distant sites. No such control over labor had previously existed in the Soviet Union or any other nation in time of peace or war. The Chief Administration of Labor Reserves and draft boards dispatched millions of teenagers and enlisted men unfit for the front to vocational schools and to work. The entire able-bodied population in town and country was subjected to compulsory labor mobilization. As the invasion set millions of people in motion—evacuees, refugees, newly mobilized soldiers, deportees, and workers—the Commissariat of Health struggled to contain typhus, dysentery, tuberculosis, measles, and other deadly epidemics that swept through crammed trains, railway stations, and ports. Industrial managers assumed responsibility for housing, feeding, and clothing millions of refugees, evacuees, and mobilized workers, caring for their children, and replacing much of the reproductive labor women did in the home. Mobilized and unfree workers lived in hastily constructed barracks without kitchens, sanitary facilities, heat, or running water. Family life was remade around the workplace. As the food supply contracted and starvation threatened, the family stove was replaced by the collective canteen kitchen.

Many of these mobilizing efforts would have faltered without broad popular support and participation. Evacuation rested wholly on the willingness of workers, even under bombardment, to dismantle, pack, and load the machines. After long and arduous journeys, these same workers reassembled their factories under open skies. Labor mobilization proved more complicated, dogged by desertion and evasion as the war ground on. But millions of people remained at their jobs under horrific conditions. Scientists and canteen cooks invented and experimented with substitute foods as an increasing number of people suffered from starvation. Party, Komsomol, union, and soviet activists organized a broad array of civilian volunteer organizations, including the *opolchenie* (home front militia). People volunteered to build defense perimeters, spot planes and extinguish fire bombs on rooftops, check ration weights and measures, and gather wood and wild greens. Although these collective efforts could not shield the home front population from the terror of Nazi bombing or extreme shortages, they enabled people to turn individual panic and despair into crucial contributions to the war effort.

Fortress Dark and Stern views the war from the perspectives of the state and of ordinary people. It draws on rich, newly discovered archival sources to reveal state policy as well as its challenges and consequences: chaos and panic on the front lines; the shortage of boxcars for evacuation; epidemics along the rail lines; starvation in the rear; the ubiquity of black and gray markets; official thievery; desertion; popular responses to propaganda; the use of forced labor; and the crisis of the labor system. Multiple *proverki*, or investigations, expose in shocking detail the extreme privations ordinary people faced. The records also allow us to move beyond speculative assertions about coercion to assess how the labor laws actually worked in daily life. Alongside testimonies and memoirs, they illuminate a variety of collective popular responses.

The war marked the Soviet Union and Russia in ways that are evident to this day. The Soviet Union lost more people, in absolute numbers and as a percentage of its population, than any other combatant nation: an estimated 26 million to 27 million people, about 13.5 percent of its prewar population. More than 8.6 million Red Army soldiers were counted as "irrecoverable losses," almost 3.4 million of them missing or taken prisoner. Many prisoners of war were deliberately starved to death or murdered in German camps; only 1.8 million returned. Approximately 19 million civilians died: 8.5 million from infectious disease and famine imposed by the Germans, including between 700,000 and 1 million in the siege of Leningrad; between 6.4 million and 11.3 million through deliberate extermination, including almost 2 million Jews; and between 2.1 and 3 million sent to forced labor in Germany.[26] In contrast, the United States lost 418,500 people or 0.32 percent of its 1939 population; the United Kingdom and its colonies lost 450,700, or 0.94 percent; and France, 567,000, or 1.35 percent. Axis deaths were higher, but still not comparable: Japan lost 3.1 million (3.67 percent); and Germany, between 6.6 million and 8 million (7.9 percent).[27] Almost every Soviet family lost a relative or was affected in some terrible way by the war.

Nonetheless, this history remains less well known in the West in part because of the Cold War that followed.[28] The Soviet contribution to the victory over fascism was gradually erased in the narratives of politicians and mass media. Many people never knew or forgot that the vast majority of Hitler's troops were arrayed on the eastern front. The United States and Britain did not open the second front in Europe until June 6, 1944, well after the Soviet Union had already suffered devastating losses and its victory over the Nazis was almost assured. Even after the Normandy landing, two-thirds of the German army remained in the east. As historian Rodric Braithwaite aptly noted of the Germans, "Indeed, had they not been fighting the Russians, they would have been in France, and there would have been no D-Day."[29] Meanwhile, in the Soviet Union and then Russia, the state-sponsored narrative of the war assumed ever more heroic and unassailable dimensions.[30] Initially focused on the leadership of Stalin, the narrative of the Great Patriotic War then shifted to the organizing prowess of the Communist Party, and finally to a post-socialist, national emphasis on the victory of the Russian state and people. All popular iterations erased any subjects that might tarnish the heroic myth of a nation united and rising as one.

If the war was a litmus test of support for the Soviet state, research on the occupied areas reveals that many peasants initially welcomed or at least accommodated the Germans, nationalist groups collaborated actively in ethnic genocide, and some Communist Party members who remained behind proved willing to serve the new authorities. Proponents of what has come to be called the "resistance genre" see such defeatist or pro-German reactions as responses to the brutalities of Stalinist rule, reviving an older totalitarian thesis that established moral and political equivalence between

Nazism and Stalinism.[31] Yet in researching the home front, we have found little evidence of pro-German support or activity. In meetings and discussions, ordinary people were at times skeptical of the state's information, but they showed strong interest in the front and support for the war effort. Those who had benefited most from the revolution and Soviet policies on gender, labor, education, and industrial development felt an intense identification with the socialist project. A relative of Lazar I. Korduner, the chief engineer at the Khar'kov Tractor Factory, later described Korduner's reaction as the Germans approached:

> He had worked on the plant's construction from the first day, and had bitter feelings when the plant was to be blasted. Katia, his mother, always waited up for him to return from the plant, and never went to bed until he got home. When the Germans were very close to Kharkov, Lazar received an order to blast the plant. He came home and literally fell onto Katia, crying. "Why are you crying?" she asked him. He replied, "Mama, I did something three hours ago that was almost like killing my own daughter."[32]

Some historians argue that the state relied heavily on coercion and repression to mobilize the Soviet population, and the primary motivation for soldiers and civilians was fear. Others note that coercion cannot explain the state's ability to mobilize people under such difficult conditions and win the war. Certainly, prisoners were forced into critical wartime construction and production, and workers were bound to their workplaces under harsh conditions by strict labor laws. Yet this book shows that the state's ability to maintain control through coercion was limited and that the vast majority of people participated willingly in the war effort. Some workers initially refused to dismantle and evacuate "their" factories, but many more risked their lives to make evacuation possible. Some evaded compulsory mobilization, but most stayed on the job despite the inability or unwillingness of prosecutors, industrial managers, and collective farm managers to enforce labor laws. People engaged in illlicit forms of redistribution and theft that reconfigured the state's strict rationing hierarchy, but ordinary people protested official privilege, not the system itself. These acts, sparked by panic, self-interest, or the imperatives of survival, were not motivated by anti-Soviet or pro-fascist aims. While most historians agree that popular attitudes, which varied over time and by social group, nationality, personal experience, and political orientation, should not be reduced to a simple binary of "for or against" the

Soviet regime, there is, in the end, scant evidence of anti-Soviet resistance on the home front.[33]

The home front developed in tandem with the military front, shaped by the exigencies of territorial loss and liberation. The chapters to come follow the contraction and expansion of the home front through the first demoralizing retreats of the Red Army to the victory at Stalingrad and the hard-fought liberation of the occupied territories. Beginning with the frenetic effort to evacuate and resettle people and industry, and ending with the first attempts to reincorporate the newly liberated territories, the book is structured both chronologically and thematically. The chapters are built around the defining policies of the wartime state—evacuation, resettlement, rationing, labor mobilization, public health, and propaganda—and the popular responses that supported, limited, and reshaped these policies. The Soviet state produced, in the words of a leading economic historian, "a wartime production miracle" on the home front.[34] How did the state and people accomplish this miracle? What policies enabled the country to win the war and what conditions did these policies create? How did people respond, and why? These questions lie at the heart of this book.

1

Panic, Scorched Earth, and Evacuation

Very strained work lasted in the SE from July 1941 until the beginning of 1942. The officials literally lost count of the days. Every Soviet person, listening to the bulletins of Informbiuro, painfully lived through the reports about the retreats of the Red Army, and the occupation of new Soviet towns and villages by the enemy. Those were bitter and difficult days. We had to leave nothing for the enemy.

L. I. Pogrebnoi, plenipotentiary of the Soviet for Evacuation

In the late summer of 1941, as German panzers rolled toward the industrial city of Dnepropetrovsk and fierce fighting engulfed Ukraine, the Soviet for Evacuation (SE) dispatched a representative to help with removal of people and industry. When he arrived on August 10, evacuation was in full swing. Officials from various industrial commissariats, factory directors, and workers were already dismantling and loading the machinery and raw materials of the city's metallurgical and defense factories. Workers and their families, part of organized convoys, crowded into railway coaches and boxcars. The vital heart of industry was to be temporarily stilled and transplanted thousands of miles to the east.

All did not proceed as planned. Officials in the Commissariat of Railways failed to provide as many boxcars as were needed for the massive operation. The Voroshilov munitions factory (factory No. 79), for example, required about 200 boxcars per day, but received only about half that number. Loading proceeded in fits and starts. Boxcars allocated to one factory stood empty as their workers hurried to dismantle and pack, while workers in another factory waited impatiently to load the crates they had already brought to the station. On August 15, the workers desperately tried to find a crane powerful enough to lift 50 tons of presses. The platform was jammed with crowds of people waiting to evacuate. The next day, the Germans bombed the station. People scattered, screaming, in every direction. The SE, working closely with local party and soviet officials, hastily improvised a new station on the eastern bank of the Dnepr River and ferried thousands of people to the other side of the city.

Refusing to succumb to panic, workers staunchly continued loading. Nine days later, the Germans occupied Dnepropetrovsk, taking control of both the eastern and western banks of the river. But the job was done: between August 8 and 22, three days before Dnepropetrovsk fell, workers, laboring around the clock, shipped out 10,000 boxcars, and more than 200,000 people left the city by rail.[1] After journeying many weeks and thousands of miles, the workers would disembark in freezing winter weather in strange towns and empty fields. Unloading the machines, they would reassemble the factories beyond the reach of German bombers. The evacuation of Dnepropetrovsk, with its central planning, mass participation, close calls, and unexpected obstacles, was repeated in countless towns across the frontline zones.

The very idea of such an evacuation was without precedent in the history of warfare or disaster. The territory the Germans occupied between June 1941 and autumn 1942 contained 40 percent of the Soviet Union's prewar population and almost 32,000 industrial enterprises, including iron and steel, machine-building, agricultural equipment, textile, food, chemical, paper, lumber, and other essential factories; mines; oil wells; and large electric power stations.[2] Together they accounted for 33 percent of the USSR's 1940 industrial output.[3] Little of this industry would remain. By the end of 1941, the state had adopted a plan to transfer the foundation of the industrial economy to the east. During the last six months of 1941 around 12 million people were evacuated, rising to at least 17 million by late 1942; during this time 2,593 industrial enterprises were shipped east.[4] According to one historian, 37 percent of the prewar value of the occupied territories' industrial assets was rescued.[5]

The SE, established within two days of the invasion, had little time to master the challenges it faced. Evacuation targeted not only the most valuable assets, but also the most vulnerable people, including children, the ill, and the elderly. It targeted vast herds of animals, grain, and raw materials. Some areas were evacuated well in advance of German occupation, but others had little time to prepare. In many areas, the front approached quickly, and people had to move fast. Workers in the Donets coal basin (Donbass) planned to dismantle the generator of the region's largest electric power station over seven days and nights but accomplished the job in ten hours.[6] The urgent work of evacuation often occurred under heavy bombing, amid deadly fires and deafening explosions. State and economic officials understood, moreover, that evacuation would create a sharp temporary drop in the production of desperately needed armaments. Machinery in boxcars could not produce.

As the Red Army retreated, local officials panicked in towns and villages throughout the frontline zones. What were they supposed to do with the people, farm animals, food, and industry in the path of the invading army? Amid the mayhem and confusion, soldiers lost touch with their units, and thousands were killed, wounded, and captured. Stalin and the General Staff could not get up-to-date, reliable information. Local officials were unsure what to do or even whom to contact. Where was the front, and where was it expected to be within the next week, days, or even hours? In rural areas and small towns without access to railroad stations, many people had no way to leave. Those who remained, particularly Jews and Roma, would be murdered by the Germans within days or weeks of occupation.

Throughout the terrifying summer and fall of 1941, the SE, supported by tens of thousands of workers, railroad troops, and local soviet, party, and industrial officials, struggled to rescue as much of the industrial and agricultural base as possible.[7] Evacuation lasted more than eighteen months and fell into two phases. The first began with the invasion and ended in December 1941, reaching its height between July and November. A second, shorter phase followed in the summer and fall of 1942.[8] In the Baltic countries, among the first to be invaded, only an insignificant number of people and industries could be rescued. In Belorussia, intense fighting slowed the German advance, and evacuation lasted from June through August, ending only with occupation of the entire republic in September. In Leningrad and its environs, the SE began sending out people and machinery in July but, once the German ring closed around the city in September, its efforts faltered. In late fall, as soon as the ice over Lake Ladoga was thick enough to bear the weight of trucks and horse-drawn carts, the SE tried again to evacuate the starving population.[9] In Ukraine, evacuation began in July and proceeded at a frantic pace until mid-October: the right (western) bank of the Dnepr was evacuated in July and August, and the left bank between August and October. In western, central, and southern Russia, the SE undertook a partial planned evacuation in July and August, followed by a larger effort as the front drew closer from September into November. In Moscow, a mass evacuation of the city began in mid-October prompted by the German advance on the capital, and workers continued to dismantle the factories through mid-December. The smaller evacuation, from the middle of May until October 1942, resulted from new losses of territory as the German army advanced toward Stalingrad.[10] Although evacuation proved essential to eventual Soviet victory, when it first began, much remained contingent and unclear.[11] How far would the Germans advance? How many people and how much of the industrial and agricultural base would need to be rescued? The extent of the mission was unknown.

Planning for Evacuation

Many republics and provinces had rough evacuation plans on the eve of the invasion, but they were badly outdated. The industrial commissariats had created evacuation plans for their respective sectors in 1928. Soviet state officials in the provinces and republics were instructed to update their plans in 1934, and the government's Military Industrial Commission began drawing up additional plans five years later.[12] In April 1941, the government created a special Commission for Evacuation (Komissiia po evakuatsii) for Moscow's population. Led by V. P. Pronin, the head of the Moscow soviet, the Commission delivered its draft on June 3, less than three weeks before the invasion. But the government never approved it. Stalin allegedly told Pronin, "Comrade Pronin, I consider your suggestion for the partial evacuation of Moscow's population in wartime untimely. I ask you to liquidate the Commission for Evacuation and stop all conversations about evacuation. The Central Committee and Soviet of People's Commissars will inform you when and if it will be necessary to prepare an evacuation." Pronin had consulted numerous state, party, and industrial officials, prompting much "conversation" about the likelihood of invasion and the possible loss of Moscow, but Stalin, anxious not to provoke the Germans or spread panic, evidently considered this more harmful than helpful. A national draft plan aimed at evacuation of factories, institutions, people, and property was still pending government approval on the day of attack.[13] One Russian historian later critically noted that evacuation "had to be decided once the war had already begun, often in haste, at a time without a clear sense of the concrete situation. This could not help but have negative consequences."[14]

More important than Stalin's failure to plan was the fact that logistics made peacetime planning for evacuation difficult. It made no sense to evacuate areas that were not under threat, and the SE's main challenge once war began was the coordination of multiple evacuations along a thousand-mile, rapidly retreating front under severe time and transport constraints. The prewar plans, aimed at the evacuation of a single province, city, or industry, would have had little practical value. As one official explained to the SE in August, when evacuation was well underway, the prewar plans "in no way reflect the conditions and demands of the present time."[15] Dubrovin admitted that no one expected such a large and rapid loss of territory: "We did not arrange beforehand concrete, worked-out evacuation plans in the event of an unfavorable military situation."[16] Yet even had the government anticipated the military debacle, the challenge was not how to evacuate any single enterprise or area, a task the SE mastered quickly, but rather how to organize and coordinate evacuation along a broad, rapidly moving front. Communication between officials from the SE and the Commissariat of Railways reveals their intense focus on available routes, passenger and freight cars, destinations, and traffic limits at the stations and on the lines, problems not subject to predetermined solutions.

The first evacuations occurred as emergency responses to the invasion. P. K. Ponomarenko, Secretary of the Belorussian Communist Party, called Stalin the day after the invasion to request permission to evacuate the republic. He later wrote, "He [Stalin] was surprised and asked, 'You think that this is necessary? It isn't premature?'" Stalin was still unsure about the German advance, but Ponomarenko understood that the western Belorussian provinces were already lost, and they needed to move promptly to evacuate Minsk and the eastern provinces.[17] In the north, the Germans planned to take the Latvian city of Liepaia on the first day of the attack but were delayed by fierce resistance. With no time to spare, the Latvian Central Committee and government developed a plan aimed at rescuing people rather than industry and began moving people out of Liepaia, Riga, Daugavpils, and Elgava. Their first concern was to protect children and the elderly from air attacks by moving 115,000 people within 24 hours by rail and road to rural areas in the northeast. Their second concern was to transport party and soviet officials, military officers, and NKVD personnel to Russia. Many of the provisions of the Latvian plan were later adopted throughout frontline zones, including the organization of convoys, worker-guards, and medical services and food stations on the rail lines.[18] Officials did manage to send off multiple convoys in rail cars crammed with workers, metal, machinery, and food before Liepaia fell on June 29, Riga three days later, and the entire republic by July 10.[19] By this time, Latvian officials were no longer acting alone and had already sent the newly created SE a stream of reports.

The Creation of the Soviet for Evacuation

In a very brief, "strictly secret" decree issued on June 24, 1941, the Central Committee and Soviet of People's Commissars (Sovnarkom) established the SE "to direct the evacuation of the population, institutions, military and other loads, the equipment of enterprises, and other valuables."[20] Soviet leaders hoped that the enemy would be quickly driven out, and had not yet considered the possibility of a transfer of industry to the east. Not until August 16, when evacuation was already in full swing, did the Party and government make the bold decision to reconfigure the economy and create a new productive base in the regions of the Volga, Urals, Western Siberia, Kazakhstan, and Central Asia.[21] This new plan, covering the last quarter of 1941 and all of 1942, was adopted, as N. A. Voznesenskii, the head of Gosplan, later obliquely noted, because the earlier plan "was still insufficient" to cope with "the ever increasing impact of the war."[22] In other words, the existing plan had failed to foresee just how much territory would be lost by July.

Eight state and party leaders were appointed to head the SE, including L. M. Kaganovich, Commissar of Railways, A. N. Kosygin, Deputy Chairman of the Soviet of People's Commissars, N. M. Shvernik, head of the All-Union Central Council of Unions, and B. M. Shaposhnikov, Chief of the Red Army's General Staff and Deputy Commissar of Defense. Over the next week, they were joined by A. N. Mikoian, Commissar of Foreign Trade, L. P. Beria, head of the Commissariat of Internal Affairs (NKVD) and member of the State Committee for Defense (GKO), the highest wartime body, and M. G. Pervukhin, Deputy Chairman of the Soviet of People's Commissars and Commissar of the Chemical Industry. Over time, the composition of the SE changed slightly—Shvernik assumed its leadership—but it retained its links to the railroads, the GKO, the Soviet of People's Commissars, the unions, the commissariats, and the NKVD.[23] The group met frequently, at least once a week and often every day. It delegated major operational tasks to its members who, in turn, prepared plans and draft decrees to be affirmed by the group or the relevant government bodies within a set deadline.[24]

A small, highly flexible body with great power, the SE relied on the local soviets, institutions, and the economic commissariats to implement its decisions.[25] The deputy commissars of coal, iron and steel, and heavy industry served as plenipotentiaries of the SE, appointed up to five officials within their own commissariats to develop plans for evacuation, and sent their own plenipotentiaries to supervise the dismantling and resettlement of their industries.

The heads of the local party committees supervised housing, construction, space, and feeding at the destination sites.[26] At moments of crisis, the SE also dispatched its own troubleshooters or plenipotentiaries to large railroad stations and ports. Invested with extraordinary temporary powers to override local authorities, they acted on their own initiative to resolve problems. Local administrations for evacuation were established in republics, provinces, and regions, along with evacuation centers (*evakopunkty*) at major railroad junctions and destination towns to assist convoys. Evacuation bases (*evakobazy*), equipped with heavy-lifting cranes, barges, and rafts, were created in ports to transfer loads between train and boat.[27] The SE was thus a paradoxical body: highly centralized, it depended on a vast local base of soviets and party committees to implement its decisions. A wartime creation, it relied on the prewar state and industrial infrastructures. Composed of powerful leaders, it gave its local troubleshooters almost unlimited power to resolve crises. The paradoxes it embraced were largely responsible for its success.

As the government ordered the SE to "begin work immediately," Kaganovich called a meeting of the group the very day it was created.[28] Dubrovin, Deputy Commissar of Railways, later remembered that, after the first meeting, everyone hurried off and "searched the archives and Lenin library in Moscow for any information about evacuation during the First World War, but we found almost nothing." "All our experience was acquired in the course of military action."[29] During its first days, the SE did not give particular attention to the evacuation of the industrial base, limiting its scope to "valuable property in a few towns and districts in the frontline areas."[30] In view of the full horror and loss that would soon unfold, its first meetings revealed the group's inability to foresee just how monumental its mission would become.

Evacuation and Scorched Earth

As the SE was just beginning its work, local officials in the frontline zones were desperately seeking instructions from Moscow. On June 27 and 29, the Central Committee and Sovnarkom issued two decrees aimed at providing direction. The first, sent to party and soviet officials in the frontline zones, was classified as "strictly secret." In contrast to the newspapers, which remained vague about the disasters unfolding on the front, it acknowledged that the country was rapidly losing territory and valuable industrial and agricultural assets. Calling for a policy of "scorched earth," it declared: "All valuable property, raw materials, food stocks, and grain in the field which cannot be shipped out and is left in place can be used by the enemy. Following the instructions of the military soviets at the front, it should all be quickly ruined, destroyed, or burned." In light of the "complex" military situation, Soviet leaders recognized that the SE might not have sufficient time to act. They prioritized four categories for evacuation: industrial machines, raw materials, food, and state valuables; skilled workers, engineers, and white-collar employees with their enterprises; youth of draft age; and leading soviet and party officials.[31]

The second decree provided instructions to the wider population:

> If the Red Army is forced to retreat, drive off the railroad rolling stock, do not leave the enemy a single locomotive, a single boxcar. Do not leave the enemy a kilogram of bread, not a liter of gasoline. Collective farmers: drive off the cattle, deliver grain to the state for shipment to the rear. All valuable property, including nonferrous metals, grain, and gasoline, which cannot be shipped out should be unconditionally destroyed.

It instructed local officials "to defend every bit of Soviet soil, fight to the last drop of blood," and "to show courage, initiative, and daring." It also gave them enormous discretionary power.[32]

In terse language, the two decrees set priorities for evacuation and established a chain of command. If conditions did not allow the SE to make decisions, the military soviets at the front were to take over. If the military soviets had already retreated, local party and state officials were to evacuate what they could, destroy what remained, and fight to the death. The Red Army was in rapid, disorganized retreat, the military soviets lacked reliable information, and the SE had difficulty maintaining contact with the frontline zones. Under these conditions, local officials faced agonizing choices. The policy of "scorched earth"—to set fields afire, drive off the livestock, and blow up factories–had irrevocable consequences for those left behind. If no agricultural produce, farm animals, or industry remained, how would the people not evacuated survive? Although the government encouraged everyone to leave, peasants in remote villages had no way to reach a railroad station, and some family members were too old or sick to travel.

For the Jewish population, the choice to leave or stay had particularly fateful consequences. Some heard rumors about the murderous behavior of the Germans but discounted the stories as exaggerated. Others, who had lived through World War I, remembered the Germans as "cultured" and "polite."[33]

As a young Jewish girl in Kiev, Raissa Smelaya remembered the split in her family when her aunt placed them on her factory's list for evacuation:

> My grandparents refused to evacuate. They said that they weren't afraid of the Germans and didn't believe what people said about their brutalities. Besides, they were too old to leave their home. And they stayed. My mother's older sister, Shura, and her two daughters evacuated to the Urals with the plant where Shura's husband was working. She also tried to convince her parents go with her, but in vain. My mother's brother, Munia, also stayed in Kiev. He was responsible for all the preparations at the factory for evacuation. After the war we got to know that on 29th September 1941 my grandmother, grandfather, and Uncle Munia were shot by fascists in Babi Yar.[34]

The historian Yitzhak Arad notes that Soviet evacuation authorities rescued about 1.63 million Jews who otherwise would have been murdered by providing a safe haven in the east.[35] But, in the face of the rapid German advance, neither soviet officials nor ordinary people had the time or the knowledge to make what would soon become life-altering decisions.

Figure 1.1 Evacuation of people from frontline zone, 1941. Courtesy of RGAKFD.

Responding to Crisis

The SE initially aimed to rescue people and industry in areas under immediate threat of bombing or occupation. Within five days of the invasion, it ordered the evacuation of children, along with key defense factories and their workers, from Moscow, Leningrad, and other cities exposed to aerial attack.[36] Freight cars of machinery and workers, followed by railway cars filled with more than 200,000 children, rolled out of Moscow and Leningrad. The children, separated from their parents, went to nearby rural areas presumed safe from bombing.[37] Working under intense pressure, the SE shipped out people, food, and equipment under "rapid evacuation," an official phrase that denoted the urgent need to rescue and dispatch without a set destination. The people aboard had no idea where they were headed. As SE plenipotentiary Pogrebnoi later noted, provisional destinations often had to be decided "operationally" at the front and in action.[38] Amid the haste of loading, the SE could not always control what local officials chose to ship out. Dubrovin later remembered:

> In the first months, due to great objective difficulties, we made many mistakes. A large number of boxcars did not have destinations, were directed to very great distances, and were loaded with things of small value. The wish that nothing would remain for the enemy resulted in boxcars being loaded with household furniture, office papers and tables, common metals, and personal items to the exclusion of more valuable industrial equipment.

The situation was further complicated by heavy traffic. The loads directed to the rear met "great streams of trains" headed toward the front, creating giant tangles and gridlock.[39]

In the first ten days, the SE's telephones rang endlessly with frantic calls from the commissariats about shipments. V. P. Zotov, Commissar of the Food Industry, recognizing that critical food factories were threatened, lobbied the SE to transfer the "most valuable equipment from the most threatened districts."[40] But Zotov's requests vied with equally desperate pleas from other factories.[41] Phone connections were frequently disrupted, and the SE lost contact with local officials in the frontline zones. A plenipotentiary from the Commissariat of Shipbuilding had to travel in person to the northern town of Kandalaksha, strategically located along the Moscow–Murmansk railway, because the telephone line to Moscow no longer functioned, and nothing had been heard from the town since it had received its evacuation orders. Kandalaksha also contained a large aluminum factory and Severonikel, a nickel mining and production operation run by the NKVD with prison labor. NKVD officials managed to send a terse note to the SE explaining that the factories were being loaded at that very moment, and a full written summary would follow.[42]

A comprehensive national plan for industrial evacuation and reconstruction was still tentative. The Red Army was desperately in need of tanks, ammunition, guns, and other equipment, and the government was reluctant to dismantle defense factories unless they were under immediate threat. Only half the workers and machinery from Krasnyi Vyborzhets, an ammunition factory in Leningrad, for example, were evacuated to the Urals while the remainder continued to produce for the front.[43] Dubrovin later noted that the Red Army was so short of ammunition and arms in 1941 that factories had to produce until the last possible moment. "As a result," he explained, "it was necessary to prepare industrial equipment for dismantling and evacuation while at the same time under artillery shelling and enemy bombardment."[44]

When defense production was not at stake, the government was better able to take preemptive measures. Within the first week of the invasion, it decided to transfer the majority of commissariats and other state organizations out of Moscow.[45] Motivated in part by fear of bombardment, this move ensured that the leadership of the state and economy would continue to function even if the capital was damaged or occupied. Yet preemptive measures appeared prescient only in retrospect. In some cases, local officials opposed preemptive evacuation because they considered it alarmist. In Leningrad, for example, the SE ordered the dismantling of electric power stations on July 3, but the city soviet balked and refused to allow the Commissariat of Electric Power Stations to cut off electricity without a direct order from Sovnarkom.[46]

Panic and Confusion

Throughout the summer of 1941, the Germans swiftly conquered one town after another. Military commanders, party officials, and ordinary citizens sent a stream of desperate telegrams, reports, and bulletins to Stalin, Georgii Malenkov, and other party leaders. The decree of June 29 urged local soviet and party officials to show "initiative, courage, and daring." Yet the Terror of

1935–1939 had inculcated different rules of survival: to make no decisions without a written order from a superior, to distance oneself from anyone under suspicion, and to denounce others preemptively to protect oneself.[47] None of these strategies was useful for promoting the initiative and solidarity necessary to create a strong, unified resistance. The Political Administration of the Red Army (Politicheskoe upravlenie RKKA or PURKKA) regularly updated the Central Committee about political and military activity at the front, and ordinary citizens and party activists, too, considered it their duty "to write."[48] Observers of the panic and confusion asked Stalin and the Central Committee for help in punishing the guilty and reestablishing order. Others had little interest in retribution, but pleaded for instructions amid the collapse of military and governmental authority.

A citizen of Mozyr', for example, a Belorussian town of about 17,500 people in Polesskaia province on the banks of the Pripiat River, sent an angry telegram to Stalin denouncing local soviet, party, and NKVD officials. He noted that Mozyr' was overrun by fleeing soldiers and refugees. After issuing an order urging the inhabitants of Mozyr' to remain, many leading officials, including the head of the NKVD, sent their families out of town and fled in the dead of night. Their actions provoked "panic and rage" among the people who remained.[49] About one-third of the town was Jewish, and most would soon be murdered by the Nazis. Similar instances of panicked flight occurred in towns and villages all along the front. A member of PURKKA on the northwestern front informed the Central Committee that in the village of Glubokoe, Opochka district, local party officials, the director of the vodka factory, the judge, and the sole militiaman "all ran in panic" on July 6 although the front line was still 60 miles (100 km) distant. "As a result of this criminal behavior," the report read, "the villagers began looting the stores, and the milk and vodka factories."[50]

On July 1, members of the Defense Staff and district party officials in El'nia in Smolensk province wrote to the Politburo, noting that, "as a result of temporary successes of the Germans in various sectors of the western front, in particular in the direction of Minsk, panic rules in the command of various military areas and panicked inactivity rules the local party and soviet organs." The informants explained that, as soon as the first Luftwaffe planes appeared, the provincial military command in Smolensk sent their wives east to El'nia. The following day, the head of the provincial military command called the duty officer in El'nia to relay greetings to his wife, but this personal message constituted the full extent of the military instructions transmitted along the chain of command. The aviation unit in El'nia had received no orders, and its commander "rules in total confusion," the officials noted. Enemy planes were flying overhead all night, and people were terrified that German troops might be droppping behind the front lines. On the night of June 26, wild shooting broke out and continued until morning. The rising sun revealed two dead Red Army soldiers, victims of a panicked exchange of friendly fire. Party and soviet officials in El'nia received no instructions from their superiors in Smolensk, who had stopped answering the telephone. The El'nia district officials added sarcastically, "On June 27, we received a single directive dated four days earlier, in which the provincial executive committee of the soviet asked about the status of churches in the area. Is it really possible that they have nothing else to occupy their attention now?" Every district of Smolensk province, they noted, was "left to resolve the situation on its own."[51]

Yet officials in El'nia had pressing problems to solve. A mass of evacuees, including families of the frontline command, had arrived in need of food and shelter. Newly drafted soldiers were drifting back to town because they could not locate their units. Volunteers for the army were arriving every day. "What should we tell people?" the local officials asked. "We have no instructions, and no light is shed on this business." They noted that they had mobilized about 2,000 people in the district for the army, provided them with some military training, and even created a regiment, but they desperately needed arms and lacked "even the most basic information about the closest front." Terrified refugees streaming into El'nia were "screaming that Minsk had already fallen, and that the Germans were overrunning Smolensk province." How could they distinguish "truth from provocation?"[52] The commanders and party officials asked the Politburo to create a body that could organize an orderly evacuation of wives and children based on reliable military information and to send all party members to the front, leaving only a small staff in the district. They firmly stated, "We do not have the right to evacuate ourselves . . . Our place is at the front." And they insisted on order and collective organization: "If every commander or leading representative of the soviet or party is concerned only with the evacuation of his own family, then no one will protect the motherland." Finally, they asked the Politburo, and Stalin personally, "to strike down all the panic-mongers."[53]

Smolensk was not the only frontline province where military commanders and civilian officials were operating without information or instructions. And even when officials had these, they still faced terrible dilemmas. In Rechitsa, a town in Gomel' province in southeastern Belorussia, district officials received orders from their provincial superiors to evacuate the population on June 28. The very next day, the district prosecutor penned a furious denunciation of local officials to the USSR's chief prosecutor for their hysterical response. They had burned some secret documents and thrown the remainder into the courtyard and, in some cases, had abandoned their offices, leaving the files intact and the doors wide open. They evacuated their own families in the morning, told everyone to evacuate at noon, and promptly fled. Groups of women and children were sent off without any food. By early afternoon, workers had abandoned the factories. A large crowd formed a line to a pier on the Dnepr River in the hope that boats would arrive, others swam to the far shore, making their way east on foot. By nightfall, no boats had come, and the weary would-be evacuees trudged home in the rain. They did not know where else to go.[54]

The prosecutor's first inclination was to accuse the district officials of treason. "I think this invention of evacuation created panic and obviously was done by enemy elements by intention." However, in the very next sentence, he softened his view: "even if this possibility is excluded, then we still need to charge those who are responsible for creating such disorganization and panic." Following the dictates of an earlier time, he demanded an investigation. "I ask you to send to the locality a representative of the All-Union Procuracy to investigate these facts because my appeal to the provincial prosecutor has found no support, and where the prosecutor of Belorussia is located now, I do not know. I cannot investigate because I am now in a defense detachment with a rifle in hand."[55] The prosecutor failed to grasp how much the situation had changed. A judicial investigation was unlikely to hold off the looming occupation. On July 10, local officials returned to Rechitsa, but the town fell to the Germans six weeks later. Similar panics and mismanaged evacuations occurred in other small towns and rural provinces. As the Germans advanced through Belorussia, the head of the Nasvinskii rural soviet received orders from the district to evacuate immediately. The orders, however, did not include any information about where to go or how to transport the people, food stocks, or animals.[56] In the village of Medved' on the northwestern front, local officials escaped with their families, leaving children and old people from the collective farms to wander around in the forest. One elderly collective farmer declared, "Our authorities have abandoned us."[57]

Local officials vacillated over what to do with the harvest, animals, and equipment from the collective farms. The scorched earth decrees were of little help to those who remained behind. In the countryside around Tikhvin and Volkov in the north, district officials instructed the peasants to stop sowing and the collective farm leaders to distribute the stored seed grain to the peasants. A battalion commissar in the region, having little sympathy for the peasants, wrote to the Central Committee criticizing this choice, "I consider it my duty as a communist to inform you about the mess created here," he wrote. "It would have made more sense to give this to the army." He indignantly noted that the collective farmers "are eating everything."[58] In Kursk province to the southwest of Moscow, a local court judge and party member charged that rural officials had failed to gather the harvest or deliver grain to the state. Although they were warned by the NKVD and the district military command not to commandeer trucks and tractors and to evacuate the machine tractor stations, they instead used the motorized vehicles to evacuate their families. The charges, however, proved impossible to verify: the Germans took Kursk in early November, and all allegations were subsumed by a far greater threat.[59]

When local officials fled, "looting" frequently followed. Local inhabitants, fearing imminent occupation, broke into stores and warehouses. Yet was it wrong for people to take property if an area was about to be occupied? One state farm director in Volot district, following the guidelines set out in the decree of June 29, released and drove off about 1,000 head of cattle and pigs. Some residents took his action as a signal to loot the state farm of any remaining food or valuables. Many state farm workers were astounded by this behavior.[60] A member of PURKKA observed of the northern front, "These are not isolated instances. They exist in other districts and villages."[61] In many places, valuable agricultural equipment was abandoned in the machine tractor stations or the fields because military officers and fleeing officials had already commandeered all the oil and gasoline.[62]

Rural officials did not know how to interpret or act on the scorched earth decrees of June 26 and 29. Some destroyed valuable property unnecessarily, others dithered and allowed equipment to be seized by the Germans. A member of PURKKA penned a long, harsh critique in early August of officials throughout Ukraine for "doing nothing." "They are not destroying things of value, which are falling into enemy hands." They were "sitting on their suitcases," "sitting on wheels," waiting to roll out. Evacuation in Shpola district of Cherkassy province in Ukraine ended in a "disordered stampede."

The mill director and head of the fire brigade ran off, and the collective and state farm chairmen absconded with as much property as they could carry. The peasants promptly auctioned the remaining horses, carts, and ammunition. In other places, peasants were furious at local officials for taking their goods and animals. In Sumy province in northeastern Ukraine, officials took the best horses and consumer goods from the stores, leaving the collective farmers with nothing. The peasants flatly regarded their actions as theft, but a representative of PURKKA was concerned at what had been left. Surveying the considerable amount of livestock and grain that remained, he noted that the enemy had "achieved a solid productive base of food supplies." In the absence of officials capable of organizing resistance, he feared the peasants would have no choice but "to adapt to the Germans."[63] Some peasants looked forward to German rule and openly proclaimed the end of Soviet power and the liquidation of the collective farms. One peasant in a group mobilized to dig anti-tank ditches announced, "Let's stop this work. Hitler will free us. I will soon get my 30 hectares of land, my horses, cows, and other things."[64] In mid-August, the Germans reached the ports of Nikolaev, on the Bug River, and Kherson, on the Dnepr. Efforts to move large herds of cattle across the Dnepr and Bug Rivers proved difficult, and many farm animals remained in territory that was soon occupied; boats carrying grain out of Kherson were repeatedly bombed. Local inhabitants looted the warehouses when local officials fled.[65] On August 6, the head of PURKKA on the southern front, viewing the collapse of local soviet authority, suggested to the Central Committee that "all power in the area 70 to 100 kilometers from the front line be transferred to the military command." His proposal openly acknowledged that local party and soviet officials had lost control.[66]

A similar state of disorganization prevailed in the frontline zones north of Ukraine. At the end of July, N. I. Iaksharov, a party member from Kalinin, wrote in angry desperation to Stalin, "There is no discipline in the rear. . . . Each person decides everything according to what he wants. Is this how it is supposed to be?" He pleaded for "the methods of the Civil War and the restoration of discipline in the rear. We must end this abominable mess, which exists in the frontline area. Comrade Stalin, take measures to restore order."[67] Iaksharov noted that, while traveling through Kalinin province, he saw fleeing soldiers and panicked district officials everywhere. Retreating soldiers stole vehicles and gas stocks belonging to local soviets. Groups of soldiers threatened collective farm chairmen with guns, demanding food. When asked to show their documents, they told the peasants, "Now power belongs to the military." Iaksharov wrote, "Everyone is shocked but silent." Livestock, driven off in accordance with the state's earlier decrees, were stampeding in the fields and trampling the harvest. Wild rumors spread, including claims that General S. K. Timoshenko had escaped abroad after being removed from his post. Iaksharov closed his letter, "I am ashamed that we have such an abominable lack of discipline."[68]

Local officials were not entirely to blame for the collapse of authority. A fine line existed between timely evacuation and premature flight, between distributing goods to the population and looting. When was grain to be destroyed and livestock driven off? How was the remaining population to survive?[69] I. V. Kovalev, a former commissar of railways and Soviet historian, later referred indirectly to these dilemmas:

> In some cases, local organs soberly considered the situation, and took measures to evacuate the civilian population and material valuables; in others, they vacillated, and as a result Soviet people, not by choice, remained in territory occupied by the enemy. Material valuables at the last moment had to be either destroyed or, worse, fell to the German fascist occupiers.[70]

What Kovalev left unsaid was that timely action depended entirely on the location of an enemy that was moving so fast that no one knew where the front was located.

Planning, Packing, and Tracking

Throughout the summer and fall, the SE struggled to create order as bombings, accidents, and blockages on rail lines, at transit points, and in the ports heightened the fear and pressure. Railroad workers and volunteers worked around the clock to clear lines and stations and repair and reset bombed track.[71] Railway troops under the Commissariat of Defense, working under bombardment, helped load and direct military and industrial transports, civilian evacuees, and wounded Red Army soldiers. They were also responsible for evacuating the railways themselves, including equipment in the depots and warehouses, rolling stock, and more than 3,000 miles (5,000 km) of track.[72] Trained as soldiers as well as skilled workers, they fought fierce battles with the Germans for control of the railways, junctions, and yards as they repaired and dismantled the lines.

An efficient organized system for planned evacuation began to develop. By July, a vast map of rail lines in motion, created by detailed reports from every station, line, and commissariat, emerged from the early darkness and confusion.[73] The SE established a system of accounting and enumeration that enabled it to track every convoy. It set limits for traffic on the rail lines to coordinate separate evacuations along a broad and moving front, organized the dismantling of massive industrial complexes, assigned boxcars to each enterprise, and approved destinations for resettlement. It also implemented plans for food, water, and medical and veterinary services. The SE functioned as an intermediary between the commissariats and the Commissariat of Railways, a process Dubrovin described: "The contents of every boxcar were registered by number in a book signed by the head of the route, and packing and unpacking were to occur under supervised conditions. Every convoy was to be accompanied by foremen and workers who would assume responsibility for reassembly; each machine was tagged with the name of the person who dismantled it and instructions for its reconstruction."[74]

Yet even the most detailed instructions could not overcome certain iron constraints. Any given route could carry only a set number of cars, worked out mathematically by railway specialists, within a given period without creating gridlock. The number of railway cars available for evacuation was limited by troop movements, food deliveries, and other essential traffic.[75] Such limits forced the SE to prioritize evacuation according to the severity of the German threat as well as the country's railway capacity. So too did the ability to provide food, water, and services along the route. The SE planned, for example, to evacuate more than 1.6 million people from threatened zones within the first ten days of July. The logistics were daunting, requiring coordination of embarkation points, routes, and railway cars and boats.[76] Despite careful tracking, many loads went astray. Workers often packed amid intense bombing and fire and did not have time to ensure that the convoys stayed together. In response to this problem, the SE established bases where unidentified loads could be inventoried, and information on their contents sent to Gosplan. The number of undocumented loads was large enough that Gosplan established a separate working group to account for them and a special category for them within its economic plans.[77] Throughout the summer and fall, the Commissariat of Railways sent the SE regular bulletins that included the number of convoys en route, the number of railway cars per convoy, and their destinations based on daily reports from the heads of the rail lines. The bulletins allowed the SE to pinpoint the location of every convoy at any given moment and were considered so important that copies were forwarded to the GKO.[78]

Between August and October, 80 percent of Soviet war industry was "on wheels," stacked in boxcars headed east.[79] The SE was forced to balance two irreconcilable imperatives: the long-term need to rescue industry and the short-term need to maintain defense production until the last minute, thus risking the possibility that industry would fall into German hands. The decision when to evacuate had serious repercussions not just for the front, but also for defense factories in the rear. The metal industry, essential to defense, embodied this quandary. On July 18, the SE ordered the evacuation of nonferrous metal factories from Leningrad and Khar'kov. Once they ceased production, Moscow's defense factories had to rely solely on metal produced locally. So desperate was the SE that it even considered melting the bronze church bells in Moscow and Leningrad for use. Some factories had to be evacuated simply because they could no longer be supplied.[80]

Figure 1.2 The evacuation of cattle from frontline zone, 1941. Courtesy of RGAKFD.

Grain, Herds, and Food Factories

The SE's main target in the summer and early fall was the agricultural base, including machinery, herds, food-processing factories, and, most importantly, grain. The Commissariats of Agriculture and State Farms, working closely with the SE, developed detailed instructions about the transfer and resettlement of equipment and herds, while also encouraging the collective farms to continue producing until the last possible moment. The ripening fields and retreat of the Red Army shaped the priority lists for evacuation: livestock were shipped out first, followed by freshly harvested grain, and then reaping and threshing machinery. According to the SE's instructions, peasants were to drive herds to safety; mechanics were to ship out motors from combines; and tractor specialists were to drive the tractors to the rear. These instructions often proved impossible to fulfill once the heavy rains and deep mud of autumn made the roads and swollen rivers impassable. The GKO and Central Committee eventually ordered local party and soviet officials to construct special crossing areas over the Don, Volga, Kuban, and Terek Rivers. Yet only a tiny number of tractors and livestock from Kirovograd, Odessa, and Kamenets-Podol'skii provinces managed to reach the Dnepr River and fewer still to cross it, although the eastern provinces of Belorussia fared somewhat better.[81] Many drivers were forced to abandon equipment on the roads after they ran out of fuel or broke down.[82]

Tremendous urgency surrounded the evacuation of food stocks. Everyone understood that the loss of the agricultural base and food factories spelled starvation for the army and the home front. The SE instructed local officials to ship out sugar, grain, and food from areas under attack.[83] In mid-July, it launched a campaign to evacuate cattle, pigs, food, and food-processing factories from all areas threatened by occupation or bombing.[84] Sugar and grain received priority over all other shipments from the frontline zones, including those of the defense industry. The SE ordered the heads of every railway: "Ship out sugar from the frontline areas within five days no matter what the conditions, and from all remaining districts within eight days." Boxcars carrying sugar beets were to be dispatched with or without a destination. A special operational group was created within the Commissariat of Railways solely to ensure the evacuation of sugar, and Zotov, the head of the food industry, ordered the immediate evacuation of the sugar refineries.[85] With the rapid loss of territory, the SE was engaged in desperate triage. The heads of the rail lines were "to sharply decrease the transfer of people" to enable the shipment of food.[86]

As food-processing factories were evacuated, the availability of jams, canned goods, meat, milk, butter, oil, and other processed food was expected to fall. To offset the losses, the SE pioneered a strategy of phased evacuation, instructing the commissariats to dismantle only part of each factory while still maintaining production. Once production began at the new site, the remaining workers and machines would leave. The strategy, however, was often ineffective given the long journeys east and the rapid German advance. By the time the evacuated factories started up production, the original sites had already fallen.[87]

The SE also attempted to evacuate herds, which proved the least successful of its endeavors. The GKO decreed the evacuation of farm animals in mid-July.[88] In Ukraine, local officials had already dispatched great columns of tractors and herds toward the steep right bank of the Dnepr. They organized the construction of forty-six crossing areas and commandeered a motley flotilla of boats, including steamships, motorboats, and barges. The Germans, however, repeatedly bombed the crossings, killing people and animals and destroying equipment. Terrified animals stampeded in all directions. Bloody limbs, severed animal parts, and mangled machinery littered the banks and the water. But the exodus continued. By the light of the sun and the moon, a steady stream of people, herds, and machinery was ferried across the river. By October, thousands of tractors, combines, vehicles, and almost three million cattle, sheep, horses, and pigs had successfully made the crossing. Many collective farms were forced to move twice: crossing the Dnepr to the relative safety of the left bank, and then moving again after the Germans occupied the provinces to the east.[89] Of the animals left behind, many were given to the Red Army, and others were driven off toward the east in the hope they would be found, fed, and sheltered. The SE tracked the columns, set up veterinary stations, and tried to quicken the pace, but the routes were subject to heavy bombing and the herds difficult to move.[90]

In one exceptional case, an entire collective farm made the long trek to safety together. K. P. Shovkoplias, a member of a collective farm near Dnepropetrovsk, remembered that, on the morning of August 27, they packed up their belongings, gathered their livestock, and moved out in a steady rain. Three herders drove about 300 cattle, which were followed by 64 supply carts carrying children, invalids, elderly people, and valuables in a caravan stretching for more than a mile. The people and their animals walked together for almost four months, finally settling near the Volga River in December. When the Germans reached the Volga in the late summer of 1942, the group was forced to evacuate again. They made their second move to Kazakhstan, where they remained until the Red Army liberated Dnepropetrovsk province. In 1943, they returned home, bringing with them almost all their original livestock.[91]

In mid-August, the deputy chairman of Gosplan informed Voznesenskii, its head, that the cattle drives had "occurred in a thoroughly unsatisfactory manner" and many animals had been lost.[92] Rural officials "were completely unprepared" and did not know where to send the animals or how. Veterinarians were not evacuated with the herds, and there were no services en route. Often peasants simply drove the animals from one district to another. When district officials in Kalinin province received the orders to evacuate the herds, each decided individually how to respond. Some evacuated the livestock on state and collective farms but allowed peasants to keep their household cows. Others drove the poorer stock out of the area and kept the better milk producers. Some sold the animals to the collective farmers, who then resold them to peasant refugees flooding the area. Still others did nothing. In Kalinin and Smolensk provinces, teenaged and elderly collective farmers, instructed by local officials, drove off the herds only as far the neighboring district rather than to their assigned destinations. Dressed in rags, with no money or food, the old people and teenagers were sent off with no way to survive the journey. The cows were not milked; the herds not watered or fed. Informed of the difficulties, Gosplan, the SE, and Sovnarkom drafted detailed instructions in mid-August explaining that herders were to take their families and personal property with them. Like workers, they would be paid for their time in transit and receive tickets for rail and river transport. The instructions laid out clearly marked routes with veterinary services, water, and food for the animals at established stations.[93]

Animals, agricultural machinery, and foodstuffs poured into Odessa, a port on the Black Sea, and were successfully sent out by rail and boat. In early August, however, fighting blocked the rail lines out of the city, and refugees and loaded boxcars piled up at the station. The SE successfully evacuated almost 40 percent of the 65,616 tons of grain brought into the city.[94] After a seventy-three-day siege, Odessa finally fell to German and Romanian troops in mid-October, leaving several hundred thousand refugees, evacuees, and local inhabitants trapped in the city.[95] After the Romanians and Germans took control, about 25,000 Odessans were murdered on the outskirts and more than 35,000 deported in what became known as the Odessa Massacre. Of the city's 210,000 Jews, 80 percent were murdered in forced death marches, ghettos, and camps.[96]

In mid-August, the shipment of grain became the first priority in the frontline regions.[97] The SE set specific loading targets for every region with the aim of forcing the Commissariat of Railways to deliver the necessary boxcars and "to forbid their use for anything else."[98] At the end of August, Zotov sent the SE a plan for evacuating food enterprises from Crimea, including canneries, wineries, breweries, flour mills, distilleries, olive oil presses, and tobacco factories.[99] The SE told Zotov to start packing and shipping.[100] Anxiously monitoring the retreat of the battered Red Army, Zotov had a long list of enterprises he hoped to evacuate by October 10.[101] By early October, however, the SE's priorities shifted toward defense. Zotov's requests carried an increasing sense of urgency. On October 4, he wrote to the SE with a plan to evacuate the food enterprises from Khar'kov and its environs. On October 12, he pleaded for boxcars to ship out bacon fat and rosin from Khar'kov. On October 13, with the Germans within reach of Khar'kov, the SE gave Zotov the order to begin loading.[102] It was not a moment too soon. On October 24, the Germans occupied Khar'kov. The loss of this major transport hub was a terrible blow, forcing the Red Army and the SE to rely on Voronezh and Stalingrad for rail and river transport. The only good news was that Zotov had successfully managed to rescue desperately needed food factories, and the diversion of German troops to Khar'kov contributed to the Wehrmacht's defeat in the battle for Rostov in early December.

By the beginning of December, the evacuation of the agricultural base and food-processing enterprises was complete. Almost 8.8 million animals had been successfully evacuated.[103] Large stocks of grain, piled in warehouses, at wharves, and at railroad stations, had to be abandoned, but there were not enough boxcars to rescue both food and heavy industry. As the Red Army retreated, part of the grain was distributed to the population, while thousands of tons were destroyed.[104] Millions of horses, cattle, and sheep entered the Volga region. As temperatures dropped and the mighty river froze, the animals, arrayed along the right bank, awaited shipment to collective farms on the home front.[105]

The Industrial Base: Emergency and Planned Evacuations

Evacuating industry, the SE proceeded simultaneously along parallel lines: emergency rescue and planned transfer. In western Belorussia, which was occupied within less than a week of the invasion, most industry was lost. Yet in Gomel', Belorussia's second-largest city, the SE had a little more time and success. The battle for Gomel' began in July, but the city was not occupied until August 21. Evacuation began in early July and continued through the beginning of August under intense bombardment. Workers managed to ship out 42 industrial enterprises and 80,000 people, including Gomsel'mash, an agricultural machinery factory already converted to defense. By September, Gomel''s enterprises had been resettled in the east and were once again producing armaments.[106]

Unlike in Belorussia, which required an immediate emergency response, the SE began evacuating industry around Moscow and Leningrad in early July, well before either city was threatened by occupation.[107] The evacuation of Kiev and its surrounding province also began within a week of the invasion. Workers slept in the factories, working around the clock to dismantle and pack the machines. The SE also targeted metallurgical industry in Ukraine in advance, but the Germans moved so quickly that the Petrovskii iron and steel plant in Dnepropetrovsk and other plants were evacuated under intense bombardment.[108]

The Central Committee and Ukraine Soviet of People's Commissars ordered local officials to prepare industrial enterprises on the right bank of the Dnepr for evacuation on July 3, but this preparation began only on August 7. The region was considered so critical to the war effort that no fewer than twelve deputy commissars flew into Dnepropetrovsk to supervise the massive operation, and the SE halted military conscription of young workers from the metallurgical factories so they could dismantle and load.[109] The SE focused on Zaporozh'e and Dnepropetrovsk, major centers of heavy industry that stood as western gateways to the Donbass, the heart of the coal industry. All along the right bank, in town after town, workers loaded thousands of boxcars with heavy machinery, metal, coke, and iron ore.[110] The transport of rolling mills, transformers, and generators, each weighing up to 150 tons, required special transporters and reinforced platforms. Since the railways had only a limited number of such transporters, workers began adapting normal platforms to bear the increased tonnage and using coal cars coupled to locomotives as transporters.[111] In mid-August, the SE ordered the iron and steel plants on the left bank to "advance to loading-ready production," a state of partial disassembly that enabled them to produce as they were dismantled.[112] Evacuation of the left bank proceeded so rapidly that the SE dispensed entirely with destinations, sending the boxcars east to the Volga River.[113]

In Zaporozhe, aviation factory No. 29 was the first to begin evacuation.[114] On August 17, only the day before the Germans reached the western outskirts of the city, the SE ordered the evacuation of its massive iron and steel plants, including Zaporozhstal' and Dneprospetsstal', from the left bank of the city.[115] As the Red Army retreated, it blew up the hydroelectric dam and the massive three-arch railway bridge spanning the Dnepr, causing a massive flood. In factory No. 29, workers, who were still packing and loading, fled. The director called a halt to loading and refused any further delivery of boxcars. The deputy commissar of railways was furious, noting that crucial machinery and metal still remained because the director was "a completely weak-willed person," who had "totally fallen apart." Two days later, the railroad workers stepped in to finish the job.[116] Over the next five days, amid flooding and bombing, they loaded and shipped most of the factory to Omsk.[117]

On August 23, the Germans launched an operation aimed at capturing Kiev and the provinces east of the Dnepr. If they could capture Stalino (now Donetsk) province, the coalmining center of the Donbass, they would secure a vast supply of energy. Pogrebnoi, an SE plenipotentiary in Kiev, remembered:

Conditions were exceptionally difficult. Kiev was under bombardment from morning until night. Evacuation was in a terrible hurry. However, the workers, despite such strain, showed unparalleled heroism and managed to ship out of Kiev all the main equipment and raw materials.[118]

As the battle for Kiev raged into September, the Red Army fiercely defended the left bank of Zaporozhe, as workers continued to load the metal factories. Workers streamed into Zaporozhe from all over the Donbass, mobilized by the Party, to help.[119] A. G. Sheremet'ev, Deputy Commissar of the Iron and Steel Industry, recalled:

The enemy saw that the equipment from Zaporozhe's factories was being shipped out, and they bombed and shelled the territory of the factories daily with artillery and mortar fire. Every day, people were wounded and killed. But people worked and they pushed on.[120]

Workers on the left bank exited the factories when they came under fire and then returned to continue the work.[121] By October 3, the Red Army was unable to hold the eastern part of the city any longer. Yet the loading was done. The workers joked that the only thing left for them to do was to sweep the empty machine shops.[122] They decided, however, to leave the janitorial work to the Germans. By the time the Wehrmacht took the left bank, the metallurgical plants had been saved.

Beyond the Dnepr: Evacuating the Coalmines

The Germans captured Dnepropetrovsk on August 25 and Konotop on September 3. The Red Army continued to hold a long western salient or strip of land with Kiev at its tip between Dnepropetrovsk in the south and Konotop in the north. The salient was threatened by a pincer attack, but Stalin refused to authorize a retreat. The failure to pull back resulted in a massive encirclement of about 655,000 soldiers, the largest number of POWs ever taken. Five Soviet field armies were virtually annihilated, and the southwestern front had to be recreated almost from scratch. Kiev was finally occupied on September 19. While Khrushchev later blamed the appalling losses on Stalin's intransigence, some military strategists claimed that the Red Army's stubborn defense of the Kiev salient forced Hitler to divert troops from the central front, enabling the Red Army to save Moscow and hold Zaporzh'e long enough to evacuate its iron and steel industry.[123] All agree, however, that the loss of Kiev was a terrible blow, allowing the Germans to advance to Stalino province and the Donbass coalfields. Mining equipment and raw materials could be evacuated but, in the event of occupation, the mines would have to be flooded, blocked with debris, or blown up.[124]

The SE first began a partial evacuation of Stalino province on August 26.[125] Dismantling the large power stations was a particularly delicate task. Once the electrical equipment was dismantled and the dam blown, the industrial base of the region went dead. Success hinged on an almost clairvoyant ability to predict movements at the front. Too early would cost the state much-needed defense production; too late would risk loss of the power stations to the enemy. The decision required nerves of steel. Most of the power stations, including those in Kiev, Odessa, and Stalino were dismantled in the very last days or even hours before the Red Army pulled out. In Dnepropetrovsk, local officials had only enough time to remove some turbine parts before they blew up the dam, while in Zaporozhe the dam was blown as the workers were still loading.[126]

As the military situation worsened, the Commissariat of Coal prepared to evacuate its equipment and demolish the mines.[127] On September 13, M. Gorshkov, Deputy Commissar of Coal, informed the SE that the commissariat had issued instructions to the directors of all its industrial combines and machine-building factories to prepare to dismantle the equipment and disable any machines that could not be rescued. Any equipment left behind was to be destroyed, buried, or thrown into the pits or mine shafts. The mines were to be flooded or blown up; machine shops and gas and electric power stations were to be burned down or blown up.[128] On September 25, V. V. Vakhrushev, Commissar of Coal, presented a plan to the SE for the evacuation of enterprises, mining equipment, and coal from Stalino province, including the Stalinugol' combine. All mining, with the exception of forty-seven mines producing coking and gas coal needed for the iron and steel factories, was to cease on October 1. The workers of Stalinugol' would be evacuated along with their families. The evacuated enterprises would be divided among sixteen already-existing mining operations in the east.[129] That same day, the SE ordered the disassembly of the electric power stations.[130] The evacuation of the Donbass was to be carried out from October 11 to 17, but the Wehrmacht was advancing rapidly, and the Commissariat of Railways could not deliver enough freight and passenger cars in time.[131] Late in the evening on October 6, a military officer wrote to explain that there were not enough boxcars to evacuate Stalino province. Workers were loading 500 boxcars per day on each of the southern and northern Donetsk rail lines, but at that rate it would take more than 100 days to evacuate the province.[132]

With the Germans fast approaching, the GKO approved the destruction of all remaining equipment on October 9. The SE immediately instructed all mine directors to flood the mines and blow up the main tunnels. All aboveground machines and structures, nonferrous metal, electrical supplies, water pipes and faucets, grease, oil, and ventilators were to be burned or destroyed. Party members, local officials, managers, and workers loaded everything they could, and the rest was destroyed by fire, cutting, or explosion and thrown onto mountains of mine rubble or into the pits, which were flooded and blocked. Petroleum products were either sent to the army, burned, or poured out.[133] On October 8, the Germans captured Mariupol' and reached the Sea of Azov, which promised access to the oilfields of the Caucasus. The following day, Otto Dietrich, Hitler's press chief, crowed to foreign journalists, "Soviet Russia has been vanquished!"[134]

After Mariupol' fell, the Wehrmacht advanced eastward along the northern shore of the Sea of Azov into Rostov province, which contained the major industrial centers of Taganrog and Rostov-on-Don, and the coalfields of the Russian Donbass. It was the gateway to Krasnodar Territory and, from there, the oilfields of the Caucasus. The Germans occupied Taganrog on October 17, but the hard-fought battle for Rostov raged from late September through mid-November. The Commissariat of Coal planned to evacuate Rostov province on October 11 but active mines, machine-building and enrichment factories, two power stations, and other enterprises, employing 40,000 people, still remained.[135] The German advance, slowed by heavy autumn rains, did not reach the outskirts of Rostov until mid-November.[136] The Germans occupied the city on November 21, but could not hold it. Only a week later, the Red Army, with the help of partisans and the people's militia (*opolchenie*), forced the Germans to withdraw. It was the first liberation of a major population center.[137]

By December, the evacuation of industry began to wind down. Pogrebnoi later noted,

> In these difficult circumstances, there were mistakes and blunders. They occurred primarily because we did not have experience of this type of work under wartime conditions. For example, in the beginning, we evacuated industry from one part of Ukraine to another .... We were so late in evacuating the machine-building factory Krasnaia Zvezda from Kirovograd, and a series of metal factories from Donetsk [Stalino] province that there were large losses.[138]

Yet the SE managed to save the most important enterprises of heavy industry and defense.[139] Metallurgical and chemical plants, food-processing factories, light industry and textiles, power stations, mining equipment, and thousands of tons of coal, raw materials, and finished and specialty steel were headed east. The Nazis, expecting to capitalize on the region's substantial industrial base, found instead a landscape of flooded mines, blown bridges, and twisted metal.

People: Evacuation by Category

The SE did not target people for evacuation as individuals, but rather as members of occupational and social groups. Individuals were not supposed to "evacuate" themselves, but they were also not supposed to remain in occupied territory. In the absence of a place on a train, many fled on their own, with friends, or in family groups. Yet the state made a distinction between "evacuees," who left in organized convoys, and "refugees," who escaped independently. The state provided resettlement, employment, and ration cards at the destination site for evacuees. Refugees, however, needed to find employment and housing before they could be added to the ration rolls.[140] *Evakopunkty*, established to aid both groups, were quickly overwhelmed by the number of people in need of help. Amid the chaos and massive numbers of people in motion, the distinction between the two groups broke down.

In the immediate wake of the invasion, the SE first targeted children in threatened areas. It followed with a broader order in the first week covering all people in frontline zones; families of party leaders, soviet officials, and military officers; and workers and white-collar employees in industrial enterprises together with their families.[141] But the front moved so fast that this order proved impossible to fulfill, and many people either chose to stay or were stranded in the frontline zones. Children were often sent to nearby areas that were soon engulfed by fighting.[142] The SE then began targeting groups with greater specificity: workers and employees in particular factories, institutions, and organizations; trade-school apprentices; psychiatric patients; and orphans. It never explicitly targeted the elderly, peasants (other than those who accompanied evacuated herds), or workers in small rural workplaces except as part of the larger category of people living in frontline zones. Elderly people were most often evacuated as family members of designated occupational groups. The order to evacuate was mandatory for employees of targeted workplaces or institutions, but their family members, who also received train tickets, could choose to stay behind.

Most tragically in retrospect, the SE did not evacuate people by nationality. Neither the Soviet leadership nor the population had foreseen the Nazis' genocidal intentions toward the Jews and Roma, and information from the occupied areas was initially patchy and incomplete.[143] Party leaders of Belorussia and Ukraine sent reports to Moscow in August 1941 about massacres of the Jewish population, and the partisan movement reported waves of killing in the summer and fall of 1942.[144] Yet the early reports dealt with local incidents, and by 1942 rescue from occupied territories was no longer possible. The full extent of the Holocaust did not become clear until the Red Army began retaking those areas in 1943. Novelist and war correspondent Vasily Grossman left his family in Berdichev, a small town in Ukraine with a large Jewish population. About one-third of Berdichev's Jewish population, including refugees from Poland, managed to evacuate or escape, but those who remained behind were murdered in successive massacres between August 1941 and June 1942. After Berdichev was liberated in January 1944, Grossman visited the town and learned that his mother had perished in a mass killing on September 15, 1941. After the war, he wrote her a posthumous letter:

> Dear Mama,
>   One night at the front I had a dream. I entered your room. I knew for sure it was your room, and I saw an empty armchair, and I knew you had slept in it. A shawl with which you'd covered your legs was hanging down from the armchair. I looked at it for a long time, and when I woke up, I knew that you weren't any longer among the living. But I didn't know then what a terrible death you had suffered.[145]

Grossman was not the only person haunted by terrible premonitions. Many Soviet citizens drafted into the army, evacuated with their factories, or separated from their families lived with horrible uncertainty about the fate of relatives and loved ones. Of the six million Jews killed by the Nazis, almost two million were killed on Soviet soil. The Einsatzgruppen covered the occupied territories with shooting pits, holding anywhere from a few hundred to tens of thousands of people. In Belorussia alone, they incinerated more than 600 villages along with their inhabitants who were accused of aiding the partisans.[146]

The first evacuations of people took place in the Baltic republics, western Ukraine and Belorussia, and Karelia amid bombing and battles that often blocked the roads and rail lines. Organized evacuation was very limited, and people were sent out by the military soviets rather than the SE. In Lithuania, for example, the government succeeded in evacuating only 42,500 people; most of the Jewish population was later herded into ghettos by the Germans and eventually murdered. In Belorussia, where the enemy advance was slower, more than one million people were rescued, roughly one in six of the population. Later, mass evacuations from Moscow, Leningrad, Ukraine, and western Russia were more successful. Most groups were sent either to provinces along the Volga River or further east to the Urals, Siberia, and Central

Asia where they went to work in factories, on the railroads, in canteens, and on collective and state farms.[147]

In addition to the frontline zones, the SE targeted people in Moscow and Leningrad for immediate attention. Employees of governing bodies and the diplomatic corps were evacuated to Kuibyshev, as were those employed by Moscow's leading cultural institutions, including the Bol'shoi Theater. The SE sent away thousands of employees of the industrial commissariats toward the end of June, along with scientists, scholars, doctors, and cultural figures, who left with their workplaces.[148] In July, the Academy of Sciences, headquartered in Moscow, was evacuated, followed by the Commissariats of Defense and the Navy, Moscow's scientific and medical institutes, Leningrad's Geophysics and Hydrology Institute, the Soviet information bureau TASS, the theaters, and other organizations.[149] In a practice known as "packing together the population," evacuees were billeted with local inhabitants. A result of the severe housing shortage, the practice often proved difficult for both guests and hosts.[150] Although evacuees from Moscow and Leningrad retained their privileged ration status, at least one ornery academician refused an order to evacuate with the Academy of Sciences, declaring, "It is better to perish from a German bomb than to go to a slow death in Kazan."[151]

Within the first three weeks after the invasion, almost 1.8 million people were evacuated from Moscow, Leningrad, and the frontline zones. Of the 900,000 evacuated from Moscow and the 341,000 from Leningrad by mid-July, more than 80 percent were children.[152] Leningrad's factories were still churning out armaments, so children of factory workers were frequently sent out in separate groups to be joined later by their parents.[153] Other vulnerable populations in the two cities were also targeted, including around 2,000 patients and staff from Leningrad's psychiatric hospitals. And as a precautionary measure, on August 12, the predatory beasts were evacuated from the Moscow zoo.[154]

Evacuation everywhere was fraught with danger and risk of death. In Shostka, a town in Sumy province in northeastern Ukraine, evacuation occurred barely one week before the Germans occupied the town on August 27. People thronged the railroad station but, as the last trains moved out, the Germans bombed the rail lines. Hundreds of people were killed or wounded, the survivors running from the wreckage and scattering in every direction. Some fled to nearby villages; others continued east on foot. The station, too, was bombed. A group of workers and their families, waiting in an alley next to an ammunition warehouse, ran screaming in terror after the Germans bombed the warehouse and triggered massive explosions. Local leaders and railway officials finally managed to quell the panic and board the group.[155]

By the end of December, the German offensive slowed in the south and halted on the northern and central fronts. Most of the key enterprises, along with millions of people, had been evacuated. Requests from the commissariats to the SE for boxcars dwindled to single digits. The SE made special efforts to rescue the starving from Leningrad in emergency convoys. In mid-December, 10,000 textile workers were transported out of the dark, frozen city in horse-drawn carts across the ice on Lake Ladoga and transferred by rail to Babaevo, a town about 150 miles (240 km) to the southeast. The SE telegrammed its plenipotentiary at the Babaevo station: "Immediately inform how many and where (and to which factory) workers and apprentices of the factory schools are being sent. STOP. Further, provide such information every ten days. STOP. Send textile workers to Ivanovo province. STOP."[156] The telegram, in its brief bursts, captured months of experience. In Ivanovo, the workers would be nursed back to health; most would recover to join the war effort. As a result of evacuation and labor mobilization, the wartime labor force would grow significantly in the Urals, the Volga region, Western Siberia, Kazakhstan, and Central Asia, the evacuated workers as critical to the war effort as the machinery they rescued.[157]

Evacuees and refugees were joined in the east by social and national groups suspected by the state of potential collaboration and deported en masse. The mass and national operations of 1937–1938 had targeted some of these same groups for imprisonment or execution. Many Communists had fled repression in their own countries only to be executed in the USSR as "spies." Beginning in 1939, the government promulgated a new wave of arrests against "unreliable elements" from the newly incorporated territories of eastern Poland (renamed Western Ukraine) and the Baltic republics. Some 383,000 people of multiple nationalities from these territories were sent to "special settlements" in the USSR, a form of exile earlier applied to kulaks and others who resisted collectivization in the early 1930s.[158] When the Soviets established diplomatic relations with the Polish government-in-exile in London, the Poles who had been arrested earlier were amnestied and designated as "Polish subjects."

After the German invasion, a new spate of "prophylactic cleansing" began in the rear. Following the October revolution, the Soviet state had created a Volga-German autonomous republic composed mainly of peasants with ethnic German heritage rooted in the area since the eighteenth century.

Fearing that these ethnic German Soviet citizens might collaborate, Soviet leaders issued a cascade of orders between August and October deporting some 800,000 of them to Kazakhstan and Siberia, where they were reclassified as "special settlers." At the end of November 1941, the NKVD did a mass check of Moscow's population and uncovered about 7,400 "anti-Soviet and socially dangerous elements," informing the SE that these people "must be immediately evacuated to clean the town." The majority were people living in the city without jobs or residence permits, including many refugees who had settled in evacuation centers because they had nowhere else to go. In December, the SE ordered these refugees, criminals, vagrants, and others lacking residence permits to the Mordovian autonomous republic and Gor'kii province to be resettled and employed.[159] Unlike the mass sweeps of the cities in 1937–1938, which resulted in imprisonment or execution, those groups deported from Moscow in 1941 were sent to work, like millions of other evacuees and refugees. The category of "vagrant," used by the state in the early 1930s to control population movement into the towns, and in 1937–1938 during the mass operations, lost all meaning amid the crowds of homeless people in transit.

Moscow: Evacuation in Twenty-Four Hours

The Germans launched Operation Typhoon, a strategic offensive aimed at capturing Moscow in early October. The Soviet command had constructed elaborate ringed defenses around the city, but as the Germans advanced the GKO made the decision on October 10 to evacuate metal and defense factories, and party activists held meetings to prepare the workers. Moscow was placed under martial law.[160] Less than one week later, as the military situation continued to worsen, Soviet leaders made an emergency decision to evacuate the population, factories, and state, cultural, and social organizations within the next twenty-four hours. On the afternoon of October 16, Dubrovin and G. V. Kovalev, Deputy Commissars of Railways, were summoned to the Kremlin. As they entered the great hall, Dubrovin noticed that it was filled with the heads of commissariats, institutions, and departments. Everyone sat silently, contemplating the very real possibility that Moscow could fall to the Germans. The country's wartime leaders, Stalin, Voznesenskii, Shvernik, Kosygin, Mikoian, and Kliment Voroshilov, quietly exited a side door, leaving Viacheslav Molotov to address the group. Molotov spoke frankly, and his instructions were brief.

The military situation was dire: the enemy had reached the outskirts of the capital. The assembled leaders would be directing the evacuations of their organizations, which would begin immediately and proceed through the night. They were to destroy their records. Every commissariat would leave one deputy commissar and a small operational staff behind to maintain contact with the evacuated enterprises.[161] Dubrovin remembered, "It was declared that Moscow would not fall to the enemy but, in order to avoid victims, the majority of the population had to be evacuated." Over the next half-hour, Kosygin met individually with each leader to work out the time and place of embarkation and destination for their enterprise, organization, or institution. A schedule was set for the trains. In Dubrovin's words, "Everyone and everything was to be shipped out of Moscow by 9:00 a.m. on October 17."[162]

After Molotov finished speaking, Dubrovin and Kovalev went to meet with Stalin. His question was brief and pointed: Could the railway workers send the necessary number of trains out of Moscow that night? After a short consultation, they replied that they could provide 100 trains. The difficulty, as Dubrovin later recalled, was that they would need 5,000 to 6,000 boxcars. When the meeting was over, Kovalev immediately rushed to the commissariat to mobilize all reserves in the depot, organize the formation of convoys, and set the order of dispatch out of the city. Dubrovin went to see Kosygin about the plan of evacuation. By the time Dubrovin left the Kremlin at 4:00 that afternoon, the streets were packed with people streaming toward the railway stations:

> Kirov Street and Dzerzhinskii Square and all the large and small streets surrounding them were thronged with people. Women with small babies in their arms, older children and elderly people with baby carriages, suitcases, and baskets moved in long streams toward Kalanchevskaia Square to the trains, not knowing where they would be sent. But there was no crying. Their faces were harsh and stern.[163]

Workers lined up to receive their last wages. Elena V. Bersenevich, a cashier in the Frunze spinning and weaving factory, remembered October 16 as "the worst day of my life":

> Arriving at the factory I learned that the factory was closing, and all the workers were to be paid off. Everyone was troubled, upset, saying the enemy was very near, that tonight they probably would blow up the factory.

Along the street, refugees from Moscow's suburbs were dragging carts loaded with their belongings. Many were rushing to leave Moscow. The chief cashier, Il'ia Sergeevich Kuznetsov, handed me a huge sum of money for the workers' wages (he himself went to the labor front, where the women from the factory were digging anti-tank ditches).

I'll never forget that day and night. A crowd of people stood around the glass partition of the cashier's window, pressing on it with such force that the walls shook. They rushed me, shouted at me, begged me to hurry and give them their money, but my trembling fingers, not used to this kind of work, refused to obey. Only with a great effort of will did I compel myself to concentrate on what I was doing, and not to think about the imminent danger. I kept repeating to myself, "It can't be. It can't be. Don't allow the enemy into Moscow!," but the growing agitation of the crowd was contagious and unbidden teardrops rolled down my cheeks. I didn't wipe them away, and they fell onto the packets of money . . . .

Late in the evening I returned home. Every now and then there would be the blaze of incendiary bombs, shells would explode with a huge bang, and along the way I'd come across groups of armed people. Our capital was in a state of alarm but just as beautiful as ever. I never loved her as strongly as I did that night, when she was threatened by a terrible danger.[164]

Figure 1.3 Women digging anti-tank ditches, 1941. Courtesy of RGAKFD.

Despite the plan to evacuate in orderly convoys organized by workplace or institutions, the railroad stations were packed with crowds of people desperate to escape. Mary Leder, the American-born spouse of a Soviet officer, remembered the scramble:

> October 15, 1941. No one who lived in or near Moscow will ever forget that day. Panic gripped the city. All over Moscow, in government offices, research institutes and factories, staff members were burning papers to keep them from falling into German hands. The great evacuation of Moscow had begun, both organized and unorganized. The organized evacuees departed by train. The unorganized took what they could carry and walked or hitched rides whenever and by whatever means they could. For days, a stream of Muscovites moved eastward along Highway of Enthusiasts, one of Moscow's main roads. But unaware of the situation, that morning I set out for the station.... Tickets were useless. The trains had been commandeered by various organizations for their employees and their families. It was a madhouse.[165]

The railway workers at the Moscow junction commandeered every conveyance remotely resembling a train car, including suburban train cars, trams, and even subway cars, which they repurposed for the railroads. Every railway car that arrived in Moscow was immediately emptied and reloaded. Soldiers, rushed to the front from Siberia, no sooner stepped off the trains than the civilian population crowded in. The first convoys pulled out at 6:20 in the evening. By 10:00 the next morning, 100 trains had been loaded. Dubrovin remembered proudly, "In one night, we shipped about 150,000 people out of Moscow." The Germans had bombed the Moscow stations earlier and would continue to do so, but that night not a single bomb fell on the Kazan' railway station and the Northern river boat station, the two embarkation points. According to Dubrovin, "The enemy never knew about the evacuation."[166]

In the following weeks, convoys continued to leave Moscow. Although the Germans shelled and bombed the rail lines, an average of eighty trains filled with people, goods, and machinery rumbled out each day. In late October, G. I. Zeziulev, a worker at the Stalin motor vehicle factory (zavod imeni Stalina or ZiS), received the order to evacuate with his factory to Ul'ianovsk with four hours' notice. He described the landscape as his train departed Moscow:

> Convoy after convoy moved slowly as far as the eye could see, stopping for a long time, and then suddenly moving again. Red lightning lit the horizon of the front, and at times we could hear a resounding rumble, like distant thunder. We passed deserted stations with no trains, passengers, or service personnel, only one or two railway workers with weary, uneasy faces. We were filled with anxiety during this time, constantly fearing enemy planes flying over the endless convoys, crowded with people, healthy and sick, young and old.[167]

Although Stalin announced that the government would not abandon the city, residents were terrified by what appeared to be imminent occupation. The mass flight was later jokingly referred to as the "*bol'shoi drap*" or "great skedaddle." The state subsequently awarded a medal, "For the Defense of Moscow," hung on a traditional ribbon. Cynics punned that some of the medals should have been suspended instead on a *drap*, a word that meant both a piece of cloth and "skedaddle."[168] Although tens of thousands of people either evacuated or fled, many chose to stay, some refusing direct orders to leave with their workplace, others joining the armed mobilization to defend the city.

On November 30, the temperature dropped to –49°F (–45°C). Wehrmacht soldiers were completely unprepared for the dangerous cold. Hitler, confidently expecting to take Moscow in October, had refused to order winter gear for the troops, and hundreds of thousands suffered from frostbite. Vehicles stalled, grease on the shells froze solid, the Luftwaffe was paralyzed. On December 5, the Red Army launched a counteroffensive, retaking Kalinin (Tver'), Klin, and several other towns to the north of Moscow, and Naro-Fominsk, Kaluga, and Maloiaroslavets to the southwest. Soviet leaders ended evacuation in December, confident that Moscow and its surrounding provinces were no longer in danger. In total, almost 500 enterprises and more than 1.5 million railway cars in 30,000 trains had been evacuated.[169] The Red Army's offensive halted on January 7, 1942, after pushing the freezing German army back between 60 and 155 miles (100–250 km) along a wide front around Moscow. It was the Wehrmacht's first major defeat since the war began, the first sign that the Nazis were not invincible.

"They Are Leaving Us Here without Bread!"

The SE's unparalleled feat would have been impossible without the support of workers. At the same time that officials and workers were evacuating Moscow, factory directors and party officials in Ivanovo, a textile region northeast of Moscow with a long revolutionary history, sparked riots and wildcat strikes when they tried to evacuate machinery without consulting the workers. The standoff began in mid-October when the Germans approached Ivanovo province as part of the campaign to capture Moscow. The town, situated in a frontline zone, was fortified with multiple lines of defense, including pillboxes, bunkers, anti-tank ditches, crossed iron bars (known as "hedgehogs"), and towering mounds of tree trunks and forest debris. Reminders of the front were everywhere. Thousands of wounded soldiers were brought straight from the battlefield to Ivanovo's railroad station, and schools, hotels, and buildings were converted to military hospitals. Women and teenagers were mobilized to build bomb shelters, dig earthen dugouts, and construct defense installations. One eyewitness recorded:

My first impression was painful. The war had left a heavy mark on the city and its people. On the platform, they were unloading a convoy with the wounded. The railroad station was packed with thin, worn-out women with small children in their arms, sitting amid bundles and suitcases. Forcing their way through the crowds, people carried stretchers with evacuees from Leningrad who were half dead from hunger. The city also seemed abject and immiserated. Overcrowded tram cars, with people hanging onto the steps, ran occasionally through the darkened streets, and long lines stood at the bread shops.[170]

When the Germans reached the border of the province, the Commissariat of the Textile Industry told Chastukin, the director of the mélange yarn combine, that evacuation was imminent. Chastukin promptly called a meeting of the combine's managers, department heads, and party committee members to develop a plan. But the group, fearful of sparking panic, signed a pledge not to divulge it. On October 16, Chastukin got the order to dismantle and pack the machines. On October 17, a day of rest for the workers, the group entered the factories and, working in secrecy, began to dismantle the machines. When the first shift arrived the next morning, they saw their machines lying in pieces and crates in the halls. In the weaving factory, the workers began yelling, "They've taken away the equipment and left us without work." Within fifteen minutes, the director and the head of the party committee hurried over to explain: workers would be evacuated with the machines, no one would be left behind, and everyone would be paid while in transit. But the workers were not convinced. People began shouting, "All the leaders are fleeing town, and we'll be left here alone." "Our leaders together with Chastukin have sent out their families, but no one sends us. They want us to stay here without work." The gathering grew increasingly raucous, furious that the decision had been made without them. As the group broke up, they called to one another, "Don't let them dismantle and ship out the equipment." Meanwhile, a few officials had already sent their families out of town, while others were hurriedly distributing consumer goods to the town's residents, which seemed to confirm the rumor that occupation was imminent.[171]

In the early afternoon, local party leaders tried to quell the rising panic by calling a meeting to explain the pending evacuation. People appeared to accept the situation. They asked questions about wages and the evacuation of children and family members. But the group was still fearful. One woman called out, "All the same, we're not letting them dismantle the machines!" Even a party member declared, "If you care so much for the machines, you first must ship out the families." As the meeting ended, a small group ran to the finishing factory and began to break open the crates with axes and hammers. When the head of the party committee and the deputy director hurried over, the workers scattered, but three weavers then ran to the winding factory and began to break up the crates there. In some shops, workers calmly continued production. In others, they came to blows as some tried to break up the crates and others tried to stop them.[172]

The next morning, the disturbances spread. Groups of workers went from one factory to another, calling to their coworkers to stop dismantling the machines. Managers, foremen, and even Chastukin were unable to stop them. Furious at their actions, Chastukin only escalated tensions when he referred to the earlier scorched earth decrees. He shouted, "If you don't let us ship out the equipment, we'll blow up the plant anyway. The enemy will not get the machines." A few workers then ran from shop to shop, yelling, "They're going to blow up the plant together with the workers, the mines are laid, Chastukin ordered it." Rumors swept the factories: "They're leaving us here without bread. They're shipping the bread out from Ivanovo through the sorting yard." "The bank has already left Ivanovo, and they won't issue any more money." Hearing this news, many panicked and left the factory. Women marched into the office of the head of the spinning factory and demanded that he immediately calculate their wages. Terrified, he ran and hid under a tarpaulin. The shop heads scattered, and the head of the weaving shop ran home after the workers threatened to kill him.[173]

As pandemonium spread, the provincial party leaders called a meeting with more than 1,000 weavers, the head of the local NKVD, and the leaders of the town and district party committees on the factory grounds. Wild rumors swept the crowd: Hitler was within 3 miles (5 km) of Ivanovo, the workers would lose the machines, bread rations would be reduced to only 100 grams. People yelled, "We built this combine and we're not going to let anyone destroy it or ship it out." When Pal'tsev, the head of Ivanovo's provincial party committee, mounted the podium, he attempted to mollify the workers. He promised to stop dismantling the machines and to reassemble those in crates. People clapped and cheered. Many had just begun to return to work, when new cries rang out. "You want to blow us up!" "Where did you send the bread?" "Where did you send the bank?" Chastukin stepped up, but his appearance only provoked a new wave of anger: "Let Chastukin tell us where he laid the mines," people yelled. "Look, here's the man who wants to blow us up. Beat him!" Some of the weavers tried to pull him down, and in the melee the podium was overturned, and a small group grabbed him. Most of the crowd rushed out through the factory gates and into the street. For about two hours, they milled around. At the same time, party activists began circulating through the crowd, speaking calmly. Slowly, the crowd broke up. Some workers left to go home. One party activist led 300 workers to the railroad station to see if the town's bread supply was actually being shipped off. Persuaded that the rumor was untrue, they turned back toward the factory. By the next day, the disturbance was over.[174]

From October 17 to 19, similar demonstrations, short strikes, and disturbances occurred throughout the province, although all petered out quickly.[175] Pal'tsev later wrote a long report to the Central Committee about the disturbances. He blamed newly hired workers, "agents of German fascism," "spies," and "panic-mongers, provocateurs, and screamers." A small number, mainly women, were arrested for acting as "direct agents of German fascism and enemy individuals." Several either had arrest records, had been fired from other workplaces, or had relatives who had previously been arrested. At least one did not work in the factory. Yet whether these people were actually the most active agitators or were chosen as scapegoats because of their backgrounds is unclear. The charges against them, for which there was little to no evidence, echoed those of the mass repressions of the late 1930s.[176] Yet as Pal'tsev himself pointed out, managers and party officials also bore a large share of the blame. They had mishandled the situation by imposing "naked administrative power." A woman worker later noted, "If they had explained all this earlier, this disorder never would have happened." Many workers expressed embarrassment, noting, "We did not expect this, and we did not want this." The vast majority who participated were not punished. That the disturbances were easily quelled suggests that managers could have avoided the trouble had they bothered to enlist the support of the workers. Local leaders, however, paid a high price. Chastukin was censured by the Party and removed from his job for "provocative declarations about the explosion of the factory" and "separation from the workers." The heads of the party committees in the combine and the town, and other local officials, were removed as well.[177] Ivanovo was never occupied by the Germans. The town remained critical to the war effort in terms of textile production and care for the wounded, and provided a safe haven for refugees and evacuees, including the starving inhabitants of Leningrad.

Railway Cars: The Insurmountable Obstacle

The single greatest constraint that the SE faced was the limited availability of boxcars. In addition to the regular transport required by an integrated industrial economy, trains were also needed to transport soldiers, armaments, and food to the front. The records of the SE reveal that the shortage of railway cars quickly became the main obstacle to evacuation. Mediating among the demands of thousands of organizations and enterprises, the SE tried to hold the Commissariat of Railways to a strict plan that would enable enterprises to fulfill their loading targets. Between July and December 1941, the SE ordered and recorded the shipment of no fewer than 1.5 million cars linked together in 30,000 trains loaded with evacuated machinery, food, and people.[178] Yet its data also revealed a considerable gap between the number of cars the SE allocated to almost every enterprise and the number they actually received, loaded, and sent.

The initial plan for evacuation of an enterprise was based on its director's estimate for the number of boxcars needed for its people and equipment. The director then sent this information to its respective commissariat, which transmitted it to the SE, which, in turn, sent it to the Commissariat of Railways. In the 1930s, directors had learned to inflate their requests for all inputs in the hope of receiving the amount they actually required. This strategy—commonly practiced by officials at every level—was built into a planning process that operated under conditions of scarcity. The vast gap between the requests for railway cars and the allocations by the Commissariat of Railways, however, suggests that the shortfall was no mere element of the planning "game." Indeed, the gap was so great that much equipment, already dismantled and packed, never made it onto the railroads. A significant number of enterprises did not get even half of the railway cars they required. Aviation and ammunition factories, both given high priority for evacuation, showed the biggest gap between what they requested and received: sometimes less than 20 percent of their requested number arrived.[179] Armaments factory No. 232 in Leningrad, for example, required 2,950 boxcars for its machinery; only 503 were actually loaded and shipped.[180] This gap between demand and supply made full evacuation of the targeted enterprises impossible.[181]

During the intense rush to evacuate Ukraine, the Commissariat of Railways could not deliver enough boxcars in time. In Poltava, a city to the northwest of Dnepropetrovsk, tons of food and machinery were ready to be loaded, but the freight was lost to the Germans despite desperate telegrams from local party officials to the SE.[182] Local officials and managers everywhere faced the same difficulties.[183] By late September, officials all along the southern and western fronts were anxiously clamoring for railway cars.[184] Massive crowds of people and mountains of goods were piled up at stations all along the Orel–Kursk line.[185] The head of the provincial soviet in Kursk sent a beseeching telegram to the SE on October 8 that the decision to evacuate an orphanage and vocational schools had left crowds of children and young teenagers at railway stations while the Germans were bombing the stations. The telegram read: "Among the crowds of children there are victims. STOP. I ask for your immediate involvement in providing railway cars to Belgorod Station."[186]

River transport was also under intense strain. Every barge, ship, and boat that could float was pressed into service. In late August, the SE instructed the Commissariat of the River Fleet to evacuate more than 17,000 people and the textile factories from Kalinin, a major hub on the Volga River, 100 miles (160 km) northwest of Moscow. The Commissariat of the River Fleet, however, was short of boats, the water level was too low to accommodate large ships, and the sluices would not permit heavy loads.[187] When the Germans reached the outskirts of the town in mid-October, the people and factories were only partially evacuated. More than 20,000 soldiers and thousands of civilians perished in the battle for Kalinin, and the Red Army was forced to withdraw. The Germans occupied the town until December 16, when the Red Army retook it in the offensive to defend Moscow. Yet most of the textile industry was destroyed. The impact of this loss and others reverberated throughout the war in the lack of clothing, warm outerwear, and bedding in hospitals, orphanages, and dormitories.

Pogrebnoi later revealed that his coworkers on the SE grumbled constantly about the organizational failures of the Commissariat of Railways. Yet he admitted that the commissariat faced an objective and irremediable obstacle: the shortage of rolling stock. "It must be said," he explained, "that the railroad workers worked under exceptionally difficult conditions and the position of transport was very strained."[188] In August, the need for railway cars in the frontline zones was so urgent that the SE temporarily unloaded boxcars before they arrived at their destinations and sent the emptied cars immediately back to the front lines.[189] Temporary unloading was not without its costs: it delayed reassembly and production, increased the risk of loss, and left thousands of people stranded.[190] At times, the economic branch of the NKVD applied pressure to force the Commissariat of Railways to meet specific needs.[191] Yet the number of freight cars was not elastic, and sending cars to one sector reduced those available to another.[192] The Commissariat did not have enough rolling stock to cover a 1,000-mile (1,600-km) front in retreat. Two weeks after the "great skedaddle" in Moscow, the head of the city NKVD listed millions of cartridge shells, mines, missiles, and thousands of tons of bullets, lead, machine diamonds, and various types of steel rusting outside the station and still waiting to be loaded.[193]

By December, the frantic urgency of the previous months subsided. Loading slowed considerably, and the number of convoys en route fell: in July, there were 300,000 railway cars filled with evacuated loads and people traveling along the rail lines, and in December only 71,000. The two greatest peaks for rail traffic and evacuation were July and October. After October, the numbers dropped by more than half. The main work was done.[194] On December 25, the GKO dissolved the SE and transferred its organizational apparatus to a new Committee for Unloading Goods in Transit (Komitet po razgruzke tranzitnykh gruzov), which functioned for another four months. Its responsibilities were reduced to a cleanup operation: to clear the warehouses and sort and process undocumented loads.

The Second Rescue

In spring 1942, the front lines around Moscow stabilized, and the Germans began a great push through the Caucasus with the aim of conquering Stalingrad, gaining control of the Volga River, and cutting off northern Russia from its oil supply in the south. The offensive prompted a second, smaller evacuation of the threatened territory between May and October 1942. A new Commission for Evacuation, similar to the SE, was formed with much of the previous leadership, including Shvernik, Mikoian, and Kosygin.[195] In July, the Germans reached the Volga River, prompting a mass evacuation of the western districts of Stalingrad province. There were no bridges and the bank was crowded with thousands of people, more than one million head of livestock, and towering piles of machinery waiting to cross the river. On July 13, the Stalingrad defense committee and provincial party committee organized the construction of twenty-three crossings, and small river craft ferried people, animals, and tons of machinery across under heavy and repeated German bombing.[196]

Later that summer, Dubrovin was appointed as a GKO plenipotentiary to direct evacuation from the North Caucasus. Fighting and occupation had blocked the rail lines through Rostov province and Krasnodar Territory to the north, and thousands of people and tons of machinery were rerouted through the ports of Makhachkala, Baku, and Krasnovodsk. The Commission for Evacuation needed to move great cisterns filled with oil and petroleum products from Groznyi and Baku to factories in the Middle Volga region, the Urals, and Siberia, but the route through Stalingrad had already been severed in fierce fighting. The railroad workers once again invented a bold, new method: after testing to see if the cisterns would float, they capped them, linked them together like train cars, and, using a tugboat, pulled them through the Caspian Sea from Makhachkala to Krasnovodsk.[197] They also worked out a method to rescue grain from Kuban, the area between the Don steppe and the Caucasus, when they lacked sufficient covered rail cars. Party activists on the North Caucasus line mobilized every possible means of transport, and railway workers loaded grain into cisterns, locomotive tenders, and coal cars. No train rolled without grain. Many of these inventive containers puzzled the workers at the other end of the line. When Dubrovin was dispatched several months later to investigate slow unloading on the Kuibyshev line, he discovered that evacuated grain had been lying in huge cisterns by the grain elevator for two months, since the workers could not figure out how to empty them into the elevator. After Dubrovin ordered the grain unloaded immediately, workers climbed down into the cisterns, shoveled the grain into small pails, and climbed back out. Each cistern took between two and three days to unload, but the task was done. By the beginning of November 1942, workers successfully evacuated about 30,000 railway cars packed with people, industrial and agricultural equipment, and grain from Rostov province and Krasnodar, Stavropol', and Ordzhonikidze Territories, along with about one million head of livestock. Grain that could not be shipped was doused with kerosene and burned. In one town, Dubrovin and Deputy Commissar of Agriculture V. A. Ershov supervised the explosion of the grain elevator, fleeing the great fire just as the Germans marched in.[198]

****

Within the first few months of the invasion, the SE had developed a clear and efficient model for evacuation. Yet, as Pogrebnoi later wrote, "It is hard to remember without agitation those painful days filled with anxiety and worry."[199] The scorched earth decrees and the retreat of the Red Army created panic in the frontline zones, forcing local officials to make hard decisions in the absence of reliable information. At the same time, the SE provided a collective alternative to panic, successfully mobilizing state and party officials, managers, and workers to rescue millions of people and the industrial and agricultural bases. By the end of 1942, the SE had mastered an assignment it had not anticipated. As the disturbances in Ivanovo showed, the cooperation of workers was essential. Factory and railway workers worked around the clock without rest under intense pressure and often under fire. No such feat had ever been accomplished before, nor has one been repeated on such a scale since.

Initially, the SE acted in response to the military threat of aerial bombardment and occupation. Yet it quickly began to act preemptively and to plan evacuation in advance. Economic and industrial officials, local soviet and party activists, and workers drew heavily on the experience of planned industrialization that transformed the country in the 1930s. However much industry was beset by shortages and poor-quality output, the experience in planning proved invaluable on the railways and in reconfiguration of the industrial base in the east. Military historian John Erickson considered this transfer "little short of a second industrial revolution."[200]

The rescue of industry was arguably the single most significant factor in the Soviet victory. Yet children and food were also among the SE's most important targets. Children constituted the overwhelming majority of the more than one million people evacuated from Moscow and Leningrad in July. By December 1942, more than 1.8 million children had been evacuated to safer provinces in Russia, Kazakhstan, Uzbekistan, and other republics.[201] In midsummer, grain and foodstuffs took priority over every load, even those of the defense factories. The SE recognized that, without food to keep civilians on the home front alive, the war could not be won. Not until early October, when the great industrial centers of Ukraine were threatened by the German advance, did the SE shift to prioritize rescue of the metallurgical and mining combines over food.

Evacuation, occurring in tandem with a retreating front, represented a peculiar dialectic of victory. Every rescue, a response to military defeat and retreat, helped build the new base for defense production in the east, which, in turn, provided the Red Army with the equipment it needed to regain the territory it had lost. In February 1942, a party instructor in Cheliabinsk province, a growing industrial center, proudly reported that, despite output lost during evacuation, "Many of the dismantled and reconstructed factories managed to fulfill the 1941 plan." Workers, he noted, were selflessly carrying out double and triple shifts.[202] Evacuation was a contradictory mix of planning and improvisation, of timely shipments and frantic, last-minute loading. The process, built on centralized command, complex coordination, and the courage and initiative of workers and local activists, was hardly perfect, but it worked.

2

Rolling East and Resettlement

One factory took over the shops of another in its new place. Two huge enterprises with complicated, many-faceted economies! And yet there was neither chaos nor disorder. Around the clock, day and night, the reconstruction of the factory continued. All night long, fires blazed throughout the area. People forgot about sleep, rest, and food, working twelve to fourteen hours a day in succession, and sometimes not returning home for twenty-four hours. The equipment was still being placed on its foundation when workers and engineers, under an open sky, in terrible frost, began assembling the components of the first tanks from the Urals.

E. O. Paton, eyewitness of the reconstruction of a tank
factory evacuated from Ukraine to the Urals

Soon after the German invasion in June 1941, thirteen-year-old Frieda Val'dman and her mother began the long road into evacuation from their home in Kiev. After a prolonged and perilous journey to Makhachkala in the North Caucasus, they traveled by boat to Astrakhan' in southern Russia, and then by train to Central Asia. By then it was winter, they had been on the road for many months, and they were cold and hungry. Val'dman recalled:

They put us on a train going to Central Asia. It was a long trip. We hardly had any clothes that could be bartered for food. Sonia, the wife of my mother's brother Iosif, was with us. She had a baby girl named Fiera, after my mother's sister who had died. Sonia didn't have any milk. We were starving. At one point, when the train stopped my brother ran to the fields to get some snow and melted it on our little stove. We gave this drink to the baby, but Firochka, the baby, died. Sonia held her, afraid that somebody would take her baby away. Our neighbor who was traveling with us asked her "Why is Fiera so silent? Why isn't she crying?" and Sonia said "I don't know. She may be asleep." The neighbor looked at the baby— Dear Lord! She was dead! And she began to cry saying that Fiera had died.

Soldiers came immediately and said they had to take the dead baby to a special car of the train—many people were dying on the train, and their bodies were taken to a special car. It took my brother some effort to take the dead girl from Sonia. He took her to that car. At one point, the train stopped and all the dead people were buried in a common grave. And our Fierochka stayed there too, in a common grave somewhere, we don't even know where it is.[1]

Similar heartbreaking stories were repeated countless times during the first twelve months of the war. The transfer and resettlement of millions of people, including children, invalids, and elderly, posed a considerable challenge to public health officials, factory managers, and local soviet authorities. People fled the German occupying forces in organized convoys connected to workplaces and institutions, but also individually and in family groups. The state made a distinction between people who were ordered to evacuate and traveled with a convoy, and those who made their own decisions to flee. The first group, designated "evacuees," often found it easier to register for rations and housing because the group was expected at its destination. Those in the second group were in reality refugees, and were overwhelmingly made up of women, children, the elderly, and infirm. They had to sort out routes, find shelter, and search for work by relying on their own ingenuity and the goodwill of those they encountered along the way. Yet for both groups the journeys east were chaotic and often derailed by bombing, illness, and death. People were forced to change routes, make long stopovers in unanticipated places, and break up their families. Under these conditions, hard distinctions between the two groups blurred. Journeys were lengthy and involved unpredictable and terrifying twists of fate. Those who were lucky traveled by rail in passenger cars, but the vast majority crammed into *teplushki* (heated freight cars adapted for passengers), unadapted freight and cattle cars, and open flatbed and semi-covered cars. Workers sometimes squeezed around the equipment from their factories. Convoys encountered holdups, gridlock, and endless delays along dangerous routes. Boxcars were sometimes rushed back to the front lines, leaving people to wait for replacements in which to continue their journey.

Health authorities were deeply worried about epidemics, but lack of proper sanitation and hygiene, lice, and contaminated water proved difficult to remedy amid the masses of people in motion. By 1942, after the first great wave of evacuation was over, health authorities put strict protocols in place but two epidemics had already taken their deadly toll: child measles, followed by typhus. Many people never reached their final destinations, and families were forced to leave their dead at unknown stations along the way. Evacuees from Leningrad during the siege were half dead already: starving, sick, and in no condition to travel.

Safe arrival was no guarantee of rest for the weary. The hungry, dirty, and exhausted people who reached their destinations in the eastern towns found that they had to summon new reserves of energy and strength. Municipal authorities required the local population to accept newcomers into already cramped rooms, but the existing housing stock could not accommodate all those in need of shelter. Enterprise managers began erecting barracks and digging *zemlianki* (earthen dugouts) to house the massive overflow. Conditions were harsh, and newcomers and natives often blamed each other.[2]

Evacuated factories were forced to share space with existing factories, and managers, shop heads, and workers battled over space and production methods. Often several different factories were crammed into a single structure, leading to new, hazardous emissions and conditions. Factories were combined in new ways, and vastly expanded. Construction crews built their own rough shelters before they could lay new electricity, water, and railway lines, erect new structures, and build blast furnaces in areas lacking infrastructure. New, more efficient production methods replaced older ones, and factories were forced to modernize rapidly. In short, the war proved a powerful crucible, forcing every branch of administration—from public health to municipalities to industrial enterprises—to confront challenges of epic proportions.

Journeys East: Evacuees and Refugees

The number of people either evacuated in convoys organized by the SE or fleeing as unregistered refugees was, not surprisingly, difficult to count. Estimates range from twelve million to twenty-five million people.[3] The great range in estimates is complicated by a statistical anomaly, namely that the numbers who left their homes greatly exceeded the numbers registered as settling in central and eastern regions. Records show that, as of February 1942, after the first great wave of evacuation was over, only around 7.4 million people were registered in new areas: 5.9 million evacuees registered in the RSFSR; 600,000 in Uzbekistan; 796,000 in Kazakhstan, including

360,000 ethnic Germans deported to Kazakhstan from their homelands in the Caucasus and along the Volga; and the remainder in other Central Asian republics.[4] The discrepancy between those leaving and those arriving may have been the result of deaths en route, long lags in registration, the failure to register refugees, or overall slippage in accounting amid the exigencies of war. Moreover, evacuation was not a one-time, uni-directional event. From 1942 on, small groups began returning home, even as a second wave of evacuation was underway in the south.[5]

The journeys were physically arduous and frightening. People were commonly crammed into unheated boxcars with a single bucket serving as a toilet. Almost 8,000 shipbuilders and their families traveled out of Moscow in unheated boxcars, prompting the deputy commissar of shipbuilding to reprimand the SE for not sending "a single railway car for the evacuation of people."[6] Agnessa Margolina, a young worker, was evacuated with her extended family in August from Kiev. She remembered:

> We boarded a cattle freight train at the railway station. There were three-tier plank beds along the walls in the carriage. People crowded in the passage and on the platform. There were no toilets. When we were leaving, Kiev was being bombed. We were bombed on the way, too. Then the train stopped and people scattered around hiding under carriages. When the planes left we returned to our carriages and the train moved on. Some people got killed and wounded during air raids. We didn't know our point of destination. When the train stopped at stations we could get off to get some water or go to the toilet. We were scared to get off the train not knowing when it was going to move again. Sometimes we could buy some food from locals at stations. I don't remember how long our trip lasted, but it was very long.[7]

The composition of the evacuees created significant challenges for the local authorities responsible for feeding, housing, and caring for them. A significant percentage were children, invalids, and elderly, who needed special care and were not capable of work. Roughly a third of evacuees were children under the age of fourteen, the age at which most children left school and entered employment. Around half were older teens and adults deemed to be "work-capable," defined as able to perform at least some form of labor. The remaining 15 to 18 percent were adult dependants, invalids, or elderly. Even in the Urals, the region that received the largest number of evacuated factories, and the heart of the USSR's defense industry, about half of the evacuees were unable to work.[8]

Workers who evacuated together with their factories went to urban areas, primarily to the Urals and Western Siberia, but also to the large industrial cities of central Russia, such as Gor'kii, Kazan' in the Tatar Republic, and Kuibyshev, which became the center of the wartime aviation industry. Evacuation transformed some smaller cities, such as Penza and Kirov, into major industrial centers. The remainder of the evacuated population—women, children, men too old or not fit to be drafted, and the elderly—was mostly sent to rural areas to help in agriculture, although many with secondary or higher education found jobs as rural schoolteachers, nurses, paramedics, agronomists, or bookkeepers. The draft was already depleting collective and state farms of working-age men, and the state hoped that the new arrivals would perform much-needed agricultural labor. They would not need to be placed on ration rolls like urban dwellers and could grow food not just for themselves, but also for those living in towns. The countryside gave children a better chance of survival, as they were closer to food supplies and less exposed to urban health risks. For all the state's efforts to control evacuation, a very large percentage of people made their own way east. Even in the Urals, a major site for evacuated factories, those who belonged to what officials called the "nonorganized evacuee population" were in the majority. In Cheliabinsk, the Urals province with the largest number of evacuees and host to multiple evacuated enterprises, including Leningrad's famed Kirov factory, those who arrived outside an official convoy significantly outnumbered those who traveled with their factories. Only in Sverdlovsk province did workers and their families who accompanied their factories make up the majority.[9]

All journeys east, officially sanctioned or not, took weeks and even months. Only 30 percent of the country's rail lines were twin-track, which impeded the scheduling of heavy traffic moving in both directions. Trains crawled along at a snail's pace. Convoys were supposed to cover between 300 and 375 miles in 24 hours, implying an average speed of around 15 miles an hour, but in reality, average speeds barely attained 5 miles per hour in late 1941. Holdups at stations and junctions could last days or even weeks. Sometimes station staff simply could not keep track of the volume of traffic they were handling. One carriage with 151 children going from Tambov to Cheliabinsk idled for four days on a siding in Sverdlovsk because station personnel forgot it was there. One group of twenty-seven workers took thirteen days to cover just 28 miles on a train that traveled barely 2 miles a day. Stations sometimes refused to receive a transport because they lacked space, requiring the train to be redirected to another destination. One convoy carrying a home for disabled people from Kalinin province was refused access to Sverdlovsk station and rerouted to Cheliabinsk. When it arrived there it was sent back to Sverdlovsk, a round trip that took more than a month. Many of the passengers were too weak to survive the arduous journey. Twenty of the original seventy-six passengers died during the first trip to Sverdlovsk, and two more died of starvation on the leg to Cheliabinsk. A similar fate befell a group of weavers evacuated from Smolensk province to Ufa. In one notable case, a convoy made up of twenty-seven railcars arrived in Cheliabinsk en route to Novosibirsk. When officials in Cheliabinsk tried to reroute the train to Sverdlovsk, the passengers climbed down from the coaches and began to protest. After a tense sixteen-hour standoff, the passengers prevailed, and the train was permitted to pass.[10]

Travel disruptions played havoc with provisioning. Food, issued to passengers before the journey on the assumption that transports would reach each station more or less on schedule, was soon depleted due to long delays. A worker from Leningrad's Kirov factory described his evacuation: "Our transport took twenty-nine days to get to Cheliabinsk. We idled more than we traveled. The weather got colder and colder as we went. Soon our provisions ran out and, when the train stopped, we scattered in different directions looking for food, sometimes five or seven kilometers from the rail line."[11] Evacuees from Leningrad who traveled by boat along the Volga from Iaroslavl' to Gor'kii, and then on to their final destination in Kazan', faced the same problem. Not only were boats designed for 800 passengers carrying 2,000, but the passengers were also not issued enough food to cover the delays and consumed most of it before the journey was half over.[12] As a result of these difficulties, trains frequently reached their final destination with fewer than half the original number of passengers. People died in transit, were removed if they fell ill, or sometimes were arrested for crimes. Most of the missing either intentionally abandoned the train or wandered off during a long stopover and missed the departure. Some hoped to reunite with family or stay with relatives in the area; others stayed behind with sick or injured family members.[13] Many would move on later by whatever means they could.

As the SE gained experience, the local organizations it relied on learned to manage the process of evacuation more effectively. Yet many elements could not be controlled. Ports, river crossings, and railway junctions were crowded with people, animals, and machinery held up by bombing or lack of transport. Tens of thousands of people, lacking food, shelter, or sanitary services, were caught in massive jams. Railway workers invented numerous techniques to repair and make use of bombed lines. When German bombers hit the rail lines out of Leningrad in August 1941, railway workers created impromptu methods to keep traffic moving. They arranged themselves within visible distance of each other to create an ordered priority of train movement in and out of crowded or blocked stations, a method they called "live blocking" that was soon adopted throughout the frontline zones.[14]

Trains were often dispatched hastily from frontline zones with mixed loads of multiple convoys and stray boxcars, all with different destinations. They had to be sorted and recomposed as soon as they reached a station of relative safety. The sorting process, which could take five or more days, created massive backups and delays. The Kuibyshev Railway, one of the oldest in Russia, served as a transit channel for 19 million boxcars, some headed east to the Urals and Western Siberia with machinery from 1,360 large industrial enterprises and 10 million people, and others headed west with ammunition, military equipment, gasoline, food, and troops for the front. Convoys could be idled there for days. The SE dispatched a plenipotentiary to Kuibyshev to try to sort out the mess, but again it was the intervention of railway workers that proved most effective. They experimented with new methods that allowed them to recompose trains rapidly, repair boxcars, drive heavily loaded trains, and dispatch doubled trains.[15]

Large jams commonly occurred in port cities and at river crossings. In early August, huge numbers of refugees crowded into Odessa, on the northwestern shore of the Black Sea, as battles raged on the outskirts. Evacuees, refugees, and local inhabitants were all frantic to escape. The evacuation, in the words of two officials from the Commissariat of State Control, was organized "exceptionally poorly," occurring "spontaneously" and "without order." Orphanages and other children's institutions were evacuated only at the last minute, and up to 6,000 skilled workers, children, and refugees from Moldavia remained.[16] After the Red Army pulled out in mid-October, tens of thousands of people fled southeast toward the ports of Baku and Makhachkala on the Caspian Sea. In October, the head of the NKVD in Dagestan wrote to Beria, Commissar of the NKVD, that 30,000 people, fleeing Rostov and other places, were crammed into the railroad stations and the port in Makhachkala, and 70,000 more were expected to arrive shortly.

Awaiting rescue, the crowds slept under open skies, living without shelter, food, or sanitary and medical services. No boats were available to move them out, nor could new arrivals be prevented.[17] The influx of hundreds of thousands of desperate, hungry people into the Caucasus overwhelmed all attempts at planned, orderly evacuation. Equipment and people without documents or destinations were placed on dangerously overloaded boats. Ida Kristina, a twenty-two-year-old who left Ukraine with her parents, sister, and three children, remembered:

> At the station we got on a train that took us to Makhachkala . . . 2,500 kilometers from home. We stayed there on the ground near the seaport for about two weeks. There were tens of thousands of refugees, there was no food or water. Later we boarded the "Derbent" tanker; there were tanks with oil in the ship's belly and about 5,000 refugees on the deck. There was no water and many people were seasick. There were only two toilets on the tanker and after using it one had to stand in line to the toilet since it took two to three hours before one could get there again. We were sitting on the very top. We crossed the Caspian Sea to Kazakhstan. When we got off the tanker I saw that dead people were being taken off the tanker. The trip had been too hard for them.[18]

Worried about the security of the region, the deputy commissar of defense requested that the SE send plenipotentiaries to the railroad stations and ports to manage the crowds, establish services, and create weight limits for the flotillas. The SE immediately dispatched several plenipotentiaries to implement a plan to reduce the chaos.[19]

As the Red Army continued to retreat, the flood of people desperate to escape swelled. By November 1941, the railroad junction at Stalingrad was packed with more than 200,000 evacuees and soldiers awaiting river or rail transport. These included 32,000 ethnic Germans, who had been expelled from the provinces north of the city along the Volga River, and 15,000 soldiers waiting to be sent to the front. The railway lines were completely blocked with boxcars carrying defense material, food, and people. K. Pamfilov, a deputy chairman of the Soviet of People's Commissars and SE member, and I. Pronin, the deputy chief of the Transport Department of the NKVD, arrived in Stalingrad on November 2 to survey conditions.[20] They found masses of people, some very sick, camped under open skies in and around the railway station and on the streets and squares. There was little food, no boiled water, and no medical services. The lack of even the most rudimentary sanitation facilities created the threat of mass epidemics of typhus, cholera, and other diseases. The head of the provincial Department of People's Education had gathered 300 orphans, many as young as six, and sent them off on a ship. Local party officials, according to one report, had tried to "shove out" people without providing food or services. Local residents were also overwhelmed by the influx as hungry evacuees created massive lines in food stores, forcing everyone to queue for hours for bread rations. Wild and contradictory rumors swept the crowds: Stalingrad would soon be cleared of refugees; everyone would be pushed toward a wharf 50 miles (80 km) distant; people would be sent back to the front. In truth, the rumored wharf was 54 yards (50 m) away, and authorities had no plans to send anyone except soldiers to the front.[21]

The SE, aware of the crisis, had already dispatched a group of plenipotentiaries to Stalingrad on November 1, and mobilized the region's party activists. Over the next two weeks, they organized food and sanitary stations, dispersed the crowd, and sent various contingents to destinations up and down the Volga. More than 75,000 people were sent to the nearby wharf where they boarded ferries to take them to places of resettlement, and an additional 145,000 were dispatched by railroad. Once it became clear that the SE and local officials were attempting to create order, people cooperated with them and with each other. The crowds became orderly, and there was remarkably little crime. And although most were grateful for the help, not all went willingly. The ethnic Germans who had been expelled were sent off to Astrakhan', and other evacuees were sent north to be resettled on their vacated farms. By November 15, the crowds, wharves, and railroad station of Stalingrad were cleared. The boats pulled out just before November 13 when the Volga began to freeze and river transport became impossible.[22]

The Perils of Flight

Journeys for both refugees and evacuees in organized convoys were vulnerable to unanticipated and uncontrollable forces.[23] Refugees from the cities frequently received food, shelter, and fresh clothing from local peasants and repaid their generosity by helping with farm work. In this regard evacuation was a great leveler. People with professional training or from white-collar backgrounds cleaned railway station toilets, threshed grain, and did odd jobs. The families of Red Army officers or lower-level NKVD officials rode in cattle cars and suffered the same hunger as ordinary citizens.[24] Large numbers of people simply fled toward safety on foot. Klavdiya P. was a typical refugee. Born into a poor peasant family in Ivanovo province, as a teenager she moved to Orekhovo-Zuevo, a textile town outside Moscow, to look after her aunt's children. She soon found a better job in Moscow's aviation factory No. 22, where she learned to read and write, completed her education, and was promoted to foreman. When the factory was evacuated to Kazan', she and her husband did not join its convoy but instead set out on foot, aiming first for Gor'kii, 280 miles (450 km) east of Moscow, and from there to Kazan'. They made it about two-thirds of the way, to her family's home in Ivanovo province, more than 185 miles (300 km) away. Only several weeks later did she and her husband, traveling separately, manage to reach Kazan', where Klavdia reclaimed her old job.[25] Many like her walked, slept along roadsides, and hitched rides on whatever transport was available. Archivist L. G. Dvorson recalled in her memoir:

> On horse-drawn carts, with bombs falling from bombers flying overhead, we made our way in the direction of Baku or, more precisely, to the sea. We traveled by day, worn out by the heat, and at night we slept wherever we could find. A whole month we went on foot; from time to time we'd take turns sitting on the cart. In Baku they put us on a tanker. Three days we floated along the sea, and one night we were hit by a storm, the boat listing so badly [the deck] was practically touching the surface of the sea. The poor passengers were seasick to the point of fainting, their heads swirled. Finally we reached Krasnovodsk, where the evacuation center was located. There they sorted the refugees. They put my mother and me in a freight car of a convoy; we all slept on the floor side by side, covering ourselves with straw. We set out ... [and] in November 1942 we arrived in Berezniki in Molotov province.[26]

Even more daunting, and yet equally common, was the odyssey of Viktor K., a fifteen-year-old Jewish boy, and his family. In June 1941, Viktor was living with his parents in Odessa. His older sister was spending the summer with her fellow university students on a farm outside Kiev, helping the peasants to bring in the harvest. When war broke out, the students were instructed to return to Odessa on foot, a trek of more than 370 miles (600 km). When Viktor's sister finally arrived home, she found only her father, who stayed behind to wait for her. They left the city together, heading south on foot, hoping to reach Chechnya in the Caucasus. Meanwhile, Viktor and his mother had already been evacuated on a coal boat. Two days out of port, the boat was attacked. The passengers were rescued and taken to Mariupol', a port city in the southern Donbass, where they caught a heated freight train (*teplushka*) as far as Gul'kevichi in the Krasnodar district, just north of the Caucasus. The journey took many days of hard traveling, but in Gul'kevichi they were fortunately taken in by a colony of ethnic German collective farmers. Viktor observed that while the farm itself was very prosperous—it consisted of 136 households, with brick buildings and excellent livestock—the farmers themselves were terribly poor. One day the NKVD showed up, rounded up all the Germans, and carted them away, leaving the entire farm in the hands of five evacuee families, plus three German women who had been allowed to remain because their husbands were in the Red Army. Although Viktor did not know this at the time, the farmers were part of the larger roundup of ethnic Germans who were deported to the east. One of the minor feats of the Soviet government was that the postal service continued to function despite the vast turmoil. Like countless other families, Viktor's parents kept track of each other by mail, using the addresses of relatives or friends as intermediaries. And so it was that Viktor's mother received a letter from a relative in Rostov with news that Viktor's father and sister were in Kizliar, a small town about 350 miles (560 km) from Gul'kevichi. Viktor and his mother set out to join them but, when they went to the nearest rail station, they learned that all trains were being deployed to evacuate local factories and only passengers in organized convoys could board. Viktor snuck his mother onto one of the trains, while he stayed behind. Again, to his good fortune, another evacuee family took him in. They survived the winter of 1941–1942 by sewing traditional Cossack cloaks from old clothes and material provided by local Cossacks, who paid them in vital milk and meat. In the spring, when the thaw set in and the roads were again passable, Viktor's father came to retrieve him. He paid the host family for caring for him and took Viktor back to Kizliar, where Viktor worked at the local post office.

In August 1942, the Germans broke through to Rostov and began advancing into the Caucasus. Viktor's family was again forced to separate. Viktor's father, along with other men of working age, was initially barred from leaving, but Viktor, his sister, and his mother departed on a horse-drawn cart with the family of the local postmaster. The roads were clogged

with panicked refugees fleeing the front and columns of soldiers moving toward it. The cart broke down repeatedly, and there was no water for people
or horses. To make matters worse, Viktor came down with malaria, and the
family—now reunited with his father—had to make yet another detour to
Makhachkala to find medication. At last, with Viktor still quite weak, they
managed to catch a boat to Krasnovodsk in Turkmenistan, where they caught
a transport to Kagan, a town near Bukhara in Uzbekistan. Now they faced a
new setback. Viktor's father fell ill with acute dysentery. The local hospital
flatly told his mother that they were unable to help him, and it fell to her to
try to nurse him back to health. Like evacuees everywhere, she sold some
of the family's possessions. With some of the money she bought a chicken,
from which she made a broth that Viktor's father could digest. With the rest
she bought ingredients to make small pies, which she sold in order to continue buying food for her husband. Eventually, Viktor's father, emaciated
and on crutches, was well enough to leave Kagan. On the advice of a doctor,
the family moved to a nearby collective farm, hoping that it would be easier
to acquire food. Viktor's father found a job as the local bookkeeper, while
Viktor worked in the village buffet. Life for the family was made harder by
local anti-Semitism, but at least they were safe. Once Viktor reached draft
age, he volunteered and was sent to a sniper training school near the Soviet–
Afghan border, where he remained as an instructor until the end of the war.[27]
Viktor's story, with its narrow escapes, separations, illnesses, and unforeseen
strokes of luck and misfortune, was typical of the travails of countless Soviet
families. Indeed, home front civilians, like soldiers, were on the move, each
group headed in opposite directions, but both toward futures dangerous and
unknown.

One of the most vulnerable groups the SE attempted to rescue was the
starving inhabitants of Leningrad. The German blockade of the city began
in September 1941, and by late fall its inhabitants had begun to starve. The
first "hunger winter" claimed some 800,000 lives. The evacuees—primarily
women and children—were severely malnourished and weak. For those who
crossed Lake Ladoga and reached a rail line, the trains traveled 370 miles
(600 km) east to Vologda, and then 87 miles (140 km) south to Iaroslavl',
a port on the upper Volga and a major rail junction. Between January and
June 1942, around 330,600 Leningrad evacuees passed through Iaroslavl', including around 88,000 children. Some 13,500 evacuees of all ages remained
in Iaroslavl', the vast majority in an advanced stage of starvation, or ill with
tuberculosis, dysentery, pneumonia, and coronary disease. Overall mortality

among this group was 17 percent. March and April were the worst months—
health officials in Iaroslavl' were carrying up to 200 sick people a day off
the trains. This rapid influx quickly outstripped the city's ability to feed,
bathe, disinfest, and treat the sick. Local officials coped as best they could,
converting twenty-six schools into makeshift inpatient units. The volume of
Leningrad evacuees slowed after April. The most serious cases of starvation
disease had been evacuated first, and those who arrived later were in better
health. Within several months, the city had improved its ability to treat,
shelter, and transport the new arrivals.[28]

Vologda, the first stop for the Leningrad evacuees, was much smaller than
Iaroslavl' and even more hard pressed. It took in far fewer evacuees than
Iaroslavl'—in excess of 5,400 through May 8, 1942—but more than one-
quarter of them died. Initially, the town could provide only emergency accommodation. It began to organize a network of evacuation hospitals, but
in the interim evacuees lived in dormitories which, in the words of one of
Vologda's senior health officials, resembled a train station. Every room held
several families. There was no furniture or sanitary facilities. People heaped
their dirty parcels and suitcases on the floor next to buckets of excrement and
chamber pots, or on the beds where they slept and were served their meals.
No regular doctors and only a single nurse were on call. The pipes had burst
from lack of heat, a problem that was rampant throughout the country. One
public health official wrote,

> There was a great deal of lice infestation and filth, since there was no sani-
> tary block, and there was nowhere for them to wash and nothing for them
> to wash with. One set of linen was not sufficient, since these were people
> seriously ill with starvation disease, who in 80 percent of cases also suffered
> from gastro-intestinal problems (colitis, entero-colitis). There were no dis-
> infection chambers.

There was no kitchen, showers, or bath. Canteen workers were too
overwhelmed by so many sick people to provide regular meals. Most of the
people were suffering from starvation. The health official noted with pity:

> On little scraps of paper they had written the last names, but no first names
> or patronymics, no address, no indication of age, or whom to inform about
> the patient or if the patient died, and sometimes even without a diagnosis,
> the doctor's signature, a record of the time the patient was admitted or

indication of the progress of the disease (whether the patient recovered, died—nothing was known at all).

The doctors tried to do what they could, but "There were no regular supplies of medication. There were no medical instruments. There was no operating room whatsoever—at a time when a large number of those who were ill had frostbitten limbs or gangrene." Most of Vologda's hospitals were so full they could not admit additional patients. Sick people "were all piled into a bus, and taken from hospital to hospital, until one of the hospitals took pity on them and admitted them." When people died, the health official reported, "Bodies lay in a barn, heaped up in a pile, without any name tags (it was impossible to establish who the dead person was), and a long time elapsed before documentation on the death was drawn up or the bodies were buried."[29] Medical personnel struggled valiantly to save the starving evacuees from Leningrad but the science of refeeding was still in its infancy, and the entire country was desperately short of food.[30] Yet, like Iaroslavl', Vologda coped more successfully with the next wave of evacuees: local officials established more hospital facilities, and the smaller number of evacuees were in a less precarious state of health.

The child evacuees from Leningrad were an especially piteous sight. The head of the kindergarten at Moscow's factory No. 45, which took in Leningrad children during 1942, recalled:

> The children were extremely weak, with no teeth. Anichka Pasynkova, five years old, no teeth, short in stature. Even now her teeth are not growing properly. Nina Goncharova, her mother went blind from starvation, the child was emaciated and swollen. Tolya Durkin, had acute rickets, was swollen, had no teeth. He was four years old but couldn't walk. Over the course of a year he began to walk. He had been unable to speak–he began to talk. He'd watched his father and two sisters die from hunger. He came here with his mother.

She proudly concluded, "Now all these children have recovered."[31]

Cities further east encountered similarly distressing scenes. In April 1942, the city of Kirov was receiving between 350 and 400 Leningrad evacuees a day, many in need of extensive medical care. Among a group of seventy teenagers from a vocational school, more than half were so weak that they had to be carried off the train on stretchers; several eventually died. Sometimes local hospitals were reluctant to treat evacuees in need of such specialized nutritional care and sent them back to the evacuation center.[32]

The strain of travel weighed most heavily on the very young, the sick, and the elderly, as shown by the astronomical increase in both adult and infant deaths during 1942. In 1940, Vologda recorded 2,473 deaths; during 1942, this leapt to 13,737. In Iaroslavl', the number of deaths jumped from 6,872 in 1940 to 16,337 in 1942. Some of this increase occurred among natives due to worsening wartime conditions, but most was attributable to evacuees who died in transit. Infant mortality spiked during the months when the influx of Leningrad evacuees was at its height. In Iaroslavl' during April–June 1942 there were 1,388 births and 900 deaths of infants under one year of age, an average of 648 per 1,000 births. Most of the babies who died were born in Leningrad although their deaths were registered in Iaroslavl'. In Vologda, during these same months, there were 564 births and 423 infant deaths, averaging 750 deaths per 1,000 live births, again, astounding figues mainly due to loss of evacuated babies.[33] This pattern was repeated across the country as the Leningrad evacuees moved from west to east.

Of particular concern to evacuation and public health officials were infectious diseases such as typhus, gastro-intestinal infections, and childhood droplet infections, the most serious of which was measles. Although public health officials perceived the risks and dangers almost immediately, the speed of the German advance and the enormous number of people in motion meant it was not until late 1942 that they successfully implemented epidemic controls. Public health conditions, however, were difficult even before the invasion. Industrialization and mass migration in the 1930s created ubiquitous overcrowding, which in turn had significant health effects. The country had a high incidence of tuberculosis, and measles was second only to pneumonia as a killer of toddlers. The country also suffered periodic epidemics of typhus, an often-fatal disease transmitted by lice.[34] Outside Moscow and Leningrad, few people had indoor plumbing, and waste disposal was a constant problem. Outhouses, used by the majority of urban inhabitants, were emptied irregularly, and raw sewage frequently spilled onto sidewalks and streets or seeped into groundwater. Even in the central districts, it was essential to boil water before drinking it. Dysentery was endemic, easily spread, and potentially fatal; in 1940, it accounted for 3 percent of all deaths in urban areas of Russia. Acute gastro-intestinal infections were a leading cause of the Soviet Union's high prewar infant mortality.[35] Under such conditions, personal hygiene was essential, but most city dwellers lacked indoor piped water. People drew water from cold-water street pumps, which they then lugged home in buckets. In outlying districts people drew water from wells, rivers, and streams, which were often polluted by industrial effluvia and human waste. People relied heavily on public bathhouses. During the 1930s the government ran imaginative health education campaigns to teach people about microbes, the importance of hand-washing after using the toilet, and the need to wash and boil vegetables and the bottles and utensils used to feed infants, but public knowledge about hygiene nonetheless remained rudimentary.[36]

The country's elaborate network of public health controls was overseen by two related authorities: the State Sanitary Inspectorate (Gosudarstvennaia Sanitarnaia Inspektsiia, or GSI) and the Sanitary-Epidemic Stations (Sanitarno-epidemicheskie stantsii, or SES). To control typhus, for example, they developed systems and procedures to eradicate lice. Anyone living in a dormitory or barracks, or who was suspected of carrying lice, had to undergo "sanitary processing" (*sanitarnaia obrabotka*, or *sanobrabotka* for short), carried out at a sanitary processing station (*sanitarnyi propusknik*, or *sanpropusknik*), a small-scale bathhouse with a disinfestation chamber. Upon entering, people surrendered their clothes to be disinfected and disinfested in the laundry and/or subjected to high dry heat. At the end of the process, they collected their clean clothes, although the underwear they received was not necessarily their own. Health officials understood that notification and quarantine were central tenets of epidemic control: anyone with a potentially infectious disease was to be isolated; all carriers and contacts were to be identified and if necessary quarantined, and living quarters thoroughly disinfected.

The health authorities were thus alert to the problems inherent in the mass movement of people.[37] On June 30, 1941, one week after the German invasion, the USSR People's Commissariat of Public Health issued detailed instructions on evacuation. Local medical personnel were to inspect all local gathering points, which were to be regularly disinfected and, most critically, provided with sufficient toilets or field latrines. All evacuees were to undergo medical inspection, and anyone running a fever or suspected of being ill was to be prohibited from joining a convoy. Authorities were to ensure that evacuees had warm clothing, underwear, and food. All trains and boats were to have medical personnel on board: paramedics would accompany smaller transports, and a doctor, nurse, and paramedic would accompany larger ones. The medical personnel were charged with regular inspections on trains to identify and isolate anyone who was ill and ensure hospitalization at the next stop. Anyone found with lice, but not yet ill, was to be taken off the train at the first station that had a *sanpropusknik* or a bathhouse. If there was a mass outbreak of disease, the entire train was to be quarantined and all passengers and their belongings were to be disinfected.[38]

By the end of August, however, the volume of evacuees and the perilous conditions had overwhelmed health authorities. Many train stations could not even provide clean drinking water. Mothers traveling with infants and small children were forced to use contaminated water, which contributed to the high mortality during late 1941 and the first half of 1942. Evacuees unable to find a place in a passenger coach or *teplushka* crammed into freight and cattle cars. Every convoy was supposed to have one railway car set aside as an isolation unit but, given the shortage of railway cars, most trains lacked them. Convoys traveled without medical staff and, under the pressure of the rapidly approaching front, passengers left without sanitary processing. As a result, infectious passengers were not screened, no one on board was able to detect typhus or other infectious diseases, and ill passengers were not isolated from the healthy. The crowds were so great and the facilities so limited at stations that people defecated on the railway tracks or on the surrounding ground. Many stations did not have washrooms. And basic health regulations governing troop travel went unenforced. Soldiers and civilians mingled in the stations and at sidings, and used the same unsanitary boxcars: troops had no sooner disembarked for the front than the wagons were reloaded with evacuees heading in the opposite direction. Like civilian passengers, soldiers with lice or illness were not isolated and removed from the trains.[39]

Despite the difficult conditions, officials did sometimes manage to keep disaster at bay. In July 1941, the SE evacuated 500 children of workers in Trekhgornaia Manufaktura, a textile factory in Moscow, to Kineshma, a textile town 250 miles (400 km) to the northeast in Ivanovo province. The group included at least 100 babies in the high-risk under-three age group. The factory, affectionately known as Trekhgorka, was one of the country's oldest textile mills and its mainly female workforce had played a prominent role in the 1917 revolution. The children reached Kineshma safely, but in October the military situation worsened, and the SE decided to evacuate the children to Cheliabinsk province, about 1,000 miles (1,600 km) to the east. The factory sent its own representatives to Cheliabinsk in advance to organize the children's reception. The journey took more than three weeks, yet all the children arrived in good health, a point of justifiable pride for factory officials and great comfort to their worried mothers. The factory officials offered the following explanation for their success. All the carriages had been equipped with cast iron stoves, and the children were accompanied by 120 kindergarten and nursery staff as well as one doctor and one nurse for every two wagons. The staff washed the children's hair and feet every day and provided a complete body wash and change of underwear once every seven to ten days. Not a single child arrived with lice. At the larger stations they were able to take the children out for fresh air and a walk. Moreover, the convoy had an isolation car, and when two children came down with measles the staff was able to prevent its spread.[40]

Yet few convoys took this kind of staff or sanitary precautions. As a result, the country suffered a mass epidemic of measles in fall–winter 1941–1942, followed by a typhus epidemic in winter–spring of 1942, both spread along the routes of evacuation.[41] Only beginning in the spring of 1942, after the bulk of evacuees had already passed east, were local health officials able to implement the procedures necessary to prevent more epidemics and deaths. Officials shunted transports onto sidings, near *sanpropuskniki*, to prevent large crowds from forming at junctions and stations. Passengers were examined, sent for sanitary processing, and provided with food, clean water, and access to toilets; stations received vats for boiling drinking water, more than 2,500 chlorination units were installed, and the number of field latrines expanded. As a result, public health officials succeeded in preventing the outbreak of further epidemics despite continuing large-scale population movements. From 1942 on, the state mobilized millions of people to work in the Urals and Western Siberia, organized a second, smaller wave of evacuation, and began sending evacuated workers back to the liberated territories, but the crisis of 1941–1942 was not repeated.

Housing New Arrivals

Evacuation centers or *evakopunkty* were created with the intention of caring for those in transit. At the destination points, they were to provide medical screening, sanitary processing, temporary accommodation, and food. If the arrivals were able to work and had not arrived as part of a factory convoy, the centers were also responsible for finding them employment, usually in the countryside. Many urban people, seeking to escape the collective farms, found work on their own through local soviets, factories, or other institutions. Initially, the *evakopunkty* coped well with the large numbers of new arrivals. On a single day at the end of July 1941, for example, more than 15,500 evacuees, including 349 children without parents, arrived in the Marii Republic on the Volga River from Estonia, Latvia, Lithuania, Moscow, and other places. The secretary of the provincial party committee later provided a lengthy and somewhat self-congratulatory report on their processing and settlement. The evacuees were welcomed at an *evakopunkt* in Ioshkar-Ola with ten dormitories, bathhouses, dining halls, and buffets. Special brigades were mobilized to meet them at the railroad station, transport their luggage to the dormitories, care for the children, and staff the canteens and bathhouses that had been created for them. Political instructors were stationed in the dormitories to answer questions and update the evacuees on the latest news from the front. After the evacuees bathed and passed through disinfection, families were sent to collective farms and single men to logging camps.[42]

Yet this tale of hot baths and clean beds soon came to resemble a wishful fairytale of warmth and plenty. Even the largest cities found it difficult to cope with the influx, while smaller towns and villages were simply overwhelmed. Towns and villages that first welcomed refugees grew resentful under the strain. As one Jewish former refugee recalled:

> The local residents in Pokrovka [a village in Chkalov province] were very sympathetic with us. They tried to help with whatever they could. However, there was a constant flow of people coming into evacuation. The population of Pokrovka became forty times bigger than it originally was. Life was getting very hard. There wasn't enough food, so it became very expensive. Some people had money or valuables with them, which they could sell to buy food at the market. The local population was poor. Gradually their warmth towards those in evacuation faded and they developed open hatred towards us. They blamed those that had come to the village for the change of the situation. Besides, anti-Semitism was demonstrated by other nationalities that were in evacuation and local residents learned promptly that Jews were to blame for everything negative. I heard the word "zhyd" [kike] for the first time there.[43]

Such tensions were not difficult to understand. Some evacuees made impossible demands, claiming they could not live without sugar or electricity.[44] Many urban dwellers knew nothing of farm labor or considered it beneath them. Peasants, for their part, were faced with a group that did little useful work. Local soviets were overwhelmed by the sheer number of arrivals. It was as if a bustling host and hostess had carefully prepared dinner for ten guests, only to discover tens of thousands of starving, sick, ragged people waiting outside their door.

Sometimes local soviets sought to offload responsibility for evacuees onto other towns. One battalion commissar accompanied 2,000 family members of the military command from Rostov to Mineral'nye Vody, a city on the main rail line between Rostov and Baku. No sooner had they arrived than the secretary of the town party committee sent the families to another town, then another, and finally to a place where 2,000 other people still awaited housing. While the military and civilian authorities quarreled furiously over the destination of the convoy, hundreds of people, including mothers, children, and elderly, spent three days "languishing in a freight car" waiting to learn where and when their journey would end.[45] They were not the only unwelcome "guests." In August, before the siege of Leningrad began, the SE ordered the evacuation of 2,000 patients and staff from Leningrad's psychiatric hospitals to Penza. The response from the secretary of the Penza provincial soviet was swift and unequivocal: "We cannot settle them here."[46] Such incidents were not uncommon.

Population shifts were occurring on a huge scale as shown by a comparison of the populations of major cities in 1939, January 1942, and January 1944, when reevacuation back west was already underway (see Table 2.1). Within the space of just eighteen months, Kuibyshev, Chkalov (Orenburg), Cheliabinsk, Molotov, and Novosibirsk saw their populations swell by 40 percent or more. Omsk and Ufa grew by nearly a third; Kazan', Sverdlovsk, and Nizhnii Tagil by well over a quarter. Mobilized workers also poured into the industrial towns, continuing to replace those who left even after reevacuation began. As a result, many cities in the Urals and Western Siberia grew steadily throughout the war. On the other hand, Moscow, under threat of occupation, and Leningrad, under siege, lost almost 40 percent of their inhabitants. The great shift in population from west to east required a vast organizational response from the localities.

The newcomers also arrived in a compressed period of time. By the beginning of August 1941, barely six weeks after the German invasion, Cheliabinsk province had already received 92,500 evacuees, less than a quarter of the total number the province would take in by the end of 1941. Its main evacuation center was initially well prepared to accommodate 1,000 people with a medical isolation unit and two experienced physicians, but quickly broke down under the strain. The SE was unable to alert the center to the arrival of convoys, which were often delayed, and public health staff could not meet the trains, screen passengers, or carry out "sanitary processing." One train destined for a small town in the province passed through Cheliabinsk with a number of people suffering from measles, virulent infant diarrhea, and colitis, all of whom should have been identified and removed.[47] Similar plans in Molotov province also collapsed under the sheer number of new arrivals. Many people, including refugees, convoys of workers, and people disembarking outside the city, never passed through an evacuation center and were not officially registered as "arrivals."[48]

Medium-sized cities with less infrastructure faced even greater challenges. At the start of the war, Kamensk-Ural'skii, 93 miles (150 km) north of Cheliabinsk, was a single-industry town with 50,000 people, home to a pipe factory and, more importantly, the country's only aluminum factory, essential for aircraft production. In 1942, it took in metallurgical factories evacuated from Moscow and Rostov. Within weeks of the invasion, its population doubled to 100,000. The newcomers were mainly evacuees from Dnepropetrovsk and Moscow, including mothers, young children, and pregnant women, as well as workers in newly formed construction battalions. Neither its housing stock nor its infrastructure could absorb such a rapid increase. People were housed in tents or in buildings with hurriedly installed, three-tiered plank bunk beds lining the walls of every room. The town, lacking a sewer system, had to dispose of twice as much waste as before the influx. Its bathhouses were only able to provide each resident with one visit every thirty-seven days, far from the three visits a month necessary for epidemic prevention. Moreover, the city was so sprawling that any evacuee with an infectious disease had difficulty getting to a hospital. The epidemic-control station responsible for evacuees had just one horse, and its only truck was sidelined for lack of fuel. At one point medical personnel took a diphtheria patient to the hospital on a crowded bus.[49]

Although evacuees were permitted to bring several kilograms of luggage, clothing shortages were a serious and widespread problem. People were often told they would be away from home for only a few weeks.[50] More often, they survived their long journeys by trading their clothing—which the peasants preferred to money—for food. Thus many arrived at their destinations just as winter was setting in with only a few items of summer clothing. In late September 1942, evacuation and resettlement authorities across the country reported acute shortages of clothing and footwear. Textile, footwear, and garment production was shifted to military needs, and little clothing was produced for civilian consumption. Workers were often without a change of underwear. Especially critical was the severe shortage of overcoats, shoes, and warm felt boots (*valenki*) that prevented workers from reporting for work and children from attending school. Lack of shoes and outerwear was in fact officially accepted as a legitimate reason for absence.[51]

The huge population increases were not solely attributable to evacuees and refugees. Local and evacuated factories significantly expanded their production capacity, and sectors such as coalmining, peat, timber cutting, and construction relied heavily on workers mobilized from afar. All of these newcomers poured into towns whose prewar housing stock was already inadequate or, in the case of new workers' settlements in rural areas, nonexistent. In most central and eastern towns, a large part of the prewar housing stock consisted of small private dwellings with no access to water supply, sewerage, or central heating. Towns that underwent significant expansion during industrialization in the 1930s accommodated most new workers in dormitories or barracks which, like private homes, also had no amenities, and many of which were so badly built that by the end of the decade they were in need of major repair. In Nizhnii Tagil, the second-largest city in Sverdlovsk province, private homes provided just over a quarter of living space and barracks just under one-third. About 40 percent of housing was in brick apartment blocks, but only a small percentage of these had water supply (mostly nearby outdoor street pumps), sewerage, or heating.[52] In Molotov, housing sprang up in workers' settlements located around the city's factories in a widely scattered pattern that later proved an obstacle to providing centralized utilities: about 60 percent of the city's inhabitants had neither sewerage nor piped water.[53] Simply put, none of the central and eastern industrial cities was prepared to cope with these vast changes during the early phase of the war.

Nizhnii Tagil was typical of most industrial cities in the east. With just under 160,000 inhabitants in 1939, the population had ballooned to 243,000 by the end of 1943. Employment was dominated by a number of large enterprises: the Urals Coach Factory, which became the Urals Tank Factory during the war; a chemical works; the Ordzhonikidze machine-tool factory; the Kuibyshev Novo-Tagil iron and steel works; and the Tagilstroi construction trust. The city also received forty additional factories evacuated from Leningrad, Moscow province, and Ukraine, and acquired a Gulag labor camp known as Tagillag. During the last six months of 1941, Nizhnii Tagil took in more than 60,000 evacuees, most of whom arrived with their factories. To make room for the new arrivals and keep families together wherever possible, city authorities decreed that every resident with a four-room house or apartment was obliged to let out two rooms to evacuated families, and those with three rooms to let out one. Every privately owned home would have to take in at least one family. Single people would be housed in dormitories. Evacuees with small children and those too old to work in industry or construction would be relocated to rural districts. Yet even this policy, which compelled the native population to double or even triple up with incoming families, did not create sufficient housing for all the new arrivals.[54]

Soviet leaders immediately understood that the housing infrastructure was inadequate for the mass influx. A decree of the Soviet of People's Commissars on September 13, 1941, ordered commissariats and republic and provincial authorities to build structures for evacuees of the simplest design—dormitories, barracks, and earthen dugouts known as *zemlianki*—as quickly as possible using local industries and materials. Construction organizations were to build for arriving factory convoys, and officials were to mobilize the new arrivals, together with the local population, to build dwellings for those arriving outside organized factory convoys.[55] Construction was to be basic: barracks were to have a simple wooden frame with rooms holding up to twenty-five beds, allowing up to 3 square meters per person. Floors were to be wattle and daub or wooden planks.[56] *Zemlianki*, even more primitive, were to consist of a trench about 3 meters deep partitioned into four to six "rooms," each about 6 to 8 square meters in size, covered with boards, and earth piled on the roof for insulation. Each room was to have a stove, with an exhaust pipe going up through the earthen ceiling.[57] Much of this construction would be done by Gulag prisoners.

Yet new construction, too, quickly proved insufficient. In 1942, the Urals Tank Factory (factory No. 183) in Nizhnii Tagil was ordered to build a settlement for 40,000 evacuated workers but managed just 173 *zemlianki* for 11,000. Building quality both before and during the war was so poor that by 1945 the amount of totally derelict housing in Nizhnii Tagil exceeded all the new housing space that had been added.[58] By 1944 almost half the tank factory's workers lived in hastily built wooden-frame barracks without heat, running water, or indoor toilets. Others lived in *zemlianki* or other rickety structures made of scrap materials. None of these dwellings were properly heated because the factory, which was responsible for supplying the workers with fuel, received only a fraction of the wood it was allocated according to the plan. None of the dormitories included places for washing. In two of the settlements, 15,000 people used six outdoor water pumps; in another, there were five kettles for 8,000 workers. The factory had communal baths, a few laundries, and a number of shoe repair shops, but not enough to meet the needs of its workers or those from other enterprises living in its settlements.[59] As union leaders noted, the main obstacle was not funding, which the state provided, but the lack of construction materials, transport, and construction workers. In Sverdlovsk, for example, doors, window frames, hinges, and even nails were impossible to procure. Motorized vehicles had been requisitioned by the military, and even carts and horses were scarce.[60] Factory directors and commissariats erected barracks, no more than wooden shells, as quickly as possible, but the structures, often built of unseasoned wood, soon had gaping cracks between the planks and leaking roofs and windows. Most barracks and *zemlianki* were unheated: even if they had stoves, they had no fuel to burn.[61]

The state hoped to alleviate the housing crisis at least in part by encouraging workers to build their own homes. The Soviet of People's Commissars provided substantial sums to willing builders but did not provide materials. Factory directors and local soviets were supposed to contract with local industry for building materials, allocate transport, and provide individual workers with the supplies they would need.[62] The state offered various financial incentives, including low-interest loans. Workers would carry out the construction themselves. Managers at the Urals Aluminum Factory quickly pointed out that this was impossible: workers spent long hours in the factory, and in the summer many devoted their free time to growing food.[63] Between long working hours, overtime, and the walk to and from the barracks, they did not even have time to pay their rent. In May 1942, 70 percent of the 20,000 workers housed in the dormitories of the aviation industry in Kuibyshev were behind with their rent. The workers did not lack money; they lacked time and repeatedly petitioned their union to allow the factory bookkeepers to deduct the monthly payment from their wages.[64] More important than money, neither the state nor the factories were able to provide construction materials or the transport needed to deliver them. Not surprisingly, the campaign to encourage individual home construction yielded few results in any of the industrial towns.[65]

Although union, soviet, public health, and other officials all protested the housing situation to central authorities, no one had a viable solution to the problem. An official in Sverdlovsk province wrote:

The worst situation is that of single workers settled in newly built barracks and dugouts (opened up for occupation with enormous defects and not fully finished). Roofs, floors, ceilings haven't been sealed, there are chinks in the walls everywhere, the stoves have been badly installed, there are no cesspits or gutters for waste water.[66]

The Union of Armament Workers complained in 1942 that at Kuibyshev's factory No. 525 more than 85 percent of workers were living in tents or dugouts, in filth and damp. The tents had no bedding, the workers slept on bare wooden boards, and there were no baths. A letter about this same factory from a medical correspondent to the editor of the journal *Meditsinskii rabotnik* (*The Medical Worker*) observed in January 1943, "We saw a worker who had just spent a double shift standing on his feet, having worked 24 hours without a break. He came home, stood in front of a cold stove, shaking all over. He wouldn't allow himself to lie down on the bed, because it was cold and filthy."[67]

Similar conditions prevailed everywhere, especially for young workers, evacuees and refugees, and others mobilized from afar to work in industry. In August 1942, the Komsomol received a report on the housing of 1,200 graduates from Labor Reserve schools at the Stalin iron and steel works in Zlatoust, one of the most important factories in Cheliabinsk province. The windowpanes in their barracks were broken, there was no heat, and the washrooms—located outside in the courtyard—were out of order. Workers washed their clothes in a nearby stream when weather permitted. There were no tanks for boiled water, which was just as well because there was no fuel with which to boil it. The inspector noted:

The shortage of soap, washrooms, and water, and the lack of regular visits to the bathhouse has led to workers going about dirty, often not washing for several days at a time. Workers can't change their underwear sufficiently often because most of them don't have another pair to change into. No one has organized the regular laundering and change of bed linen. The bed linen that exists is far from enough. Moreover, because workers don't have a change of clothing, most of them go to bed in their work clothes. All this leads to a situation where bed linen is in an exceptionally neglected state, especially in the general barracks. Sheets and pillowcases have literally turned black with dirt; there are infestations of lice (barracks No. 2).[68]

Figure 2.1 Workers in an aircraft factory, Altai Territory. Courtesy of RGAKFD.

The hard truth was that the country was diverting every resource to heavy industry and armaments, and even the most eloquent protests and pleas could not conjure up lumber, nails, fuel, and bedding.

Industrial Space: Construction, Expansion, Merger

The SE, the GKO, the Soviet of People's Commissars, and the industrial commissariats were all involved in determining destinations for evacuated factories.[69] At times, the commissariats sent out their own roving representatives to try to locate viable spaces. The GKO took up the issue of factory resettlement well before evacuation was fully underway but, as more factories were forced to evacuate, the conflicts over space intensified.[70] By September 1941, there were already so many difficulties in delivering convoys that the Commissariat of Railways got involved in choosing destinations.[71] Plans for both people and factories were made in terms of "*ploshchad'*" or space in cubic meters rather than rooms or structures. New factories frequently doubled or tripled up with host or native factories, sharing the same structures and machine shops.[72] Factory No. 77 (the Kirov factory) in Leningrad, for example, which manufactured the KV-1 tank, shared space with the Cheliabinsk Tractor Factory (ChTZ).[73] Although the Kirov workers were only a small minority of ChTZ's overall workforce, the factory was known during the war and early postwar years as the Cheliabinsk Kirov factory. Some factories remained intact and autonomous within a shared space; others combined production methods, workforces, and management teams. Factories were also split up, their machinery parceled out to others. Much machinery from light industry, for example, was transferred to defense.[74] Some factories were redistributed among multiple towns. The Stalin motor vehicle factory in Moscow was broken up, and its various subunits sent to Ul'ianovsk, Miass, Cheliabinsk, Shadrinsk, and Molotov. The main part of Moscow's Krasnyi Proletarii factory went to Cheliabinsk, where it then became host to the Molotov machine-tool factory from Khar'kov.[75] The rapid organizational changes required directors, foremen, and skilled workers to adapt to new machinery, production methods, and even products, and the division and recombination ultimately resulted in a sweeping reconfiguration of industry.

Local authorities often made decisions about sharing space under extreme pressure, and their choices were not always practical or safe. When the Commissariat of Ammunition evacuated a gunpowder factory from Ukraine to Krasnoiarsk, it was assigned space with a paper factory, an obvious hazard given the volatility of gunpowder and the flammability of paper. At the same time, the SE ordered the Commissariat of the Paper Industry to send its other evacuated factories to the same space. The commissar of ammunition promptly complained. "Tell the Commissariat of the Paper Industry to stop sending its evacuated machinery to the grounds of the Krasnoiarsk paper factory, and get a special representative out here to pack up their stuff and get it out."[76] He was undoubtedly imagining the huge conflagration that a single spark might ignite. A less dangerous but equally bad decision to place a rubber chemical complex in a meat factory in Sverdlovsk drew the ire of A. I. Mikoian, a member of the SE and later of the GKO. Understandably, the rubber factory, with its poisonous emissions and toxic chemicals, was a poor partner for a food factory.[77]

Officials from the provincial party committee, the SE, and the commissariats, all seasoned wheeler-dealers, were involved in elaborate swaps to site the evacuated factories. Highly placed officials from the Commissariats of Aviation and Ammunition both claimed the space occupied by a small furniture factory in Sverdlovsk province. An ammunition factory had already moved in and begun producing armored missiles. The Ammunition officials were promised a brewery if they would vacate the furniture factory, but the head of the provincial party organization would not relinquish the brewery, claiming that it could be repurposed to produce bread, which was desperately needed by the arriving workers. He suggested instead giving the Commissariat of Aviation the Institute of Journalists, whose members had already been pushed out of their premises.[78] Tram and railroad depots, warehouses, schools, and every unoccupied square meter were all repurposed to house evacuated machinery. In Tambov, equipment from an evacuated machine-building factory was dumped without any cover on the grounds of a defense factory. The machines could not be moved into the defense factory, so workers were running machines as construction workers built a structure around them, which was expected to take at least four months. The secretary of Tambov's provincial party committee asked the SE to tell him where to put the machines that were lying "under open skies," "so as to preserve them from ruin."[79] Unprecedented combinations created other problems as well. Each factory had its own specifications for emissions, safety, ventilation, and disposal of hazardous materials. When factories were combined, they created more intense and sometimes unique chemical emissions. The hazards were even greater when workers were sleeping in the shops or residents living in the same building.[80] A big garage in Tashkent, for example, became the new home to two factories, evacuated from Moscow and Khar'kov, each making different products. The workers and their families lived among the machines.[81]

Arguments, delays, and difficulty in assigning destinations complicated the urgent task of resuming production. Sometimes factories were rerouted several times before they could be reassembled. Moscow's Kalibr factory, for example, which manufactured measuring instruments, was sent in mid-October 1941 to Tashkent, where workers began to unload and reassemble the equipment in a new building in early November. As they were doing so, a new order arrived directing the factory to Cheliabinsk. By mid-January, only about three-quarters of the evacuated machinery had reached Cheliabinsk, much of which was stranded near the railway station in boxcars. Of Kalibr's original workforce of 2,700 workers and specialists, 820 went to Cheliabinsk with their families (about 1,500 people in total). Of this number, 530 were housed in the classrooms of the local primary school. The factory itself was to occupy the site of a new, and as yet unfinished, drama theater, but the move was delayed because the structure was already being used as a storage facility for party archives evacuated from Leningrad. It took most of December to decide what to do with the archives. Not until mid-January did Kalibr finally take possession of the building and begin installing its equipment. At this point, the workers discovered that the space was too small and needed to be expanded by two-thirds, which they did by building an annex. Despite its trials, the factory had resumed turning out instruments by the end of January 1942.[82] Other factories, too, arrived only to discover that the space they were assigned was insufficient.[83]

Upon seeing their destinations, many factory managers from Moscow immediately wired the SE, their commissariats, and even Stalin requesting they be allowed to return. Eight shop heads from defense factory No. 266 were evacuated with their factory from Moscow to Tomsk. Shocked at the conditions, they quickly bypassed the head of their commissariat and sent Stalin a telegram:

Arrived in Tomsk 2/3 of equipment located in railroad station and on frozen ground of unconstructed unheated structure STOP Remaining equipment part en route, part in Moscow forbidden to load. Great majority of packers still in Moscow STOP Shops cannot be constructed in space provided STOP Lack tools STOP Energy is 20 percent of that necessary to build line 5 kilometers to bring water to living space STOP

Lacking electricity lines, loaders, part of their equipment, housing, water, and a structure for the factory, they requested return to Moscow to inhabit their old premises. Stalin, the recipient of torrents of complaints, passed their telegram to the appropriate authorities in the Commissariat of the Electrical Industry, which told the crestfallen shop heads in no uncertain terms that they were to remain in Tomsk and that their former space had already been occupied by another factory.[84]

The breakup and redistribution of factories were partly dictated by the logistics of evacuation and the needs of the military, but the process was also facilitated by the structure of Soviet industrial complexes, which contained multiple factories and subunits and tens of thousands of workers. The workforce at the Magnitogorsk and Kuznetsk iron and steel combines fluctuated between 25,000 and 26,000.[85] The giant Uralmash machine-building factory, which manufactured large-scale tank components, employed 23,000.[86] Many enterprises contained a mix of production and auxiliary shops, with the latter often employing as many workers as the former. As a legacy of the shortages and imbalances of rapid industrialization, many factories had their own machine shops and foundries to produce spare parts.[87] These features helped ease the divisions and new amalgamations that evacuation and the lack of infrastructure in the east initially required. Although some structures housed unlikely combinations, the eastern industrial base also received evacuated machinery that allowed it to upgrade and expand.

In addition to new structures, the eastern towns had to build water and electricity lines, spur rail lines, and roads. The massive construction effort rivaled the industrialization drive of the 1930s, but operated under the severe constraints and shortages of wartime. Much of this construction was carried out by Special Construction and Erection Units (Osobye stroitel'no-montazhnye chasti, or OSMCh). During 1942, there were some seventy OSMCh throughout the USSR, more than half of them in the Urals. OSMCh functioned as mobile militarized labor detachments, also known as labor battalions or construction labor columns, employing mostly men of draft age unfit for combat. Later their ranks were supplemented by workers and peasants mobilized from Central Asia and members of the Labor Army, who were under NKVD control. Of the 700,000 workers mobilized in construction columns by the end of 1941, about 40 percent worked under the auspices of the Commissariat of Construction.[88] Many industrial commissariats used OSMCh and also had their own construction units. In December 1942, the iron and steel industry, for example, employed more than 63,000 people in construction, only 20,000 of them through OSMCh.[89]

OSMCh took responsibility for building many of the new structures to house the evacuated factories. In Sverdlovsk in 1941, for example, the OSMCh was charged with constructing a new tank factory, to be designated as factory No. 37, from the evacuated machinery of three different enterprises, and parts from two factories already in Sverdlovsk, neither of which produced tanks, as well as a new building to house the Bol'shevik factory evacuated from Kiev. The OSMCh workers labored outdoors throughout the harsh Urals winter as temperatures plunged to –40°F (–40°C). They lacked essential building materials, and even blueprints, which were drawn up as they built. Their battalion consisted of no fewer than forty-four nationalities, including workers mobilized from Central Asia, who spoke little or no Russian and who arrived on site in open-toed sandals. Managers procured warm clothing and boots, and the battalion worked fast. Within a short period, both factories began producing armaments in their new buildings.[90]

In some areas, the OSMCh battalions were composed mainly of women. The Urals–Siberian OSMCh built railway lines and roads, installed water supplies and sewerage systems for defense factories, and laid a new railway line for the North Urals bauxite mines. It also served some of the largest factories in the Urals, including the Cheliabinsk Kirov tank factory and the Stalin motor vehicle works in Miass, part of which had been evacuated from Moscow. For its work on the Urals Aluminum Factory and the rail line for the bauxite mines, it employed 2,500 evacuees, mainly women, from Leningrad and Kalinin, and 400 women from Bashkiriia. Some of the new arrivals were young girls and mothers with small children. Only around 1,000 were physically capable of heavy labor, especially in the harsh conditions of the taiga. Former textile workers, hairdressers, accountants, bookkeepers, or teachers learned new skills as carpenters, welders, truck drivers, blasters, or turners; others dug earthworks, felled trees, and uprooted stumps. Constantly on the move, especially when laying railway track, they had no permanent housing. Soon after the women arrived in fall 1941, the rainy season ended and the deep freeze set in. Temperatures dropped to –22 or –40°F (–30 or –40°C). Exhausting labor and wretched conditions frequently left them in tears. The women, like so many mobilized workers, lacked warm clothing and decent footwear. Ever ingenious, the women sewed warm footwear using scraps of canvas and thick felt, dug the water lines, and built the railways.[91]

Sometimes OSMCh battalions, like other evacuated workers, received unexpected assignments. In April 1942 the GKO ordered the construction of several new iron and steel works in the Urals to be carried out by construction organizations from multiple cities. OSMCh 63, previously employed constructing aviation factories, was assigned to erect the blast furnace in Chusovoi, a town in Molotov province along the Chusovaia River. The first obstacle the battalion faced was that Chusovoi was almost impossible to reach. An advance party consisting of 360 workers quickly realized that the city could be accessed only by river boat. They found a vessel and managed to get as far as Molotov, but then got stuck in the shallow river; eventually they found a smaller vessel and completed their journey. The advance party had to find housing for 5,500 workers, some of whom had already arrived and were living in tents, with the rest due to arrive shortly. In the words of the head of the battalion, A. V. Tishchenko, not a single square meter of housing space was available anywhere in the city. The local party organization could offer no help. The workers were eventually housed in primitive barracks that they built themselves. The next difficulty was food. Those workers already in Chusovoi were temporarily fed by the iron and steel works. Yet once the Commissariat of Construction opened its own Department of Workers' Provisioning, the iron and steel plant expelled the OSMCh workers from its canteens. The OSMCh workers now had food, but no way to store or cook it until they built their own canteen and facilities. At the same time, the workers began work on the blast furnace but lacked workshops to manufacture tools or cut timber, stables for their 300 horses, and places to park and service their 120 trucks. Mobilized from three different localities—Kazan', Kirov, and Ul'ianovsk—each group suspected the others of receiving better treatment amidst the harsh conditions. Senior managers, fed up with the rivalries and bickering, finally explained in no uncertain terms that henceforth there were to be no more "Kazan' people," "Kirov people," or "Ul'ianovsk people," just people working for OSMCh 63. Out of these seemingly intractable difficulties emerged a new blast furnace just nine months after the battalion first received its assignments.[92]

Evacuation helped modernize the eastern industrial base by placing more technologically advanced factories on the premises of those using older technologies. Yet the melding of factories, workers, managers, and production methods did not always run smoothly. The combination of factory No. 22, a large aviation factory evacuated from Moscow, and the smaller and less advanced factory No. 124 already sited in Kazan' reveals the difficulties such mergers often produced.[93] The initial plan to evacuate factory No. 22 laid out an orderly removal in two stages, the first to begin in August 1941. The second stage was accelerated by the rapid advance of German troops on Moscow and began on October 16, during the chaotic emergency evacuation of the city. Most of the factory's personnel arrived in Kazan' by early November. The machinery did not arrive until January, after having been loaded onto barges in Moscow and being frozen en route along the Volga and Oka Rivers. Some of the stranded machinery never reached Kazan' and was reassigned to factories closer to the front. The rest arrived only after the factory sent a team of 400 horses—no small achievement given wartime requisitioning—and a group of workers to pull it out of the frozen Volga to a rail line. The striking juxtaposition of hundreds of horses and people straining to haul technologically advanced machinery over a frozen river and rutted rural roads captured the essence of the Soviet war effort. Once in Kazan', however, the machinery turned out to be too corroded to be useful for anything but salvage. So factory No. 22 began its new life in Kazan' with only a portion of the equipment the workers had laboriously crated, dispatched, and then rescued from the frozen Volga.

The workers meanwhile had difficulties of their own. When they arrived, many were temporarily billeted in Kazan''s Kremlin, because there was nowhere to house them. Pelagiia Davydova, a twenty-two-year-old worker who made her way to Kazan' via a torturous route, explained her struggle to get settled:

> Having arrived in Kazan' they quartered us in the Kremlin. I spent three days registering at the factory. There was nowhere for me to live. From the Kremlin they shunted us over to the city soviet, but the city soviet would not register us, just drove us away saying, let factory No. 22 give you housing. From my very first days at the factory I was pursued by misfortune: they took away my documents, my bread ration cards, my Komsomol membership card, [and] my factory pass. I went to my shop head, Comrade Rekhtman, and told him what had happened. He said, you've had a whole bunch of misfortunes, now go and talk to them and get your bread ration card. Then they gave me an authorization for living space in Koz'ya sloboda [literally, "the goat settlement"], I went there but they wouldn't let me in, saying they were already crowded. I went back to the factory—I didn't abandon my job. I refused to leave the city soviet until they gave me somewhere else to live. Then they gave me an authorization for the Socialist City [*sotsgorod*]. I went to look at the place, but it was already occupied by other people. I went back to the factory, and again asked for a housing authorization. Finally, I moved into the basement of building No. 10. My neighbors looked after my things while I went to work every day. Then they gave me yet another authorization. I went there and the landlord and landlady took me in, they had nothing against me, and I lived there for a year. When my sister arrived it was too cramped there, and we moved to another apartment. Now I've got used to our apartment, I've organized life in the Socialist City just as I had in Moscow and feel myself at home. I don't think about Moscow and don't dream about it.[94]

For all her travails, Davydova was relatively lucky in eventually finding somewhere to live. Many of the factory's young workers remained homeless: some lived in the factory, others ran away, and some begged to join the Red Army—a request management refused because it was so short of labor. The factory placed workers wherever they could, but not all of them had access to water supply, and very few had indoor toilets or heating. The winter of 1942 was unusually harsh in Kazan' and elsewhere (temperatures fell to –49°F [–45°C]), and workers in factory No. 22 received no fuel deliveries at all that winter.

Conditions in the combined factories were equally difficult. The heating system at factory No. 124, the host, had a very limited capacity, and temperatures in many of its shops barely rose above 21–23°F (5–6°C). Until April 1942 it did not have a single heated toilet stall or washroom, although it did have a bathhouse. The managers of factory No. 22 took the lead, installing toilets, shower rooms, medical stations, water fountains, tanks for boiled water, a *sanpropusknik*, a delouser, and a second bathhouse. The harsh winter took its toll in other ways. The bulk of the factory's workforce lived some 5–9 miles (8–14 km) from the factory and walked to work because the city's tram system barely functioned. Many suffered frostbite, and some days literally thousands of workers showed up late or not at all. The factory solved the problem by effectively expropriating the tram line. It used its workshops to make the spare parts needed to get the line running again and took over responsibility for regular maintenance. The canteen in host factory No. 124 was too small to feed the new combined workforce. For several weeks, the Moscow evacuees lived on cold sandwiches until managers at factory No. 22 built a large-scale kitchen, which by December 1941 was serving 100,000 hot meals a day. To supply the kitchen, the factory's Department of Workers' Provisioning created links with three state farms. The farms were not in good shape: they had no fodder for their animals, no seed grain for planting their next crop, decrepit barns, and equipment in need of repair. The factory soon began to bring the farms into working order in order to provide its workers with adequate food.

As the problems of food, housing, and transport were slowly resolved, new conflicts developed between the managers and workers of the two enterprises. Facilities at factory No. 124 were already poor and sharing them with several thousand new arrivals led workers to resent each other for overcrowding. More serious conflicts arose between managers and skilled workers over production methods. Moscow's factory No. 22 was a modern, technologically advanced factory that produced aircraft on an assembly line and stamped parts out of templates. Kazan''s factory No. 124 had no assembly line and used more labor-intensive, skill-based methods for making parts. The attempt by the Moscow newcomers to impose their methods on No. 124

infuriated its managers and skilled workers. Shop heads came to blows. The situation became so tense that the directors of the two factories had to call an emergency meeting of all the workers to calm everyone down. A direct order from Moscow to subsume Kazan's factory No. 124 under the single management of Moscow's No. 22 "resolved" the conflict in December 1941.

Factory No. 22's arrival in Kazan' thus transformed No. 124 into a modern enterprise perhaps decades before it would otherwise have become one. An assembly line, built by factory No. 22, was installed. Workers either made the parts themselves or found substitutes. The assembly line cut the labor invested per unit of output and increased production, but it also undermined the power of Kazan's older skilled workers. New workers who came to the factory during the course of the war, and indeed for years afterwards, entered a modern work culture and environment, with an assembly line, toilets, showers, medical stations, and large-capacity canteen. The managers of factory No. 22 maintained that many factories had similar wartime experiences with modernization. Their suppliers, for example, increased output as well as quality, a legacy that would last long after the war ended.

Although the process of modernization was marked by reversals, the advocates of speedier and more efficient production tended to prevail. The Kirov factory, evacuated from Leningrad to join the Cheliabinsk Tractor Factory, exemplified the difficulties in supplanting older with newer methods. The Cheliabinsk Tractor Factory, constructed in the 1930s, assembled its tractors and tanks on an assembly line. The old and venerable Kirov factory assembled its tractors separately, each built start to finish as a discrete unit. After the Kirov factory and its 7,000 evacuated workers arrived, the combined factory started to produce tanks using the newer Cheliabinsk system. However, troops at the front soon encountered problems: engines that overheated, failing brakes, and badly designed optical instruments. The head of Kirov's design bureau, Zhozef Kotin, insisted that the factory return to Kirov's older, individual approach. After considerable argument, Kotin prevailed, and the production of heavy tanks was totally reorganized. Yet, later in the war, production shifted toward the lighter T-34 tanks, a machine so fast and so effective that it gained fame throughout the world. The T-34, designed with the demands of the battlefield in mind, was made on an assembly line.[95]

****

Figure 2.2 Assembly shop at the Kirov Tank Factory, Cheliabinsk, 1942.
Courtesy of RGAKFD.

The SE's orderly statistics represented the messy, dangerous, and unpredictable journeys of millions of evacuees and refugees. People arrived in sponsored convoys and independent groups to face new problems of housing
and work in towns ill equipped to absorb them. Stripped of every comfort,
they suffered conditions far inferior to those they had left behind. Hosts and
arrivals fought over space, methods of production, and scarce resources.
Accommodation was not easy, and evacuees often wore out their initial
welcome. Despite the great difficulties, the war proved a crucible, forcing
public health officials to adopt increasingly effective prophylactic methods,

construction workers to build new industries and infrastructure, and municipal authorities to install power grids and roads. The demands of the battlefield forced industry to modernize rapidly. Startup times, normally lasting months, were telescoped into mere weeks. In Saratov, workers began operating machines as walls were being built around them. Two weeks after the last machine was unloaded in Saratov, the first MiG fighter rolled out. Workers from the Khar'kov tank factory turned out their first tank less than ten weeks after they packed and loaded their factory and rolled east.[96]

In the end, evacuation proved a potent force for modernization, combining less developed with more technologically advanced factories, creating streamlined processes of production, and forcing new construction. It required a massive investment in transport as well as the building of new structures designed to house the vastly expanded and combined enterprises that melded the industrial bases of west and east. In 1944 the Soviet Union produced nearly four times as many combat aircraft as it did in 1940; ten times as many combat vehicles (mainly tanks); eight times as many heavy guns; and twice as many small arms. At the same time, every sector other than defense was starved of resources. The majority of what was still produced by light industry went to the military, including building materials, textiles, footwear, tools, and transport. The sharp decline in metal, machinery, railway locomotives, rolling stock, motor vehicles, bricks, cement, timber, textiles, and footwear left the country with a vastly weakened base to begin its postwar reconstruction.[97] It would be many years before ordinary people were adequately clothed, shod, housed, and fed. These, however, were long-term concerns, unimaginable in light of the threat to the country's very existence. For the moment, the only task was to drive the fascists out of Soviet territory and win the war. Evacuation and the resettlement of industry and people made this possible.

3

The Staff of Life: Feeding the People

"Do we have enough bread given the loss of territory or will there
be hunger?"

Question asked by an audience member at
a meeting in Kalinin province

The evacuation of millions of people and the loss of the agricultural
base in the occupied territories dealt a double blow to the Soviet Union.
Major grain-producing lands were lost to the Germans, severely disrupting
the distribution network of collective and state farms, retail stores, food-
processing factories, and transport. The territories occupied by November
1941 had accounted for 38 percent of the country's prewar production of grain, 84 percent of sugar, and 38 percent of cattle. Production of
processed foods dropped by 58 percent between 1940 and 1942.[1] At the
same time, millions of evacuees and refugees had to be fed despite transport being under terrible strain.[2] People housed in barracks and *zemlianki*
had no access to private kitchens. Other residents, still occupying their
own apartments or houses, had dwindling access to cooking fuel. Home
cooking everywhere gave way to communal dining in canteens, where the
vast majority of workers, students, children, and others received their only
hot meals.

The state established a rationing system for urban residents and waged
workers within three weeks of the invasion. Over time, an increasingly complex hierarchy for the distribution of various food groups emerged. Rationed
food was highly subsidized and inexpensive. Unlike other combatant countries that adopted rationing, shortages were so great that the state was forced
to halt almost all commercial sale of food through retail stores. Yet rations
alone were not sufficient to feed the army and the civilian population. Raisa
Roitman was fifteen when she fled east with her family from Moldavia to
Uzbekistan, where she found work in a cotton oil factory. She remembered
one of the perks of the job:

I worked as a loader at the cotton oil factory. Before I left the factory I was allowed to soak my clothes in cotton oil. I put on as many clothes as possible and soaked them in oil very well. The members of my extended family were waiting for me by the entrance. There was a considerable lack of fats in our diet, so they had to suck cotton oil from my clothes. I was standing there and crying. Almost all the factory workers were taking the cotton oil the way I did, and there were other people close to us, who were saturating in oil like my relatives. . . . I tried to leave some oil for my little brother. Motle took the hunger really hard.[3]

During the war's grimmest years, many workers subsisted on bread and gruel. Hunger and starvation-related mortality, so well documented in the besieged city of Leningrad, also claimed many lives in the Soviet rear.[4] The full extent of deprivation, however, known to everyone who lived through the war, was hidden from the West and later omitted from Russia's own heroic accounts.

Hungry citizens on the home front have overthrown more than one regime struggling to finance war.[5] In France, years of war created the fiscal crisis that led to revolution in 1789. During World War I, women's bread riots in Russia toppled the tsar in February 1917 and helped bring the soviets to power in October. And in Germany women's food protests merged with the rebellions of workers, sailors, and other groups to bring down the Kaiser in 1918. In each of these revolutionary moments, hungry people lost faith not only in their leaders but also in the systems they represented.[6] Yet despite hunger in the Soviet Union being fiercer and more widespread than in 1917, there were no mass protests, food riots, or rebellions. On the contrary, state food policy effectively organized scarce resources and had widespread popular support.

The food system that emerged during the war differed from the grain requisitioning of War Communism, the market exchange of the New Economic Policy (NEP), or the developing retail trade network of the 1930s. Central state stocks provided the bulk of calories consumed by the civilian population, and a parallel decentralized system of subsidiary farms, local procurement, gardens, and collective farm markets supplemented the ration.[7] State, party, and union organizations played an essential role in provisioning, fighting to ensure that planned allocations reached the groups they represented, and organizing collective initiatives that enabled people to supplement their rations. Scientists, nutritionists, and canteen workers experimented with substitute foods to alleviate the worst effects of nutritional deprivation. This combination of rationing, state-sponsored collective activities, and individual efforts allowed the country to manage and survive the terrible food shortages of the war years.

The Wartime Rationing System

The Soviet state was able to respond to the food crisis so quickly in part because of its previous experience with rationing. During the Civil War years, the embattled Bolsheviks employed both grain requisitioning and rationing to guarantee food to the cities and the Red Army. In the early 1930s, the state returned to rationing during the upheaval of collectivization and industrialization as it struggled to eliminate private middlemen and develop a network of retail state stores.[8] Soviet leaders, however, never viewed rationing as a permanent or desirable feature of socialism. Its implementation resulted from the need to ensure an affordable and stable supply of food to the cities amid extreme shortage.[9] As soon as shortages eased, the state abolished rationing in favor of a system based on wages and retail trade.[10] In 1939, as the country shifted resources into defense and food shortages intensified, the state again adopted a limited form of rationing through "closed network" stores for the officer corps and workers in leading branches of industry.[11] In 1940 food shortages became even more severe. Although the Politburo refused to sanction the introduction of rationing nationwide, many local officials instituted their own ad hoc rationing systems to ensure the basic distribution of bread.[12]

Soon after the invasion, Soviet leaders responded to the growing needs of the army and the losses in the occupied territories by slashing central state stocks of food for distribution to the retail trade network. A new "Mobilization Plan for the National Economy" placed the country on wartime footing and replaced the food figures of the Third Five-Year-Plan: central state stocks of flour dropped to 70 percent of their already low 1940 level, grain to 67 percent, and sugar to just 34 percent.[13] In mid-July, the state introduced a rationing system to be administered by the Commissariat of Trade that soon encompassed all urban inhabitants and waged workers. First introduced in Moscow, Leningrad, and their surrounding provinces on July 18, it included bread, pasta, meat and fish, sugar, candy, and fat. A more limited ration for bread only was introduced in all towns and workers' settlements in the industrial provinces of Sverdlovsk, Cheliabinsk, Molotov, Gor'kii, Iaroslavl', Tula, and Ivanovo, and the autonomous republics of Bashkiriia and Tatariia on August 15. A week later, rationing for bread, as well as sugar and candy, was extended to a wider list of towns and settlements. On November 1, the ration system expanded again to include provisioning of meat and fish, fats, grains, and pasta to a total of forty-three towns and workers' settlements, as well as to many industrial enterprises in areas that were guaranteed only bread and sugar, and to some occupational groups, including teachers and medical personnel. On November 10, bread and sugar rationing was decreed for all towns and workers' settlements.[14] By late fall 1941, every urban area was guaranteed, at minimum, bread and sugar.

A. V. Liubimov, People's Commissar of Trade, remembered how the Commissariat's employees calculated ration amounts at night in a bomb shelter in Moscow:

> In this first period of the war, there was much that was unclear about the situation in the frontline areas, the status of food stocks, and their movement. The necessary information only reached us, as a rule, at the end of the normal working day, in the evening or at night. To delay decisions on this or that question was impossible . . . At the sound of the air raid siren, people with packs with slide rules and adding machines would descend to the underground shelter, equipped for work. There we had typewriters and a working telephone line. Above, the bombs tore through the sky, exploding randomly, and the anti-aircraft guns shot back. But here, underground, work continued. The time could not be lost . . .[15]

Rationing set limits on consumption, but more importantly it ensured a fixed minimum. As food stocks dwindled and commercial sales ended, people who possessed ration cards for fish, meat, pasta, fats, and grains were better provisioned than those entitled only to bread and sugar. State farm and rural waged workers received rations, but peasants did not, under the assumption that they could provision themselves directly through their collective farms and private plots. Bread was the very heart of the ration system. The state was committed to providing all towns with an uninterrupted, daily norm of fresh-baked bread. Unlike meat, fats, or other foods, bread was rarely subject to substitutions. The state treated a bakery stoppage as a crisis meriting immediate attention. Urban residents greeted the rationing system favorably. It ended panicked buying, long lines, and the speculative practice

of buying in bulk and reselling. It also stopped the common peasant practice of feeding cattle and pigs with state-subsidized bread, which was cheaper
than fodder.[16]

The Commissariat of Trade, originally established to oversee retail trade,
was repurposed to manage rationing and distribute food stocks through
its organizational pyramid at central, republic, provincial, and town levels.
Its provincial and town trade departments (*obtorgotdely* and *gortorgotdely*)
were the primary distributors of central stocks to industrial enterprises,
institutions, and stores. The state also allocated central stocks directly to
other recipients, including institutions, provincial and district executive
committees of the soviets, and industrial enterprises. The Commissariat of
Trade calculated norms of provisioning based on the size of various population groups. Initially, ration cards (*kartochki*) were printed by the republic-
level Soviets of People's Commissars or provincial soviets, and distributed
through factories, schools, institutions, and the managers of houses and
apartment buildings. In 1943, an Administration of Rationed Provisioning
under the USSR Commissariat of Trade was established to take over
printing and distribution through its local bureaus.[17] The apparatus of the
Commissariat of Trade grew steadily with the development of the ration
system. By January 1946, there were 3,100 ration card bureaus employing
more than 14,000 people, and an additional 400,000 people helped to distribute cards.[18]

People received a ration card and coupons (*talony*) each month entitling
them to buy a set amount of bread, foodstuffs, and consumer items. Bread
cards, however, were printed in categories ranging from a daily ration of
100 grams to one of 600 grams.[19] Many people also received at least one hot
meal daily in their factory canteens through coupons entitling them to set
amounts of fat, meat, bread, etc. The state also issued coupons for consumer
items, which were sold only on ration. Each item required a certain number
of coupons: a wool dress—60, leather shoes—50, children's sandals—20.[20]
Yet coupons did not guarantee availability. By the beginning of 1942, for
example, the Commissariat of Rubber ended production for the civilian
market, and it became impossible to buy rubber boots.[21] Clothing, shoes,
needles, thread, and many other items were also very difficult to obtain.

In 1942, the Germans conquered more territory, and the demands of the
army increased with vast new mobilizations. Despite heroic efforts at evacuation, the overall picture was grim. The loss of food-processing factories
resulted in a sharp decrease in jams, oil, butter, margarine, meat and fish

products, and canned vegetables.[22] Planners were again forced to cut central state stocks for the home front: flour was reduced to about half the 1940 level, grain to one-third, and sugar to 15 percent.[23] By spring, the state recognized that central stocks would not cover the food needs of the urban population. It encouraged local trade organizations and enterprises to develop four additional decentralized sources of food. First, it instructed local soviets to distribute unused land to all enterprises and organizations for subsidiary farms where their employees could grow food for their canteens. Many factory officials organized piggeries based on canteen swill. The state also "attached" already-existing state and collective farms to specific enterprises and industrial commissariats, which would receive part of their harvest. Second, it encouraged factories and town trade departments to purchase food from local food producers and processors. Managers might negotiate a contract with a fishing trust, for example, allowing workers to fish in their waters and deliver the catch to the canteens. Factories set up workshops to produce consumer items from cast-off materials to trade with peasants. And union representatives bought food in bulk in the collective farm markets on behalf of factory canteens. Third, the state launched a nationwide gardening movement, providing workers with small plots, implements, and seed. And, fourth, the Commissariat of Trade actively promoted collective farm markets where peasants could sell food from their private plots. Of all these sources, only the collective farm markets sold food at free market prices.[24]

Despite the push toward alternate sources of food, the state continued to supply the vast majority of the calories consumed by the urban population throughout the war (see Table 3.1, p. 382). Central state stocks contributed by far the greatest share: in 1942 nearly 80 percent of the calories consumed, and in 1944 more than two-thirds. Subsidiary farms provided only a small percentage of calories consumed by the population overall, but played a greater role in provisioning factories, children's homes, and other institutions. Decentralized procurement provided less than 1 percent of food consumed, although this source, too, greatly benefited workers in certain enterprises. Over the course of the war, individual gardens and collective farm markets increased their combined contribution to consumption. Garden plots were a key source of potatoes, a lifesaving source of calories and protein. Collective farm markets were important for providing scarce foods such as milk, eggs, and meat, which were often not available on ration. Taken together, state organizations provided at minimum almost three-quarters of the calories consumed.

State food policy, no matter how broadly diversified, could not compensate for the loss of prime farmland, agricultural machinery, herds, and draft animals captured in the occupied areas (see Table 3.2). By 1944, the total grain harvest (47.2 million tons) was only 49 percent of the harvest in 1940; wheat, 42 percent; and sugar beets, a mere 30 percent. Even potatoes, the staple crop of gardens, were only 77 percent of the amount produced in 1940. Similar drops occurred in the number of cattle, pigs, sheep and goats, and horses. The availability of food reflected these decreases. In 1944, the amount of meat available was 55 percent of its 1940 level; milk, 79 percent; and eggs, 40 percent. The food industry showed even sharper decreases, with most foods, including flour, reaching their low points in 1943 and 1944. In 1945, after the liberation of the occupied territories, not a single index of agricultural production had reached its prewar level. Personal consumption of food and consumer goods dropped by 40 percent in comparison with the already difficult prewar years.[25] At that time, with the shift of resources to defense, the war with Finland, and exports of food to Nazi Germany, bread and staples had already begun to disappear from the shops, and mortality, particularly in the towns, to increase.[26]

According to the calculations of U. G. Cherniavskii, a Soviet economist, the nadir of food consumption for the urban and wage-earning population was 1942, but most qualitative accounts suggest that conditions continued to worsen throughout 1943.[27] In either case, the difference between the two years was small. People were hungry, many were chronically malnourished, and some starved. Scurvy and other diseases caused by vitamin deficiencies were common. Significant improvement in diets came only toward the end of 1944, yet even then consumption remained well below the prewar level and people's biological needs (see Table 3.3).[28]

The array of foods also shrank. People substituted potatoes for other basic foods, but the protein in potatoes could not fully offset the loss of dairy products, meat, and fish, or the lower protein content of adulterated wartime bread. Starvation disease, as doctors in Leningrad and the Warsaw ghetto discovered, was linked not just to hunger but also to severe protein deficiency and, in the latter stages, the body's consumption of its own muscle.[29] Despite improvement in provisioning throughout 1943 and early 1944, the cumulative deficits took their toll. More workers proved unable to work due to severe malnutrition and starvation, and more working-age adults, primarily men, died of starvation. Only after mid-1944 did food stocks sufficiently improve to place workers and other groups on refeeding programs scientifically designed to restore their weakened systems to health.[30]

Hierarchies of Provisioning

The ration system, based on differentiated rather than equal distribution, operated according to a labor principle, which rewarded those who expended more calories at work with more food, and a social principle, which protected the most vulnerable groups independent of their labor contribution. Soldiers were fed better than civilians. Both the military and the civilian spheres, in turn, were divided into their own hierarchies of provisioning.[31] On the home front, ration cards were divided into four groups: workers received the largest rations, followed in descending order by white-collar employees, dependants, and children under twelve. Able-bodied adults of working age, who were not caring for small children, and teenagers were expected to work or attend school or vocational training. In accordance with the labor principle, workers in industries most important to defense or who expended the largest number of calories received the highest ration. Dependants were defined as nonwaged housewives, the ill or disabled, elderly, orphans, and those in state institutions. In accordance with the social principle, young children, nursing mothers, workers in hazardous occupations, people suffering from tuberculosis, malnutrition, and starvation disease, and teenaged workers were to receive supplemental calories or access to scarce, nutritious foods such as milk.[32] Officials channeled milk and special foods to orphanages and young children.[33]

The rationing system, deceptively simple in its four categories, was soon subdivided into finer gradations of privilege. Workers and employees, for example, were also divided by economic branch. The state allotted the highest norms (*povyshennye* or *osobo povyshennye normy*) to those in Category I, which included the defense, coal, peat, chemical, rubber, cement, machine-building, and metallurgical industries; electric power stations and the electrical industry; rail and sea transport; construction of defense, metallurgical, machine-building, and railroad installations; and seasonal work in forestry, fishing, and peat. Category II included all other branches of industry, transport, municipal services, and any remaining urban inhabitants not included in Category I. By the end of 1944, most industrial employment was concentrated in Category I, and more than 60 percent of workers received these higher norms.[34]

Every food group was subject to differentiation. Bread provided the largest source of calories for everyone by far: 75 percent for workers in Category I and 80 percent for adult dependants. While the difference in bread allocation between workers and engineering/technical personnel (ITR) in Categories I and II was relatively small, the differences among workers, dependants, and children were much greater: workers received twice as much bread as Category II clerical employees, adult dependants, and children. These differences, negligible to a well-nourished person with a varied diet, assumed much greater importance under conditions of deprivation where bread was the predominant source of calories, and could even determine survival over time. Sugar and confectionery had the least differentiation in allocation, meat and fish (protein) the greatest. The highest groups (Category I workers and ITR) received more than five times as much protein as the lowest (children). The distribution of fats, essential to the body's ability to synthesize vitamins, was also sharply differentiated: the best-provisioned workers received three times as much as the lowest category (dependants). Most significantly, the daily calorie intake from the ration ranged from a high of 2,015 for the best-provisioned workers to a low of 944 for children. No one, however, could live for an extended period on 2,000 calories a day, let alone half that amount, without suffering severe weight loss and nutritional deficiency. In short, no group could survive on the ration alone (see Table 3.4).

Over time, gradations within the ration system multiplied further. Defense workers had the coveted "O" for "Oborona" or "Defense" stamped on their ration cards, entitling them to a larger amount and wider array of foods. Unions maneuvered to get their workers into this category. When Leningrad's shipbuilding factories were evacuated to Kazan', for example, they were not categorized as defense factories although they built and repaired ships for the Baltic Fleet. As a result, their canteens served meager meals and their ration cards did not include meat, sugar, grains, or fats. The Union of Shipbuilding Workers sharply protested that the factories should be reassigned and the workers receive the precious "O" on their cards.[35] Yet even workers who carried the "O" stamp were subdivided. Both aviation factory No. 47 (the Maksim Gor'kii factory) and the Stalin garment factory in Chkalov, for example, were designated as defense factories. Workers in factory No. 47, evacuated from Leningrad in July 1941, produced rocket launchers and were relatively well provisioned with meat, butter, and grains.[36] Those in the Stalin garment factory, almost all women, produced uniforms and received soup, groats with no fat, and 100 grams of bread. The "soup" was so thin that many preferred to stay in the workshops and eat their bread with a mug of water. According to popular opinion, the canteen was not a place to eat but "to waste money."[37] There were other divisions as well. Peasants who were temporarily mobilized for lengthy stints in peat bogs and forests received lower rations than workers permanently employed in these sectors. Skilled workers were fed better than unskilled. Stakhanovites (norm busters) fared better than ordinary workers. In aviation factory No. 19, for example, Stakhanovites could choose between a glass of milk or two eggs with their dinner.[38] Whether these entitlements were actually available in practice was questionable: the Central Statistical Administration estimated that the average member of a worker's family in 1943 saw one egg every fifty days.[39]

The provisioning of officials added another layer of complexity to the system. Officials were supposed to be supplied at the same level as white-collar employees, but some took advantage of their power to provision themselves well above the highest categories. Many also received special food supplements (paiki) in addition to their ration cards. Up to July 1943, when the Soviet of People's Commissars issued a decree detailing how much food the various ranks of party, union, soviet, and Komsomol officials would receive, their norms and categories were not fully regulated by the state.[40]

At the very bottom of the ration hierarchy were those groups that were temporarily excluded from or poorly protected by the ration system. Evacuees were supposed to receive rations once they settled and began work.[41] Yet many new arrivals, particularly refugees who were not part of an organized convoy, struggled to find jobs and register for rations. Free market prices were prohibitively high, and people soon exhausted their limited savings and personal belongings in the peasant markets.[42] Those housed in barracks or zemlianki, including teenaged workers and apprentices, people mobilized for work in distant sites, and prisoners, were completely dependent on canteens for their meals. At the height of the food shortage, many lived on little more than thin "soup." Forced laborers were fed at the expense of stocks allocated through the Commissariat of Internal Affairs (NKVD) rather than the Commissariat of Trade and were at the very bottom of the ration hierarchy. In many cases, managers allocated part of the stocks belonging to workers to prisoners working in the factories. Yet these emaciated prisoners still haunted the canteens, hovering behind the workers as they ate, staring with wolfish intensity at the food, and waiting to lick the discarded plates.[43]

The ration system did not differentiate by gender, although some nutritional scales assumed that women needed less food then men.[44] Under wartime conditions, many women performed the same heavy labor as men, and their equal ration probably offered little advantage. Families tended to share food, which may have had a leveling effect on all hierarchies.[45] Despite performing heavy labor, caring for children and dependants, and enduring difficult living conditions, relatively few women starved to death in the rear.[46] One Russian demographer attributes women's higher survival rates to greater biological "hardiness." And if women were hardier than men in general, they were considerably hardier than men in the rear, many of whom were exempted from the army due to physical defects and chronic illnesses.[47]

The ration system allowed the state to direct food to groups fulfilling emergency tasks or in need of special supplements. At the beginning of 1942, for example, the state allocated extra food to railway, river, and maritime workers who were laboring around the clock under the strain of evacuation.[48] In May 1942, it introduced a second hot meal, soon known as the "second hot" (*vtoroe goriachee*), for workers who met or exceeded their output targets in defense, did heavy labor, or put in long hours of overtime. In May 1943, it extended the "second hot" to prisoners working in industry and on construction sites. Between December 1943 and January 1945, the number of people receiving it expanded from about one million to six million. Miners, too, received special consideration. During the first half of 1943, when the Germans still held the southern coalfields and the metallurgical factories were desperate for coal, the state increased rations for miners in the Kuznetsk coal basin (Kuzbass), providing not only the highest ration (*osobo povyshennyi norm*), but also a "cold breakfast" of bread, lard, and sugar. Access to the cold breakfast soon expanded to workers in other coalmines, nonferrous ore pits, and metallurgical factories. Workers in hazardous jobs in chemicals, defense, and metallurgy were allotted special supplements of milk, white bread, cream, meat, fish, and other foods. Malnourished workers were to receive high-protein, high-calorie meals, as were wounded veterans, blood and breast-milk donors, pregnant women, infants and children, and those with tuberculosis and ulcers. Infants and children between the ages of one and three were entitled to milk, fat, rice, and other foods in addition to their rations. In 1943 these promises proved impossible to deliver due to acute milk shortages throughout the country, but by the end of 1945 special milk kitchens were serving about 960,000 children. Almost 2.6 million children in childcare facilities also received extra food, and all students in towns and workers' settlements were supposed to receive a breakfast of bread, sugar, and tea in school.[49] All too often, however, these special allotments, although highly sought and urgently needed, proved unavailable.

The state also used the ration system as a tool of labor discipline "to stimulate conscientious labor" and to punish those who "harmed production" through absenteeism or lateness. Workers who overfulfilled their output norms, for example, received an additional 100 grams of bread, while those who failed to meet their quota received 100 grams less. A law of October 18, 1942, granted workers who overfulfilled their targets extra vegetables, eggs, and milk from subsidiary farms and, at the same time, stipulated that any worker convicted of absence without a valid reason and sentenced to compulsory labor in their workplace could have their bread ration reduced by between 100 and 200 grams a day.[50] Many directors fully understood that absence or lateness was often not the fault of the worker and that such a loss was a severe deprivation, so never imposed the penalty.

As critical as the hierarchy of provisioning was to the population, in order to determine how any group might have fared, the calories it received had to be measured against the calories it expended. Considered over time, this provided the best indicator of which groups were most vulnerable to nutritional deficiency and starvation. Soviet citizens understood this energy calculation well. Diarists and memoirists often mentioned the energy required to work, walk daily distances, haul water, and climb stairs. When the factories in Leningrad shut down for lack of fuel, those groups that received less bread than workers bitterly resented a continuing differential that could no longer be justified by labor.[51] No group, with the exception of leading political and economic officials, received enough food through the ration system to cover its biological needs. Among workers, only miners came close. For those in the lower ration categories (children, dependants, white-collar employees), the ration met less than half of what they needed to sustain life (see Figure 3.1). By the end of the war, the vast majority of workers had been placed on lists for higher norms and thus had a caloric shortfall of only about 25 percent or less. Yet everyone depended on other sources of food sources outside the ration—mainly potatoes—to supplement their daily consumption. And even with this supplement, most Soviet citizens expended more calories than they consumed. Most of the country went hungry, and in the hardest years, in regions with a weak agricultural base, many starved.

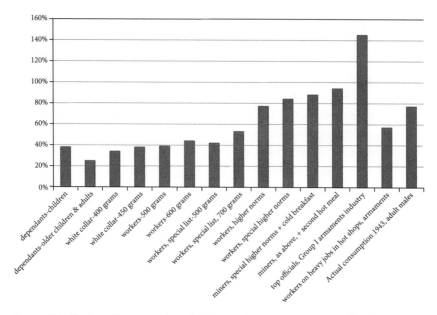

Figure 3.1 Ration allowances in calories per day as a percentage of biological need by group, November 1943. Source: Goldman, Filtzer, eds., *Hunger and War,* pp. 15–16.

Bread Cards and Canteens

As the food crisis deepened, the state halted the commercial sale of food and converted retail stores to use by ration only. In many industrial towns, food was increasingly distributed through canteens.[52] In early 1942, the state prohibited all off-ration commercial sale of bread in an attempt to consolidate and control stocks.[53] People were "attached" to particular stores or canteens where they used their ration cards to buy food and consumer goods.[54] Above all, the state guaranteed the bread ration, promising daily, reliable deliveries of fresh-baked bread. Over the course of the war, as the urban population swelled and the Red Army liberated the occupied territories, the number of people provisioned with bread increased steadily from 61,778,000 in December 1942 to 80,586,000 in December 1945.[55] The state's role in providing bread, far from diminishing through the war, increased significantly.

At times, however, even the bread ration could not be guaranteed. After the Germans occupied the coalfields in the Donbass and Moscow regions in 1941, the shortage of fuel forced the closure of water pumping stations, flour mills, and bakeries. Throughout fall 1942, tens of thousands of people in the industrial town of Gor'kii waited patiently each day, clutching the ration cards that entitled them to 500 grams of bread. Once the stores ran out, however, those still waiting were turned away. In October and November, fully 30 percent of Gor'kii's bakeries were not working, and in November 50,000 to 60,000 people each day failed to receive their rations.[56] Lack of fuel also forced bakeries in Saratov, Ufa, and other towns to close for several days at a stretch and to dispense flour instead of bread. The Soviet of People's Commissars took disciplinary actions against the officials responsible, considering their attitude toward rationing "impermissible." It sternly warned them that, "whatever the difficulties with fuel, they must guarantee uninterrupted supply for the provisioning of bread."[57] Throughout 1942, only seven of the forty-three bread stores and stalls in Kirov and its surrounding province were in operation. The situation improved toward the end of the year when the town and provincial party committees declared that it was "categorically forbidden under any condition to turn off the electricity to the flour mill, the bakeries, and the water pumping station."[58] After 1943, new problems arose in the liberated territories as party and soviet officials struggled to reconstruct bakeries, pumping stations, dams, and the electricity grid. Khar'kov, for example, was liberated in August 1943, and by fall 1944 its inhabitants required more than 171 tons of bread per day. Yet the bakeries struggled with recurring shortages of flour, fuel, and transport, which left many without their daily ration.[59]

For workers in particular the factory canteen served as their main source of food. Using their ration cards, they paid for hot meals that were supposed to contain the amounts of food to which they were entitled. Some got their bread ration outside the factory in stores; others received it in the canteen or in more convenient, closed-network stores within the factory. Construction and railway workers and temporary workers mobilized for peat and timber cutting also ate at communal kitchens on site. The factories were provisioned with central state stocks through various channels, including the Commissariat of Trade, local trade departments, and the industrial commissariats. Yet the gap between planned and actual deliveries was considerable, and canteens could not meet the needs of their workers with central state stocks alone. Throughout 1942, before subsidiary farms, decentralized procurement, and gardens were fully organized, cooks responded to dwindling stocks and burgeoning numbers of diners by cutting portion sizes, watering down the soup, and adding inedible fillers. In the first quarter of 1942, for example, aviation factory No. 29 in Omsk received well below half of the fish, groats, pasta, and fat it was allocated by plan, and none of the dairy products, meat, or potatoes. At the same time, the number of meals served by its canteens jumped from 23,200 to 31,100. As a result, workers received one meager, low-calorie course a day.[60] Factory managers scrambled to procure food from nearby collective and state farms, but even these additional stocks were insufficient.[61] In December 1942, twelve of the canteens in Kirov received just 16 percent of their planned potato allotment and nothing else. For 10 kopeks, workers received one bowl of thin potato soup each day, containing 100 grams of potatoes, 20 grams of flour, and 5 grams of salt. The workers in Kirov's fur/sheepskin factory subsisted on soup made from cabbage and flour, and those in aviation factory No. 19 in Molotov were forced to live on soup made from flour or grain with a small amount of fat and salt. At 190 calories per serving, this meal was 50 percent lower than the norm established by the Commissariat of Trade.[62] Workers gave bitterly humorous names to these canteen concoctions, dubbing the soup from stalks and stems "Blue Night," the mix of water and peas "Autumn," and the strange brown liquid that appeared to be made from roach (the fish, not the insect) "Brown Eyes."[63]

Between 1940 and 1944, the number of meals served by canteen kitchens almost doubled from 8.1 billion to 15.7 billion.[64] Canteen cooks struggled not only with shortages of food but also with lack of equipment. Before the war, the Commissariat of Trade managed four factories that produced canteen kitchen equipment. Once the war began, their machinery was transferred to the defense industry. The commissariat began creating workshops in 1942 to repair equipment and utensils, but production was hampered by lack of fuel and materials.[65] The canteens at aviation factory No. 26 outside Ufa could seat 3,300 workers, but had only 2,300 plates and bowls. Workers stood in line for up to two hours to be served. Shop heads tried to circumvent the lines by allowing their workers to leave for meals 30 minutes early. Nevertheless, huge crowds would block up the entrance to the canteens, creating "unbearable" conditions for the waiters. Kitchen staff washed dishes and pots in cold water, the food was often spoiled, and food poisoning and stomach illnesses were endemic. Workers had no place to wash their hands, which were covered in oil, dirt, and toxic chemicals.[66] Defense factory No. 200 in Cheliabinsk had no trucks to move food stocks from the railway station to the canteen's kitchen so the workers used a KV tank, produced in the factory, to pull a wooden sleigh piled with produce.[67] The canteens in the renowned Kirov tank factory in Cheliabinsk were located in the production shops, and crowded with workers as well as people from outside the factory. Workers brought their own spoons and wiped them off on their work clothes. Great lines formed before meals, and people pushed, shoved, and fought to get served.[68] One canteen in ammunition factory No. 15 in Chapaevsk, responsible for feeding 1,400 people, had a total inventory of 40 spoons, 40 small plates, 40 bowls, 15 glasses, and 60 metal mugs. No less than 90 minutes were required to get food, and workers often returned from their meal break without having eaten. In another factory, the storehouse was so damp and poorly ventilated that everything, including the food, was covered in mold. Coal gas smoke billowed from a broken stove. Kitchen staffers, regularly overcome by toxic fumes, had to be carried out on stretchers.[69]

Party, union, and factory officials made strong efforts to stagger meal breaks to reduce lines, enforce basic hygiene, and provide cooking equipment, dishes, and utensils.[70] In early 1944, the first self-service system, replacing seated diners and waiters, was introduced in a canteen in a Moscow defense factory. Immediately, lines disappeared, meal time dropped to twenty minutes, and the numbers employed in food service decreased.[71] Yet the self-service system spread slowly, and efforts at improvement were often overwhelmed by the challenge of feeding millions of people under conditions of extreme scarcity.[72]

In many industrial towns, factory canteens became the most reliable source of food. Shortages of fuel, lack of kitchen facilities, continuous shift work, large amounts of overtime, and women's employment all made home cooking difficult. In the textile towns of Ivanovo province most workers had their own apartments, but ration cards covered only bread, sugar, and sweets so workers lacked ingredients for home-cooked meals.[73] In October 1942, the Soviet of People's Commissars decreed that all primary and secondary school students must receive a hot breakfast with tea in school, but an investigation in Kirov showed that the majority of schools did not receive enough food to provide it.[74] In Vol'sk in Saratov province, there was no sale of food anywhere in the town. Desperate families of soldiers and workers petitioned to be allowed to eat at least one meal in factory canteens, but the head of the Union of Cement Workers responded, "It is not possible to satisfy this request." The canteens of the town's four cement factories were already feeding teachers, doctors, evacuees, and the neediest family members of Red Army soldiers as well as their own workers (some 6,132 people).[75] Local authorities everywhere used factory stocks to feed students, evacuees, municipal workers, officials, families of workers, and others who did not work in the factories. The multiplication of eaters depleted the already meager stocks, forced cooks to dilute meals, and created sharp resentment. Unions protested, but in many cases the factories were feeding the children of their own workers. Five daycare centers in aviation factory No. 29 cared for 350 children, and the town trade department provided them with less than half the norms they needed for proper nutrition.[76] No workers objected to the painfully thin, abnormally quiet children seated at nearby tables. The Stalin garment factory provided nursing mothers a little extra food through the factory's crèche. Although it served almost three times as many children as it was designed for, both mothers and babies were in good condition.[77] The union factory committees (*zavkomy*) also helped the families of workers who were mobilized into the army, providing material aid and wood for fuel.[78] The factories, sometimes the only sites in town with access to hot water and electricity, became centers of domestic life. Children took their baths there, workshops offered repair services, and town residents ate hot meals. While all these groups were in desperate need of help, they depleted the stocks designated for workers.

Meager diets took a toll on the health of workers, especially in industrial towns in poor agricultural areas in the east and Far North. The head of the union committee and the factory doctor in factory No. 200 in Cheliabinsk wrote a worried letter in February 1943 to N. M. Shvernik, head of the All-Union Central Council of Unions (VTsSPS): "We have an increase of cases of protein-deficiency edemas, vitamin deficiency, and first- and second-degree starvation, leading to a high rate of illness and death, especially among single workers living in the dormitories. If measures are not taken quickly to improve the feeding of single workers and those suffering from starvation, then we will come to a catastrophic position with the labor force because the factory is already very short of workers." They pleaded with Shvernik to find enough food and vitamin C so that the union could provide two meals a day for the factory's 1,600 workers and special supplements for those in various stages of starvation.[79]

As the food crisis deepened, the unions, Komsomol, and Party launched a series of hard-hitting investigations, which led to some improvements in the canteens.[80] In November 1943, the same month that ration allowances were sharply reduced in response to a poor harvest, the Soviet of People's Commissars passed a decree requiring a "minimum choice" of two offerings for the first course; three for the second; one sweet; and one hot drink in all Moscow canteens. This mandated meal was gradually implemented everywhere. Cooks were encouraged to vary the menu, which they could more easily do if their enterprise was able to draw on supplementary stocks from subsidiary farms and gardens. The Commissariat of Trade ordered that people suffering from advanced malnutrition and semi-starvation receive reinforced nutrition (*usilennoe dieticheskoe pitanie*, or UDP). In Moscow, the number of children receiving reinforced meals almost doubled to more than 46,000, and adults to almost 57,000. In Penza, 2,275 starving workers in ammunition factory No. 50 were transferred onto three canteen meals per day.[81] The efforts were not immediately successful. In early 1944, about one-third of the factory's 18,000 personnel were still suffering from varying stages of starvation, and the special UDP dining room had only 165 places. The factory, like many others, did not receive its full allocation of central stocks, and its subsidiary farm yielded little. Management tried to resolve the crisis by redirecting food intended as bonuses for Stakhanovite workers to those who were starving, creating tension between the two groups.[82] Reflecting on the successes and failures, Liubimov explained, "Of course, not all canteens worked in the same way—some were better, some worse. But in the end we can only conclude that communal dining helped the Soviet people to endure the burdens of the war, to nourish children, and to live and work toward victory. This was true in the farthest reaches of the Siberian rear, in blockaded Leningrad, and on the railway lines that stretched over thousands of kilometers."[83] Liubimov had perhaps an overly rosy view of canteen dining and its accomplishments, but he was not wrong that this system of communal dining was central to people's survival.

Subsidiary Farms, Gardening, and Decentralized Stocks

As central state stocks dwindled, local sources of food provided critical supplements. On January 5, 1942, the All-Union Central Council of Unions issued two decrees that launched the gardening movement. The first established collective factory gardens for use by canteens; the second made small plots available to individuals.[84] In February, the Commissariat of Trade established Departments of Workers' Provisioning (ORSy) in leading defense, coal, chemical, and iron and steel enterprises intended to improve provisioning for workers, ensure full delivery of allocated stocks, and procure additional sources of food. Throughout the spring of 1942, ORSy were established in every industrial sector. By the end of the war, 7,720 ORSy served almost half of the population covered by the rationing system, delivered to workers more than half of their allocations from the state's central stocks, and managed 30,000 subsidiary farms.[85] They established fishing brigades, gardens, and piggeries, and contracted with state and collective farms and local food processors.[86] In some industrial towns, ORSy took over the stores once run by town trade departments.[87] In many factories, they created subsidiary enterprises, including workshops to repair clothing, footwear, and furniture and to manufacture crockery, barrels, building materials, leather, and baked goods to serve the needs of the workers and to trade with peasants in collective farm markets.[88]

On April 7, 1942, the Soviet of People's Commissars and the Central Committee directed local soviets to transfer all unused land around the towns to factories and other institutions for subsidiary farms and personal gardens.[89] Piggeries, which proved easy to maintain, accounted for one-quarter of all subsidiary farms attached to canteens, others provided workers with potatoes, vegetables, and other types of meat.[90] The state also permitted the industrial commissariats, enterprises, and local food producers and processors to trade and conclude contracts.[91] The farms were not always successful. In the Urals, the quality of land was often poor, and shortages of labor, transportation, and storage limited how much acreage workers could sow.[92] Besides vegetables and potatoes, many of the farms also grew grain, a portion of which they had to deliver to the state.[93] On the larger farms, the state stipulated the amount of acreage to be sown, the selection of crops, the percentage of the harvest to be set aside for livestock, and regulations for storing and sprouting seeds, tool maintenance, composting, irrigation, and the use of fungicides and insecticides.[94]

The state also organized the distribution of land for individual and collective gardens through union and local soviet officials. Between 1942 and 1944, the number of collective and individual gardens more than tripled to 16.5 million. In 1942, about one-third of all urban inhabitants worked in an individual or collective garden, and in 1944 about one-half. Among workers, the share was even greater: more than 90 percent of workers employed in iron and steel, mining, and the railroads participated in the gardening movement.[95] By 1945, more than 18 million people had their own gardens, and many also raised animals and poultry to provide scarce eggs, milk, and meat. Almost two million cows were living in towns.[96] Millions of workers planted potatoes, cabbage, and other vegetables, and gardening commissions, created by the unions, supervised weeding, terracing, and harvesting, and provided packing materials and winter storage. When factory No. 29 received about 495 acres (200 hectares) of land to be divided among its workers, the director was deluged by more than 8,000 eager requests for plots.[97] Inventive workers in Magnitogorsk plowed their large collective plot with captured German tanks they converted to tractors.[98]

The most popular garden food was the humble potato, which quickly became "the signature food" of the war.[99] In 1943, for the USSR as a whole personal garden plots and subsidiary farms attached to factories and institutions provided each urban resident about 69 kilograms of potatoes. Yields in Siberia, where workers had more land to till, were much higher: 148 kilograms in Omsk, 201 in Novosibirsk, and in Kemerovo province a hefty 274 kilograms per person. The potato provided on average an additional 159 calories and 3 grams of protein per person per day nationwide, and 631 calories and 11 grams of protein for residents of Kemerovo. These were substantial amounts, and in some regions the potato saved many lives.[100] Yields from the gardening movement peaked in 1944, although not all families, and evacuees in particular, had access to a plot.[101] Taken together, the subsidiary farms, decentralized procurement, and gardens made a substantial contribution to the food available. For the urban population as whole, the most important of these three sources were gardens although, for workers in enterprises that managed or were attached to large and productive farms, the food supplements were considerable. All these local food sources, however, were part of a central food policy organized and overseen by state, union, and party organizations.

"Free" Trade and Collective Farm Markets

The economic arrangements most similar to a "free" market in food were the collective farm markets, known at the time as "free" (*vol'nyi*), "private" (*lichnyi*), or "peasant" markets. In the collective farm markets, access to food was determined by the consumer's ability to pay, rather than by the subsidies and principles that underlay the ration system. Yet the collective farm markets, too, were part of state food policy, actively promoted as a valued supplement to central stocks. A Department of Collective Farm Trade, under the Commissariat of Trade, supported them, tracked their numbers and sales, and calculated their contribution to the overall food supply. As of January 1, 1944, for example, the Commissariat of Trade counted almost

2,700 collective farm markets in Russia. Local party and soviet officials set up the markets, providing space, sanitary facilities, advertising, and contacts with the urban population in order to boost their sales.[102]

The harvests of the collective farms were procured by the state at state-mandated prices and served as the main source for central state stocks. Each collective farmer's share of the sale was determined by the number of "labor days" they contributed during the year. Yet the prices set by the state were low, and labor day payments were too small to provide subsistence. In 1942, for example, they amounted to no more than 200 grams of grain and 100 grams of potatoes per person per day.[103] Collective farmers relied on their private plots, which the state expanded in August 1941, and poultry stocks to survive.[104] Using the surplus from their private plots, peasants traded produce and cooked food with workers in and around factories, at train stations, and along railroad routes. The collective farm markets provided a significant and growing share of the food consumed by the urban population, and were especially critical sources of milk and meat.

Although the share of food provided by collective farm markets to consumption increased over the course of the war, the amounts delivered to market by the peasants fell. The collective farms were systematically stripped of their able-bodied residents who were mobilized for waged work, vocational schools, and the Red Army. By 1944, the vast majority of those who remained were invalids, mothers, children, and the elderly.[105] With little to buy, peasants had few incentives to market the food from their private plots, choosing either to plant less or to consume more. Between October 1941 and October 1943, sales of meat, milk, butter, eggs, vegetable oil, and even potatoes dropped sharply. Milk sales fell from more than 57 million liters to just over 48,000, and meat from more than 20 million tons to about 4 million. Only the sale of rye and wheat flour rose steadily. The increasing share of the peasant markets in urban consumption despite the drop in marketing was a painful indicator of the dwindling intake of urban consumers.[106]

Prices in the markets were based on supply and demand, yet they were also affected by the low, state-subsidized prices set by the ration system. When state provisioning increased in 1943, for example, market prices dropped. Likewise, when in November 1943 the state cut the bread ration, collective farm market prices for flour increased.[107] The gardening movement also constrained market prices, particularly for potatoes and vegetables, by reducing demand. Bulk purchases by buyers from industrial enterprises also reduced prices. Workers received the food at lower prices than if they had

purchased it individually. The state also consciously sought to curb price inflation by removing money from circulation through state loans (war bonds),
lotteries, taxes, and levies.[108] In June 1943, for example, the state increased
taxes fivefold on private plots, cows, and poultry to reflect increased peasant
earnings in the collective farm markets.[109] Finally, local officials made strong
efforts to eliminate middlemen and speculators, who bought up large quantities of food for resale at higher prices. Food policy produced some paradoxical results. Over the course of the war, the collective farms increasingly
paid peasants for their share of the harvest in cash rather than precious flour
or grain. Yet grain was difficult to grow on small private plots and to mill by
hand. Peasants, ineligible for ration cards and lacking access to grain or flour,
often sought to exchange produce from their private plots in the market for
bread or bread cards. In Leningrad province in late fall of 1943, for example,
peasants and workers frequently exchanged milk for bread.[110] The war thus
created a strange reversal: the main producers of grain were frequently forced
to buy their bread from workers.

Prices in the peasant markets were often too high for ordinary people.
Wages rose during the war, but so did prices in the collective farm markets,
along railway routes and in areas inundated by evacuees.[111] Peasants in the
collective farm markets around Kazan' were selling meat at 200 rubles per
kilogram, butter 570, potatoes 40, onions 60, milk 40, and cottage cheese
120. The head of the Union of Shipbuilding Workers noted that such "speculative marauding prices" were "absolutely out of reach" for the workers evacuated from Leningrad to Kazan'.[112] In early 1942, the price of a kilogram of
meat was more than one-third of a worker's monthly wage. The most affordable food item in the market was potatoes. Prices varied from one region
to another, fluctuating between a high of 50 rubles per kilogram and a low
of 3, but they dropped in all regions as individuals and collectives began
growing their own.[113] Cabbage, beets, carrots, and onions all showed similar declines.[114]

With few consumer goods available for purchase, peasants were increasingly interested in bartering. In one market in Ivanovo province, more than
half of the collective farmers would trade food and wood only for kerosene,
soap, vodka, or tobacco. The workers were so hungry that "streams of town
inhabitants" regularly set out in large groups from Ivanovo to the village
of Palekh, 40 miles (65 km) away. Many collective farmers abandoned the
market altogether. "We have no need to go to the collective farm market,"
they said. "They [the workers] bring everything that we need to us."[115]

The greatest obstacles to trade with the peasantry were the lack of consumer goods and transport. In 1943, the Moscow soviet tried to encourage
peasants to bring more food to market by sending 250 activists into Moscow
and Riazan' provinces to conclude contracts with collective farms. By providing transport, it succeeded in increasing the tonnage of meat, pork fat,
dairy products, vegetables, and fruit that the peasants were able to bring.
Officials happily reported that deliveries were almost double the plan for
some items.[116] Yet success depended entirely on transport, which was generally unavailable at any price. Markets almost universally lacked scales and
measuring equipment and even paper for receipts. And the markets were
not immune from the dangers of war. In Moscow, the Krasnobogatyrskii
market in the Sokol'niki neighborhood was bombed by the Germans.[117]
The state's efforts to incorporate the markets into larger food plans proved
overly ambitious. Peasant deliveries to the market arrived haphazardly, and
almost no provinces or regions could make reliable plans. Contracts, even
when they were signed, were frequently not met. Although almost 25,000
people nationwide were employed to service the collective farm markets,
most had little experience, and the local trade departments were constantly
short of *sborshchiki*, or those who worked with the peasants to collect the
produce. The Commissariat of Trade was more successful at organizing holiday bazaars, a more limited venture, on May Day and the anniversary of the
October Revolution.[118]

Forage, Substitute Foods, and Culinary Experimentation

As the country grew hungrier, people turned to forage and food substitutes,
common practices during times of famine. More unusual was the state's
sponsorship of research, collective forage, and culinary experimentation
among people from many occupations, including scientists, canteen cooks,
bakers, and officials in the Commissariat of Trade. The first experiments
began in the canteens as cooks were forced to substitute raw ingredients for
processed foods. The Soviet Union got most of its sugar from the white, fleshy
root of the sugar beet, which grew in colder climates and required processing
in order to crystallize the "juice" into sugar.[119] By 1942, the sugar available
to the home front was a mere 15 percent of its prewar level. In July 1942,
Liubimov announced that the remaining sugar mills could no longer process sugar beets due to a shortage of machine parts, and the food-processing

factories stopped producing jams, jellies, and syrup. The Commissariat of Trade began shipping unprocessed sugar beets directly to factory and municipal canteens.[120] Cooks soon began producing a variety of boiled, semi-jellied preparations that passed as "dessert." By September 1942, similar problems affected salt, and town trade departments were unable to provide local pickling, preserving, and dairy processors with the salt they required.[121] The loss of preserved meats and fish was disastrous, and once again canteen cooks were forced to invent substitutes for processed foods. Flour stocks, too, were cut repeatedly, sending the bakeries into crisis. When central stocks of flour were cut for the third time in spring 1943, the state compensated by substituting potatoes for flour.[122] The Commissariat of Trade began experimenting with new bread recipes that used potatoes, barley, corn, oats, and millet instead of flour and distributing them to bakers.[123] The soggy, coarse, gray admixture resembled "bread" in name only, provided fewer digestible materials, was lower in calories, and contained more fillers. Yet it was baked and distributed daily.

The state also sponsored campaigns to gather wild greens, an important source of vitamin C, through ORSy, the unions, canteens, and local trade departments. The Union of Workers in Public Catering and ORSy organized workers into large foraging teams to gather wild apples, mushrooms, sorrel, nettles, and dandelion leaves to add to soups and salads in canteens.[124] The director of canteens in Moscow sent out detailed instructions in 1944 about the best way to use nettles: "I suggest collecting only the nettle leaves, add salt, cook it fresh, and do not store it too long." Nettles could also be salted and preserved in chilled tubs. Canteen cooks received recipes for soup made from 200 grams of nettles, 50 grams of sorrel, 80 grams of potatoes, 5 grams of flour, 10 grams of onions, 15 grams of carrots, and egg and sour cream (although the latter two items were often unavailable). The canteens, unions, and ORSy collected tens of thousands of tons of edible wild greens for collective consumption.[125] In Leningrad, when the daily bread ration dwindled to 200 grams in the fall of 1941 and thousands of people began to die of starvation, the Union of Workers in Public Catering launched various initiatives to save as many people as possible. In November 1942, the second autumn of the blockade, Mikhailova, the head of the Leningrad union committee, summarized their efforts: "We took the initiative into our own hands. We held meetings with the canteen employees and the people who ate there. We gathered the cooks." Together, canteen workers, students, and pensioners gathered plantain weeds and wild greens, and prepared ash to fertilize the gardens.[126]

In 1942, at the nadir of food provisioning, the state also began using "invented" foods as supplements. Pine needle extract, a bitter concoction made from boiled pine needles and containing high amounts of vitamin C, was used as a "juice" to counteract scurvy. It was known simply as *khvoia* (pine needle), and millions of people dutifully downed glasses of the foul-tasting stuff in canteens throughout the country. When workers in defense factory No. 19 in Molotov began suffering from scurvy in May 1942, the local union met with a professor from the Pharmaceutical Institute to organize a vitamin shop to produce *khvoia* and other anti-scurvy juices. Using fir trees, the shop produced up to 3,000 liters per day, providing every employee with a daily dose. These effective anti-scurvy juices were also distilled from birch leaves and rosehips.[127]

The Commissariat of Trade took an active role in searching for new sources of vitamins, and "vitaminizing" basic canteen fare. The nascent vitamin industry had few resources, and most of what it produced went to the front. Food service workers learned to make their own concentrations of vitamin A (carotene) from wild greens, including alfalfa, clover, Timothy grass or meadow's cat's tails, and the tops of rutabaga, beets, and other root vegetables. They also used black currents, rosehips, nettles, orache, plantain weed, rhubarb, and other flowers and greens. Rosehips were used in both the Soviet Union and Britain as a substitute for citrus fruits to combat scurvy. By 1944, canteen diners were receiving more than 4.3 billion doses of vitamins A, B, and C.[128] The plants that canteen workers used were well known to peasants and folk healers, and many of these workers, no more than one generation removed from the village, likely combined their own folk knowledge with the instructions from their union and the Commissariat of Trade. Although they lacked scientific knowledge, they recognized the plants, roots, and preparations that could alleviate certain ailments and deficiencies.

The state encouraged scientists and cooks to experiment together. Uralmashzavod, the machine-building plant in Sverdlovsk that produced components for the famed T-34 tanks and other armaments, became the site of a special experimental food combine. One of its most successful products was a concentrated vegetable bullion from nettles and ashweed or goutweed, optimistically named "Springtime." It also experimented with substitutes for tea and coffee, including a tea called "Novinka" or "Novelty," brewed with willow weed and dropwort leaves. A "coffee" drink, made from burdock root and mixed with saccharine, was added to whatever small stocks of real coffee were available. The combine also provided recipes to canteens for purées from wild greens, pâtés popularly known as vegetable "caviar" (*ikra*), and vegetable cutlets.[129]

Home cooks also experimented. One woman who spent the war in Sverdlovsk later remembered, "Let me tell you, we tried absolutely everything." She noted, "You could eat burdock root, but only in springtime, because then it was thick. You can also eat nettles, but it is best if they are still young, although we ate them even after that. Chickweed, too. We picked them all, and if you chop it up you can even put it in soup – it is good." People stripped the trees in the city. She explained, "this shows you how far we were prepared to go—there wasn't a single bud left on the linden trees, and not a single pine tree grew (we gathered the young shoots). We picked it all and carted it home."[130] Parents and grandparents who had survived earlier famines passed on their knowledge. The state encouraged gardeners to use parts of the plants they normally discarded and disseminated advice widely through popular magazines and lectures. One writer for the women's journal *Rabotnitsa*, for example, explained that even the leafy green tops of carrots could be dried and used to produce a vitamin-rich tea.[131]

The initiatives launched by the state also aimed to wring every precious drop of nutrition from scraps or leftovers. Water used to soak or boil foods in the canteens was repurposed into new edibles. The Union of Public Catering Workers taught canteen cooks to boil down the water left after cooking potatoes to create jelly-like "desserts" from the potato starch by adding sugar or saccharine. In Moscow, food service workers produced eighty-seven tons of potato starch extract, which was then distributed to the factory canteens. Canteen cooks also made a sweet gelatin drink (*kisel'*) from water used to boil beets and other vegetables. By the end of 1943, the state had access to various dried foods, including powdered milk and eggs. One food service worker explained, "When these products showed up in the canteens, the comrades did not know how to use them." After large packages were sent, "the phone calls start. 'What are we supposed to do with this? How are we supposed to prepare it?'" Food service workers took state-sponsored cooking courses in the use of these new "foods," and their union sent recipes to canteens throughout the country.[132]

The holy grail of food substitutes was protein, given the short supplies of meat, fish, dairy products, and eggs. In the absence of sufficient protein, the body first devoured its own fat, and then tissues, muscles, and organs. Doctors in Leningrad and the Warsaw ghetto identified this condition as a distinct stage in what they came to understand as starvation disease or what Soviet doctors called *"alimentarnaia distrofiia"* or "nutritional dystrophy." The two groups, unbeknownst to each other, meticulously observed and recorded the changes they saw in their own bodies and those of their patients. Starvation, they discovered, was not simply an extreme case of food deprivation, but a disease with specific stages that required more than simple refeeding to reverse.[133]

Soviet researchers seeking a new form of protein soon discovered the potential of nutritional yeast. When a group of specialists met in Leningrad in October 1941 to discuss the possibility of creating food substitutes for the starving city, V. I. Sharkov, a young professor and head of the Department of Hydrolyzed Production in the Leningrad Forestry Academy, suggested that protein might be produced from yeast. Engineers turned out the first useable batch of yeast protein in the winter of 1941–1942.[134] Yeast could be grown on various bases, and it contained as much protein as meat and more B vitamins than many vegetables and fruits. Soon factories everywhere were growing yeast for their canteens. In the textile factory Trekhgornaia Manufaktura, canteen staff grew it on the industrial starch used for sizing the warps.[135] Local trade departments grew it on solutions made from the hydrolysis of water used to clean potatoes and vegetables. In Leningrad, it was grown on sawdust, in Moscow on millet husks. Produced as both a paste and a milky liquid, the yeast could be added to any food, or even served as a food itself, formed into cutlets or pâté jellies.[136] In Moscow, the Culinary Soviet developed and sent detailed instructions to the canteens on growing, processing, and adding yeast to meals. Canteen cooks began adding tons of the stuff to soups. In ammunition factory No. 50 in Penza canteen cooks added up to 500 kilograms of yeast protein every day to the meals they served.[137] The main challenge was how to disguise its foul taste.[138]

In 1942, employees of Optbakaleia, a food combine under the Commissariat of Trade, collaborated with nutritionists to produce albumen protein from plant remnants. Although they lacked the proper machinery—acid autoclaves—they developed alternate means of producing albumen bullion cubes from oil cake, the mass of compressed linseed, cottonseed, sunflower seed, soybean, and other plant material left after the oil was extracted.[139] Oil cake, most commonly used for fertilizer or fodder, was repurposed for human consumption. Tens of millions of these cubes were shipped to the canteens. In 1943, the Commissariat of Trade created ten more enterprises to produce the bullion extract, each producing 50,000 pellets per day. In Optbakaleia, researchers also began producing other artificial food products including semi-prepared "Noodle Soup" (*"Sup Lapsha"*) from vegetable leavings and a coffee substitute made from oil cake.[140] Canteen cooks also experimented with bone extract to make soups and sauces. Fish that were too small to eat were descaled and boiled to make jellies. Cooks in railway canteens extracted fat from bones, which they then pulverized to produce hundreds of kilograms of "flour."[141] Vitamin factories prepared a variety of supplements and preparations. By 1945, canteens throughout the country provided a "vitaminized course" as a compulsory part of the meal designed to meet deficiencies in the diet.[142] Although individuals also foraged and gathered, most of these experimental efforts were collective. The connection between food substitutes and victory was captured in a short poem by L. Markarov, written after the war.

> We ate everything we could possibly eat,
> And of poison were not afraid.
> I can still count all the grasses,
> With which our meals were made:
>
> Wormwood, nettles, orache,
> Young leaves of the birch tree,
> To banish forever and always
> The hanging misery.
>
> We boiled the belts of soldiers,
> Ate grasses, and joiner's glue.
> Growing stronger than the enemy
> We broke him through and through.[143]

The Organizational Struggle over Food

The system of allocation and allotment was constantly contested by industrial commissariats, enterprises, unions, and local soviets, party committees, and trade departments, all of which struggled to get food for the people they represented.[144] Food from central state stocks was distributed through the Commissariat of Trade, which sent it to the republic Commissariats of Trade, which delivered it to ORSy and local trade departments, which in turn provisioned the industrial enterprises and institutions. Officials at the highest levels fielded a steady stream of appeals on behalf of needy groups. People were incorporated into the ration system as members of contingents or categories entitled to set allocations. After food stocks improved slightly in 1943, for example, state decrees incorporated new groups, including workers in hot shops in foundries, forges, optical glass, and ammunition, into higher levels of provisioning. The decrees, which each targeted a specific group ranging from 400 to 5,000 people, eventually encompassed almost 29,000 workers.[145] Toward the end of the war, the Commissariat of Trade established a special commission just to address claims for provisioning. The requests were specific: to provide cold breakfast for 12,000 people, including 7,000 children under the Commissariat of the Oil Industry; to provision workers in the construction camps of Krasnoiarsk Territory according to the norms of the far north; to allot supplementary food for starving workers and their dependants.[146] The requests revealed not only the elaborate gradations within the ration system, but also how people attained more privileged positions.

Despite the elaborate distinctions within the ration system, planned allocations were often more aspirational than real. In reality, chronic shortages undercut the plans and prompted fierce struggles among officials. Actual deliveries from both central and local stocks frequently fell short of the plan and even of the minimum required to feed the target population. The Commissariat of Trade had a shortage of stocks at every level of its vast organizational pyramid. In spring 1942, for example, the Commissariat of Trade sent strict instructions to the republic-level Commissariat of Trade in Tatariia to improve provisioning for the residents of Kazan', yet Tatariia never received its full allocation of stocks. In March, no canteens in Kazan' received any deliveries of their planned allocations of meat or fish.[147] In May and June, republic officials sent a mere fraction of the grain and flour that Kazan''s trade department was supposed to receive. Most of the food was delivered directly to factories, orphanages, and schools, leaving little for those outside these institutions. The city was flooded with evacuees and refugees, all struggling to get employment and access to a canteen. As in many areas, trade officials in Tatariia were forced to make painful choices about which needy group would receive priority. The evacuees, for example, were fed in canteens but received only one bowl of noodle soup a day. Written protests from the Union of Shipbuilding Workers ultimately led to an investigation that resulted in the release of additional food from central state stocks.[148] Such protest letters from organizations representing specific constituencies were common, and relief depended on the intercession of powerful officials. Yet every organization had similar claims to make, so a gain for one only meant a loss for another.

Officials sometimes seemed to be in the business of distributing hunger rather than food. The 1,000-plus shipbuilders evacuated from Leningrad to defense factory No. 402 in Molotovsk, a port city in Arkhangel'sk province, fared even worse than the group evacuated to Kazan'. Leaving Leningrad in a weakened state, their condition deteriorated further once they arrived. Central stocks of potatoes and vegetables were inadequate, and local officials had little supplementary food available. Factory No. 402 received land for a subsidiary farm in April 1942, but the soil was poor and the climate harsh. Union and industrial leaders interceded repeatedly, pressuring higher officials to authorize the release of more food. In October 1942, Shvernik and I. I. Nosenko, Commissar of the Shipbuilding Industry, pleaded with A. I. Mikoian, a deputy head of the Soviet of People's Commissars, to take 2,450 tons of potatoes and vegetables from adjoining provinces and deliver them to factory No. 402, but the request was denied. In November, the Soviet of People's Commissars finally ordered the Commissariat of Trade to deliver 20 tons of onions and garlic, a small portion of the original request, to the factory. In December, a party organizer from the Central Committee wrote to Shvernik again about the failing health of the workers and their families, noting that the vast majority were suffering from scurvy and starvation. He again begged Shvernik to intercede. Local officials continued to squabble over who should feed the workers and their children, but no one had any provisions to offer.[149]

Local officials also argued over responsibility for feeding vulnerable groups, including orphans, invalids, and disabled workers.[150] The plight of the Spanish orphans was typical of the difficulties such groups faced. At the end of 1942, an older party member, R. Kostyleva, wrote a desperate letter to the secretary of the Moscow party committee. Kostyleva was deputy director of an orphanage housing children whose parents had fought and died in the Spanish Civil War. Rescued from Spain and brought to Moscow, the children were placed in a special orphanage staffed by Soviet and Spanish pedagogues, which was evacuated to a small village in Saratov province in October 1941. Kostyleva, who also cared for her own teenaged daughter and blind sister, wrote, "As a party member, I cannot be silent about what is being done in this district." Local officials had settled the children and teachers in ruined huts with no doors, windows, roofs, or floors, and provided no construction materials for repair. Although the teachers and children tried to prepare the huts for winter, local officials supplied no firewood. The children soon became ill, and their school was forced to close for lack of heat. Initially, the children received a daily bread ration of 400 grams, but within a short time it was cut to 300, and then to 200. Neither the orphans nor the teachers received any other food. The teachers wanted to sow potatoes in the spring, but Kostyleva explained, "To buy or barter for potatoes is not possible for goods or for money." The closest market was 15 miles (25 km) away. Abandoned in the countryside, the children and staff were sick, freezing, and malnourished. When the teachers begged the district party head for help, he refused, saying that, "there is nothing more to give us. And that he was sick of the orphanage." The peasants regarded the group as "freeloaders and parasites." The chairman of the village soviet told one of the Spanish communist teachers, "Why are you hanging around here, and not protecting your own motherland from the fascists?" Kostyleva's letter brought results. The Moscow authorities remanded the letter to the Saratov provincial party committee, which promptly launched an investigation. The head of the district party committee was removed from his post for "self-provisioning, drunkenness, and discrediting himself before party activists," and measures were taken to improve the housing and provisioning of the orphans and staff.[151] Yet such complaints were common, and most were not so favorably resolved.

Conflicts among officials over food also extended to local sources. Central stocks were based on food appropriated by the Commissariat of Procurements from state and collective farms. The policy of decentralized procurement, however, placed officials from the center and the localities in sharp conflict. In March 1942, provincial party and soviet officials in Omsk set up collective farm markets. Union representatives from factory No. 20 quickly collected one million rubles from the workers and fanned out through the markets to buy meat, butter, cottage cheese, potatoes, grain, flour, and wheat for the factory canteen. But when they tried to take the food they purchased back to the factory, representatives of the Commissariat of Procurements claimed that the collective farms had failed to meet their delivery quotas, and therefore the union's purchasers had bought food that rightfully belonged to the state. The factory director and the officials from State Procurements, arriving at an impasse, each appealed to higher authorities in Moscow. Meanwhile, the objects of their squabble began to spoil. Officials from the State Procurements then announced that the union could take the spoiled produce, but threatened arrest if they removed the grain. After receiving appeals from the factory's director, the union, and the provincial party committee, the All-Union Central Council

of Unions in Moscow remanded the problem to the Omsk provincial soviet. In the meantime, the workers discovered they had spent their hard-
earned wages on spoiled meat and milk.[152] As in most of these disputes, no
one group had a greater moral claim on food than any other. Everyone was
hungry.

****

The food crisis on the home front began to abate only toward the middle of
1944, as the ability of the Red Army to provision itself outside Soviet territory, together with Lend-Lease food aid from the United States, Canada,
and Great Britain, made more food available to the civilian population
inside the USSR.[153] Until that time the home front had to survive on the
country's limited internal resources. Although at least one historian of the
war suggests that the state played a negligible role in feeding the people,
the basic facts of the wartime food system belie this view.[154] Central state
stocks provided the bulk of food for the urban population, although the majority could not live on the ration alone. The problem was simple: given the
loss of the agricultural and food-processing base in the occupied territories,
the state did not have enough food to feed the Red Army, waged workers,
and the urban population. It faced the unenviable task of creating a hierarchy for central allocations. The principles it adopted, to channel food to
those most valuable to the war effort and most vulnerable to hunger, were
widely accepted by the population despite extreme privation. Once more
food became available, increasing numbers of people were incorporated
into the ration system at higher levels, and efforts were made to target those
suffering from starvation.

   The state was not an abstraction but was, rather, concretely embodied in
the Party, GKO, VTsSPS, soviets, unions, Commissariat of Trade, industrial commissariats, and other organizations. The entire ration system was
predicated on state-created categories, encompassing constituencies whose
members were represented and defended by state organizations. Wartime
survival cannot be understood solely through the efforts of individuals to
trade, forage, or garden. The shift to decentralized purchasing and collective
farm markets only increased the role of central state institutions. Once new
sources of food became available, officials argued heatedly over access and
appealed to higher state authorities to resolve their disputes.

State strategy, built on a combination of central and local provisioning, and collective and individual efforts enabled people to survive the extreme privations of the wartime economy. Food policy was, however, limited in its success. As the state channeled resources from every economic sector to defense, factories were forced to produce their own food and consumer items. As a result, a substantial part of the workforce in every factory was employed outside production in auxiliary jobs. Peasants, mobilized from afar to work in industry, often did the same work on the factory's subsidiary farms as they had done on state and collective farms. The blurring of work lines played havoc with nationwide pay scales based on differentials among economic sectors. Industrial workers, for example, who gathered peat for fuel were paid 2.03 rubles per cubic meter; state farm workers, who did the same work, received 1.10.[155] Workers in low-waged sectors complained when they found themselves working alongside others who did the same work but received higher pay. Yet wage discrepancies were only one symptom of a larger change in the economy as industrial workers took on the full panoply of jobs required for subsistence.

The wartime economy embodied a peculiar paradox: as defense production became more efficient and technologically advanced, each unit of production became less differentiated. Factories assumed the full array of reproductive tasks normally performed by women in the home for free (mending, cleaning, cooking, gathering wood for fuel, gardening, repair, washing). The division between agriculture and industry, between consumption and production, so pronounced in advanced industrial societies, began to dissolve. Barter replaced money, wood replaced coal, and the garden potato replaced the food-processing industry. The simplest and most primitive economic relationships supported the mighty, industrial economy that defeated the German war machine. Factories, like peasant households of an earlier, premodern era, became units not only of production but also of consumption, replacing the family and the home.

The Soviet economy was stretched to the breaking point. In December 1942, officials protested the lack of food and cloth for workers in Irkutsk, who never received the tons of meat, fish and fats they were allocated from the Commissariat of Trade's centralized stocks. Yet as Liubimov patiently explained, central stocks were based on deliveries from other enterprises. The textile and food commissariats had failed to meet their planned quotas to the Commissariat of Trade.[156] The reason for their failures was simple. Hungry and poorly clad textile and food workers were too weak to meet their own production targets. Workers could not produce, walk to and from the factories, and gather fuel on bread and gruel alone. In the final analysis, the breaking point of the economy was set by the collective energy of the workers and peasants. This energy, determined in part by caloric intake and in part by sheer will, proved sufficient to achieve victory but the human cost was very great.

4

Illicit Provisioning: Inequality, Leveling, and Black Markets

Arbitrariness and thievery rule the canteens. The workers are robbed twice. First, other contingents are fed on the stocks set aside for workers, and second, in all the investigated canteens, workers are short-weighted in the rudest and most impudent manner.

Report from the Central Committee on conditions in the eastern factories and mines

In the spring of 1943, Ivan Aleksandrovich Bednov, a Civil War veteran and worker in ammunition factory No. 62 in Cheliabinsk, sat down and wrote an angry, six-page letter on frayed gray paper to the Central Committee. Bednov did not seek to conceal his identity, but confidently stated his full name, home address, and the name and address of his factory, which had been evacuated from Iaroslavl' in the fall of 1941. An older worker, he quoted Maksim Gor'kii's famous revolutionary novel, *Mother*, and averred his commitment to Soviet power. His letter, subdivided into sections describing food, housing, consumer goods, and workers' views, resembled an official investigatory report. It read as a scathing indictment of official thievery and workers' suffering.[1]

Conditions in Bednov's factory were similar to others: most workers lived in *zemlianki* located miles from the factory. The bathhouses did not function, and the workers had no soap. Bednov's letter differed little from the angry reports issued by the unions, the Komsomol, and the Party, yet his concerns went beyond wartime deficits. While he understood that shortages were unavoidable, he blamed trade officials in the factory's Department of Workers' Provisioning (ORS) for systematically stealing the food and consumer items allocated to workers:

Workers as a rule are fed in the canteens once in twenty-four hours, and what do they feed us? One course which consists of a half-liter of some kind of stirred-up water called soup and nothing more because ORS rules as a circle, they thieve and pilfer and divide the planned foodstuffs among themselves. The allocated food and consumer goods, which we are allotted by ration card, have not been distributed to the workers now for almost a year. In the factory canteen, as a rule, there is a system of substitutes; in other words, they may tear off the coupon for bread from the workers' ration cards but they give them cabbage or stewed turnips, or very, very rarely potatoes, and then most of those are frozen. The workers are dying from hunger and malnutrition. We have special *zemlianki of death* where about five to seven sick people are dying each day. Often, we have seen cases where workers die in the shops and at the gates of the factory.

Only a few days earlier, a sick, hungry, and exhausted worker had stumbled toward the union's office to plead for help. Bednov wrote, "He died in the doorway." In his judgment, poor provisioning of workers was not only the result of objective scarcity, but also systematic, large-scale theft by local officials who subverted the ration system to benefit themselves. He was not wrong.

Throughout the war, the pyramid of the ration system was made and remade through three illicit practices: self-provisioning, leveling, and theft. Many officials created steep new hierarchies through self-provisioning, a practice known as *samosnabzhenie*. They took advantage of their control over stocks to establish elite canteens, stores, and special parcels (*spetspaiki*) for themselves and their associates, while cultivating patronage networks by granting privileged access to stocks that rightfully belonged to others. At the same time, officials also redistributed stocks, mainly those allocated to workers, to ensure that vulnerable groups were fed. This form of illicit redistribution, known as *razbazarivanie* or "squandering," leveled or erased distinctions within the ration hierarchy. Finally, theft, both petty and large-scale, occurred at every site where food was stored, moved, or served. Trade officials, food service workers, and anyone with access to stocks or ration cards siphoned food from warehouses, railways, subsidiary farms, canteens, and bakeries. Employees in ration bureaus, coupon collection points, and print shops forged, altered, reused, and stole ration cards. Shortage created a large market for stolen goods, and theft in turn drained the ration system and increased shortage.

Gray and black markets sprang up everywhere: on street corners, in alleys and entrances, around collective farm markets, and in factory yards. Hungry workers, thieves, disabled veterans, and pensioners turned to markets to trade, supplement their meager rations, and sell stolen goods. As money lost its value, ration cards replaced rubles as the preferred currency.[2] Markets bolstered the ration system by allowing goods to circulate in the absence of retail stores. They also destabilized the system by offering an easy outlet for stolen goods. As such, they diminished the stocks that belonged to ordinary people and forced them to buy back at vast markups what they should have received by right.

Officials and "Self-Provisioning"

According to the ration system, managers and officials were supposed to be provisioned as white-collar employees, which placed them in a category directly below workers. Although some did live on these meager rations, others exploited their position to ensure that they received extra canteen meals, supplements, and special parcels from stocks allocated to workers or other groups. Until July 17, 1943, when the state set precise norms for party, union, soviet, and Komsomol officials, this group was loosely permitted to determine its own level of provisioning.

Ordinary people deeply resented those officials who took advantage of their position and considered the appropriation of provisions a form of theft. Bednov articulated this view in his description of managerial abuse in his own factory:

> In regard to consumer goods, there is a system of *talonchiki* [coupons], which the ORS gives out to the shop heads. These coupons never reach the workers but stick to the hands of idle people such as foremen, fixers, bookkeepers, accountants, and favorites, secretaries, and similar factory "intelligentsia" who manage to receive consumer goods several times a month. But the basic worker, the production worker, who directly puts out products, has only a passbook [*zabornaia knizhka*] which entitles him to 400 grams of salt and one box of matches.[3]

For Bednov, this unsanctioned hierarchy was an egregious violation of socialist principles. In trying to understand the disparities he saw between officials and workers, Bednov turned to the older narratives of revolutionary literature, quoting one of Gor'kii's characters: "We are the workers, who forge the flails and coins, build palaces and factories, feed those countless parasites, but to protect us, care for us, there is no one, because they do not consider us as human beings." Bednov hesitated to compare Soviet socialism with prerevolutionary capitalism, yet he perceived certain parallels. "Perhaps it is not exactly so now," he wrote, "but in a sense it is the same. The majority of workers were evacuated from Iaroslavl' and brought from Kazakhstan and other republics and provinces, and here, under this 'system' of provisioning, everything is cut off, worn out, they go around barefoot and in rags, and the factory does not manage to provide the state orders for shoes and clothes for those who are due them." Bednov's sense of justice was offended by those officials who improved their positions at the expense of others. "The truth is that the 'leadership' is all more or less shod and clothed," he wrote. "But the workers trade their only change of underwear for a potato."[4]

Of course, not all officials took advantage of their position. Many accountants, record keepers, and secretaries lived very poorly on white-collar rations. Members of the central committees of the unions, for example, were more poorly provisioned than the workers who elected them. The Central Committee of the Union of Iron and Steel Workers of the East received white-collar ration cards and were permitted to eat one meal a day in a factory canteen. As a result, the head of the union complained, union members preferred to remain in the factory as defense workers and refused to stand for election.[5]

Beginning in 1942, the Komsomol, Central Committee, and unions launched investigations into provisioning in the eastern industrial towns. Their reports uniformly described abuse of the ration system by local managers and officials. Letters to newspapers and various authorities complained of similar problems. A member of the Central Committee of the Union of Aviation Workers, one Lisitsyn, wrote a detailed letter to N. M. Shvernik, head of the All-Union Central Council of Unions, about aviation factory No. 95 in Verkhniaia Salda in Sverdlovsk province. Food, he explained, was distributed "apart from any plan, but according to the discretion of the factory directorship."[6] Workers, for example, were supposed to receive 270 liters of milk daily from the factory's subsidiary farms, but they received none. The factory director instead sent about 60 percent of the milk to children's institutions, 20 percent back to the farms, and the remaining 20 percent to party officials. Similarly, officials appropriated almost half of the meat. Lisitsyn asked, "Is it not correct that the meat and other food from the subsidiary farms be distributed first to the workers, their children, and families, so that they receive the full amounts that they are entitled to according to their ration cards?" He noted that, if the meat had been added to central state stocks, workers and their families would have received the full amount they were guaranteed by the plan, and extra meat would still have remained to reward the best workers. Lisitsyn asked for some guidance as the union was caught between the director's appropriation and the workers' anger about their meager rations. He wrote, "This situation raises great discontent among the workers of the factory and criticism about the lack of help from our union factory committees. I ask you to explain."[7] Party leaders recognized that "self-provisioning" not only promoted resentment, but also encouraged corruption. Mikhail A. Shamberg, the head of the Organizational-Instructional Department of the Central Committee, wrote to the Central Committee in spring 1943, "In practice, local organizations decide for themselves the norms and contingents of provisioning and feeding at the expense of stocks received by the towns, as well as the distribution of additional parcels." In other words, local trade officials and factory managers determined both the size and content of their special parcels and the extra food they dispensed to associates, relatives, and friends. Shamberg reported, "This creates great discord and leads to individual cases of illegality."[8]

The most common method of self-provisioning used by managers within the factories was differentiated canteens. Rather than all canteens serving the same food to all employees in accordance with their ration category, managers created a hierarchy: a director's canteen served a small circle of managers and party officials, a mid-level canteen was reserved for a larger group of engineering and technical personnel, and a main canteen was used by ordinary workers. The food served in each differed in amount, assortment, and quality. Directors defended this system, which existed in almost every factory, by claiming that they did not want shop heads, engineers, and other valuable personnel to waste time waiting in line. These highly skilled employees worked around the clock to repair machines, resolve supply problems, and ensure that targets were met, and directors sought to reward their service with food. The food stocks that factories received from the state, however, made no allowance for special canteens or any other forms of differentiation. The better-provisioned canteens thus drew their extra provisions directly from stocks allocated for workers.

An investigation of the canteens in aviation factory No. 32 in Kirov in May 1942, for example, revealed no fewer than four canteens, each serving a different clientele. The most privileged canteen served three abundant meals each day to the director, chief engineer, three deputy directors, head bookkeeper, party officials, and two officials from the design office. For breakfast, they received two eggs, 25 grams of butter, cheese, ham, fried doughnuts (*ponchiki*), and sweetened tea. Dinner consisted of borscht with meat, ham with potatoes, cheese cakes, and coffee with milk. Supper brought goulash, more cheese cakes, hot doughnuts, and coffee with milk. The meals, moreover, were free and off ration. The second-tier canteen, serving shop and department heads, also provided three meals, but of a lower quality. Breakfast consisted of doughnuts from dark flour, a lump of salted sheep's milk cheese (*brynza*), and tea without sugar. Dinner was 200 grams of bread (for commercial sale off ration), lentil soup, a meat cutlet, and half of a pickle. Supper was two dark flour doughnuts and a glass of tea with sugar. These meals required ration coupons and were not free. The third-tier canteen provided only one meal of lentil soup, 200 grams of bread (for sale), and oatmeal to engineering and technical personnel and the best Stakhanovites. At the bottom, a fourth-tier canteen served one meal per shift of a thin porridge from flour and pickled cucumbers to thousands of workers.[9] Rather than reward those who expended the greatest calories with the largest amount of food, the director of factory No. 32 turned the labor principle of the rationing system on its head, ensuring that caloric intake was in inverse proportion to caloric expenditure.

The system of differentiated canteens was widespread throughout industry. In spring 1943, Klavdiia Nikolaeva led a special commission created by the Central Committee and Soviet of People's Commissars to investigate canteens in factories and mines in Cheliabinsk, Magnitogorsk, Kopeisk, and Miass. Born in 1893, Nikolaeva was the daughter of a worker and a washerwoman. She went to work in a printing plant, was arrested for revolutionary activity at the age of fifteen, and joined the Bolshevik Party one year later. After the revolution, Nikolaeva led the Zhenotdel, the Party's first mass organization for women workers. She later became a member of the Central Committee and leader of the All-Union Central Council of Unions. Her commission's report documented the extensive use of differentiated canteens with undisguised repugnance. The report emphasized that "workers receive significantly less food than established by norm" at the same time as the "top" canteens received significantly more.[10] Managers in the Kirov factory, for example, created a three-tiered canteen system. According to the ration system, workers, technical personnel, and leading managers should all have received 20 grams of fats per day. In fact, workers received only 10 grams while diners in the top canteens received nearly three times their allotted norm and nearly six times what workers were eating. The allocations for meat and fish showed the same patterns.[11] The report emphasized: "All this is done at the expense of centralized stocks allocated for the workers."[12] Investigations in other factories supported the same conclusion. One investigator noted, "Short-weighting the workers has taken on such a mass character that it has become a system." When a cook in Magnitostroi was asked, "Where are the stolen sausages?" she shamelessly replied that she had "to feed the director of the canteen, the head of the workers' settlement, she herself needed to eat three to four portions, and she had to feed her assistants."[13]

The investigators maintained that workers' stocks were substantially depleted by the practice of differentiated canteens. They proved that 55 percent of workers were receiving portions that were short-weighted by 10 to 15 grams. These losses were not solely the result of managerial self-provisioning. Food was siphoned at many points in the journey from production to canteen, and the full allocation from central stocks rarely arrived in factory kitchens. At the same time, the food the managers appropriated for themselves would have made a significant difference if it had stayed in the common pot even though the canteens for managers served only a handful of people, while the canteens for workers served thousands.[14] More importantly, their behavior would have demonstrated that the sacrifices required of workers were shared by all.

Managers and officials, however, practiced blatant self-provisioning in every area. They also created a steep hierarchy within the network of "closed" stores available to factory employees. In aviation factory No. 381, for example, the best and scarcest foodstuffs—butter, compote, chocolate, cocoa, and sausage—as well as one-third of the factory's flour allotment, were diverted to a store open only to the secretary of the party committee, the head of the union, and the heads of shops and departments. Not surprisingly, as one investigator noted, "This situation raises a great deal of discontent among the workers and criticism of the union's factory committees."[15] Managers extended shopping privileges to local officials who had no relationship to the factory. These "circles" or patronage networks, built on mutual ties and reciprocal "favors," facilitated their work, but the favors they dispensed came from stocks that belonged by right to workers. As a woman weaver in the Nogin textile factory noted angrily, "We go about hungry. We are not able to work properly, but the leadership gets food in closed stores; for them it is possible to live."[16]

The practice of allotting special parcels of food or consumer items was another important element in the creation of unsanctioned hierarchy. This practice, which predated the war, rewarded officials in high-level posts with products unavailable to ordinary consumers in retail state stores. Until 1943, officials determined both the contents of their own special parcels as well as the "subscription lists" of those they deemed entitled to extra food.[17] The state's policy of putting ORSy in charge of subsidiary farms opened new opportunities for enlarging special parcels and strengthening patronage networks.[18] Factory managers dispensed parcels to local party, trade, and soviet officials as well as managers of other enterprises who could help resolve economic or administrative problems. In the Kirov factory, for example, in the fall of 1942, managers distributed special parcels "by note" (po zapiskam) or "by warrant" (po orderam) to 515 local officials and other "favored" people. The parcels were generous: from 3 to 5 kilograms of meat and 2 to 3 kilos of butter each month. Both groups also received an array of scarce items, including caviar, jam, dried fruits, eggs, herring, honey, vitamins, tobacco, and vodka.[19]

Although the number of officials who received special parcels was small compared to the overall workforce, the amounts taken from the workers' stocks were not insignificant and markedly reduced the amounts available to workers. Evidence suggests that special parcels removed a larger percentage of the food allocated to workers than differentiated canteens. An investigation of one factory store revealed that out of the 5,185 kilos of butter the store received over four months, only about half was distributed by ration cards, with the remainder given out to managers, officials, and "favorites." Similar losses affected meat and fish stocks.[20]

Many officials used the collective or state farms attached to their enterprises as their personal storehouses. The canteen for workers in aviation factory No. 19 in Molotov "did not receive one gram of food" from the prosperous state farm attached to its factory. Instead, the factory's deputy director set up stalls at the farm for the exclusive use of "circles of factory and state farm officials." In March 1942 alone, 583 kilograms of meat, 7,540 eggs, and large amounts of butter, cream, and sour cream were sold while the farm delivered to the factory only 12 percent of the plan for meat, 31 percent for sour cream, 62 percent of the eggs, and 73 percent of the butter. The factory's deputy director had a close relationship with the head of the Department of Subsidiary Agriculture (OPKh or Otdel podsobnogo khoziaistva) and sent him hundreds of notes instructing him to release food to his cronies, including his chauffeur and the head of the garage. The trade official, in turn, ordered packers at the farm to release the food. The notes, no more than a few scribbled lines, stated only the first name of the recipient and the amount of food to be released. People arrived in cars at the state farm at all hours of the day and night, often waking up the packers to demand their orders. This "trade" naturally infuriated both the farm and factory workers. The investigator quickly stopped the sales and referred the case for prosecution. "This 'trade,'" he wrote, "can definitely be understood as a form of theft."[21]

The inclusion of a chauffeur and garage manager in patronage circles was not uncommon. Officials frequently used state vehicles for their personal convenience, an illicit practice that infuriated workers who were forced to trudge long distances to and from work after fuel shortages halted trams and trolleybuses. Workers in Ivanovo, for example, were enraged at the sight of officials using state cars and rationed gasoline to cart home extra food. Solov'eva, the wife of a Red Army soldier, wrote an indignant letter to the Central Committee after reading an article in *Pravda* stressing how local officials cared for workers. She charged, "in Ivanovo we have several officials of the provincial party committee who care only about themselves." Solov'eva provided a long list of abuses: the secretary of the provincial party committee transported potatoes, cabbage, and other vegetables by car to a special closed store in the center of town he had established for officials. "There is no gas for ambulances," Solov'eva fumed, "but their wives travel by car, and create great bitterness among people." The food was brazenly distributed in front of everyone, although "workers and white-collar employees cannot get these foods and must buy them in the market at very high prices." Solov'eva emphasized that she understood the need for sacrifice. "I am not against that," she said firmly. She even acknowledged that managers might deserve more than workers. "We do not want to be equal with officials who work honestly and give themselves wholeheartedly to work, but here what do we wives of Red Army soldiers receive?" The press lauded soldiers' wives for their loyalty, but the head of the party committee was conducting an extramarital affair, eating well, and providing food to his mistress. "There are conversations throughout town," she wrote, "in the stores and on the trams and in the bathhouses, and in other places. People are saying, 'Here is a person who holds a responsible position, and what kind of example are we supposed to take from him?'" Local officials and their wives, in her opinion, benefited from the sacrifices of others, dressing stylishly in clothing from closed stores when ordinary people and their children wore rags. Solov'eva explained that she had refrained from telling her husband at the front about the situation "because I do not want anything to upset him. He should be at ease and smash the German bastards in order to destroy them quickly. And, anyway, he cannot do anything about this shocking mess." Other women, equally disgusted, said, "Our husbands will come home from the front and pay them back for everything." Solov'eva, however, had faith that the Party's leaders could "put this mess in order," and appealed for more ethical and egalitarian behavior: "We need to be served by other principles," she insisted, "then the people will have bigger food parcels and the difficulties will be easier to bear."[22]

Workers throughout the country shared her view. Workers in a defense factory in Nizhnii Tagil wrote a joint letter stressing the importance of shared sacrifice:

> Our people love our country very much and are glad to take on deprivations and sacrifices for her, to endure patiently all the deprivations and difficulties of war. We fully recognize that there is not enough food, clothing and other things in our country, and that this is because our native soil is occupied by the German invaders. We are leading a great war of liberation and people in the rear are working with redoubled energy in order to give the front what it needs. But it is insulting and painful to realize that precisely while we are working and protecting the motherland, many officials have climbed on the bandwagon, so to speak, found a warm place, and are embezzling food and deceiving the state.[23]

The belief that officials were pilfering stocks was widely held, even by young and inexperienced workers. Recent vocational graduates working at factory No. 76 (Urals Engine Works) in Sverdlovsk wrote a joint letter to the regional newspaper in January 1943, charging that officials were stealing food and goods allocated to them. Another letter noted, "We are living like dogs. The dormitory is cold, we have no clothes or shoes ... All the clothing—felt boots, tall boots, and padded jackets—is taken by the bosses, those who sit in the offices."[24]

By spring 1943, state investigations and popular disgust with self-provisioning prompted the Party and Commissariat of Trade to end self-provisioning and distribution by note and by list. On July 17, 1943, the state set norms for rations, canteen meals, and special parcels for approximately 262,200 leading officials in the Party, Komsomol, soviets, and unions based on position and location.[25] Groups I and II received food from three sources: ration cards, canteen meals, and special parcels. The allowances were generous: roughly 300 grams of meat or fish per day, between 60 and 80 grams of fats, and large helpings of grains or pasta. They also received substantial allocations of potatoes, vegetables, dried fruit, milk, and eggs in parcels. Group III received no parcels but was partially compensated with a large bread allocation and extra canteen meals that increased its consumption of meat and fish, fats, and grains by roughly one-third.[26] Unlike workers, none of the groups had to use their ration cards to eat in canteens. The decree gave local trade departments the right to open special stores and canteens for officials and to provide them with special parcels. In terms of calories, the new allowances were enough to provide Group I with more than 4,600 calories a day; and Groups II and III with 3,500 and almost 3,200 calories respectively. In addition, each month, officials in Group I received 300 grams of tobacco, 1 bar of household soap, 1 bar of toilet soap, 50 grams of tea, and either 3 bottles of vodka or 1 bottle of wine.[27] The differentials between officials notwithstanding, all officials were far better provisioned than workers, even those in defence sectors at the top of the rationing hierarchy. The differentials in bread were fairly modest. The real chasm between officials and workers was in other essential food groups (see Table 4.1).

Officials in Group I were allotted more than twice the calories afforded to defense workers and three times the calories for workers in other sectors. Even Group III officials, the lowest category, consumed 50 percent more calories than defense workers and double the number of calories of other workers. The differentials were even greater between officials and white-collar workers or dependants.

The main aim of the July 1943 decree was to stop the practice of self-provisioning and end the more flagrant raids on workers' food stocks. While the decree codified the allocations of officials, it also categorically banned any additional provisioning above the stated allowances.[28] In effect, it systematized and legalized the generous privileges of top officials, but in a way that would no longer provoke the resentment of workers. It promptly resulted in a stream of petitions from groups who sought inclusion into the higher levels of provisioning. More than 20,000 union officials, for example, were covered by the decree in late 1944 after repeated petitioning.[29] In early 1944, Commissariat of Trade inspectors launched a nationwide investigation to review whether the decree had achieved its aims. Fifty trade inspectors and workers in Saratov province fanned out through factory canteens, railway buffets, and ORSy to check portion sizes, ration receipts, and records.[30]

They were stunned to find that the decree had not ended the practices of self-provisioning or distributing food to patronage networks. Investigators in other places came to similar conclusions. In Rostov province, an investigator wrote to the deputy commissar of trade noting that, although no more than eight officials were covered by the July decree, leaders of the provincial soviet had listed up to sixty people for extra food from stocks earmarked for workers. About twenty-five of these "officials" also received an additional monthly monetary supplement of up to 1,500 rubles, along with highly prized special items. The inspector was astounded. "I ask you to inform me whether this decision of the executive committee of the provincial soviet is legal or not."[31]

In some places, officials blocked investigators from reviewing their provisioning arrangements. When the head of the Commissariat of Trade's Inspectorate in Tatariia, I. O. Kadyrov, launched an investigation of the canteens in March 1944, and was shocked by the meals and allocations local officials received, he asked, "Are there any norms set for these officials?" Yet his question was rudely rebuffed. The deputy secretary of the provincial party committee sneered, "This is not your business. You do not have the right to investigate the activities of the Soviet of People's Commissars and the provincial party committee." Kadyrov then turned to his supervisor for guidance, but his supervisor warned him, "Do not go there, this is not your business." When Kadyrov persisted, his supervisor flatly declaimed, "I do not report to you." Kadyrov understood that officials in Tatariia were protecting each other. Appalled by their brazen behavior, he appealed beyond the republic's elite to the deputy commissar of trade. Signaling that an investigation could get uncomfortable, he noted, "a large number of violations are committed by high-standing officials served by these canteens."[32] Kadyrov's experience suggested that even trade inspectors, charged with supervising official behavior, could be blocked by powerful networks.

Leveling by Local Officials

Not all officials who took stocks allocated for workers did so for personal gain. Many managers and local officials, responsible for the welfare of poorly provisioned groups, redistributed stocks earmarked for others to ensure the survival of as many people as possible. As food shortages worsened in 1942, the state channeled central stocks from local trade departments to ORSy for allocation to industrial workers. Faced with hungry groups outside the factories, local officials either reallocated food from one group to another or placed groups from outside the factories in its canteens. The state termed these efforts "*uravnilovka*" (leveling) or "*razbazarivanie*" (squandering or illicit redistribution). Although both terms implied a violation of state norms, *uravnilovka* was part of a long socialist tradition of egalitarianism, while *razbazarivanie* connoted negligence and waste. The Bolshevik Party program of 1917 had supported *uravnilovka*, proclaiming that no official should be paid more than a skilled worker, a principle that opposition groups within the Party continued to support through the 1920s. During the early part of the First Five-Year Plan tens of thousands of workers joined production communes, where they shared earnings according to various egalitarian methods. In June 1931, however, Stalin launched an attack on egalitarian wage systems in favor of steeper wage differentials and piece work. The new policy was designed to impose speedup, encourage workers to raise their skills, and increase production in the factories. *Uravnilovka* lost its previous positive connotations, and evolved from a revolutionary rallying cry to a state epithet.[33] Yet municipal authorities, faced with starving children and other needy groups, often had no choice but to redistribute stocks.[34]

The most common method of redistribution was to assign groups unconnected with the factory to eat in its canteens. Workers in a defense factory, for example, might find themselves seated amid orphans, evacuees, and their own children. Union investigators found that more than 1,000 people who did not work in aviation factory No. 19 in Sverdlovsk received coupons entitling them to eat in its canteens. Unions, defending the interests of their members, took a strong stand against this practice.[35] In some instances, workers were actually displaced from their own canteens by other groups. A large number of workers in ammunition factory No. 15 in Chapaevsk, for example, were removed from their own canteen to make room for hundreds of officials from municipal organizations and the Commissariat of Textiles and their families, and thirty-five members of an evacuated Moscow operetta ensemble. Moreover, the workers who remained received less food than the newcomers. The workers, served a single bowl of soup or millet porridge without butter, stared resentfully at the plates of the operetta singers, who scarfed down three or four servings of fried ham and potatoes, noodle soup, pickles, and tea with pastries. The union factory committee repeatedly protested the situation but was overruled by Chapaevsk's party committee. The All-Union Central Council of Unions finally took measures to rectify the differentials, providing singers and workers with the same meals and barring officials from other organizations from the canteens altogether.[36]

Tens of thousands of NKVD prisoners labored alongside free workers and also received supplementary food from workers' stocks. Prisoners were supposed to be fed from separate stocks through the NKVD, but their norms were so low that they were too weak to work. Factory directors, in desperate need of labor, supplemented their paltry rations with stocks designated for free workers. Managers at the Kirov factory, who employed around 2,000 prisoners, provided each with about 240 calories, taken from workers' stocks.[37] Managers in other factories did the same.[38]

In fall 1943, the food situation improved slightly as a result of gardening, the liberation of the occupied territories, and the capture of "trophy resources" or stockpiles from the Germans.[39] As more food became available, the state rewarded workers who exceeded their norms with a second hot canteen meal and provided supplementary nourishment to single workers in barracks and those suffering from starvation and tuberculosis. No worker, however, was to receive more than six coupons per month for the second hot meal, and those suffering from tuberculosis or starvation had to be certified by a medical commission.[40] Managers widely flouted the guidelines. The director of ammunition factory No. 572 in Saratov province, later accused of "gross violations," provided the factory's poorly provisioned auxiliary workers with more food.[41] In Stalingrad province, trade inspectors visited fifteen factories and construction sites and found that fully 80 percent of the stocks allocated for starvation sufferers was given out to people without medical certificates. Officials were not stealing the food, but redistributing it to sick workers who had not seen a doctor because those responsible for certification were either absent or overwhelmed by cases. Directors also gave supplemental food earmarked for norm busters to all workers who put in compulsory overtime, a humane practice that allowed workers to eat two canteen meals in a shift that lasted fifteen hours or more. Even the stocks allocated for officials were redistributed: 55 percent of the total went to other groups. Directors thus disbursed food to the needy, but not in precise accordance with state instructions. Although inspectors criticized directors for not using the extra food to raise labor productivity, the actions of the directors were in fact well aligned with production. Although many may have acted from humane motives, they also understood that a weakened workforce could not produce.[42]

Supplemental food was also channeled from production workers to white-collar employees. In Kuznetsk (Penza province), the director of a shoe factory gave meal coupons to the head bookkeeper, who in turn passed them out to the factory's white-collar employees, including telephone and radio operators, norm setters, bookkeepers, cashiers, cleaners, packers, water line workers, cooks, weighers, and economists whose rations were well below those of production workers. Some directors, swamped with other tasks, gave shop heads and foremen the coupons to distribute as they saw fit. In other workplaces, special supplements for those suffering from starvation went to any worker in poor health. Tens of thousands of coupons were not distributed in the month for which they were issued. One investigator noted critically, "Leaders of the enterprises consider any leftover coupons or cards to be their personal reserve and use them as they choose."[43]

Like coupons for the "second hot," extra ration cards were widely dispensed by managers and local officials to people within and outside the factory. The food allotments were significant. In fifteen tank and chemical factories in Gor'kii province surveyed over two months in 1944, tens of thousands of kilograms of bread, grain, meat, fish, fat, and sugar, along with 160,135 coupons for the "second hot," were redistributed to groups not entitled to these stocks. Almost 38,000 people who were not in defense industries received cards with the defense stamp "O," entitling them to higher rations. Officials working in ration bureaus dispensed cards reserved for workers in hot and dangerous shops to ordinary workers and officials. They gave workers in the peat industry the better cards of industrial workers and stamped the cards of workers laboring in forests and state farms with the city mark that entitled them to more food. Factory managers redistributed supplemental stocks to factory clinics and the local newspaper.[44] All these activities leveled the ration hierarchy and benefited workers at the lower end. Yet because food stocks were fixed, they also ensured that workers at the higher end received less.

Such illicit redistribution was widespread. Almost half the directors of 204 enterprises in Moscow province were found guilty of "gross violations." Out of more than 3.7 million coupons allocated, about 20 percent were diverted from designated workers to bookkeepers, machinists, hairdressers, and laundresses or not distributed at all.[45] In the defense factories of Tatariia, similar practices prevailed. One inspector concluded that state instructions for supplementary food were "grossly violated by leaders of the enterprises investigated."[46] Yet the "gross violations" also fed the hungry and kept the workforce on its feet.

Theft

Outright theft, unlike the more ambiguous practice of redistribution, involved taking food or goods allocated for others for personal gain or profit. Anatolii A. Volin, Chief Prosecutor of the RSFSR, noted that theft was committed mainly by people with access to stocks of food and goods. Volin, responsible for prosecuting food as well as other crimes, collected data showing that petty pilfering and large-scale embezzlement flourished in town trade departments, ORSy, rural consumer cooperatives, canteens, control and ration card bureaus, food processors, consumer goods factories, transport points, and storehouses.[47] Trade officials convicted for theft amassed a total of 167 million rubles in 1942, 212 million in 1943, and 560 million in 1945. In several republics, including Dagestan, Tatariia, and Mordoviia, a substantial percentage of the food and consumer goods allocated for workers and the urban population was stolen.[48] In a secret report to A. N. Kosygin, head of the Soviet of People's Commissars in Russia, Volin presented data supporting the common opinion of workers that theft, illicit distribution, and "criminal self-provisioning" were pervasive. Based on numerous investigations, he took a dim view of managers, maintaining, "The directors of enterprises think that they are the masters of the stocks they distribute and, in fact, they squander them according to their own estimation."[49]

Officials used a variety of ruses to cover up the illegal diversion of stocks. In Ivanovo province, a ring of rural officials organized a "black storehouse" where they stockpiled pilfered vodka, salt, and baked goods for sale to other officials at low state prices. In choosing not to charge the free market price, the officials declined big profits, but instead used the stocks to support a valuable patronage network. They channeled about 80 percent of the stocks designated for the local population through two crooked consumer unions, leaving the village stores and rural population with nothing. Similar schemes proliferated throughout rural districts.[50] In Tula province, trade officials set up a stall where they sold thousands of kilograms of embezzled food. The food was falsely invoiced to twenty-three rural consumer cooperatives, which never received a single gram.[51] Thieving trade officials concealed missing stocks by forging invoices for fake deliveries, inventing fictive contingents, and inflating the number of coupons they claimed to distribute. In Saratov province, the militia uncovered a scheme that involved the trade inspector himself. Colluding with the heads of ORSy in the oil refineries, the group created false categories of recipients and stole supplementary food designated for workers' canteens.[52]

Thieving officials in the town trade departments and ORSy, however, were only responsible for losses at the very end of the food chain. In actuality, the ration system leaked food at every point from production to distribution. Tons of meat, fish, sugar, and vegetable oil disappeared from the Novosibirsk railway junction, never reaching the town trade departments or ORSy. As a result, the residents of Novosibirsk and its surrounding province consistently received less food than their ration cards allotted. One investigator of the Tomsk rail line noted in late 1944, "On the railroad, the practice existed of giving out so-called gifts to officials." Food "gifts" were dispensed to speed up services, repairs, loading, and unloading. "Most of the best goods," the investigator wrote, "were distributed by lists." The railway trade administration used food to bribe and incentivize officials and workers to meet their targets.[53] Food disappeared from food-processing factories and storage facilities. Managers of salt depots, milk and meat factories, granaries, flour mills, bread factories, and warehouses were frequently involved in theft and illicit distribution. In Kursk province, an expediter working in the salt trust (Glavsol') "systematically plundered" tons of salt every month and gave it to relatives who sold it in the market. A search of his apartment revealed 45,000 rubles.[54] A group of officials in Molotov who managed production and distribution of meat, cream, milk, and eggs was charged with embezzlement in 1944 after years of thievery.[55]

Managers passed out food waste products to some staff, which complicated the definition of theft. Dar'ya Markovna Rakhina, evacuated with her sister and children from Kursk to Penza, remembered that her sister, who worked in the Livestock Procurement Administration, received "unlimited quantities of heads, feet, liver, lungs, heart" from the slaughterhouse which they boiled up in a big pot every day. Some people traded their offal in the market. Rakhina wrote:

> The more experienced and prudent employees who received large amounts of "offal" sold what they didn't need and used the money to buy milk, sour cream, bread. It was wartime. Pava and I, as former Komsomolki and

patriots, didn't think we had the right to sell meat at a speculative price in order to buy the foods the children needed. Whatever we couldn't use we gave away for free to our neighbors and acquaintances, but our children went hungry. How naive we were! Having become accustomed to a peaceful, honest life, we couldn't go against our conscience.[56]

Bread, considered the lifeblood of the ration system, was supposed to be measured at every stage of production, from threshing to milling to baking, yet it vanished in kernels, flour sacks, loaves, and slices. Bread store clerks who short-weighted consumers merely took the final cut.[57] In Molotov province, the head of a granary and his deputy conspired with two carters, who embezzled more than 1,300 kilograms while transferring grain from one warehouse to another and then resold it in the market at steep prices.[58] Officials in Gor'kii province embezzled forty-five tons of flour and grain when fuel and flour shortages forced the bakeries to close and people were starved of bread. Large-scale thefts also occurred in Cheliabinsk and Ulan-Ude. When a group of twenty-one officials in Chistopol' were found guilty of systematically stealing 13,665 kilograms of grain from a storage facility in 1944, the two ringleaders received the death penalty, a sentence that was applauded by many hungry people who regarded food crimes as an indirect form of murder.[59]

Theft also occurred in hospitals, orphanages, and schools. The doctors, bookkeeper, and managers of the subsidiary farms attached to a psychiatric hospital in Ul'ianovsk province created fictive lists of patients, hid the extra food in a warehouse, and then sold it. Managers in other hospitals allowed "dead souls" to linger on the ration rolls in order to inflate the number of patients entitled to food. In one tragic instance of "theft," starving doctors and officials in hospital No. 4 in Leningrad placed all medical and service personnel on sick lists so they could survive and continue to treat their patients. Officials in collection centers for breast milk and blood also created lists of fictive donors and pilfered the extra food allocated for them. Pharmacy officials embezzled products used to mix medicines, including oil, pork fat, vitamins, and sugar. In 1943, a military tribunal sentenced the director of the Medical Trade Department (Rosmedsnabtorg) and other officials to six years in prison for thievery and "self-provisioning" of clinical foods and medicines.[60]

Local party and soviet officials were often enmeshed in circles of corruption. In Ul'ianovsk, trade inspectors discovered that leaders of the district party committee and soviet "not only did not take measures to stop criminal illicit distribution of goods, but themselves received a large quantity of food items illegally."[61] Corruption flourished in the NKVD, the organization responsible for policing food crimes. In 1944, the head of the Main Inspectorate of the Commissariat of Trade wrote to Zaveniagin, the deputy commissar of internal affairs, about an investigation of Dal'stroi construction camps in the Far East. Trade investigators discovered that NKVD officials stole shamelessly from starving prisoners, selling consumer items and thousands of kilograms food "by list" and "by note" at low state prices to favored officials.[62] Party officials also stole from the Kolyma transit camp connected to Dal'stroi. The massive cache of food and goods, which should have been distributed to the starved, freezing prisoners, included more than 8,500 kilograms of meat and fish, 1,600 kilograms of bread, felt boots, warm clothing, wooden shoes, and padded jackets.[63]

The most common and simplest form of theft occurred in the factory canteens. Liubimov, the commissar of trade, noted "mass violations in the rules of trade, short-weighting, and overpricing of consumers" as early as June 1942.[64] In one factory canteen in Omsk, cooks pilfered large amounts of flour, rice, and butter from food "remnants." The portions the workers received weighed considerably less than the norm: cutlets that should have weighed 110 grams, for example, weighed only 75.[65] Bread for workers was also commonly short-weighted in canteens. An investigation of factory No. 200 in Cheliabinsk, which manufactured tank armor and components, revealed that pieces that should have weighed 400 grams weighed only 300. Portions of fish weighed 30 grams rather than 45. Over time, the losses created by short-weighting were considerable: more than 3,000 kilograms of bread disappeared from aviation factory No. 19 in Molotov over three months in the winter of 1941–1942, allegedly pilfered by the canteen bread cutters.[66] Weighers would surreptitiously place a few kopeks on the scale under the food to convince consumers they had received the full weight.[67] Deliberate short-weight was facilitated by the widespread lack of measuring equipment. Slicers often used kopeks when they lacked proper weights for scales. In many canteens, apportionment occurred largely by guesswork.[68] When inspectors in the Primor'e Territory in the Soviet Far East checked the status of scales in 215 stores and factory canteens, they found that more than one-third of consumers received short-weight or measure in rationed goods.[69]

The coupon system, despite its elaborate procedures for distribution, tabulation, and receipt, was also easily scammed.[70] The head of ORS in factory No. 299 in Kurgan embezzled goods, forged allocations for fictive contingents, and even fooled the accountant in the control bureau. A search of her apartment found piles of coupons for hundreds of kilograms of meat, fat, sugar, grain, and vodka as well as almost 3,000 ration cards.[71] People were caught forging bread cards and allocation orders, and reusing coupons that were redeemed or expired.[72] A group of sixteen people, including heads of stores, canteens, buffets, and even the workers' control commission in Molotov province, embezzled almost 3,700 kilograms of bread from stocks for workers and urban residents by colluding to recycle cards and enabling "favorites" to double-dip.[73] Reusing coupons that should have been canceled or collected allowed people to access food stocks multiple times, thereby reducing the overall amount available to others. Officials partnered with store clerks, who were paid in food or money, to overlook coupon scams. Others stole from food stocks by writing fraudulent order forms. In Ivanovo province in 1943, officials stole blank forms, wrote fictitious orders for food, and then sold the food in the market. In Novosibirsk province, thieves stole 13,700 cards in 1943 and resold them. Theft of food cards even led to murder. A shop foreman in factory No. 38 in Irkutsk broke into the apartment of the party secretary with the aim of stealing the key to the shop safe. He killed the secretary, took the key, and stole almost 1,000 ration cards designated for workers.[74]

Scams also proliferated in printing shops where cards were produced. On January 22, 1943, the GKO established stricter control over printing as part of a broad state campaign against food theft, but people continued to steal print type and plates to forge cards. In Vladivostok, artists teamed up with the head of a printing works to forge cards, which they sold in the market for up to 800 rubles apiece. In Cheliabinsk, the militia discovered no fewer than five underground printing presses devoted to forging ration cards, and in Omsk employees of the local newspaper printed cards on its press and used them to steal 1,000 kilograms of bread.[75] In a district near Ufa in Bashkiriia, an investigation of factory No. 26 revealed that coupons for 200 grams of bread were doctored to show 400 grams.[76] Petty thieves stole ration cards from workers in factories and dormitories. Some scammed the system by applying for a replacement for a "lost" ration card, and then using both or selling one.[77]

Ordinary people were not immune to the temptations of theft. The amounts tended to be small, and the acts motivated by hunger rather than profit or patronage. Workers in the factories of Magnitogorsk filched bowls and soap, both items in short supply. They took scrap metal from their shops to make combs and cigarette lighters for personal use and market barter.[78] Authorities were reluctant to prosecute workers for common petty theft. An investigation of nine factories making highly prized consumer items in Moscow showed that only a small number of workers were arrested for theft. The numbers, however, were not indicative of the prevalence of the practice. When managers in Krasnaia oborona (Red Defense), a garment factory, announced a surprise search of workers leaving the factory, guards discovered that the floor by the exit was littered with trim, cloth, reels, bobbins, thread, and buttons, all items eagerly sought in the market. The loot on the floor gave some indication of the small haul that occurred with every shift change. Yet when searches were introduced in the famed chocolate factory, Krasnyi Oktiabr' (Red October), the district prosecutor sharply objected to the practice as demeaning to the "dignity and honor of the workers" and convinced Moscow's prosecutor to abandon it. Directors frequently refused to press charges when they caught workers stealing, preferring internal disciplinary measures.[79]

Volin, Chief Prosecutor of the RSFSR, kept a record of the money and goods that the militia confiscated from thieves in 1943: millions of rubles and kilograms of food, 1,500 liters of vodka and wine, and valuables, including tens of thousands of gold and silver tsarist coins, gold and metal watches, silver pieces, grams of gold, coats, and other personal consumer goods. The objects revealed what people traded for food and exposed the limits of accumulation.[80] Most of the ill-gotten gains were in the form of food or money. Ordinary people had few valuables to trade for stolen items. Amid all the goods confiscated, there were only 212 gold and 725 metal watches; indeed, most ordinary people did not own a watch. More importantly, large-scale food embezzlers had trouble converting their profits into stable capital. Cash and food stocks were both insecure forms of accumulation, subject to inflation, devaluation, or spoilage. Large amounts of cash could not be banked, and food was difficult to store. Theft did, however, foster the market, which provided a relatively safe place for officials and ordinary people alike to offload purloined goods. Without markets, stolen stocks would have been far more difficult to parley into even the limited form of accumulation that flourished in the Soviet wartime economy.

Gray and Black Markets

Throughout the war, markets flourished at any site, official or unofficial, open or closed, where people bought and sold items at prices determined by supply and demand.[81] Collective farm markets were promoted by the state, but others operated in zones ranging from partial legality to outright criminality. Large markets, filled with people hawking every imaginable item, often surrounded collective farm markets and existed in full view of the militia and any passersby. Others, located in warehouses and apartments, were open by invitation only. In many places, collective farm markets were taken over by petty exchange and gray and black market sellers. In Krasnoiarsk, the collective farmers made up only 13 percent of the trade in the markets. In Irkutsk, the collective farm market, entirely devoid of peasants, was populated solely by urban residents exchanging or reselling goods.[82] Peasants, discouraged by the lack of consumer goods, stopped bringing produce to market or contracted with factories and other state institutions.[83] The state encouraged factories and municipal workshops to produce small consumer items, including metal tools, to trade with peasants for food, an activity it called "counter trade" (*vstrechnaia torgovlia*). Managers, however, hampered by shortages of labor and raw materials, were not very successful. The Commissariat of Trade noted in 1943, "counter trade in markets is very poorly organized, and requests, particularly for tools and implements, are not met."[84] Rather than produce their own items, factory managers and local trade officials sometimes took matches, soap, and vodka from central state stocks allocated to workers to trade for food for the canteens.[85] Although workers urgently needed extra food, the loss of these consumer items, especially soap, was a serious hardship. Unable to wash off the dirt, grease, and toxic chemicals from work, they suffered constant rashes, abscesses, and infections. The Commissariat of Trade, aware of this practice, prohibited any trade of workers' consumer stocks for food. The schemes, designed to keep workers and urban residents from starvation, were not aimed at personal gain, but rather constituted a form of trade in the gray zone between legal and criminal.

Other forms of trade also existed in this gray zone. While trade of personal items was legal, workers sold or traded items issued by their factory, including pillows and blankets, which they technically did not own. Such trade, which forced the state to repeatedly resupply the already poorly equipped dormitories, bordered on "theft of state property," a serious crime. The sale of ration cards and coupons, both highly coveted items, was another gray area. Such sales undermined state categories of provisioning, entitled people who had no relationship to the factory to eat at the expense of its stocks, and encouraged theft. The state initially criminalized sale of ration cards in July 1941 and replaced criminal sanctions with a fine in 1943, but then instructed the militia to turn a blind eye to petty hawking and swapping of all types.[86]

Prosecutors were unsure how to treat many gray areas of market activity, but they regarded large-scale theft and resale for profit as unambiguously illegal. When the head of the provincial trade department in Rostov colluded with other officials to remove vodka, matches, and tobacco from ration stocks, resold these highly coveted items, and then divided the profits, the group was prosecuted more harshly than officials who appropriated these same goods and exchanged them for food for factory canteens.[87] Other examples of outright illegal activity included officials in Riazan' province who appropriated food coupons and sold them in the market for more than 25,000 rubles. Two trade officials in North Ossetia took food from the Commissariat of Trade's storehouses, hosted large banquets, and provisioned their relatives who sold it in the market.[88] Many perpetrators of large-scale theft, however, were embedded in patronage networks and did not sell goods in open markets. In Molotov province, ORS officials at factory No. 33 systematically embezzled workers' provisions and used an official's apartment as a "store," where they sold the food at vast markups. A liter of vodka, which cost only a few rubles on the ration card, sold for 1,000 to 1,200 rubles.[89] Regardless of whether goods were sold openly or secretly, directly by officials or indirectly through their relatives, the sale of appropriated goods for profit was treated as a crime.

In the absence of retail stores, people turned to huge "secondhand markets" (*tolkuchki*), where they bought, sold, and bartered firewood, clothing, shoes, food, and ration cards in what was known as "hand-to-hand trade" (*torgovlia s ruk*). In Moscow in 1943, these tumultuous trading sites, teeming with peasants, workers, craftsmen, invalids, beggars, criminals, orphans, veterans, and speculators, were so crowded that they spilled out over tramways and stopped traffic.[90] The Commissariat of Trade strongly disapproved of these congested, chaotic sites. One investigator wrote: "These secondhand markets are not only unsanitary but also, when they encircle the main markets, it is impossible for the militia or controllers to catch thieves who snatch goods from consumers and collective farmers. When people call for help, we cannot get to them through the crowds." Wounded soldiers gathered on the outskirts, drinking heavily and "acting like hooligans." The Commissariat of Trade was particularly concerned about unregulated vendors of cooked food, *samogon* (home brew), and tobacco. Dressed in rags, they handled their wares with dirty hands and prepared it under unsanitary conditions with unsafe ingredients.[91] Yet the markets provided an essential venue for ordinary people to find goods they needed. When a shipment of shoes arrived for workers in the Kuznetsk iron and steel combine, the women received men's canvas shoes with torn soles in large sizes. They quickly took them to the market. Delighted to find even this substandard item in high demand, they exchanged the shoes for items they desperately needed.[92]

Unofficial markets or trading sites sprang up everywhere. In Penza province, peasants traveled from the villages to towns, stayed with friends or relatives, and sold their produce directly from apartments.[93] Secondhand markets also materialized in the yards, corridors, staircases, and production shops of factories. According to one investigator, "Officials declared that they did not have the strength to struggle with this phenomenon." In one defense factory in Saratov, a bazaar formed in the canteen to trade coupons as well as bread and consumer goods.[94] Near the Magnitogorsk iron and steel combine, crowds of several hundred people gathered from morning until evening, trading stolen food cards and various materials and items.[95] Hundreds of workers in the Kirov factory in Cheliabinsk gathered every day around the building that housed the administration and personnel department. They nicknamed the site "Tricky Market" ("*Khitryi rynok*"), a popular nod to the shady business transacted in direct sight of factory officials. Workers and outsiders gathered there to trade clothing, bedding, and ration cards. Local officials did little to police sales until the summer of 1943, when the "Tricky Market" and other unsavory market sites were shut down as part of a larger effort to stop theft in the dormitories.[96] The trade in ration cards proved impossible to stop. The ruble could buy little, but cards held real value, namely, a fixed amount of food, and were easy to steal, conceal, and resell.[97] As the country reverted to barter, ration cards became the most widely traded commodity in the markets. Trade was so common among workers in the Kirov factory that each card and coupon had a commonly accepted monetary value. A card for 100 grams of bread, for example, cost 10 rubles, a monthly bread card, 500. A coupon for the first course of a canteen meal cost 5 rubles, the second course, 10.[98]

Secondhand or unofficial markets supported a growing group of small traders who lived solely on the wares they bought and resold. The state deemed them "middlemen" or, more pejoratively, "speculators." Many "enterprising" people from all occupations dabbled in this petty trade, including war veterans. Peasants who arrived with their produce on market days often did not have a clear idea of pricing. Middlemen (*perekupshchiki*) bought their goods quickly and then promptly resold them at a considerable markup.[99] Both workers and peasants tended to view "middlemen" with hostility. They drove down the potential earnings of peasants and increased the prices for workers. Yet middlemen also offered a needed service: they saved peasants long trips to town and workers time in lines. When district leaders in Ordzhonikidze in 1943 forbade peasants from using horses and carts for any purpose other than spring sowing and the militia forced peasants in horse-drawn carts to return to the collective farms, the vacuum was quickly filled by an army of middlemen and bagmen (*meshochniki*). Fanning out from the towns, they bought produce in the villages, hauled it back in sacks on foot, and resold it for a profit. Food arrived in the markets, albeit at a steep price.[100]

Party and state authorities disapproved of the omnipresent unofficial trading but could not stamp it out. Commissar of Trade Liubimov informed L. P. Beria, head of the NKVD, in September 1944 that private, hand-to-hand trade had "assumed a mass character" in Moscow. People traded from morning to night on the streets. Railroad stations and main thoroughfares were clogged with petty traders. Liubimov wrote, "Trade goes on openly, from early in the morning until late at night, in full view of the militia. I ask you to entrust the head of the militia in Moscow to end this speculation." Yet the militia took little action. One month later, the head of the Commissariat of Trade's Inspectorate wrote to the head of Moscow's militia complaining about the "particularly brisk" hand-to-hand trade in the central squares, streets, and metro and railroad stations, and asking the militia to "suppress the speculation in food and consumer goods."[101] The problem, according to the Commissariat of Trade, was not trade itself, but rather that most of the goods on offer were stolen from the ration system and then resold at "speculative" prices.

The great prevalence of markets suggested that they played an essential role. Yet how important was the market to workers? How often did they use it, why, and for what purpose? In September 1942, in-depth interviews with eighty-four young workers in Cheliabinsk revealed their budgets and provided a detailed view of their survival strategies.[102] The majority of workers interviewed were concentrated in the middle range of the wage scale, receiving an average of 437.5 rubles a month. Yet investigators focused on one month only, thus creating a snapshot that did not capture the fluctuations resulting from bonuses, overtime, and one-time sales of personal property. As a result, some workers received far more money in the month under investigation than usual. Plishko, a machinist at grade five, for example, had an income of 1,115 rubles in September 1942, while Khabarov, a mechanic at a higher pay grade, earned his regular 518 rubles. The investigators calculated the budgets on "rubles in hand," or the sums the workers received, rather than their official wage rates.

Most of the workers were teenagers who had been mobilized to work in Cheliabinsk and were living far from home in *zemlianki* or dormitories. According to the investigators, on average, their necessary monthly outlay came to 352 rubles, considerably less than their average wage of 437 rubles. The young workers' largest outlay—over one-third—was on food provided on ration through canteens and state stores. Their other needs—housing, basic consumer items, baths, haircuts, clothing and shoe repair, and daily transport—were also state-subsidized and negligible in cost, together amounting to 19 percent of their expenditures. Dues to the union, Komsomol, or Party, for those who were members, took another chunk of the paycheck, amounting to about 5.4 percent. The remaining 40 percent of their expenditures was devoted to a range of items (movies, newspapers, theater visits), the most important of which was tobacco. More than half of the workers bought small amounts of loose tobacco, costing between 30 and 50 rubles for a small glass. For smokers, tobacco was as desirable and necessary as extra food. Indeed, had food rations and canteen meals been adequate, workers' wages would have easily covered all of their other basic needs and additional spending. Rations and canteen meals, however, were not adequate even though 80 percent of the young workers surveyed received a "second hot" meal. As a result, the majority of the group, 76 percent, supplemented their canteen meals and rations with food purchased in the market.[103]

The budgets, however, disclosed a conundrum: on average the workers spent 311 rubles per month in the market, an amount that well exceeded the average monthly wage when added to their other expenditures.[104] How was this possible? In this case, the investigators' snapshot of "average" market expenditure was somewhat misleading. It represented not what each worker regularly spent each month, but an average of all surveyed workers, some of whom made large, one-time purchases with money they received from the sale of personal belongings. As such, it reflected two different practices among workers who used the market. About half of the group sold personal items and then spent money that well exceeded their wages. This group spent a lot in the market, on average 649 rubles per person, a sum greater than the entire average monthly wage. But these were one-time spending sprees, unsustainable from one month to the next. The other group, slightly more than one-third of market users, spent a much smaller amount, on average 118 rubles, but still more than they had left over after meeting necessary expenditures.[105] None of the workers, regardless of whether they used the market or not, put money in the state bank. During the war, workers were hungry and spent whatever they had.

The budget snapshot revealed another counterintuitive fact about market behavior. The lower-waged workers, not the better-off, were more likely to spend large sums in the market. They found it most difficult to survive on the combination of wages, ration cards, and canteen meals and thus were forced to sell personal or state-issued items, such as clothes, underwear, or bedding. The market, in this sense, was more important to the poor. Yet the personal property of all workers was meager: a coat, a pair of shoes, a shirt, pants or skirt, and a set of underwear and perhaps some state-issued bedding and work clothes. Once workers sold these possessions, they were very difficult to replace. They resorted to the market as an act of desperation, selling goods they could ill afford to lose in exchange for food. While the market may have helped poor workers to survive, it also made them poorer.

T. V. Shemelov, a twenty-year-old who earned the pitifully low wage of 236 rubles a month, provided a good example of one such worker. In September 1942, Shemelov boosted his income by 3,280 rubles by selling at the market a bread card, coat, and padlock, which factory administrations provided to secure workers' individual cupboards against theft. Like many items that workers hawked in the market, it was unclear whether the padlock was state or personal property. In return for the money Shemelov received, he bought potatoes, carrots, tomatoes, sunflower seeds, onions, apples, turnips, and milk.[106] His use of the market was a one-time act driven by hunger. Although Shemelov would get a new bread card the following month, he would find it impossible to replace the coat and padlock. He might wander the market again in the wintry months to come, but he would have little left to sell or barter.

Other one-time expenditures had the same character. E. I. Babenko, an impoverished seventeen-year-old electrical mechanic, sold a shirt, two pairs of socks, a sheet, blanket, two notebooks, a pillow, and some towels for 1,936 rubles, almost five times his monthly wage, in exchange for bread, potatoes, and vegetables.[107] N. P. Bulavin, another seventeen-year-old electrical mechanic, also sold his belongings, including a pillow, two towels, pants, a cloak, two bedsheets, a pair of socks, and two pillowcases, for 3,290 rubles. He bought in exchange pencils, a notebook, milk, vegetables, potatoes, butter, four cutlets, a stack of pancakes, and a second monthly bread card. The card alone cost 600 rubles.[108] Bread cards provided good value, but the markup was huge. Using a bread card, a worker spent about 20 rubles per month to buy about 12 kilograms of bread. The same card, however, when sold in the market, cost 600 rubles, a markup of 2,900 percent.

In general, workers' market purchases displayed few of the latter-day pleasures of consumption. Mainly they consisted of supplemental food, especially the items their daily diet lacked. Very few shoppers bought clothes or shoes, although they were likely in need of both. They were forced into hard choices between food and personal belongings. Wandering among stalls and hawkers, most had too little money to assuage their hunger. Others, driven by desperation, anxiously traded the few possessions they had. Even the most naïve teenager understood that the sale of a coat in autumn would result in a winter of suffering. For workers, the market was filled with coveted produce, but satiety was bought at the price of future hardship or, more commonly, was not within reach.

State Investigations and Workers' Control

The state, aware that a significant percentage of stocks was lost to theft, pursued various strategies to protect the ration system. Liubimov, Commissar of Trade, later wrote, "Not all went smoothly, there were mistakes, violations, corruption, even outright crimes, and to struggle with this, and primarily to prevent it, honest, vigilant, daily control was needed."[109] The Commissariat of Trade, the unions, the Komsomol, and the Party carried out investigations of canteens, stores, and warehouses to ensure that full allotments reached their intended recipients.[110] The State Trade Inspectorate (Gostorginspektsiia) under the Commissariat of Trade was devoted to monitoring local trade officials. The militia and the judiciary investigated and prosecuted large-scale theft and embezzlement of stocks, arresting and trying those accused of food crimes, and sentencing those convicted to harsh prison terms. Finally, the GKO organized workers through the unions to oversee food distribution points.

Workers' complaints, particularly if they were put in writing, signed by a group, and addressed to leaders in Moscow, often prompted investigations that resulted in improvements and punitive action against responsible officials. The letter that Ivan Bednov, the ammunition worker in Cheliabinsk, sent to the Central Committee, for example, launched a major investigation. Given the centrality of workers to the war effort and the burdens they bore, party leaders were sensitive to workers' complaints. Bednov's suggestion of a split between workers and local party officials immediately raised alarms:

The Bolsheviks in the factory are afraid to get out among the workers with explanations of this or that insufficiency, particularly now with painful questions such as the feeding and provisioning of the workers, and why party leaders are all mixed up with this or some other unsavory business of self-provisioning or, simply to say, barefaced embezzlement of foodstuffs. Where have we ever seen this in the history of the Bolshevik Party that Bolsheviks were afraid of the workers? This was never so. Bolsheviks, on the contrary, always went to the working masses and explained to them the essence of this or that question. Shame on those Bolsheviks who fear the workers.

Bednov noted that relations in Cheliabinsk had become so tense that "We have many Bolshevik leaders who fear to meet comrade workers even in the street, i.e. fear those who scream directly in their faces, 'bloodsucker,' 'drunkard,' 'potbelly,' 'you drank yourself sick on our blood.'"[111]

Bednov's letter was forwarded to B. L. Vannikov, Commissar of Ammunition. Vannikov, like many party members of his generation, had his own troubled history. Rising rapidly through the industrial ranks in the 1930s, he was appointed deputy commissar of defense at the height of the purges, a position he retained until early June 1941, when he was arrested. Freed one month later in a startling twist of fate, he went from prison to the post of deputy commissar of armaments, in which he assumed responsibility for the evacuation of the artillery factories. In 1942, he became commissar of ammunition, a post he held until 1946.[112] Apprised of Bednov's letter, Vannikov quickly established a commission to investigate factory No. 62, and report its findings to the Central Committee and the GKO. Vannikov acknowledged that conditions were "exceptionally difficult." The factory was placed in a warehouse after it was evacuated, and its workers were housed miles away. The Soviet of People's Commissars twice ordered the Commissariat of Construction to build housing for the workers to no avail. As Vannikov pointedly noted, "It is not possible to improve conditions at factory No. 62 without construction materials." The commission concurred with Bednov's allegations of food theft, and the head of ORS was fired. Although Vannikov attributed most of the difficulties in factory No. 62 to "objective" conditions that existed throughout Cheliabinsk province's defense industry, he did what he could to ensure that the factory received its full allotment of stocks, found extra coupons to provide 350 dinners daily, and provided 1,000 sets of bedding.[113] Shamberg, head of the Organizational-Instructional Department under the Central Committee, summed up the results in a letter to Georgii Malenkov later that summer, noting that "Bednov's facts are supported" and the measures taken by Vannikov had improved conditions. The head of ORS had been expelled from the Party and charged with embezzlement and waste, and his staff had been replaced. Shamberg ended his brief summary, "I suggest we consider this question resolved."[114] Other investigations were triggered by similar complaints.[115] Investigations acted as a check on the behavior of local managers and officials. Yet, as Vannikov noted, conditions in one factory did not differ appreciably from those in the next. Intervention from the highest level could stop blatant thievery, but it could not eliminate the shortages that existed everywhere.

The Commissariat of Trade also policed its own local officials, who were frequently at the center of food crimes. In the first months of the war, a significant portion of its staff left for the front. These employees were replaced by a much smaller staff of inexperienced people, and supervision over food distribution weakened.[116] In June 1942, the state created the State Trade Inspectorate within the Commissariat of Trade to ensure that consumers received full weight and measures at state-mandated prices and that the clerks, cooks, and servers in the stores observed regulations on hygiene. Each inspector-controller was responsible for a group of stores, stalls, or booths, and reported directly to the trade director.[117] One month later, in July 1942, the local trade departments also established Monitoring and Accounting Bureaus (Kontrol'no-uchetnye biuro) to check the numbers of every contingent receiving ration cards and to ensure that the correct norms for food and goods allocations were met. By the end of the war, there were about 1,900 bureaus employing 12,000 people.[118]

Despite increased oversight, food theft proved hard to stop. The GKO took more vigorous action, issuing a decree on January 22, 1943, expanding the Inspectorate to all republics, regions, and provinces and urging local prosecutors "to strike a blow against embezzlers, squanderers, and criminal elements who use the difficulties of wartime to speculate and deceive consumers." In practice, prosecutors continued to distinguish between theft and illicit redistribution, subjecting officials convicted of "squandering or *razbazarivanie*" to fines rather than criminal prosecution.[119] During the first six months of 1943, inspectors, working closely with the militia and prosecutors, helped the courts convict almost 36,000 people for theft, illicit redistribution, speculation, and deception of consumers. Most of the cases involved large-scale crimes; only about 2 percent of the convictions were for short-weight and measures, offenses that usually involved petty pilferage.[120]

Party leaders, however, were not pleased with the results. In spring 1944, USSR deputy chief prosecutor G. N. Safonov noted that neither the Inspectorate nor prosecutors were pursuing food crimes as aggressively as they should. The Inspectorate sent its reports to the prosecutors only after long delays. In some republics such as Tatariia and Tadzhikistan where embezzlement and illicit redistribution were rife, no action was taken at all. Safonov urged his judicial subordinates to more actively bring violators to justice.[121] He also complained about the "unsatisfactory work" of inspectors who failed to turn violators over to the courts, but instead removed them from their posts or levied small fines or reprimands.[122] Inspectors, prosecutors, and judges, however, remained reluctant to pursue food crimes and, even when officials were charged, conviction rates were low. In July, the provincial party committee in Irkutsk noted that, of forty cases, only fifteen were brought to trial, and of these a mere five convicted.[123] Inspectors, prosecutors, and judges all understood that illicit redistribution, which fed hungry contingents at the expense of workers' stocks, differed from self-provisioning and theft. Yet the line was often blurred, and officials responsible for enforcement had difficulty parsing the finer distinctions.

The Inspectorate faced other problems as well. As part of the Commissariat of Trade, it supervised its own officials, who were protected by powerful patronage networks. In Iakutsk, for example, an investigation by the Inspectorate in fall 1944 charged thirty-one trade officials with violations, yet only seven people were convicted. The trial resulted in a nasty fight. The head of the Inspectorate charged that Iakutiia's commissar of trade, one Lavrov, retaliated against the inspectors by expelling them from their headquarters and depriving them of housing, firewood, and water. The accused trade officials were also furious with the inspectors and demanded a new investigation. The head of the Inspectorate refused to back down, insisting that the provincial party committee create the necessary conditions for his investigators to do their job and, moreover, that the court reexamine those it had failed to convict.[124] The Inspectorate created enemies everywhere, sowing charges and countercharges in the wake of its investigations.[125] Illicit redistribution and theft were so firmly embedded in the system of patronage that inspectors found the practices almost impossible to eradicate.

Given the difficulties the Commissariat of Trade faced with self-policing and local power circles, the GKO also established a parallel system of external control from below. The unions were charged with organizing elections among their members to serve on newly established Commissions for Workers' Provisioning (Kommissii po rabochemu snabzheniiu) to supervise ORSy. These democratically elected representatives, known as "social controllers," would work as unpaid volunteers to check stocks in canteens, stores, and subsidiary farms, measure portions, and ensure that no food was disbursed "by note" to anyone who was not officially assigned to a store or canteen. Social controllers were to report suspected malfeasance directly to their local union committee, which in turn would dispatch the information within three days to the judiciary. Every three months, the controllers reported to the workers who elected them. The unions were charged with overseeing scales and measures, creating workshops to repair broken equipment, and calling regular meetings of social controllers in every workplace to exchange information. The social control movement grew steadily. More than 600,000 controllers were elected nationwide, and large factories had as many as several hundred controllers each.[126] As the movement grew, the unions convened nationwide conferences of social controllers from across the country.[127]

Social controllers improved the system of provisioning, but they often clashed with factory managers. Controllers shared the view of their fellow workers that managers, focused obsessively on production, cared little about the people who did the producing. At a large meeting of social controllers, Baranova, a delegate from a cotton-spinning factory in Alma-Ata, declared: "If you see some problems and inform the leadership of the factory, they do not consider it worth their attention." She noted that social control was especially needed in childcare centers. "There is no kind of control there," she said angrily, "and I know of childcare centers where the children are literally starving." She suggested that the weight of all provisions in daycare centers and crèches also be continuously monitored. Controllers like Baranova were closely attuned to their own canteens because they ate in them. They knew when the cottage cheese was watered down, a detail easily overlooked by an external inspector.[128] At the same time, controllers were more likely to overlook more elaborate schemes. In Kirghiziia, for example, managers bought wood to fuel the canteen kitchens at a vast markup in the market, rather than send workers into the forest to cut and haul it. Paying thousands of rubles per cubic meter, they concealed the cost by raising the price of kasha in the canteens from 30 kopeks to 1 ruble. This scheme, designed to circumvent the shortage of transport, was a form of illicit redistribution. The cost of wood was borne by the workers through a 70-kopek "tax" carefully concealed in every bowl, a ruse that eluded the social controllers.[129] By empowering the victimized to police those most likely to transgress, social control was able to place real constraints on the scale and incidence of theft, even if it too had its blind spots.

****

Within the basic framework of the ration system, self-provisioning, illicit redistribution, and theft leveled state categories and established new hierarchies. These practices built up some hierarchies and tore down others but did not increase the aggregate stock of food. On the contrary, all redistributed a fixed and scarce resource, creating benefits for some only at the expense of others. They also worked at cross-purposes. Self-provisioning created new, steeper hierarchies of privilege; illicit redistribution leveled those that already existed. Theft worked in both directions, depending on the status of the thieves and the size and disposition of the haul. All three practices, however, siphoned stocks that were designated for workers and ordinary people, who recognized that local officials often profited at their expense. Central state and party leaders intervened frequently on behalf of workers to redress the more egregious violations. The struggle over food thus put central state and party leaders in opposition to local patronage networks, while pitting workers and ordinary people against local managers and officials. It also set different groups of workers against each other and against more vulnerable groups.

Central party leaders, including Nikolaeva and Shvernik, both leaders of the All-Union Central Council of Unions, N. A. Mikhailov, head of the Komsomol, and Volin, the RSFSR's chief prosecutor, as well as thousands of social controllers and trade inspectors, fought actively against theft. Their investigations aimed to safeguard workers' stocks against the countervailing forces of unsanctioned privilege and leveling. They believed that, if local officials stopped pilfering or reallocating stocks, "the combination of subsidiary farms and central stocks would improve the workers' provisioning considerably."[130]

At the same time, many managers and local officials also leveled hierarchies by redistributing stocks to feed those vulnerable groups most disadvantaged by the ration system. They redistributed food meant for workers to white-collar, service, auxiliary, and prisoner workers, transferred malnourished workers in peat and timber to the higher category of defense, and passed out coupons for supplementary food to the uncertified sick and starving. Their activities, motivated by a humane impulse, could hardly be seen as profiteering. And inspectors and prosecutors were reluctant to judge them as criminals.

Workers and ordinary people were divided in their opinions on illicit redistribution. Those at the lowest end of the wage scale were deeply grateful when local officials transferred them to a higher category, and vulnerable groups welcomed the extra food they received. Workers in higher ration categories, on the other hand, lost food through leveling. At the height of the food crisis, their stocks were the largest and most reliable and, as a result, the most likely to be used for redistribution. Workers in aviation factory No. 29 in Omsk, for example, subsisted on less than half and sometimes less than one-third of the stocks allocated for them.[131] Workers did not speak out against leveling or redistribution, but they hotly resented the differentiated canteens, special parcels, distribution by list and by note, and all the other unsanctioned hierarchies invented by local managers and officials. Provisioning was so poor that even small differentials had an impact on survival.[132] In Sverdlovsk province, starvation was so widespread it merited a special note from Beria, the head of the NKVD, to Stalin, V. M. Molotov, Malenkov, and A. I. Mikoian, explaining that local medical facilities were treating 22,400 people for starvation, the majority urban residents and mainly workers at industrial enterprises.[133]

State and party investigators concluded that if workers had received their full allotment of food from the ration and subsidiary farms, their provisioning would have been "completely sufficient."[134] Yet the gains for the workers would have also meant a loss for other groups. In Kazan', for example, in spring 1942, not a single factory canteen received any grain, flour, meat, or fish. The stocks were sent instead to provision orphanages, hospitals, and other institutions. The commissar of trade in Tatariia explained in a letter to Liubimov that allocations from central stocks "were not sufficient" and that he had decided to divert food from the subsidiary farms from the factories to these vulnerable groups.[135] Distribution was so fraught with political and ethical meaning precisely because there was not enough food to provision everyone.

Black and gray markets were essential to the practices that undermined the state-sanctioned categories of the ration system. The role of the market in the ration system was mixed. On the one hand, it provided an incentive to peasants and gardeners to produce more food for sale and allowed ordinary people to exchange the items they had for those they needed. On the other, the market was a parasite on the ration system, serving as an inducement to thievery and speculation, and reducing the fixed stocks allotted for ordinary people.

Several historians view the war years as a critical incubation period for a new class of black market "dealers."[136] Historian V. S. Pushkarev argues that officials "privatized" or stole so many stocks from the ration system that ordinary people were compelled "to acquire at market prices the food and consumer goods they should have received on their ration cards." These black market "dealers," composed of interconnected trade, state, and party officials, continued to flourish after the war, solidifying into a privileged "new class" that would eventually "privatize" social property and foster the collapse of socialism. Known in popular parlance as the "trade mafia," they treated state stocks as their personal property, a form of "shadow capital."[137] This argument, however, does not fully account for the obstacles to Soviet wartime accumulation. During the war years, local officials benefited themselves and their patronage networks, but they were never able to convert their gains into "capital." As Volin's list of confiscated items showed, officials guilty of large-scale theft realized their gains mainly in the form of food and money, both unstable forms of accumulation. Hoarded food spoiled, and money could not be invested in nationally owned and managed industry, land, banking, or real estate. In short, neither money nor food could constitute the basis for the creation of a new class.

On December 14, 1947, the state intentionally wiped out many of the ill-gotten gains of the war years through a mandated currency exchange of old for new rubles. Acknowledging that "speculators" had "accumulated great profits at the expense of the population," the state decreed that all cash in hand was subject to exchange at the rate of one new ruble for ten old ones.

Bank deposits were more protected: savings up to 3,000 rubles were to be exchanged one to one; deposits of 3,000 to 10,000 rubles exchanged at the rate of two new rubles for three old, and deposits over 10,000 rubles at a rate of one for two. The reform had only minimal impact on workers and ordinary urban residents, who had little savings or cash in hand, although they did lose two-thirds of the nominal value of the state bonds they had purchased during the war and early postwar recovery. Those with large bank deposits (only 3.7 percent of depositors had more than 10,000 rubles in the bank) and loose cash, on the other hand, lost heavily. Few peasants had savings accounts and, while the vast majority were desperately poor, all lost 90 percent of whatever cash they had gained through trading at the markets. Hardest hit were thieves and speculators: they did not bank their plunder and their large holdings of cash were subject to sharp devaluation. In one fell swoop, the state wiped out the hoarded loot of the war and, with it, those groups who had profited at the expense of others.[138]

It is impossible to calculate precisely how much food missing from workers' stocks was attributable to each of the practices of self-provisioning, illicit leveling, or theft. The workers were many, and the officials few: tens of thousands of workers would have benefited little even if the stocks appropriated by managers and officials for their special canteens were returned to the common pot. Losses from subsidiary farms and illicit redistribution were likely greater. In the main, however, the hunger that wracked the country was the result of an absolute shortage of food imposed by the fascist invasion. The sacrifices required were great, and the vast majority of people bore them patiently in the belief that they were necessary. What could not be borne, however, was the fact that some people chose to profit personally at the expense of others. The anger that workers and ordinary people felt was rooted in a deeply held ethos of egalitarianism. Ivan Bednov captured this sentiment in the final lines of his letter:

> For a long time, I vacillated about whether to write this declaration, but an accidental conversation with a worker convinced me decisively in the opinion to describe this in brief and send it to the Central Committee. Indeed, the workers heap all this on Soviet power, they curse it and blame it. But I fought for Soviet power and won it in October 1917 and, for me, it is dearer than anything in the world, i.e. it belongs to me and I would give my life for it.[139]

5

"All for the Front": Free Labor, Prisoners, and Deportees

"Our front and rear are a single, undivided military camp ready to surmount any difficulty on the path to victory over the enemy."
Stalin, quoted on Soviet poster titled
"The Socialist Contract"

The popular slogan, "All for the Front!" was everywhere during the war years, on posters, in newspaper articles, and on broad banners festooning streets and factories. The slogan was more than just an enthusiastic rallying cry to encourage Soviet citizens to support the Red Army. It was a literal description of how the needs of the front would upend the daily lives of ordinary people. During the war, the Soviet state created a labor system that was unique among the combatant nations and unprecedented in its own history. At no point before or after the war did the Soviet state hold so much power to command the labor of its citizens. Over the course of the fighting, the state mobilized almost fifteen million free workers for permanent or temporary work. At the height of mass mobilization in 1942, it sent almost four million people to work, and the numbers in 1943 and 1944 were only slightly lower.[1] It enrolled millions of youth in vocational schools. It exiled entire national groups, transformed them into "special settlers" enrolled in a "Labor Army," and employed prisoners in Gulag camps in defense industries, construction, mining, oil, and timber felling.

All the combatant countries faced a shortage of labor, but none so acutely as the Soviet Union. Both the United States and Britain were able to staff their defense plants with waged workers who chose, voluntarily and individually, to take new jobs. Although their governments sponsored mass campaigns to encourage people to enter the workforce, the choice and place of employment remained voluntary. The Nazi government, ideologically committed to keeping women at home and fearful of provoking a repetition of the revolutionary unrest of World War I, replaced its soldiers with up to 5.5 million *Ostarbeiter* or slave laborers from the occupied territories as well as inmates of concentration camps and Jewish ghettos.[2] Japan also used slave labor, deploying captured Korean and Chinese civilians. Only in the Soviet Union, however, was the entire able-bodied population subject to a compulsory wartime labor draft based on central planning, levies, and mass deployment.[3]

By 1943, nearly one-quarter of the Soviet workforce was in uniform.[4] Yet the labor shortage was not due solely to the loss of the draft-age population. Rapid industrialization in the 1930s had created a pressing need for workers, which only became more acute with the preparation for war. After the invasion, the country's population decreased by one-third as a result of the German occupation.[5] Five million young people were drafted into the army within the first week, and 40 percent of Russia's skilled workers went to the front.[6] Even petty criminals were released from prison camps and sent to the front. Women, a common wartime reserve of labor, had already entered the labor force in record-breaking numbers in the 1930s and already held fully 40 percent of all industrial and white-collar jobs on the eve of the war.[7]

The evacuation of industry demanded a new labor force: in June 1941, 18 percent of the defense industry was located in the east; one year later, that figure had risen to 76 percent.[8] The eastern towns, however, were sparsely populated, and most evacuated factories were accompanied by less than half of their original labor force. The new industrial base needed workers, but residents and evacuees alone could not fill the gap.[9] The bold move of evacuation carried inevitable and not entirely foreseeable consequences, demanding that people be transferred to work far from their homes. While evacuation enabled the country to win the war, it also set a new challenge: where would workers come from?

The Great Mobilizing Machine

During the war, the state took control over labor as a resource in the planned economy for the first time in Soviet history. Although it had relied on central planning during industrialization in the 1930s, it had not succeeded in controlling the distribution of labor. Labor exchanges (*birzhy truda*), established to match workers with jobs, were ineffective. Workers changed jobs often in search of better living and working conditions, and factory managers, desperate to fill vacancies, hired directly from crowds gathered around the factory gates.[10] After the invasion, the state quickly recognized that individual volunteers, vocational school graduates, and the unemployed might not be sufficient to meet the needs of industry.[11] Within a week, on June 30, 1941, it created the Committee to Distribute the Labor Force (Komitet po raspredeleniiu rabochei sily), known simply as the "Komitet." Headed by P. G. Moskatov, who also led the Chief Administration of Labor Reserves (GUTR), which oversaw the vocational schools, the Komitet was composed of representatives from the Soviet of People's Commissars, the NKVD, and Gosplan. At the start of 1943 Moskatov was replaced by N. M. Shvernik, head of the All-Union Central Council of Unions. The Komitet also had three deputy chairmen, L. I. Pogrebnoi, who headed its Special Department (Spetsotdel) and also served on the Soviet for Evacuation, G. N. Zelenskii, who managed industry and transport, and B. I. Telepnev, responsible for construction and seasonal work.

The Komitet initially took on the limited task of mobilizing high school graduates, housewives, pensioners, and employees in nonessential sectors to fill jobs in industry. Early policy suggested that its leaders hoped the country's labor needs might be met with these groups, coupled with strategic shifts from one sector to another.[12] Within six months, this hope had completely evaporated. The Komitet was renamed the "Committee to Enumerate and Distribute the Labor Force" and charged with counting the able-bodied unemployed in every village, town, province, and republic, filling requests for labor from the industrial commissariats and the State Committee for Defense (GKO), and recruiting vast contingents of people from provinces and republics it selected. Responsibility for mobilization fell to the local soviets, plenipotentiaries from the Labor Reserves, and older commissions for recruiting labor (Orgnabor). The Komitet also had the power to transfer workers from one industry to another, to issue binding instructions to the industrial commissars, and, later, to draft youth into vocational schools. To assess how many able-bodied unemployed existed in every province and town, the Komitet established local bureaus in the towns that collected monthly data from house managers and ration card bureaus, and from collective farm managers and village soviets in rural areas.[13] By mid-1944, the Komitet had built a powerful organizational pyramid composed of 148 bureaus in republics and provinces and 279 in towns and urban districts.[14]

The entire population, barring specified exemptions, was subject to mobilization. Between July 1941 and December 1944, the Komitet, the vocational schools, and the local draft boards (*voenkomaty*) sent almost eight million workers to permanent jobs in industry, mining, and construction (see Table 5.1). They mobilized an additional 6,751,200 people, mainly peasants, between January 1942 and July 1945 for temporary jobs, such as cutting peat, logging, floating timber, chopping firewood, and carting fuel.[15] The Komitet was responsible for mobilizing 40 percent of the permanent workforce; the remainder were mobilized by the draft boards, which sent draft-age people unfit for the front to permanent jobs, and the vocational schools, which sent young graduates from factory training schools (shkoly fabrichno-zavodskogo obucheniia, or FZO) and trade schools (remeslennye uchilishcha, or RU) and their counterpart on the railways (zheleznodorozhnie uchilishcha, or ZhU). While the vocational schools targeted youth, and the draft boards mainly (but not exclusively) men, the Komitet targeted the entire population on a scale unprecedented in either war or peace.

The Early Search for Labor

The state had begun placing workers on wartime footing one year before the invasion. On June 26, 1940, new legislation extended working hours and criminalized absenteeism and job-changing.[16] In June 1941, four days after the invasion, the Supreme Soviet canceled all holidays and gave directors the right to impose compulsory overtime of up to three hours (with exemptions for teenagers under sixteen, and pregnant or nursing women).[17] An eleven-hour, six-day workweek became the norm. The Komitet began mobilizing workers immediately to replace the skilled workers sent to the front. It requested that the vocational schools provide groups of 50 to 5,000 graduates for the aviation, armaments, and ammunition industries, while commissariats were instructed to prepare dormitories for them. Over the course of the summer, the Komitet forwarded the requests it received from the defense industry to the Labor Reserves, which in turn sent off newly trained young mechanics, milling machine cutters, turners, chauffeurs, and shipwrights to industry. The teenagers were often sent to work before they finished their courses.[18]

The number of vocational students, however, proved insufficient to fill the thousands of vacancies created by increased production and the military draft. To supplement the young graduates, the Komitet turned to workers in those sectors deemed "nonessential" to defense: municipal services and handicrafts. In Moscow, for example, the Komitet transferred 2,750 handicraft workers to a ball-bearing factory and to Kompressor, the factory that produced the renowned truck-mounted, multiple "Katiusha" rockets.[19] Most of these workers continued to live at home, though some groups, harbingers of the vast transfers to come, were forced to move from outlying areas into the towns. The Komitet possessed the power to transfer workers between industries, as well as from place to place.[20] The systematic stripping of the "nonessential" industries would eventually impact the entire country. Sewing and repair workshops, along with soap, needles, thread, shoes, clothing, bedding, paper, and hundreds of other items essential to daily life, disappeared. Only one consumer sector was not stripped of skilled workers. The Komitet mobilized about 100 coopers from various provinces to work in breweries and vodka distilleries, a branch of light industry the state still considered "essential."[21]

Labor mobilization, like the military draft, was compulsory. Yet in the first months of the war, most mobilized workers did not have to leave home. By mid-summer 1941, the need for workers on distant sites began to grow. The Commissariat of Railways required workers to build and repair roads, railway lines, supply depots, and stations damaged or destroyed by German bombers. On the single day of July 18, 1941, the Komitet approved the mobilization of more than 30,000 people to work on various railway sites far from their homes. Spreading the levy over multiple Russian provinces and Central Asian republics, the Komitet instructed local and republic-level soviets to assemble people who were unemployed or working in nonessential industries.[22] Military construction also demanded labor for distant sites, and the Komitet provided 11,500 workers from Azerbaidzhan, Moscow, Novosibirsk, and other areas, in groups of about 1,000 each, to these projects.[23]

The labor shortage was partially alleviated by pensioners, who volunteered and even demanded to return to their old factory jobs, and women. Managers promoted women already working as cleaners, white-collar employees, and auxiliary personnel into production jobs. Women, eager to contribute to the war effort, receive training, and earn more money, took jobs that had previously been held by skilled men. Fired by feminist enthusiasm, women at one machine-tool factory pledged in the summer of 1941: "The machines should run, and will run. They will be managed by us."[24] With the slogan, "For Every Girl – an Industrial Skill!," the state launched a mass campaign to move women from white-collar jobs into production. Women at one Moscow factory wrote the party committee, "Let our soldiers go to the front without worry. In the rear, an army of women and girls will replace them, picking up their tools, standing at the machines, and sitting behind the steering wheels of the automobiles." In the fall, women in Arkhangel'sk province moved en masse into the lumber factories. By October 1941, women constituted fully 45 percent of workers throughout the country.[25]

Despite the wave of enthusiastic volunteers, the Komitet began to exhaust the labor reserves in the towns by the end of July. On July 29, Moskatov sent a memo to G. I. Zelenko, the deputy head of Labor Reserves, asking him to supply figures for able-bodied evacuees and the unemployed, and to tally the labor needs of every factory and construction site. The local departments of Labor Reserves and planning commissions were to gather the data, update it weekly, and establish "groups for the accounting of labor resources" in twenty-two provinces, including the eastern industrial centers.[26] With these instructions, Moskatov took a major step toward mapping and controlling the labor force. In early September, the Komitet made its first foray into calling up the rural population. It mobilized more than 11,000 collective farmers in Moscow province, mainly women, for work in defense factories. The group, which had already been temporarily deployed over the summer to dig peat for fuel, was transferred to defense factories and construction sites for the winter. Their collective farms were forbidden to recall them before April 1, 1942.[27] The largest deployment of seasonal workers thus far, it signaled the Komitet's expanding reach into the country's largest pool of labor: peasants. It also signaled the end of agricultural rhythms of work and rest: the women moved from sowing in the spring to peat bogs in the summer to defense factories in the autumn, and back to the collective farms for spring sowing. Their exhausting schedule of hard physical labor was a direct expression of the slogan, "All for the Front! All for Victory!"

By the end of 1941, massive encirclements and losses of Red Army soldiers led to new callups of draft-age men and further depletion of the industrial workforce. As of January 1942, the evacuated factories alone were short by 500,000 workers.[28] On December 26, 1941, the Supreme Soviet, anxious to stabilize the workforce, significantly increased the penalty for any worker in the defense industry or defense-related sectors who quit a job. Leaving work without permission would henceforth be considered an act of desertion to be judged by a military tribunal. Punishment, too, became harsher, leaping from two to four months in jail as provided for in the law of June 26, 1940, to five to eight years in prison or a labor camp.[29] Yet even draconian labor legislation to fix workers in place could not fill the growing labor shortage.

On February 13, 1942, the Presidium of the Supreme Soviet issued an edict, unprecedented in the history of modern warfare: the urban population became subject to labor service analogous to the military draft. All able-bodied unemployed inhabitants of the towns, including men between the ages of sixteen and fifty-five, and women sixteen and forty-five, were subject to mobilization for the defense industry in their place of residence. Students in secondary school or higher education, nursing mothers, and women with children under eight who did not have another family member to care for them were exempt. Teenagers between sixteen and eighteen who were not in school were subject to mobilization into factory training schools. Failure to obey a mobilization order was punishable by compulsory work in one's place of residence for up to one year.[30] The Komitet was now charged with vast new responsibilities: enumerating and mobilizing a greatly enlarged pool of potential workers and distributing them to meet the needs of industry. The Soviet of People's Commissars and the GKO were responsible for setting and approving the orders, dates, and size of the mobilizations. In practice, however, these leading bodies were dependent on the commissariats and the Komitet for data on the needs of industry and availability of workers.[31] As such, the Komitet served as the ultimate arbiter, the only organization able to judge whether requests from the commissariats could be fulfilled.

Mass urban mobilizations began immediately throughout provinces and republics targeting the able-bodied unemployed, mainly housewives, unskilled evacuees, and teenagers.[32] The conscriptions were large: by June 1942, more than 28,000 people were mobilized in the province of Novosibirsk and 18,000 from Sverdlovsk. Requests from the commissariats, appealing for tens of thousands of workers, poured in to the Komitet. In April, for example, the Commissariat of Medium-Sized Machine-Building alone requested 34,000 workers.[33] Most factory directors were reluctant to hire unskilled people, yet few possessing industrial skills remained. In March, several directors of defense factories in Moscow refused to hire the unskilled workers sent to them by the Komitet. Acceding to the power of the directors, Moskatov asked the Soviet of People's Commissars to rescind the orders, although he added that factory directors would soon have to accept that most of the people subject to mobilization were unskilled. That same month, when the Commissariat of the Chemical Industry made a specific request for skilled labor, the Komitet firmly explained that it could no longer accommodate requests for specialized occupations and would accept only numerical requests.[34]

The February 13 Edict triggered a growing tussle over labor. As the Komitet pulled workers from "nonessential" sectors into the defense factories, local soviets tried to use the edict to refill the jobs vacated in local consumer goods factories, on streetcars, and in public baths and canteens. When the Chkalov soviet requested the Komitet provide workers for a local garment factory, the Komitet responded that local factories could be staffed only through individual volunteers. Yet local soviets often flouted the rules. The head of the Novosibirsk soviet took advantage of the edict to mobilize almost 6,000 people for its "nonessential" enterprises, leaving the town's defense factories short by more than half the workers they needed. The head of the soviet received "a sharp reprimand," but his machinations were not the only cause of the shortfall. Labor in the towns was rapidly vanishing as the unemployed were quickly absorbed into the labor force.[35] When the Commissariat of Ammunition requested 7,880 people for its factories in Chapaevsk, a center of military production 25 miles (40 km) south of Kuibyshev, only 700 unemployed people were left in the town, and the chemical plants had already commandeered 400 of them. The Komitet noted that the situation in other towns and provinces "was very strained."[36] In April, it informed Gosplan that "the possibilities for further mobilization were extremely limited" in all towns in the Urals and Siberia.[37] Many of the orders for mobilization remained unfulfilled. In early April, for example, the Komitet ordered a large mobilization for the Commissariat of the River Fleet, instructing towns to mobilize 15,000 workers for loading and unloading in the ports. The deadline came and went, and the ports remained without dock workers.[38]

In March 1942, in honor of International Women's Day, the Party called on women to replace their fathers, husbands, and brothers who were at the front, declaring, "Not a single women in either the countryside or the towns should remain outside socially useful labor."[39] Yet, as the Germans advanced, the Red Army made its own incontestable claims on the female civilian population. Sending male soldiers in the rear to the front, it filled noncombatant positions at the front and rear with women. On April 13, the GKO decreed that all able-bodied women between the ages of nineteen and twenty-five in jobs, schools, or unemployed in urban and rural areas were subject to mobilization for the communications sector in the army. Only pregnant women, mothers, and women caring for invalid relatives were exempt. In place of the local draft boards, the job of mobilizing these women fell to the Komitet. The initial callup involved 40,040 women from 46 provinces and various republics, many of whom left industry to fill jobs as radio operators, clerks, cooks, and draftsmen in the army.[40]

Many of the newly mobilized factory workers were too ill to cope with long hours of manual labor. Of the 5,240 unemployed people who remained in Kuibyshev province in April 1942, for example, 3,668 were not healthy enough for work.[41] Moskatov, however, was focused on meeting the targets set by the Komitet. Concerned by the increasing numbers of people that the medical commissions deemed unfit for work, he wrote a sharply worded letter to the head of the Commissariat of Health, claiming that the percentage of people receiving exemptions was too high. In Moscow, almost 4,000 people passed through local medical commissions, but only 587 were certified for physical labor. In Kuibyshev, of more than 5,000 people mobilized, fully 70 percent were certified as incapable of physical labor; in Chapaevsk, Voronezh, Stalingrad, and Sverdlovsk, about one-third of the people who appeared at the factories were deemed unfit. Moskatov requested that the Commissariat of Health issue new instructions to the medical commissions "to approach the question of incapacity for physical labor among citizens subject to mobilization more strictly."[42] Yet Moskatov's desire to meet the mobilization targets overrode a more realistic assessment of the remaining unemployed, namely that most were unable to work at a machine or shift heavy loads for eleven hours a day, six days a week.

As the last of the urban unemployed were absorbed into the labor force, the state, like a vast suction machine, began searching for new, untapped reserves. A large pool of able-bodied people existed in rural areas, but the February 1942 Edict specified that only the urban population was subject to mobilization and they were to be deployed in the same place they lived. The Komitet soon found these stipulations a growing impediment to its larger charge. The construction industry, which encompassed sites in outlying areas lacking public transport and unreachable on foot by urban residents, was the first to breach the edict. When the soviet of Penza province was ordered to mobilize 500 people between March and August 1942 to construct an armaments factory located miles from any town, the Komitet appealed to the Soviet of People's Commissars to allow it to mobilize peasants around the site.[43] And, as the Komitet increasingly turned to rural labor, it began sending urban residents, mainly students and white-collar employees, to work for short stints on the collective and state farms. On April 13, 1942, the Soviet of People's Commissars and the Central Committee decreed that able-bodied men between the ages of fourteen and fifty-five, and women between fourteen and fifty, would go to the countryside to help with the spring sowing. Workers in industry and transport were exempt, as were nursing mothers and mothers with children under eight.[44] According to Soviet labor historian A. V. Mitrofanova, the decree marked a turning point in the mobilization of labor. Henceforth, the villages would give up their residents for permanent work in the defense industries of the towns and receive in exchange a temporary labor force to help with the sowing and harvest.[45] The arrangement carried considerable costs. Peasants sent to the towns needed to be housed and fed, and students and white-collar employees proved poor substitutes for peasant farmers.

The Komitet increasingly disregarded the urban requirement of the February Edict. Evacuees billeted with peasants were one of the first rural groups to be mobilized. In May 1942, the Komitet received a request for labor from the Commissariat of Ammunition, an industry that received top priority. The Komitet, however, was forced to explain that the two factories in need of workers, located in Gor'kii and Molotov respectively, were in provinces in which "all contingents were exhausted according to earlier mobilization orders." It could meet the requests only by using urban evacuees settled in rural areas.[46] Similar breaches of the edict soon became common.[47]

The needs of the coal industry soon swept away the edict's stipulations completely. Coal was the basis of defense production, yet the industry constantly struggled to retain workers and meet its output targets. Mines were located outside towns, and new workers had to be brought in from other places. Underground work was grueling and dangerous, and living conditions were poor. Many people mobilized for the mines worked for a brief period and promptly fled. After the Germans seized the Donbass coalfields, the government began expanding the Kuzbass in Western Siberia, an effort that depended on additional miners and construction workers. In April 1942, the

Commissariat of Coal and Gosplan drafted a plan to develop the eastern coal industry that required almost 15,000 workers, but the Komitet responded that the towns targeted had no able-bodied people left.[48] If the Komitet was to meet the labor demands of the coal industry, the residency stipulations of the February Edict would have to be eliminated.

The labor crisis in the coalfields intensified through the summer and early fall of 1942. Calling on party members, Komsomoltsy, and military recruits, the state ordered 27,000 emergency workers to the Kuzbass. Even this group, firmly bound to its task through party or military orders, was not easy to muster. By November, less than half the total number had arrived, and about 70 percent of them were deemed medically unfit to work underground.[49] More difficult than finding workers was retaining them. Despite the harsh punishment for desertion, a significant portion of the labor force simply refused to stay. Mining was hard, and wartime shortages exacerbated the dangers. Worn-out machinery and pumps, along with persistent shortages of reinforcing rope, metal cable, timber, spare parts, and metal guards, led to frequent accidents and stoppages. Mine directors routinely tried to fulfill their output plans through "storming," a practice that required workers to make up lost time at the end of the plan period in a short burst of intense and continuous labor, and that led, in the words of one investigator, to "mass accidents." Not only did miners lack warm clothing and footwear but they slept in bunk beds on bare boards without mattresses, linens, and blankets in overcrowded, rickety barracks.[50] In September 1942, the Party made a concerted effort to reorganize the Kuzbass mines, assigning 100 party activists to improve living and working conditions, allocating more horses and tractors for underground work, cleaning up the dormitories, and providing more barracks, bedding, kitchen equipment, and stores. The provincial party leaders found a local factory to produce tens of thousands of trousers, hats, mittens, and shoes, and launched a lecture series around "the struggle for coal." Despite those efforts, workers continued to flee the Kuzbass: almost 4,800 people, about 45 percent of the new recruits, deserted the mines in October and November.[51] The labor shortages in the coalfields were replicated in the construction, timber, and other industries. The Komitet tried to fill the gaps through temporary mobilizations carried out by local soviets, but there were so few able-bodied people available that the soviets sometimes resorted to "gross violations" of the law. In some districts, people's passports were confiscated and returned only after they boarded the trains. The Komitet strongly opposed such coercive approaches.[52] Yet coercion by the local soviets was itself a desperate response to the fact that the people who remained to be mobilized were often ill, caring for disabled family members, or otherwise unable to work.

In late summer 1942, the government issued a series of decrees eliminating the stipulations of the February Edict and broadening the categories of those subject to mobilization. On August 10, the Soviet of People's Commissars decreed that all citizens, rural as well as urban, were "subject to compulsory labor duty" for up to two months and not necessarily in their place of residence. Children under sixteen, men over fifty, women over forty-five, pregnant women, the disabled, and mothers with nursing infants or children under eight were still exempt.[53] On September 14, the Supreme Soviet lowered the age of mobilization for factory training schools (FZO) from sixteen to fifteen for boys and, for the first time, included girls aged sixteen to eighteen.[54] Shortly thereafter, the Supreme Soviet raised the age of exemption from forty-five to fifty for urban women.[55] The country was on the brink of a vast labor mobilization that would place ever larger numbers in barracks and canteens far from home.

Figure 5.1 Two women workers at a munitions factory. Courtesy of RGAKFD.

Figure 5.2 Young workers making bombs, Siberia, 1943. Courtesy of RGAKFD.

Mobilizing Teenagers for Vocational Schools

In the expanding search for labor, the Komitet targeted hundreds of thousands of teenagers for vocational schools. The local soviets, pressed to meet numerical targets, often rounded up youth who were too young or too sick to qualify. One investigator later observed, "a large number of the mobilized are physically disabled." Out of the 800 youth sent from the provinces of Kalinin, Smolensk, Voronezh, and Moscow to vocational schools hundreds of miles to the north in July 1942, 70 percent were younger than fourteen, and one-quarter had serious chronic illnesses. New arrivals for vocational schools in other provinces had similar medical problems. When the teens boarded trains in their home provinces, no one checked to see if they were properly clothed, shod, and provisioned for the journey. Convoys with hundreds of teenagers were accompanied by a single adult.[56] Often they did not receive enough food for the journey. Two teenaged boys remembered their trip:

> On the fourth day they gave each of us a piece of bread smaller than the palm of your hand, plus half a bucket of soup for forty-four people. We were on the road for nearly twelve days, and everyone's food had run out. In our boxcar people began to steal, taking food from each other, from anyone who still had something left. It got to the point where they no longer stopped our convoy at major stations or towns, since the boys had started pillaging the bazaars, they were so hungry. It was horrible to watch, how the entire gang would swoop down on the peasant women.[57]

Unsurprisingly, many fled home. Of the 1,000 teenagers mobilized in Voronezh in August 1942 for the 1,400-mile (2,250-km) journey east to Omsk, for example, only 35 remained when the train arrived at its destination. Three different people headed the convoy in the course of its two-week journey, but not one received a list of those on board. Authorities were often unable to trace the missing because the mobilization lists contained last names only and no addresses.[58] One young girl recalled how her convoy melted away on the journey to Kazan':

> They gathered us from our settlement and sent us to the railway station of Toropets [about 250 miles (400 km) northwest of Moscow]. We lived at the station for an entire week . . . we lived on the streets. Then they placed us in a cowshed and took us away. They gave us nothing en route, we only had what we took with us, dried rusks, bread . . . .There were 112 people in the railway car, but then some ran away, and only 86 were left. The entire convoy had 1,000 people, but only 700 arrived in Kazan'.[59]

N. A. Mikhailov, the head of the Komsomol, later noted that her story was replicated "in the majority of provinces."[60]

The vocational schools were often woefully unprepared to receive the new arrivals. After weeks of hard traveling, one group arrived in the eastern industrial town of Molotov at 5:00 a.m. They waited, cold and hungry, in the train for hours. When the school directors finally arrived, they took the youngsters to drafty barracks with broken windows, where the boys and girls slept together in a heap on the bare, dirty floors. About fifty of the new arrivals had scabies, a highly contagious skin disease, but they received no medical attention and were not isolated from the others. On the first day, the teenagers received uniforms, but no food. Over the next few days, they received some soup. One boy explained, "I decided to run away because they fed us very poorly, water and water. They didn't talk with us, and there were thieves in the dormitory."[61] Mikhailov blamed the leaders of the Labor Reserves who had been repeatedly notified of "soulless treatment by school directors," but did nothing to rectify the situation. "No one takes responsibility for the runaways," he fumed, "not the recruiters, not the head of the convoy, and not the directors who fail to welcome the arrivals ... The head of the convoy does not consider himself responsible for escapes en route, and the director simply declares, 'We were still not ready to receive these young people. What do you want from us? We are not to blame for the fact that they ran away.'"[62] Even after the teenagers settled in, the vocational schools continued to have problems with retention. An investigation of 18 provinces and republics in 1942 showed that almost 49,000 teenagers had fled.[63]

Collective farm leaders, eager to have the teenagers return, often overlooked the reappearance of runaways. They wrote repeatedly to multiple authorities to rescind mobilization orders. The chairman of the collective farm "Frontier Guard" in Kalinin province requested the release of twenty-nine teenagers by name "in view of the fact that the harvest campaign has begun but we have no labor force. The main thing is that the flax on the collective farm is plentiful, but there is no one to carry it." Another chairman wrote, "They have taken our young people from us .... The harvest is good, but there is no one to gather it."[64] Agriculture was barely mechanized on the eve of the war, and after the invasion the military and industry commandeered horses, tractors, and motor vehicles. Much of the work of sowing and harvest was done by hand by women and teenagers. One collective farm chairman pleaded with the recruiters, "Urgently and truly, I ask you not to refuse to release the children of the collective farm. We have no draft power in the collective farm, and there is a great shortage of people. Pulling up the flax depends completely on the children."[65]

Mobilized teenagers were also under pressure from their families to return to help the elderly, invalids, and mothers with small children survive. Family members begged authorities to release their children from vocational schools, while others wrote or telegraphed their children directly. One sibling told her brother, "Mama has broken her leg, come home quickly." Sometimes recruiters mobilized the only person in a family who was able to work. One collective farm chairman wrote on behalf of a teenager sent to vocational school, "His father is at the front, and his mother remains at home with small children. On this basis, we ask the director of the vocational school to return the citizen named above." Teenagers also begged to be released. One young man first wrote to ask permission to flee: "Urgently, I ask the director of the school to let me go home. I left a seventy-year-old father sick with stomach cancer and a six-year-old little sister, who require much care in feeding, clothing, and shoes. If you, comrade director, do not permit me to go, then I must leave anyway as many others are doing. I cannot leave my father and little sister to the mercy of fate."[66]

The percentage of runaways was also high among vocational school graduates and young workers mobilized for jobs far from home and, in many industrial sectors, significantly exceeded 50 percent.[67] Among the 1,000 young workers mobilized for mines in the Urals, almost the entire group fled. The turnover rates presented a serious obstacle to training and production. During the first nine months of 1942, the Kirov tank factory, for example, took in almost 13,0000 workers, of whom about 9,500 left.[68] Workers who were accompanied by their families in general fared better than single workers, a testament to women's selfless contribution to the family.[69] Many wives of evacuated skilled workers, for example, worked for wages and maintained the home, even if it was only a *zemlianka*: cleaning, mending and washing, and caring for the family. This extra labor, performed for no remuneration and often after a long shift, made a significant difference to the lives and even survival of family members. Young workers who were mobilized to distant sites without their families faced the greatest difficulties. In Sel'mash in Uzbekistan and factory No. 714 in Saratov, no barracks could be built in time so young workers slept "in various corners of the factory" or any place where "they were not driven away."[70] In the Kirov tank factory, factories No. 200 and No. 78, and the Magnitogorsk iron and steel combine, workers slept on staircases, in the offices, and in the corridors. In one horrific case, two young workers in Magnitogorsk fell asleep by the blast furnace and were burned to death by a shower of flaming cinders when the molten metal was poured out.[71]

In the summer and fall of 1942, the Komsomol and All-Union Central Council of Unions launched a series of investigations into the living conditions of young workers. The first investigators arrived in Cheliabinsk province in June to discover that, of the 9,500 young workers sent to 17 enterprises, 5,830 had fled. The reasons were clear. The dormitory for trust No. 22 had no ceiling. In the winter, the workers slept in the factory so they would not freeze to death. The dormitory in the Koliushenko defense factory, fitted with tiers of plank beds, was crammed with fifty people per room; the young people "slept in heaps." In the Kirov factory, the girls' dormitory was a narrow, poorly equipped room located in a cellar. The more fortunate girls slept on planks; the remainder slept in the factory.[72] One investigator noted:

> The outrage which characterizes the dormitories of the Kirov factory is literally beyond my ability to describe. And all this is because neither the factory director, nor the shop heads, nor the party or union organizations even bother to look at the dormitories, and they cannot even imagine what is being done there and who is living there . . . The barracks where the adult workers live are like an open courtyard where any random person, not having any relationship to the factory, can enter at any time of the day or night and occupy a cot.[73]

Accommodation in other factories was no better: filthy lice-infested spaces without oversight or control. The dormitories were unlocked, open to anyone and rife with theft, bullying, and hooliganism. Many young workers had no change of underwear or clothing. As one investigator noted, "They go everywhere in the same dirty greasy smocks and jackets that they work in at the factory." There was no place to wash or mend clothing, and no needles or thread available for personal use. When the workers went to the public bath (bania), they dressed in the same soiled clothes they took off before bathing.[74]

The unremitting cold, lack of bedding, filth, bugs, poor food, and physical stress of work made many youngsters sick, but most doctors and nurses had been called to the front. Medical services were poorly funded and staffed. Unaccustomed to caring for themselves, some teenagers died of lack of attention and care. One teenager, trained in a Leningrad vocational school and shipped to Cheliabinsk, lay ill in a dormitory for three days before a doctor diagnosed severe pneumonia. Several days later, he was taken to a hospital where he died. At Magnitostroi, the vast construction site for the Magnitogorsk iron and steel combine, a young worker with lice was sent to the disinfection station. When he returned, he discovered that another worker had taken his bed. He went to the factory to find a place to sleep. After eight days, exhausted and barely able to stand, he crept back to the dormitory, where he lay on the bare floor. Two days later, he died.[75] These stories, relayed by the investigators, were among the most horrific examples of common wartime difficulties and managerial neglect. Some cases of negligence, in the words of one investigator "were so disgusting they bordered on the criminal." When one young worker lost his eye, his foreman filed charges against him for absence while he was in the hospital, and the court sentenced him to a 25 percent deduction in wages. Neither the foreman nor the judge appeared to be aware of the extenuating circumstances. Foremen, overwhelmed by turnover and preoccupied with production, had little time to investigate reasons for absence. In Magnitostroi alone, more than 1,000 young workers were sentenced for absence, many due to circumstances beyond their control: illness, lack of shoes or outerwear, family tragedy. The investigators' report placed responsibility directly on the directors and managers, insisting on punishment not only of "violators of labor discipline," but also of "managers who show a heartless attitude toward young workers."[76]

The Komsomol had earlier blamed the leaders of the Labor Reserves for poor conditions, but the summer's investigations showed that the conditions in the vocational schools were replicated on work sites. In response, the Komsomol and Labor Reserves joined forces to demand improvements. In a letter to the Commissariat of Trade about the lack of food in factory canteens, Mikhailov and Zelenko, the deputy head of the Labor Reserves, pointed to a predicament that affected all mobilized workers: industrial managers had to assume the functions provided by the family. They wrote, "Not having their families near, living in dormitories of enterprises and private apartments, young workers are deprived of the possibility to organize a household, food, clean clothing, and to repair their shoes and clothes as core [kadrovye] workers do. As a result of the unreliability of personal services, they are not attached to the enterprises, and they run away." Mikhailov and Zelenko were clear: as long as the war demanded that young workers live far from home, managers had to provide decent care for them outside work and, until they did so, they would not succeed in retaining workers.[77]

Throughout the summer and fall of 1942, the Komsomol pressured the commissariats to improve conditions. It launched new investigations in August and September into the aviation, tank, and coal industries. One investigator noted, "The worst conditions for young workers are in the factories of the Commissariat of Tank Production, and the Kirov factory in particular." Almost 45 percent of the roughly 35,000 tank workers in Cheliabinsk were young graduates of vocational schools. Yet factory directors placed them in poorly paid jobs incommensurate with their skills. Trained mechanics, for example, were deployed in loading and unloading. Shop heads could not keep track of their workers, and attendance and timekeeping records were in "complete chaos." People who did not work in the factories roamed the shops and slept in the halls.[78] Production schedules were in disarray, undermined by late deliveries, lack of transport, and other disruptions. To meet their targets, shops "stormed" toward the end of every month, and workers did not leave the factory for days on end. Solomatov, a young brigade leader in the cold press shop, enthusiastically rallied his brigade to work for two weeks without leaving the shop, stopping briefly only to eat and sleep. In this time, they overfulfilled the norm for the entire month. The head of the nonferrous metals foundry of the Kirov factory, inspired by the brigade's success, launched what he called the "Solomatov movement." The "success," however, was illusory: most of the tank missile housings that the brigade produced were unusable, and the workers were "completely worn out." Other young brigades had similar results. When one foreman kept his brigade in the shop for weeks working in temperatures over 100°F (38°C), the young head of the brigade was temporarily crippled. An investigator from the Central Committee later noted, "The managers and party leaders of the factory do not see that such work creates more harm than good."[79] The Solomatov experiment, first launched on the initiative of workers, clearly could not be sustained.

Mikhailov summarized the findings of the investigations in a scathing report sent to A. A. Andreev, Secretary of the Central Committee, and V. M. Molotov, the deputy chairman of the Soviet of People's Commissars. The report was subsequently published in the mass-circulation newspaper *Komsomol'skaya Pravda*. Mikhailov emphasized that conditions in the aviation, tank, and coal industries were no better than those discovered earlier in Cheliabinsk. The dormitories were filthy, beset by thieves, and "completely unsuitable for habitation." Unidentified people, who did not work in the factory, took up residence, drinking and playing cards. A gang of hooligans moved into one dormitory and terrorized the young women living there. In the defense industries, too, vocational graduates were placed in unskilled work, subsidiary jobs, or forced to retrain. In factory No. 466, for example, turners were retrained as drillers, and drillers as turners. Clearly, foremen deployed them in whatever job needed to be filled at the moment. "The whole business," in Mikhailov's words, "was absurd." Young workers lacked winter clothing and footwear. Mikhailov angrily suggested that factory directors stop waiting for the state to deliver consumer items and establish their own workshops.[80] A few dormitories proved exceptions, suggesting that managerial attention could make a difference, despite shortages of building materials, bedding, and fuel. Those in ammunition factory No. 68 were clean and bright. The beds were the same wooden planking, but the boards were painted and fitted with clean straw mattresses, pillows, flannel blankets, pillowcases, and sheets. The youngsters had towels, a washbasin with warm water, a boiler, and a communal bath. Watchmen were on duty day and night, and the dormitories closed to all but their residents. Yet even under these conditions, shortages were ubiquitous. One worker explained, "I am practically barefoot. They gave me some laced boots in the shop, but someone stole them." Footwear remained a severe problem. The workers had access to a shoe workshop, but it had no leather for repairs. One sixteen-year-old lathe operator explained, "I am an orphan. No one sends me anything. I have worn out everything I own. I am hungry. I fulfill the production norm. In March, I received 520 rubles in my hand. I have been working for a total of two months. I don't know what to do with the money." Officials from the party organization, the union, and the factory administration all pleaded with the Commissariat of Ammunition for clothes and shoes.[81]

By fall 1942, protests and angry reports forced central authorities to address the squalid living conditions.[82] The government responded by ordering a new round of investigations aimed at ensuring compliance. Managers struggled to rectify the worst problems but were not often successful. In the Novo-Tagil iron and steel and byproduct coke factories in Nizhnii Tagil, and in Uralmashzavod, the giant machine-building factory in Sverdlovsk, they used their own scrap metal to build bunk beds to replace the ubiquitous wooden planking, as well as providing cots and clean bedding. They sanitized the dormitories regularly and equipped them with secure storage boxes for personal belongings. As clothing and footwear remained in short supply until the end of the war, everyone improvised, using footcloths or rags in place of socks and even shoes.[83] Yet conditions did not improve significantly in 1943, and continuing investigations replicated the bleak findings of the previous year across the country, not only in eastern industrial towns. When the manager of one textile factory in Ivanovo province was asked why, in the middle of 1943, young workers were still living in an unheated barn and sleeping without bedding on wooden planks on a concrete floor, she allegedly replied, "There's a war on. They just have to put up with it."[84]

Investigators were genuinely outraged at what they discovered. Klavdia Nikolaeva, a leader of the All-Union Central Council of Unions, noted that many young workers had fathers at the front and mothers living under German occupation. Far from home, they were unable to communicate with their families and deeply anxious about their fate. Both Mikhailov and Nikolaeva wrote to Stalin, Molotov, and Andreev to emphasize the connection between mobilization and turnover. Nikolaeva wrote, "The enterprise heads scream about not having enough workers to meet the plan, but the commissariats do not know the actual situation in the enterprises and blindly support the incorrect demands of the enterprise directors for more labor."[85] Mikhailov concurred, noting that managers were "accustomed to considering people as hundreds or thousands, but were not interested in the fate of any individual worker." Mobilization provided them with a seemingly endless supply of labor. The defense industry, in Mikhailov's biting words, was "accustomed to easily satisfying their demands for labor, while paying no attention to the real value of workers." Despite "unending mobilizations, and the transfer of huge numbers of people," the factories and mines could not retain the people they were sent.[86]

As Mikhailov and Nikolaeva pointed out, the mass mobilization and transfer of workers to faraway sites could be seen as the cause of labor turnover rather than its solution. Their trenchant critique, however, went unanswered. Factory managers and local party leaders were not judged on the basis of the living conditions they provided, but rather their ability to meet production targets. In the Karaganda coalfields, after the mines failed to meet their targets for the first half of 1942, the head of the provincial party committee was told in no uncertain terms that he would be removed from his position and expelled from the Party if the mines did not "meet and overfulfill" the targets within the next two months. No exceptions, no excuses.[87] The country was waging an armed struggle for its very existence, and the message to leaders was that production took precedence over every other concern.

Figure 5.3 Women packing mortar shells for the central front, December 1942. Courtesy of RGAKFD.

Forced Labor: The Gulag System

The Gulag, like the larger economy, was also severely depleted by the needs of the front. Throughout the 1930s, the camps played a significant role in industrialization. Prisoners were forced into jobs that free workers were unwilling or unavailable to do on major projects in distant or inhospitable locations. They were also critical to the development of industry in the rear, creating the economic base that became central to the war effort. Yet, once the war began, the state made the decision to release hundreds of thousands of prisoners to the front. The Gulag population fell sharply from more than 2.7 million prisoners in 1941 to more than 2.1 million by 1945. Between July 1941 and September 1944, more than 1 million inmates of camps and prisons were sent to the Red Army. These releases accounted for a substantial part of the nearly 30 percent net reduction in the overall Gulag population during this period (see Table 5.2).[88]

The camps were sharply depleted of able-bodied workers. The Presidium of the USSR Supreme Soviet issued two edicts, on July 12 and November 24, 1941, announcing that any person serving a sentence of less than one year was to be released immediately: those of draft age to local draft boards, and those over draft age to work in industry or agriculture. Two months later, on January 22, 1942, the Supreme Court broadened the release orders to cover those serving sentences of less than two years, and subsequent orders of the GKO expanded the categories further. Local authorities in the central and eastern industrial cities were not pleased by the orders, which required that they find employment, housing, and rations for former prisoners. In December 1941, the Kuibyshev city soviet, asked to resettle tens of thousands of newly freed prisoners, demanded that the SE provide railway cars to ship at least 20,000 of them to their former homes. The problem was not only their convict backgrounds. Younger and healthier prisoners were sent to the front; among those who remained were 5,000 invalids and elderly who were incapable of work.[89] While the NKVD was not concerned by the release of its invalid population, it objected to the loss of its stronger prisoners. After some bureaucratic wrangling, the NKVD reached a compromise with the USSR Procuracy in July 1942: anyone of draft age convicted after January 1942 would be automatically subject to conscription, while those convicted of petty crimes earlier were to be reviewed on an individual basis.[90] In short, after July 1942, petty criminals of draft age went directly to the front or to industry.

The Gulag was in many ways an extreme microcosm of the difficulties that beset the larger economy.[91] Prisoners suffered, albeit far more intensely, from the same shortages and grim conditions that affected mobilized workers. The Gulag, like the commissariats, was tasked with contributing to the war economy with a vastly reduced labor force. Both mobilized workers and prisoners were shipped far from home and family, housed in barracks, fed in canteens, and entirely dependent on the state for their upkeep. Both populations became increasingly debilitated as food stocks dwindled. And both the camps and the enterprises suffered from rapid turnover. The statistics in Table 5.2 are static snapshots of the Gulag population at given points in time, but fail to reflect just how fluid that population was. Over time, new people were arrested, including many for labor desertion, while others were released to join the Red Army, for incapacity for work, and after completion of their sentences. Many died while in custody. During 1942, for example, more than 544,000 new prisoners entered the camps while nearly 1 million left, including 509,000 who were freed and 249,000 who died, equivalent to one out of every five camp prisoners.[92]

The camp system consisted of three branches: corrective labor camps, corrective labor colonies, and special settlements. Both camps and colonies held people convicted of crimes. The main distinction between them was administrative: the camps were managed centrally and the colonies locally. The special settlements, however, contained social and national groups who were exiled to remote regions. These people, often deported as families or, later, as entire communities, became known as "special settlers" (*spetsial'nye poselentsy* or *spetsposelentsy*). The best-known example of these "special settlers" was the peasant families who were targeted as kulaks and exiled during collectivization in the early 1930s.[93] In the mass and national operations of 1937–1938 and again during and after the war, new social and national groups, suspected of potential disloyalty or collaboration, were exiled, including Latvians, Lithuanians, and Estonians; Poles from eastern Poland after the Nazi–Soviet Pact (later released after the German invasion); Soviet citizens of German, Finnish, Romanian, Italian, or Greek ancestry; Crimean Tatars, Chechens, Ingush, and other Caucasian minorities; and, toward the end of the war, suspected collaborators from the Baltic states, Romania, and Hungary.

Mortality in Gulag camps depended on whether or not a camp was deemed to be of high or low priority. High-priority camps, such as Noril'sk, Vorkuta, and Kolyma, despite their severe conditions, received more food, and mortality rates were well below the all-Gulag average. Low-priority camps received less food, and deaths soared as a result.[94] Among the worst conditions were those in Glavpromstroi, the sub-administration of the Gulag responsible for industrial construction, which during the early years of the war saw far higher mortality rates than the Gulag labor camps and colonies as a whole. In 1941, nearly one out of every five prisoners working under Glavpromstroi died, a rate three times that in the Gulag at large. In 1942, as food supplies throughout the country contracted, death rates accelerated throughout the Gulag. A quarter of all prisoners in the camps and colonies perished, but in Glavpromstroi the figure was even higher, more than one out of every three. Only when food supplies improved during 1944 and 1945 did Gulag mortality show a significant fall, although not as much as the official statistics might suggest.[95] Despite these improvements, the great privations of the earlier years created a labor force that was increasingly too debilitated to work. In the short term, Glavpromstroi completed its projects, but in the longer term the debilitation of the labor force contributed to the labor shortage (see Table 5.3).

The number of able-bodied prisoners in the camps was never great. Even before the war, only about 60 percent could perform some level of physical labor and, of these, barely more than a third were able to do heavy physical work. Nearly a quarter were too disabled or weak to work at all. As the camps sent their younger and healthier prisoners off to the front, the proportion of prisoners able to work in construction, timber felling, and coal and ore mining dropped from more than one-third in 1940 to less than one-fifth in 1942, and the percentage of prisoners capable only of light work more than doubled. The capacity of the prison population for work dropped over time: a large percentage of those able to do heavy work in 1940 fell to the "moderate work" category in 1942, those doing moderate work dropped down to "light work," and those doing only light work fell into the weak and disabled category. By 1942, almost two-thirds of prisoners were either completely incapable of working or capable of light work only. The Gulag had become a system of destroying rather than deploying labor (see Table 5.4).

The Gulag mobilized workers through three channels: in contracts with industrial commissariats, in camps sited near industry, and within the "Labor Army." Prisoners contracted out to the commissariats were most often concentrated in dangerous jobs involving heavy, unskilled, or semi-skilled labor in construction, factories, coal and ore mining, timber felling, and other jobs. They were supposed to be segregated from free workers in the dormitories and canteens and at work, but this regulation was often ignored. They received smaller rations than free workers, although managers often tried to provide supplementary food. The contribution of contracted prison labor to the industrial commissariats was relatively small. In 1943 and 1944, an average of around 200,000 prisoners was contracted out to the industrial commissariats. This was only about 10 percent of the total Gulag population. In most, but not all, cases prisoners were a small percentage of the overall workforce: in January–June 1944 they accounted for just 2 percent of workers in the tank and coal industries, but a far more significant 12 percent in nonferrous metals. Given high levels of labor turnover in the metallurgical industries, prisoners filled an important gap.[96]

The vast majority of prisoners, more than 90 percent, worked within the camps, colonies, and special settlements under the direct control of the NKVD. Those deemed fit for work were marched out each day to labor on various industrial projects. In his 1944 summary report, V. G. Nasedkin, Chief of the Gulag, claimed that, from mid-1941 to mid-1944, a total of 1,517,000 prisoners worked on such projects: more than two-thirds in construction of railways, industry, and aerodromes and highways; the remaining third in logging, mining, and metallurgy. These figures, however, were cumulative, and the numbers employed in any sector at a given point in time were much lower.[97] Over time, the state shifted Gulag priorities away from construction, logging, and mining to direct manufacturing for defense. During the first thirty-six months of the war, for example, Gulag labor produced as much as 15 percent of all shells.[98] Prisoners were also responsible for building important defense installations, including aircraft factories in Kuibyshev; iron and steel works in Nizhnii Tagil, Cheliabinsk, and Aktiubinsk; the Noril'sk nickel combine in the arctic Far North; the Bogoslovskii aluminum factory in Sverdlovsk province; and numerous highways and rail lines.[99]

As the labor shortage and the needs of the front intensified, the debilitation of the camp population mirrored, albeit on a more extreme scale, the experience of free workers, and the camp administration, like the Komitet, was forced to mobilize ever weaker and less able groups. Bezymianlag, a camp in the city of Kuibyshev, exemplified these pressures. At least a year before the invasion, the state decided to build a new base for the aircraft industry in Kuibyshev, along the eastern bank of the Volga River. New aviation factories were to be built in the outlying district of Bezymianka, east of town. The work was entrusted to the NKVD, which established Bezymianlag, a network of enclosures. Between February and April 1941, the number of prisoners more than doubled, to 88,600, declining to around 77,000 prisoners by the end of the year. With the outbreak of the war, the construction tasks assigned to Bezymianlag, in particular to its Special Construction unit (Osobstroi, the Administration of Special Construction of the NKVD, or Upravlenie osobogo stroitel'stva NKVD), increased substantially to include new sites for aircraft factories evacuated from Moscow and Voronezh, barracks for newly arriving workers, and the construction or adaptation of buildings to house government bodies evacuated from Moscow. As the camp's workload increased, the target dates for completion of its assignments were also moved forward. Work shifts were extended to twelve hours. Camp authorities offered incentives, including the promise of early release, to workers who could exceed their norms, but food rations were reduced. Between November 1941 and January 1942, 6 percent of the camp's prisoners died from disease or starvation, equivalent to an annual mortality rate of 24 percent. A quarter of all prisoners in Bezymianlag were so debilitated that the camp's medical commission declared them either wholly or partly unfit for work. The pressure to produce was so great and the mortality so high that prisoners and their immediate supervisors resorted to falsifying output records in order to receive extra rations, maintain an endurable pace of work, and survive. As construction neared completion over the course of 1942, Bezymianlag began to downsize, and its workforce was shifted to projects outside Kuibyshev.[100] At its peak, Bezymianlag, one of the largest units in the Gulag, was critical to the success of the Soviet aviation industry. Yet success came at a terrible cost. Bezymianlag was one of the first camps to display the astronomical rates of mortality and morbidity that were to characterize the Gulag as a whole during 1942 and 1943. A similar situation developed in Tagillag, the camp established to expand the iron and steel works and defense industry in Nizhnii Tagil, the second-largest city in Sverdlovsk province.[101]

In addition to the camps and colonies, the NKVD also commanded the labor of groups sent into exile. Considered unfit for military service, the able-bodied members of these groups were mobilized into an entity known popularly as the Labor Army (Trudovaia Armiia), and more officially as "labor army-ites," or "*trudarmeitsy*." The term "*trudarmeitsy*" appeared repeatedly in state orders and documents, although the term "Labor Army" was less common, suggesting that this so-called Army was not a unified entity, but rather an agglomeration of disparate brigades, columns, and battalions.[102] As a category of labor, members of the Labor Army fell somewhere between free citizens mobilized by the Komitet and Gulag prisoners working in industry, or, as historian Grigorii Goncharov put it, members of the Labor Army were expected to live like prisoners but work like free workers. Like mobilized free workers, they received wages, were deployed at sites far from home, and were not able to leave their jobs at will. Nor had they been convicted of any crime. Like prisoners, however, they lived in guarded quarters or camps under the control of the NKVD. Unlike either group, they were members of social or national categories distrusted by the state, and were presumably under the control of the NKVD only for the duration of the war. Their wages were set at around three-quarters of the rates for civilian workers, and they paid the same taxes as free workers, but the NKVD deducted sums for their accommodation, food, clothing, bedding, and social insurance to offset the cost of running their camps. Their wages were disbursed at the discretion of camp authorities and depended on behavior. They received the same rations as free workers, but they had to fulfill their targets by a higher percentage to earn them. Those who failed to meet their daily targets could receive as little as 300 or 400 grams of bread, or at most 800 calories. Moreover, unlike the factories, their camps received no supplementary food from gardening, collective farm markets, or subsidiary farms. Survivors recalled how people made desperate by hunger would offer cooks or food servers their wedding rings or the gold fillings from their teeth just for an extra bowl of porridge. The very weakest who could no longer meet their production targets were reduced to picking fish bones and offal out of garbage bins.[103] In tank factory No. 183 (the Urals Tank Factory) in Nizhnii Tagil, the 12,000 Labor Army conscripts arrived in "extremely shabby clothes" with no shoes or coats, and lived in the worst barracks, without beds or bedding, heat, or water. Many were already sick, and some starving. Several were caught stealing from the fields of a nearby state farm, but neither the militia nor the district prosecutor had the heart to prosecute them.[104] Yet the living conditions of the Labor Army were not significantly worse that those experienced by many young free workers, and their mortality rates, while high, were nonetheless considerably lower than those of prisoners. In camps that housed both prisoners and Labor Army conscripts in 1943, mortality among prisoners was 21.3 percent, close to the overall Gulag average, while mortality among Labor Army conscripts was half that. Yet these averages concealed great variation among camps, suggesting that the attitudes of camp management played a significant role in the fate of their inmates.[105]

Isaac Serman was a Jewish soldier from Estonia who, after evacuation to Omsk, was tasked with helping to form a division of Estonian troops, which would eventually grow to become the Estonian Corps. There he discovered that many of his new recruits had spent time in the Labor Army. He recalled their condition when they arrived for military training:

> At that time the Estonian corps had not been formed yet, there was only a division. Thousands of Estonian guys were coming from everywhere. At the beginning of the war they were mobilized in the army and then called off the front as per order of Stalin and sent to the labor army. They worked under severe conditions in the North, starved and died from emaciation and overwork. More than a third of the Estonians who were there died in the first winter. Those who came to us were exhausted and sick. We had very good doctors, and thanks to their care and good food those guys got well. The Siberian climate was very auspicious for us—dry and clean air, aroma of pine forest. Doctors made sure that we had the infusion from pine sprouts. That is why we did not have scurvy and beriberi. Of course, there were severe frosts, which was hard on us. I was to conduct military training for the guys and teach them army discipline. Of course, it was very hard to do—as those who came back from the labor army had difficulty walking,

even slowly. It was way too hard for them to march, go hiking. I understood that and did not force them. Things gradually got better.[106]

The division eventually fought on the Kalinin front where it suffered many losses. Serman received the "Order of the Red Star" in the battle of Velikie Luki in December 1942.

Historians A. A. German and A. N. Kurochkin estimate that, over the course of the war, more than 315,000 ethnic Germans, or 30 percent of all those in exile, were enrolled in the Labor Army.[107] The deportations of the ethnic Germans began within two months of the invasion. On August 28, 1941, the Supreme Soviet issued an edict stating that the community of Volga Germans was harboring tens of thousands of subversives and spies and was to be deported en masse to rural areas in Siberia, Kazakhstan, and neighboring localities. That same day, an additional 96,000 citizens of German and Finnish nationality were deported from Leningrad and its surrounding provinces. Three days later, the Politburo decreed that ethnic German males between the ages of sixteen and sixty living in the main industrial provinces of Ukraine were to be mobilized into construction battalions. The swift advance of the Germans in early September cut short the implementation of this decree, but not before 18,600 men were sent to labor camps in Molotov and Sverdlovsk provinces. A cascade of orders followed: on September 6, 30,000 Germans were expelled from Moscow and Rostov provinces; on September 8, ethnic Germans were removed from the military ranks and sent to work in military construction units in the rear; on September 11, they were expelled from the Red Army altogether and transferred into workers' battalions under the supervision of the coal, iron and steel, nonferrous metals, and timber commissariats or the NKVD. The territorial expulsions continued through September and October.[108] By the end of the war, more than one million ethnic Germans had been sent into exile. They would be joined by other national groups deported later in the war, the largest of which were Chechens and Crimean Tatars.[109]

In exile, about half of working-age ethnic Germans were initially placed in agriculture, but over time growing numbers of both men and women were conscripted into the Labor Army. The first order, issued on January 10, 1942, transferred 120,000 ethnic German men between the ages of seventeen and fifty in exile in Siberia into workers' columns under the control of the NKVD to work in timber felling and construction or under the Commissariat of Railways to construct new rail lines in Siberia, Kazakhstan, and the Urals.

In mid-February, the order was extended to include all able-bodied Soviet German men between seventeen and fifty. The following fall, on October 7, 1942, the group targeted for workers' columns widened again to include men between fifteen and fifty-five as well as all able-bodied women between sixteen and forty-five. The only women excused from mobilization were those who were pregnant or had children under the age of three. Those with older children were required to place them in the care of immediate family members or relatives or, if no family was available, in ethnic German collective farms. The collective farms in Kazakhstan, however, were liquidated as their adult inhabitants were mobilized. The hapless children were then moved again to be resettled with non-German peasants in other districts or placed in orphanages. The men were sent to the coal industry; the women to the oil industry. On October 14, 1942, ethnic Hungarians, Romanians, Italians, and Finns between the ages of seventeen and fifty were also mobilized for workers' columns. The mobilizations continued until the end of the war.[110] In line with the growing labor shortage, no group, free or unfree, at home or in exile, was immune to mobilization for labor.

Over the course of the war, a large number of ethnic Germans in the Labor Army were transferred from NKVD camps to the industrial commissariats where conditions were considerably better. By the end of the war, almost half of those working for the commissariats—56,000—were deployed to far-flung coalmining or oil sites.[111] Their contribution to the labor force in these industries was considerable: about 10 percent of all workers in the coal industry in January 1944, and around 20 percent in oil, most of whom were women.[112] Their mortality rates in coal, oil, and munitions were roughly on par with those for the general civilian population during 1942 and 1943.[113]

Ethnic Germans working in the camps fared worse. At least 182,000 were sent to NKVD camps over the course of the war, the majority in the Urals, and almost all were deployed in either timber felling or construction.[114] Although many camp commandants considered camp labor both expendable and replaceable, the state was concerned about the loss of the labor force. By mid-1942, G. M. Granovskii, the head of the Department of Accounting and Distribution of Prisoners (OURZ), had already raised the alarm about death rates. At Bogoslovlag, for example, fully 17.6 percent of the ethnic German workforce died between January and July 1942, while another 34.6 percent had to be removed from work because of ill health. Granovskii wrote, "The reason behind such high losses is the debilitation of the labor stock, driving it to a state of disability and unsuitability for work. If action of a preventive nature is not taken in time, such losses, if they proceed at these tempos, will within a very short time lead to a sharp contraction of the labor stock among these contingents [ethnic Germans]."[115] Granovskii made his report at the very nadir of food provisioning. Workers in the defense factories were suffering along with children and other vulnerable populations, and the state was unable to redress the shortages in the camps without depriving other groups. In 1944 and 1945, the crisis in provisioning eased, and the state began shipping more food to the camps. Yet the effects of malnutrition and harsh working conditions were cumulative. Despite the increase in provisions, death rates among the ethnic German Labor Army members in NKVD camps and the percentage of those demobilized as too weak to work did not fall in 1944 and 1945.[116] Granovskii's concern with the "labor stock" of ethnic Germans, rather than their human suffering, captured the attitude of many officials toward camp inmates and, often, to the free population as well.

✳✳✳✳

The experience of people on the home front cannot be separated from the state's exhaustive search for labor. During the war, the state assumed its greatest power, drafting and moving millions of people around the country to serve the needs of defense. By the end of 1942, the mass mobilization of labor had thoroughly changed the composition of the labor force. As the more physically able and skilled male workers left for the front, the labor force became increasingly female, with a larger percentage of both teenaged and elderly workers. In 1942 alone, half a million housewives entered production.[117]

Within one week of the invasion, the state recognized that volunteers and vocational graduates alone were unlikely to fill shortages created by the military draft and expansion of the defense industry. It established the Komitet immediately, yet it had no idea how much of the industrial base would be evacuated or how many workers would ultimately be required to replace those drafted into the army. As the labor shortage intensified, the power and reach of the Komitet steadily increased. The state also mobilized prisoners and deportees for the war effort. The Gulag, like the industrial towns, was drained of men as prisoners were released en masse to go to the front. Although the Gulag population dropped precipitously, prisoners and the Labor Army made significant contributions to the war economy.

Forced labor, however, proved a limited solution to the labor shortage. The vast majority of prisoners and deportees were not capable of heavy work, and conditions were so bad and rations so low that the strong and able-bodied were quickly turned into invalids. Death rates were high.

The state relied overwhelmingly on the mobilization of free labor. Initially, the Komitet tapped the most obvious reserves in the towns: workers from nonessential sectors, vocational graduates, housewives, teenagers, and the unemployed. Teenagers constituted one of the first large groups to be mobilized for training and permanent work away from home. Too young for the Red Army, they were old enough to be mobilized for vocational schools and then dispatched to essential economic sectors in the east. In the absence of the families of these teenagers, the enterprises assumed responsibility for housing, feeding, clothing, and caring for them. They were the first group to signal a systemic crisis. Conditions were frighteningly bleak, and hundreds of thousands illegally quit their jobs and tried to return home. By the beginning of 1942, the Komitet was unable to satisfy industry's voracious demands through these limited channels. The February Edict subjected all able-bodied people in the towns to mobilization for work in their place of residence, but its target populations were exhausted almost as soon as it was passed. The Komitet began to exceed its mandate, reaching into rural areas and expanding the age range for mobilization.

Mobilized workers would become the very foundation of the war effort, but they would also pose the state's greatest domestic challenge: to fix workers in place and provide services traditionally performed by the family. Cooking, laundry, cleaning, and repair—all jobs assumed by women for no remuneration—fell to the industrial enterprises. Poor organization, pressure to produce, managerial indifference, and persistent shortages created appalling living conditions, which drove mobilized workers to flee. In the camps, colonies, and Labor Army, a turnover of a more horrific nature reigned: unlike free workers, prisoners could not flee; rather, they became incapacitated for work or they died.

Although prisoners and deportees were subject to far harsher conditions than mobilized workers, the three groups shared much in common. All made significant contributions to industrial production and construction. They often mingled in canteens, and at times managers provided prisoners and deportees supplementary food from workers' stocks. Although the death rates in the camps were far higher than for mobilized workers, the dearth of food was so great in 1942 and 1943 that both groups suffered from malnutrition and starvation. All lived in unheated barracks and ate their meals in canteens; all suffered from a lack of bedding, soap, hot water, decent medical care, and bathhouses. And all were forbidden from leaving their jobs. If wartime labor was arrayed on a continuum from prisoners to skilled free workers, young, mobilized workers were only marginally better off than members of the Labor Army and camp inmates.

This bleak ground nevertheless nourished the seeds of eventual victory. The lowest age for entry to the schools was fourteen, but younger children entered both the vocational schools and the factories. Indeed, mothers of twelve- and thirteen-year-olds in Moscow asked the head of the vocational school at the Frunze spinning and weaving factory to take their children so they could receive larger rations, and almost all the school's students were aged twelve to thirteen. After training, the children took on responsible jobs, including repairing machinery. Nonetheless, they remained children. One supervisor poignantly recalled one cold day when the children who repaired roving machines disappeared from the shop. Their supervisors found them out in the factory yard playing in the first snowfall of the winter.[118] The head of the tool shop at Moscow's factory No. 45, a large aviation factory, made a similar observation:

> At that time, 1942–1943, you could observe the following picture. Instead of all of them working at their machines, the children—and they were children in the literal sense of the word—would forget that they were at work and, as befitted their age, would ride around on dollies and wheelbarrows during work time, collect whatever parts they could find, and build every conceivable kind of merry-go-round. All the same, these kids worked, although obviously it was very tough for them.

One young teenager was so small he could barely reach the machine. One day, not realizing he was being watched, he stopped machining and began playing with some of the cams, pretending they were tanks. When he realized someone was looking, he ran off in embarrassment. Later he became a skilled fitter.[119] In this way, hundreds of thousands of young teenagers spent the last years of their childhood.

The mass mobilization of teenagers, peasants, prisoners, and deportees allowed the state to build and staff a new industrial base in the east. By mid-September 1942, the Germans reached the Volga River north and south of Stalingrad. As the Red Army fought, in General V. I. Chuikov's words, for "every brick and stone, for every yard of Stalingrad earth" and massed outside the city for the first great encirclement of the Wehrmacht, it wielded a fourfold superiority in equipment, produced by workers in summer and early fall. Soldiers ferried ammunition and supplies across the Volga at night into the battered city and, after the river froze, they crawled on their bellies, pulling little sleighs over the ice.[120] Throughout the occupied lands, people in concentration camps and ghettos waited in tremulous hope for news from Stalingrad. And on boxcars rumbling west from the industrial towns to the Volga River, from the frostbitten, blackened hands of mobilized workers, prisoners, and deportees, came the armaments, tanks, and aircraft that the Red Army needed to win.

6

The Labor System in Crisis: The Limits of Mobilization

Here in Kopeisk they do not consider Kirghiz, Uzbeks, and Kazakhs to be people. They call them "bogeyman," "sheep," and "dog." If *natsionaly* are walking down the street the Russian lads throw stones at them and call them all kinds of names. In 1942, no matter young or old, men or women, all the Russians displayed nationalism (great power chauvinism), violated the Stalin Constitution, insulted *natsmeny*, created inhuman conditions.

From investigative report commissioned by the
Kirghiz Communist Party, 1943

By 1943, the labor system was in crisis. The Committee to Enumerate and Distribute the Labor Force (the Komitet) made every effort to squeeze more workers from the rapidly dwindling urban reserves of labor, but the pool of able-bodied unemployed was drained. Switching its focus, the Komitet turned to peasants, women with young children, ever younger and ever older age cohorts, wounded Red Army soldiers, and draft-eligible men unfit for the front to fill industry's needs. The turn toward the countryside stripped the collective farms of able-bodied people and left children, women, and elderly in the villages. Hundreds of thousands of peasants from the Central Asian republics—Tadzhikistan, Uzbekistan, Turkmenistan, Kazakhstan, Kirghiziia—were sent to the eastern towns. The factories, mines, and timber operations became multinational sites combining workers from every province and more than fifty different national and ethnic groups. By 1945, 70 percent of women in the Russian Republic were engaged in waged labor, and 56 percent of the entire country's waged labor force was female.[1] After the victory at Stalingrad, the Red Army began liberating large swathes of territory, and new workers were needed to rebuild devastated towns, infrastructure, and industries. Mobilization intensified along with the labor shortage.

Commissariats, the Komitet, local soviets, and collective farms began fighting fiercely over labor. The commissariats requested more levies to meet their production targets. Local party and soviet officials fought to retain the residents of their provinces. Leaders of the Central Asian republics protested the maltreatment of their citizens in the eastern industrial towns and demanded their return. The Komitet fell further and further behind in its efforts to muster the numbers demanded by the State Committee for Defense (GKO) and the commissariats. Like an assembly line speeded up beyond all human ability to keep pace, the Komitet continued to generate new demands for labor while local soviets struggled to meet unfilled orders from previous months. Backlogs reached into the tens of thousands and undermined any semblance of planning. Hundreds of thousands of newly mobilized workers fled back home; others sickened and died from illness and starvation. Industrial managers, faced with high labor turnover, ordered more workers. Mass mobilization, so critical to filling labor needs in the east and the newly liberated territories, developed a self-generating and destructive dynamic. The very solution to the labor shortage had become part of the problem. The labor system, initially a powerful weapon in the struggle for defense production, reached an impasse.

Figure 6.1 Women spinners in Kemerovo province, 1944. Courtesy of RGAKFD.

Slicing Wedges off the Block of Labor Reserves

Throughout 1943, the shortage of labor intensified as demands for production increased. N. M. Shvernik, the newly appointed head of the Komitet, energetically spearheaded an effort to create a more thorough accounting system that would presumably yield undiscovered reserves of labor. He ordered the Central Statistical Administration of Gosplan to undertake a comprehensive census of the remaining urban able-bodied unemployed and, more importantly, to include two categories previously exempt from mobilization: women with children between four and eight, and students in secondary school and higher education. The Komitet also charged the local soviets with collecting more data from housing administrators, homeowners, and the Ration Card Bureaus, which issued cards to "dependants," or people who were not working but receiving rations. The Central Statistical Administration and the Ration Card Bureaus were to transfer the lists they compiled to the Komitet's local town and district bureaus by February 15, 1943.[2] Yet by May, despite Shvernik's efforts, the Komitet was still failing to meet its orders from industry. Frustrated by the inability of the provinces to fulfill their targets, the Komitet called for "daily control" over its orders, an effort no more effective than the existing weekly and monthly control. It also planned to send inspectors with access to "exhaustive data" on labor reserves to provinces and republics that were failing to meet their mobilization targets.[3]

The Komitet tightened its own procedures by breaking down the process of mobilization into its component parts. According to standing practice, the Komitet received requests for labor from the GKO, the Soviet of People's Commissars, and the commissariats, and then spread the requested levy over numerous provinces. It issued target numbers to the local soviets, which in turn were responsible for mustering the necessary number of people. The commissariat that ordered the workers sent plenipotentiaries to the provinces to help with mobilization and accompany the convoys to the work sites. Yet the process "leaked" workers at every stage, and the number of people who arrived on site was only a fraction of the number originally targeted. In an effort to plug the leaks, the Komitet developed an elaborate accounting system, compiling figures at every stage, including the number of people required by the order, assembled for the journey, placed in railway cars, counted en route, and received by the work site.[4] Shvernik was wedded to the idea that statistical command was the key to control. In June 1943, the Komitet ordered its local bureaus to issue monthly and quarterly reports with detailed data about the labor force and developed new forms to complete with the date of the mobilization order; the period for assembly; and the numbers subject to mobilization, actually mobilized, and remaining to be mobilized.[5] Despite all these efforts, the Komitet still could not ensure that the number of people subject to mobilization actually equaled the number delivered.

In the spring of 1943, the Komitet began including groups for mobilization that had previously been exempt. In April, it drafted 500 deaf people in the rural areas of Cheliabinsk, Kurgan, and Kirov provinces for work in ammunition factories. The mobilization of the deaf from the rural eastern provinces continued into 1944.[6] It targeted younger teenagers and mothers with small children. The government shifted the new mobilization of millions of youngsters from the Chief Administration of Labor Reserves (GUTR), which handled recruitment for vocational schools, to the Komitet. The age subject to mobilization into the factory training schools (FZO), lowered first in September 1942 to fifteen for boys and set at sixteen for girls, was dropped again to fourteen for boys and fifteen for girls, thus placing the FZO in direct competition with the two-year trade schools (RU) for the youngest students. In June 1943, the Komitet mobilized 81,000 rural and urban teenagers from more than fifty provinces and republics into vocational schools for the mining and metallurgical industries. If local officials could not meet their designated quotas with youngsters who were not in school or at work, they were permitted to remove students from secondary schools and higher education. Officials from the Komitet were dispatched across the country to help the localities complete the assignment.[7] In August 1943, the Komitet targeted mothers with children between the ages of four and eight, a group that had previously been exempt. Women with children younger than four were exempt only if they could prove that no other family member was available to look after them, and the Komitet ordered its local bureaus to make an immediate accounting of how many additional women would be eligible for mobilization. As mothers with young children began arriving in the factories, directors of enterprises were ordered to create childcare facilities, along with barracks and canteens.[8]

In September 1943, following the amnesties of petty criminals that had depleted the Gulag, the Komitet and the NKVD targeted the labor colonies and urban reception centers for juvenile offenders. Teenagers, fourteen and older, who finished their sentences were sent directly to vocational schools and industrial enterprises. The local branches of the NKVD were charged with sending information about all teenagers under their jurisdiction to the local bureaus of the Komitet, and the two organizations together were instructed to compile data on the numbers available each month for mobilization.[9] Many of these tough youngsters, who had grown up around older criminals, brought habits of theft and violence into the factory dormitories and sparked complaints from other young workers. The Komitet also began targeting military recruits and wounded soldiers not fit for the front but still capable of work.[10] The Commissariat of Defense was responsible for coordinating with the Komitet to determine where these unfit draftees should be sent.[11] In October 1943 alone, 207,000 were sent to work in industry.[12] Over the following months, large numbers of draft-age recruits from Central Asia were sent east to the factories.[13]

The most important shift the Komitet made was to turn its efforts to the rural areas, including the Central Asian republics with their large peasant populations. In 1943, the rural areas became the main source for recruitment of permanent labor (see Table 6.1). Of the almost 734,000 people mobilized for permanent work in 1942, only 23 percent came from rural areas; in 1943, the balance shifted to 59 percent, and in 1944 to 62 percent. The numbers, too, increased steadily and steeply. In 1942, 168,000 people were mobilized from the rural areas for permanent work; by 1943, this group more than tripled in size to 525,900; and it increased again in 1944 to 687,000. The shift depleted the countryside of labor, separated hundreds of thousands of people from their families, and forced the enterprises to assume care for new workers arriving from afar.

Mobilizing Central Asian Workers

All workers mobilized to labor far from home experienced great hardships, but the plight of those from Central Asian was singularly painful: they were unable to communicate in Russian, forced to adapt to a new climate and foods, and subject to inhumane prejudices. These workers, along with others mobilized from Bashkiriia and Tatariia, became known as *natsionaly* or *natsmeny* (a contraction from the Russian words for "national minority"), a catch-all term used to indicate their non-Slavic ethnicity. The Komitet and the draft boards mobilized people from Central Asia throughout 1942, but the GKO ordered the largest levy, 350,000 collective farmers between the ages of nineteen and fifty from Kazakhstan, Uzbekistan, Turkmenistan, Tadzhikistan, and Kirghiziia, for jobs in industry and construction that October. The levy was divided among the republics, and local draft boards were responsible for rounding up the people within six weeks. The party leaders of the republics were instructed to organize mass campaigns around the drafts, and each convoy was expected to include native party and Komsomol activists. People were ordered to appear at the collection points with warm winter clothing, their own bedding, sheets, mugs, spoons, and enough food to last ten days (to be provided by their collective farms or the Commissariat of Trade). They were to be met and accompanied by representatives of the industrial commissariats that would receive them. The order was so large and so significant that a special commission, composed of Shvernik, E. A. Shchadenko, Commissar of Defense, V. V. Chernyshev, Deputy Commissar of Internal Affairs, and G. P. Kosiachenko, Deputy Chairman of Gosplan, was formed to supervise its implementation. The mobilized workers were to be organized into workers' columns of 1,000 each and parceled out to various commissariats: almost one-third would go to the coalmines, while the remainder would be divided among the railways, the oil industry, construction, iron and steel, nonferrous metals, the chemical industry, and munitions. The mobilization was expected to impact other groups as well: the Central Asians sent to railways would replace 27,000 ethnic Germans, who in turn would be transferred to NKVD camps. Over the following months these initial plans for deployment changed and more workers were assigned to construction, including the building of electric power stations. By March 1943, mobilization orders had been issued to about 351,000 people.[14]

The Komitet continued recruitment from Central Asia after this first massive levy was completed. More than 6,500 Central Asians were shipped to armaments factories in May 1943 where they were mainly deployed in unskilled, auxiliary jobs in construction. None of the men, many of whom were ill and unfit for work, received the mandated examination by a medical commission before being taken from their native villages.[15] Large numbers of Uzbeks arrived in Chkalov province that same month to work in unskilled jobs in construction, loading and unloading on the railroads, and the industrial enterprises.[16] Another 1,000 were mobilized for Ivanovo province to work in factories, the peat industry, and electric power stations. While some workers were placed in decent dormitories, others were housed in barracks with no water, heat, toilets, or beds, and then fell ill. Ivanovo's provincial party secretary reported that up to 40 percent of the Central Asian workers were sick with malaria and, in four months, sixteen people had died.[17] More than 15,000 Uzbek workers were also sent to Cheliabinsk, working mainly in construction. These workers never received medical examinations, and many were suffering from pneumonia, tuberculosis, and stomach illnesses. Those who were too ill to work were shipped home.[18]

In January 1943, party leaders received an outraged letter from Kirghiz miners working in the Kuibyshev mine in Molotov province. The letter, composed earlier in October, and addressed to the Supreme Soviet of Kirghiziia, had been forwarded to the Central Committee. Signed by ninety-three workers, it consisted of three pages of handwritten complaints followed by the scrawled signatures and small signs of men who had never learned their letters. The miners, who referred to themselves as members of the Labor Army (*trudarmeitsy*), were part of a larger group of 150 Kirghiz collective farmers mobilized by their local draft boards in early May 1942 to clear slag at the mine. "From the moment of our arrival," they wrote, "the mine administration has looked upon us as the lowest of the low, and its attitude to us in practice, we have to say, is as if we were in feudal society." They were segregated from Russian workers during meals and provided with a separate "Uzbek" canteen that offered little more than vegetable scraps and frozen potatoes left over from the main canteen. As fall passed into winter, their clothes and shoes were reduced to rags. Housed in dormitory rooms built for ten people but crammed with up to thirty, they slept on bare boards without bedding. The workers suffered from lice and bed bugs, but the mines had no laundry and the workers had no soap. Similar conditions affected workers of all nationalities, including Russians, but language barriers exacerbated the problems. The Kirghiz workers were unable to communicate with their foremen, and their wages were too low even to cover their canteen meals. In their letter, they explained their predicament:

> our daily earnings at a maximum might reach 2 rubles, 80 kopeks, while the bare minimum you need to eat in the canteen is at least 3 rubles. This is because the mine administration won't give us any coal wagons for loading, and every day we spend five or six hours of each shift just standing around in the cold, under rain or blizzards, and these stoppages aren't paid ... From what we've said here it should be obvious that the mine administration is treating us with blatant chauvinism, the foremen shove us around and call us animals and Basmachi [Muslim counter-revolutionaries during the Civil War], which we simply do not deserve, given that many of us were Stakhanovites back on the collective farm.

The letter asked the Kirghiz Supreme Soviet to petition the Commissariat of Defense to reassign them to the Central Asian republics, "where, as honest patriots, we will serve on the labor front up until the final victory over the perfidious enemy." "Either that," they concluded, "or send a commission to investigate how we live here, for under these conditions in a harsh winter the rate of those falling ill will rise, and the number dying will go up even more." The Central Committee, following its practice, sent the letter back to party officials in Molotov with instructions to investigate its charges.[19]

Similar protests sparked investigations in other industries. One investigator of the timber industry reported that "desertion, theft, speculation, and rape" were rampant among the 2,500 Uzbeks mobilized to work in the sawmills. None of the party organizers or managers in the mills could speak Uzbek. The commissar of the timber industry asked G. M. Malenkov to send five or six party activists fluent in both Russian and Uzbek.[20] At Uralmash in Sverdlovsk and the Urals Tank Factory in Nizhnii Tagil, the Central Asian workers were housed in the worst *zemlianki* and barracks: doors and windows were not sealed for the winter, water pooled on the floors, and not a single piece of furniture was provided. Here, too, the workers could not speak Russian and could neither communicate nor complain. Many were very sick, suffering from traumatic injuries, stomach illnesses, vitamin deficiencies, and pneumonia. Some were dying of starvation. A special canteen to help all workers recover from starvation-related illness was established in May 1943, but it could not accommodate all those in need.[21] An investigation of defense factory No. 577 in Molotov province found somewhat better conditions. The provincial party secretary noted that the Uzbek workers had beds, underwear, and clothing, received two meals a day, and were given one more if they overfulfilled the norm. Those working with hazardous chemicals received milk. The prevailing standards, in his opinion, were as good or better than those applied to other workers.[22] The deputy commissar of armaments also offered an optimistic report of conditions for about 6,600 Central Asians mobilized for construction work, despite the fact that fully 20 percent were sick and unable to work. He shifted the blame to the recruiters in Central Asia, who had violated the rules of mobilization by failing to provide medical examinations for the people they drafted.[23] According to his account, the workers were sick and disabled before they arrived. While his charges were likely correct, the lack of proper housing undoubtedly exacerbated whatever illnesses they had on arrival.

Figure 6.2 Machine shop at a Urals factory, 1944. Courtesy of RGAKFD.

The investigative reports from the construction sites, where a significant percentage of Central Asian peasants was deployed, were considerably worse. During the first days of the war, the Commissariat of Construction, in accordance with an order from the GKO, set up Special Construction and Erection Units (OSMCh) for urgent projects required by the defense industry. In OSMCh-52 in Kuibyshev province, one-quarter of the workforce was Uzbek. The work was dirty and difficult: digging, earthmoving, hauling, and lifting without the aid of machines. The dormitories consisted of filthy planking, the workers were covered in lice, and there were no sinks, baths, toilets, or laundries on site. The workers had ration cards but like most people they rarely received the foods they were allotted, so were reduced to eating grass, wild greens, and peelings. Many suffered from gastrointestinal illnesses, twenty-five people had already died from poor nutrition, and many more had run away. Appalled, local party officials tried to force managers to remedy the situation. The head of Kuibyshev's provincial party committee noted that Central Asians endured similar conditions in other enterprises.[24] Yet no one took responsibility for the workers' ill health and weakened state: local party officials blamed the construction site managers, the managers blamed the recruiters in Central Asia, and the recruiters in turn cursed the high targets for labor imposed on their districts by the Komitet.

The workers assigned to NKVD construction projects suffered the worst conditions. In July 1943, more than 4,000 Central Asians were sent as free workers to Cheliabmetallurgstroi (Bakallag) in Cheliabinsk and to the iron and steel works in Zlatoust to build an open hearth furnace. Both groups lived in NKVD-run camps, in special areas set apart from both prisoners and ethnic Germans in the Labor Army. Their workloads, housing, and food rations were the same as those of prisoners and the Labor Army, although the NKVD did adjust their work schedules to the harsh Urals winters. Whereas free workers, prisoners, and Labor Army recruits at Bakallag all worked a ten-hour day and stopped work only when the temperature dropped to –31°F (–35°C), the shifts for Central Asian workers were shortened to eight hours at 14°F (–10°C), and work stopped at –4°F (–20°C).[25] Regardless of accommodation for climate, the placement of free workers under the same conditions and ration allocation as prisoners violated the law and could be explained only by discrimination.

By summer 1943, complaints, protests, and investigations had created a scandal that reached the Central Committee and the Procuracy. The state, concerned by the high rates of illness and death among the Central Asian workers, took measures to improve conditions specifically for them.[26] On July 20, 1943, A. V. Liubimov, Commissar of Trade, ordered every enterprise or construction site employing Central Asians to set up special canteens or separate eating areas, in which meals were to be prepared and served by people from their own republic using special Central Asian pots and dishware, according to recipes conforming to "national customs." Lamb, beef, fish, cottonseed oil, rice, wheat, beans, barley, pasta, potatoes, beets, onions, carrots, tomatoes, and cucumbers were to be used in place of pork, and every worker was to receive 300 grams of green tea a month.[27] Yet given the severity of wartime shortages, few foods on Liubimov's list were available. Not all managers made the effort to make separate accommodations. At Cheliabmetallurgstroi, management used the *chaikhana*, or teahouse, to house workers who had no place to sleep.[28] At the Kalinin weapons factory in Sverdlovsk (factory No. 8), food intended for Uzbek workers was diverted to canteens for engineers, clerical staff, medical personnel, and temporary workers.[29] Yet many managers genuinely tried to comply, setting up *chaikhany* and dispatching teams to Central Asia to bring back native ingredients and warm clothing. Others allocated their Central Asian workers extra meals or ration cards.[30] The

Central Committee ordered all factories and construction sites to provide the Central Asian workers with beds, bedding, and clothing; instructed local officials to report on their status; and requested interpreters at all labor sites employing Uzbek and other Central Asian workers.[31] The government also lifted postal weight limits for packages so that Central Asian families could send warm clothing to relatives on distant sites.[32]

Republic officials, however, were still dissatisfied. In August, A. Ia. Romanov, Chief Procurator of the Tadzhik republic, sent an angry report to V. M. Bochkov, Chief Prosecutor of the USSR, about the mistreatment of mobilized Tadzhiks. The litany of suffering was all too familiar: poor food and housing, unsafe working conditions, and no medical care. Eight workers on one farm had lost toes due to frostbite yet were forced to continue working. Sick workers received no medical attention, were declared truants, and then had their meals docked. Romanov wrote, "the mobilized workers have been reduced to a state of extreme emaciation."[33] At the same time, Bochkov wrote to L. P. Beria, the head of the NKVD and GKO member in charge of armaments, about the abuse of Uzbek workers. Focusing on a group of 239 Uzbeks placed in armaments factory No. 65 in Novosibirsk, Bochkov described unheated barracks with no access to clean drinking water, little bedding, and no protective work clothes. According to him, the majority of Uzbek workers did not even have shoes. Many were swollen with hunger. Like their Tadzhik counterparts, the Uzbeks were peasants with no factory experience. Given the least-skilled jobs, dressed in rags, and lacking protective work clothes, they suffered burns and cuts from red-hot flying metal as well as frostbite in the unheated barracks and shops. Between April and June 1943, seventeen members of the group had died of starvation, pneumonia, or tuberculosis. The full death toll was unknown because the factory kept no records of workers who fell ill. Bochkov wanted to prosecute the manager of the factory, but the case was blocked by the commissar of the ammunition industry, who claimed that the Uzbeks were already ill when they arrived, and that the manager had no extra stocks of food and clothing at his disposal. Local party officials, under sharp pressure from the judiciary, quickly found some extra resources, providing the Uzbek workers two meals a day, bedding, and work clothes.[34] As in other cases, pressure produced some amelioration.

Although the charge that many of the Central Asians were in poor health on arrival was true, it was also used by managers to evade responsibility for the high rates of illness and death. The orders to the republics for labor were so large that local recruiters mustered people who suffered from tuberculosis, venereal and coronary artery disease, and malnutrition.[35] At factory No. 309 in Chapaevsk, so many Central Asian workers arrived suffering from malnutrition and active tuberculosis that a large number had to be sent home or moved to light work.[36] At OSMCh-23 and other construction sites in Molotov province, most of the Bashkirs, Tatars, and Kazakhs showed signs of heart disease, emaciation, and "other diseases that render them unfit for physical labor."[37] A majority of the 12,200 Uzbeks drafted for construction work in Cheliabinsk were sent home because they were too weak for heavy physical labor.[38] Local party leaders were informed about the health status of the Central Asian workers, and the secretary of the Cheliabinsk provincial party committee telegraphed Malenkov, Secretary of the Central Committee, noting that "an extraordinarily great number" were suffering from pneumonia, tuberculosis, and gastric illnesses.[39] A similar situation prevailed in other provinces.[40]

Doctors who examined the workers tried to find interpreters and organize special office hours and separate hospital wards. But treating such a high volume of very sick patients proved difficult. The interpreters were themselves poorly educated and struggled to explain complaints or relay medical instructions. Nor were Central Asian workers, who were mainly peasants, accustomed to seeking medical help. Doctors, foremen, and managers only knew they had been sick after they returned to work or died. Doctors noted that every worker who received a medical discharge was also malnourished, and starvation was the leading cause of death. The doctors themselves concluded that mobilization of peasants from Central Asia had been a mistake.[41]

The problems faced by the Central Asian workers were exacerbated by prejudice and discrimination. Supplementary rations were tied to norm fulfillment, but many became trapped in a downward spiral: unable to overfulfill the norms to earn extra calories, they became still weaker, making it less likely that they could fulfill their norms in the future.[42] Their lack of Russian made it easy for them to be swindled or short-weighted by canteen staff.[43] Like other workers, they lost access to food when they violated laws against lateness and absenteeism. Workers convicted of absenteeism were penalized by up to six months of compulsory labor and a considerable cut in their bread ration: 200 grams a day if their daily allowance was 800 grams, and 100 grams a day if it was lower.[44] Yet many did not understand the laws. Their foremen, poorly educated and accustomed to dispensing rough discipline, insulted them, swore at them, and even beat them.[45] One foreman in Kuibyshev province was arrested after he marched into a hospital where a group of Central

Asian workers lay ill, tore up their sick notes, and rousted them from their beds.[46] In his opinion, they were malingering and being coddled by the medical staff.

Not all factory employees shared management's indifference and hostility. Ia. E. Gol'dshtein, the chief metallurgist at the Kirov factory, recalled the workers' plight with deep empathy:

> They poorly understood the orders that rained down on them and were even worse at fulfilling them. Often they got down on their knees, folded their arms, and prayed. The chief of the fettling shop, under whose command they had fallen, treated them worse than the Spaniards treated the slaves when they conquered America. He beat them if they failed to complete a job, took away their meager meals and bread rations. The Uzbeks wilted right before your eyes; many of them died right there in the shops.[47]

More common than empathy was tragic mutual incomprehension. Officials, for example, were puzzled to discover at times large amounts of cash on the bodies of workers who died of starvation.[48] The finding encouraged customary racist stereotypes of the miserly "Uzbek in a robe," who would rather die of hunger than spend his hoarded money. Indeed, a common joke among the workers at Uralmash (Urals Heavy Machine-Building Factory) was that the factory's Russian initials, UZTM, stood for "*Uzbek, zdes' tvoia mogila*" or "Uzbek, here is your grave." A report from Sverdlovsk province also noted the problem: "The Uzbeks and Tadzhiks do not eat fish, salami, mushrooms, or pickled cabbage, and meals are made only from these foods. Many *natsmeny* sell off their main course to Russian workers right there in the canteen. This trade in dinners and bread takes place on a vast scale." It was not only the unfamiliar food that prompted this behavior. As historian Vera Solov'eva explains, many of the Central Asian peasants were earning wages for the first time and hoped to accumulate cash for their families so they could expand their holdings when they returned. The head of personnel at Nizhnii Tagil's Khimzavod expressed a common view when he callously remarked, "in any case, the Uzbeks and Tadzhiks will all die off in the winter."[49] Memoirist M. M. Kovalevskii coined the striking phrase "involuntary genocide," noting that the workers in their desperate desire to save unwittingly precipitated their own death. Kovalevskii was most angered by the fact that managers, who were aware of the behavior and its consequences, took no action to stop it.[50] The prevalence of starvation among the workers, intimately linked to victimization, food customs, and future hopes, was dismissed at best with bewilderment and at worst with racist disregard.

Abused by their foremen, Central Asian workers were also spurned and harassed by other workers. One investigator, in a report compiled for the Central Committee of the Kirghiz Communist Party in September 1943 concerning Central Asian workers in the coalmines of Kopeisk in Cheliabinsk province, wrote:

> One night, last year Russian youths beat one *natsmen* to death, a man who was guilty of absolutely nothing. Abdukarimov, a cobbler working for the Construction Administration, went into the dining room one day and three Russian youths encountered him and badly beat him; the other Russians passing by laughed at him instead of stopping the assault. On 10 September 1943, an Uzbek worker went to the bazaar, there two Russians beat him with the sticks, asking "who gave you permission to go to the bazaar?" He ran off and this saved him. The public prosecutor and head of the mine knew about all these facts and took no action; the city party committee also knew and also took no action.[51]

In the summer of 1943, the state not only attempted to rectify the worst living conditions and provide customary foods, but also took some limited measures against racist behavior or, in official parlance, "anti-Soviet attacks by backward workers ... who failed to understand the roots of the national unity of the peoples of the USSR." Some of the worst offenders were prosecuted and received heavy sentences intended to set an example for others.[52]

The Struggle over Labor

Within weeks of the German surrender at Stalingrad, the Komitet celebrated its own small moment of triumph when it mobilized the first group of 750 people within the battered city and province to begin reconstruction. After months of hellish bombing, scarcely a structure was left standing, although thousands of civilians were living amid the smoking ruins.[53] An additional 1,000 people were also mobilized to rebuild the city's port.[54] Throughout the spring, tens of thousands of skilled and unskilled workers arrived to rebuild, including 20,000 newly mobilized girls and women. Aleksandra Cherkasova formed a brigade of women volunteers in June 1943, an initiative soon emulated by tens of thousands of other young women who formed "Cherkasova brigades."[55]

After the victory at Stalingrad, the Red Army moved steadily west, liberating territory along a broad front stretching from Orel in the north to Novorossiisk on the Black Sea. Khar'kov was liberated in the winter of 1943, retaken by the Germans in March, and then freed again. By March, Voronezh was liberated, along with Voroshilovgrad in the Donets coal basin. In the summer of 1943, the Germans launched Operation Citadel, an offensive aimed at expanding the territory they held around Kursk. The Red Army took Orel to the north and Belgorod to the south, defeating the Germans at Kursk in August in the largest tank battle in history, a stunning victory that some historians consider the decisive turning point of the war. A short communiqué from Stalin was read over the radio, and the victory celebrated with 12 artillery salvos from 120 guns in Moscow. It was the first of more than 300 such announcements and salutes that would mark the progress of Soviet forces.[56] In fall 1943, the Red Army forded the Dnepr, pushed the Germans off the right bank, and liberated most of Ukraine. Kiev was freed in November 1943, and by December two-thirds of the occupied territory was freed.

The armaments factories were swamped with orders and forced to meet ever higher targets of production.[57] Labor needs of the eastern factories intensified at the same time as reconstruction of the liberated territories began. Among the first steps in every newly liberated province was restoration of the power stations, which had been blown up twice, first by the Red Army when it withdrew, and then by the Germans when they retreated. The Komitet mobilized 18,000 peasants from Kazakhstan, Tatariia, and Bashkiriia for construction work on electric power stations throughout the country.[58] Factories that had been evacuated east began to be rebuilt in their home provinces.[59] In July and September 1943, the Komitet launched two women-only drafts following its February initiative that had replaced all male postal workers with women and sent the men to industrial jobs. Newly mobilized women would serve as guards for armaments, ammunition, and chemical factories.[60] Guard posts in key installations, including airports, aerodromes, and military enterprises of defense, were soon staffed exclusively by women.[61]

Most civilians in the occupied territories greeted liberation with joy, but the war was far from over. The urban inhabitants and peasants who had survived occupation and refused to collaborate lived a semistarved, hand-to-mouth existence.[62] The population had been cruelly decimated through genocide, murderous reprisals, disease, and slave labor. Survivors provided the Komitet with a new reserve pool of labor. A veritable exodus of able-bodied teenagers, women, and older men streamed out of the front-line zones, mobilized by the Komitet to work on sites near and far.[63] In July 1943, the Komitet ordered a mass levy of 34,000 people from the recently liberated provinces and Kazakhstan to reopen the coalmines of the Donbass that had been blown up, blocked, and flooded.[64] By fall, reconstruction of the liberated territories was well under way. Workers mobilized by the Komitet swarmed the ruins, tools in hand, clearing rubble, rebuilding, and restoring telegraph and telephone lines.[65] In October, the GKO ordered huge new mobilizations of tens of thousands of urban and rural recruits to the iron and steel industry. The same month, the first major mobilization began to restore the byproduct coke plants in Stalino.

Although the system of mass mobilization was highly effective in staffing the defense industry in the east and rebuilding the newly liberated territories, the Komitet was increasingly challenged by factory and mine managers in the liberated areas who bypassed its authority by sending word to rural areas that people were needed locally to rebuild. Those who had fled the cities during the German occupation voluntarily made their way back singly and in small groups to the gates of the mines and factories.[66] Plenipotentiaries from the factories fanned out through the rural districts to recruit others, many of whom were former workers.[67] The commissariats, too, understood that the Komitet was facing ever greater difficulties in procuring labor and began to bypass the Komitet by sending their requests for labor directly to Shchadenko, Commissar of Defense, or the GKO. The Komitet had become a bureaucratic obstacle to their immediate demands for labor. Local soviets also began contesting the mobilization orders. Claiming that they had no more able-bodied unemployed people, rural or urban, in their provinces, they requested to be released from the levies. In some instances, the Komitet, based on its own accounting, was forced to concur. In March, Shvernik wrote to Stalin to complain.[68] The Komitet was keen to preserve its control over labor, but its ability to meet the demands of the industrial commissariats was weakening.[69]

The economy was beginning to resemble a giant emergency room, and the Komitet a frantic doctor triaging to meet the needs of its competing industrial patients. Much of the energy sector—wood, coal, and peat—relied on temporary deployments of peasants along with their horses and carts.

Without energy, the factories were at a standstill. The Commissariat of the Timber Industry urgently needed woodcutters, draft animals, and carts, but so did the collective farms. If the Komitet granted the requests of the timber industry, it would strip the farms of the people they needed to produce the nation's food. The high rates of starvation already attested to the strain on the farms. In July 1943, the Timber Commissariat requested 3,250 people on foot and 2,000 carters with horses to haul wooden blocks to produce rifle stocks. The provincial soviets opposed the mobilization because the peasants and their horses were busy with agricultural work. Shvernik attempted to mediate between the competing demands, offering the commissariat a smaller number of people, carts, and horses "in view of the strained state of the labor force and draft animals." He ordered newly mobilized peasants to work for three months in the forests "during their free time," a phrase they likely received with angry astonishment.[70]

Almost all motorized vehicles had been commandeered earlier by the military, and now even the most basic conveyances—carts and horses—had become objects of fierce contention. In January 1943, there were more than 4.2 million horses in the Soviet Union. By December, almost 10 percent had been mobilized by the Komitet, mainly for work in hauling timber.[71] Provincial officials responsible for agriculture and food production were desperate to retain control over their carts and horses. In September 1943, for example, officials in Karelia requested that the Soviet of People's Commissars reduce the numbers for its mobilization of horses and carters for the timber industry. Only about 1,500 horses remained in the entire republic, and these last few were essential to the fishing industry. Again, the Komitet advised that the horses could work in the forests during their "free time" from November to December when they were not needed to haul fish and equipment.[72]

Provincial officials also resisted the military's unending demands for horses. After the great tank battles for Kursk and Orel in the summer of 1943, General K. K. Rokossovskii commandeered horses from local peasants and then demanded 1,000 additional horses in October. The provincial party secretary flatly refused; only 2,500 horses remained in the province, which had no other form of transport. Moreover, Rokossovskii never returned the horses he had commandeered earlier, and it was unlikely he would hand back this second group either. The Komitet ruled that Rokossovskii could take 500 horses but had to return those that the army had borrowed earlier.[73] Unfortunately, the Red Army had the habit of supplementing its rations with horse flesh, so the first group had probably already disappeared into the vast iron cauldrons of the mess kitchens.[74]

Throughout the summer and fall of 1943, provincial and republic officials also fought to retain peasants on the state and collective farms.[75] After the party secretary of Krasnoiarsk Territory "categorically refused to meet an order for mobilization" in view of "the strain on the labor force in the district," L. I. Pogrebnoi, a member of the Komitet, wrote one terse line to Beria, head of the NKVD and member of the GKO: "Make him do it."[76] The Komitet consistently favored industry over local agricultural needs. When officials in Mordoviia, an autonomous republic located between Moscow and the Volga, petitioned the Komitet to decrease a mobilization order for almost 9,000 peasants, Shvernik flatly refused, explaining that deployment of peasants to industrial towns and the peat industry "cannot be disrupted by the needs of agricultural work."[77] The interdependence of town and country was starkly laid bare: the food shortage was exacerbated by the labor drain from the countryside, and the inability to retain labor in industry a consequence of the lack of food. Although not all officials grasped the connection, they well understood the sharpening struggle over labor. The wartime economy, which privileged defense production over all other sectors, was stretched to breaking point.

The pool of draft-eligible men and wounded veterans not fit for the front was also dwindling. When the GKO ordered the Komitet in July 1943 to mobilize 2,000 people, half of whom were to be servicemen from Central Asia, local officials failed to deliver a single person.[78] Provincial and republic officials routinely requested extensions, knowing they could not possibly produce the numbers requested in the time set.[79] As a result of the growing failures to meet mobilization orders, the Komitet was repeatedly forced to deny the commissariats their requests. As the commissariats began preparing to meet the production plan for 1944, factory directors anxiously began placing their orders for labor in September 1943. The director of the Gor'kii auto factory, converted to making tanks, for example, requested 7,000 new workers. At best, the Komitet could promise 2,000 servicemen who were too disabled either to fight or to do construction work.[80]

In response, factory directors and officials developed various schemes to bypass the Komitet's centralized control. The head of the Novosibirsk soviet, for example, worked out a deal in November 1943 whereby the director of a local textile factory would send him 5 meters of cloth in exchange for every worker the soviet sent to the factory, as well as 10 additional meters to each worker as incentive. Given the terrible shortage of cloth, the offer was attractive to all parties involved. The commissar of the textile industry even got involved and promised to provide cloth to the factory's director for the deal. Shvernik, who discovered the scheme, immediately informed the head of the soviet that bargaining with state goods was tantamount to theft and asked the USSR procurator to charge him with "illegal mobilization and squandering state stocks."[81] Despite the Komitet's acumen in exposing various hidden ruses for labor, managers and officials increasingly resorted to new "fiddles" to outwit it.[82]

As reserves disappeared and the struggle over labor intensified, the Komitet and the Commissariat of Defense informed the GKO of the difficulties. Shvernik and Shchadenko sent a joint letter in February 1943 requesting the GKO temporarily to stop issuing new orders to mobilize draft-eligible men from Central Asia. Prior mobilization orders had still not been filled, and the republics were hard pressed to fill new ones.[83] The coal and peat industries were desperately short of workers but, of the 50,000 draft-eligible young Central Asians promised to the Commissariat of the Coal Industry, only 21,000 were sent.[84] In September, a new mobilization for the coal industry from multiple provinces, including the newly liberated territories, also failed to meet its target, and the Komitet issued a flurry of telegrams to the provincial soviets chastising them for their failures.[85] Similar shortfalls in mobilization occurred for the peat industry. Work in the bogs was crippling, and the living conditions harsh. By March 1943, January's mobilization order for workers in peat had still not been met, nor had the two prior orders. Officials from the Ivanovo soviet had sent out mobilization orders to 10,030 people, but only 2,000 appeared at the transit stations; soviet officials in Gor'kii and Kirov provinces did not even bother to report their numbers.[86] Shvernik, in an attempt to compel local soviet officials to fulfill their obligations, dispatched activists to help round people up. Despite the extra effort, the mobilizations for the peat bogs were not met until October, when large cash prizes were distributed to those local bureau officials who had succeeded in meeting the targets.[87] At the end of March, the need for fuel was so urgent that more than 215,000 people were ordered to leave the factories to gather peat. Yet the emergency transfer, too, fell far short of the target. Only about 144,700 people appeared, of whom only about 56,000 arrived at the peat sites.[88] New efforts at mobilization were also unsuccessful despite special commissions created by party activists in every province to help with the levies. As the fuel crisis mounted, this mobilization, too, fell short.[89]

Throughout the summer of 1943, great lags developed between the mobilization orders and the actual appearance of people at their destinations. In June, 2,450 people were mobilized for gunpowder factories, but only 227 showed up. In Gor'kii, 200 people were mobilized for defense factory No. 222, but only 46 began work.[90] Each month, mobilization deficits from the previous months were carried forward and new orders were added. Almost 180,000 people nationwide received mobilization orders in May 1943, although the orders from April were still short by 108,000 people. In June, the backlogs continued to mount. The combination of unfilled orders from April and May, plus new orders for June, totaled almost 286,000 people, of whom 117,000 were actually mobilized. In short, in June, the commissariats were still waiting for workers who were supposed to have arrived in April and May. And in July new mobilizations added hundreds of thousands more to the backlog. By this point, the commissariats no longer knew how many people had been ordered, who would show up, or when. Amidst the growing failure to reach target numbers everywhere, many people, registered on lists that were never filled, escaped mobilization altogether.[91]

By January 1944, the shortfalls in previous mobilizations for some industries actually surpassed the target figures for new mobilizations. The machine-building factories, for example, were waiting for 4,800 people from previous mobilization orders when the Komitet ordered 2,800 more.[92] A similar situation prevailed for the electric power stations.[93] The backlogs naturally gave rise to great confusion in the provinces. Local officials were mobilizing almost continuously, but which people filled what orders? Were officials required to generate a new list of recruits with each new order, or could older names be repurposed to serve the new targets? No one knew.

By November 1943, the Komitet was juggling vast numbers in a rapid sleight of hand, moving backlogs forward and, at the same time, generating new orders. Of the 3,700,400 people mobilized in 1943, more than 1.5 million were supposed to be mobilized in only two months, October and November. Yet the backlogs were staggering. As of mid-November, 1.6 million people still remained to be mobilized according to earlier orders. Soviet and party officials in the provinces responded that the targets were impossible to meet by the deadline. The Komitet simply extended it, carrying forward at least 588,000 people targeted for earlier mobilization into the first quarter of 1944. The number of people actually appearing at any given site bore no relation to the numbers originally requested. The system was veering out of control.

The Komitet itself recognized that there were no more people to mobilize in either rural or urban areas. All those able to perform some kind of labor (of whom many were incapacitated) were working—in factories, forests, peat bogs, or mines; on construction sites; or on collective or state farms. Children were either in school or vocational training. Men not fit for the front were at work, as were mothers with young children. Shvernik openly admitted that there was no labor left to mobilize. He wrote to V. M. Molotov, "I ask you to limit the new orders to cases of sharp need, and allow us to satisfy need at the expense of redistribution of the labor force through contingents that have already been provided to the commissariats."[94] The main function the Komitet could serve, in his opinion, was to shift workers from one sector to another. It could not conjure workers out of thin air. Yet the Soviet of People's Commissars and the GKO continued to generate new orders to fill, and the commissariats continued to press their demands. The numbers began to lose all meaning. The standard form used by the Komitet to track mobilizations showed the growing backlogs. In 1944, the Komitet added a new column: annulment of unmet targets. The system of labor mobilization, one of the war's most powerful weapons, had run out of human ammunition.

The lags and backlogs made it impossible for factory and construction managers to plan housing and rations for those workers who did arrive. Managers never knew how many to expect or when the overloaded rail system might deliver them. The Komitet recognized that there was little coordination between the GKO, the industrial commissariats, and the factory directors. In July 1943, for example, the Komitet notified the GKO that armaments factory No. 710 in Podol'sk was unprepared to house the 3,000 workers the GKO had ordered for the Commissariat of Armaments. The workers were scheduled to arrive from the countryside in ten days. In this instance, even the Commissariat of Armaments, normally an insatiable consumer of labor, agreed to cancel the mobilization.[95] Yet most orders were not countermanded, and peasants and young vocational graduates arrived at factories that were not prepared to house, clothe, or feed them. In the summer of 1943, V. N. Merkulov, Commissar of State Security, received several letters signed by young workers, mainly girls, who had been mobilized in Iaroslavl' and sent to Miass, in Cheliabinsk province. The teenagers were sent to work in the Stalin motor vehicle factory (UralZiS) and were housed about 8 miles (13 km) from the factory. The walk took so long that many slept at work to avoid the harsh penalties for lateness. One teenager wrote, "We arrived to bare walls, and we sleep on the floor. We received nothing, neither mattresses, nor blankets, nor pillows." One young worker summed up the plight of the group: "We are living very badly. We have sold everything we had. You come home from work, but there is nothing. I go hungry all the time. Nothing is clean, but there is no money to buy soap. They feed us only greens, and we are very hungry. We are often sick. Many have run away." Yet the hardest part of daily life, one young girl noted, was the repeated victimization by local criminals, who entered the dormitories at night to rob the girls. Penning her letter at night, she wrote, "Now, we are sitting here in the dormitory and waiting for an attack." "They show up around midnight, and they begin to search us, to take our ration cards and money, remove our good belts. They take anything they want. . . . The local guys come to the dormitory and steal and beat us, and then, because of this, people run away to go back home."[96]

The teenagers knew that desertion was illegal, yet they explained to the state security organs that they had little choice. As one young vocational graduate asserted, "I am so hungry, and I am beginning to swell up. We are getting together to return to Iaroslavl', and I too will run away."[97] Signing their names and addresses to their letters, the teenagers showed little fear of prosecution but, rather, assumed the authorities would remedy their plight. They stressed that they shared the same goals as the state: to win the war. They asserted proudly that they were willing to work, but the authorities also needed to meet their obligations: to create conditions that would make work possible. The letters eventually had an impact. About a year later, the provincial party committee in Cheliabinsk reported to the Central Committee that measures had been taken to improve daily life for the vocational graduates.[98] By that time, however, many of the teens had already fled.

As the war continued, many people simply refused to heed the summons from their local soviet for mobilization. Evasion was a criminal offense, yet the law was difficult to enforce. The procedure for prosecution for evasion, at least on paper, was clear. If a person failed to appear for mobilization, the Komitet's local bureaus were required to ascertain "the facts of evasion" or the reason within two days. They then had another day to forward their findings to the district prosecutor with the evader's full name, date of birth, home address, time of appearance set by the mobilization order, and the original mobilization summons. Bureau officials thus had three days to investigate, document, and forward the case file to the prosecutor. The district prosecutor, in turn, was to review the materials, forward the case to People's Court, and append an order on sentencing.[99] If a person was found guilty, the court sent a note back to the head of the local bureau, who then informed the local NKVD within ten days where the violator would serve a sentence of compulsory labor at reduced pay.[100] In principle, officials established clear punishment for evasion of mobilization with time limits for every stage of the procedure. In practice, it was unworkable. The local bureaus did not have the staff to investigate hundreds, or sometimes even thousands, of evaders, nor the transport to go to remote villages to ascertain "the facts of evasion." The two-day term set for investigation scarcely sufficed to reach many villages on foot, let alone return. With mobilization orders rolling over provinces in mighty and unstoppable waves, officials barely managed to round up one group before another order appeared. And as NKVD officials pointed out, the final step required the NKVD to detain the evaders while awaiting instructions about where to send them, but local jails had neither the space nor the ration allocations to hold such large groups. In short, the process of prosecution and punishment was as backlogged as the mobilization orders. Local bureau and NKVD officials, under pressure to act quickly, soon found a quicker way to treat convicted evaders: they put them to work doing compulsory labor in local factories. Evasion was therefore rewarded: convicted evaders were allowed to stay in their home province. The state quickly put an end to this practice so convenient to lawbreakers and enforcers alike. In November 1942, the Supreme Court decreed that anyone sentenced to compulsory labor for evading a mobilization order had to be sent to the enterprise for which they were originally mobilized. In the end, however, the law was barely enforced: there were only 21,786 convictions during the entire war.[101]

Local soviet officials, under pressure to meet mobilization orders, sometimes committed egregious abuses in their efforts to produce bodies, and many citizens filed complaints. In Khabarovsk, a soviet official attempted to meet a mobilization order for the vocational schools with children aged twelve and thirteen. After the local prosecutor protested, the official explained, "We don't have enough people and the party's city committee decided to call up those born in 1930." Youngsters with chronic diseases and handicaps were sent off without medical exams and then had to be returned. In January 1944, K. P. Gorshenin, Chief Prosecutor of the USSR, angrily informed Shvernik that mobilizations were occurring with "administrative despotism." The militia took children from their homes without permitting families even a moment to say goodbye, hustled them off to central callup points, and put them on trains. Sometimes the militia arrived at night, rousing the family and taking children from their beds. Gorshenin cautioned Shvernik to stop local officials from treating mobilized teenagers like criminals. "Such a mobilization," he wrote, "provides no positive results." Yet local officials, caught between Moscow's orders and the lack of able-bodied people to mobilize, saw few options. Favoritism also undermined strict enforcement of the law as some district officials shielded their own relatives and friends. In Gor'kii province, collective farm chairmen removed certain names from the mobilization lists for timber cutting and substituted others, who were supposed to be exempt, including the elderly, women with babies, and the disabled. Gorshenin tried to steer a middle course between permitting local officials some leeway and prosecuting abuses.[102] Yet neither leniency toward, nor repression of, errant officials could alter the objective shortage of labor.

Figure 6.3 Women packing artillery shells, Altai Territory. Courtesy of RGAKFD.

Pressure and Opposition

The state was aware that the labor system was becoming ever more chaotic. In February 1944, the Commissariat of State Control launched an investigation into the Komitet and its work. Beginning with the premise that the main obstacle to mobilization was not depletion of labor reserves, the investigators focused instead on the Komitet's bookkeeping and organization. Charging that the Komitet had failed to maintain up-to-date records, the investigators sought a solution in better accounting and stricter enforcement. They noted that the monthly data the Komitet received from its local bureaus were often late and data from the rural areas unreliable. As data from rural areas were reported only once a year, the Komitet was forced to calculate the number of able-bodied people who remained in any particular province through successive deductions for prior mobilizations, a method subject to gross inaccuracy. Those mobilized for seasonal labor, for example, were deducted from the numbers available, although they might have already returned to the village.[103] In the opinion of the investigators, the statistics "were obviously underestimated," and the rural areas contained substantial reserves hidden by poor assessment practices.[104] The registry (*kartoteka*) in every province, which listed the unemployed, was so outdated that it "had no real function."[105]

The investigators were most concerned by the lags and backlogs, which threatened to undermine the entire system of planning. At times, the Komitet did cancel backorders, but in general, targets that the localities failed to meet in one quarter were, in the words of the investigators, "mechanically carried forward to the next." Records for seasonal mobilizations, such as peat cutting, were especially chaotic.[106] The Komitet was too sympathetic to excuses from provincial officials that their labor reserves were in a "strained position," and, as a result, "those provincial organizations that showed resistance received a lighter plan or were totally released."[107] Finally, the Komitet was undermining its own work. It often sent people out of their native provinces and replaced them with those mobilized from elsewhere. In January 1944, for example, the Komitet sent 3,500 people out of Stavropol' Territory to Stalingrad, and then, fifteen days later, 1,500 people out of Stalingrad to Arkhangel'sk. What was the purpose of sending workers to Stalingrad at the same time that Stalingrad's workers were sent to other towns?[108] Finally, the overall statistics uncovered by the investigators showed a poor record: in 1943, the defense industry received only 70 percent of the workers that were supposed to be delivered; transport and communications—65 percent; construction—58 percent; and all other branches combined—53 percent.[109]

Pogrebnoi sharply rebutted the charges. Acknowledging that the Komitet had problems with data, he offered suggestions to improve assessment, but above all stressed the complexity of the Komitet's task. He reminded the investigators that the Komitet could not meet an order until it received information from the industrial commissariats about where they planned to send the mobilized workers. Yet the commissariats were often late in responding. Data on labor reserves were based on multiple sources but, given the great disruptions of wartime, none were entirely accurate or up to date. Pogrebnoi proposed that every person who was not working be compelled to register with the local bureau of the Komitet.[110] Local bureaus would no longer depend on ration bureaus, collective farm chairmen, or house managers for their data, but would instead become the civilian analog to draft commissions. Labor service, already compulsory for the civilian population, would become fully "militarized." This proposal, however, was never implemented. By 1943, the majority of mobilized labor was drawn from rural areas, and peasants were not able to travel to provincial centers to register with local bureaus. In short, the Komitet did not have the staff, transport, or reach to militarize the civilian labor force.

The investigators from the Commissariat of State Control presented an accurate assessment of the Komitet's failings. Yet their fundamental premise, that better data would yield substantial hidden reserves of labor, was wrong. By early 1944, every sector that was not producing directly for defense had been stripped of workers, along with the reserves of mothers, teenagers, handicapped, and elderly in both towns and countryside. Although more female and elderly peasants might be drafted into industry, further losses to the collective farms would leave no one to do agricultural work and put an already malnourished waged labor force on the brink of starvation. The situation, in its starkest form, was a textbook illustration of the Marxist principle that the creation of value ultimately stems from labor. Yet, in the midst of war, Soviet leaders took scant comfort in having their more abstract theoretical precepts affirmed. Not surprisingly, attempts to improve accounting practices had little effect on lags and backlogs, which continued through 1944.

In February, the demand for fuel increased and the energy crisis deepened. More than 81,000 peasants were mobilized to work in peat enterprises of the Commissariat of Electric Power Stations.[111] The peasants would cut and process peat in February and March and return to their collective farms in time for spring sowing. Yet the need for fuel was so great that the peat mobilizations continued into spring: 300,000 more people were mobilized in March and April. The mobilization was considered so critical that officials from the provincial and republic soviets and local bureaus of the Komitet were summoned to a national meeting for instructions.[112] Local party and soviet officials, frantic to meet the quotas for spring sowing, petitioned the Komitet to release them from the never-ending mobilizations. Moscow provincial officials, among others, begged the Komitet to reduce the recent levy of more than 13,000 peasants for the peat industry.[113] The loss of labor to the collective farms was insupportable: more than 60 percent of people mobilized for permanent work in 1944 came from the countryside, and temporary mobilizations of more than 400,000 carters with horses further undermined the ability of the farms to reach their agricultural targets.[114] Yet collective farms were compelled to surrender their peasants, carts, and horses. In exchange, the Komitet sent more than 3.3 million people, mostly secondary school students, to the collective farms to help with spring sowing and the fall harvest.[115] Pleas poured in from rural officials throughout the country begging to be released from various levies, but Shevnik repeatedly refused. In his view, local agricultural interests could not be allowed to prevail over the national needs of defense.[116]

In August 1944, the Commissariat of Defense ran out of recruits for industry and construction. By this time, any man deemed unfit for the front was unlikely to be capable of physical labor. The industrial commissariats had begun refusing those who arrived: they were too sick or too weak to work. The Commissariat of Coal in particular complained steadily of its labor shortage. After Rostov province was liberated, the mines were cleared of rubble, and workers were needed underground. The head of the military soviet of the North Caucasus district, tasked with delivering draft-age recruits, wrote to both the Komitet and the Soviet of People's Commissars to explain that he had no men fit to work in the mines. The Commissariat of Defense had already sent 1,800 men to the mines in Rostov, but the mine directors deemed only 38 of them capable of work. The head of the military soviet noted with exasperation that the representatives of the commissariats demanded "completely healthy" men, but this group was at the front.[117] The head of the Komitet's local bureau in Rostov affirmed what everyone already knew: a medical commission had determined that not a single one of the men mobilized for the Rostov mines was capable of mining.[118] Yet the Komitet still insisted that the order for the mines be met. It refused to accept the assessment of the North Caucasus military soviet, its own local bureau in Rostov, or the medical commission. Pogrebnoi wrote to Malenkov, the secretary of the Central Committee, requesting that he support the Komitet's decision. "We have huge mobilization tasks in Rostov," Pogrebnoi stated flatly.[119] In December 1944, the head of the military soviet of the North Caucasus district again requested a reduction in the mobilization orders, noting that the backlog for his district had reached more than a quarter of a million people. "It is not possible to mobilize more than 45,000 men per month," he said. Even if the military soviet received no new requests for labor, it would still not be able to clear the backlog until May 1945.[120]

Consent for mobilization was also rapidly eroding among Central Asian leaders. The GKO had halted mobilizations of Central Asians for work beyond the borders of their republics in October 1943, but smaller mobilizations continued into 1944. Those who had already been mobilized were unaffected by the order, although some enterprises sent the Central Asian workers home due to their poor health. In 1944, the Soviet of People's Commissars issued an order for the demobilization of the bulk of Central Asians still working outside their home republic, yet many still remained at their jobs.[121] In April 1944, a group of twenty-five Uzbek and Tadzhik workers, first mobilized in early 1943 for a railway factory in Ivanovo province, petitioned to return home, citing the deaths of 20 percent of their original number.[122] Kazakh officials received many similar appeals. In August, Nikolai Skvortsov, head of the Kazakh Communist Party, and Nurtas Undasynov, chairman of Kazakhstan's Soviet of People's Commissars, wrote a joint letter to Malenkov. They noted that since 1942 the Commissariat of Defense had mobilized more than 87,000 residents of Kazakhstan for work in industry outside the republic, the overwhelming majority consisting of men deemed unfit for the front. Sent to enterprises in Siberia and the Urals, they were employed "in the most difficult, unskilled work." Indeed, none of this information was new. Skvortsov and Undasynov, however, made an unprecedented request: "We ask that you return the Kazakhs to their republic."[123] Many provincial and republic officials pleaded with higher authorities to reduce their mobilization targets, allow them to retain people in their provinces, and cancel backlogged orders. Yet these pleas still recognized the right of the Komitet, the GKO, and the Soviet of People's Commissars to mobilize and move millions of people. The letter from Skvortsov and Undasynov marked the first time that the heads of a republic had the temerity to request that the Central Committee return their people to their republic.

Skvortsov and Undasynov attached a lengthy report to the letter detailing the results of their own investigations in the eastern industrial provinces. The findings were by now all too familiar: most of the recruits were not fit for heavy labor, and many had already been returned "due to sickness or exhaustion." The factories were ill prepared to house, clothe, or feed them, leading "to mass desertion, illness, exhaustion, and death." Local party organizations and managers displayed a "soulless attitude toward Kazakhs." The Party had failed to provide political activists who were able to speak with them, read newspapers aloud, or provide information in their native language. Unable to communicate, and scattered among hostile people, the Kazakh workers suffered from terrible depression, and they lost limbs and lives to work accidents. Many failed to meet their work norms, and as a result their pay was low and irregular. Some were reduced to selling their bread cards so they could pay for canteen meals. Accustomed to a meat- and rice-based diet, they were malnourished, and some were dying from starvation. Attempts to provide them with special food had failed. Perhaps most poignantly, the workers were scorned by the general population. On trams and in the streets, people looked at them "as if they were bogeymen [kak babai]," something not even human. Moreover, these conditions were unlikely to change. Small groups of evacuees were being mobilized to return home, and it was time to send the Kazakh workers home as well.[124]

The request was denied. Four months later, in December 1944, the Central Committee responded that "with the exception of those older than fifty and or ill, we consider it inexpedient to send them home." Instead, it reaffirmed the need to improve conditions, a pledge that in the past had resulted in little concrete change.[125] As late as July 1945, two months after the war ended, republic leaders were still asking for the return of their workers. D. Z. Protopopov, head of the Tadzhik Communist Party, wrote to Malenkov requesting that the mobilized Tadzhik workers be allowed to return to their collective farms. During the war, Tadzhikistan had provided about 50,000 workers, almost half of whom were still working in the Urals and Siberia.[126]

By 1944, the strain of mobilization for reconstruction and wartime production was becoming increasingly insupportable. In the fall, N. A. Mikhailov, the head of the Komsomol, visited Stalingrad. After the victory in January 1943, the Komsomol mobilized more than 21,000 young people to rebuild the city. Most considered it an honor to be sent to the storied battlefield. They worked on huge construction sites and in factories, including the famed Stalingrad Tractor Factory, where the Red Army had battled the

Wehrmacht floor to floor in close combat.[127] The Tractor Factory, nothing more than a smoldering shell in early 1943, was once again producing tanks. The workforce was very young: more than 60 percent were under eighteen.[128] In Mikhailov's report, which he sent directly to Malenkov, the secretary of the Central Committee, he noted that almost 60 percent of the 7,600 young people who worked in the Tractor Factory were living in the ruins of buildings, which lacked even the most primitive facilities. For those housed in barracks, living space for each person was estimated at between 1 and 2 square meters, a space barely larger than a coffin, and the young workers had no access to hot water, kettles, sinks, or laundry facilities. They lived "in the same dirty clothes literally for months." Another 3,000 were housed in drafty tents. The canteen food was meager and monotonous: millet soup, millet porridge, herring, and a dollop of margarine. Although the majority of the young workers mobilized to rebuild Stalingrad's defense factories stayed, thousands had deserted. Of the initial 21,000 mobilized by the Komsomol, more than one-third had disappeared. Mikhailov blamed local party officials and industrial managers, while pointing again to the problems inherent in the system of labor mobilization. The industrial commissariats had no incentive to keep workers because they could easily appeal to the Komitet for another levy to make good their losses. He wrote that even "mass cases of desertion do not produce a serious response from the leaders of the enterprises." Mikhailov's opinion of S. Z. Ginzburg, Commissar of Construction, was particularly harsh. "When Comrade Ginzburg found out that the GKO had decided to mobilize the Komsomol'tsy and youth to reconstruct the Tractor Factory, he called the Central Committee of the Komsomol several times a day to speed the process of sending people. However, Comrade Ginzburg did not demonstrate the same energy when it was necessary to improve the lives of the young people on site." As a result of his report, Stalingrad's district and factory party officials received a strict warning from their provincial superiors: if they failed to remedy conditions within one month, they would face party strictures.[129]

In 1944, the unions created housing and service committees in many factories to improve the dormitories, stop theft, and ensure that workers had access to baths, laundries, and shoe and clothing workshops. By this time, the country was bearing the debts accumulated over four years of total war. Workers had been transferred from municipal services, including laundries and baths, to work in defense, and consumer industries had been repurposed to serve the military. The country was no longer producing leather shoes; workers had no footwear, and tens of thousands of children were unable to attend school in the winter. In response, the Commissariat of Light Industry began producing wooden clogs, which many people were already making for themselves.[130] Factory workshops, lacking sewing machines, needles, spare parts, and raw materials, could not do even simple repairs. Workers had to bring their own nails to fix boots and their own needles and thread to mend clothing. Needless to say, these items were not available through ration cards or at almost any price in the markets.[131] Workers were deserting the defense factories in droves.[132] Investigators everywhere echoed Mikhailov's critique: "the lives of workers cannot be separated from production."[133]

In the summer of 1944, state and party organizations once again pressured local officials and industrial managers to take action. In June, the Soviet of People's Commissars decreed that union inspectors could impose a 500-ruble fine on industrial managers who violated labor and occupational safety rules. The decree, part of a wider campaign to improve living and working conditions, gave the unions some leverage against foremen and shop heads in eliminating the more egregious abuses.[134] The Commission of Party Control reprimanded party officials and managers for their "failure to be involved in the lives of workers" and ordered the delivery of fuel, clothing, and shoes.[135] Yet both labor mobilization and desertion continued, each now linked to the other by the inability of managers to improve conditions amid severe wartime shortages. In 1944 alone, the Komitet mobilized 1,113,350 for permanent work and 2,227,700 for seasonal labor—more than 3.3 million people in all. More than half of those mobilized for permanent work, 630,500, came from newly liberated territories in Ukraine, Belorussia, and Rostov province. Yet these figures, impressive as they were, were only two-thirds of the Komitet's planned target.[136] Not a single republic or province in the country was able to meet the Komitet's orders in full. Most areas were either tapped out of able-bodied unemployed, or the local soviets were unable to pull any more peasants out of the rural areas.[137] Given the failure of the republics and provinces to meet their targets, every industrial sector other than munitions and the meat and dairy industry fell short of the labor it needed: coalmining received only 59 percent of the workers it requested; the timber industry just 56 percent.[138] The figures laid bare the labor crisis.

****

Very few Soviet citizens awoke on Victory Day, May 9, 1945, in the same beds they slept in the night the war began. The home front, often imagined as a stationary, stable bulwark, was in reality composed of vast mobilized contingents in motion. Red Army soldiers may have dreamed of the homes and families they left behind, but so did the millions of civilians mobilized to work in distant towns and sites. The war years encompassed not one but two great fronts in motion, both under military discipline, both fed, housed, and clothed by the state. Labor mobilization, which extended to virtually the entire population, was a powerful weapon in the war. It enabled Soviet leaders and workers to staff the evacuated factories, build a new industrial base in the east, and reconstruct the liberated territories. Yet, by 1943, the Komitet was forced to move beyond its original mandate to mobilize only urban unemployed in their place of residence. The draft boards, the Labor Reserves, and the Komitet drew labor from the Far North and Central Asia, from herders and nomads, from collective farms and remote villages. Only 23 percent of those mobilized came from the countryside in 1942, but the share had risen to 62 percent by the end of 1944.[139] With the liberation of the occupied territories, hundreds of thousands of survivors became subject to mobilization to staff industry in the east and rebuild the ruined towns in the west. Mobilization and labor turnover were intimately connected: industry's inability to create decent conditions led vast numbers of people to flee, which created in turn more demands for new workers.

The Komitet became a perpetual mobilization machine, charged with the task of searching out new reserves of labor to replace those who ran away, fell ill, or died. The pool of labor, however, was not inexhaustible. Mass backlogs resulted from the inability of the provinces and republics to meet the Komitet's levies. Local officials mobilized without end, but the people mobilized were too old, too young, too sick, or too weak to work. The plight of the Central Asian workers and the teenage vocational graduates were but extreme examples of the hardships faced by workers of all nationalities and ages. The country had reached its limit: every able-bodied person was working in industry, agriculture, or both.

The Komitet functioned as a sort of *deus ex machina*, exercising vast powers to solve what was arguably the war's most important challenge: to equip the Red Army to defeat the Nazis. The state was able to call up millions, distribute great levies over multiple provinces and republics, and send people where they were most needed. Civilian recruits were not asked to do a job but, like soldiers, were drafted and moved about in great convoys with no control over where they would go or what they would do. Under painful conditions, they applied themselves to their jobs, sending tanks and armaments to the front, and rebuilding the territories that had been destroyed. Yet even a "god" of such power as the Komitet proved unequal to the task of controlling labor. Although most mobilized workers stayed in place, the sheer number of evaders and runaways overwhelmed the courts. The mighty state achieved a great feat, but it had finally encountered an obstacle that no orders or exhortations could overcome: the limits of what ordinary people, mere children in many cases, could endure.

7

Coercion Constrained: The Wartime Labor Laws

As for the return of those urban youth who have willfully fled, this
is exacerbated by the fact that the Procuracy refuses to assist in their
return. Thus, for example, when juveniles who have abandoned their
vocational studies find work in a factory, the Procuracy as a rule
refuses to bring charges against them.

Official from the Moscow Administration of Labor
Reserves, December 1942

Come, Frosia, ditch the factory, everything will be done to set you
up here.

A woman worker urging another to run away

In June 1940 the legal status of Soviet workers changed dramatically.
Previously free to change jobs whenever they wished, both absenteeism and
unauthorized job-changing became criminal offenses. In December 1941,
six months after the German invasion, the severity of the penalties escalated: workers in defense and defense-related sectors who left their jobs were
branded "labor deserters" to be punished by long prison terms. Workers,
like soldiers, were soon subject to compulsory mobilization as well as trial
by military tribunal. The militarization of labor was complete. Between 1941
and 1945, more than seven million workers were convicted for absenteeism
or illegal quitting. Yet coercion had its limits. Despite the draconian penalties, millions of vocational trainees and workers defied the law and fled the
schools and enterprises to which they had been mobilized. Painful working
and living conditions prompted workers to flee, while multiple authorities
showed themselves either unable or unwilling to enforce the law, thus weakening the threat of punishment. Although nearly one million defense workers
were sentenced to the Gulag over the course of the war, this was just over half
of all those who fled their jobs, and of those convicted and sentenced the state

was only able to arrest and imprison 40 percent. Those still serving a sentence at war's end were amnestied in July 1945.[1]

High labor turnover had plagued Soviet industry since the beginning of the five-year plans. The breakneck speed of industrial development soon exhausted the large pool of urban unemployed and led to an acute labor shortage. Millions of peasants, eager to escape the impoverishment of the collective farms, left the countryside to take up work in construction and industry. Jobs were plentiful, but migrants and older workers alike had to cope with overcrowded housing, a collapse in real wages, and intense speedup. Workers had few ways to redress their grievances. Strikes, while not uncommon, tended to be short-lived and met increasingly with state repression. Deprived of avenues for collective action, workers were thrown back on individual responses: disregard of orders, slacking, or absenteeism. For many workers, the most effective way to better their living or working conditions was to move to another job or town. Factories, mines, and construction sites became revolving doors: during the First Five-Year Plan (1928–1932) managers were renewing their entire workforce every eight or nine months. Although turnover declined toward the middle of the 1930s, at the end of the decade workers still changed jobs every twelve to fifteen months, and the instability of the workforce remained a serious obstacle to industrial production.[2]

Throughout this time the state reacted with relative caution. As much as it railed against absenteeism and job-changing, both in law and in practice it maintained a sharp distinction between free and prison labor. Workers who disappeared or changed jobs faced various economic sanctions and administrative impediments but retained the right to move from one job to another.[3] This right ended abruptly in June 1940 and was curtailed even further in December 1941. The line dividing free and unfree labor blurred. Workers were not prisoners, but they were bound to their place of employment.

The draconian wartime regulations aimed to eliminate the production problems created by high turnover. Yet, for all their harshness, they failed to curb labor mobility. Every stage of the process of recruitment, mobilization, and retention leaked workers. The Komitet met only 64.5 percent of its plan for mobilizing workers to permanent jobs in 1943 and 67.7 percent in 1944. One out of every three people targeted for mobilization never appeared.[4] Many of those mobilized fled while en route to their Labor Reserve schools or factories, mines, or construction sites. Enterprise directors lost hundreds and even thousands of workers after they arrived. The military draft, illness, and death also took a toll, but most troublesome to the state were the many workers who simply fled. During 1943 and 1944, there was a steady increase in both legal and illegal labor turnover. In 1944, it became common for enterprises to lose as many workers as they had hired, if not more.

Enforcement of the laws broke down because of a complex interplay of competing interests. Some factory managers reported labor deserters out of personal fear of prosecution or to deter other workers from quitting, while others were highly negligent in reporting. The collective farms, where most workers who fled took refuge, benefited from their labor and refused to surrender them. Urban and rural prosecutors, police, and party and soviet officials also had their own interests, depending on where they were situated. The Procuracy itself, responsible for enforcing the laws, was divided over their efficacy. Each group saw their actions as essential to their ability to meet their obligations to the war effort, but by pulling in different directions they undermined the effectiveness and rationale of state policy. As for the workers who defied the law, they remained within the war economy, taking up work in agriculture or in other factories. There is scant evidence that they viewed desertion as an act of resistance. The collision of the efforts of the state to enforce harsh legislation and the attempts of workers to meet their personal and family needs speaks directly to broader questions, namely, the limits to state coercion and the role of repression and fear in promoting mass participation in the war effort.[5]

Labor Turnover, Desertion, and Legal Constraints on Movement

In September 1944, N. A. Voznesenskii, head of Gosplan, a man accustomed to viewing reality above all through statistics, sent a letter to V. M. Molotov, L. P. Beria, G. M. Malenkov, and N. M. Shvernik in which he highlighted what seemed to be a strange conundrum. Between the creation of the Labor Reserve vocational training system in October 1940 and July 1, 1944, the Labor Reserves had sent almost 1.7 million young workers to jobs in industry and construction. However, according to the Central Statistical Administration employment returns, only 465,000 of the former trainees were still working. The numbers suggested a staggering attrition rate

Figure 7.1 Young turner in a defense factory in the Urals, 1942. Courtesy of
RGAKFD.

of 72.6 percent. The authorities were genuinely puzzled. Where were these
young workers?[6] Moreover, the same puzzle that emerged from the data on
vocational students was replicated for all mobilized workers. During 1942–
1944, the Labor Reserves, the Komitet, and the Commissariat of Defense
mobilized 5,771,800 workers. Yet during this same period, the number
of workers in industry, construction, and transport increased by only
1,820,000. In other words, the state had to mobilize more than three people
in order to add just one worker to the permanent workforce. The other two

had seemingly disappeared.[7] The problem was so pervasive that industrial commissariats, expecting high attrition rates, routinely inflated their requests for labor. The mortar industry, for example, estimated that, in order to add 12,000 extra workers during April–June 1944, it would need to mobilize 20,000.[8] There were many factors behind such large attrition. Workers died, became disabled, or were drafted into the army. Factories also surreptitiously hoarded extra workers to employ on essential tasks outside the labor plan dictated to them by Gosplan. And of course many workers simply fled their jobs to whereabouts unknown.

The legal clampdown on job-changing began a full year before the German invasion, at a time when, from the Soviet point of view, the war in Western Europe took an ominous turn. Following the Hitler–Stalin Nonaggression Pact, the Soviet press, while allegedly neutral, was in tone pro-German. In May 1940, after Hitler occupied the Netherlands and Belgium, and an attack on France became more imminent, this tone began to change.[9] Reporting grew increasingly wary of German actions. With the fall of France in June, the likelihood that Hitler would turn his attention eastward grew greater, and Soviet leaders substantially increased defense spending. Indeed, the Edict of June 26, 1940, which extended the working day from seven to eight hours and the work week from six to seven days, and criminalized lateness, absenteeism, and quitting one's job, was issued just a few days after France's defeat.

According to the edict, workers who left their job without the permission of enterprise management would, upon conviction by a People's Court, face a jail term of between two and four months. Anyone who was absent for more than twenty minutes without permission would be penalized by up to six months' corrective labor at their enterprise with loss of pay of up to 25 percent.[10] Given the need to retain workers, dismissal was not considered a useful penalty. On the contrary, the law plugged a loophole created by an earlier law of November 15, 1932, which required factories to fire a worker for even a single instance of unsanctioned absenteeism. Workers who did not wish to work for the period mandated after giving notice to quit or whose managers refused to release them would often intentionally be absent to force management to fire them. At the Frunze factory in Penza (factory No. 50), of the 10,378 workers who left the factory during 1940, 43 percent or 4,457 were dismissed for unsanctioned absence.[11] The June 1940 Edict made such tactics obsolete. Absenteeism was no longer penalized by dismissal but by a reduction in wages.

During the first months following the edict, the state had inordinate difficulties compelling managers and the courts to enforce it. Managers refused
to report truants, local prosecutors did not press charges, and judges handed
down acquittals or light sentences in contravention of the law. When trials
were held in People's Courts, rank-and-file workers disrupted the proceedings and shouted in defense of the accused. Resistance to the law persisted
until the end of the summer, at which point the state launched a harsh campaign against managers and judges, including putting some on trial. Only
then did enforcement "normalize" and convictions swell.[12] Between the
edict's promulgation in June 1940 and its de facto replacement by more
draconian penalties in December 1941, more than 636,000 workers and
white-collar employees were convicted of illegal quitting, and a staggering
3,253,000 were convicted of unauthorized absenteeism.[13]

On December 26, 1941, the state enacted even stricter legislation that effectively brought workers in the defense industry under military discipline.
Defense workers who quit their jobs without permission no longer faced a
brief jail sentence imposed by a People's Court but, rather, a trial before a
military tribunal and, upon conviction, between five and eight years in either a camp or a prison.[14] The edict initially covered the core defense industries of aviation, weapons, ammunition, mortars, tanks, shipbuilding, and
chemicals, along with their respective construction organizations. Between
1942 and 1944, the list of industries and enterprises steadily expanded to include medium-sized machine-building (primarily motor vehicle and coach-
building factories); nonferrous metallurgy; coalmining; oil; iron and steel,
textiles, and the electrical industry; copper smelting; paper and cellulose;
selected machine-tool factories; synthetic rubber; and gas.[15] In April and
May 1943, rail and then water transport were also militarized under a separate edict: transport workers who were more than two hours late to work
could be sentenced to between three and seven years in a labor camp; those
who left their jobs, or were absent for more than one day, faced three to ten
years in a labor camp, or an even harsher penalty (including execution) if
their actions resulted in an accident.[16] The less harsh Edict of June 26, 1940,
continued to govern absenteeism in all nontransport enterprises, as well as
illegal job-changing outside the defense sector. The differential punishments
were denoted by a change in language. Quitting a job in defense or transport was labeled labor "desertion"; leaving a job in other branches of the
economy continued to be described as "willful quitting." The wartime edicts
against labor desertion remained in force until well after the war ended.

The militarization of transport was lifted in March 1948, and the Edict of December 26, 1941, was finally repealed two months later.[17]

Wartime Convictions for Labor Desertion

Despite the harsh penalties for labor desertion, millions of people flouted the legislation and illegally quit their jobs. According to USSR Procuracy reports, between January 1, 1943, and November 30, 1944, almost 1.3 million people deserted their jobs in defense-related industry, the overwhelming majority of them workers. Taken together, the number of convictions for "desertion," "willful quitting," and absenteeism was large: just under 3.9 million during the first eighteen months of the Edict of June 26, 1940, and 4.7 million for the three full war years, 1942–1944 (see Table 7.1). Between 1941 and 1945, convictions under these laws accounted for nearly half of all criminal convictions in the USSR, most of these for absenteeism rather than desertion. Regardless of whether conviction was for the lesser or the greater offense, 28 percent of all those employed in the state sector ended the war with a criminal record as a result of these laws.[18] Penalties for absenteeism were hardly negligible. The loss of 25 percent of a paycheck for up to six months was serious enough, but in October 1942 the state punished absentees further with a cut in their bread ration: by 200 grams for those on an 800-gram ration, and by 100 grams for those on a lower ration.[19] During the six and one-half years in which the Edict of December 1941 was in force, a total of 1,157,992 people were convicted for labor desertion. Of these, 74 percent occurred during 1942 to 1944. Convictions during 1943 and 1944 accounted for about one out of every eight defense workers.[20] In addition to these figures, people were also tried and convicted under the Edict of February 13, 1942, for refusing or avoiding mobilization to work in industry or construction. A summons to appear for labor mobilization, like an order from a draft board, had to be obeyed. During 1942–1945, 21,786 people were convicted, almost all of whom were either sentenced to corrective labor at a workplace or received a conditional discharge; only 113 people received a custodial sentence.[21]

The number of convictions for labor desertion was high, but they provided a deceptive view of the reach and power of the state. The vast majority of people who fled the workplace either never went to trial, were not convicted at trial, or, if convicted, were never punished. Judicial enforcement proved ineffective and erratic, increasingly so as the war wore on. A large proportion of labor "deserters" escaped detection altogether. Prosecutors had so little information about them and their whereabouts that they could not hold a trial, even in absentia. Many deserters had their cases quashed at the pretrial stage due to mitigating circumstances or errors during investigation and, in a small number of cases, were acquitted. In the two years between January 1943 and December 1944, the Procuracy recorded 1,334,246 cases of labor desertion, of which just 52 percent resulted in conviction. Moreover, both the number and percentage of convictions fell over time. In 1943 there were 532,891 reported cases and 386,846 convictions—a conviction rate of 72.6 percent. During 1944, however, the number of reported cases increased by 50 percent, to 801,355, but total convictions fell to 310,258—a conviction rate of just 38.7 percent. If in 1943 just over a quarter of alleged offenders escaped conviction, in 1944, more than 60 percent did.[22]

A conviction, however, still did not guarantee that someone served a sentence. On the contrary, a striking percentage of those convicted never served a single day. The authorities were unable either to locate them or to bring them back, so they were tried and convicted in absentia. Having been convicted, they remained at large, entering the statistics as meaningless "convictions," testifying less to the power of the state than to the inefficacy of the police and judicial system. Between January 1942 and March 1944, only 40 percent of those convicted were actually apprehended and made to serve their sentence. The remaining 60 percent were never caught.[23] Of the 386,846 people convicted during 1943, only 154,738 were captured, or 40 percent of those convicted and only 29 percent of the 532,891 people originally reported as deserters. For 1944, assuming that the 40 percent "capture rate" remained stable beyond March, the authorities would have apprehended only 124,103 out of that year's 310,258 convictions, a mere 15.5 percent of the 801,355 reported deserters.[24] Thus the "capture rate" in 1944 was barely more than half that of 1943. In short, many workers understood that the likelihood of getting caught, convicted, and actually punished for labor desertion was slim, a fact that partially explained their willingness to risk such severe penalties (see Table 7.2). Finally, the number of reported cases underestimated the actual numbers of workers who ran away. Managers concealed their knowledge of runaway workers, never noticed their absence, or simply failed to report them. This was especially noticeable in 1944, when enforcement of the edict effectively broke down, leading to an amnesty of that December.

Application of the Wartime Labor Laws during 1942 and 1943

According to the law, if a worker failed to report for work and was absent for more than a few days, the factory had first to investigate the reasons. Yet, the very conditions that drove many workers to run away—lack of decent housing, heat, sanitation, food, clothing, and shoes—could also serve as mitigating circumstances to justify their actions. If it turned out that the worker had fled, the factory was required promptly to notify the local prosecutor, so that the latter could begin an investigation. Notification did not, however, automatically lead to prosecution. The prosecutor had to verify that the accused was indeed the person who had fled and that flight had actually occurred: the worker, for example, might have been drafted into the Red Army, taken sick, died, been mistaken for another with the same name, or had a legitimate reason to be absent. Yet assuming none of these possibilities was valid, the prosecutor had to find the worker who had run away. Without a body, the prosecutor could either drop the case or the military tribunal could try the deserter in absentia.

Even if the procuracy fulfilled all the formal conditions of investigation, and passed the case to a military tribunal, a more than one-in-five chance existed that the tribunal would either reject it or remand it for further investigation. The statistics told the story of the prosecutor's multiple challenges. Between January 1, 1942, and March 1, 1944, the Procuracy received 859,394 cases accusing workers or employees of deserting a military enterprise.[25] Of these, the Procuracy referred 75 percent to the military tribunals, and dropped the remaining quarter. Convictions by military tribunals tended to be almost automatic. Yet of the 645,827 cases sent for trial, the military tribunals convicted only 502,990. The rest, more than one-fifth of all those to be tried, were either sent back for further investigation, dismissed, or tried and acquitted.[26] In other words, fully 41.5 percent of all alleged "desertions" that factory directors forwarded to the Procuracy during this period failed to lead to conviction.

All of these various statistics reveal that the Edict of December 1941 was strikingly ineffective. Indeed, at every level of the process for identifying, locating, and punishing deserters, a combination of wartime chaos, benign indifference, and active antipathy to the law blocked its implementation. At the factory level, timekeepers and line managers often did not know who was working in their shops, where these workers lived, or how to distinguish workers with the same or like-sounding names. Large numbers of new arrivals, rapid expansion, and high turnover interfered with their ability to know the workers in their shops and maintain regular attendance records. In late 1942, the authorities had to abandon the prosecution of literally hundreds of workers, many of them from Central Asia, who openly admitted to having fled from factories in Cheliabinsk and other provinces, but could not or would not recall the factories' names or locations. For those who did name their workplaces, the identified factories had records for only a tiny number of the deserters. As a result, none of the workers was tried. The best the judicial authorities could do was to press local draft boards to remobilize them back into industry.[27]

Industrial managers, focused primarily on production, were not always eager to prosecute evaders and alienate the workforce, and local prosecutors, especially in rural areas, were disinclined to take on cases of dubious validity or anger local constituents. The prewar experience of the Edict of June 26, 1940, had already exposed the potential problems. Numerous managers, local prosecutors, and People's Court judges questioned the economic rationality of the law and either acted to subvert it or tolerated those who did. Their prevarications were no doubt reinforced by the overt hostility that the edict produced among ordinary workers. It was only when the state retaliated by shaming, firing, and even prosecuting lax officials—including People's Court judges—that enforcement became more or less routine.[28] Managers and judicial authorities faced similar dilemmas when confronted with the much harsher penalties of the December 1941 Edict. Some, fearful of being accused of being too liberal, referred any case where there was even a suspicion of "desertion," "willful quitting," or absenteeism for prosecution. Such self-protection also carried risks, as was most clearly evidenced in the case of absenteeism. Already by mid-1943, around a quarter of all Soviet workers and employees had received convictions for absence without permission, which caused considerable alarm among leading labor and judicial officials. A joint appeal from Shvernik, the head of the Komitet, V. M. Bochkov, Chief Prosecutor of the USSR, P. G. Moskatov, the head of the Labor Reserves, N. M. Rychkov, Commissar of Justice, and F. M. Butov, deputy head of the Central Committee's Personnel Administration, to Molotov, blamed managers for being too quick to refer cases without investigating the circumstances and criticized the People's Courts for their perfunctory rulings. They wrote:

> As a result of these distortions a significant number of innocent people
> are being made subject to judicial repression for *progul* [absenteeism],

including cadre workers who have worked for many years at one and the same enterprise and have shown a conscientious attitude toward their work, a fact which undoubtedly weakens the struggle against genuine disorganisers of labor discipline.

The fault, according to the authors, lay with enterprise directors who "don't trouble themselves with the need to investigate carefully the real causes of *progul* and take upon themselves no responsibility for deciding whether or not these reasons are warranted." They also stressed that many workers were absent "not due to malice or criminal negligence" but because of difficult living and working conditions, "something which not only factory directors, but also People's Courts sometimes find no need to take into consideration."[29]

The authors no doubt had in mind cases such as one cited by the Komsomol, in which a girl working underground at a coalmine missed work for nine days because she had no shoes. Her foreman, who had expressly forbidden her to work barefoot, then had her prosecuted for absenteeism.[30] Similar concerns surrounded unwarranted prosecutions for labor desertion. A draft of a decree from the Central Committee attacked managers for bringing cases against workers who were transferred from one shop to another within the same factory, joined the Red Army, were recovering from illness, or were already dead. Managers ignored family circumstances that might compel workers, especially women, to miss work. In one instance, a woman at Moscow's Stalin motor vehicle factory received five days' leave from her manager to care for her wounded brother and sick father in Orel province. Knowing full well she could not complete the round trip in five days, he prosecuted her for desertion as soon as she returned to the factory.[31] The dilemma for managers was that, if they took workers' actual circumstances into account, and treated cases with empathy and common sense, they could quickly find themselves on the wrong side of the law. During the brief crackdown of mid-1944 some of those accused of excessive softness received heavy Gulag sentences for "concealing deserters." These conflicting pressures and fears explain in part why managers sent so many borderline or unwarranted cases to the local procuracy or military tribunals.

In May 1943, S. G. Berezovskaia, a member of the USSR Procuracy's General Oversight Department, analyzed a series of cases from Ivanovo province, a textile region. The textile factories became subject to the Edict of December 1941 only in October 1942. The immediate impact of the law was a drop in the number of cases of illegal quitting, but the numbers soon began rising again.

Between January 1 and April 30, 1943, managers referred to the province or district prosecutors 2,436 cases of alleged desertion. During this time, military tribunals heard 1,574 cases, either at full trial or at preliminary hearings, but sent a quarter of these back to the Procuracy for further investigation. In doing so, the tribunals cited such legal technicalities as missing personal documents; lack of information about previous convictions; failure to locate the accused at their place of residence; and lack of communication with the accused about the punishment prosecutors would seek at trial. But the point of most concern to Berezovskaia was the failure of procuracy investigators to determine whether there were extenuating circumstances that might have compelled a worker to break the law. While Berezovskaia argued that the tribunals were wrong to hold up cases for legal technicalities, extenuating circumstances, such as lack of clothing, shoes, or childcare, were legitimate reasons to reject a case. She derided enterprise directors for their "extremely formal, indeed bureaucratic approach when deciding requests by one or another woman worker to be released from her job." And she noted that women's family circumstances often required them to seek permission to leave. The proper response was not punishment but "an offer of major assistance." She wrote, "The consequence of such a formal attitude to these women's requests is that they willfully leave their jobs. Procuracy agencies, receiving case materials on women workers who have willfully quit in this manner, refuse to instigate criminal proceedings, which creates the impression that willful quitters are going unpunished." Berezovskaia thus shifted the blame from workers and prosecutors to managers who refused to acknowledge legitimate requests to be released from work. Women, especially those with husbands at the front, often bore sole responsibility for ill relatives and children, and had no choice but to leave work to care for them. Local procuracy officials were right not to proceed with these cases, but the impact was nonetheless dangerous insofar as it gave workers the idea that they could leave their jobs without fear of judicial reprisal.[32] In short, Berezovskaia understood the difficult position prosecutors occupied: responsible for enforcing the laws on wartime discipline and, at the same time, being attuned to the pressures workers faced. Her solution was to encourage managers to select the cases they chose to prosecute more carefully.

Indeed, judicial authorities throughout the country were unsure how rigorously to apply the December 1941 Edict. Military tribunals in the Volga region rejected a number of cases from defense factories when they discovered extenuating circumstances. In one case, a male worker at factory No. 204, a munitions plant in Kotovsk, Tambov province, requested permission to return to his collective farm to fetch warm clothing and footwear. His foreman refused his request, but he went home nonetheless. Although he returned to his job a week later, management prosecuted him for labor desertion. The tribunal threw the case out. In another case, a group of workers on a construction site received no pay, housing, or food for three months. Instead of bread, site managers provided raw flour. After the workers ran away and the local prosecutor brought charges, the military tribunal upbraided the Procuracy for having ignored the dire conditions that prompted the workers to flee.[33] These and similar cases revealed a system beset, even paralyzed, by a welter of contradictions. Strict adherence to a law that proved difficult to enforce, coupled with harsh underlying conditions that prompted repeated violation, placed prosecutors and judges in an untenable position. Many were keenly sensitive to mitigating circumstances and were reluctant to punish workers who were the sole support of the household, whose husbands were at the front, who had to care for ill children or disabled dependants, or who lacked clothing, housing, footwear, or food. The Procuracy at all levels cited these factors as legitimate reasons for absenteeism, and, to a lesser extent, for illegal quitting.[34] At the same time, prosecutors understood that, regardless of their inclinations, they were responsible for enforcing the law and would be held accountable for the gap between the large number of runaways and the relatively small number of actual convictions.

Flight from the Labor Reserve Schools

The plight of teenagers mobilized, mostly from rural areas, into vocational schools far from home was similar to that of mobilized workers, although the teenagers were far less equipped to deal with separation from their families.[35] With few exceptions, conditions in all the vocational schools were grim, especially during the early years of the war, and students often fled from them en masse. Evasion frequently began as soon as the teenagers received a summons. Youngsters were dragged from hiding places in attics and cellars by the militia or local party officials. The state responded by arresting parents whose children failed to report for mobilization. One fourteen-year-old girl, who was actually below the legal minimum age for conscription, recalled her experience:

> If a person didn't show up, their father or mother, whoever was at home, was taken to a prison and held there until their daughter put in an appearance.

They forced you, as though it was a military draft. I wanted to hide, lived at my aunt's for a week. Mother came one day, crying ... I had nothing to wear, and Kirov was ten kilometres away. Halfway there my shoes fell apart. I tied them together with a piece of rope and walked on ... it was autumn and very muddy. And if you don't go, they will take you to court. Some lads ran away and received six-month sentences. They enrolled me in a FZO, found me new shoes size 40 (for a girl of fourteen).[36]

Although many avoided mobilization or fled the convoys, most obeyed the summons for mobilization and enrollment. During 1941–1944, the FZO managed to mobilize between 80 and 90 percent of their planned callup; the RU and ZhU fared even better, and in 1942 actually exceeded their plan by nearly 30 percent. The real problems for the schools began after the students arrived. Virtually all had difficulty retaining students. An inspection of Labor Reserve schools in the Volga region, carried out in early 1943 by V. S. Tadevosian, head of the Juvenile Section of the USSR Procuracy, and Smoliakov, an official in the Commissariat of Justice, claimed that the schools in Kuibyshev province were losing a minimum of between 10 and 25 percent of every quarterly or semi-annual intake. They warned, however, that school records were so slipshod and incomplete it was not possible to know the true figure.[37] Retention proved most difficult in 1942, when conditions in the schools were at their worst: more than 35 percent of all students enrolled in the FZO failed to complete their training and move to a job.[38] Not all these students ran away, but many did. FZO training courses ran for three to six months, and the schools accepted a new cohort every three or four months. Some 27 percent of the students in the FZO in Sverdlovsk province ran away in September 1942, and an additional 36 percent left in October, totaling almost two-thirds of their quarterly intake. The FZO in Cheliabinsk province shared the same dismal record: 29.5 percent of their students ran away in September 1942 and another 24 percent in October.[39]

Conditions in FZO No. 14 in Saratov in December 1942 illustrated the difficulties schools had with attrition. Of the 352 students the school admitted in August 1942, almost half fled within a month. Another seventy-one were either excluded for disciplinary violations or transferred to other schools, so that by September just over a third of that cohort remained. Conditions were bleak: the dormitories and classrooms were freezing cold, and many of the windows had no glass. Students slept in their street clothes and overcoats because their beds lacked sheets, pillows, pillowcases, and blankets. Unable to bathe, they were filthy and infested with lice. The food was inadequate in quantity and quality; even potatoes and cabbage were rarities.[40]

In addition to the hardships of work and daily life, the state created new difficulties when it ordered the transfer of teenagers in juvenile corrective labor colonies and homeless and unsupervised children on the streets to Labor Reserve schools in the fall of 1942 and again in the summer of 1943.[41] Between 1943 and 1945, local militias sent more than 100,000 of these teenagers to Labor Reserve schools in the hope they would learn a skill.[42] The delinquents released from the colonies created serious discipline problems in the schools. During the first three months of the new policy, the Labor Reserve schools in Sverdlovsk province, for example, took in 1,791 freed delinquents, of whom 270 ran away, and another 360 were rearrested for new offenses. FZO No. 1 in Gor'kii received 223 delinquents from juvenile corrective labor colonies, of whom fully 60 percent absconded. The schools of Cheliabinsk province had a similar record.[43] The teenagers from the streets and the colonies were sent to the schools without shoes or clothing, and they were sometimes physically abused by the staff when they arrived.[44] The deliquents not only worsened the retention rates of the schools with their own propensity to flee, but their habits of heavy drinking, fighting, theft, and physical bullying had an allegedly "demoralizing" effect on the other students. Procuracy officials claimed that they often so terrorized the rural recruits that many of the latter fled.[45] Finally, many of the teenagers, especially from the countryside, were frightened by the conditions they witnessed in the eastern industrial towns. The factories were cold, crowded, and chaotic. Vocational students from the collective farms were overwhelmed by the lack of ventilation, noise, and dangerous machinery. They noticed that many workers were hungry, and some suffering from starvation disease. The cities, locked in the grip of wartime shortage, were filthy, dark, and grim. Frightened by what they witnessed and experienced, many fled home. In 1943, conditions in the schools began to improve, and those students who did their practical training in the factories, as opposed to the schools themselves, often benefited from the tutelage and generosity of older workers, who helped them improve their skills and increase their production.[46] Incentives to run away diminished, and turnover from the schools dropped considerably.[47]

Authorities took a markedly different attitude toward prosecuting Labor Reserve students than they did toward labor deserters. The Labor Reserve system came under a separate, prewar set of rules. As with workers, it was illegal for vocational students to quit their schools without official authorization, yet teenagers were never subjected to the same harsh penalties as adults. According to the Edict of December 28, 1940, vocational students who ran away faced a penalty of one year in a juvenile corrective labor colony. This penalty remained unchanged throughout the war years and applied even to Labor Reserve schools that were attached to defense factories.[48] In sharp contrast to the laws against quitting and absenteeism by workers, the number of convictions was small, just 50,179 between January 1941 and December 1945. Of these, nearly a quarter (23.8 percent) received a noncustodial sentence, either corrective labor at the student's original place of work, or a conditional discharge.[49]

Authorities in the Labor Reserves were at odds with the USSR Procuracy over whether, and under what circumstances, to apply the criminal penalties set down in the Edict of December 28, 1940. Local procuracy, militia, and state and party officials were often unwilling to take any action against runaways at all, while some highly placed officials in the USSR Procuracy favored a policy of automatic prosecution. A procuracy report from late 1942 or early 1943 on enforcement of the December 1940 Edict in the Urals complained that the "unprincipled, illegal, and harmful policy" of merely returning runaways to the schools from which they fled encouraged more young people to run away, undermined discipline in the schools, and "created unhealthy attitudes" among the population at large. The report was not wrong. Letters from runaways found at the schools encouraged their friends who remained to follow their lead and return to the village, assuring them that there was no danger of prosecution. Students received similar letters from their parents.[50] The report urged that the runaways be punished in accordance with the law. The policy of the Labor Reserves, on the other hand, was not to prosecute runaways, but to track them down and return them to the schools. Moskatov, the head of the Labor Reserves, cautioned at an October 1942 session of its Collegium, "Don't forget, to hand a young boy over to the courts is the highest measure of punishment you can give him. He goes to court, they stick him in a camp, and there he meets recidivists, criminal elements. So he already starts to learn how to climb through windows, and the like."[51] In line with this approach, the Labor Reserves encouraged the schools and local Labor Reserves administrations to send representatives to the localities to locate runaway students, round them up, and return them to the schools. The main complaint of the Labor Reserves was not that local procuracy officials were too keen to prosecute, but rather that they refused to help round up the runaways and return them.

Yet the main problem facing officials from the Labor Reserves and the Procuracy, regardless of their approach, was the extreme difficulty they faced in recovering rural students who fled home. Local soviet and party officials, as well as local prosecutors, were reluctant to help round students up and, indeed, did much to obstruct their return. A member of the Moscow City Administration of Labor Reserves discussed this problem at its Collegium in December 1942:

> The return of those who have willfully abandoned their studies is proceeding very slowly. In all cases where teenagers who left had been called up from the provinces, the schools have dispatched staff to try to ensure their return. In October they sent twenty-two people, in November twenty-four; however, this did not produce much of a result. Local district executive committees, party organizations, and the Procuracy take no genuine action to return them. Beside this, some of the teenagers who willfully fled have been mobilized a second time in their localities and been sent to other provinces; some have volunteered for the Red Army; others, together with the [general] population, have been resettled away from territories near the front; and so on.[52]

Railway militia, preoccupied with more pressing concerns than policing teenagers, also tended to ignore the runaways picked up during the periodic roundups of homeless and unsupervised children, As the Gor'kii provincial procurator noted, "Often the railway militia just put them on a train and send them back. But everyone knows they don't go back. They hang around the stations and add to the ranks of homeless waifs."[53]

Urban prosecutors, especially in the eastern industrial towns, tended to take a stricter line toward runaways, often seeking prosecution even when painful extenuating circumstances existed. Deeply invested in maintaining the Labor Reserve schools and production at the factories, they differed from their rural counterparts, who were more aware of the difficulties of rural families and needs of the collective farms.[54] The collective farms, having lost the bulk of their draft power and men of working age, wanted their young people back. So great was the shortage of horses, it was not uncommon for women to harness themselves up to harrows and plows and pull them through the fields.[55] Collective farm managers tried to protect their strongest youth from mobilization and replace them with teenagers who were ill and disabled, in the hope they would be rejected and returned.[56] They were also not above encouraging the teenagers to run away and hiding those who returned to the village. In this way, rural and urban prosecutors, managers, and collective farm chairmen reflected the larger, intensifying tussle between industry and agriculture over labor.

This conflict was graphically illustrated by the travails of RU No. 9 in Molotov province. The school's deputy director, a woman named Litovskikh, wrote a detailed report to the USSR Procuracy in December 1943 describing her experience of trying to retrieve a large group of runaway students who had fled her school back to their homes in Dzerzhinskii district in the eastern corner of Smolensk province. RU No. 9 was located almost 1,250 miles (2,000 km) to the east in Chusovoi, a grim industrial center in Molotov province that was home to a large iron and steel works.[57] Along with the rest of Smolensk province, Dzerzhinskii district, about 93 miles (150 km) southwest of Moscow, had been occupied by the Germans early in the war. The province was fully liberated by September 1943, but some of its eastern areas had been freed earlier in the spring. As in all newly liberated areas, the survivors were incorporated into the wartime labor system and subject to mobilization. The teenagers in Dzerzhinskii district were mobilized to Labor Reserve schools in Kuibyshev province in the middle Volga region, Sverdlovsk and Molotov provinces in the Urals, and Novosibirsk province in Western Siberia. According to Litovskikh, in December 1943, Dzerzhinskii district was sheltering roughly 400 runaways from these regions. She further alleged that the "overwhelming" share of runaways from Molotov province were hiding in Smolensk province. As far as her own school was concerned, Litovskikh maintained that Dzerzhinskii district was the runaways' primary destination.

In June 1943, Litovskikh's school mobilized a group of 300 fourteen- and fifteen-year-olds, 36 of whom subsequently fled back to Dzerzhinskii district. The problem began to engulf the entire school, however, when the parents of the mobilized teenagers began writing letters, over collective signatures, to the directors of Labor Reserve schools throughout Molotov province asking them to grant their children temporary leave to return home. They also sent requests to the militia in these localities to arrange passes for the children to travel the long distance by train. Their letters were clearly part of a coordinated effort. At the same time, the teenagers began to receive "summonses" (*vyzovy*) from the chairmen of their village soviets and collective farms, requesting their return home to help with agricultural work. Chairmen also sent letters to the school directors, listing the students whom they wanted released. Finally, parents wrote to the teenagers citing changed family circumstances (disabled or ill parents, large families in need) that required the teenagers to return home. Some of the letters even gave advice on how to run away. All this caused considerable unrest among the students, who announced that they would be extremely angry if the schools did not release them.

With encouragement from so many quarters, many teenagers soon made their own way back to Dzerzhinskii district. Once they returned, village authorities immediately issued them documents certifying that they either had jobs on collective farms or were back in school, while those among them who were not part of a collective farm received ration cards and internal passports. The local authorities ignored every request to return the teenagers and concealed the fact that such requests had ever been received. When the Labor Reserve schools drew up paperwork to pursue the runaways under the Edict of December 28, 1940, most of the documents were returned, with a note from the head of the village soviet, "Doesn't live in this village." According to Litovskikh, this may have been true; local officials simply moved the runaways from one village to another in the same district.

Some cases did land in People's Court, but were heard only after long delays, and then not under the December 1940 Edict. A few sentences were imposed, then suspended, and finally forgotten. Indeed, not a single runaway returned. The Labor Reserve schools sent their own representatives to Dzerzhinskii district to bring back the runaways, but when they arrived they received no assistance from local authorities. Meanwhile, the runaways sent letters back to their friends in the Labor Reserve schools explaining that they were now living at home, suffering no penalty, and urging them to run away. Litovskikh herself made the long and exhausting trip to Dzerzhinskii district in October 1943 to retrieve the runaways from her own school. When she informed the local procuracy and village soviets of her mission, twelve students, some with their parents, showed up at district procuracy headquarters. Three categorically refused to return, boldly proclaiming that they would not work in the factory, that nothing would happen to them, and that if they went on trial they would receive only a suspended sentence. They seemed to have an accurate, albeit brazen view of the current state of law enforcement. In fact, these three, penalized perhaps for their outspokenness, became the objects of a highly publicized show trial in October, and were convicted under the Edict of December 28, 1940, although it is not clear that they were ever sent to a juvenile labor colony. The remaining nine teenagers pledged in writing to return. However, before their scheduled departure date a second trial of runaways from another Labor Reserve school was held, which ended in a conditional discharge. The original nine promptly changed their minds and never reported for return. As for the rest of the runaways from Litovskikh's school, none of them bothered to go to the local procuracy office. Their village soviets continued to shield them, and no one attempted to locate, return, or prosecute them.

During her visit, Litovskikh made heroic organizational efforts to reclaim her students. She organized a meeting with the chairmen of the village soviets and collective farms, and provided them with lists of the students. She explained that she had booked a carriage on a train and that the teenagers should be ready to leave in two days' time. On the appointed day, however, no one showed up. Instead she was handed numerous parcels from parents of teenagers still attending the Labor Reserve schools, which she graciously agreed to deliver. The students, she claimed, were so grateful that they later boosted their production output. But the train came and left without either Litovskikh or the runaway teenagers.

District officials understood that, although they had done nothing to help Litovskikh locate or round up the teenagers, they had to appear responsive to her efforts. The heads of the district soviet and the local NKVD thus told the district prosecutor, one very reluctant Orlov, to order the runaway teenagers to return. Orlov, citing lack of permission from his boss, the Smolensk provincial prosecutor, Bakharov, did nothing. Bakharov in turn brusquely rebuffed all of Litovskikh's protestations. Only when Litovskikh threatened to go over his head to the USSR Procuracy did Bakharov phone Orlov and tell him to issue the order. Orlov, careful to appear to be in compliance with the letter of the law, advised Litovskikh to prosecute the runaways under the December 1940 Edict, knowing perfectly well that it was the school's policy not to prosecute because it saw no benefit in putting large numbers of children in jail. Rejecting Orlov's advice, Litovskikh turned to the USSR Procuracy, which issued her a directive to take directly to Orlov. Finally Orlov acceded and wrote to the local NKVD head, telling him to round up the teenagers on Litovskikh's list and bring them to the district procuracy office.

On November 19, one month after the original departure date had come and gone, twenty-eight teenagers arrived to accompany Litovskikh. Four others failed to turn up and disappeared from their homes. The teenagers were supposed to spend a night in the local hotel and leave the following day. The journey was complicated: the group would travel by train to Kaluga, and from there to Moscow, where they would then drive by truck across Moscow to another railway station to board a train east to the Urals. The children would also need food for their journey. In order to complete these arrangements Litovskikh had to travel to Moscow, leaving the local prosecutor, NKVD, and militia in charge of taking the teenagers from the hotel room to the train. Yet as soon as Litovskikh departed, the plans collapsed. The teenagers refused to leave, and Orlov sent them home. All of Litovskikh's efforts to arrange local transport, accommodation, train tickets, and food came to naught. The journey to the Urals was canceled.

Orlov, who had done everything in his power to undermine the spirit of the law, took refuge in its letter. He claimed he was trapped in a legal loophole. Because Litovskikh had declined to prosecute the runaways under the Edict of December 1940, he had no legal means to hold them. Nor could he have prosecuted them under the edict, because he had not received the necessary legal documentation from the school. Indeed, Orlov was correct. He had no power to force the teenagers to return to school or to prosecute them. His superior finally advised him to issue separate orders for each student, interrogate them, refer the cases to court, and organize a show trial of two or three runaways, which presumably would convince the rest to return voluntarily. Orlov then ordered the head of the local NKVD to round up the teenagers one more time and bring them back to the Procuracy. In the meantime, he disappeared on "other business." The NKVD officer dutifully toured the district, gathered the teenagers, and brought them back, only to find that Orlov was gone. He promptly released the teenagers, who once again disappeared. Whether or not Orlov ever staged a trial or Litovskikh succeeded in bringing a single runaway back to the Urals is unknown. The story's ending was in keeping with its long and frustrating plot. Its message in any case was clear: neither local prosecutors, soviet representatives, NKVD officials, nor collective farm chairmen had any desire to return runaways to distant schools or work sites when they were desperately needed by their families and the depleted collective farms. Even the most dogged administrator of a vocational school was likely to return empty-handed.

While Litovskikh's misadventures were unusually well documented, the failure of her efforts was common. In weapons factory No. 88 in Kaliningrad, Moscow province, in mid-1944, the workforce was made up almost exclusively of young workers taken from various sources, and turnover was very high. The efforts of the factory's union committee to locate and return runaways met the same local intransigence that Litovskikh described. The head of the factory's union committee wrote:

> One of our comrades traveled down to Kamskii district in Moscow prov-ince, and wrote: "Having arrived in the district, I turned for help to the dis-trict prosecutor and the secretary of the Komsomol district committee. On May 11, I handed over materials to initiate proceedings under the Edict of December 26 [1941]. On May 15, the procurator summonsed eleven people. Only one of them, Kurochkina, showed up. After this I traveled down into the district and established that all eleven of them were living at home. I then went to Spasskii district. There the chair of the district soviet, who knew about these deserters, declared, 'we need these people ourselves, the spring sowing's just started and we've got nobody to work on the col-lective farm.'" Gathering her information on the whereabouts of all those who had deserted to Spasskii district, the comrade went to the procurator with the aim of taking decisive measures. The prosecutor once again issued a summons for [the deserters] to appear on May 19. But nothing came of it. After this our comrade came back to the factory.

In this case, the head of the union committee provided a clear-eyed assess-ment of the "help" he received from the close, interlocking network of local officials in the soviets, procuracy, and party. He explained:

> This just goes to show how certain prosecutors, instead of helping the fac-tory to call the guilty to account, shield those district soviet executive com-mittee chairs and secretaries of district party committees, who know full well that deserters are living in their districts and draw no conclusions from this fact.[58]

1944: The Failure of Repression

By 1944, the scale of labor desertion had increased enormously, and its geo-graphic location broadened to include the liberated territories. The attitudes of workers as well as judicial officials changed. With the end of the war now in sight, people became restive. Everyone longed for normality. Mobilized workers wanted to go home. The number of reported "desertions" in 1944 increased by 55 percent over 1943. As the Red Army liberated more territory, some evacuated workers were sent home, while others in the liberated territories were mobilized to work in both the newly freed western provinces and the eastern industrial towns. Great movements and countermovements of people crisscrossed the country. "Special contingents" composed of those suspected of disloyalty and collaboration, repatriated but dubious Soviet prisoners of war, and distrusted groups in the Baltic republics and parts of Finland were mobilized for work in the Urals and Siberia.

These vast population deployments both increased the number of people who wanted to flee their jobs and heightened the chaos inherent in transfer and resettlement. In 1942 and 1943, the motivations behind labor desertion were closely linked to harsh conditions and difficult family circumstances. Yet most workers, whether mobilized or not, stayed at their jobs. Evacuated workers felt strong loyalty to their enterprise, coworkers, and managers, and older workers made conscientious efforts to teach and guide the young vocational graduates. By 1944, however, many workers had grown impatient with the mobilization of labor and the freeze on job-changing. Evacuated workers, Central Asian herders, collective farmers, teenagers, and others mobilized to distant sites all longed to return home. The Red Army was winning, the western provinces were being slowly freed of occupation, and the sense of emergency and duty that had animated people earlier began to dissipate. Local militia, NKVD, and judicial and soviet officials were all eager to be rid of the burden of labor mobilization and its enforcement. Many authorities recognized that the entire system, so effective in building the eastern industrial base, was beginning to collapse under the weight of its own contradictions.

As a result, desertions accelerated. In both 1943 and 1944, they peaked from July to September. The warmer weather made it easier to run away, and this was the time when the collective farms were most in need of labor. In the summer of 1943, 161,264 workers were reported by their managers to have fled; during the same period in 1944 the number almost doubled.[59] The increase was driven mainly by mobilized workers. The legal authorities insisted that the bulk of labor deserters were teenagers, rather than the mobilized workforce as a whole. Yet this was a convenient fiction that allowed them to skirt the systemic nature of the problem: namely, the growing failure of labor mobilization. It was true that the percentage of teenagers convicted for desertion was considerably greater than their share of the industrial workforce as a whole, but even at the highest point, teenagers never made up more than 30 percent of labor deserters. The state was invested enough in this notion, however, that it redefined "young" workers to include people up to the age of twenty-five, although anyone of that age had probably been working in either agriculture or industry for at least ten years. Reclassification allowed authorities to demonstrate that a majority of deserters were "young," but did not solve the social and structural problem.[60] The issue was not "youth" but mobilization. Local workers had little incentive or opportunity to flee. They had homes and families, dependants to look after, and often a private plot on which to grow food. They also had nowhere to run to. Mobilized workers, on the other hand, endured the worst conditions. Separated from their families and far from home, these workers were an intrinsically unstable element, yet the state relied heavily on them to staff its factories, mines, and construction sites.

Not all the hemorrhage of workers was due to desertion. A substantial percentage of workers died or had to leave their jobs due to ill health. In 1943, the iron and steel industry, which saw nearly 15 percent of its workers desert their jobs, lost another 10 percent of its entire workforce to death and illness, and 4 percent to the Red Army; another 5 percent received legal permission to leave. In all, iron and steel factories lost around 40 percent of their workforce in both 1943 and 1944, a figure that was common across a range of industries. All of these workers had to be replaced through mobilization.[61] In 1944, these losses created a genuine crisis for the economy. Turnover among the newly mobilized could be so high as virtually to nullify the effort and cost of rounding up and transporting people to distant sites. During the first half of 1944 the ammunition industry lost 3,000 more workers than it hired; nearly 8 percent of its entire workforce deserted (not just the new arrivals). From January to May the armaments industry lost three out of every four new workers, and here, too, 8 percent of all its workers fled. Figures from individual factories were even more striking. Ammunition factory No. 63 in Nizhnii Tagil hired 507 workers but lost 1,589, of whom 460 deserted and 174 died of starvation. Ammunition factory No. 50 in Penza, where one-third of all workers suffered from starvation, hired 2,459 workers, but lost 2,586, including 1,633 deserters. The Komitet refused to send any more workers to either of these factories until conditions improved. Armaments factory No. 8 in Sverdlovsk, and ammunition factories No. 259 in Zlatoust and No. 557 in Moscow, saw more workers flee than they hired; turnover simply dwarfed the number of new arrivals.[62] Turnover in the tank industry showed a similar pattern. During the period June–August 1944, tank factories, including the giant Uralmash factory in Sverdlovsk and the Kirov works in

Cheliabinsk, hired 14,762 workers, and lost 14,370. Of those who left, the overwhelming majority (9,062) deserted.[63] Between January and September 1944, Uralmash, probably the most important factory in Sverdlovsk, with more than 18,000 workers, hired 4,362 new workers and lost 4,262, giving it a net gain of just 100 workers. Two-thirds of those who left either deserted or exited the workforce due to death or illness. Starvation took a heavy toll on the workforce in Uralmash, and workers were increasingly unwilling to remain under conditions of great strain.[64] At the Kirov factory in Cheliabinsk, turnover in some shops during the winter and spring of 1944 reached an annual rate of more than 100 percent, and even the most stable shops lost the equivalent of a quarter of their workforce a year. The Cheliabinsk city procuracy claimed that the high rate of desertion was directly linked to the mobilization of disabled war veterans and young workers from the liberated territories. The work was heavy and dirty, and beyond the physical capabilities of the newly mobilized workers, many of whom were elderly and, in the words of the procuracy, "totally emaciated."[65] Starvation mortality in Cheliabinsk was even higher than in Sverdlovsk, accounting for roughly 30 percent of all deaths in the city in 1943 and 1944.[66] As the war neared its end, the workforce was becoming weaker and an ever larger percentage of those mobilized were already starving, disabled, or otherwise too frail to do factory work.

High rates of desertion among the newly mobilized, most acute in the Urals, affected enterprises everywhere. Between October 1943 and September 1944, the textile industry, which manufactured cloth for the military, hired 81,659 workers, but lost 71,500. Nearly a quarter of those who left quit illegally. At Moscow's October Revolution textile factory, more than half the workers who arrived during 1944 ran away. Originally from Leningrad and Kalinin, these workers were mobilized earlier in the war to work in Udmurtiia and then transferred in 1944 to Moscow. Many took advantage of their new proximity to home to abandon the factory. The cumulative effect of these losses on the textile industry was severe. The Commissariat of the Textile Industry had planned to install new spinning equipment by May 1944, but as of September, five months after the anticipated installation, half of the new spindles were still not operational because factories did not have enough workers to run them.[67]

The reconstruction of the coalmines and iron and steel factories in the Donbass region of Ukraine also relied heavily on mobilized labor, mainly from other newly liberated, rural provinces. Here, too, rural officials selected people for mobilization who were infirm, underage, or lacking personal documents that would make them easier to trace.[68] During 1944, 45 percent of all those hired to rebuild and staff Donbass iron and steel factories deserted, a desertion rate only slightly worse than that of iron and steel in the interior regions. In the Donbass coalfields 70.9 percent of those hired during 1944 left their jobs, nearly half of whom "deserted." Desertion from the coalmines was highest at the start of the year. If the winter trend had continued throughout 1944, two coal trusts, Voroshilovugol' and Rostovugol', would have lost the equivalent of their entire workforce to desertion. By late summer, however, the situation began to stabilize, and desertion in the Donbass approached the coalmining national average of about 25 percent.[69]

As workers fled back to their home regions, factory managers, also acting in contravention of the law, were quick to hire them. Aviation factory No. 26, for example, had been evacuated from Rybinsk in Iaroslavl' province to Ufa (Bashkiriia) in 1941.[70] Between January and June 1944, 2,500 workers and other staff fled from the Ufa factory, many returning home to Rybinsk, where they took up jobs at a new factory on the site of their former workplace, where managers were eager to hire them. Eventually the authorities caught around thirty of these workers and discovered that they all had papers from the Ufa factory giving them temporary permission to travel on "a special mission." Armed with these documents, they had gone to Rybinsk and never returned. Managers at both factories colluded in this process. Rybinsk managers needed workers, and the managers in Ufa reported that their workers were missing only after a very long delay. When the Procuracy questioned shop foremen in Ufa, they responded, "Why should I report him to the Procuracy, he was given leave. So maybe suddenly he gets sick or dies." Managers in Ufa did send letters to some of the missing, indicating that they should return, but did not really expect them to do so. During the second half of 1944 this practice became widespread. Workers asked for unpaid leave under various pretexts and management acceded, knowing full well that a large percentage of them would never return.[71]

The state, however, was still heavily reliant on mobilized workers for the defense factories in the east and reconstruction of the newly liberated provinces in the west. Mass flight from the factories was threatening to undermine production at a time when the war was far from over. The state's initial response to the rising number of desertions in 1944 was to compel enforcement of the law by speeding up and setting time limits for investigation and trial. On June 29, 1944, the Soviet of People's Commissars ordered enterprise managers immediately to report cases of alleged "desertion" to their local procuracy, prosecutors to investigate and forward cases to military tribunals for trial within three days of receiving allegations, and the tribunals to conduct the trials no more than three days after receiving case materials from prosecutors. Most significantly, the decree banned in absentia trials.[72] The new decree was followed by a brief but intense flurry of activity. Managers, procuracies, and military tribunals rushed to clear their vast backlogs of cases and to refer cases to the Procuracy. The number of cases received by local prosecutors leapt from a monthly average of 56,540 for the period from January to March to 104,950 in July. Tribunals convicted more deserters: between January and June 1944, they convicted an average of 5,925 deserters each month; in July they convicted 12,384.[73] There was a brief but substantial surge in the number of deserters still at large who were tracked down and arrested.[74] For those workers unlucky enough to be caught, the results were tragic. The small number of deserters caught in Rybinsk, for example, received labor camp sentences of five to seven years.[75] Most striking was the sudden drop in the huge number of cases that had been put on hold due to the inability of the militia or Procuracy to determine the runaways' names and whereabouts. The USSR Procuracy proudly claimed that their local agents had cut the number of such cases from more than 209,000 in July to just 22,900 in August.[76]

Yet the flurry of energetic law enforcement soon subsided, and the claims of success proved wildly inflated, if not entirely mythical. The high rejection rate of the military tribunals actually increased. After the June decree, between July and November 1944, the tribunals sent back for further investigation 20.2 percent of the cases they had received from local procuracies, and either quashed, acquitted, or reclassified as a lesser offense an additional 3.8 percent, bringing their overall rejection rate up to 24.0 percent, even higher than in the period up to March.[77] Figures from the fifteen largest industrial regions of the RSFSR show that during this same period the authorities managed to arrest a mere 25 percent of newly reported desertion cases, while the number of deserters convicted but remaining at large once again began to rise.[78] More importantly, deserters had become a vital source of new workers in the factories, coalmines, and peat bogs of the western USSR. The decree now pitted new against former managers in the struggle to retain labor. In late July 1944, not even a month after the decree appeared, G. Toropov, Chief Prosecutor of the USSR Procuracy's General Oversight Department, reported that the militia had arrested more than 2,000 deserters working in the coalmining and peat-digging industries of Sumy province in Ukraine. These were not the only deserters in the region, merely the ones they caught. The applause for the militia, however, was brief. The party provincial committee immediately protested the arrests because the province's peat-digging enterprises turned out to be wholly reliant on workers who had fled from defense enterprises. If these workers were arrested, peat digging would have to shut down. Even worse, managers of the peat bogs had also been arrested for concealing deserters, an unacceptable consequence of the decree. The provincial party committee requested that the policy be relaxed and only "malicious deserters" (that is, people who had fled repeatedly and refused to work locally) be prosecuted. However, this was not the only question vexing Toropov. The USSR Procuracy knew that, if all prosecutions proceeded as they should, the military tribunals in Sumy province would be unable to cope with the sheer volume of cases.[79]

Sumy was a relatively small and economically insignificant province, but the issue of what to do with deserters who had taken other jobs affected the entire country. In August 1944, K. P. Gorshenin, the newly elevated procurator general of the USSR, wrote to Molotov proposing a change in policy. Gorshenin placed the emphasis not on deserters, but on a smaller subset of evaders to whom the state was likely to be more sympathetic: workers who deserted but then returned voluntarily to factories from which they fled. He offered the example of Stavropol' Territory, where local authorities had picked up 1,250 deserters as of July 20, 1944. These deserters were mostly young women, aged between seventeen and twenty-four, who had been mobilized from local collective farms for jobs in the Donbass, Stalingrad, the Urals, and Moscow province in early 1944. Several had been tried in absentia, but only after they had returned to the factories from which they had fled. According to the law, former deserters who went back to their workplace were still subject to the Edict of December 26, 1941, and, if convicted, subject to a lengthy term in prison or a labor camp. Gorshenin maintained that "local party and soviet bodies" did not see the sense of this. If a worker voluntarily returned to her or his original job or, after deserting, took a new job in the defense industry and worked there "conscientiously," to prosecute or execute an existing sentence for desertion would result in the loss of labor and discourage other workers from returning. Local party and state officials believed, and Gorshenin concurred, that such workers should be sent back to the enterprise from which they had absconded and, upon their arrival, the military tribunal there should alter their sentences to conditional discharge or reclassify the offense from "desertion" to absenteeism, penalized under the Edict of June 26, 1940, by a temporary reduction in pay.[80]

Molotov's response to Gorshenin's appeal was unknown. Yet some military tribunals began to act as if Gorshenin's suggestions had already become law. While some continued to apply the June decree vigorously, others either permitted deserters to remain at their new place of employment or offered lighter sentences to those who returned voluntarily. Armaments factory No. 92 in Gor'kii, for example, received a large contingent of workers mobilized from Stalingrad who were eager to return home after the city's liberation. The Gor'kii managers refused to release them, but all of the workers left anyway, and their home factory in Stalingrad readily hired them. When the Gor'kii managers protested, the province's military tribunal simply refused to prosecute, noting that the workers were all working conscientiously at their previous place of employment. Further appeals to the Stalingrad procuracy also got them nowhere. The workers stayed in Stalingrad.[81] Indeed, Gor'kii's military tribunal had moved well beyond Gorshenin's modest suggestions: it did not hand down a lighter sentence or insist on return, but rather simply ceased to prosecute or pursue deserters from its own province who found jobs in other places.

As summer 1944 gave way to fall and early winter, judicial practice spontaneously shifted away from the repressive philosophy of the June decree toward de facto acknowledgment that desertion—and the concealment of deserters—would continue so long as conditions drove mobilized workers to flee. Once again the procuracy reports began to stress the hardships for mobilized workers, and, in a few extreme cases, judicial authorities even prosecuted managers, who received heavy sentences for neglect and abuse.[82] At the same time, prosecutors and local officials failed to search for or locate those who ran away. People had been mobilized from every republic and province in the country, and local procuracy offices simply did not possess the staff, the means, or the reach to oversee searches stretching thousands of miles in every direction. Energetic prosecutors in Magnitogorsk, for example, sent out search orders to Udmurtiia, Stalinograd province in Kazakhstan, Odessa oblast in Ukraine, and Smolensk, Saratov, Tula, Rostov, Orel, Moscow, Tambov, and Kirov provinces in the RSFSR. None produced a deserter.[83] District prosecutors received scant cooperation from their colleagues, even when seeking deserters within their own or a neighboring province. In October 1944, the procuracy in the Kalinin district of Dzerzhinsk, the second-largest city in Gor'kii province, sent out nearly 150 search orders for deserters still known to be in the province, yet hardly any were found. Similarly, the prosecutor of Kopeisk city, in the heart of the Cheliabinsk coalfields, sent forty-six search orders for "deserters" in neighboring Kurgan province, but the Kurgan authorities failed to act on a single one. Not surprisingly, attempts to track down deserters farther afield in Odessa, Moldavia, and Orel met with the same spectacular lack of success.[84]

By every measure the June crackdown had been a failure. The decree of June 29 was, in effect, the state's last-ditch effort to stem illegal labor turnover and to enforce the mobilization and militarization of labor. The state had a choice: it could continue wasting scarce procuracy and militia resources in the fruitless hunt for labor deserters, or it could find a way to regularize their situation. On December 30, 1944, the state declared a limited amnesty for labor deserters who had thus far avoided capture or incarceration by granting total amnesty to any worker who had fled from an enterprise governed by the Edict of December 26, 1941, if they had already returned or returned voluntarily by February 15, 1945.[85] The edict made no mention of workers who had taken jobs elsewhere, and thus provided only limited recognition of the magnitude of desertion, the shifting mood of the workers, the Procuracy's own recommendations, or the actual practices of local prosecutors and officials. The aim of the amnesty was to encourage the many hundreds of thousands of still hidden deserters to return to the jobs from which they had fled. Yet this limited recognition persisted only for another six months. On July 7, 1945, in honor of the victory over Nazi Germany, the state declared a general amnesty for numerous crimes, including all those convicted under the Edict of December 26, 1941.[86] All criminal proceedings against labor deserters who had not yet been tried were halted, anyone already serving time under the edict was released, and the criminal record of all those convicted (imprisoned or not) was expunged. In short, on July 7, 1945, the balance of labor deserters was reset to zero. The Edict of December 26, 1941, however, remained in force, initiating a new round of fruitless pursuit and evasion. Postwar reconstruction saw the continuing mobilization of millions of workers, most of them young and from the countryside, to work in regions and industries where conditions were still extremely harsh. Given the terrible losses at the front, the great destruction wreaked by the Nazis, and the burgeoning Cold War, the state faced an urgent imperative to rebuild and rearm amid a sharp and ongoing shortage of labor. Labor desertion continued, but local prosecutors, officials, and militia, especially in rural areas, largely lost interest in pursuing errant workers. The cycle was broken only in

1948, when the state finally repealed the Edict of December 26, 1941, and its corresponding edicts governing rail and water transport.[87]

****

The strict wartime laws proved a weak bulwark against the driving imperatives of survival among workers and were never fully embraced by the authorities responsible for their enforcement. Managers, prosecutors, collective farm chairmen, and militia proved unable or unwilling to enforce the law at every stage from the first report of desertion, to the verification of identity and collection of evidence, to the location and return of the deserter. Their mounting reluctance in the face of rising numbers of deserters was a strong factor in the state's decision to issue a partial amnesty on December 30, 1944, and then a blanket amnesty on July 7, 1945. The response of officials was deeply affected by a shift in workers' mood. By 1944, people yearned to return home and were less willing to endure the horrific conditions in the dormitories and canteens.

Managers and local officials had their own interests, which encouraged them to overlook or even abet labor desertion. When managers reported a deserter this was as much for their own self-protection as out of a desire to enforce the law. If they reported cases, they often failed to provide prosecutors with sufficient information to proceed. In reality they found it easier to order new contingents from the Komitet than to pursue long and often pointless prosecutions. Prosecutors were stymied by poor record keeping in the factories and rural areas, as well as the vast territory from which workers had been mobilized. Collective farm chairmen and factory managers in the provinces to which workers returned welcomed the runaways by quickly putting them to work and quietly concealing them. Finally, the Procuracy, the organization on the front line of law enforcement, was riven by conflict at every level. Within the central apparatus, hardliners who insisted on its rigid application proved less powerful than more pragmatic leaders. At the local level, rural procuracy officials refused to cooperate with their urban colleagues. Prosecutors in one town ignored the search orders sent by those in another. Every official tried to protect the interests of his or her own domain, whether a village, a town, a collective farm, or an industrial enterprise.

At the root of all these conflicts lay the actions of the labor deserters, the "willful quitters," and the absentees. Their disobedience required the creation of a huge bureaucratic apparatus involving the police, the Procuracy, and civil and military courts to expend considerable time, energy, and resources to track, try, convict, and punish them. Much of this effort and expenditure was in vain. Wartime labor legislation proved more repressive on paper than in practice. Perhaps as many as 385,000 labor deserters served time in the Gulag, but this proved an ineffective deterrent.[88] Managers, overwhelmed by the chaos of labor mobilization, failed to report deserters or to forward sufficient details to prosecutors, who in turn failed to compile the information needed to pursue the cases. Military tribunals threw out any number of cases for lack of documentation or mitigating circumstances, or were forced to try people in absentia. Convictions resulting in capture were only a tiny fraction of the number of reported cases, which in turn were an even smaller fraction of the numbers who fled. Only 29 percent of those reported in 1943 were captured, and only 15.5 percent in 1944. Over these two years a mere 21 percent of reported runaways actually served a sentence.[89] If the saga of labor mobilization demonstrated the limits of the wartime state's control over labor, the fruitless pursuit of deserters was that saga's apotheosis. Workers, motivated by hunger, family circumstances, painful conditions, and, toward the war's end, the mounting desire to return home, flouted the harsh labor legislation in vast numbers. After years of hardship and patient endurance of wartime discipline, they carefully weighed the risks of return. Desertion, however, was never synonymous with a lack of support for the war. The vast majority of deserters quickly took jobs in their home provinces, either in industry or in agriculture, and continued to contribute to the war effort. Repression played a surprisingly small role in the willingness of Soviet workers to endure so much and contribute so mightily to the victory.

8

The Public's Health

I know now what a mistake I made coming to this hell. The hunger is terrible, and every day they carry eighteen or nineteen coffins out of the factory.

Mariia Pechenegovksaia, a Komsomol member mobilized
to work at the iron and steel plant in Zlatoust

The war saw a protracted mortality crisis among the country's civilian population. The movement of millions of refugees and evacuees through teeming railroad stations and in crowded boxcars with little access to sanitary facilities, clean water, or medical care created dangerous conditions for the development and spread of epidemics. Widespread hunger and nutritional deficits took a terrible toll on the health of people of all ages. Defense production exposed workers to new, toxic chemicals, and the combination of multiple factories within a single, poorly equipped structure posed serious risks to workers' safety. The war made unprecedented demands on the infrastructure of public health, posing extraordinary challenges to the control of epidemics, child mortality, starvation disease (*alimentarnaia distrofiia*), and occupational health. At the same time, health officials and medical staff lacked almost everything they needed to diagnose and treat the sick, the wounded, and the starving. The needs of ordinary people in the rear were subordinated to those of soldiers fighting at the front.

Doctors, nurses, and public health officials faced public health threats unknown in scale or intensity since the Civil War of 1918–1920. The majority of medical professionals were quickly drafted into the Red Army, leaving only a "skeleton staff" to cope with the mounting crises. Elena Skriabina, evacuated with her two children and elderly mother from Leningrad in early 1942, described the trail of filth and human excrement along the evacuation routes:

The stations and railroad line are especially dirty. Indeed, freight trains full of evacuees are moving without interruption; of course there are no latrines

on these trains and everything occurs en route, between the cars, and there
is no one to clean up.[1]

Yet unlike World War I and the Civil War, when Russia was engulfed by vast
epidemics of cholera, typhoid, and typhus along the refugee routes, public
health officials managed to contain the worst outbreaks of lice- and water-
borne diseases.[2] Despite a shortage of personnel, health practitioners and
officials worked diligently to establish basic procedures for disinfection that
meant the difference between life and death for millions.

Evacuation took an especially heavy toll on small children. The first major
killer was the measles epidemic that advanced from west to east along the
rail lines used for evacuation.[3] An even greater number of children died of
starvation, diarrhea, and pneumonia contracted during evacuation or soon
after arrival at their destination. Mary Leder, a young American communist
who was evacuated from Moscow to Engel's, described what happened to her
baby girl:

> Disaster struck. First it was pneumonia at the end of January. She was taken
> to the hospital and I stayed with her day and night until she pulled through.
> Then on February 12, she started breathing with difficulty. I recognized the
> signs of croup . . . With my child in my arms, I went on foot from one hos-
> pital to another . . . No room—the hospitals were overcrowded with war
> wounded. Finally, at the end of the day, a hospital admitted us and the doctor
> made the necessary incision. But it was too late. Four days later, on February
> 16, my daughter stopped breathing. She was seven months and fifteen days
> old. The death certificate gives diphtherial croup as the cause of death. But
> she was as much a casualty of the war as anyone who died in battle.[4]

Once evacuation was over, the new and much-feared epidemics did not
materialize despite extreme overcrowding, poor hygiene, and the lack of sanitation. Sanitary (public health) physicians employed by the State Sanitary
Inspectorate and other health workers managed to impose strict controls as
a result of the lessons they learned during evacuation and resettlement. Yet
just when the mortality crisis connected to the vast population movements
from west to east had subsided, a new danger emerged: hunger and malnutrition. Starvation deaths were already noticeable in 1942, but in 1943 and 1944
starvation and tuberculosis—a disease highly sensitive to malnutrition—
together became the largest single contributor to nonchild mortality.

Moreover, for every death caused directly or indirectly by starvation, many more people suffered serious debility, although they did not die. Starvation and hunger heightened the impact of chronic diseases such as tuberculosis and heart disease. Adult deaths, especially among urban men, rose sharply. In 1942 the Soviet Union controlled a far smaller territory with a much-reduced population than in 1940, yet deaths among men aged between twenty and forty-nine were nearly a third higher for the country as whole, and 76 percent higher in the towns.[5] During the final years of the war, starvation and malnutrition, not epidemics, were the country's primary health hazard.

Hunger and disease were not the only hazards that confronted the population. Working conditions deteriorated markedly, especially in the defense industry, coalmines, and other sectors central to the war effort. Illness rates among workers rose to such a level that they canceled out much of the gain in production anticipated by the imposition of longer wartime working hours. Work accidents increased as exhaustion and long hours took their toll. The exposure of workers to toxic chemicals was made more dangerous by the lack of protective work clothes, baths, and sanitation. Shortages of guard rails, goggles, and other safety equipment created a spike in industrial accidents.

The health crisis of the war had deep historical roots. After the revolution, the Soviet Union made significant strides in improving the population's health. Substantial increases in the number of doctors, nurses, paramedics, and midwives, health education campaigns, and mass immunization programs contributed to significant reductions in overall mortality. Despite these gains, the state of the country's health remained poor. The huge growth of towns and cities during the 1930s was not matched by the necessary investments in infrastructure (decent housing, indoor piped water, citywide sewerage systems), which left the population highly vulnerable to epidemics, water- and louse-borne diseases, and such highly contagious, and often fatal, diseases as tuberculosis and dysentery. These problems were compounded by the uneven distribution of medical resources. Forty percent of all doctors were in Moscow, Leningrad, and the cities of Ukraine, and peasants in rural areas still had little access to care. Moscow alone had the same number of doctors as the entire Volga region, the Urals, and Western Siberia combined. The countryside had just 1.5 doctors for every 10,000 people. Rural residents relied on paramedics, nurses, and midwives.[6] Health education campaigns notwithstanding, people in both cities and villages knew little about hygiene, microbes, and food safety. The lack of a safe living environment and access to medical care was reflected in the country's high rates of mortality and illness.

By almost every measure of societal wellbeing—infant and child mortality, and deaths from tuberculosis, measles, pneumonia, and other infections—Soviet metrics on the eve of the war were considerably worse than those of the United States, England and Wales, and Western Europe, which had invested heavily in sanitary reform forty to eighty years earlier.[7]

Unable to prevent, or at least curb, the root causes of disease, the country relied on basic public health measures: rapid identification and isolation of those who fell ill, contact tracing and quarantine, and disinfection of actual and potential sites of infection. Such measures were far cheaper than investing in sanitation and housing but were highly labor-intensive and dependent on well-functioning systems of diagnosis, reporting, and followup, which could not always be guaranteed. These systems were to come under enormous pressure early in the war but would prove vital later on.

At the time of the German invasion the population was already in precarious health and vulnerable to shocks, weakened by pressing food shortages and a fall in consumption during 1939 and 1940, which led to a sharp rise in mortality.[8] At the very moment when the risks people faced increased, however, the healthcare system contracted. Doctors were called up to the front, hospitals and clinics in the frontline zones and the rear were transferred from civilian to military use, and vital medical supplies, from bandages and antiseptics to X-ray film, were commandeered by the army. To conserve resources, medical authorities shuttered much of the network for diagnosing, containing, and treating two of the country's most ravaging diseases—tuberculosis and malaria. In many towns and rural areas, paramedics assumed physicians' duties, including those requiring specialist training. Of the doctors left to treat civilians, a growing percentage—over half by 1945—were recent medical school graduates with little clinical experience.[9] A conflict arose between the needs of the front and the civilian population, especially workers, whose efforts were critical to defense. Health officials, limited by the shortage of medical facilities, medicines, and personnel, could not do what they knew needed to be done.

Saving the Children

During 1942, every town that received evacuees saw a fundamental shift in its demographic structure. Despite the fact that the new arrivals swelled their populations, what the Soviets called "natural population growth," or the excess of births over deaths, sharply reversed. Everywhere the number of deaths exceeded—and in the majority of towns vastly exceeded—the number of births. The city of Gor'kii, for example, registered 13,072 births and 26,653 deaths; Sverdlovsk, 10,970 births and 17,234 deaths; Kirov, 3,352 births and 10,586 deaths; Izhevsk, 5,145 births and 24,691 deaths; and Kazan', 9,400 births and 24,354 deaths.[10] A large proportion of these deaths were of young children, particularly infants under one year of age. Towns across the country witnessed very high levels of infant mortality, in some cases reaching 500 infant deaths for every 1,000 live births.[11] Not all of those who died were born in the town where their death was registered. Many were evacuated children who became so weak and ill during their journey that they succumbed either in transit or soon after arrival. Others died because of infections they acquired amid the unsanitary conditions of their new homes. Public health officials and Soviet leaders, aware of the high mortality levels, and the impact on children in particular, understood the need to protect these most vulnerable members of the population. Children would eventually have to replace the teenagers and adults who were lost at the front or died in the rear. The rising death rate, coupled with a collapse in the birth rate, created a demographic shortfall, causing leaders to see the protection of children as both a humanitarian and a demographic imperative.

Before the war, the Soviet Union had significantly reduced mortality from three of the major childhood infections: diphtheria, whooping cough, and scarlet fever. Measles, which every year took tens of thousands of lives, mainly of the very young, proved an exception. During the 1930s, Soviet doctors and public health officials attempted to follow the latest Western practice for containing measles through prompt isolation and quarantine of infected children and their contacts, and the rapid administration of plasma antibodies drawn from those who had already had the disease. However, these techniques were applied effectively only in the largest cities; outside Moscow and Leningrad infection and fatality rates remained high. The country suffered a measles epidemic virtually every winter.[12]

After the invasion, the normal summer abatement was already underway when the Soviet for Evacuation began moving children and evacuated families out of the threatened areas, and refugees began fleeing east. Children spread the disease from west to east along the evacuation routes, eliminating all possibility of isolation, containment, or treatment. By mid-1942 the epidemic burnt itself out, but not before taking more than 100,000 lives. After the summer of 1942, measles ceased to be a major health hazard. As long as children remained stationary, they were unlikely to be exposed to new sources of infection. Yet toward the end of the war, as the evacuated children began to return home, major outbreaks of measles once again recurred. At this point, however, the most vulnerable group—infants and very young children—had contracted in size, and older children were better able to cope without developing life-threatening complications. Fatalities were relatively few.[13]

The second major risk to children came from poor sanitation, overcrowding, and the general lack of public knowledge about basic hygiene. Almost two-thirds of infant deaths were the result of just two hygiene-related causes: gastrointestinal infections, caused by exposure to fecal bacteria, and pneumonia, a common complication of respiratory infections, including the common cold, whooping cough, or measles, all easily spread within cramped childcare centers, schools, apartments, and dormitories.[14] The third and greatest risk to children was inadequate nutrition, which was not only debilitating in its own right, but also exacerbated the severity of other diseases and conditions and increased the likelihood of death. Infantile rickets, for example, heightened the risk of pneumonia and impeded the ability of babies to fight off lung infections.[15] Malnutrition also increased vulnerability to tuberculosis. As a result, when children fell ill, they suffered from more than one life-threatening illness either simultaneously or in rapid succession. A. I. Perevoshchikova, in her detailed study of nurseries in wartime Izhevsk, cited one mother whose infant fell ill with influenza complicated by pneumonia, followed by suppurative otitis, dyspepsia, diphtheria, chickenpox, and whooping cough. Miraculously the child survived. Another infant was not so lucky: she first came down with chickenpox, then dysentery and influenza, complicated by otitis and pneumonia. She managed to recover from all of these, but then caught whooping cough, complicated by severe pneumonia, from which she died.[16]

Public health officials received the first warning signs of a developing nutritional crisis among children within a few months of the invasion. In late 1941, even before the mass evacuation of starving children from Leningrad, major cities, including Saratov, Molotov, Penza, Kirov, Sverdlovsk, and Novosibirsk, reported rising rates of infant disease and mortality as a result of the influx of child evacuees, overcrowding in children's institutions, and shortages of protein and fats for older children, and milk, semolina, rice, and sugar for formula and baby food. Commenting on the growing danger sometime during early 1942, A. F. Tret'iakov, Commissar of Public Health of the RSFSR, warned in early 1942:

> The selection of foods covered by the ration cards cannot be deemed sat-
> isfactory, since it cannot ensure the normal development of the child and
> does not create the necessary conditions to prevent the onset of high rates
> of disease and high rates of mortality among children, not to mention that
> in a significant proportion of towns these ration cards are completely unre-
> deemable and the children for all practical purposes are eating nothing but
> bread.[17]

In 1942, the consequences for children of the nationwide food shortage became more severe. The daily fare at one boarding school for preschool children, evacuated from Leningrad to Cheliabinsk province, consisted of a breakfast of tea and bread, a lunch of soup made from groats and oil, and a dinner of sweetened tea and bread. A children's home for evacuated children in Gor'kii province reported in mid-May 1942 that it had received no food for all of April; at other homes in the province, the children were subsisting on nothing more than black bread.[18] By the end of the year, cities were re-porting growing numbers of cases of acute malnutrition, many of them fatal. In Kirov, which received a large number of child evacuees, the nutritional state of the city's children reached a crisis point by the end of 1942. The city had 4,500 infants under the age of one, and 10,500 children between one and three, all of whom needed milk from the city's milk kitchen, a special dis-tribution center established in all the major towns exclusively for children. In July, the kitchen received only enough milk to provide each child with 250 ml a day or about one cup; in October this dropped to 160 ml or 5.4 ounces, and in November to just 45 ml or 1.5 ounces. In early December, the city opened a special canteen for 3,000 especially malnourished chil-dren, designed to replace a much larger canteen for thousands of school-age children who had no access to stocks. The schools were supposed to provide pupils with a hot breakfast but could offer only a single roll. The children who were not in a childcare center, children's home, or school, or were not fed through an institution, subsisted on little more than their bread and sugar ra-tion. In December, the city granted children a small bread ration, but this was to come out of their mothers' own allowance. Yet neither children at home nor those provisioned through institutions fared well. Kirov's children's hos-pital for somatic diseases reported that 95 percent of children admitted were suffering from advanced malnutrition. Between September and November, 30 percent of all children admitted died, half of them directly from starvation, and in the other half with starvation as an aggravating factor.[19] In 1943, the situation continued to worsen, especially among the youngest children. An inspection brigade dispatched from the Soviet of People's Commissars found that 13 percent of all children in Kirov's nurseries suffered from acute starvation and between 11 and 12 percent from tuberculosis.[20] Throughout the country, most children depended on their families and their individual ration, the size of which was insufficient to keep them at even a minimal level of health. Parents, at great risk to their own health, often tried to sustain their children by sharing part of their own rations.[21]

Even before the war, infants in prerevolutionary Russia and the Soviet Union suffered high mortality due to the common practice of early weaning.[22] The period that mothers could nurse was further decreased after the mass entry of women into the workforce in the 1930s. During the war, many mothers were unable to nurse because of poor nutrition. Mary Leder noted that, although she was able to nurse, her baby did not develop "at a normal rate." She explained, "I myself was thin and haggard and my nursing could not have provided her with much nutrition and no supplementary food was available."[23] The survival of infants and toddlers therefore depended in large part on external supplies provided by milk kitchens.

The kitchens, first established in the 1920s to provide safe milk, baby formula, and baby food during the summer months when infant diarrhea was at its height, suffered from numerous shortages and organizational problems, including a lack of refrigeration and sterile receptacles, and poor knowledge of hygiene among the kitchen staff, nurses, and doctors.[24] Although the state greatly expanded the network during the war, it still met only a small proportion of the population's need. At the end of 1942, the Commissariat of Public Health estimated that in the RSFSR alone more than 550,000 infants and more than 1.1 million children aged between twelve months and thirty-six months had no access to a milk kitchen or nursery that might provide them with milk and food. Even for those who had access, the kitchens had an acute shortage of milk, semolina, rice, and easily digestible grains for babies. They resorted instead to a range of substitutes, including "malted milk," a concoction made from whole milk diluted with water, often in a ratio of 1:9, with some sour cream, wheat flour, or vegetable oil. Only older children could consume the mixture, which was too acidic for babies, and its nutritional benefit was questionable. After nutritional experts began experimenting with yeast as a source of protein for adults, the kitchens began dispensing a concoction known as "yeast milk" in the hope of providing children with vital protein.[25]

During the summer of 1942, the medical authorities in Moscow province invested considerable effort expanding their network of milk kitchens and special child nutrition stations allowing them to meet the needs of all children up to the age of four. In the autumn, as the food crisis intensified, all progress came to a crashing halt. By early 1943, almost every town reported an acute shortage of milk. One health official from Moscow province noted in despair,

> At present our work to develop the milk kitchens and feeding stations has slowed down due to the catastrophically small amount of milk. If in summer the average child in a nursery or milk kitchen was receiving 250 to 300 grams of milk a day, now they are receiving just 10 or 15 grams [two to three US teaspoons]. They are issuing just 3 or 4 liters of milk for 150 or 200 children. Thus in Babushkin, they received 20 liters for 400 children; in Pushkin, 15 to 20 liters for 350 children; in Orekhovo-Zuevo, the children have been getting no milk at all; in Balashikha the milk kitchen serves 353 children, and has been receiving 2 liters a day. Recently they have begun to issue malted milk, although no one knows what's in it, to which children you can give it, or how to dilute it. We need the Commissariat of Health to issue an instruction on this question.[26]

A report from the health authorities in Bashkiriia in early 1943 noted, "The situation with regard to the nutrition of Bashkiriia's child population is now exceptionally serious. Recent months have seen a whole range of nurseries in towns and districts going without essential foodstuffs, especially milk, as a result of which we have a significant number of children suffering from starvation."[27] In Chkalov province, managers of the milk kitchens resorted to buying a few liters of milk each day at the collective farm markets. In Udmurtiia, the only town to obtain any milk at all was Izhevsk: roughly 20 liters a day, a mere 5 percent of what its residents needed. Officials in Sverdlovsk province reported that deliveries of milk had stopped altogether, forcing milk kitchens to close. Only the milk kitchens in Sverdlovsk city still received limited supplies, and these arrived only sporadically.[28] Kitchen employees began preparing baby foods with just water and a bit of semolina. Whole milk and protein-rich dairy products were simply unavailable.[29]

Even children's hospitals could not obtain milk. In February 1943, the infectious diseases hospital in Kuibyshev received just 1 liter of milk each day to feed 120 children, less than 2 teaspoons for each child, while the infectious diseases hospital in Kirov gave each of its children about 3 teaspoons.[30] The reasons for the shortage were directly linked to the loss of dairy herds in the occupied territories, and the lower yields provided by herds in the rear. The animals, lacking fodder, were also starving.[31] Children competed with other groups who, according to prevailing medical beliefs, also needed milk, including tuberculosis patients, and workers exposed to toxic metals and other hazardous substances.[32]

Oddly, the milk crisis occurred at the same time as infant mortality was falling. Following the calamity of 1942, infant mortality in most major urban regions fell, not just to prewar levels, but below them, a trend that continued into the postwar years. The reasons for the drop are not clear, especially as parental knowledge of hygiene was still low and food supplies did not appreciably improve before the second half of 1944. Despite the fall in infant mortality, the milk crisis did have an adverse long-term effect, leaving many children weak, malnourished, and vulnerable to infection.[33] Children suffered widely from rickets, a skeletal disorder produced by a lack of vitamin D, calcium, and phosphate, as the foods that would have prevented it—fish, eggs, and milk—were unavailable. In Zlatoust, 35 percent of all children in nurseries had rickets, and in Ivanovo, 41 percent. In Sverdlovsk, the disease took its toll: 27 percent of babies younger than six months, 52 percent of babies aged between six months and one year, 48 percent of those aged twelve months to twenty-four months, and 9 percent of those older than two were seriously underdeveloped.[34] Rickets also began to affect older as well as younger children in severe forms.[35] While mortality among infants fell, among one- to four-year-olds, more than one-quarter of deaths in 1943 were due to either starvation or starvation-aggravated tuberculosis.[36] Insofar as the milk shortage contributed to the general state of malnutrition of this age group, it contributed to these deaths.

Nurseries, which took in children up to the age of three, should have provided a haven for those who were weak and ill, but the staff, including doctors and nurses, were ill equipped to cope with the many challenges. The children were already suffering from weight loss and malnutrition, and nursery staff found it difficult to reverse the damage. Surveys of nurseries attached to defense factories in Sverdlovsk province during the first half of 1942 found that, although a large percentage of their children were of a normal weight at birth, they were seriously underweight by the time they entered the nursery and continued to lose weight there. Some nurseries achieved a temporary reversal by marshaling extra resources during the summer, but the gains could not be sustained. By the end of 1942, some nurseries were recording tragically high death rates. The nursery attached to the Verkh-Isetskii metallurgical factory in Sverdlovsk, for example, recorded a death rate of 11 percent during the second half of 1942. In Lys'va in Molotov province, roughly 16 percent of children in the city's nurseries died during the first six months of 1942, the vast majority from pneumonia or gastrointestinal infections.[37] In Iaroslavl' at the end of 1942 the "very best nurseries" found that between 13 and 18 percent of children were suffering from starvation and between 20 and 30 percent had rickets. Tuberculosis was common. The children's diets consisted almost exclusively of carbohydrates, since the nurseries received very little milk, vegetables, fats, or protein. Most children did gain weight, but slowly, remaining well below the normal range for their age group.[38] Despite isolated pockets of good practice, most nurseries did not have the food necessary to combat widespread nutritional deficiencies. As the war progressed, the conditions that affected children's health shifted from infectious diseases to chronic conditions, such as malnutrition, rickets, and tuberculosis. As with adults, fundamental recovery for children would not occur until major improvement in the food supply at the end of 1944.

Occupational Health

The First Five-Year Plan (1928–1932) saw a major reorientation of Soviet healthcare as an earlier accent on preventive medicine and universal access gave way to what historians have called the "industrial principle." The new goal of healthcare was to advance industrial production and thus provide industrial workers with preferential allocation of medical resources. This new orientation brought much-needed improvements in the organization of factory medicine, but it also had ominous implications for workers who fell ill. The obligation of the factory doctor was not to heal the worker for the sake of his or her wellbeing, but rather to enable the rapid return to productive labor even where this jeopardized the worker's long-term health. Over the course of the 1930s strict adherence to the industrial principle weakened, as large investments were made in other areas of public health.[39]

The principle came back into favor during the war, when the Commissariat of Health created a new department to focus exclusively on the health of workers in defense and its related industries of iron and steel, nonferrous metallurgy, coalmining, building materials, textiles, light industry, and food processing. Numerically these workers constituted less than 10 percent of the total working population, including agriculture, but, since the state saw their output as critical, it concentrated medical attention on them.[40] The logic followed that of the ration system: channeling scarce resources to those workers most essential to the war effort.

Throughout the industrialization drive, shortages of safety equipment, high tempos of production, and an inexperienced workforce all contributed to high rates of occupational illness, injury, and death.[41] The war heightened these problems. Evacuation led almost everywhere to a sharp deterioration in working conditions. When evacuated factories were compelled to share space with each other and with local enterprises, and local soviets resettled or transferred factories into schools, municipal buildings, warehouses, and other structures unsuited for industrial production, a raft of new dangers emerged, especially for workers in hazardous occupations vulnerable to poisoning.[42] Many new and hastily erected structures had major construction defects.[43] The pressure to meet urgent war orders also encouraged workers to ignore safety regulations, while the large number of young or inexperienced mobilized workers received insufficient training on the proper use of equipment and materials. The Chief Administration of Labor Reserves did not issue instructions on labor safety and work hygiene until February 1944, by which time tens of thousands of young workers had already suffered injury, illness, and occupational disease.[44]

With the rapid expansion of new lines of production, most notably munitions and aviation fuel, workers were exposed to a range of highly toxic substances, including tetraethyl lead, TNT, and corrosive emulsions used for cooling machinery. By 1942, the impact was clearly demonstrable in the data on workdays lost to sickness, injury, and poor health. Surveys of lost work time carried out by the Central Statistical Administration in October 1942 showed that workers in most branches of defense and defense-related industry lost on average from two and a half to four weeks a year to illness and injury. The stunning statistic was two to four times the all-industry average recorded in June 1941 before the German invasion, and more than eight times what factories lost to absenteeism, a violation of labor discipline that the state devoted great efforts to eliminating.[45] Indeed, the figures suggested that the occasional unexcused absence of workers was hardly the main problem. Moreover, the figures did not account for those workers who were sick with serious illnesses such as tuberculosis and malnutrition but reported to work anyway, nor did it include the large number of prisoner-workers and deportees, who were in even worse health but not covered by the surveys.

Acute respiratory, gastrointestinal, and skin infections constituted three of the four leading causes of absence for sickness. The fourth cause was workplace and domestic injuries, which also leapt upward.[46] Part of the time lost to sickness was the result of workers' sheer exhaustion. The wartime working day was mandated at eleven hours, and all holidays were canceled.[47] Depending on the branch of industry, workers were limited to two days off per month, although in reality these, too, were frequently canceled. Workers could be called in at short notice to work as many as sixteen hours on a day off. Few workers could sustain such a grueling, unrelenting schedule. Exhaustion increased the likelihood of accidents, weakened resistance to infection, prolonged recovery from infection and injury, and, combined with food shortages, led to high morbidity and mortality from malnutrition. In addition to the long working day, as the Union of Armaments Workers complained in September 1942, workers were also gardening, hauling firewood, caring for children and other dependants, and walking long distances to and from work.[48]

Respiratory, gastrointestinal, and skin infections spread easily in crowded dormitories and *zemlianki* in the absence of sanitary facilities, boiled water, and soap. Most industrial commissariats saw time lost to skin infections increase between 50 and 100 percent compared to 1940.[49] The majority were bacterial—furunculosis, pyoderma, carbuncles, and erysipelas—but some were caused by parasites, the most common of which was scabies. Poor hygiene, the shortage of protective work clothes, soap, and basic first-aid and antisepsis could quickly turn even the most innocuous microtrauma—a scratch, nick, or break in the skin—into a major illness. At the Gor'kii Motor Vehicle Factory (GAZ), each year between 1942 and 1944, roughly one out of every five workers suffered a skin infection serious enough to keep them off work, with the average sufferer laid up for nine or ten days. Nor was GAZ exceptional. The Stankozavod machine-tool factory in Gor'kii lost nearly twice as many days to skin infections as did GAZ.[50] Workers in a number of industries handled highly corrosive emulsions used to lubricate equipment or to cool machinery, which caused chemical burns and, if not filtered regularly, became breeding grounds for bacteria.[51] The shortage of clean bandages for dressing wounds was ubiquitous, and wounds either went untreated or workers covered them with dirty rags.[52] Antisepsis was generally seen as an innovative medical intervention. In March 1943, twenty-one months after the outbreak of war, factory No. 45 in Moscow introduced the "novel" measure in its machine shops of treating every cut and scratch with iodine. During one month alone they treated more than 3,000 such injuries.[53] A few perceptive factory doctors observed a close association between skin infections and severe malnutrition, an observation later verified by scientific research on nutrition.[54] Without fats, protein, and zinc, even small wounds took a long time to heal, increasing the possibility of infection.[55]

The most dangerous industries were coalmining, iron and steel, machine-building, and basic chemicals.[56] In 1943, the Kuzbass coalfields recorded one accident for every six workers, while chemical plants recorded one for every twelve in 1942 and one in every thirteen in 1943. Many of the accidents were serious, even fatal. The average accident cost a worker twelve workdays in the Kuzbass, fourteen days in basic chemicals, and fourteen and one-half days at the Gor'kii Motor Vehicle Factory, almost twice the number of days the Gor'kii factory lost to accidents in the months leading up to the German invasion. In the Kuzbass mines, 275 miners lost their lives in 1942 and 365 in 1943.[57] The reasons behind such high accident rates were apparent to even the most casual observer. Factory shops were cluttered with piles of metal, machinery, and scrap. Given the shortage of warehouse space, finished output turned shops and passageways into hazardous obstacle courses. In an effort to conserve electricity and fuel, workplaces were poorly lit. Light bulbs were scarce, and many shops had little natural light because windows and skylights were not cleaned; broken panes were boarded up with plywood in the absence of glass. At the giant Kuznetsk iron and steel combine less than 15 percent of sockets had light bulbs.[58] In coalmining the shortage of timber for pit props increased the risk of cave-ins.[59] Amid these heightened dangers, young, inexperienced, and often unfit workers began work with minimal instruction. In coalmining, a dangerous occupation in the best of circumstances, workers received little preparation. The prosecutor of Rostov province complained in late 1943 that teenagers, some as young as thirteen or fourteen, were sent into the mines. The youngest worked underground for a full eleven-hour shift, despite the fact that labor legislation limited shifts for younger teens to six hours. Many youngsters were seriously injured, some of them permanently, and at least one young boy was killed when he fell under the wheels of a truck. Not surprisingly, these dangers led to high desertion rates in mining.[60]

In other industries, the main risk was not physical injury but poisoning. Workers were exposed to a host of hazardous chemicals and substances, many of which were specific to war production: new types of solvents derived from the wood chemical industry; chlorinated benzol and benzine compounds; chemicals used in the production of ammunition; aromatic nitrogen compounds; arsenic compounds; asbestos dust; lead dust; and tetraethyl lead used as an antiknock compound and ignition retardant in aircraft fuel.[61] In factories forced to share the same structure, the vapors of each combined to form new, unknown lethal compounds. These new chemicals were added to a long list of well-established hazards, such as mercury, aniline dyes, sulfuric acid, fine metal particles, and the gases and high heat produced in iron and steel production. All of these chemicals and byproducts damaged liver, skin, eyes, nerves, and lungs. The production of ammunition, including TNT and nitrocellulose, polluted the air with nitric oxides, dinitrobenzene, ether, cyclonite, and other chemicals. Work areas were not hermetically sealed, and gas leaks could force the temporary closure of entire shops.[62] In munitions factory No. 56 in Nizhnii Tagil, workers in hazardous processes were constantly exposed to toxic gases because the ventilation system was so poor. In 1943, half of workers in the factory's hazardous shops were found to be suffering from industrial poisoning, and by 1944 the figure was nearly 100 percent. Local and health officials tried repeatedly to force the factory's managers to remedy conditions, but the imperatives of production overrode their complaints. Only after the head of the Sverdlovsk provincial party committee intervened did managers take action.[63]

Another serious hazard was lead poisoning, which damages the central nervous system. Strict regulations, dating from 1928, required factories to have special shower rooms, laundries, washrooms, sanitary processing stations, and separate locker rooms for street and work clothes. Washrooms were supposed to be equipped with soap, scrub brushes, and mouthwash, and workers were to have their own towel, toothbrush, and tooth powder. Consumption of food was allowed only in areas carefully isolated from production shops.[64] The 1944 health education instructions issued to vocational schools set out additional measures, including maintaining ventilation ducts free of lead, the use of respirators, regular cleaning of premises, and careful disposal of lead-contaminated water.[65] Yet few factories met any of these requirements. Lead dust was the most prevalent cause of poisoning, but not the only one.[66] The aviation fuel additive, tetraethyl lead, had devastating effects on workers' health. In at least two factories producing antiknock compounds in the city of Dzerzhinsk in Gor'kii province, workers were repeatedly sickened by lead. During the first half of 1942, workers at the Iava chemical works lost on average two working weeks to illness. In factory No. 365, the Oka chemical plant, workers were doubly exposed through their production of tetraethyl lead and munitions. During the first half of 1942, each worker was out sick an average of eighteen days, adding up to more than 10 percent of the factory's entire stock of work time. Nearly half of these sick days were due directly to industrial poisoning. In 1942, more than one of three Oka workers was signed off sick because they had been poisoned, and each poisoning victim was out for an average of thirty-three days. Fortunately, conditions at both the Iava and Oka factories improved significantly during the second half of the year.[67]

Ventilation was especially important to removing the fumes produced by tetraethyl lead, but ventilators were frequently broken or inadequate. The situation at factory No. 636 in Tiumen' in Omsk province in Siberia reflected the tragic consequences of placing the demands of production over health. The factory was set up in an abandoned winery after its evacuation from Moscow. Despite the fact that the building lacked the necessary safeguards for tetraethyl lead production, the factory began operations in April 1942. As of January 1943, workers were still waiting for the ventilation system, showers, and sewerage for contaminated waste. Managers instead substituted an underpowered distilling system to remove toxic vapors, but it was too weak to cope with the load. Fumes built up inside the half-finished ventilation system, releasing high concentrations of tetraethyl lead into the air. Several workers suffered serious brain damage. A doctor from the factory's medical unit described the shocking consequences:

> Given the specific illnesses of our workers, what we need most of all is to send patients to the neurological department and the closed psychiatric unit. This is one and the same place, in which there are only four wards for violent patients; the confinement of patients in these solitary confinement cells is, one has to say, disgusting. Violent patients are housed in these wards completely without any linen, mattresses, or robes, there are no straitjackets in the entire hospital, and so they roll around on the floor in a cold room, and as a rule in addition to their existing illness they come down with pneumonia. There are not enough staff and the sum total of these conditions

leads to patients dying. In this way Bondarev, a fitter of ours from Shop B, died on December 28, 1942.

The factory's medical team refused to refer any more workers to these hellish wards and appealed instead for the construction of a small inpatient facility for workers "with [our] specific illness." In the meantime, they tried to treat brain-damaged patients at home or in the dormitories, an effort that required extra staff, which they did not have.[68]

Alarmed by the inexorable rise in absence for illness, but unable to alter the fundamental conditions that caused it, the state sought to cut down on lost work time by making it harder for workers to receive sick leave. In mid-1942, the Commissariat of Health, which supervised doctors who wrote sick notes, and the unions, which managed the social insurance funds that issued sick pay, launched a campaign to crack down on sick notes, treating illness less as a matter of health than of labor discipline. The campaign had three targets: doctors, who allegedly wrote unnecessary sick notes; workers, who were accused of feigning illness; and factory timekeepers, who supposedly ignored strict instructions to accept only validated medical certificates when excusing workers from work.[69] In some places the NKVD and Procuracy convened meetings with doctors to "focus their attention" on the need to issue fewer sick notes.[70] Union representatives toured the dormitories to root out alleged malingerers and send them back to work.[71] Although the campaign's intentions were clearly coercive, it did compel factories to improve their medical services and record keeping, two areas that benefited patients who bore the consequences of incorrect diagnosis and spotty case histories. Good records were essential for identifying the exact causes of accidents, poisoning, and infections, without which factories or public health officials could not attempt corrective measures. On balance, however, the campaign was economically and medically counterproductive. By denying sick leave to at least some workers who genuinely needed it and forcing others back to work before they had properly convalesced, it only postponed the looming crisis posed by a rapidly weakening workforce. The statistics revealed the struggle of exhausted and debilitated workers to maintain production. Despite more rigorous control over the dissemination of sick notes and significant improvement in factory medical services, absence for sickness did not decline. Central Statistical Administration surveys in May 1943 and May 1944 found rates of absence for illness virtually unchanged and about double the prewar rate.[72] Although the 1942 campaign claimed to have unmasked countless malingerers, union representatives were forced to acknowledge during 1943 and a renewed campaign in 1944 that the workers who were lying in the dormitories and hospitals were very ill and clearly unable to work.[73] If rates of illness and injury remained stubbornly high, it was because conditions remained so very difficult.

During the war, female workers became a significant presence in the factories. In the 1930s, women entered industries and trades from which they were excluded in the West, at the same time as they gained ever greater predominance in traditional "female" industries (most notably textiles and garments).[74] The war intensified these trends. By the end of 1942, women had dramatically increased their share in heavy industry, constituting the majority of workers in the munitions, mortar, electrical, and timber industries; just under half in weapons, chemicals, and most branches of machine-building; and a sizable minority in other core industries, such as iron and steel, nonferrous metals, shipbuilding, tanks, aviation, and coalmining. At the same time, 40 percent of all women workers were still concentrated in traditionally "female" and low-waged sectors, such as textiles, light industry, meat and dairy, food processing, local industry, and small-scale producers' cooperatives.[75] Women also increased their skills, becoming a majority in the lower ranks of the skilled professions, most notably turners, milling machine operators, and capstan lathe operators, but were still strongly underrepresented in highly skilled jobs such as fitters, repair mechanics, and electricians. They were also a majority in many semiskilled jobs, composing more than 80 percent of core-makers in foundries, as well as more than 80 percent of storeroom attendants, sorters, and quality controllers, jobs that often involved heavy lifting. They continued to shoulder a disproportionate share of unskilled jobs, constituting more than two-thirds of the vast army of unskilled, ancillary, or support workers in industry, and 93 percent of shop floor cleaners.[76] Regulations dating back to the early 1930s limited the amount of weight that women were allowed to lift at any one time but, as women replaced men in heavy manual auxiliary jobs during the war, these limits were widely ignored. In the ammunition industry, women routinely lifted and carried weights of 110 pounds (50 kg) or more; and in the textile industry, up to 175 pounds (80 kg). Most women, and many men, found it difficult to cope with such loads, and their norm fulfillment and pay suffered.[77]

Tremendous losses at the front, coupled with grim maternal statistics, prompted the state to focus new attention on the care of women and children. By late 1943, the state was thoroughly alarmed by a looming demographic crisis fueled by the falling birth rate, an increase in stillbirths and miscarriages, and high infant mortality. After prolonged planning and discussion, the USSR Supreme Soviet promulgated a new family law in July 1944 aimed at raising the birth rate and creating greater stability within existing families. Women at the front had entered into liaisons with married men that were often hotly resented by wives at home, who tarred them with the phrase "frontline whores." Moreover, the number of men available for marriage was drastically reduced by the terrible losses at the front. The new law made divorce more difficult and imposed a tax on men and women who had fewer than two children. Most significantly, it absolved married men from responsibility for providing child support for children they sired out of wedlock, and shifted the burden of support to the state, which encouraged women to have children whether or not they were married. Special payments and medals were awarded to mothers who bore large numbers of children. The Commissariat of Health pressed for important provisions on maternal healthcare, including an extension of maternity leave, limits on the hours and workload of pregnant women and nursing mothers, and an obligation on every enterprise to provide them with extra food and childcare.[78]

Until 1944, the state focused mainly on the amount of time women lost from work to look after sick children, but managers, union officials, and health authorities gave scant attention to the personal needs of women themselves. Only in the wake of the new family law did factories begin to monitor the health of women workers. Reviving prewar practices, managers reestablished "personal hygiene rooms," where women could rinse or change the cloths they used during menstruation. They also reinstituted medical examinations at the hygiene rooms or in specially designated examining rooms for women. Although the emphasis was on pregnant women, doctors also treated other gynecological problems, including genital infections, hernias, venereal disease, cancers, and amenorrhea, a wartime phenomenon that contributed significantly to the falling birth rate. Many women, due to nutritional deficiencies and low body fat, ceased menstruating. In Magnitogorsk in 1944, 40 percent of women working in one of its turning shops suffered from amenorrhea, and the condition was likely widespread.[79] Most of the new health measures were concentrated in the defense factories. Although services remained insufficient in other enterprises and almost nonexistent in rural areas, hundreds of thousands of women and wives of male workers employed in large industrial enterprises finally had access to basic healthcare.

Although health officials in the industrial towns were constantly stymied by shortage, they actively worked to improve public health by substituting mass mobilization for medical supplies whenever possible. By the end of 1943, the Commissariat of Health recruited 370,000 "public sanitary in-spectors," mainly ordinary citizens and shop floor workers. Placed under the guidance of sanitary physicians and state sanitary inspectors, these newly trained inspectors provided public health education and enforced health regulations in the workplace and factory dormitories. They supplemented the thin, overextended ranks of sanitary physicians and inspectors and pro-vided a sizable core of people well schooled in public hygiene who could dis-seminate knowledge to the general population.[80] Public sanitary inspectors mobilized urban residents to clear away the vast accumulations of garbage and human excrement that built up over the frozen winter and again during the summer, and posed a grave threat to health. Medical personnel intensi-fied efforts to identify and isolate carriers of typhus, typhoid fever, and dys-entery before they could infect others and lead to major epidemics. These different policies and initiatives combined from 1943 onward to prevent epidemics, bring down rates of infant mortality, and halt the large increase of adult deaths due to gastrointestinal infections. The wartime health emer-gency and the critical shortage of doctors also led to a massive expansion of the training of new doctors. Between 1941 and 1944, medical schools turned out 57,300 new doctors, equivalent to nearly half the number of doctors al-ready working in the Commissariat of Health on the eve of the war. The pro-duction of new doctors accelerated further after the war: by 1950 there were nearly twice as many doctors practicing within the civilian system as there had been when the war ended.[81]

Public Health Problem No. 1: Malnutrition and Starvation

In the early years of the war, adults, like children, suffered the impact of evac-uation, overcrowding, and poor sanitation. In 1942 there was a sharp rise in deaths from acute gastrointestinal infections and dysentery: in urban areas alone they caused one out of every six deaths or more than 116,000 deaths among those aged five and older.[82] Once evacuation ended, deaths from gas-trointestinal infections in 1943 returned to prewar levels and fell further in 1944. Although sanitation in most cities deteriorated throughout 1943 and 1944, the improvement was a testament to the vigorous efforts of public health workers to improve surveillance, isolate the ill, and rigorously enforce epidemic control measures.[83] If the reduction in gastrointestinal infections was a partial success, the achievement was quickly overshadowed by the rise in other causes of mortality. Unlike infant mortality, which dropped after the first chaotic years of the war, adult deaths continued to rise sharply. In 1943, deaths among those aged five years and older in the major home front cities were up to five times the number recorded in 1940, an increase so large that it could not be explained by the growth in population alone. During the war, the city of Cheliabinsk, for example, grew by 46 percent, but deaths in the five and older group increased by 571 percent, more than ten times the increase in population. In Zlatoust, the population increased by just under 20 percent, but deaths in this same group shot up by 335 percent, more than fifteen times the increase in population. And in Saratov and Kirov, the disparity between population growth and the increase in deaths was more than twentyfold.[84]

The single greatest reason for the increase was the combined impact of starvation and tuberculosis. In the pre-antibiotic age, human tuberculosis, caused by the bacterium *Mycobacterium tuberculosis*, had no cure. Infection rates among the general population were nearly universal.[85] Most people were exposed to the bacteria by their late teens, but not everyone became ill. Some people fought off the disease, while others displayed a mild illness after which the bacteria lay dormant in the lungs, encased in protective casings called tubercles. The vast majority of people thus exposed might live their entire lives asymptomatically. If, however, the immune system suffered an insult due to malnutrition or serious infection, the body's protection would break down. The bacteria would escape their encasement and proceed to produce active disease (usually in the lungs) which was highly contagious and almost always fatal. Environmental factors therefore played a major role in both the virulent recurrence of the disease and its spread. Historically, a collapse in nutrition quickly led to more cases of active disease and a higher likelihood of fatality, while overcrowded housing and poor hygiene led to its rapid spread. In the absence of effective drugs, the only methods available to health specialists were isolation of carriers, identification and close observation of their contacts, and rest and improved diet for those already ill. The war created perfect conditions for a deadly resurgence of TB. Overcrowding and poor sanitation fostered its spread and facilitated the contraction of other serious infections that reduced the immune system's ability to keep latent tuberculosis in check. I. A. Shaklein, a Soviet tuberculosis specialist, explained:

> During the first phase of a war the epidemiological danger of tuberculosis increases. The number of those carrying the bacillus increases as

tuberculosis patients are evacuated to the rear. The network of hospital and sanitorium beds contracts. It becomes difficult to isolate the carriers from barracks, and the number dying at home increases. Many of those disabled by tuberculosis go back to the work bench, to the factory, to the institution . . . These, in essence, are the conditions brought about by war.[86]

Most evacuees, like the population at large, already carried latent tuberculosis, and the harsh conditions of evacuation and resettlement heightened the risk of the disease becoming active. The mass mobilization of workers imported still more tuberculosis into urban areas. Many Central Asian collective farmers, rural teenagers, and men ineligible for the front arrived in the towns carrying undetected latent or even active infections. At the same time, the anti-tuberculosis infrastructure built after the revolution effectively collapsed. Badly depleted medical teams and the large increase of people needing surveillance meant that fewer people were screened and isolated, leaving a large pool of sick people living among the general population in overcrowded dormitories and apartments. While the numbers needing treatment continued to rise, the number of tuberculosis beds and specialists sharply declined throughout the country, including major industrial towns such as Irkutsk, Omsk, Novosibirsk, Sverdlovsk, and Cheliabinsk, all of which had a high incidence of TB before the war and relatively weak networks of anti-TB facilities.[87]

Lack of screening and increased risk of exposure were not the only factors that sparked rapid growth in the rates of the disease. Hunger and starvation weakened the body's immune system and its ability to fight off infection. In the case of tuberculosis, severe malnutrition suppressed that part of the immune system that contained the infection and allowed it to remain asymptomatic. Doctors in Germany and Austria during the severe food shortage of World War I, in the Warsaw ghetto during World War II, and in Leningrad during the siege all observed the increased frequency and virulence of tuberculosis as acute starvation ravaged the population.[88] At the same time, tuberculosis itself caused weight loss and emaciation (cachexia), and, in this way, accelerated the process of starvation and increased the number of starvation deaths. The two conditions were so closely intertwined that in times of severe social crisis it could be nearly impossible to distinguish the primary cause of death, a fact that remains just as true today as it was during World War II.[89] In the wartime USSR the two diseases were inseparably linked in a single deadly phenomenon: a "starvation–tuberculosis complex."

Home front cities were devastated by the starvation–tuberculosis complex.[90] In 1943, in urban areas of the USSR starvation and tuberculosis together accounted for 40.9 percent of all male deaths, and 27.5 percent of
female deaths. Although the overall number of deaths fell in 1944, the
starvation–tuberculosis complex still accounted for 39 percent of urban
deaths among males and 29.4 percent among females.[91] In the major cities
of the Urals, where starvation was especially acute, in both 1943 and 1944
more than half of all deaths of those aged five years and older were due to
starvation or tuberculosis.[92] In fact, in every major region of Russia, with the
exception of the city of Moscow, the starvation–tuberculosis complex was
the largest single cause of death in both 1943 and 1944. Only in the older age
groups—women over fifty and men over sixty—was it surpassed by coronary artery disease, which was also aggravated by starvation.[93] Deaths alone,
however, understate the true cost of starvation and malnutrition. For every
person who died, there were many more who were too debilitated to work.

While the prevalence of starvation was concealed in the statistical forms
and suppressed in the newspapers, the issue was openly, and often angrily,
discussed by doctors, public health inspectors, trade union officials, the
Procuracy, local party officials, and the Komsomol. Investigators from all
these groups and organizations did not hesitate to report workers who died
on the shop floor. Reports noted that in the Kirov factory in Cheliabinsk
during December 1942–January 1943, 16 workers died from starvation while at their machines, and another 143 died in the hospital. Union
officials were closely attuned to the problem. Thousands of workers in the
Kirov factory were provided with sick leave because of starvation: 1,426 in
November 1942, 1,407 in December, and 1,572 in January 1943, as well as
an additional 265 given extended leave, and 149 discharged altogether on
health grounds.[94] In May 1943, the Union of Aviation and Defense Workers
frankly described the situation at factory No. 63, the Vysokogorskii Machine
Factory, in Nizhnii Tagil:

The most widespread ailment among the factory's workers right now is
starvation. Thus during February, the medical station saw 240 people with
this illness, 70 in March, and 250 in April. A significant number have died
of it. Thus, 38 died during the first quarter of the year, 25 of them in the
hospital—and 21 of these died within a day of being admitted. The remaining 13 died in the dormitories. In April 14 people died—in all, 52
people between the beginning of January and 30 April 1943. But these

figures do not include those who died at home with their families, since no records are kept of them.[95]

By the middle of 1944, factory No. 63 had lost an extraordinary number of days to sickness: at its peak in July, absence for illness was running at an annualized rate of an entire month of lost work time per worker, and 43 percent of these missed days were due to starvation, far and away the largest single cause.[96] Many reports attributed the bulk of starvation cases to highly vulnerable "Uzbeks" and other Central Asian workers, but by January 1944 all the Central Asians had been sent home from factory No. 63, yet starvation continued to worsen over the next six months. As one doctor noted, starvation was inevitable, since workers received no more than 1,700 calories a day versus the 4,000 they needed. Moreover, beginning in 1942, the state channeled its decreasing stocks to the factories; retail stores closed, and dependent family members of workers were unable to redeem their ration cards. Assessing the period up until mid-1944, the doctor noted:

> One of the major reasons for the increase in sickness absence is, in my view, the thoughtless attitude of the ORS [Department of Workers' Provisioning] to provisioning workers' dependants. What happens is that the ORS doesn't redeem dependants' ration cards and so the worker has to feed his own family out of his personal ration. It's hardly surprising, therefore, that we see cases of starvation among workers who are receiving "kilogram" rations [that is, 1 kilogram of bread a day, the highest ration category]. Naturally the worker leaves for himself 500 or 700 grams of bread and the rest he gives to his family; it's clear that when he's given the dinner to which he's entitled he doesn't eat it all, but part of it, maybe as much as 50 percent, he takes home. I've personally witnessed cases where a worker eats only soup, but his main course he wraps up in paper or stuffs into a small container and takes home.[97]

Although the doctor attributed starvation among workers to the negligence of the ORS, in fact, the department did not receive food stocks for workers' dependants, who were supposed to be provisioned through local organizations under the Commissariat of Trade. Yet when stocks failed to arrive in the towns, workers took the task of redistribution on themselves, and they also bore the painful consequences. A garden plot was essential to supplementing the diet. As the doctor noted, "The shop simply isn't able to feed [workers] normally for an entire month, and if a given worker doesn't have support from his own garden plot then he starves."[98]

Garden plots were critical to workers throughout the country. Local residents often had access to land, but evacuees and mobilized workers were often solely dependent on the canteens. In early 1943 officials at armaments factory No. 314 in Mednogorsk in Chkalov province noted that, in the absence of garden plots, so many workers were starving that the production plan was threatened:

> The difficult supply situation is threatening to disrupt the factory's production program, since the main body of the factory's workers are evacuees who, aside from what they receive in the factory canteen or get on their ration cards, have no other sources of food; at the market prices are such that they can't pick up anything there. At present we have a number of cases of cadre workers suffering from emaciation due to malnutrition (especially fitters, forge hands, and workers on heat treatments).[99]

Potatoes, grown widely in collective and individual gardens, provided a critical supplement to the ration, especially after November 1943 when the state cut ration allowances in response to the poor grain harvest. Yet for workers in Sverdlovsk province that difficult autumn, the potato was of little help, as the province lost most of its crop to blight and widespread flooding.[100]

The toll taken by starvation began to diminish everywhere in the second half of 1944, as food supplies improved. The "second hot" meal and special dietary programs began to reverse some of the worst effects of the earlier period. In factory No. 63, for example, starvation began to abate after July, and by the end of the year it recorded no cases at all.[101] Starvation, however, was a cumulative process, and it took time to reverse the damage. In the city of Krasnoural'sk in Sverdlovsk province, for example, factories and mines in the town still recorded exceptionally high numbers of workers suffering from starvation in the fall of 1944: 50 percent at the copper-smelting factory, 55 percent at one ore mine and 60 percent at another; 35 percent at factory No. 758; and 20 percent at factory No. 595.[102]

A major contributing factor to malnutrition was the wartime system of payment and rewards. Workers who overfulfilled their targets earned both extra money and extra food, the so-called Stakhanovite rations. Workers, however, did not always receive the extra portion. Many managers used the extra allocations to improve the diets of those most in need, rather than the most productive.[103] But when the policy was enforced, it trapped weaker workers in an inescapable spiral of decreasing fitness and productivity. The Union of Ammunition Workers in Cheliabinsk province described the consequences of the policy in a letter to the union's leaders in April 1943:

> Despite the rapid growth of workers falling ill with protein-deficiency edema, factory heads, shop chiefs, and foremen are deciding the question of how to distribute the food intended to provide extra nutrition incorrectly, solely on the basis of production indicators. If a person is physically weak and as a result starts to give lower norm fulfillment, they take away his extra food. Thanks to this the percentage [of workers] falling ill with emaciation is going up. Thus, for example, Comrade Cherepanov, a young worker in shop No. 32 of the Ordzhonikidze factory, used to be a record-breaker, overfulfilling his norms three- and fourfold. In March he became weak and started fulfilling them only by 120 percent, and for this they took away his extra food. Worker [name illegible] in shop No. 32 was also one of the best Stakhanovites, overfulfilling his norms by two- and threefold, but when he got sick with first-degree starvation [the mildest form] he began to fulfill his norms by only 110 percent, and they took away his extra food. In April both these comrades were signed off work with protein-deficiency edema.[104]

As the union pointed out, depriving weakened workers of food only enfeebled them further until they were unable to work at all. Using food as an incentive for a vulnerable, exhausted workforce struggling with chronic and long-term nutritional deficiencies had the effect of lowering, not boosting, productivity. Workers themselves faced a terrible dilemma as long as they were still fit and able: to expend the extra energy to achieve a bonus or to cut back on their exertions and make do with less food. For many workers, the effort to become a Stakhanovite could actually set them on the path to starvation.[105] Nevertheless, workers able to vie for Stakhanovite rations were in a better position than those who could not or would not fulfill their norms.

Rationed foods and canteen meals were not free, and very low wages were also a factor in malnutrition. Some low-waged young workers who were unable to meet their norms did not have enough money even to cover their canteen meals. Stoppages due to shortages of supplies or equipment breakdowns also cut into workers' earnings. At factory No. 99, an aviation plant in Ulan-Ude in the Buriat-Mongolian republic, stoppages had cut earnings so much that workers in two shops—148 workers in all—owed the factory an average of 133 rubles each, equivalent to around a week's average pay in the aviation industry.[106] But the largest pressure on workers' finances, aside from low gross pay, were the numerous deductions that the state took out of their monthly earnings. The Ammunition Workers' Union reported on the plight of young workers at the Ordzhonikidze factory (factory No. 78) in Cheliabinsk in late 1942, who were unable to cover their basic subsistence needs. The workers, ranging in age between thirteen and nineteen, made up nearly a quarter of the factory's workforce. A small percentage were unable to meet their norms and earned so little that by the middle of the month they had no money left. Yet even those who overfulfilled their norms were left struggling to pay for meals after state deductions.[107] Every month, the state took deductions for a cultural tax, income tax, the mandatory state loan, a mandatory contribution of one day's pay on behalf of the front, social insurance, union dues, and even the occasional raffle to raise money for the front.[108] Workers often had to reimburse the factory for their protective work clothes and pay back any advances the factory provided at the start of employment. A young woman turner in the Ordzhonikidze ammunitions factory earned just 280.58 rubles, including payments for overtime, in September 1942, barely half the industry's average wage. Out of this small sum, the state deducted 218 rubles, including 130 rubles for repayment of her advance, 46 rubles for doing her laundry, and smaller amounts for taxes and loan subscriptions. At the end of the month she was left with 62 rubles, not enough to cover her basic rations. The Union of Ammunition Workers, protesting the situation, cited several similar tales.[109] Some young workers, in particular recent graduates from the Labor Reserve schools, had so little money that they could not even redeem their bread ration cards. Their letters home described take-home pay of a mere 20 or 50 rubles after deductions. Some complained of going long periods without bread; others openly admitted that if they did not resort to stealing they could not survive.[110]

Such instances of extreme poverty were most often documented by the unions in the Urals, but investigators found similar difficulties among low-paid workers in other places as well. Reports from Orekhovo-Zuevo in Moscow province noted that many low-paid textile workers were too poor to pay for their rations. The wage of the average textile worker in 1943 was just 351 rubles a month, roughly half the earnings of workers in the tank industry, the sector with the highest average wage. Eighty percent of textile workers were women, and many had family members at the front and were the sole supporters of their families.[111] The town's textile combine employed more than 13,000 workers. In 1942, the food crisis hit the factory hard: the average worker lost an entire month to illness. In July, the worst month, one out of every six workers was off sick, and doctors estimated that between 25 and 30 percent of these lost days were due to acute malnutrition. Mortality in the town spiked, double that of 1941. In June and July one out of every forty people in Orekhovo-Zuevo was diagnosed with some form of starvation illness: scurvy, pellagra, edema, or cachexia. Workers ate only around 1,300 calories per day, almost all from bread, and many mothers sold their bread cards to buy milk for their children.[112]

By 1943, as starvation deaths climbed steadily higher, doctors developed a common standard for classifying degrees of starvation illness and appropriate treatments for each stage based on Leningrad doctors' work with starvation victims during the siege.[113] The new protocols spread slowly to general practitioners, who often found it difficult to distinguish one stage of the disease from the next. Factory doctors were under pressure to reduce the number of sick notes and to send patients back to work. When people in an advanced stage of the disease were misdiagnosed and prescribed lighter work and more rest in place of immediate hospitalization and refeeding, the condition quickly proved fatal. Doctors also commonly and fatally misdiagnosed starvation as a vitamin deficiency.[114] But the main difficulty, even for a well-versed diagnostician, was the lack of food. Thus, despite greater knowledge among experts, starvation mortality and morbidity continued to afflict large numbers of people until the middle of 1944, when factory medical services had access to enough food to remove workers from their jobs and put them on refeeding programs. Many workers were out of work for long periods, but the majority now recovered.[115] Starvation abated more slowly outside the defense factories, and doctors were still treating people with milder stages in late 1945, although the numbers dying from starvation now fell sharply.[116]

One reason for the improvement in food supplies was Lend-Lease food aid from the USA, Britain, and Canada. Allied food aid began to arrive in large quantities in the middle of 1942, under the proviso that it would only be used to feed the Red Army. In theory, this would then free up domestic food stocks for the population in the rear. In practice, however, food shortages were so severe that even with Allied aid the state was initially unable to boost civilian consumption. Despite Lend-Lease food aid, the state was forced to cut civilian rations in November 1943 as a result of harvest shortfalls, and starvation continued to worsen through early 1944. Only from spring and summer 1944 did Lend-Lease make a sizable contribution to civilian diets.[117]

Until that time hunger and ill health proved enormously costly, not just in terms of mortality and morbidity, but because they dramatically lowered workers' productivity. Long hours and limited rest often proved counterproductive by weakening workers over the long term and making it difficult for them to recover fully from illness. With shorter hours and a less intensive expenditure of energy, malnutrition and starvation might have been held at bay, and a healthier workforce might have recorded higher productivity and produced the same total output in less time. Yet in the early years of the war, when the country's very existence was threatened and workers needed to resupply the Red Army after its disastrous losses, the human costs of this great "production miracle" were disregarded.[118] But the state could not disregard them forever. Over time, hunger and starvation became a driving force behind desertion and the growing difficulties of labor mobilization. After callups to the Red Army, the two largest contributors to turnover on the labor force were "desertion" and physical incapacity, including death. The two were intimately linked. The very fear of starvation and incapacity drove many workers, especially teenagers, to flee at the same time as the growing debilitation of the workforce demanded more workers. The lack of food and progressive weakening of the workforce beginning in 1942 and lasting into 1944 added to the self-generating and destructive dynamic of labor mobilization. In the final analysis, hunger and overwork actually increased the pressure on food supplies by enlarging the number of those on the ration rolls who were unable to work. When peasants mobilized from the countryside to work in the eastern industrial towns fell ill with starvation, the Komitet mobilized new workers to take their place. In the main these new workers also came from rural areas. The collective farms lost their most active food producers, while the state had to feed two people, the malnourished worker and the mobilized replacement. The cycle was finally broken during the second half of 1944 when the gardening movement, the liberation of the occupied territories, and Lend-Lease food aid made more food available in factory canteens, on the ration, and through refeeding programs.

****

Unlike many hardships the population faced during the war the health crisis was not solely the result of extreme wartime conditions. Prewar imbalances in the distribution of medical resources, the failure to invest in essential sanitary infrastructure, and the attempt to subordinate medicine to the goals of industrial production all left the population vulnerable to the shocks brought by the Nazi invasion. At the same time, the wartime emergency prompted important initiatives and reforms. These had only a modest impact on mortality and general health during the war but produced much more tangible benefits later on. The evacuation and the urgent need to deal with a threatened sanitary disaster along the railway lines, train stations, and waterways led to the development and increasingly strict implementation of sanitary controls along transport routes. These controls played a key role in preventing a recurrence of the typhus epidemic of 1942 and became a permanent part of population-wide typhus-prevention measures in the postwar period. The pressures on urban sanitation systems—already inadequate before the war and overwhelmed by the influx of evacuees and mobilized workers—led to the twice-yearly cleanup campaigns that became a regular feature of postwar urban life. The war greatly enhanced the role and authority of the State Sanitary Inspectorate, which prior to the invasion had been the stepchild of Soviet medicine with few enforcement powers. All of these were important achievements focused on containment of disease rather than eliminating the conditions that produced it. Clearing cities of their accumulated filth twice a year was no substitute for investing in comprehensive sewerage. Mass surveillance for lice was no substitute for providing every household with indoor plumbing, hot and cold running water, and adequate supplies of soap.

It was in the field of sanitary education that the lessons of the war made perhaps their most durable contribution to later improvements in health and mortality. The Bolsheviks had launched concerted programs in sanitary education from the earliest years after the revolution, and these efforts intensified in the 1930s when sanitary education became part of the civil defense effort. The training encompassed a significant part of the population. By 1945, some 13 million adults and 5.5 million children had completed substantive courses in hygiene, first aid, and disease prevention. Vocational students, schoolchildren, and wounded soldiers in evacuation hospitals in the rear received similar instruction tailored to age. These efforts were supplemented by concerted and often highly imaginative propaganda campaigns, including posters, factory newspapers, and radio broadcasts, aimed at teaching the general public the importance of basic hygiene. Although people had difficulty putting their new knowledge to use given the acute shortage of soap, fuel, and bathhouses, the educational programs had a major impact after the war. The millions of schoolchildren who took training courses and received lessons in hygiene eventually became parents. And, unlike their own parents, who did not know about microbes or how diseases spread, the young parents of the early and mid-1950s put the new knowledge into daily practice. Under Khrushchev, Soviet infant mortality fell to levels close to those in Western countries. The decrease was due not only to the discovery of antibiotics, but also to the success of wartime educational programs.[119]

9

"Our Cause Is Just": Loyalty, Propaganda, and Popular Moods

> I am 50 years old. I am healthy and vigorous. I am a participant of
> the armed uprising of 1905. I participated in the imperialist war,
> and I routed the Germans. I was a volunteer in the Red Guard, and
> in the October Revolution, I marched off against the Junkers. I was
> wounded at the battles at the Red Barracks. But now my wounds are
> healed. I am able to protect the Soviet land and I strongly stand up
> for Soviet power. I ask you to enroll me in the ranks of volunteers.
>
> F. B. Denisov, worker at Moscow
> machine-building factory, July 8, 1941

Throughout the war years, the state's mobilizing efforts could not have been
sustained without the support and sacrifices of ordinary people. The initial
military losses were so demoralizing and daily conditions so difficult that
the state's ability to deploy "propaganda" and to convince people of its message assumed even greater importance.[1] Both state propaganda and people's
responses changed over time in accordance with events at the front, the liberation of the occupied territories, and conditions on the home front. Although
at times communication broke down, a unifying wartime culture did emerge
based on political education, newspaper and radio reportage, poster art, poetry, and song. Collective activities also bound people together in common
purpose. Workers pledged to meet production targets and initiated norm-
busting campaigns, all-female brigades taught women workers new skills,
and ordinary people trained in civil defense, worked together on anti-tank
construction and roof-top fire-spotting, and joined the volunteer militia
(*opolchenie*). All these state and popular initiatives helped create the *levée en
masse* spirit evident to so many observers at the time.

Historians differ over the extent of, and motivations for, home front support. While many argue that the majority of people shared "a fervent, cru-
sading patriotism that transcended the risks and miseries of everyday life,"

others maintain that the country was split into "those looking forward to an 'easy occupation' and those who would sooner die than let this happen."[2] Indeed, collectivization and the repressions of the 1930s turned many against the regime, and some peasants and nationalist groups initially welcomed the Germans.[3] Some historians assert that Russians were the strongest supporters of the war effort as a result of "age-old traditions of selflessness, self-renunciation, and self-sacrifice," a view rejected by those who emphasize the state's skill in creating a new "Soviet patriotism" that encompassed multiple nationalities and even briefly promoted national martial mythologies of the non-Russian republics.[4] Others link loyalty to class rather than nationalism, noting that ordinary people of many nationalities, particularly workers, saw the war as part of the international struggle against fascism and the defense of socialism.[5] There are comparable disagreements over the efficacy of propaganda in mobilizing people.[6] For all their different approaches, however, most historians concur that the majority of people on the home front, for whatever reasons, remained loyal to the state and strongly supported the war effort.

Wartime propaganda was generated through a strong, deeply rooted organizational structure. In 1920, the Party created the Agitation-Propaganda Department under the Central Committee. The department, whose name changed several times over the years, was called during the war the Administration of Propaganda and Agitation, or by its catchier moniker, "Agitprop." The Organizational-Instructional Department, also under the Central Committee, trained and dispatched party instructors to disseminate Agitprop's messages in factories, in cultural and educational institutions, and on collective farms. Both departments compiled talking points, based on the speeches of party leaders and current events, for political leaders at the front (*politruki*) and for party instructors and discussion leaders (*besedchiki*) in the rear. The most widespread form of propaganda was these "conversations" or *besedy*, which covered international politics, military objectives, daily life, and production.[7] In addition, the Party organized lectures, talks, newspaper readings, and larger meetings between people on the home front and frontline soldiers (*frontoviki*) and survivors of occupation.

Propaganda was also generated more spontaneously "from below" by artists, writers, musicians, and workers in articles, sketches, poetry, and radio transmissions that the state endorsed and encouraged. Many initiatives to support the war effort originated on the shop floor, beginning as small experiments by brigades of young workers, which were then expanded by

Figure 9.1 Woman electrician reading *Pravda* to women workers at the Voikov factory, Moscow, 1941. Courtesy of RGAKFD.

the state into nationwide movements. People found public outlets to express personal feelings of sacrifice, loss, and grief. Propaganda proved most effective when it was able to imbue individual experience with meaning based on a larger, collective political narrative. Personal experiences merged powerfully with the state's ideological view of fascism, for example, after the Red Army began liberating the occupied territories. War correspondents and photographers, especially Jewish journalists, infused their reporting from the newly liberated areas with a visceral hatred of Nazism that proved deeply moving and convincing to Soviet citizens.[8]

State propaganda did not remain static over the course of the war but changed in tone and message alongside the military situation, demands of production, and liberation of the occupied territories. After the first shock of the invasion and the painful retreats that followed, the state adopted a more honest tone in response to people's demands for greater clarity about events at the front. Political abstraction and sloganeering gave way to more emotional and personal expressions, and the discovery of Nazi atrocities produced rage and passionate calls for revenge. In April 1945, as the Red Army crossed into Germany, party leaders called a halt to "vengeance propaganda" and reasserted a class approach that emphasized the differences between the German people and their Nazi rulers.

If propaganda helped to shape popular opinion and moods, the reactions of ordinary people also shaped the state's message. Party leaders were keenly interested in how workers, peasants, and other social groups thought about the war. After meetings, discussion leaders and instructors made detailed notes of people's questions and responses, which they forwarded up the chain of command to the Central Committee. These compilations, once considered top secret, reveal not only how the speeches of Stalin and other party leaders were distilled into "talking points," but also how ordinary people reacted to them. Popular moods shifted over the course of the war, from the first panicked shock of invasion, through the hard years of sacrifice and retreat, to rising pride and anticipation of victory. The state's message, too, shifted over time. Mood and message, both keyed to events at the front, production needs, and conditions of daily life, each in turn shaped the other.

The Shock of Attack: Turmoil and Resolve

Most Soviet citizens were asleep in their beds when German bombers attacked Sevastopol at 3:15 a.m. on June 22, 1941. In the absence of an official declaration of war, the screeching bombers proclaimed the invasion. For the vast majority of citizens, who were not privy to secret intelligence, the attack came as a complete surprise. They knew war was likely but did not expect it to arrive without warning. Throughout the 1930s, the newspapers were filled with anti-fascist rhetoric and reportage: news of the Spanish Civil War, Hitler's march east, and the Nazi occupation of Europe. Party activists held regular meetings in schools and factories to explain events. Poet E. Dolmatovskii later wrote, "Spain was like an extramural university in anti-fascist struggle, presaging the four-year course of the Great Patriotic War."[9] Schoolchildren drilled for war, and their parents worked under strict new labor legislation. Yet the Hitler–Stalin Pact, signed in August 1939 and designed to last ten years, allayed fears that invasion was imminent. Jacob Mikhailov, a teenager in 1941, later remembered his thoughts at the time:

> We were brought up with propaganda. We were raised with movies as "Esli Zavtra Voyna" [If War Comes Tomorrow, USSR 1938] and such like. We were convinced if somebody dared to attack our country, he

would be defeated [on foreign territory] and there would be little bloodshed . . . Frankly speaking, I wouldn't have imagined that such a powerful
state could be attacked. I couldn't even think that Germany would attack
the USSR after the Molotov–Ribbentrop pact had been signed.[10]

Most people held an unrealistic idea of how long or how painful such a war
was likely to be. Soviet media disseminated a confident, even boastful, view of
the Red Army's prowess, assuring the population that the war would be brief
and fought beyond the country's borders. Popular films such as *Alexander
Nevsky*, *If War Comes Tomorrow*, *Tankist*, and *Naval Post*, reinforced this
idea. Even military leaders were filled with false optimism, promising the
population an "easy victory" achieved "with little bloodshed."[11] Immediately
after the invasion, people more distant from the front still clung to this naïve
belief. One Leningrad metallurgical worker explained to a coworker, "it will
all be over in a week." His coworker replied, "No, it won't be over in a week.
We will have to go to Berlin. We will need three or four weeks." Many who
remembered the fraternization and revolutionary solidarity of World War
I expected that German workers would refuse to fight for Hitler. Another
worker explained, "Of course the German workers will support us, and other
people will rise up as well. How could it be otherwise?"[12] These illusions were
all quickly and brutally dispelled.

On the day of the invasion, people gathered around radio loudspeakers
mounted in the streets to listen to V. M. Molotov, Deputy Chairman of the
Soviet of People's Commissars and Commissar of Foreign Affairs, address
the nation. Molotov's announcement was brief: the German army had
crossed the border and bombed numerous cities. The people stood, hushed
and still. Molotov ended the announcement with three short sentences that
would become a rallying cry through the next four years: "Our cause is just.
The enemy will be beaten. Victory will be ours."[13] Molotov's speech resonated
strongly with the grave crowds. A few embittered people were heard to mutter
comments welcoming the invasion. One former kulak recently released from
prison noted, "Finally and good, at last what we have been waiting for." There
were other isolated expressions of anti-Soviet sentiment and even a few
scattered cases of arson, but the vast majority of people were eager to partic-
ipate in the war effort.[14] The following day, the newspapers printed a longer
version of Molotov's announcement. It stressed the distinction between the
German people and their fascist rulers: "This war was imposed on us not
by the German people, not by German workers, peasants, and intellectuals,

whose suffering we well understand." Yet at the same time that Molotov drew a class line between the German people and their Nazi rulers, he also evoked a tsarist past that erased the class line between the people of the Russian empire and their tsarist rulers. Drawing a parallel between Napoleon and Hitler, he revived the older phrase of 1812, deeming the coming conflict a "fatherland [*otechestvennaia*] war." Yet Molotov made no special reference to Russians, but rather addressed "all our people," "real Soviet patriots," "closely knit and united as never before." Although the text referenced a previous invasion, it appealed to a new Soviet patriotism.[15]

The country rallied quickly. Tens of thousands of people volunteered for the army, showing up unbidden at draft boards and district party headquarters. Young women besieged the recruiting stations, demanding to be sent to the front. In Krasnoiarsk alone, on a single day, the district party committee and draft boards were inundated with more than 2,600 requests to enlist, split almost evenly between men and women. Komsomol and party members were among the first to volunteer in large numbers.[16] Thousands of soldiers and factory workers, recognizing that the Party would lead the war effort, applied for membership. Party organizers throughout the country reported a swell of "great patriotic feeling at meetings in factories and on collective farms." Workers requested subscriptions to state loans, a form of fund raising that had often provoked resentment in the past. Party organizers reported some drunken revelry among new recruits in Kuibyshev, Ul'ianovsk, and other towns, and regional authorities temporarily halted the sale of vodka, but the mood overall was sober and committed.[17] Stalin addressed the nation on July 3 in a quiet speech that emphasized the struggle against fascism. He explained that the war was a battle of ideologies "of all Soviet people against the German fascist army." People were fighting for a goal greater than "the elimination of the danger directed at our country": to "help all people of Europe groaning under the yoke of German fascism."[18]

The early flush of optimistic resolve, however, was soon followed by disturbing news from the front. Newspapers and radio bulletins were initially vague about the losses. Jacob Mikhailov remembered the first days following the invasion:

All day long we were discussing when our troops would be crossing the border. People outside had likewise talks. The next day we would ask each other with hope whether our troops had crossed the border. There was no information on the radio for a while, only optimistic promises that the enemy wouldn't cross our territory. Only a few days later we found out that Minsk had been captured by the Germans. They didn't even say a thing about the battles with the enemy on this territory. Then, when the Germans were deep in the country, for thousands of kilometers, there was nothing to say, but, "After severe fighting our soldiers had to retreat from such and such city."[19]

People soon learned to read the phrase, "fighting in the direction of" as a euphemism for the loss of a town or area. Radio, a new mass medium capable of up-to-the-minute reportage, was initially unsure of its role. One historian later noted, "radio met the invasion with silence."[20] Not surprisingly, the lack of reliable information generated panicked rumors. In the countryside, some angry and alienated peasants told their neighbors, "Don't believe the newspapers, it is all lies." Others expressed defeatism, claiming, "We cannot compare with Germany and we will not fight," and "It is better not to resist fascism, it is not worth it to go to the front." The Germans deliberately encouraged this view in their leaflets and propaganda. An engineer in a defense plant told the workers, "Hitler is clever, Germany is strong, and it would be better not to go to war with Germany, but to put down our weapons." A carpenter and party member in a timber factory echoed these sentiments, telling his coworkers, "The USSR has no business tangling with Germany. Their technical level is higher than ours. The radio is not telling the truth, and you should not believe the newspapers." Some even suggested that the country would be better off under German rule. A former kulak in a tool shop asked a fellow worker, "Why should blood flow, to annihilate our people, if the Germans have already conquered so much? Let it be as they want. Let us come to terms and obey them. Indeed, it is all the same to us, the workers, who will rule. Under every power, it is necessary to work."[21]

These defeatist sentiments, expressed during the first months of the war, suggested that their proponents still had little understanding of German occupation policy. They disliked the Soviet state, distrusted the press, and held the misguided hope that damage might be averted by acquiescence. For a small minority of the non-Jewish population in the occupied areas, such accommodationist inclinations blossomed into active collaboration, but for the vast majority they were quickly dispelled by German brutality and contempt.

Collectivization and the mass repressions of the 1930s had created groups throughout the country that felt deeply aggrieved by Stalin's policies. Some peasants told the chairman of one collective farm, "Soon your heads will roll." Another spitefully told a rural brigade leader, "Soon you won't be in charge here anymore." Some officials working in the district party committees and draft boards received anonymous letters and threats. In the northern town of Molotovsk, a former kulak working in a factory was charged with spreading fascist propaganda over the factory's internal radio system. Some former party members, purged in the mass repressions of the 1930s, hoped for the fall of the government. One former member in exile, hearing about German bombing of Moscow, exclaimed, "It is a pity that the bombs fell on the central polyclinic, and not the Kremlin itself or on our leaders." A few individuals even hoped for Soviet defeat. One embittered person declared, "In the coming days, we will await the fall of Kiev, Leningrad, and Moscow. The fall of these towns will bring the immediate fall of Soviet power. I will then devote my soul to killing communists. I have lead bullets, which I am keeping for this purpose: to shoot communists. Not a single bullet will miss its target." In Arkhangel'sk and Solombal, passersby found five hand-written leaflets calling for the overthrow of Soviet power and the massacre of communists.[22] These stray comments and notes, reported to local party officials by NKVD employees or ordinary people, were not representative of the majority.

Yet even the most loyal citizens struggled to maintain their initial optimism in the face of the summer's defeats. Some felt betrayed by the earlier propaganda that had promised a quick victory on foreign soil. An official in the communications administration of the navy, regarding the success of the German army, noted despondently, "We all said that we would never allow war on our territory, but now all military activity is occurring only on the territory of the USSR." Unsure whom to reproach, or how to explain the losses, many people, including party members, blamed the country's leaders. One organizer in Arkhangel'sk complained that the state had not been honest: "The state allowed boastful speeches, claiming we had inexhaustible stocks of everything, that we would beat the enemy only on his own territory, but the facts have been otherwise." Many became angered by the Pact, which had provided valuable material to the enemy. A doctor noted, "For two years, our government fed the Germans. It would have been better if we had provisioned our own army and people, but now everyone is expecting hunger."

One former party member, listening to a bulletin about the Red Army's most recent retreat, referred to the "friendship" Pact in a sarcastic aside, "Soon Hitler will show such friendship to our communists that they will not know where to run." Some believed the invasion had caught the country "unaware." Others, recognizing that the propaganda of the Pact years was false, mistrusted all the news. One white-collar employee reasoned, "The Germans are advancing rapidly, almost without stopping. Now it must be said straight out that our leaders are busy only with nonsense and not serious business, assuring everyone that the army is well armed and invincible." Negative coverage of Britain and the United States between 1939 and 1941 also left its mark. One collective farm chairman doubted whether the two countries would prove reliable allies. Channeling the view that prevailed during the Pact (and the later Cold War years), he noted darkly, "In my opinion, we will wait for nothing. In the end, England and the United States will [make a] pact with each other."[23]

Although few Soviet citizens were rash enough to discuss the purges openly, some attributed the failures at the front to the repression of the officer corps in 1937–1939. They spoke euphemistically of the "change in command." A bookkeeper in a garment factory noted, "The spirit of our army is completely shattered. Our soldiers are giving up towns to the Germans because there were so many changes among the officer corps." And the purges and mass repressions shaped the outlook and explanations of ordinary people in other ways as well. The chairman of a collective farm stated, "I am simply bewildered by why the Red Army is retreating. Obviously there are traitors and wrecking in the Red Army." Repeating a common trope of the 1930s, he believed that behind every failure lay a "wrecker." He clearly felt that the purge of the military had not gone far enough.[24]

Whatever explanations people sought for the continuing retreats, they found little reliable information in the daily press. One soldier said dispiritedly, "Since yesterday, I have been very depressed. They write and say one thing, but in fact something else happens. They said that we would fight only on foreign territory, but in fact we are giving up town after town." Party leaders still had not found a way to make the unfolding disaster comprehensible to a stunned population.[25] At the height of the panic in Moscow in October 1941, one diarist overheard an old man say aloud to no one in particular: "Why didn't anyone speak on the radio . . . . Just let them say something . . . Miraculous, good, no matter . . . But we are completely in a fog, and each one thinks for himself."[26]

The damaging communication gap between state and people was particularly pronounced in the textile province of Ivanovo, where workers later rioted against the efforts of local officials to evacuate the factories. In the months after the invasion, many textile workers experienced a 30 to 40 percent reduction in wages with the shift to the production of military cloth.[27] Difficulties at work were accompanied by sharp reductions in food, and workers threatened strikes throughout the region. In the Nogin factory, a woman worker spoke contemptuously of the Pact. "Hitler did not take the grain," she said, "We gave it to him ourselves, and now they give nothing to us. Why did they protect him?" Workers, most of whom were women with children, were particularly furious at the large food allocations for officials and managers. Even party members on the shop floor were unwilling to defend the ration cuts. After another inadequate dinner in the crowded canteen, one party member gathered a group of fifteen workers and marched them straight to the canteen director. "Feed them," he said brusquely; "They are hungry."[28]

In August and September 1941, the textile factories seethed with discontent. A total of about 450 workers in 8 factories went out on strike to protest the lack of food, falling wages, and problems with production. The strikes, short-lived and easily quelled, were provoked by fear and hunger. But some party organizers noted that "strike moods" were inflamed by "enemy elements." Workers gathered in small groups in washrooms, corridors, and staircases to discuss the war, listen to anti-Soviet anecdotes, and trade rumors. One young Komsomol member said to a fellow worker and party member in the Shagov factory, "If someone would only start a strike, we would support it."[29] Many textile workers did not understand the deepening impact of German occupation on the food supply, and the loss of local party activists to the front made it difficult to explain the need for ration cuts. More than 2,000 workers lived in dormitories, but there were no organizers to answer questions or lead discussions, and printed materials, including wall newspapers and posters, were unavailable. The director of the Shagov factory noted the poor morale: "For some time now, the mood has not been good, people are not unified and there is no sense of rising, no fighting spirit, but the opposite, a decline." In the absence of reliable information, workers substituted "all kinds of idle talk and religious rumors." The director noted that some even wondered whether food provisioning would improve under the fascists. A similar situation prevailed in other textile factories. Inexperienced party organizers seemed stymied by even the simplest questions. When a woman worker asked, "Will we win or not in the struggle against fascism?" the organizer equivocated, "It is hard to say who will win, but according to the newspapers, it is clear that our forces are still retreating."[30] His answer was honest, but hardly inspiring.

Party leaders made strong efforts to improve communication. The Organizational-Instructional Department sent activists to organize party members "who are wandering around the factories, not knowing how or where to apply their energy." Factory directors were authorized to buy horses to speed deliveries of raw materials, and thus reduce stoppages and increase wages.[31] Pal'tsev, the head of the provincial party committee, permitted the commercial sale of bread (over the amount set by the ration card) in the factory canteens even after such sales were banned nationwide, eliminated cuts that ended "double" feeding of children in daycare centers and on ration at home, and refused to implement the order that tied provisioning to output. His actions split the provincial party committee. Later in 1942, Pal'tsev's deputy sent two long complaints about him to the Central Committee, claiming that he had "discredited himself" earlier in October 1941 during evacuation and had subsequently lost authority with the workers. The secretary wrote angrily, "He knows this. This consciousness generates in him confusion, uncertainty, fear, and hesitancy." Pal'tsev, in his opinion, was too quick to conciliate the workers. The complaints were investigated, but Pal'tsev remained in his post, and the deputy was removed.[32] Like Pal'tsev, the more flexible local officials recognized that workers were enduring great deprivation and that their support was critical to the war effort.

"You and I—as Before—Are One"

At the same time that the shock of retreat engendered doubt, millions of volunteers also embraced the state's mobilizing initiatives. Within two days of the invasion, A. Aleksandrov and Vasily Lebedev-Kumach wrote the music and words to "Sacred War," the stirring hymn that captured the spirit of "people's war." The chorus ran:

> Let noble wrath Boil over like a wave! This is the people's war, a
> Sacred war![33]

Sung at railroad stations as volunteers left for the front, the song's lyrics inspired soldiers and civilians alike. Hundreds of thousands of women, teenagers, and pensioners stepped in to fill jobs vacated by men leaving for the front. Local soviets organized additional childcare facilities so that mothers could go to work.[34] People contributed their beloved jewelry, wedding rings, watches, and heirlooms to state collections of gold and silver, as well as parting with meager savings that might have bought extra food in peasant markets. Collective farmers donated milk, eggs, meat, and grain. The Party organized surveillance posts on the roofs of buildings for residents to extinguish incendiary bombs, and small groups on every block to guard bomb shelters, establish fire commands, and mask windows through the civil defense organization Osoaviakhim (Society for the Promotion of Defense and Aviation and Chemical Construction). Millions joined the *opolchenie*, or volunteer civilian militias, which were deployed to protect railroads, bridges, and communication lines and, in the most desperate circumstances, to fight alongside the Red Army.[35]

Figure 9.2 "Presents for the Fascists" scrawled on bombs. Courtesy of RGAKFD.

In Leningrad, the front lines ran only 2 miles (3 km) from the famed Kirov factory, and battalions of soldiers, workers, and students walked to the front through the streets of the city. Olga Berggol'ts, a poet and party member, captured the poignancy of this march to battle in her poem, "The Road to the Front" ("Doroga na front"):

> We walked to the front through streets so familiar,
> Remembering each, as if in a dream:
> Here, picket fencing before Father's house,
> Here, rustling, wind-tossed, a great kindly tree.
>
> I walked to the front through the years of my childhood—
> On that road, where I ran to school long ago.
> I walked through my youth, through its cares and worries,
> Through joys that were mine, before the war's woe.[36]

An outpouring of poetry and music captured a mood of grim determination in the face of the ongoing losses. Konstantin Simonov's "Russian People," A. E. Korneichuk's "Front," and L. Leonov's "Invasion" were among the songs most popular during the war years. Nikolai Tikhonov's poem, "Kirov Is with Us [Kirov s nami]" described a vision in which S. M. Kirov, the former head of the Leningrad party committee, assassinated in 1934, still walked through the bombed-out city:

> The factory, blacked-out and frozen,
> Looks like a fortress, dark and stern.
> There are no breaks, no smokes, no chatting.
> All thought of rest and sleep is gone.
> The workers' faces, strained and sweating,
> Are grimly purposeful and strong.[37]

Simonov penned "Wait for Me [Zhdi menia]" the iconic poem of the war, written in the voice of a soldier to his beloved and known by heart by every soldier and civilian:

> Wait for me, and I'll come back!
> Wait with all you've got!
> Wait, when dreary yellow rains

Tell you, you should not.
Wait when snow is falling fast,
Wait when summer's hot,
Wait when yesterdays are past,
And others are forgot.
Wait, when from that far-off place,
Letters don't arrive.
Wait, when those with whom you wait
Doubt if I'm alive.

Its verses gave hope to soldiers that they had not been forgotten and served as a magical talisman for those who waited, replacing helpless anxiety with the promise that the very act of waiting would bring a beloved soldier home:

Wait for me and I'll come back,
Dodging every fate!
"What a bit of luck!" they'll say,
Those that would not wait.
They will never understand
How amidst the strife,
By your waiting for me, dear,
You had saved my life.
Only you and I will know
How you got me through.
Simply—you knew how to wait—
No one else but you.[38]

The emotional and political landscape of the country was scarred by the mass repressions of the late 1930s, and many people struggled to reconcile their bitterness with support of the war. Olga Berggol'ts became one of the strongest voices of Radio Leningrad, which broadcast during the siege. Berggol'ts was also a victim of the Terror. Both she and her husband had been arrested, and she miscarried her third child after a beating in prison.[39] Yet Berggol'ts remained a committed communist, reading her poetry on the radio and giving hope to the city's starving inhabitants. She dealt with the deep conflict she felt between her love for the country and her anger about the mass repressions in her poem, "We Expected the

Blaze [My predchuvstvovali polykhan'e]." In the poem, she understands in a "blinding flash" that her "motherland" was neither Stalin nor the state, but rather, the people, including those condemned as enemies in the 1930s:

I, on this day, did not forget
the bitter years of persecution and evil,
but in a blinding flash, I understood:
It did not happen to me alone, but to You too,
It was You who took courage and waited.

No, I forgot nothing.
But even if I were dead, condemned—
I would rise at Your call from the grave,
All of us would rise, and not I alone.

I love You with a new love,
bitter, all-forgiving, alive,
My motherland with a crown of thorns,
and dark rainbow over Your head

Our hour has come,
and what it means—
Only You and I are given to know.
I love You—and I cannot do otherwise,
You and I—as before—are one.[40]

In the poem, Berggol'ts reconciled the bitterness of the Terror years with a newfound commitment to the war effort and the country, a choice made, perhaps with less elegance but no less dedication, by countless others.

In the late summer, a few glimmers of hope finally lightened the unrelieved gloom at the front. In August 1941, the Red Army succeeded in halting the German *Blitzkrieg* on the road to Moscow. The line stabilized and, although Smolensk fell, the Germans were forced to retreat from the El'na salient, a small area, but in the words of war correspondent Alexander Werth, "the first piece of territory—perhaps only 100 or 150 square miles—in the whole of Europe reconquered from Hitler's Wehrmacht." In a visit to the newly liberated area, Werth noted that soldiers had already developed a different view of the enemy. One officer explained, "This is a very grim war, and you cannot imagine the hatred the Germans have stirred up among our people."[41]

The German failure to capture Moscow in October also lifted morale greatly. The Party adopted a new policy, encouraging any soldier who distinguished him- or herself in battle to become a member. As a result, almost 50,000 soldiers on the Moscow front joined the Party or the Komsomol.[42] Local and regional party organizations also mobilized civilians throughout the frontline zones west of Moscow. In Kursk, people built barricades in the streets, joined the *opolchenie*, and established a ring around the city. When the Germans entered the city on November 2, the *opolchenie* fought alongside soldiers in the streets.[43] Similar initiatives with broad popular support were replicated in many towns.

On November 6, deep underground in the Mayakovsky metro station in Moscow, hundreds of military officers and party, soviet, and union officials celebrated the anniversary of the Revolution. The capital had been saved, at least temporarily. In a widely disseminated speech, Stalin sounded themes that would become central to the state's mobilizing message: the unity of front and rear, the need to increase defense production, the nature of fascism, and the struggle against German aggression. Nor did he obscure the losses: "The enemy has seized a large part of the Ukraine, Belorussia, Moldavia, Lithuania, Latvia, Estonia, and a number of other regions, has forced his way into the Donets Basin, hangs like a black cloud over Leningrad, and is threatening our glorious capital." He explained the retreat of the Red Army by the power of its enemies, "the absence of a second front in Europe," and the lack of sufficient tanks and aircraft. Despite the losses, Stalin conveyed optimism, contrasting the Soviet cause, defending one's native land, with German aims, an empire to be built, in Hitler's own words, on "the extermination of the Slav peoples." Stalin continued to assert his faith in class, maintaining that the German people would rise up against the Nazi state. And, if Germany was rent by class divisions, the Soviet Union was united. Striking a balance between Russian nationalism and Soviet patriotism, he invoked "the great Russian nation, the nation of Plekhanov and Lenin, Belinsky and Chernyshevsky, Pushkin and Tolstoy, Glinka and Chaikovsky, Gorky and Chekhov, Sechenov and Pavlov, Repin and Surikov, Suvorov and Kutuzov!" and called for "all the peoples of the USSR to organize into a single fighting camp." The speech ended with the slogan first proclaimed by Molotov: "Our cause is just—victory will be ours!" After the cheering died down, the assembled group, hundreds of feet below ground, sang the "Internationale," the anthem of workers all over the world. With the exception of Stalin's single sentence invoking a pantheon of cultural and military luminaries familiar to every Soviet schoolchild, little else in the speech suggested a return to Russian nationalism. In fact, throughout the war Stalin's speeches would continue to invoke Lenin, the October revolution, and the multinational character of the war effort.[44] The tenor of the celebration, including the final rousing rendition of the "Internationale," remained overtly Soviet and socialist. The speech was widely disseminated, printed in newspapers and brochures, and distributed to construction sites, factories, and collective farms. Hundreds of thousands of people listened to it on radio loudspeakers, and then read and discussed it at meetings with party instructors. Its emphasis on production launched a wave of mass meetings at which workers pledged to overfulfill their output norms to provide the Red Army with the armaments it needed to win.[45]

The most inspirational war reporting in these months was devoted to acts of suicidal resistance. In mid-November, the Germans launched their second offensive against Moscow, advancing to within 15 miles (25 km) of the capital. Fierce fighting and bitter cold, however, soon slowed their progress. A small group of soldiers, in an anti-tank division under the command of Major-General Ivan Panfilov, crippled fifteen German tanks using rifles, grenades, and bottles filled with petrol (Molotov cocktails) on the road to Moscow after Panfilov himself was killed. According to the story, in an act of suicidal resistance, their severely wounded party leader (*politruk*), threw himself under a German tank, blowing it up with hand grenades. The German breakthrough failed. The actions of the "Panfilov Men" soon became one of the great heroic tales of the war. Nikolai Gastello, the aviator who rammed his burning plane into a German panzer column, and a young partisan girl, Zoia Kosmodemianskaia, who was captured, tortured, and hanged by the Germans, were also lionized as heroes. All three tales, central to what would become the heroic narrative of the war, were later investigated, challenged, and debunked.[46] Yet as wartime journalist and historian Alexander Werth pointed out, these publicized acts were but a sample of numerous self-sacrificing actions that went "unrecorded for posterity."[47] The tales, first told to war reporters, and then embroidered and disseminated by the press, captured the public imagination in a way that other mobilizing exhortations did not. Nor was it accidental that all three stories emerged from the early period of defeat and despair. Celebrating suicidal resistance, they not only inspired courage, but also captured the desperate mood of the time.

Figure 9.3 Women workers at the Krasnyi Bogatyr' factory, Moscow, after adopting children orphaned by the war, January 1942. Courtesy of RGAKFD.

Vengeance and Political Education

As the Red Army liberated the towns and villages west of Moscow in the winter of 1941–1942, it discovered sickening scenes of devastation. Accompanied by journalists, the soldiers were soon joined by state and party officials, who assessed the damage. Stalin had received the first NKVD reports on German atrocities in July 1941. By 1942, the Red Army began actively collecting photographs, survivor testimonies, eyewitness accounts, and captured Nazi documents. In July and August 1942, the Central Committee ordered war correspondents to do the same. Agitprop created the Jewish Anti-Fascist Committee in January 1942, which collected material about the extermination of Soviet Jews. Its letters to Stalin, which provided extensive documentation, were published in the press on May 24, 1942, and February 24, 1943. The information was also disseminated to the public through articles in *Einikait*, the Jewish Anti-Fascist Committee's Yiddish-language weekly. The mainstream press, however, emphasized the mass murder of civilians without reference to nationality, adhering to the rule, "we do not divide the dead." Party leaders justified the policy by the losses suffered by many national groups and the German intent to promote anti-Semitism. In the press and in official reports on mass murder, Jews most often appeared as one group among many, including Ukrainians, Belorussians, Latvians, and Soviet POWs, and sometimes were not mentioned at all.[48]

In spring 1942, both *Krasnaia zvezda*, the Red Army newspaper, and the civilian press began featuring a new genre of articles based on interviews with local survivors. These tales of humiliation, murder, and torture shocked their readers, providing a vivid human dimension to more abstract discussions of fascist ideology. In April, Molotov published a bill of indictment against the Germans in *Krasnaia zvezda*, which included accounts of extreme violence against civilians. In Belorussia, the Germans applied the death penalty for any minor infraction and responded to partisan attacks with fierce reprisals against civilians. "Children were beaten in front of their parents, adults killed before children, people were hunted, tortured, murdered with grenades, machine guns, set on fire; they were burned, buried alive; drenched with water in the freezing cold, turned into icy poles; corpses were mutilated; the living and the dead violated, transformed into bleeding hunks." Young girls were stripped and raped, their corpses found frozen in village streets, with eyes gouged out, breasts cut off, faces disfigured. Each crime was documented by date, village, district, and province. Molotov also listed mass shootings of tens, hundreds, and thousands. In Khar'kov alone, 14,000 people were murdered in the first days of occupation. "Hundreds of thousands of Ukrainians, Russians, Jews, Moldavians, and people of other nationalities" had perished in the towns of Ukraine. The Soviet government possessed irrefutable proof that Soviet POWs, deprived of warm clothing and food, were dying in concentration camps. The Germans had systematically destroyed cultural, social, and education institutions. They had looted and burned the museum-house of the great writer, A. S. Pushkin, destroying invaluable paintings by employing them for target practice. They used the books of the great library of Khar'kov as paving stones for German automobiles on the muddy roads. In the historic Russian town of Staritsa, they burned the ancient monastery and heaped the naked, mutilated corpses of Red Army prisoners in the ruins. Molotov's report contrasted fascism, which was based in "race hatred," with the Soviet principle of multinational unity. Yet despite the litany of crimes, Molotov, like Stalin, still maintained the distinction between the Nazi state and the German people. The soldiers of the Red Army, he noted, "had no wish to destroy the German people or annihilate the German state."[49]

Figure 9.4 Painting by F. Reshetnikov, "Germans in Kerch," part of exhibit at the Tretiakov Gallery on December 7, 1942. Courtesy of GARF.

The Party arranged speaking tours for civilians from the newly liberated areas. District party leaders organized collective farmers from Klin, which was briefly occupied between November 21 and December 15, 1941, to visit thousands of peasants and factory workers. Their audiences, anxious to know about life under the Germans, asked simple practical questions: Where did people hide when the Germans arrived? Did the Germans give people food and pay workers their wages? They were also concerned about those still under occupation: Could the Soviet government help them? Was there a partisan movement? Could the ruined factories be restored? Almost everyone in attendance had relatives in the army, and they were eager to know how their soldiers compared to the Wehrmacht: Who was better dressed? Beneath the simple questions lay more controversial concerns that could not be addressed directly: Was it possible to live decently under the Germans? Was the Red Army as well equipped as the newspapers claimed? The speakers, in turn, related their experiences. One peasant from Kalinin province replied, "The fascists turned us into their slaves. All the people of our village were treated like working cattle, nothing but numbers, and deprived of every human right." The speakers made a deep impression on their audiences. The chairman of a rural soviet, for example, noted that some collective farmers, initially skeptical about German brutality, were convinced

after the lecture. Among workers, the tours linked the horrors of occupation with the Red Army's need for armaments. Many audience members
expressed gratitude to Stalin and the Red Army for saving Moscow and for
providing the opportunity to meet with people who had first-hand experience with the Germans.[50]

On May 1, 1942, Stalin issued an order in lieu of the traditional May Day
greeting, which was soon converted into new "talking points" for party
activists. The country, he proclaimed, had become "a single and undivided
military camp," uniting front and rear. Working people had refused the traditional holiday in solidarity with soldiers and would provide the front with
an extra day of labor, a May Day gift of ammunition, weaponry, tanks, planes,
bread, and food. Stalin made no reference by this point to Russian nationalism
or tsarist heroes. Continuing to insist on German class distinctions, he inti-
mated that the German people, "disappointed, hungry, and impoverished,"
might overthrow Hitler. Despite the continuing losses, his account of the
past year conveyed hope. The victories around Moscow had ended "idle talk
about the invincibility of the German troops." The partisan movement was
growing in size and organization. The "complacency and carelessness" that
had characterized the army in the first months of the war had vanished, and
it had "truly learned to hate the fascist occupiers." Ending with a resolutely
socialist rallying cry, he concluded, "Under the invincible banner of the great
Lenin, forward to victory!"[51]

The hopes Stalin invested in the German working class proved groundless,
but his observation that Soviet "soldiers had learned to hate" was becoming
ever more true. Class analysis was soon swept aside by a great outpouring of
what Werth later called "hate propaganda," or the avenging spirit of horror
that seized soldiers, journalists, and others who saw the newly liberated territories.[52] By the summer of 1942, journalists such as Ilya Ehrenburg, Vasily
Grossman, and Konstantin Simonov were reporting regularly about violence, rape, and mass murder. Agitprop sanctioned the publication of these
accounts along with the glorification of individual heroes and martyrs.[53]
In June, on the first anniversary of the invasion, renowned writer Mikhail
Sholokhov published "The Science of Hate [*Nauka nenavisti*]," the story
of a Soviet POW sadistically tormented by his German captors.[54] The article had a powerful impact on both soldiers and civilians. The phrase "Kill
a German!" was widely adopted on posters and leaflets. First coined by
Simonov in his poem, "Kill Him!," published on July 18, 1942 in *Krasnaia
zvezda*, the poem was republished in other newspapers as well as *Sputnik
agitatora*, the journal for party instructors. Werth noted later that the poem

"became like Russia's Ten Commandments all in one."[55] Combining powerful feelings for family and home with images of German defilement, the poem concluded with the repeated refrain: "Kill him!"[56] A selection from its many verses read:

If your mother is dear to you
And the breast that nourished you
Which has had no milk for many years
But now is where you lay your cheek.
If you cannot stand the thought
Of a German doing harm
Beating in her furrowed face
With her braids wound round his arm.

If you don't want to give away
The girl you strolled with, but never touched
Who you never dared to kiss
But loved so long, so very much.
And the Germans cornering her
Taking her alive, by force
Three crucifying her
Naked on the floor
With coarse moans, hate, and blood
Those dogs, taking all
You sacredly preserved
With your strong manly love.
If you don't want to give away
To the German with his black gun
Your house, your mother, and your wife
All that's yours as a native son.

No, no one will save your land
If you don't save it from the worst
No, no one will kill this foe
If you don't kill him first.

If your brother killed a German
If your neighbor killed one too
The vengeance taken belongs to them

It is not revenge for you.
You cannot sit behind another
Allow him to take your shot
If your brother kills a German
He is a soldier, you are not.

So kill one at the very least
As soon as you will
Kill each one you chance to see.
Kill him, kill him! Kill![57]

The publication of Simonov's poem was followed on July 24 by Ehrenburg's article "Kill" in *Krasnaia zvezda*, which repeated the same forceful, primal message:

We know everything. We understand everything. We have understood: Germans are not human beings. From now on, the word "German" is the most terrible curse. From now on, the word "German" is the shot of a gun. We will not speak. We will not be shocked. We will kill. If you do not kill at least one German a day, that day has been wasted. If you think that your neighbor will kill the Germans for you, you have not understood the threat. If you do not kill a German, he will kill you . . . If you let a German live, he will hang Russian men and shame Russian women. If you have killed one German, kill another. For us, there is no greater joy than German corpses. Do not count the days. Do not count the miles. Count only one thing: Germans you have killed. Kill the Germans! Your elderly mother begs you. Kill the Germans! Your child prays for this. Kill the Germans! This is the cry of your native land. Don't blunder. Don't miss. Kill![58]

Along with other talented journalists, Ehrenburg successfully channeled grief into rage and resistance. The journalists received thousands of letters from readers, thanking them for their work.[59] Posters featuring arresting graphics of dead children, terrified mothers, burning huts, anguished elderly people, and dead civilians swinging from German gallows visually captured the twin themes of atrocity and vengeance. After the liberation of the territory west of Moscow, posters were emblazoned with such captions as "Blood for Blood! Death for Death!," "Death to the Child Murderers," "Revenge!," and "Papa, Kill a German!" Illustrating the brutalities of the Nazis, they appealed to people's deepest emotional ties.[60]

Popular Moods and Opinions: "Why Are We Still Retreating?"

As the Red Army continued to retreat through the bleak summer of 1942, Agitprop distilled Stalin's May Day speech into twenty "talking points." Part exhortation, part ideological explanation, the talking points stressed military successes, the brutalities of occupation, and the Red Army's need for armaments. Stalin's hopes for an uprising of German workers was dropped. Activists were informed that "1942 would be the year of decisive rout," a point that would soon prove true at Stalingrad.[61] Within a short time, local party officials reported back to the Central Committee on popular reactions to the talking points. Their reports revealed, not surprisingly, that people were deeply worried about the military situation. Remembering the boastful promises of the prewar years, people questioned whether 1942 would in fact be "the year of the great rout." Bewildered by the continuing losses, they asked repeatedly, "Why did we retreat?" and "How do you explain the success of the Germans in the south this summer?"[62] Many older workers and peasants, veterans of World War I and the Civil War, posed questions about strategy that reflected their military experience. One asked, "In order to lead, one must be able to predict. Why did no one predict the gathering of enemy forces in various sectors, and why did we not counter-attack?" Ordinary people, accustomed to viewing frontline maps in newspapers, storefronts, and workplaces, knew that the Germans had crossed the south shore of the Don, and expressed concern about the threat now posed to the Caucasus. Why had Rostov been abandoned? What happened to the Black Sea Fleet in the surrender of Sevastopol? They displayed detailed knowledge of military movements: "Why have we not been more active on the Kalinin and northern fronts?" "What is the situation in Leningrad?" They wanted to know why the Red Army was unable to dislodge the Germans from the Rzhev salient despite numerous attempts and vast losses, and the impact of those battles on the now-stalled Kalinin and western fronts.[63] Although discussions among military leaders over strategy were not publicized, people were surprisingly well informed about strategic differences. They asked, for example, "Why did so many people die in the battle for Khar'kov?," the very question that Khrushchev posed in his searing critique of Stalin's wartime leadership in 1956.[64] In an effort to reconcile the high figures of reported dead and wounded with the small Finnish population, someone asked skeptically, "Given its small population and large losses, what is Finland now fighting with?"[65] The questions revealed an underlying suspicion that the government was not being frank about the military situation. After one lecture, a written question read, "All the time, in the press and on the radio, they contemptuously call the German army 'scaredy-cats [*boiaki*],' nonentities, petty, and inconsequential. Then why are we messing around with them so much, even retreating, giving up towns? Doesn't this mean the Red Army is weak?" In response to the feedback collected by party instructors, G. F. Aleksandrov, the head of Agitprop, wrote to the Central Committee that the Party's tone misled people: "In fact, it does not make sense that the Red Army forces are battling 'scaredy-cats' and at the same time, still surrendering towns." In his opinion, more "accuracy" was required.[66]

Ordinary people at lectures and in meetings also focused intently on the second front, the single most urgent issue in the summer of 1942. The British were fighting in North Africa, and the United States in the Pacific, but the vast majority of German divisions were concentrated on the eastern front. The United States and Britain promised to open a second front in Europe in 1942, but, despite Roosevelt's urging, Churchill was more reluctant, daunted by the difficulties of a Channel crossing. After repeated delays, the second front was finally opened after the landing in Normandy on June 6, 1944, very late in the war and well after vast Soviet losses. Throughout 1942, people were deeply concerned by the unmet promises. Women textile workers in Ivanovo asked forthrightly, "Why don't our allies open the second front?" Others demanded, "What are our allies doing to honor their commitments?" and "What is the explanation for the delay?" Some cynical observers questioned whether the delays were solely a matter of logistics. "Is it possible to see the delay in the second front as motivated by England's desire to weaken the Red Army?" asked one speaker. Another commented angrily, "For an entire year, our allies have considered that it is better not to open a second front and now to delay so as not to open it until the end of the war." Although the Soviet government insisted that the Red Army was strong enough to counter the Germans without the second front, everyone understood the human costs. One questioner anxiously speculated, "Will we die waiting for them because we cannot cope with Germany and all its allies alone?" The questions revealed a growing anger at the failure of the Allies to assume greater responsibility. In Moscow, an audience member passed a sarcastic note to the lecturer: "When and in which month will the second front be opened? Perhaps on December 31, 1942, they will send fifteen soldiers with a broken tank?"[67]

Special meetings on production were also held in the factories. As the Germans advanced toward Stalingrad, defense production assumed ever greater urgency. Party instructors centered discussions on the close connection between military success and production targets. Workers, too, were intensely focused on the monthly plan and did not hesitate to blame managers publicly for any obstacles. In their view, the main impediment to meeting the plan was not workers' lack of motivation or labor discipline, but rather management's failure to provide a steady, uninterrupted supply of materials. In meetings with party activists, they boldly demanded, "What measures has *the administration* taken to increase the productivity of labor?" "Why do we not get orders [for production] in a timely manner?"[68] Fearless in criticizing management, they demanded "more order" and stronger punishment for those who profited from wartime shortages. Many posed questions related to food provisioning and health. Workers in the port city of Arkhangel'sk impudently challenged the party organizer, asking, "How can you explain the lack of fish in our factory canteen when we are surrounded by water?"[69] Above all, the reports from party instructors showed that ordinary people wanted the truth about the military situation. Instructors had trouble explaining the retreats and the delay in the second front. Popular mistrust of the state's pre-invasion arrogance still lingered. At the end of August, provincial party officials wrote to Aleksandrov, requesting that he send them "skilled speakers" from the Central Committee. Given the bewildered, even skeptical reception of the Party's latest talking points, perhaps more sophisticated propagandists would have greater success explaining "the current moment."[70]

Party leaders responded to the feedback from the instructors, propagandists, and discussion leaders. On July 28, 1942, Stalin issued the order that would become known as "Not One Step Back," which provided the flat, unvarnished truth that people demanded. The retreats could not continue. "Our territory," Stalin stated plainly, "is not empty but filled with people—workers, peasants, intelligentsia, our fathers, mothers, wives, brothers, and children. The territory that is given up means the loss of bread for the army and the home front, of metal and fuel for industry. We have lost 70 million people, 800 million poods [13.1 million metric tons] of grain, and more than 10 million tons of metal. We no longer have mastery over the Germans in terms of either human reserves or stocks of grain. To retreat further means to ruin ourselves and to ruin our motherland." Any more talk of limitless reserves of land or people was a lie. The Red Army, "covering its banner with shame," had abandoned Rostov and Novocherkassk in panic. "It is time to end the retreat," Stalin declared. "Not one step back!" From here on, the Red Army would apply "iron discipline": anyone who retreated without an order would be considered a traitor. The army would establish blocking brigades that would shoot those who retreated without orders or created panic in the ranks. Punishment battalions, composed of those who violated discipline or showed cowardice, would be placed on the most dangerous sectors of the front "to allow violators to expiate their crimes against the motherland with their blood." Yet Stalin also assured the country that victory was possible: the military finally had the equipment it needed to fight and to win.[71]

In the wake of Stalin's order, the resistance of the Red Army assumed an almost suicidal intensity between the Don and Volga Rivers. As the Germans advanced through the Caucasus toward the Baku oilfields, everyone wondered, "How much farther *can* we retreat?"[72] By mid-September, the Germans had broken through to the Volga in the north and south, encircled Stalingrad, and trapped the 62nd Army. General V. S. Chuikov took command, declaring, "We shall either hold the city or die there."[73] As the battle for Stalingrad raged, Agitprop developed new talking points based on Stalin's "Not One Step Back" order. Party instructors were told, "Don't whitewash the danger, don't downplay the difficulties."[74] Pushed to the precipice of defeat, the state appealed not to Russian nationalism but to a shared socialist community: "the fate of our motherland, the great gains of the people in the October revolution, the fate of socialism and Soviet construction" were at stake. The message was straightforward: "Every soldier, commander, political activist, every working person and party member should clearly understand that there is nowhere further for us to retreat, that the loss of the districts directly beyond the front line will threaten the very existence of the Soviet state."[75] Party propagandists now aimed to lower people's expectations, to introduce the possibility that the Red Army might have to do most of the fighting against Germany alone. The output of tanks, aviation, and armaments had increased by almost 50 percent between June 1941 and July 1942, but the sectors of iron and steel, electric power stations, and coal—the building blocks of defense—were still hindered by stoppages and fuel shortages. Local sources of peat, shale, and wood, used

to heat barracks, homes, and workplaces, would have to be diverted to industry. Everyone could expect daily life to become harder. Despite the painful
truths and grave tone, the talking points conveyed a genuine conviction that
victory was possible.[76]

"A Single and Undivided Military Camp"

With Stalin's pronouncement that the Red Army had the equipment it needed
for victory, the great burden for meeting output targets was assumed by the
workers. The slogan "a single and undivided military camp" acknowledged
their profound importance to military success as well as the deep deprivations
and dangers experienced by the home front population. Party agitators focused intensely on production. New slogans were introduced: "Not a Single
Minute of Absence in Production! Anyone Who Blows Off Work in These
Days of War Undermines Supplying the Front with Armaments!," "Workers!

Figure 9.5 Workers assembling machine guns under a banner reading "Let's take
revenge on the German fascist bastards for the plunder and devastation of our
towns and villages, for the violation of our women and children. Blood for blood.
A death for a death." Courtesy of RGAKFD.

The Machines and Tools Are Your Weapons. Preserve and Conserve Them Like the Apple of Your Eye," and "Every Saved Kilowatt of Electric Energy, Every Saved Kilogram of Fuel, Increases the Output of Arms and Ammunition for the Front."[77] Workers in every factory attended meetings where propagandists explained the importance of each unit of production for soldiers at the front. They signed pledges, vowing: "Victory will not come by itself. We need to seize it. A tripling of energy, a high level of organization, firmness, and iron discipline, are required from us now."[78] The state awarded medals and decorations, similar to those given out to soldiers, to workers and engineers who overfulfilled norms in coalmining, defense, and transport.[79]

Workers closely followed the front, tracking every gain and loss. Galina Barskaya, a twenty-eight-year-old metal worker evacuated to Pervouralsk, made her own front maps which she posted in her factory. She remembered her foreman's reaction:

> I made huge maps of the fronts, hung them in the office of our plant and every day marked the movement of our troops with little red flags. I listened to everything the radio broadcast and copied information on these maps. By the way, I still have those maps. One time the chief of my workshop called me and said, "Listen, you are causing every instrument in the plant to stop working." I was shocked when I heard that and scared. I was very young then. So I asked him, "How come?" He said, "Every day when you show new information about our troops people stop working!" I got very anxious and thought I was in trouble, but he patted me on the hand and said, "You are doing a great job! Afterwards they all work even better."[80]

Campaigns from above often sparked new initiatives from below. Workers participated in shock work and Stakhanovite campaigns, but also organized their own initiatives to overfulfill output norms, becoming known as "200-percenters," "300-percenters," and even "1,000-percenters." Sofiia Polovina led a brigade of young female drillers who produced tanks and consistently doubled and even tripled their output norms. During the battle of Stalingrad, they devised a nonstop schedule whereby they staggered their dinner breaks and kept each other's machines running, each girl simultaneously tending three machines. One young driller, when asked how she managed to cope, replied thoughtfully, "You think to yourself, is it easier at the front? And the strength to do it appears."[81] Many women workers learned more than one skill, enabling them to do several jobs. The idea of mastering "adjacent skills," first pioneered by workers, was soon elevated into a nationwide campaign with competitions, conferences, and prizes. At a congress on socialist competition organized at the beginning of 1943, Arshipov, a young brigade leader and *tysiachnik* or "1,000-percenter," told the delegates, "My father and mother died in Smolensk in 1942. I would have gone astray if I did not have such a tightly knit factory family, such good comrades. Much work lies before us young bricklayers. I think about the towns we will build, and about the houses that will adorn these towns." In the words of another young brigadier, "my father and two brothers went to the front. One of my brothers died. I want to avenge my brother and I'll work without stop."[82]

Party activists used the slogan "a single and undivided military camp" to forge stronger links between front and rear. Radio, for example, began transmitting news in both directions. By 1943, Soviet radio broadcasts reached listeners at home, at the front, and even throughout Europe. One historian notes that Radio Moscow became "a trusted news source," building a relationship of "openness and intimacy" between broadcaster and audience with popular programs such as "Letters from the Front" and "Letters from the Rear." Mobile war correspondents recorded soldiers reading their letters aloud, and civilians did the same in broadcast stations. Both groups listened avidly to the programs, which also helped to reunite families separated by the war. "Dateline Western Front!" used mobile units to visit troops and broadcast directly from the front. "Dateline" was soon joined by other programs, including "Listen Up Front Lines!," "From the Urals to the Front," and "Workers of the Rear Are with You, Comrade Warriors," which reported on the lives and contributions of workers and collective farmers. The Germans considered the broadcasts so effective that they tried repeatedly to bomb Radio Center in Moscow and placed a price on the head of Iurii Levitan, one of the most popular broadcasters.[83]

Collective defense actions also built solidarity on the home front and dissolved the distance between front and rear. Although such activities were not considered part of the state's mobilizing message, they served as a form of propaganda in action. Party activists enrolled civilians between the ages of seventeen and fifty-four in defense training where they learned to use rifles, machine guns, and radio communication. Workers were encouraged to name the tanks they produced after their work brigades or groups that donated money. The inhabitants of Irkutsk, for example, raised 52 million rubles to create a tank column which was called "Irkutsk Collective Farmer."[84] People living close to the front were regularly mobilized to dig anti-tank ditches and construct perimeter defenses. About 110,000 peasants, workers, employees, and students in the Chuvash autonomous republic were temporarily mobilized to construct a 250-mile (400-km) defense line to protect Kazan' in the winter of 1941–1942. Living in barracks and earthen dugouts, they worked with shovels in extreme cold and heavy snow. Initially, people were frequently late or absent, and spent a lot of work time warming themselves around bonfires. When several hundred party propagandists were assigned to the sites to organize discussions and publish a broadsheet based on the writings of workers themselves, people began to understand how their work fit into military logistics. One of the mobilized workers, an alleged loafer, was inspired to set a shoveling record for which he received several prizes. When the project was complete, he decided to join the mobile construction organization to work on other defense lines. Women on site joined special all-female brigades, which carried their own *esprit de corps*. Even retired people, past the age of mobilization, showed up to work. Elizaveta Efimova, an older woman from a nearby collective farm, arrived at the site, picked up a shovel, and allegedly put the younger people to shame, achieving two and one-half times the expected quota.[85]

In towns under bombardment, the slogan "undivided military camp" became frighteningly real. The Germans dropped tens of thousands of incendiaries and high explosive bombs on Arkhangel'sk, a port that received materials from British convoys, in August and September 1942. On some streets, not a single building escaped bombing, and hundreds of people were killed and wounded.[86] The city, however, was prepared: party activists had divided it into quadrants and provided training in rooftop plane-spotting and extinguishing of incendiaries. Pensioners, at home during the day, were among the most active defenders. After the detonation of a high explosive bomb near a bakery, the women employees worked through the night, ignoring the shooting flames. Not a single kilogram of bread was lost, and Arkhangel'sk's inhabitants received their rations the next day. Of course, not everyone's behavior was so exemplary. When several warehouses holding sugar and other goods burned, some people looted the ruins. In the Molotov timber factory, a worker frightened everyone. His dire predictions of occupation supported the Germans, who dropped leaflets advising people to flee. Some did flee; others left their workplaces without permission. Yet, after the bombings, the head of the city's party committee reported that the overwhelming majority of the city's inhabitants had met the firebombing with "courage and resourcefulness" and a minimum of "panic and confusion." By all reports, it had the opposite effect to the one the Germans had hoped: it infuriated the city's residents and stiffened their resolve.[87]

In the newly liberated towns, party activists linked reconstruction work to vengeance and commemoration of the dead. Almost 150,000 people participated in the one-year anniversary celebration of the liberation of Kalinin. In the central square of the town, a crowd of about 15,000 workers, teachers, and schoolchildren gathered by the soldiers' cemetery to watch the erection of a new monument to Lenin, replacing the one destroyed by the Germans, and to lay wreaths to commemorate the dead. Local residents, partisans, and soviet officials spoke, transforming the call for vengeance into pledges to produce. One factory worker testified, "Among the victims was my elderly father. The Germans shot him as he was sleeping on the stove. I know I'll give all my strength to turning out lethal weapons with which I'll avenge the death of my elderly father and the mockery of our people. Up to now I've worked double the norm, but I now take responsibility to produce three times the norm."[88]

The state's mobilizing messages found strong support among the population, but they were also accompanied by repression against those deemed to be a threat. Phrases from the lexicon of 1937 such as "enemy of the people," "Trotskyite," and "wrecker" faded, but others, such as "the ability to recognize the enemy, no matter how well he may be masked," and "the impermissibility of political complacency," still circulated. The Central Committee repeatedly warned local party organizations about the possibility of diversionist acts, sabotage, and espionage in defense factories and electric power stations, on the railroads, and in areas close to the front. People were arrested for spying and collaboration and, while some were guilty, many charges had a whiff of the spurious accusations of the Terror years. A letter from the Moscow provincial and city party committee to all local party organizations noted that the Germans recruited from "anti-Soviet elements, criminals, former kulaks and White Guards who dream of restoring capitalism, from unstable local inhabitants, and Red Army prisoners of war, who are cowards and betrayers of our motherland."[89] Some of these warnings proved true: some inhabitants of the occupied areas, particularly former kulaks, did collaborate, as did General A. A. Vlasov and other Soviet POWs. Yet after so many false accusations, it was not easy to separate genuine sabotage, collaboration, and spying from accusations invented by the state.

In many cases, the state took severe prophylactic measures, exiling entire groups deemed likely to collaborate. After the war started, it deported almost 3.3 million people from 61 national groups, including ethnic Germans, Crimean Tatars, Chechens, and Ingush. The Crimean Tatars, for example, were exiled to various republics in 1944, after 20,000 volunteered to join the Wehrmacht. These national groups were neither arrested nor executed, but rather deported en masse.[90] In August 1941, the state and Party mandated the resettlement of almost 480,000 Soviet citizens of German descent from the German Volga republic and two other provinces.[91] Almost 85,000 German-Soviet citizens were sent to Omsk province, where they were divided into groups of 120 to 800 households, dispersed throughout various districts, and placed on collective farms. The exiles complained angrily about the poor provisioning, lack of compensation for their own farms and animals, and the wages owed them before they left. Their anger, however, was not centered solely on their losses. The head of the Omsk provincial party committee noted "enemy moods" among the deportees, who bragged to local peasants about the invincibility of the German army and the futility of resistance. Many of the deportees were also deeply anti-Semitic, reassuring local peasants that Nazis "loved Russians, but only hated communists and Jews." One deportee explained, "Don't be afraid of the Germans, the German people are good, they will not bully peaceful people and collective farmers, they only bully party leaders and Jews. If the Germans did not pity the people, they would step on the gas and take the entire country in one week, but they don't do this because they can be victorious over the Soviet Union without this." (Indeed, the Germans did later "step on the gas," murdering millions of Soviet POWs and Jews in mobile vans and gas chambers.) Others threatened local officials, sneering, "Hitler is coming, and then things will be bad for you. We will teach you to organize and agitate." They told the peasants that they were exiled for preparing an uprising and, "if the Germans get close, we will do it here." "Hitler will rescue us," they said, "and we, Germans, will soon rule over you Russians as your masters." Their contempt, pro-German feelings, and anti-Semitism suggested that many might have indeed welcomed the Nazis. Yet not all exiles shared these views. Party members, who were also exiled, were deeply offended that the state would deport an entire people rather than those who posed a genuine threat. One party member noted bitterly, "In general, this resettlement is an unheard-of mess. Judging from the state's decree, all 800,000 Germans on the Volga are fascists and diversionists." Another, eliding the distinction between deportation and genocide, noted that the policy of resettlement bore a striking similarity to Hitler's own

policies. He said, "Here is Stalin's national policy. And what is the difference with the fascist acts? Yes, it is even worse." All these remarks did not
go unnoticed. The Omsk NKVD arrested 119 people for treason and conspiracy and excluded 9 from the Party.[92]

If some wartime policies had links to the preemptive purges of the past,
they also held portents of purges to come. In 1946, the state launched an
anti-cosmopolitan campaign against members of the intelligentsia who
were allegedly influenced by Western liberal ideas. By 1949, the campaign
had become overtly anti-Semitic, targeting Jews as "rootless cosmopolitans."
A group of Jewish doctors was arrested and tortured for an alleged plot to
kill Stalin and other party leaders. Stalin's unexpected death in 1953 ended
the spiraling madness.[93] The roots of the postwar anti-Western campaign
could be seen early in the war. At a meeting held in Sverdlovsk in fall 1942
with evacuated scholars from the Academy of Sciences, the head of the local
NKVD carefully noted the names and comments of speakers he considered
subject to Western influence. His report, sent to Agitprop, charged that the
academics placed too much confidence in the Allies. One academic, refer-
ring to the British landing in Egypt in August 1942, noted, "Events in Africa,
this is unquestionably the beginning of the second front. Soon we will witness Italy's exit from the war, and the inevitable consequence of this, the destruction of Hitler." Some even considered the British campaign in Africa
to be the full equivalent of the promised second front in Europe, a view that
would have shocked those Red Army soldiers battling German divisions that
had been diverted from North Africa to Stalingrad. Another academic ful-
somely praised the Americans, "Finally, we have reached the moment when
Hitler is threatened with a real blow. The Americans, now here is a real ally,
an adversary with their own peculiar business-like expertise." The NKVD report noted that some academics believed that only the West was capable of
rendering "a real blow."[94] This view, while hardly tantamount to treason, was
clearly one the NKVD found worthy of report.

The strong anti-Semitic overtones that would infuse the anti-cosmopolitan
campaign after the war were also vividly apparent as early as 1942. A policy
memo from Aleksandrov, the head of Agitprop, to the Central Committee
in August on the "selection and promotion of cadres" focused on the ma-
lign influence of Jews in the arts. Aleksandrov noted, "at the head of many
institutions of Russian art are non-Russian people (predominantly Jews)."
Providing a long list of directors, administrators, journalists, critics, teachers,
and performers, he placed "(Jew)" after the names of those he sought to

remove. He wrote, "It is not accidental that students in conservatories are not inculcated with a love for Russian music, for Russian folksongs, and that the majority of our well-known musicians and vocalists . . . have in their repertoires mainly the works of West European composers." He recommended immediate measures to replace Jews—who, in his view, were disproportionately represented in the arts—with Russians. After the war, these anti-Western and anti-Semitic ideas would guide party policy in academia and the cultural realm.[95]

One of the greatest challenges the Party faced was maintaining support for the war amid extreme deprivation. Even the most inspiring slogans could not increase rations, provide clothing, or heat buildings. A reporter from *Pravda* captured the problem perfectly in a scathing letter to his editor about the visit of Mikhail Kalinin, Chairman of the Supreme Soviet and Politburo member, to Gor'kii in 1942 to pass out medals to workers. In the reporter's words, Gor'kii's streets were "befouled with trash" and piles of human excrement, which local officials were quick to dismiss "as the cost of wartime." When questioned about the filth, the head of the city soviet replied, "In other towns it is even worse. Do you really think that in Moscow they are busy cleaning the streets?" The elderly Kalinin was scheduled to give out the medals in Gor'kii's Palace of Culture, but the building was so cold and damp that he began trembling uncontrollably. The ceremony had to be canceled, and Kalinin was rushed to a doctor. The reporter also noted that "Soviet Square" had been renamed "Minin and Pozharskii Square," in honor of Prince Dmitrii Pozharskii and Kuzma Minin, who fought to expel the Poles from Moscow in 1612. In his opinion, it would have been better to stop extolling tsarist heroes, clean the streets, and provide fuel to the baths, trolleys, and bakeries.[96]

The reporter's letter was similar to the thousands sent by ordinary people to local party officials and newspapers. In Ivanovo, the provincial party committee and local newspaper received more than 8,700 letters between January and October 1942. Signed by groups (workers, evacuees, teachers, etc.), families, and individuals, the letters focused on shortages of food, fuel, or housing.[97] The provincial party committee in Rostov received almost 8,000 letters in 1944, most containing pleas for food and housing. A typical letter, from a Red Army major, read: "From the start of the war I have been at the front and not able to give attention to my family, who have lived through much difficulty. Twice, they were evacuated several thousand kilometers from Rostov. The family lost their mother on the journey; she died in a boxcar. Winter is coming, and they are living in an apartment with a leaking roof in need of repairs." After an investigation, the party committee repaired the apartment and provided aid to the family. Investigators insisted on strict time limits for the party committee to clear its backlog, and at least one local official was removed from his post for dereliction of duty.[98]

Most worrisome for some party leaders were the negative views many people expressed about "bureaucrats" who were "indifferent" to people's needs.[99] One of the principal themes of propaganda was that the war demanded sacrifice from all. This emphasis on shared hardship enabled people to believe that their sacrifices were for a "just cause." People despised those who sought personal gain at the expense of others, and their anger was even greater if such a person held a position of power. In an effort to deflect blame, central authorities encouraged ordinary people to condemn local officials and managers, and investigators and journalists berated local officials for their failure to improve conditions.[100] Ordinary people, for their part, maintained a sharp eye for what they perceived as unfair disparities. For those who lost family members at the front, in the occupied territories, or to evacuation and hunger, grief magnified their resentment. When Zhalkova, a female engineer living in Ivanovo, learned of her husband's death at the front, she wrote a long, emotional letter to Pal'tsev, the head of the provincial party committee, conveying the fury she felt at "self-seeking" officials:

Comrade Pal'stev, I can no longer postpone writing to you because the contradictions, which I am now living with in my bitterness, have simply overwhelmed me. I never thought myself capable of having such deep feelings of anger and hatred that are equal to, if not stronger than, my hatred toward fascism. These feelings are for our leaders with party cards in their pockets and military exemptions giving them the right to sit like mice in their holes, warming themselves by the labor of the people's hands. When we triumph over fascism they will be the first to broadcast their service, claiming that they are responsible for the victory, and then again, use the privilege of their positions.

Zhalkova did not hesitate to name those she considered responsible: "I refer to such leaders as Ogorel'shev, the manager of the Butter Trust, who calls himself a communist. I advise you to investigate his communist ideas in this affair, and to suggest to him that he give up his exemption from military service and go to the front voluntarily. I am sure that he will refuse and take all measures and bombard the commissariat about their mistake in sending someone who has 'an armor-clad exemption' [*bronirovannaia bron'*] from the draft." (Here Zhalkova sarcastically punned on the words *bronia* [armor], and *bron'* [a reserved list or exemption].) The crux of her complaint was that Ogorel'shev provided Red Army families of Butter Trust employees with firewood, but her family had been left off the list. She noted, "I was deeply insulted on behalf of my husband for this neglect, but I remained silent. At this time, he had been wounded but was still alive, and I firmly endured all these difficulties in the hope of a happy future, knowing that my husband would return as a father to our family, and everything would become easier for me." Then she received notice that he had been killed. Left as the sole support of two small children and her elderly mother-in-law, she wrote, "My bitterness can be understood only by someone who has gone through this. There are no tears; words pale." Ogorel'shev, head of the Butter Trust, ignored her. She wrote, "When a comrade asked him, 'What did he think about providing Zhalkov's family with fuel?,' this self-seeker with a party card answered, 'I didn't think about it and I'm not thinking about it. His wife works in the milk *kombinat*, let [its head] provision her.'" Ogorel'shev's response was typical of local officials, who sought to shift responsibility for dependants onto other providers. Focused on his refusal to help, Zhalkova begged Pal'stev to investigate the situation. Her letter ended with a plea: "Out of this soulless attitude my bitterness is multiplied tenfold, I want to scream to the entire Soviet Union so that everyone will know and shove out these Ogorel'shevs."[101] In the end, Zhalkova got help, and Ogorel'shev received a party reprimand.

The feelings that Zhalkova expressed were widely shared. The sacrifices that people made, whether through daily deprivation or irreparable loss, heightened their sensitivity to slights and abuses of power. Their letters did not suggest that the war was not worth waging, or that they would prefer a system of private ownership and free market distribution. The critique ordinary people made was simple: they expected their leaders to demonstrate the values they publicly extolled and to adhere to the country's highest vision of itself.

German Guilt: Vengeance versus the Class Line

As the Red Army liberated one province after another in 1944, the newspapers were filled with stories of mass graves, murdered civilians, ruined towns, and incinerated villages. In June, the Red Army launched its offensive to retake Belorussia, a center of partisan warfare. Minsk, Kovno, and Vilna, all scenes of horrific Nazi violence, were liberated that summer. At the front, soldiers were encouraged to keep written "accounts of revenge," and before battle they gathered to discuss a simple question: "What am I avenging against the German occupiers?" Every company kept a notebook in which soldiers logged the atrocities they saw. One soldier wrote with grim fury, "We will be in Germany . . . and we will remember everything." Workers also kept "account books of revenge," a practice started by a woman worker in Sverdlovsk. One historian later noted that propagandists did not have to invent much in order to incite feelings of hatred: "It was sufficient simply to collect and summarize the personal experience of each person."[102]

Yakov Voloshyn, a commander of a communications platoon, remembered:

> The fascists were evil enemies. Those who weren't at the front could have thought otherwise, but we saw it all with our own eyes. We saw villages burnt to the ground: only chimneys remained. We saw families coming out of cellars with their children and bags, dirty, wearing rags; they were rare survivors. We saw those people burying their dear ones, small children burnt alive for nobody knows what sins. We saw and heard it all. We marched into battles with the words "For our Motherland, for Stalin!," and they were not mere slogans or meaningless words. This was our faith, religion, a call of the heart and conscience, if you want. Nobody will take this away from me! For our Motherland, for Stalin, we marched into the battles. This was what we knew and what we believed in.[103]

The discovery of the extermination camps fueled the mounting rage. The Red Army entered Maidanek and Trostenets in July 1944, Auschwitz in January 1945, Ravensbrück in April, and Theresienstadt on May 8, shortly before the Nazis surrendered. Most of the prisoners who were still alive had already been sent out on death marches, but the barracks and grounds of the camps were piled with rotting corpses. In Auschwitz, 7,000 inmates remained, including children who had been subject to Nazi experiments. In August 1944, Simonov wrote the first article to appear in the Soviet press about the death camps. The three-page article, describing the liberation of Maidanek, was accompanied by photographs showing mountains of starved corpses, the ovens where bodies were burned, and canisters of Zyklon-B gas. Simonov wrote in furious anguish: "I do not know which of them burned people, which of them simply murdered them, who removed the boots, and who sorted the women's underclothes and the children's dresses, I do not know. But when I look at this warehouse of things, I think that any nation that produces this, that can do this, should bear and will bear responsibility for all that their representatives did."[104]

A desire for vengeance suffused the press, inflaming soldiers and civilians, but its meaning was not entirely clear. Would Nazi leaders be held accountable for their crimes in court? Or would Red Army soldiers do to the Germans what they had done to others? Simonov, shocked by the scale of murder at Maidanek, suggested that the German nation must bear responsibility. The soldiers took Simonov's message to heart. The first sign of the Red Army's rage occurred after the ferocious battle for Bucharest in February 1945. After tens of thousands of Soviet casualties, the soldiers took out their fury in pillage and rape. In April, the army crossed the border into Germany. War correspondent Vasily Grossman noted that someone had posted a huge road sign at the border: "Soldier, here it is—the lair of the fascist beast."[105] The soldiers took their revenge in a rolling wave of mass rape, which crested in Berlin between April 24 and May 5, 1945, several days before the Nazis capitulated.[106] The rapes, a phenomenon not yet thoroughly investigated, were prompted by the desire for vengeance, the willingness of officers to overlook the behavior of their men, and the atrocity reportage that permeated the press.

The press, aware of its influence, began to caution the soldiers to act with dignity and discipline almost as soon as they crossed the Soviet border. An editorial in *Krasnaia zvezda* in February 1945 emphasized, "If the Germans marauded and publicly raped our women, it does not mean that we must do the same . . . . Our revenge is not blind."[107] Yet these admonitions paled beside the continuing coverage of German atrocities. In mid-April, Ehrenburg wrote an article, "Enough!" in *Krasnaia zvezda*, which noted the killing of "millions of innocent Jews." Trembling with fury, he wrote, "I am trying to contain myself, I try to speak as softly as possible, as austerely, but I have no words. I have no words to evoke again the world the Germans made in my land. Perhaps it would be better simply to repeat the names alone: Bab'i Yar, Trostenets, Kerch', Ponar, Belzec," all place names that would soon become bywords for the mass murder of Soviet POWs, Jews, and other civilians. Ehrenburg also lashed out at the West, demanding to know why the Germans seemed to regard the Americans as "some kind of neutral force." Why did the Germans appeal to the Western allies to permit them to keep their slave laborers for spring sowing, to help them catch Soviet POWs who escaped from their camps? And why did they fight so hard against the Red Army, creating so many unnecessary casualties? Addressing the soldiers as they crossed the German border, Ehrenburg declared, "The bitterness of our Motherland, the bitterness of all the orphans, our bitterness is with us in these days of victory. It fans the fires of implacability, it will be the conscience of the sleeping, it casts a shadow, the shadow of the twisted birch, the shadow of the gallows, and the shadow of mothers weeping for the spring of the world."[108]

Three days later, on April 14, Aleksandrov demanded a halt to the anti-German "revenge" theme in the press. In a sharp rebuke titled, "Comrade Ehrenburg Oversimplifies," he signaled a new line: all Germans should not be equated with Nazis. Resurrecting the class line, which had been eclipsed by the mounting revelations of German atrocities, Aleksandrov explained, "It would be foolish to confuse the clique of Hitler with the German people, with the German state." By criticizing the country's allies, Ehrenburg was only playing into German hands. German leaders aimed to foment dissension by transferring their divisions to the eastern front and appealing to the United States for help.[109] Aleksandrov put an end to "vengeance propaganda." Journalists were prohibited from blaming Germans for Nazi atrocities, or assuming that all Germans had benefited from the exploitation of the occupied territories. The class line that had characterized Soviet propaganda through 1942 was revived in the expectation that Germany would soon have a new government built on the few anti-fascist forces that survived.

****

Throughout the course of the war, both the state's message and popular moods changed. In part, they evolved in tandem, each influenced by the other. The state was initially guarded and opaque about the situation at the front at the very moment when the invasion and the rapid advance of German forces left people in a state of shock. It wavered about how to report the retreats, and its evasions created mistrust. Older veterans of the Civil War posed probing questions about strategy, preparedness, and retreat, showing that they were closely following the news from the front and reading between the lines. In the summer of 1942, Aleksandrov responded to reports from party instructors by requesting a more realistic portrayal of German strengths and Soviet losses. Stalin's brutally frank "Not One Step Back" speech was a response not only to continuing losses but also to the popular demand for a more honest accounting. In a darker vein, Aleksandrov also reacted to growing popular interest in Western democracy and culture. Ugly portents of the postwar anti-cosmopolitan and anti-Semitic campaigns could already be discerned.

Over time, propaganda became more personal and emotional, deliberately forging ties between soldiers, workers, and peasants. Radio connected soldiers and their families in innovative ways. Beginning in 1942, reporting assumed a new passionate tone with discoveries of German atrocities. "Vengeance propaganda," based on eyewitness accounts from soldiers, war correspondents, and survivors, channeled rage and frustration into support for the war effort. The horrific news from the liberated territories aligned with the state's more abstract political education about fascist ideology. In the early spring of 1945, reportage reached a crescendo of horror with the discovery of the death camps. Yet when the Red Army finally crossed the border into Germany, the guidelines around propaganda changed again as party leaders sought to tamp down the rage within the Red Army and consider the prospect of a new German government.

As the state's message evolved, so too did popular moods and reactions, shifting from the shock of invasion and enthusiastic voluntarism to a growing anxiety over defeat, fury at the devastation wrought by the Germans, and, ultimately, growing pride in the Red Army. Workers, under tremendous pressure to produce and to sacrifice for the war effort, sought not to eliminate socialist principles, but rather to enforce them more strictly. They repeatedly stressed their disgust with the differentials between officials and ordinary people. If they were fighting to defend any particular economic system, it was a greater socialist egalitarianism.

Propaganda was most successful when it aligned with the experiences of ordinary people and elevated those experiences into a coherent political narrative about fascism. At its best, it succeeded in these aims. The slogans, "Single and Undivided Military Camp" and "United Front and Rear," for example, successfully captured the reality of frontline and industrial towns under bombardment and honored the essential role that workers played in defense. The intense campaigns for production in 1942, closely tied to Stalin's promise to supply the Red Army with the equipment it needed at Stalingrad, received mass support. Many propaganda campaigns, including teaching skills, production pledges, and experiments with continuous production, originated with young workers on the shop floor. "Vengeance propaganda" proved similarly effective. The state was less successful when its message did not accord with what people knew or experienced. Not until Stalin's "Not One Step Back" order in July 1942, for example, did the state respond to the demands of ordinary people for straightforward information. Similarly, the state's insistence on shared sacrifice backfired when local officials took advantage of their positions for personal gain.

Soviet citizens were never monolithic in their responses. Their reactions to the war effort changed over time and were shaped by social class, nationality, and personal and political experience. While some groups may have hoped for a Soviet defeat or even welcomed the Germans, there is little indication of organized resistance to the war effort on the home front. Workers and other groups who had benefited from the revolution tended to be more firmly committed to Soviet power. Peasants dispossessed in the dekulakization campaigns were more embittered. Yet peasants were also mobilized in large numbers into the army and the waged labor force, where they were exposed to new experiences and perspectives. Both the peasantry and the working class, the two largest social groups in Soviet society, were remade by the war. Citizens from all social and national groups who suffered during the Terror of 1935–1939 struggled to reconcile bitterness toward the state with support for the war effort. A few frankly hoped that the Soviet government would fall, and even committed communists such as Olga Berggol'ts experienced internal conflicts. Reports on the Volga Germans, for example, revealed among the deportees both loyal communists—who were outraged by the exile of their entire community—and others who displayed anti-Semitism, hostility toward Soviet power, and hope for German victory. Yet the overwhelming majority of Soviet citizens strongly supported the war effort and maintained a daily fortitude under conditions that might have proved crushing or incendiary in another political context.

Ordinary people had varied motives for their support: a family member in the army, revulsion at fascist occupation and brutality, Soviet or national patriotism, and pride in socialism. The revolution after all was only twenty-five years past, part of the lived experience of many. Younger soldiers had grown up on heroic Civil War stories of Stalin and the Red Army fighting to defend the same terrain they fought for at Stalingrad.[110] The one message that came through repeatedly in all the information gathered through letters, discussions, and investigations was that ordinary people did not begrudge the sacrifices they were asked to make. In the words from a letter written by group of workers in a defense plant in Sverdlovsk province:

> Our people love our motherland very much and we are happy to undergo all deprivations and sacrifices for her, to patiently bear the deprivations and difficulties of the war . . . But it is insulting and painful to realize that, while there are those who work and protect the country, many leaders have attached themselves, as they say, to a comfortable berth, and are busy stealing food and deceiving even the state.[111]

They asked only that the deprivations and sacrifices be shared.

10

"Brick Dust and Ashes": Liberation and Reconstruction

As you know in 1943, the Red Army moved as if they were wearing seven-league boots.

> Head of the Dnepropetrovsk provincial party
> committee, after liberation

The problem [with reconstruction] is that our working people have no shoes . . . .

> Activist from Public Catering Workers Union on
> the reconstruction of Voronezh, 1944

As the Red Army fought its way back west, it discovered a devastated land. In Alexander Werth's chilling words, "Nearly every liberated town and village in Russia, Belorussia, or in the Ukraine had something terrible to tell."[1] Poet Aleksandr Tvardovskii, returning to his childhood home of Smolensk after its liberation in September 1943, described the sinister emptiness of the city:

Only two years—or two hundred
Cruel poor years have passed,
But what is here in this place,
Neither town, nor village.
Wasteland dry and gloomy,
Among the ruins, an evil wind
Hurls cold brick dust
And ashes in our eyes.[2]

German policy aimed at the systematic creation of "desert zones," and the newly liberated areas lay in ruins. The power stations were dead, leaving towns without electricity, heat, or water. Transport had ceased to function: the railway lines had been bombed into twisted heaps of metal, and motorized transport demolished. Cultural and social institutions were obliterated, and the collective farms had been systematically pillaged of machinery, farm animals, and grain. Housing the population and keeping them safe from the outbreak of epidemics were major tasks. One-third of Ukraine's urban housing stock had been destroyed, and much of what remained was barely habitable. The number of horses, trucks, and waste removal vehicles needed to cart away garbage and human waste had fallen precipitously to just a fraction of their prewar level as well. Bathhouses, crucial to avoiding or controlling outbreaks of typhus and other diseases, had also suffered extensive damage. Their prewar capacity, already inadequate, had fallen by more than 85 percent.[3]

Yet the worst consequence of German policy by far was the decimation of the population. About 9,200 villages in Belorussia alone had been burnt to the ground; their inhabitants had been incinerated in barns and churches. Jewish civilians, along with millions of others accused of partisan activity or Soviet sympathies, lay dead in small and large shooting pits outside every

Figure 10.1 Street in Stalingrad showing the ruins of an apartment building, the main post office, and the children's theater. Courtesy of GARF.

town and village. Gallows hung with bodies stood in the deserted town squares, and the prisons were piled with murdered corpses. More than four million young people had been shipped off to Germany to work as slave labor. A worker wrote, "For twenty-two months, the fascist occupiers stole, thieved, and ruined our Khar'kov. They annihilated the population in mobile gas vans and torture chambers and shipped them off to Germany to hard labor. The monsters burned and blew up the best buildings . . . and blew up and burned the factories."[4]

Figure 10.2 Atrocities committed by the Germans against Jews in Belorussia. Courtesy of GARF.

Party activists following in the wake of the Red Army were faced with the daunting challenge of reintegrating the surviving population and rebuilding the economy. The survivors were rent by bloody political divisions and hatred. In the borderlands of western Ukraine and Belorussia and the Baltic states, nationalist guerrillas who had welcomed the Germans in 1941 aimed to eliminate Soviet power. They had collaborated actively with the Germans, serving as concentration camp guards, local police, and active participants in the murder of their neighbors: partisans, party members, Soviet sympathizers, and Jews.[5] Collaborators had been handsomely rewarded with food, money, and the property of their victims. Other survivors had either worked for the Germans in menial or factory jobs or had been left to starve, trading battered household goods for food scraps in impoverished local markets. NKVD officials, following in the wake of the Red Army, carried out a process known as "filtration" aimed at identifying and prosecuting the most active collaborators. The Party and the unions also carefully reviewed all members who sought reinstatement. The inhabitants of the newly liberated territories were to be incorporated into the ration system and subject to mobilization for labor and the Red Army. The war was far from over, and the defense factories in the east still clamored for workers and fuel. Yet the traumatized population resisted labor mobilization, especially for work outside their native provinces, and the tasks of rebuilding were complicated by nationwide shortages of building materials, transport, and skilled workers.[6]

The territory in need of reconstruction was vast. As the Red Army pushed the Germans back west, 1944 unfolded like a newsreel of 1941–1942 run in reverse: in January, the Red Army broke the blockade of Leningrad; in February, it forced the Germans from Rovno, the center of the Reichkomissariat Ukraine; by May, it had freed the Black Sea area, including Nikolaev, Odessa, Kherson, and Crimea; and in July it liberated western Ukraine and Belorussia. The victories continued through the fall as the Red Army drove the Germans out of Estonia and Latvia and crossed into Poland, Moldavia, Romania, Hungary, Czechoslovakia, and Norway. The occupied Soviet territories were free, but the challenge of reconstruction and integration had just begun.

Rebuilding the Party

The daunting task of reconstruction was made all the more difficult by the absence of any administrative and organizational infrastructure. Local soviets and party organizations were destroyed. Small operational party groups followed the Red Army and remained in place after liberation to rebuild district organizations.[7] The Party had increased its numbers during the war, yet it was still short of members both in the rear and in the newly liberated territories. At the time of the invasion, as of July 1, 1941, it had 3,814,409 members and candidates; by July 1943, it had grown to 4,373,727 members. The reason for the shortage of cadres in the rear and the liberated territories, however, was that the bulk of the Party's membership had shifted to the military. The number of people in the territorial (civilian) party organizations declined by 44 percent as the number and percentage in the military increased. In 1941, only 15.7 percent of members were in the military; by 1943, the figure was 58.6 percent. Party members had volunteered en masse to go the front: almost 50 percent of the members of the civilian organizations joined the armed forces. Almost all new enrollments during the war years occurred within the military: 82 percent of those accepted as candidates and 75 percent of those accepted as full members. As a result of these changes, women came to constitute a much larger percentage of the membership in the rear, making up 18 percent in 1941 but more than 30 percent in 1943. The number of women overall grew by almost 10 percent. Despite its overall increase in membership, the Party also suffered great losses: as of September 1, 1943, 1,116,000 party members were murdered, killed in action, or missing. The Party lost older, experienced activists as well as younger, newer members, but the overall impact of the losses and new enrollments was that its membership became younger.[8]

In the newly liberated territories, local party organizations were mere shadows of their former, vigorous bodies, having lost between 75 and 85 percent of their members. Those who survived occupation had gone underground, escaped to the partisans, or been tainted by collaboration.[9] Every organization had to be rebuilt. The party organization in Krasnodar Territory, a beautiful region in the north Caucasus, typified the damage. Krasnodar was occupied in August 1942 and liberated in February 1943. Although German rule was relatively brief, the Nazis wasted no time in installing a local administration and exterminating almost 7,000 civilians. Of the 61,777 party members in the territory before occupation, fewer than a third had been accounted for four and a half months after liberation. The drop in membership was the result of many factors: the largest group was evacuated; others joined the partisans, were murdered by the Germans, or joined the Red Army when it returned. The partisans suffered particularly heavy losses: about 43 percent were killed in battle. About half the party members who remained under German occupation were women, many of whom stayed behind to care for sick or elderly family members or because they were pregnant. The Germans ordered party members who remained to register with the Gestapo. Many of these either chose or were forced to serve the Germans in some capacity. Yet the statistics from Krasnodar belied a slippery reality: party members fell into more than one category and left, entered, or reentered the district before, during, and after occupation. Of the almost 4,600 party members who did not leave, party investigators concluded that the overwhelming majority— 93 percent—served the Germans, and more than 70 percent registered with the police or Gestapo; of this latter group, however, only 22 percent registered voluntarily. Moreover, the numbers did not specify what work they had done. After investigation, most members (77 percent) were accepted back into the Party. Of these, 17 percent received a reprimand in their file, suggesting that those who had served the Germans worked in some menial capacity (maids, laundresses, etc.), but had not harmed others. Those who were found to have actively collaborated, by providing names of fellow communists or Soviet sympathizers, were not only excluded but also subject to prosecution. One female worker, for example, not only registered with the police but also provided a list of forty other party members to the Gestapo. She was among the 601 people in the district excluded from the Party and then arrested for serving in German administrative or punitive organs. The 23 percent of party members excluded in Krasnodar territory was lower than the percentage excluded in Rostov (more than 60 percent) and that excluded within the liberated territories as a whole (40 percent).[10]

In every newly liberated province, the Party launched investigations of the members who remained during occupation. Verifications began on January 17, 1942, with a decree that required the re-registration of all party members found in liberated areas.[11] The process was slow, and the number of members awaiting verification and readmission mounted as the Red Army liberated more territory. Party members who remained in occupied territory were expected to have actively aided in the struggle against the Germans through either partisan activity or underground work.[12] As of September 1943, district and town party committees in 18 provinces had reviewed 36,861 of the 56,133 party members who had remained in occupied territory. Of those reviewed, about 40 percent were excluded. No small percentage, the individuals in this group had either accommodated or collaborated to some degree with the Germans.[13] The decision to expel, however, required review at multiple levels. After the district and town organizations rendered a decision, they forwarded it to the provincial committee. The provincial party committees, however, were severely short staffed, a problem that was both a cause and a consequence of delays in readmission.

In Ukraine, more than 66,000 party members remained during occupation. After liberation, the party members who returned to rebuild the party organizations were in such desperate need of help that they allowed a number of those who stayed and served the Germans to retain their managerial positions. The Party had 16,521 outstanding requests for readmission in Ukraine in fall 1944, but only a small percentage of these had been reviewed at all levels required for readmission. An external investigation showed that, despite the slow vetting process, town and district committees were moving too hastily and readmitting people guilty of collaboration.[14] Cases appeared to be decided quickly at the local level and then blocked higher up the chain of review.

Party officials in Krasnodar devised an extensive questionnaire with some fifty questions as part of the verification process.[15] The questions—some standard in all past party verifications, others aimed at uncovering behavior under occupation—fell into several categories. The first category, familiar to all party members, required basic biographical information: name, age, and place of birth; party card number; years of membership; membership in other parties before or after the revolution; service and rank in the tsarist army; former oppositional activity; relatives living abroad or in internal exile; trips abroad; criminal prosecutions, and prerevolutionary ownership of immoveable property. Many of these questions, which had ensnared party members during the Terror in the late 1930s, were not applicable to younger members who came of age after the Revolution or the fierce oppositional debates of the 1920s.

A second category of questions was carefully designed to uncover contact with or privileges bestowed by the Germans: Why did you remain on occupied territory? Did you have occupying soldiers billeted with you? Aiming to ferret out those members who had moved into the apartments of victims of the Germans, the questionnaire required members to provide the address of every residence they had occupied during the war and their reason for moving. It also asked about survival: What did you live on and where did you work during the time of occupation? Did you register for work or as a party member? Did you ever work under the Germans either voluntarily or under compulsion? Where, in what capacity? Where are you working now?

Everyone had been forced to earn a living, and the answers provided immediate clues to accommodation or collaboration.

The questions also aimed to fix the member within a wider circle of comrades, relatives, and friends: Did you live with relatives? If so, what did they do under occupation; where do they live and work now? Did you or your relatives become owners of any property or businesses during occupation? Were any of your relatives in the Red Army captured by the Germans? Do you have any relatives in concentration camps?

A third category dealt with military service. Some party members who had served in the Red Army had escaped encirclement and disappeared into the countryside where they worked on peasant farms or became forest bandits. Others were used as forced labor for the German army. A small number had escaped the deadly German POW camps by volunteering to fight against the Red Army. These questions asked: Did you serve in the Red Army? Why were you freed from army service? Did you serve in any military brigades mobilized against Soviet power? Was this service voluntary or were you mobilized? Were you in a partisan brigade? If so, why did you leave it?

The fourth category investigated whether the member had ever provided information that harmed others: Were you arrested by the Germans? What questions did they ask you; what answers did you give; what were the conditions of your release? Were you subject to repression by the Germans (beatings, searches, loss of property or living quarters, forced labor in Germany or in the occupied territories)? Were you ever called on as witness or in a face-to-face confrontation with someone accused by the police or Gestapo? What was the fate of the accused? Party members who survived a group arrest, especially if their comrades had been executed, were immediately regarded with suspicion.[16]

The last category centered on resistance, an activity expected of party members: Did you attempt to leave occupied territory? What other party members did you meet with in occupied territory and for what purpose? Did you engage in wrecking, sabotage, murder, aid to partisans, or countering German propaganda? All answers were cross-checked against information gathered from others. The questionnaire, like a finely wrought net, made it difficult for party members to pass through by concealing their activities. The final question, which rose above the minute details of residence, income, and associational ties, compelled members to account not just to the party committee but also to posterity: What did you do to make conditions in the rear unbearable for the occupiers?

Filtration

Party members were subject to particularly close scrutiny and held to a higher standard than the overall population of the occupied areas, but everyone had to register with the new Soviet administration and pass through some form of verification designed to identify collaborators. Basya Chaika was only fifteen years old when she returned from evacuation in the Urals to Konotop in Ukraine. She described the formation of the new local government:

> Bodies of Soviet power were formed from our midst, the young people, Komsomol members, who were in evacuation, that is, who did not stay in the occupied territories. Local residents, who had stayed in the territories occupied by the Germans, were not trusted with such work.

Chaika began to work in the passport department of the Konotop police and, given the shortage of qualified people, was made head of the department by the time she turned sixteen. Her work consisted of re-registering and checking the residents of Konotop. She described the procedure:

> People stood in long, several kilometers long lines to get to our department. We worked 12–14 hours a day. The flow of people did not decrease for several months. The reason was that, without the Soviet mark in their passports, Konotop residents could neither find a job, nor get bread cards. Their passports were considered invalid. If I remember correctly, there were practically no Jewish names among Konotop residents I checked and registered. Registration and checking of documents was a hard, responsible and sometimes dangerous task. Many people turned out to be without documents at all; many were hiding from the Soviet authorities or concealed their names, for different reasons, pretending to be somebody else. There were many deserters from the army and very many bandits. We had to filter out all of them, find them out and pass them on. Regularly, once or twice a week, we took part in special raids to check documents around the town.

After two months, Chaika became a court assessor on a three-person military tribunal that judged collaborators. Similar tribunals were established throughout the liberated territories. Chaika remembered:

A military tribunal was a secret, closed court hearing, but the procedure, as you can imagine, was kept very strict. There were many witnesses. Court hearings could last from two to ten or more days. We convicted a Ukrainian doctor, who was chief of the medical service of the concentration camp for prisoners of war in Konotop under the Germans and who gradually killed all the Soviet prisoners of war and betrayed those doctors who tried to save them. I don't remember ever convicting anyone for shooting the Jews in Konotop, although I'm sure there were such shootings. But we did not register such places or people who took part in them at that time. We convicted those locals who betrayed their fellow men, sending them to death. I, as an assessor, had to sign death sentences more than once. Such a responsibility really changes a girl's character at 16. I was very radical and uncompromising. Local residents treated me with caution. When my friend and I turned up to the dance club, people fled from that place, often thinking we were on another raid. Several times people tried to kill me. My poor mother cried a lot because of me. But in the eyes of the local youth we were heroes who accomplished justice.[17]

The process of filtration was complicated. Verifications proceeded slowly in various administrative organizations, including finance, housing, factory management, and trade. Many people escaped punishment or censure as a result of personal connections or difficulties in finding qualified replacements. Those who returned from the front or evacuation looked down on those who had remained.[18] The GKO first developed guidelines for the treatment of collaborators and their families in December 1941 when the area around Moscow was liberated, instructing the NKVD to send the families of individuals who served in the administrative or punitive organs of the Germans or had retreated with the German army into exile in remote provinces. Investigations were to be carried out by the Special Board (Osoboe soveshchanie) of the NKVD, an extrajudicial administrative organ that also had the right to try and sentence people accused of counterrevolutionary or anti-Soviet crimes. The decree, however, was limited to the newly liberated areas around Moscow. A second decree instructed the Commissariat of Defense to establish collection–transfer points for Red Army soldiers found in newly liberated areas who had escaped captivity or encirclement, where they would be subject to "filtration" by Special Departments of the NKVD.[19]

Policy evolved through 1942, shaped in part by the traumatic events in Rostov, a frontline city that was occupied twice. Rostov was taken over on November 20, 1941, and liberated within eight days, and then reoccupied from July 24, 1942, until February 14, 1943, a period marked by large-scale destruction and the mass shooting of 27,000 residents, almost half of whom were Jews.[20] In mid-June 1942, about six weeks before the second occupation, the head of the Rostov provincial party committee sent a cipher telegram to Stalin. Anticipating that the province might be reoccupied, he requested that the GKO immediately authorize the exile of families of individuals who had previously served the Germans and then retreated with them. Recognizing that such families were likely to aid the Germans, he requested their exile not only from Rostov but also from other provinces along the right bank of the Don River, which were also under threat.[21] The Criminal Code already stipulated that families of individuals convicted of fleeing across the border or of servicemen who had surrendered to the enemy or abandoned their units could be sentenced to exile, but it did not include families of individuals convicted of treason, spying, aiding the Germans in punitive or administrative capacities, or retreating with them. As of June 1942, the NKVD had already identified 37,350 people, mainly women and children, who fell into this category in the newly liberated territories.[22] On June 24, the GKO responded to the request from the party secretary in Rostov, decreeing that adult family members of individuals (civilian or military) who were convicted and sentenced to death either in person or in absentia by the courts or by the Special Board of the NKVD for spying, serving the Germans, or defecting to the enemy were subject to exile for five years. "Family" was defined as "fathers, mothers, husbands, wives, sons, daughters, brothers, sisters who lived with the traitor or were dependent on him for support." Recognizing that families might be split in their allegiances, the decree exempted from exile any members who had served in or aided the Red Army or partisans or been awarded medals or honors.[23] In June 1942, however, the Red Army was still in retreat. Although the decree set forth the treatment of collaborators and their families, it was less a response to large numbers of actual collaborators than a deterrent to potential collaborators in areas about to be occupied. The Soviet state still had little conception of how many such people might exist in those areas currently under occupation or the gravity of their crimes.

The mass roundups and prosecution of collaborators began in earnest after the victory at Stalingrad. On February 2, 1943, the same day that German field marshal Friedrich Paulus surrendered, NKVD and army units began arresting people who had served the Germans or denounced partisans, soviet officials, or party members to them. When Voronezh, Rostov, Stavropol', Krasnodar, and other areas were liberated in the spring and summer of 1943, similar prosecutions followed. In April, the Central Committee decreed the establishment of the Commissariat of State Security (NKGB), to be split from the NKVD and devoted exclusively to exposing spies, diversionists, and anti-Soviet elements.[24] That same month, the Supreme Soviet decreed that, after discovering "unprecedented atrocities" in the liberated areas by militia units, Gestapo, camp chiefs, and burgomasters, the German fascist criminals guilty of "the murder and torment" of Soviet civilians and Red Army soldiers were to be put to death by hanging, as would be spies and Soviet traitors. Their local accomplices were to be sentenced to fifteen to twenty years of hard labor. Cases were to be tried by military field courts and the sentences "carried out publicly before the people."[25] The state staged the first public trial for war crimes in Krasnodar in July 1943, predating the Nuremberg trials by more than two years. The eleven men on trial had worked in the SS-Sonderkommando, one of many subunits created by the Germans to carry out mass murder throughout the occupied territories. Charged with killing local residents, many in mobile gas vans, eight were sentenced to death and three to hard labor. The public hanging was attended by more than 50,000 people. Both the trial and the hanging were filmed and broadcast. Public trials, in which Germans and their Soviet accomplices were accused of multiple crimes, including gassing ghetto residents and civilians, were also held in Khar'kov, Smolensk, and other towns.[26]

Throughout 1943, NKVD troops conducted extensive purges of the liberated areas, investigating 931,549 people, including former Red Army soldiers who had deserted their units or escaped captivity or encirclement; civilians who left work without permission, evaded the draft, or refused to leave a frontline area; and collaborators. Less than 10 percent of these, however, were investigated for collaboration.[27] The process of filtration continued through 1944 and into 1945. In April 1944, the NKVD purged Crimea, detaining thousands of people who had joined Tatar, Russian, and Ukrainian nationalist groups sponsored by the Germans.[28] Despite their shared sponsorship, all these groups held different ideas about who constituted the "true" people of Crimea. By January 1945, the NKVD had checked an additional 96,956 people in "investigatory- filtration points" in Ukraine, Belorussia, Moldavia, Estonia, and Leningrad and Murmansk provinces. Of this group, 45 percent were sent to NKVD camps for further investigation, 35 percent received permission to return home, and 6 percent were drafted into the army. Only a tiny number—153—were immediately arrested as German collaborators or traitors.[29] The investigatory sweep, however, was extensive: more than 1,028,000 people passed through the filtration points, and a sizable percentage were sent to NKVD camps for further investigation. The NKVD conducted large-scale deportations from both the pre- and post-1939 Soviet territories with the aim of eliminating nationalist guerrilla bands and facilitating collectivization. In January 1945, the state revived an older Civil War strategy, deporting families of those who refused to register. The threat of deportation was open, well publicized, and effective. The property of exiled peasant families was distributed among poor and middle-ranking peasants and demobilized Red Army soldiers. In response, many peasants who had been conscripted by nationalist bands quickly surrendered to the NKVD and received amnesty if they had not been involved in atrocities.[30]

Residents also came forward voluntarily to denounce collaborators once local party committees and soviets were reestablished. Angry that families of Red Army soldiers were homeless or housed in ruins, they exposed those who had served as mayors, headmen, and police under the Germans and were still living comfortably with their families in the apartments of victims of the Germans. The political situation in the wake of liberation, however, was chaotic. Power had changed hands, but the state still did not have a clear policy toward families of people accused but not yet convicted of collaboration. Nine months after the liberation of Krasnodar, for example, district party and soviet officials were still discussing this issue. In a large, district-wide meeting, one local soviet official declared, "When we go to the factory, always the first question they ask us is, 'Look, you, chairman, tell us why do we have families of the *politsai* [local police force established by the Germans] living undisturbed among us? When will you show them? When will you let them feel that Soviet power has come back?'" He asked his fellow officials, "Can Soviet power really be so weak that it cannot clean out this trash?" Questions of property, however, were left to the courts, and the Procuracy refused to adjudicate claims without an investigation. Its stance was an obstacle to the dissemination of rough justice, but it also allowed many collaborators and their families to remain undisturbed in apartments they had received from the Germans as reward for their services.[31]

In Kiev, a city with strict prewar residency requirements, local officials struggled to implement clear rules for filtration after liberation. Thousands of people had made their way back to the city seeking work and housing. Many were authorized to return from evacuation, but others were military

deserters, collaborators, or simply former residents without official authorization. Returnees frequently invoked the Supreme Soviet decree of August
5, 1941, which guaranteed the return of a serviceman's housing to his family.
Ukrainian state officials insisted that Kiev's local leaders not permit people
to enter the city "in an unorganized manner" without authorization from
an institution or enterprise. Yet city officials were uncertain how to treat the
families of servicemen as well as collaborators who had remained in the city
but had a family member who had joined the Red Army or partisans after
liberation.[32]

Many local officials proved amenable to bribes. Yelizaveta Dubinskaya
remembered her family's return to Kiev:

> When we returned to Kiev our flat was ruined. So my father bought a wet
> basement from a landlady in Podol (a district of Kiev). Only later, a few
> years later, I was given a flat. I fought a lot for it, even though I was entitled
> to one as a participant in combat actions. But they did not want to give it to
> me first. Flats then were sold for money. Not officially, of course. People had
> to give bribes to officials.[33]

The rules on housing tended to favor people who had remained in Kiev
under occupation. Much of the housing stock was ruined, and many who
remained moved into better apartments. At the the time of liberation, more
than 350,000 people were still in evacuation and about 100,000 of the city's
residents (including 50,000 Jews) had been murdered by the Germans.
A full inventory of who was living where was not conducted until after the
war was over. Meanwhile, tensions flared between those who had stayed
and those who returned to claim their homes. Ukrainians who remained
under occupation accused Jews who returned of sitting out the war in
evacuation, while returning evacuees charged those who stayed with
collaboration.[34]

In some cases, people managed to live together amicably, sharing the
space. Naomi Deich, a music student who had worked in a defense plant in
Sverdlovsk, remembered doubling up with the people who had taken over
her family's apartment:

> At the end of 1944 our parents returned from evacuation. My father asked
> the people that occupied our apartment to move out . . . . He had a certifi-
> cate confirming that this apartment had belonged to us before the war. We

were given a corner in a room. Other tenants had put up wardrobes, and we got accommodation behind these wardrobes. We didn't have any furniture left—it had been stolen or burnt during the war. Our neighbors gave us a folding bed, a sofa, and a mirror. One neighbor had our table and low table for the samovar, another one had our sewing machine, which I got back. The hardest loss for us was the grand piano that my parents' acquaintances had given to us before the war. My brother and I were so upset that we decided to [make] every effort to find it. We asked everyone and did find it. Our neighbors from the first floor had it. They gave it back to us.[35]

In attempting to distinguish active collaborators from those who had simply accommodated the occupation regime, Soviet authorities followed rough guidelines. Those who were forced to work for the Germans in menial capacities, such as laundresses, cleaners, or forced laborers in battalions or factories, but who did not inform on others, were not prosecuted. Those, however, who had joined administrative or punitive organs, denounced others, or aided in arrests, roundups, and murder of civilians were subject to arrest, investigation, and punishment. The lines dividing accommodation, collaboration, and resistance were often blurred. People lied under investigation, concealed certain activities, and foregrounded others. Some had both collaborated and resisted at different points in time. A number of deserters from the Red Army, for example, later joined the partisans. After 1943, Jewish partisans in particular noted an uptick in anti-Semitism within their detachments with the influx of these new, opportunistic recruits.[36]

Everyone naturally sought to recast their behavior in the most favorable light. In an indignant letter to the Central Committee, one bold woman, Z. Orlikova, in a newly liberated town in Riazan' province, complained, "After all this horror, the local power is beginning to abuse us. They blame us for giving blood to the Germans, for not trying to leave, and mainly for working for the Germans .... They tell us, 'You should have died rather than work for them.'" But in Orlikova's view, working for the Germans was not "a betrayal of the motherland." "People were forced to do this!" she exclaimed. "How could people not go to work?" Making reference to the popular wartime hymn, "Sacred War," she noted, "Indeed, they could not feed themselves by the 'sacred spirit' alone. Are they also enemies? Is it necessary to destroy all of them?" She protested that the newly established district soviet had arrested many people and tried and shot several for collaboration. In fact, she casually mentioned, her own father was among those detained.

Orlikova, who clearly hoped to help her father, instead sparked an investigation of her claims. The letter was remanded to the provincial party committee, which discovered that her father had voluntarily joined the German administration and supplied them with food, shelter, and fuel. Worse still, he conducted a census of the population and prepared lists of soviet and party activists for the Gestapo. German officers were billeted in Orlikova's home; her sister, a party member no less, was seen everywhere with them. The family's fate neatly illustrated where Soviet officials placed the line between accommodation and collaboration: Orlikova and her sister were not arrested, although her sister was expelled from the Party. Their father was sent to prison.[37]

Rationing and Labor Mobilization

As the Party and soviets rebuilt local organizations, the Commissariat of Trade established new networks of food provisioning and extended the ration system to encompass all urban residents, rural waged workers, and the newly mobilized in the liberated territories. In August 1943, the Soviet of People's Commissars and the Central Committee instructed the Commissariat of Trade to count and register the population, order food from central stocks, distribute ration cards, and organize canteens.[38] In 1943 and 1944, the state added no fewer than 12,221,000 people to the bread ration rolls.[39] Kiev, like many towns after liberation, had neither electricity nor running water, which complicated the reconstruction of bakeries. Although people were soon incorporated into the ration system, there were frequent interruptions and sharp shortages in the supply of bread.[40]

The Union of Public Catering Workers played an essential role in rebuilding the canteen system. Its members cleared towering piles of garbage and filth from the few buildings still standing and set up municipal and factory canteens. Kalinin was one of the first provinces to be liberated during the winter of 1941–1942. As the city had been occupied for two months, its shops and canteens were destroyed. After liberation of the city on December 16, 1941, union members managed to open up a number of new canteens, and by January 1, 1942, fifteen were working. Soon, there were seventy-four. The head of the Union of Public Catering Workers remembered reconstructing the canteens with equipment salvaged from under the ruins:

It must be said that the reconstruction period was extraordinarily difficult and strained. When we arrived in town, we had no light, we had absolutely no transport of any kind, and absolutely no fuel. The workers in public catering had to take on the task of bringing fuel from the forest on sleds. For almost the entire winter, they also brought water on sleds because the water pipes did not work.[41]

Similar obstacles faced the largely female canteen workers after the liberation of Khar'kov, but within a month they had managed to establish almost 60 canteens, serving 20,000 adults and 4,000 children. In the absence of electricity, pumping stations, light, running water, and fuel, they hauled water from the rivers, and cut and dragged wood from the forest. Every activity had to be done on foot: the trams did not run, there were no motorized vehicles, and the few horses that remained were needed by the collective farms. The canteens had no furniture or supplies, but women workers pitched in, scavenging tables, chairs, plates, pots, spoons, and even curtains to create collective spaces where people could be fed. In Khar'kov, the union began with a staff of three, but soon recruited more than 1,600 workers. Some cooks and servers, clutching old union cards they had hidden from the Germans, came forward to reclaim their prewar jobs. The union reviewed every person who applied for work and membership, sometimes discovering compromising information about collaboration.[42]

The efforts in Kalinin and Khar'kov were replicated in other towns. A Red Army soldier later recalled entering Voronezh after the Germans had retreated. The town lay in ruins, empty, without "a single living soul."[43] The Germans had blown up the railroad station, tens of thousands of homes and buildings, and the electric trams and tracks. After liberation, every able-bodied person was required to contribute ten hours of labor each month to reconstruction but, as one canteen worker noted, "Our working people have no shoes . . . It's only this year that we started going around in footwear. We threw together some *valenki* [felt boots] and shod our own people. But look what happens when it comes to felling timber—they are working in slippers."[44] Another union activist in Dnepropetrovsk remembered, "Everything was burned, absolutely nothing remained." The local residents were living in earthen dugouts, and not a single building remained that could station a canteen. So the workers opened the canteen in a dugout. He remembered, "For the first days we had to work under such conditions! We gave out dinners, but the roof leaked, and the rain streamed onto the plates."[45]

Another union activist from Nikolaev province noted with modest pride, "we managed to feed the workers not badly."[46]

Along with the ration system, labor mobilization was extended into the liberated territories, and the Committee to Enumerate and Distribute the Labor Force (the Komitet) began establishing provincial and district bureaus. The Komitet, however, was dependent on local soviets for mobilization and was unable to meet any targets before these bodies were reestablished. In Belorussia, the Komitet set up bureaus immediately after liberation in February 1944 in Gomel', Mogilev, and Vitebsk, but was not able to extend its reach into other provinces until almost a year later.[47] Qualified, politically reliable staff, possessing basic literacy and numeracy skills, were needed by all newly formed administrative organizations, including the courts, municipal departments, ration bureaus, schools, and hospitals. Partisans were initially recruited to fill vacant positions within the local bureaus of the Komitet, but these former fighters were in high demand everywhere. Many immediately enlisted in the Red Army and others were deployed by the Party.[48] The Komitet complained that it was the last organization to be staffed: its bureau chiefs were no sooner appointed than they were dispatched to other posts. Every organization needed trustworthy people who were not compromised by collaboration but, as one representative of the Komitet acknowledged, "In a district formerly under occupation, the problem of selection of cadres is well understood." In other words, many people had either been compromised or were still waiting to be cleared. Despite the obstacles, the Komitet immediately began training new staff composed of less educated people. Provincial bureaus organized local seminars to explain the laws on mobilization and evasion and to teach how to assess the size of the able-bodied population. The provincial and district bureaus, short of staff, equipment, and even paper, scribbled mobilization summonses, lists, and records on scraps and old newspaper. The paper shortage was more than a petty hindrance. If a case of desertion or evasion came to court, the prosecutor had the right to reject any document that was not printed on official paper.[49]

The first task the Komitet confronted was enumeration: how many able-bodied people in the liberated territories were available for work? No one knew. The usual sources for data—ration bureaus, local soviets, and house managers—were either missing or struggling to reestablish themselves. And, to complicate matters further, the population was in motion. Once liberated, people joined the Red Army, moved to reunite with family members, or were dispatched to jobs in other places. The Komitet's Rostov bureau chief noted as late as January 1945 that there was still "almost no enumeration of the local population." The Kiev provincial bureau managed to collect statistics on the urban population, but had no figures for the rural areas, a predicament common to all bureaus. Collective farm managers and heads of rural soviets, determined to retain the few able-bodied people they had, refused to provide names to the Komitet and were easily persuaded by their fellow villagers to remove names from mobilization orders.[50]

The difficulties of mobilization in the rear were now reproduced in even more extreme form in the liberated territories. If basic enumeration was challenging, issuing summonses and rounding people up was more difficult still. Given the poor health of the population, people had little trouble convincing local doctors to issue exemptions. The Komitet repeatedly urged the staff of polyclinics to reduce the number of exemptions but, after the hunger and horrors of occupation, many people had good reason to claim disability. Transport posed another problem. The rail system functioned poorly, and roads and bridges were often impassable. Travel into rural areas was impossible even by horse-drawn cart. Many liberated areas remained in frontline zones, and the railroads prioritized food and ammunition for the front. Plenipotentiaries from the commissariats arrived to accompany mobilized people to their new work sites, only to wait days or weeks for an empty train. Sometimes the plenipotentiaries themselves failed to arrive. According to law, a mobilized group had to be sent home after any delay lasting more than ten days.[51] Despite the difficulties, tens of thousands of newly mobilized workers were dispatched to work throughout the liberated areas. More than 25,000 workers arrived to work in the coalmines in Rostov province in September and October 1944 alone.[52]

By 1944, the state began to pressure managers nationwide to improve housing, food, and bathhouses, and to punish those who ignored the "services of daily life."[53] On January 19, 1944, the GKO decreed that mobilized people were to travel only in heated railway cars and had to be fed regularly on the journey.[54] The decree was in part a response to several shocking deaths among two convoys of Central Asian workers, who had been sent home ill in unheated railway cars with little food and died after being delayed at various stations. Some months later, Molotov angrily criticized the Komitet for "not valuing people" and sending them to work in places without decent accommodation. After Molotov's reprimand, the Komitet and the commissariats were responsible not only for providing proper transport for mobilized workers but also for ensuring that managers were "ready to receive them."[55]

The spotlight on living conditions precipitated a new bureaucratic struggle over accountability. The Komitet refused to send mobilized workers to sites with poor living conditions, and the commissariats, unable to improve conditions significantly, refused to accept new workers. In short, the Komitet and the commissariats both refused to fulfill mobilization orders, the very engine of the labor system. The coalmines in Rostov, for example, repeatedly refused to accept workers mobilized for the mines. The system, having reached a crisis, began breaking down under the state's order to improve conditions. The Komitet, responsible for fulfilling mobilization orders, was caught between conflicting state demands: to deliver a specific number of workers to each industry and to ensure that managers of these industries created "minimally normal conditions." Komitet officials and managers each blamed the other for failure to meet the labor needs of industry and appealed to the courts. The ongoing conflict had no resolution.[56] Complaints sounded from every quarter. In Odessa, a port city, the provincial bureau of the Komitet was supposed to mobilize more than 46,000 people for work inside and outside the province. The port, however, categorically refused to accept women as stevedores, and the Black Sea Fleet demanded skilled workers only. The Komitet noted, "We cannot provide skilled workers and they categorically refuse women." One member of the provincial bureau summed up the situation with frustration: not only were there no skilled men available, but also, "In almost half the provinces, there are no people." At times, the Komitet disregarded the planning and distribution process altogether and simply mobilized people first to help with the harvest, and then to cut and cart wood.[57] The wartime practice of planning labor deployment for defense was devolving into a basic effort at survival.

In the summer of 1944, the labor legislation that criminalized job-changing without permission was extended to the newly liberated areas. Military tribunals, replicating those in the rear, were created in Ukraine to try labor deserters and managers who abetted them. More than 140,000 people, mainly peasants, were mobilized to work in the Donbass mines under very difficult working and living conditions. Tens of thousands of people ran away each month. Women and rural youth who had been mobilized for the metallurgical industry deserted in droves and returned to their villages. Although 34,376 workers were sent to the Voroshilovgrad coalmines in the spring of 1944, at the same time almost 39,000 ran away. In July alone, the prosecutor of Ukraine received material on almost 19,500 cases of desertion by mobilized workers.[58] "Mass desertion" was rampant: neither threat of punishment nor small improvements could induce people to remain in place.

Many of the newly mobilized workers, particularly in the liberated areas, were women with children, one of the last remaining reserves of healthy labor. Women with children between the ages of four and eight were exempt from mobilization if the enterprise to which they were sent lacked a childcare facility. As a result of poor communication, mothers of young children were sometimes mobilized and sent on long rail journeys to sites without childcare facilities anyway. Arriving exhausted, with small children in tow, they were then sent back home. Yet even this exemption was soon whittled down. In April 1945, shortly before the Germans surrendered, the Komitet issued instructions that the exemption would last only two months, after which the mothers would become eligible again for mobilization. Women with children under the age of four were also exempt from mobilization, but members of the Komitet hungrily eyed even this potential pool of labor. One noted that they were "the healthiest, most active, and largest part of the nonworking population." Managers, however, were far less enthusiastic about hiring mothers of young children, declaring that they could not offer "normal conditions" for women workers.[59] In April 1945, the state became stricter about exemptions for dependants, instructing the district and town bureaus of the Komitet that everyone receiving a dependant's ration card would also need an official exemption, medical or otherwise, from labor mobilization. If they did not have an exemption, they would not receive a ration card.[60] As the war neared its end, the state tossed out carrots and sticks with frantic disregard—better conditions, deprivation of rations, mobilization of mothers with young children and dependants—resorting to any conceivable administrative solution to block evasion, find workers, and maintain production.

Labor Mobilization and Armed Resistance

By 1945, every province and republic in the nation was struggling to meet its target numbers for labor mobilization. The last quarter of 1944 proved particularly difficult for the provincial bureaus, especially in the liberated territories. Some bureau chiefs no longer believed that the targets were realistic: there was no labor left. The Rovno bureau chief explained unhappily,

"We are not able to provide a labor force even for the internal needs of our province," he said. "As result of ruin by the German occupiers, the economy of the province is rebuilding slowly due to a shortage of labor, and even the restored enterprises are not working at full strength due to the absence of a labor force." When the draft board was ordered to mobilize people for the Red Army, it was able to meet its target only by pulling workers out of industry. A bureau chief from Dnepropetrovsk noted that it was almost impossible to mobilize people for industry because of the severe labor shortage in agriculture. "We can take no one," he shrugged. "The contingent has vanished." In short, everyone was working somewhere.[61]

Local mobilizers, under intense pressure to meet targets, rounded up people without an official summons and took people who were exempt, including youngsters under fourteen and women with small children. One member of the Komitet noted indignantly that local soviets exempted the relatives of officials, but "mobilize every old person or woman with kids." In Rostov province, four women collective farmers with small children, whose husbands were at the front, were mobilized to work in a factory in Taganrog, more than 50 miles (80 km) to the west. The women wrote a letter of protest to Mikhail Kalinin, the head of the government, asking for help:

> Dear Comrade Kalinin,
> We four and our little children lived and worked in the Shchedenko collective farm. After liberation from the German yoke, we immediately were taken to reconstruct the economy of our collective farm. We know that this grain which we grow on our native fields is also a weapon against the hated enemy. Sparing neither time nor strength, we have achieved good success. Our harvest is rich, and the only bad thing is that we do not have enough working hands. And here, at the very height of our work, a representative from the Stalin factory in Taganrog arrived at our collective farm and mobilized us, our families with our children, to work in the factory. He threatened that if we did not go, we would go to prison. We cried bitterly, took the children, left the households and cows with outsiders, gave some of the children to a seventy-year-old woman, and we arrived in Taganrog. Here we asked the director of the factory to allow us to go home, but he did not even answer our petition. Our hope is that you, dear one, will stand up for us, and we assure you, we will work on our fields, not sparing time or strength, still more and still better.

In pencil, three of the women signed their names in a childish scrawl, and one signed for the fourth who could not write. The letter, typical of petitions for redress, stressed the women's support for the war effort and, most importantly, their economic contribution on the collective farm. Yet the women, forced to abandon their children, farm animals, and gardens, also described the profound disruption that mobilization created. The letter soon found its way to the Komitet and to the chief prosecutor of the USSR, who launched an investigation that found the mobilization illegal and allowed the women to return.[62] Although the women received justice, their plight was typical of many others whose cases were never investigated.

People in the liberated provinces had widely divergent reactions to labor mobilization and the return of Soviet power. Sealed off from Soviet news for most of the war, they had not participated in the *levée en masse* spirit or the wartime culture that reinforced it. People in the towns, especially workers, regarded mobilization more favorably than peasants. Their livelihoods depended on the reconstruction of industry and transport, and they understood that a nationwide collective effort offered the fastest and most efficient way to rebuild. Peasants, living in rural areas with less infrastructure, were more reluctant to leave their families and farms for distant labor sites. The response to mobilization was also more favorable in the prewar Soviet territories than in the borderlands incorporated after 1939. In the industrial region of Dnepropetrovsk, for example, mobilizers were more successful in fulfilling their target numbers, while in Rovno and Volynskaia provinces many people refused to register. The Rovno bureau chief noted, "A large part of the population has a hostile attitude toward mobilization." People refused to work outside the province or ran off to the forest. Yet Komitet officials were impatient with the complaints of the new bureau chiefs and derided them for having spent the war under occupation. One official urged them to stop complaining and to enforce the law, "If you compare your situation with that of the Urals and Siberia, you would change your attitude to this business. Enormous effort was required then and, all the same, they coped with the situation and the need to resurrect the evacuated industries quickly and mobilize the maximum labor force. Now Ukraine itself must reconstruct its industry . . . It is necessary to adopt the attitude that there will be mobilization."[63]

Armed nationalist bands throughout the borderlands were openly antagonistic not just to mobilization but also to the reestablishment of Soviet power in any form.[64] They had collaborated with the occupation forces, joining the local administration and police. After liberation, those who

Figure 10.3 Rebuilding Kreshchatik Street, Kiev, May 1945. Courtesy of GARF.

did not flee with the German army harassed and murdered Soviet officials, members of the Komitet, convoys of mobilized workers, and the families of teenagers who entered vocational schools. In Ukraine, the largest of these far right, fascist groups, the Organization of Ukrainian Nationalists (OUN), and its armed wing, the Ukrainian Insurgent Army (UPA), murdered tens of thousands of Jewish and Polish civilians with the aim of creating an ethnically pure Ukraine. Before the invasion, OUN had declared, "we destroy Jews as the basis of the Muscovite Bolshevik regime." After the Red Army left western Ukraine in the late summer of 1944, OUN became more active, murdering civilians who had cooperated with Soviet power or entered the region to help rebuild, including agronomists, technicians, railroad workers from eastern Ukraine or Russia, and entire families whose members joined the Red Army or provided grain to the Soviet state. One OUN leader stated, "OUN should destroy all those who recognize Soviet authority. Not intimidate, but destroy."[65]

Armed fighters followed mobilized groups to the railway station, attacked their leaders, and urged people to run away. The Komitet's Rovno bureau chief explained the failure to meet the target numbers for mobilization in 1944: "The population is bullied and terrorized by nationalist bands that not only agitate the local people not to go to work, but even use terror against those who appear for mobilization and set fire to their property." Travel was so dangerous that soviet and party representatives could not enter the villages unarmed. Labor mobilizers traveled in groups of up to thirty people, armed with grenades and machine guns. In some areas, "even armed groups could not get through." As soon as the mobilizers appeared in a village, the entire population "with the exception of children and the elderly" disappeared into the forest. When people were mobilized, they moved out in horse-drawn carts under guard. The Rovno bureau chief noted that these armed mobilizations made a "poor impression." Most district mobilizers were local people, which conferred a certain advantage, but they were also poorly educated and had difficulty explaining the need for mobilization. Mobilized workers who were brought to district centers fled the railway stations and trains at their first opportunity. According to the Rovno bureau chief, "Most who are placed in the railway car never reach their destination." Of 635 people mobilized to work in the iron and steel industry, for example, only 46 reached the destination. In one convoy, everyone fled with the exception of one person and the two plenipotentiaries sent to accompany the convoy. As a result of the difficulties, the Rovno bureau chief asked the government of Ukraine to remove the province from further assignments until the bureau had time to educate the people.[66] In western Belorussia, too, local mobilizers encountered resistance. The villagers melted away into the thick forest as soon as the mobilizers appeared. One bureau chief explained, "There are districts in which it is completely impossible to mobilize. In Baranovich district, you cannot take a single person without a machine gun. That's how to make a mobilization there."[67]

Members of the Komitet vehemently opposed these armed mobilizations. One member described a horrific scene she witnessed in her visit to a village: "Twelve carts were carrying young girls, followed by their relatives. The bawling was awful. One man was carrying a girl of about fourteen who was sick. In the front walked our official with a machine gun, and in the rear several others with rifles. From the guns it was clear, they are not mobilizing people but arresting them. There was not a single summons or speech." When she spoke with the girl and her relatives about the mobilization, however, they replied that they were grateful for liberation and understood the need for a labor draft. The Komitet, concerned about violations, resolved to send a letter to the state prosecutor.[68]

Figure 10.4 Family of Ivan Zhelezniakov, a young Komsomol, mourning his murder by Germans in the retreat from Gomel', January 1944. Courtesy of GARF.

At the same time, it was difficult for local soviet officials to combat armed bands with explanations alone. Many local people refused to comply with Soviet reconstruction efforts simply out of fear. One member of the Komitet referred to "mass intimidation." In Belorussia, three bureau officials along with fifty families of district and village soviet activists were murdered. Local inhabitants told mobilizers that if they answered the summons nationalist bands would murder their families. In Rovno province, nationalists slit the throats of the family of a teenager who voluntarily enrolled in vocational school and burned their farm to the ground. They hanged another teenager in the yard and murdered his family as an example to others. They burned down a factory and vocational school, as well as attacking peasants mobilized to cut and cart wood. In one case, they stopped peasants on their way to the forest, stole their axes and saws, cut the harnesses from the horses, and made them pull the carts back to the village themselves.[69] Over time, however, the terror began to backfire. In the words of one historian, the terror was so brutal and indiscriminate that it "multiplied the number of Soviet supporters." Despite armed resistance, the shortage of qualified staff, and difficulties with transport, workers were mobilized throughout the liberated territories to rebuild. In Dnepropetrovsk province, the Komitet successfully mobilized workers from almost every district and met 85 percent of its target figures by the end of 1944. Mines, power stations, factories, and transport began to function again as mobilized workers rebuilt the ruins.[70]

Reconstruction

The devastation in liberated areas initially appeared overwhelming. Towns were littered with trash, corpses, human waste, and unexploded shells and mines. Water lines, sewerage, and communication systems were destroyed. There were no generators, power stations, industrial equipment, warehouses, refrigeration, medical facilities, schools, or transport of any kind.[71] In January 1944, the Soviet of People's Commissars made reconstruction a priority, calling a meeting of the commissars of light industry, timber, textile, construction, medium-sized machine-building, and construction materials, as well as officials from Gosplan and local industries.[72] The Komitet began sending home small groups of highly skilled workers who had been evacuated in 1941 to help with rebuilding. In the words of journalist and poet Tvardovskii, workers returned "to the irrevocable loss" of "everything sacred to the heart from childhood."[73] Yet there were few moments for mourning. For the second time in less than four years, they began rebuilding the country's industrial base.[74] After hard fighting, the Red Army opened a narrow land corridor to Leningrad on January 18, 1944, and the siege was lifted on January 27. The day before the liberation of the city, 300 evacuees were sent home to rebuild Leningrad's armaments factories.[75] The Komitet continued to send small groups of evacuees from Leningrad back home through the spring of 1944.[76]

With a new pool of workers available in the liberated areas, 1944 proved the height of labor mobilization nationwide: 1,113,350 workers in total, more than half from Ukraine and Belorussia.[77] Huge mobilizations from Rostov province and other places were launched to restore the coalmines and rail lines.[78] In February, 5,000 people were mobilized from Ukraine to reconstruct Dneprostroi, a massive hydroelectric station and dam on the Dnepr River that Red Army engineers had blown up in August 1941 in advance of German occupation.[79] The Komitet sent almost 12,000 Belorussians to Ukraine that same month to rebuild the Donbass iron and steel industry, transferred thousands more from one town in Ukraine to another, and sent more than 4,000 people, the overwhelming majority from Ukraine, to work in the shipbuilding industry.[80] Thousands of people left the newly liberated territories to work in the east. In March and April, the Komitet sent 8,500 people, about one-quarter of whom were women, from Ukraine to work in the tank industry in Stalingrad and the eastern towns.[81] In April and May, the first very large groups of evacuees, numbering in the thousands, returned to Leningrad and the liberated territories.[82] Great convoys of workers, some headed to the east, others returning to the west, passed each other in transit. At the end of April, the Komitet launched a massive mobilization of 625,000 people, mainly peasants from the newly liberated areas. More than 152,000 people were mobilized in Ukraine alone, of whom about one-quarter were sent to the mines.[83] The liberated territories, too, were soon depleted of labor. The Germans had murdered or shipped out millions for slave labor, and Soviet deportations of targeted national groups, including citizens of German origin, further reduced the population. More than 180,000 Crimean Tatars, for example, were deported in May 1944 to Uzbekistan.[84] That same month, when the Komitet sought to mobilize workers in Crimea for reconstruction of the food-processing factories, the heads of the Crimean Soviet of People's Commissars and provincial party committee tactfully requested that the mobilization be postponed, "due to the exit of part of the population."[85]

On June 22, 1944, the Red Army launched Operation Bagration, its strategic offensive in Belorussia. The operation, named after Piotr Bagration, the Russian prince who fought against Napoleon, lasted until August 19 and cleared Belorussia and eastern Poland of German forces. It resulted in the largest defeat experienced by the Wehrmacht thus far: more than 500,000 Germans killed or wounded. In combination with the L'vov–Sandomierz Offensive, it allowed the Red Army to regain the country's 1941 borders in Belorussia and Ukraine, reach East Prussia, and advance into Poland. Some 60,000 German prisoners of war, encircled east of Minsk, were paraded through Moscow. Marching twenty abreast, they passed through the crowds of Muscovites who lined up to watch in eerie silence. The ragged, shambling POWs were a far cry from the arrogant, jackbooted soldiers who invaded in 1941. In a final symbolic gesture, the prisoners were followed by a small fleet of sanitation trucks to clean the streets of the "Nazi filth" that had inflicted so much destruction. The liberation of each new Soviet city was celebrated in Moscow with great nighttime displays of fireworks, one celebration following the next in a quickening crescendo of victory. In September and

October 1944, the Red Army captured Tallinn in Estonia and Riga in Latvia, gateways to Germany.

The tussle over labor intensified. The Komitet continued to mobilize tens of thousands of people to work in the coal, peat, and timber industries to meet the voracious demand for fuel.[86] In November, it ordered provincial officials in Ukraine to mobilize over 43,000 more people for the coal industry. Backlogs already existed and the Commissariat of the Coal Industry explicitly demanded that November's levy not come at the expense of previous unfilled orders. The Ukrainian Soviet of People's Commissars, aware that Ukraine had almost no able-bodied unemployed left, refused the commissariat's demand and insisted that it subtract the workers from previous unfilled orders from the new levy.[87]

By 1945, members of the Komitet openly acknowledged the limits of the labor system. Its provincial bureau chiefs in the rear and in the newly liberated provinces had run out of people to mobilize. As of February, the Komitet had met its annual quarterly target (due in March) by only 11 percent for the overall economy and 14 percent for the defense commissariats. The Commissariat of the Aviation Industry was supposed to receive 1,150 people but, as one member of the Komitet noted, "not a single person has been sent

Figure 10.5 Victory fireworks following the liberation of Briansk, September 17, 1943. Courtesy of RGAKFD.

to its factories." The Commissariat of Construction was short by more than 10,000 people. Yet the war was almost over. Several members of the Komitet suggested that the time had come to replace compulsory mobilization with a new system of voluntary recruitment through bureaus that would match people with jobs in their home provinces. On May 12, three days after the war ended, the Komitet again discussed the cessation of labor mobilization. One member stated plainly, "We should make a suggestion to the government to end mobilization in connection with the end of the war. We should state that the mobilization of the urban and rural population is over." He suggested that the current system continue until the end of May and then be replaced with voluntary recruitment. The Komitet's members recognized that industries such as peat and timber rafting would need help with recruitment, but they imagined a new, limited role for the Komitet in the future. It had accomplished a remarkable feat, but all agreed that the mobilization and militarization of labor could not be sustained.[88]

****

The occupied territories were freed in stages and incorporated into a rapidly expanding home front. The systems that had sustained the war effort—the military draft, rationing, and the militarization and mobilization of labor—were extended into the newly freed areas. The long process of reestablishing Soviet power began. Reincorporation faced challenges both familiar and different to mobilization in the rear. Once again, the state struggled to feed a greatly expanded civilian population, create canteens and barracks for newly mobilized workers, and build transport, electrical power, housing, schools, clinics, and other basic infrastructure. Unlike the rear, the liberated territories were completely devastated. Factories were ruined shells, mines were flooded, the dams blown, and the towns in ruins. The cities were depopulated, and those who remained were starved, traumatized, and rent by bitter divisions. Those who returned from evacuation and those who had stayed under occupation regarded each other with a deep mistrust and suspicion that was heightened by shortage and prejudice. Yelizaveta Dubinskaya remembered:

> For Jews it was particularly hard to get a flat. Everyone expected them to pay. People believed that Jews did not fight during the war, but spent their time in evacuation and got very rich there. But both my brothers fought at the front: one was killed, another one was wounded. I personally fought,

and every Jewish family had a soldier as well. But life was very hard materially. I began to work as an emergency nurse. I worked for two salaries, in two shifts, because a nurse's salary was very small, and I had to bring up a child. I was left alone, without a husband.[89]

Soviet and party organizations had to rebuild from almost nothing. Initially, small operational groups followed the Red Army and remained in liberated territory to become the nuclei of the Party's district committees.[90] The Party also relied on demobilized partisans. But these sources provided only skeleton staffs. Union, party, and NKVD organizations established verification procedures to vet former members, and uncover and punish collaborators. The process was slow, and verification of party members continued into the postwar period. The NKVD also conducted large-scale deportations, removing entire nationalities from their homelands and sending them into exile. Amid vast population shifts, the political terrain remained fluid and chaotic. Although many collaborators were caught and punished, others successfully concealed their wartime pasts and flourished in the new order.

The wartime system, so successful in mobilizing the population for feats of production and home front defense, was stretched to the breaking point before the liberation of the occupied territories. Efforts to further extend the ration and canteen system faltered on the lack of electricity, running water, fuel, and useable buildings. Although more than twelve million newly freed people were added to the ration rolls, the delivery of bread was irregular. The canteen system became a necessity given the labor mobilization of more than half a million new workers from Ukraine and Belorussia to defense factories in the east and construction sites in the west. The problems the Komitet encountered in the newly liberated areas were sharper than in the rear. After mass murder and slave labor shipments to Germany, few able-bodied workers remained, and those who did had little desire to work on distant sites. In the western borderlands, some mobilizers and volunteers were murdered for participating in reconstruction. Nationalist armed bands continued to fight the establishment of Soviet power well into the postwar period. Yet the restoration of the liberated territories began almost immediately and continued as the Red Army moved past the Soviet frontiers and into Germany.

On May 8, 1945, the German High Command signed an act of unconditional surrender. The end to the war was announced in the Soviet Union in the early morning hours of May 9. The headline in *Pravda* read: "The Great Patriotic War of the Soviet People against the German Fascist Invaders Has Ended Victoriously. Long Live This Day of Nationwide Celebration – THE HOLIDAY OF VICTORY!" In Khar'kov, people streamed into the streets at 2:00 a.m., gathering around the mounted radio speakers to hear the announcement of the capitulation. Tens of thousands gathered in the central square of the city. Rockets were launched against the dark sky. All night, people sang and shouted. In Moscow, about three million people filled Red Square, thronging the river embankments, and crowding the main avenues. That night, the most spectacular fireworks display of all lit up the skies. In Leningrad, workers attended mass meetings in the factories, and people gathered in the squares of every district. Speakers recalled the first months of the war when the Germans besieged the city and spoke movingly of those who had died. In the eastern towns, the sun was already rising as the news reached the defense factories. In Sverdlovsk, workers in Uralmash gathered in a huge meeting, congratulating each other, shaking hands, and embracing. Throughout the country, in every town and village, people at last celebrated the day of victory.[91] Sophia Abidor, a medical student, had returned to her hometown of Odessa from evacuation. Although her husband had been demobilized after crippling wounds, she remembered her happiness at the time:

> My husband met his childhood friend and we were having a chat with him when, all of a sudden, we heard shooting. My husband and his friend ran outside telling me to stay inside. It turned out that there was an announcement on the radio about the victory over Germany and everyone demobilized from the army came into the streets and were shooting into the air. We were overwhelmed with joy. People came into the streets crying, singing, and hugging one another. We couldn't believe that everything horrible was in the past.[92]

Conclusion

After the German invasion, the Soviet state and people, confronted with a threat to their very existence, were forced to channel all human and material resources toward the war effort. The vast majority of German divisions were concentrated in the east, and here the outcome of World War II was decided. The Red Army marching westward broke the backbone of the Wehrmacht, opened the gates of Maidanek, Belzec, Sobibor, Treblinka, and Auschwitz, and freed millions of people from fascist occupation. The military prowess of the Red Army, however, was determined by the people on the home front who supplied the armaments the soldiers needed. The greatest victory of the twentieth century depended on their efforts.

Figure C.1 Soviet infantry advance alongside T-34 tanks in the summer of 1944. From http://ww2today.com/7-july-1944-t-34s-attack-panzers-cornered-in-the-russian-forest.

To create the most cursory inventory of what the Red Army required, imagine a typical frontline soldier in a uniform, helmet, and boots, carrying a gun, ammunition, a blanket, and other basic equipment. He or she went into battle supported by tanks, planes, trucks, mortars, shells, grenades, radios, and communication cables. The soldiers in the photograph, taken in the summer of 1944, were moving alongside a OT-34 tank. The tank was produced in the Urals Tank Factory in Nizhnii Tagil. After the invasion, eleven major factories and enterprises were evacuated to Nizhnii Tagil, including the factory where the famed T-34 was first created. The workers in the Urals Tank Factory built half of all T-34 tanks used during the war. In the foreground of the photograph is a Red Army soldier carrying a 1931 Mosin sniper rifle. The other soldiers are armed with Shpagin PPSh-41 automatic machine guns, the single most common machine gun. Nicknamed "Papasha," or "Daddy," the Shpagin machine gun became an iconic symbol of the front, carried by soldiers featured on posters and monuments. Due to the simplicity of its design, six million such guns were manufactured by workers in converted textile, ball bearing, and diesel engine factories.[1] Now follow the supply lines reaching back thousands of miles to the workers who manufactured this equipment and then beyond to those who produced the wood, steel, rubber, oil, engines, ball bearings, coal, cloth, and chemicals its fabrication required. Supporting these workers in turn stood others who labored in fields, forests, and peat bogs to feed, warm, and shelter those in the defense sectors. Behind every frontline soldier stretched a vast chain of invisible laborers who "produced" the soldier and made battle possible. Now imagine a transfer of resources from rear to front so complete that the laborers who produced the soldier struggled to sustain life.

The home front revealed the very limits of an economy and people involved in total war. Workers lacked clothing, footwear, soap, and food. People crowded together in unheated dormitories, earthen dugouts, and apartments without access to bedding, boiled water, and bathing and sanitary facilities. Public transportation ceased to function, forcing workers to trudge long distances to and from work. Accident rates increased along with poisoning, rashes, and abscesses from unprotected contact with hazardous materials. Prisoners died at alarming rates partly because they ranked so low in the ration hierarchy. The camps and the Labor Army provided the most extreme examples of the punishing impact of shortage, but hardship and lack of food took their toll on everyone. Children lacked calcium, vitamins, and protein essential for growth and development, their huge eyes and quiet listlessness a heartbreaking sight for parents, teachers, and public health officials. Workers, the best-provisioned category, weakened over time, and some eventually died of starvation and ill health.

The cost of total war was most deeply felt by those who lived through it. Arkadiy Redko, a veteran who fought on the Ukrainian and Belorussian fronts, reflected on the sacrifices:

> Of course, many nations and many countries suffered in this war, but I think that the heaviest hardships fell on our people. Would any other country have endured this? Not one army or state. I think any other country would have had to surrender . . . . Germans were merciless to many peoples and particularly so to Jewish people. Only the Soviet people serried [unified] by the party and Stalin could win after suffering such great losses . . . . Who made a decisive contribution to the victory? The Soviet Union and the Soviet army, of course. . . . I can say the same about my brother, who perished young, having seen or done nothing in his life. We, the living, must feel this.[2]

The story of the Soviet home front provides new answers to Redko's question: "Would any other country have endured this?" Just as the Allied victory cannot be understood apart from the Soviet contribution, the performance of the Soviet wartime state cannot be assessed apart from its record on the home front. The military and home fronts developed in tandem, but their trajectories of strength bore almost an inverse relationship to each other. On the military front, the first months of the war proved disastrous. The Red Army stumbled back in disordered retreat, massive stocks of armaments were lost, and entire divisions were encircled or wiped out. Not until the victory at Stalingrad in February 1943 did the Red Army begin to recapture the ground it had ceded. In contrast, policies on the home front were initially far more effective. The state adopted the basic pillars of the wartime system— evacuation, the ration system, resettlement in the east, public health controls, and labor mobilization—rapidly and successfully. Yet, if the Red Army realized its greatest fighting capacity after Stalingrad, the home front population was, by this time, beginning to weaken. The trajectories of the two fronts rose and fell in opposite directions, each intersecting in a common point of strength at Stalingrad. At this decisive battle, workers were finally able to provide soldiers with the advantage in armaments they needed to win. But the production campaigns and eleven-hour days had begun to take their toll. After Stalingrad, the military gained in power, but shortages of food, consumer items, and labor began to weaken the home front.

The Stalinist state reached the height of its vast powers during the war, manifesting a greater ability to command and mobilize its people than any other combatant nation. With few exceptions, all able-bodied civilians were subject to mobilization for work. Workers were placed under military discipline and subject to harsh penalties for unauthorized lateness, absence, or desertion. Millions of people were sent to work in locations far from home. The evacuation and reconstruction of the industrial base, the mass mobilization and distribution of workers, the centralization and allocation of food under starvation conditions, the aversion of a public health disaster, and the reconstruction of the liberated territories were all the result of exceptional organizational efforts. Each of these achievements drew on existing state organizations and previous experience, but also required the creation of new bodies invested with extraordinary powers. The state evacuated millions, relocated entire ethnic populations, dispatched vast contingents of newly mobilized workers to distant sites, and deployed prisoners and exiles.

Strict discipline and repression certainly played a role. Yet the ability of the state to undertake such unprecedented feats of mass mobilization was not based on coercion alone. Without the support of the vast majority of people and workers in particular, the great achievements on the home front would not have been possible. The central state relied on an extensive network of new and existing organizations that enabled local officials and ordinary people to contribute to the war effort. Decision-making was centralized in the State Committee for Defense to the exclusion of the Politburo and Supreme Soviet, but at the same time the war required an unusual devolution of power, responsibility, and participation, ranging from local officials who were forced to make hard decisions about evacuation to troubleshooters who cleared the wharf at Stalingrad to workers who invented innovative techniques to keep the rail lines open.

The Soviet for Evacuation (SE) was created within the first week of the war. The success of its mission evolved with the loss of territory and provided a stabilizing alternative to the rising panic that threatened to engulf local officials and ordinary people in the frontline zones. The evacuation of children and food stocks was its first priority but, as more territory was lost, its goals shifted. By August 1941, the state decided to create a new industrial base in the east, out of the reach of German bombers. The SE's charge progressed from an emergency response to threatened territorial loss to a comprehensive economic plan for industrial reconstruction. Relying on a powerful combination of industrial commissariats, soviets, and local party organizations, as well as the experience with planning and mass production pioneered during the industrialization drive of the 1930s, evacuation proved critical to the food supply, defense production, and the lives of millions of citizens. The support of workers was essential. As events in Ivanovo demonstrated, when party activists and managers failed to communicate with workers, their efforts floundered. The willingness of workers to labor around the clock, under bombardment, amid fires and floods, made evacuation possible. As the German Army swept with unexpected speed through Ukraine, the biggest obstacle to evacuation was the lack of railway cars. After long and perilous journeys, workers built a new industrial base that combined the most advanced production methods of multiple factories. Evacuation functioned as a forcing ground for a second wave of massive industrial development.

The German occupation of the great grain-producing agricultural lands immediately precipitated a food crisis that worsened as the Red Army retreated. Yet here, too, the state moved quickly: the Commissariat of Trade created a complex ration system that planned and delivered set allocations to waged workers and urban residents. Ordinary people accepted the essential hierarchy of the system, which privileged defense workers and provided supplementary food to the most vulnerable groups. As women went to work and retail stores closed, workers, students, and small children ate their main meals in closed canteens attached to factories or institutions. Central state stocks provided the majority of calories consumed by the population but were not sufficient to cover its basic biological requirements. By 1942, the food crisis was so severe that ordinary people and even defense workers began to starve. The death rates among more poorly provisioned groups, especially prisoners and members of the Labor Army, were horrific. As the food situation improved, as a result in part of Lend-Lease food aid, factory managers and public health officials began to provide a second hot meal in the factories, more food to vulnerable groups, and special dietary programs to nourish the starving.

Evacuation, like an earthquake, set in motion a tsunami of consequences. The vast flood of refugees and evacuees created a public health disaster along the evacuation routes. Public health workers and medical personnel struggled to contain epidemics of measles, typhoid, and typhus that took many lives en route and upon arrival. The reconstruction of an industrial base in

the sparsely populated east required a labor force. The state quickly established the Committee to Distribute the Labor Force (the Komitet), a new organization charged with enumerating the able-bodied unemployed in every
province and republic and dispatching them to enterprises in need of labor.
With the help of draft boards and vocational schools, it mobilized millions
of people. As the Komitet exhausted the reserve pools of urban labor, it
turned toward the countryside, overstepping its initial mandate and sending
millions of people to work on distant sites far from home. Mobilization was
the most expeditious solution to the labor shortage in the east, but it forced
industrial managers to feed, house, and care for mobilized workers, replacing
the services normally provided by women within the family. Under enormous pressure to produce amid an almost total absence of consumer goods
and building materials, the enterprises provided little more than unheated
barracks, earthen dugouts, and poorly provisioned canteens and childcare
centers. Repeated investigations by various state and party organizations revealed the appalling conditions in the industrial towns.

By 1944 the home front labor system was in crisis. Thousands of workers
fled the factories and mines, finding work in other places or returning to their
collective farms. Industry and collective farms competed for labor, and local
soviets were unable to meet the targets set by the Komitet. In every province,
backlogged, unmet orders surpassed new ones. Industrial managers found
it easier to request fresh contingents from the Komitet than to stanch desertion by improving conditions. The system of labor mobilization became a
self-generating juggernaut of orders corresponding poorly to both the needs
of the industrial commissariats and the provinces. Yet, despite the growing
numbers of deserters and the exhaustion of reserves, labor mobilization continued to support defense production in the eastern industrial towns and the
reconstruction of the liberated territories.

Repression played a role in enforcing discipline, but its efficacy was limited. It would be deeply mistaken to attribute the vital contribution workers
and ordinary people made to the war effort to coercion. Forced labor, the
most extreme example of coercion, had an important role in defense construction and industry but, in the wake of the mass amnesties, the camps
suffered the same shortage of able-bodied workers as the larger economy.
The state relied overwhelmingly on free mobilized labor to staff the defense
industry and construction. The most common experience of coercion came
through the draconian labor legislation. Penalties for lateness, absenteeism,
and desertion were harsh, and many people were convicted. Between 1941

and 1945, more than 5.6 million people—over a quarter of all those employed in the state sector—were convicted of lateness and absenteeism and suffered a temporary loss of pay and in many cases a cut in the vital bread ration. Penalties for illegal quitting were more severe: almost 700,000 people were convicted in 1943 and 1944. Yet only about 20 percent of the workers first reported for desertion were ever found.[3] Penalties were so poorly enforced that many workers regarded them with little fear. Collective farm and factory managers, judges, and procuracy officials proved either reluctant or unable to enforce the law. Like the members of the Komitet, the Komsomol, and the unions, they too understood that desertion could be reduced only by creating better conditions for labor.

Propaganda, which changed over the course of the war, helped to build support for the war effort. Initially, the state's message failed to connect with ordinary people despite a great upsurge in support. Over time, it more closely aligned with people's emotional needs and became more adept at infusing individual experience with political and collective meaning. The sharp switch in the summer of 1942 to franker reporting resulted in part from criticisms of party activists of the state's previous "talking points." Ordinary people reacted strongly, for example, against the obvious disjuncture between the state's claims of military prowess and the Red Army's continuing retreat. Yet in 1942, as the Red Army discovered the extent of Nazi destruction, brutality, and genocide in the liberated areas, the state's antifascist message began to resonate more powerfully. The ideal of a socialist, united, multinational collective may not have reflected how Soviet national groups treated each other in practice, but it stood in sharp contrast to the virulent race hatred of Nazism. The consequences of fascist ideology were on ample display in the piles of Soviet POW corpses, the shooting pits, and the gallows in the newly liberated territories. The state also established a strong and convincing link between home front production and military victory. Campaigns to increase production took on personal meaning for workers who had friends and family members at the front. After the state's push to increase production in the summer of 1942, workers saw their efforts redeemed at Stalingrad. Finally, many people, particularly workers, evoked the ideals of socialism in their letters, protests, and complaints. The revolution was less than a generation past. Older workers had participated in the struggle for soviet power, and younger people were raised on heroic tales of 1917 and the Civil War. Nor were Soviet citizens alone in viewing the war as a great ideological battle; they were joined by partisans, underground fighters, and allies all over the world who saw socialism as a desirable alternative to fascism and capitalism.

The great hardships on the home front resulted in multiple organizational tensions. Various state and party organizations were often pitted against each other in the struggle over food as each sought to protect its own constituency against starvation. Local officials placed contingents of evacuees, prisoners, and orphans in factory canteens and fed them from central stocks allocated to workers. These attempts at redistribution leveled the hierarchies of the ration system, and kept more vulnerable, less well-provisioned groups alive. At the same time, local officials, food service employees, and others took advantage of the system to self-provision and steal stocks. Practices of redistribution, theft, and self-provisioning made and remade the ration hierarchy through black and gray markets that both supported and undermined the ability of the system to feed the country. Similar struggles existed over labor. Local soviets resisted the efforts of the Komitet to mobilize ever greater numbers of people from their provinces, collective farm managers protected runaways, and the court system balked at enforcing strict labor laws. Trade union and Komsomol officials protested against the commissariats that ignored the health and welfare of workers in favor of the relentless drive for production. Every organization and enterprise fought to advance its own constituencies and interests, and thus inevitably came into conflict with others. There were strong limits on the state's ability to unify contending interest groups and enforce the wartime regime it envisioned.

By 1945, the main wartime policies, once so essential to home front strength, were beginning to collapse from the weight of their own contradictions. Peasants mobilized for industry were unable to sow or harvest, creating starvation among workers, labor desertion, and, in turn, the need for more labor mobilization of peasants. The ration system was beset by shortage, which led to theft and in turn generated greater shortage. The systematic starvation of every sector not devoted directly to defense—clothing, footwear, building materials, and municipal services—weakened the labor force and ultimately affected its ability to sustain the war effort. The same contradictions characterized public health and forced labor: had the state had more resources to improve conditions, desertion and death rates would have dropped, less time would have been lost to absence, and both forced and free laborers would have had more strength to contribute to production. Yet, given the imperatives of the battlefield, the country simply could not make the investments that workers, prisoners, peasants, and ordinary people so desperately needed.

When Stalin died in 1953, the country had reached its prewar level of production and repaired much of the material damage done by the Germans. The state eliminated the Komitet in May 1946, and the ration system in December 1947. To the great benefit of the population, public health measures first adopted during the war became standard practice. Yet the scars of the war were still visible everywhere almost fifty years later. Special benches on the Moscow metro were reserved for war veterans and invalids. Older men in their sixties and seventies were eerily absent from public spaces while women of the same age, *babushki*, were a vigorous presence. People continued to live in crowded individual and communal apartments, and food and consumer goods remained in short supply. A generation of children had lost their childhoods, and many grew up without fathers. Large numbers of women missed the opportunity to marry. Parents never recovered from the deaths of sons and daughters who did not return. The human losses left a lasting mark on every Soviet family.

Figure C.2 Women workers picking up children from kindergarten after the liberation of Odessa. Courtesy of RGAKFD.

For generations to come, people would continue to celebrate the victory and to mourn the dead. The victory over fascism was a monumental achievement, not just for the Soviet Union, but for the world. But, in defeating fascism, the Soviet people also enabled the Stalinist system to consolidate itself and reassert its authority. The victory, closely identified with Stalin's leadership, was popularized and accepted broadly as a great moral triumph. The spontaneous initiative of the war years and popular hopes for political relaxation and prosperity were smothered in the stultifying political atmosphere of late Stalinism.

As the years passed, the victory, gained at such great cost, would come to have many meanings. The great celebratory marches on May 9, the Day of Victory, which once included veterans, are now composed of their children and grandchildren, holding portraits of those who fought. This display of what Russians call the "immortal regiments" began in Tomsk in 2012 and spread throughout the country. For the post-Soviet, Russian state, the victory has become central to a new national, patriotic identity. Discarding the socialist, anti-fascist narrative of the war, Russia's leaders now emphasize the ability of the motherland to rally and repel an invader as it has done so many times in its long history. The victory of the Soviet people against fascism, however, also belongs to all the world's people, part of an ongoing international struggle against virulent nationalism, race hatred, anti-Semitism, and exploitation. It is an extraordinary historical legacy left to all who continue to fight for the international anti-fascist ideals it represented.

In Moscow, a monument stands to the *opolchenie*, the volunteer militia that rallied to defend the city. Made up of students and workers, the division helped liberate many towns around Moscow and in Ukraine. Inscribed on the stone is a sonnet, written by poet Mark Maksimov, in the style of Petrarch, the fourteenth-century Italian poet:

> I am with you, an equal among equals,
> I have become stone, yet I live!
> And you, who have received Moscow
> As a legacy from citizens-in-arms,
> You, who have granted me eternal life,
> You—all who will come after us—
> Do not forget for a single moment
> That I am watching you from this stone.[4]

The poem, written in the voice of a defender of the city, speaks to a younger generation of Muscovites. At a time of resurgent nationalism and hate, it also speaks to people all over the world. In the name of those who fought the war three-quarters of a century ago, it commands the living never to forget that they died so that future generations could live in a world without fascism.

Appendix

Table 2.1. Population of Moscow, Leningrad, and major home front industrial cities receiving evacuees, 1939, April 1942, and January 1944

City	1939 census	1 April 1942	% change vs. 1939	1 January 1944	% change vs. 1939
Moscow	4,238,900	2,582,300	−39.1	3,235,900	−23.7
Leningrad	3,090,800	1,912,000	−38.1	555,000	−82.0
Ivanovo	291,000	282,200	−3.0	241,300	−17.1
Iaroslavl'	302,700	285,100	−5.8	274,000	−9.5
Gor'kii	643,700	710,000	10.3	683,000	6.1
Kuibyshev	398,000	583,500	46.6	562,800	41.4
Kazan'	399,600	516,200	29.2	523,700	31.1
Saratov	372,000	428,400	15.2	403,600	8.5
Penza	159,800	184,900	15.7	191,300	19.7
Izhevsk	176,000	no data		204,000	15.9
Kirov	144,900	no data		176,400	21.7
Chkalov	171,700	252,300	46.9	225,000	31.0
Molotov	306,100	427,500	39.7	402,200	31.4
Sverdlovsk	425,500	549,000	29.0	542,200	27.4
Nizhnii Tagil	159,900	204,000	27.6	243,000	52.0
Cheliabinsk	276,200	396,600	43.6	405,500	46.8
Magnitogorsk	145,900	172,200	18.0	194,300	33.2
Ufa	250,000	328,700	31.5	406,400	62.6
Novosibirsk	405,300	567,000	39.9	609,600	50.4
Omsk	288,900	381,000	31.9	412,000	42.6
Stalinsk (Kuzbass)	165,700	179,000	8.0	206,600	24.7
Kemerovo	132,800	no data		188,300	41.8

Sources: Figures for 1939 census and January 1, 1944, are TsSU data: RGAE, f. 1562, op. 20, d. 484, ll. 32–35, 37–38. Figures for April 1, 1942, are highly approximate estimates made by Narkomzdrav, "Zdravookhranenie RSFSR v 1943 g. Statisticheskii sbornik" (Moscow, 1943), in GARF, f. 8009, op. 6, d. 1906, pp. 167–173 (the file does not have sheet/*list* numbers).

Table 3.1. Sources of food for the urban population of the USSR as a percentage of calories consumed, 1942–1944

Food source	All food products		
	1942	1943	1944
State central stocks	78.5	73.0	68.0
Subsidiary farms	3.4	4.2	4.5
Decentralized procurement	1.0	0.8	0.6
Total through state organizations	*82.9*	*78.0*	*73.1*
Individual gardens	8.0	9.4	12.4
Collective farm trade	9.1	12.6	14.5
Total consumption	100	100	100

Source: Cherniavskii, *Voina i prodovol'stvie.* p. 186.

Table 3.2. Food industry production of major foodstuffs, 1940–1945, as a percentage of 1940

	1940	1941	1942	1943	1944	1945
Sugar (granulated)	100	24	5	5	11	21
Meat (excluding kolkhoz production)	100	78	48	41	36	44
Cheese	100	–	–	–	–	60
Butter	100	91	49	45	47	52
Vegetable oil	100	86	32	27	30	37
Pasta products	100	90	73	73	64	75
Flour	100	85	54	45	45	51
Bread and baked goods	100					37
Groats	100	91	56	50	56	63

Source: Vera Valer'evna Solov'eva, "Bytovye usloviia personala promyshlennykh predpriiatii Urala v 1941–1945 gg. Gosudarstvennaia politika i strategii adaptatsii," Candidate of Historical Sciences Dissertation, Ekaterinburg, 2011, p. 76; Cherniavskii, *Voina i prodovol'stvie*, pp. 58–9.

Table 3.3. Average adult per capita daily calorie intake of the urban population, 1939–1944.

| Year | Calories | Calories in percentages | |
		1939	1942
1939	3370	100	–
1942	2555	76	100
1943	2751	82	108
1944	2810	83	110

Note: Absolute amounts and as a percentage of 1939 and 1942.

Source: Cherniavskii, *Voina i prodovol'stvie*, p. 179. Cherniavskii's calculations include data from central state stocks, collective farm markets, and decentralized purchasing.

Table 3.4. Daily ration of bread and basic foodstuffs in grams per day and kilocalories per day, October 1941

| | Bread | | Meat and fish | | Fats | | Grains & pasta | | Sugar and confectionery | | Total kcal |
	gm	kcal	gm	kcal	gm	kcal	gm	kcal	gm	kcal	
Workers and ITR Category I	800	1512	72	108	20	160	49	169	17	66	2015
Workers and ITR Category II	600	1134	59	89	13	104	39	134	17	66	1527
Clerical employees Category I	500	945	39	59	10	80	26	89	10	39	1212
Clerical employees Category II	400	756	39	59	10	80	26	89	10	39	1023
Dependants	400	756	16	24	7	56	20	69	10	39	944
Children under 12	400	756	13	20	10	80	26	89	13	51	996

Sources: RGAE, f. 7971, op. 1, d. 895, l. 62 (bread), l. 76 (other foods).

Note: Bread allocations were in grams per day; other foods are in grams per month, which we have converted into daily portions. Calorie values are those established by the Central Statistical Administration in 1925, *Trudy TsSU*, vol. xxii, vypusk 1, 1925: *Normal'nii sostav i pishchevoe znachenie prodovol'stvennykh produktov*: 189 kcal per 100 grams of rye bread; an average of 150 kcal per 100 grams of the various available kinds of meat and fish (including canned goods); 800 kcal per 100 grams of fats; 344 kcal per 100 grams of groats (grains) and pasta products; and 389 kcal per 100 grams of sugar and confectionery goods.

Table 4.1. Food allowances for leading party and state officials, workers in core defense industries (Category I), and other workers (Category II), July 1943

	Officials Group I	Officials Group II	Officials Group III	Workers Category I	Workers Category II
Bread (gm)	1,000	800	1,100	800	600
Meat and fish (gm)	309	296	168	72	59
Fats (gm)	79	59	36	20	13
Groats & pasta (gm)	164	138	128	49	39
Sugar & confectionery (gm)	102	49	26	17	17
Eggs (units)	0.33	0.33	0	0	0
Dried fruits (gm)	16	16	0	0	0
Milk (millilitres)	33	33	0	0	0
Potatoes (gm)	658	329	0	0	0
Vegetables (gm)	329	164	0	0	0
Total calories	4,659	3,489	3,164	2,015	1,527

Note: Total allowances (ration, canteens, and parcels) in grams per day and total caloric value.

Sources: Officials in Groups I–III: GARF, f. 7678, op. 8, d. 243, ll. 6, 6ob. Workers: RGAE, f. 7971, op. 1, d. 895, l. 62 (bread), l. 76 (other foods). For methods of calculation, see p. 415, n. 27.

Table 5.1. Mobilization of the civilian population to permanent jobs in industry, construction, and transport, July 1941–December 1945 (thousands)

	Total mobilized	By the Komitet to enterprises from the nonworking population		From Labor Reserve graduates		From construction battalions and workers' columns drawn from draft-eligible population (People's Commissariat of Defense)	
		Number	% of total	Number	% of total	Number	% of total
1941 (July–December)	1,288.3	120.8	9.4	439.5	34.1	728.0	56.5
1942	1,357.6	733.9	54.1	569.1	41.9	54.6	4.0
1943	2,210.3	890.7	40.3	597.8	27.0	721.8	32.7
1944	2,203.9	1,113.3	50.5	416.4	18.9	674.2	30.6
Subtotal, July 1941–December 1944	7,060.1	2,858.7	40.5	2,022.8	28.7	2,178.6	30.9
1945	858.9	272.5	31.7	457.5	53.3	128.9	15.0
Total	7,919.0	3,131.2	39.5	2,480.3	31.3	2,307.5	29.1

Source: Adapted from R. E. Romanov, "Sovetskoe gosudarstvo i rabochie v gody Velikoi Otechestvennoi voiny. Sotsial'no-trudovye otnosheniia v sfere zaniatosti," in V. I. Shishkin, ed., *Vlast' i obshchestvo v Sibiri v XX veke. Sbornik nauchnikh statei*, vypusk 6 (Novosibirsk: Parallel, Institute of History of the Siberian Division of the Russian Academy of Sciences, 2015), p. 214. Romanov constructed the table from GARF, f. 9507, op. 1, d. 211, l. 7, and GARF, f. 9517, op. 1, d. 25, ll. 85–86.

Table 5.2. Prisoners in Gulag labor camps, labor colonies, and special settlements, 1940–1945, annual averages

	Labor camps	Labor colonies	Special settlements	Total
1940	1,422,466	372,395	963,867	2,758,728
1941	1,458,060	395,326	920,969	2,774,355
1942	1,199,785	430,828	818,107	2,448,720
1943	823,784	508,217	697,093	2,029,094
1944	689,550	630,698	661,253	1,981,501
1945	658,202	850,698	652,818	2,161,718

Source: Edwin Bacon, *The Gulag at War: Stalin's Forced Labor System in the Light of the Archives* (Basingstoke: Macmillan, 1994), adapted from tables 2.1 (p. 24) and 2.3 (p. 30). The 1945 figure for special settlements is for December 1, 1944; no data are available for January 1, 1946, from which to calculate an annual average.

Table 5.3. Prisoner population and deaths of prisoners in Glavpromstroi and Gulag corrective labor camps, 1941–1945

	1941	1942	1943	1944	1945
Glavpromstroi					
Average number of prisoners	84,615	89,899	95,417	93,245	85,291
Number of deaths	16,028	31,913	19,926	9,960	3,719
Mortality rate (deaths per 100 prisoners)	18.9	35.5	20.9	10.7	4.4
Gulag corrective labor camps					
Average number of prisoners	1,458,060	1,199,785	823,784	689,550	658,202
Number of deaths	100,997	248,877	166,967	60,948	43,848
Mortality rate (deaths per 100 prisoners)	6.9	20.7	20.3	8.8	6.7
Gulag camps and colonies combined					
Mortality rate (deaths per 100 prisoners)	6.1	24.9	22.4	9.2	5.95

Sources: Glavpromstroi: A. A. Tsepkalova, "Gulag na stroitel'stve promyshlennykh ob"ektov, Rol' kontingentov Glavpromstroia," in L. I. Borodkin, S. A. Krasil'nikov, and O. V. Khlevniuk, eds., *Istoriia Stalinizma. Prinuditel'nyi trud v SSSR. Ekonomika, politika, pamiat'. Materialy mezhdunarodnoi konferentsii, Moskva, 28–29 oktiabria 2011 g.* (Moscow: Rosspen, 2013), p. 104. Gulag camps: Zemskov, "Smertnost' zakliuchennykh v 1941–1945 gg.," p. 175, citing GARF, f. 9414, op. 1, d. 1155, l. 2. Gulag camps and colonies combined: A. I. Kokurin and N. V. Petrov, eds., *GULAG (Glavnoe upravlenie lagerei) 1917–1960* (Moscow: Mezhdunarodnyi fond "Demokratiia," Izdatel'stvo "Materik," 2000), pp. 441–2. These figures are contained in a note (*spravka*) compiled from various files of the Department for the Accounting and Distribution of Prisoners (OURZ) in the main NKVD/MVD archive, but neither the sources nor the authors are specified. The figures in the note are not fully compatible with those given by Zemskov, although the order of magnitude seems to be accurate.

Table 5.4.   Labor capacity of Gulag prisoners, 1940 vs. 1942

	1940	1942
Able to do heavy physical labor	35.6	19.2
Able to do moderate physical labor	25.2	17.0
Able to do light work	15.6	38.3
Disabled or too weak to work	23.6	26.5

Note: Percentage of prisoners in each category.

Source: Zemskov, "Smertnost' zakliuchennykh v 1941–1945 gg.," p. 175.

Table 6.1.   Number of people mobilized from towns and rural areas for permanent work in industry, construction, and transport, 1942–1944

Year	From towns	Percent of total	From rural areas	Percent of total	Total
1942	565,900	77.1	168,000	22.9	733,900
1943	364,800	41.0	525,900	59.0	890,700
1944	426,300	38.3	687,000	61.7	1,113,300

Source: V. N. Zemskov, "Organizatsiia rabochei sily i uzhestochenie trudovoi zakonodatel'stva v gody voiny s fashistskoi germaniei," *Politicheskoe prosveshchenie,* No. 2 (79), 2014, pp. 4–5, accessed at http://www.politpros.com/journal/read/?ID=3167&journal=160&sphrase_id=12205.

Table 7.1. Convictions for illegal job-changing and absenteeism, 1940–1952

Year	"Willful quitting" under Edict of June 26, 1940	Edicts of December 26, 1941 (defense industry), and April/May 1943 (transport)*	Total convictions for unauthorized job-changing	Absenteeism under Edict of June 26, 1940	All labor discipline convictions	All convictions§	Labor convictions as % of all convictions
1940	321,648	not applicable (n/a)	321,648	1,769,790	2,091,438	no data	no data
1941	314,976	n/a	314,976	1,483,873	1,798,849	3,381,755	53.2
Subtotal, 1940–1941	*636,624*	*n/a*	*636,624*	*3,253,663*	*3,890,287*	*incomplete data*	*incomplete data*
1942	300,086	161,252	461,338	1,293,586	1,754,924	3,582,023	49.0
1943	160,306	386,846	547,152	974,156	1,521,308	3,222,556	47.2
1944	184,942	310,258	495,200	954,266	1,449,466	3,089,374	46.9
Subtotal, 1942–1944	*645,334*	*858,356*	*1,503,690*	*3,222,008*	*4,725,698*	*9,893,953*	*47.8*
1945	120,611	102,541	223,152	960,603	1,183,755	2,742,146	43.2
Subtotal, 1941–1945	*1,080,921*	*960,897*	*2,041,818*	*5,666,484*	*7,708,302*	*16,017,854*	*48.1*
1946	143,600	92,100	235,700	862,790	1,098,490	2,922,484	37.6
1947	215,679	73,956	289,635	685,404	975,039	2,934,810	33.2
1948	255,639	31,039	286,678	589,768	876,446	2,348,098	37.3
1949	274,765	n/a	274,765	546,818	821,583	2,224,661	36.9

1950	213,846	n/a	213,846	534,274	748,120	1,974,233	37.9
1951	137,282	n/a	137,282	327,519	464,801	1,566,963	29.7
1952	183,241	n/a	183,241	152,544	335,785	1,590,329	21.1
Subtotal, 1946–1952	*1,424,052*	*197,095*	*1,621,147*	*3,699,117*	*5,320,264*	*15,597,578*	*34.1*
Total, 1940–1952	2,826,621	1,157,992	3,984,613	11,135,391	15,120,004	31,615,432	47.8

Source: GARF, f. 9492, op. 6, d. 14, ll. 7, 11. Our thanks to Peter Solomon for making these data available to us.

Notes: *Conviction totals include those convicted on the "line courts" that operated on rail and water transport. Zemskov ("Ukaz ot 26 iiuniia 1940 goda," p. 45) lists industry and transport convictions separately, although his figures differ slightly from those in GARF.

§For 1941–1945, 81.7 percent of all convictions were in civilian courts; for 1946–1952 the corresponding figure was 90.0 percent. The figures are marked with the qualification, "Corrected for incomplete reporting."

Table 7.2. Reported cases of labor desertion, convictions, and convicted deserters actually captured, 1943–1944

	1943	1944	Total
Reported cases of labor "desertion"	532,891	801,355	1,334,246
Number of reported cases leading to a conviction	386,846	310,258	697,104
Number of convicted "deserters" actually captured	154,738	124,103	278,841
% of reported cases convicted	72.6	38.7	52.2
% of reported cases actually captured	29.0	15.5	20.9

Source: GARF, f. 8131, op. 37, d. 1844, ll. 108, 110.

Note: Procuracy figures for reported cases and convictions are for January 1, 1943, through November 30, 1944. To arrive at a total for all of 1944 we have added an estimate for December of that year extrapolated from the Procuracy's figure of 86,580 for October–November. The number of convicted "deserters" apprehended is based on Procuracy figures for the period January 1, 1942, to March 1, 1944, which show that 40 percent of those convicted were actually captured and made to serve their sentence: GARF, f. 8131, op. 37, d. 1842, l. 2. We have assumed that this percentage applies also to the period from March 1 to December 31, 1944.

Notes

The endnotes use standard abbreviations for Russian archive references, which consist of five elements:

1. The abbreviation of the archive name (the full names of the archives are given in the Bibliography).
2. f. = *fond*, or holding. These generally correspond to a particular institution or major subdivision of an institution, for example, the USSR Ministry (pre-1945, People's Commissariat) of Public Health, an industrial commissariat or ministry, or a specific trade union.
3. op. = *opis'*, or inventory. The *opisi* are the primary subdivisions of a *fond*. Sometimes the *opisi* represent subdivisions or departments within an organization; some *fondy* simply divide the *opisi* chronologically.
4. d. = *delo*, or file. These are the actual folders containing the documents.
5. l. = *list*, or sheet. Russian archives give files sheet numbers, rather than page numbers, since a file almost always contains many different documents, each of which had its own separate pagination when it was originally written.

Thus a typical reference will be something like this: GARF, f. 9226, op. 1, d. 636, ll. 52, 53. The document will be in GARF (State Archive of the Russian Federation), *fond* 9226 (State Sanitary Inspectorate of the USSR Ministry of Public Health), *opis'* 1, *delo* (file) 636, *listy* (sheets) 52, 53.

The State Archive of the Russian Federation (GARF) has two reading rooms. The central reading room, Reading Room 1, holds files from administrative divisions of the former USSR. Reading Room 2, in a different location, holds files for administrative divisions of the RSFSR. Documents from Reading Room 2 always have the letter "A" before the number of the *fond*. Thus: GARF, f. A-482, op. 47, d. 4941, l. 11, where *fond* A-482 is the Ministry of Public Health of the RSFSR.

Introduction

1. The term "home front" appeared for the first time at the beginning of World War I in German propaganda. It represented the state's recognition that the support of civilians was essential to the war effort. See Karen Hagemann and Stephanie Schuler-Springorum, eds., *Home/Front: The Military, War and Gender in Twentieth-Century Germany* (Oxford: Berg, 2002), p. 8.
2. https://www.centropa.org/biography/raissa-smelaya.
3. The leading monograph on the home front is John Barber and Mark Harrison, *The Soviet Home Front 1941–1945: A Social and Economic History of the USSR in World War II* (London and New York: Longman, 1991). Collections of essays include Robert W. Thurston and Bernd Bonwetsch, eds., *The People's War: Responses to World War II in the Soviet Union* (Urbana: University of Illinois Press, 2000); Susan Linz, ed., *The*

Impact of World War II on the Soviet Union (Totowa, N.J.: Rowman & Allanheld, 1985); David Stone, ed., *The Soviet Union at War, 1941–1945* (Barnsley, UK: Pen and Sword Books, 2010). Other important studies explore specific aspects of home front life, including evacuation, culture, propaganda, and the siege of Leningrad. This study treats rural difficulties with evacuation, and the responses of the collective farms to labor mobilization, reconstruction, and runaways, but it does not fully cover agriculture. Another volume entirely would be needed to do justice to the peasantry and its experience during the war.

4. https://www.centropa.org/biography/meyer-goldstein#During%20the%20war.

5. On life in industrial towns, see also Lennart Samuelson, *Tankograd. The Formation of a Soviet Company Town: Cheliabinsk, 1900s–1950s* (Basingstoke: Palgrave Macmillan, 2011), chs. 7 and 8; Larry Holmes, *War, Evacuation and the Exercise of Power: The Center, Periphery, and Kirov's Pedagogical Institute, 1941–1952* (Lanham, Md.: Lexington Books, 2012) and *Stalin's World War II Evacuations: Triumph and Troubles in Kirov* (Lawrence: University Press of Kansas, 2017).

6. Quote from Richard Overy, *Why the Allies Won* (New York: W. W. Norton and Co., 1995), p. 188; on loss and replenishment, see Evan Mawdsley, *Thunder in the East: The Nazi–Soviet War 1941–1945* (London: Bloomsbury, 2016), p. 47.

7. V. B. Tel'pukhovskii, "Geroizm rabochego klassa," in G. N. Sevostianov, ed., *Voina i obshchestvo, 1941–1945*, book I (Moscow: Nauka, 2004), p. 12, also cited by V. N. Zemskov, "Organizatsiia rabochei sily i uzhestochenie trudovogo zakonodatel'stva v gody voiny s fashistskoi Germaniei," *Politicheskoe prosveshchenie*, No. 2 (79), 2014, p. 3; see http://www.politpros.com/journal/read/?print=y&ID=3 167&journal=160

8. Mark Harrison, "Industry and Economy," in Stone, ed., *The Soviet Union at War*, p. 17.

9. John Erickson, *The Road to Stalingrad: Stalin's War with Germany* (New Haven: Yale University Press, 1975), p. 60.

10. David Glantz and Jonathan House, *When Titans Clash: How the Red Army Stopped Hitler* (Lawrence: University Press of Kansas, 1995), pp. 15–16.

11. See discussion of various views in David Murphy, *What Stalin Knew: The Enigma of Barbarossa* (New Haven: Yale University Press, 2005), pp. xv–xx, 6, 173–87; V. P. Baranov, N. M. Moskalenko, A. V. Timchenko, and E. P. Chelyshev, *Velikaia Otechestvennaia voina, 1941–1945* (Moscow: Ministerstvo Oborony Rossiiskoi Federatsii, 2012), vol. II, pp. 242–301.

12. Chris Bellamy, *Absolute War: Soviet Russia in the Second World War* (New York: Alfred Knopf, 2007), pp. 118–19, 126.

13. See Halder's diary notes, in Joachim Fest, *Hitler* (New York: Mariner Books, 2002), p. 649.

14. The Commissar Order was repealed in May 1942; see Jeffrey Burds, "'Turncoats, Traitors, and Provocateurs': Communist Collaborators, the German Occupation, and Stalin's NKVD, 1941–1943," *East European Politics and Societies: and Cultures*, vol. 32, no. 3 (August 2018), pp. 608, 616.

15. Adam Tooze, *The Wages of Destruction: The Making and Breaking of the Nazi Economy* (New York: Viking Penguin, 2006), p. 462.

16. On planning for the invasion, see Alex J. Kay, *Exploitation, Resettlement, Mass Murder: Political and Economic Planning for German Occupation Policy in the Soviet Union, 1940–1941* (New York: Berghahn Books, 2006).

17. Lizzie Collingham, *The Taste of War: World War Two and the Battle for Food* (New York: Penguin Press, 2012), pp. 18, 22, 25, 26.

18. Collingham, *The Taste of War*, pp. 32, 25.

19. Alex J. Kay, "Germany's Staatssekretare, Mass Starvation and the Meeting of 2 May 1941," *Journal of Contemporary History*, vol. 41, no. 4 (2006), pp. 685–9; Tooze, *Wages of Destruction*, pp. 479–80.

20. As quoted in Alex J. Kay, "The Purpose of the Russian Campaign Is the Decimation of the Slavic Population by Thirty Million: The Radicalization of German Food Policy in Early 1941," in Alex J. Kay, Jeff Rutherford, and David Stahel, eds., *Nazi Policy on the Eastern Front, 1941: Total War, Genocide, and Radicalization* (Rochester, N.Y.: University of Rochester Press, 2012), p. 113.

21. Collingham, *The Taste of War*, pp. 33, 36, 37, 38, 39, 41, 42.

22. Felix Römer, "The Wehrmacht in the War of Ideologies: The Army and Hitler's Criminal Orders on the Eastern Front," in Kay, Rutherford, and Stahel, eds., *Nazi Policy*, pp. 73–100; Christopher R. Browning, *The Origins of the Final Solution: The Evolution of Nazi Jewish Policy, September 1939–March 1942* (Lincoln: University of Nebraska Press, 2004), pp. 222–3.

23. https://www.marxists.org/archive/khrushchev/1956/02/24.htm. The critique was supported by some generals who were angry at Stalin's refusal to permit retreat in the face of what they deemed unwinnable battles.

24. Some historians believe the purges played a major role in the initial failures of the Red Army; others see their impact as more limited. Some argue that Stalin was deceived by Hitler into thinking Germany would first invade Britain; others maintain that Stalin understood invasion was imminent but was frantic to maintain peace until the country was better prepared to fight. Some stress that the Soviet Union outproduced Germany in armaments in 1941, and blame weak strategy and organization; others consider gross output an unreliable indicator of readiness given that almost one-half of Soviet tanks were in need of repairs. On purges, see Alexander Hill, *The Red Army and the Second World War* (Cambridge: Cambridge University Press, 2017), p. 76; Mawdsley, *Thunder in the East*, p. xiv; Roger Reese, "The Red Army and the Great Purges," in J. Arch Getty and Roberta Manning, eds., *Stalinist Terror: New Perspectives* (Cambridge: Cambridge University Press, 1993), pp. 198–214; Glantz and House, *When Titans Clash*, pp. 10–13. On Hitler's alleged deception of Stalin, and Stalin's views of France and Britain, see Murphy, *What Stalin Knew*, pp. 173–80, and Bellamy, *Absolute War*, pp. 145–6, 149, 150–62. On Stalin's "frantic desire" to maintain peace until 1942, see Glantz and House, *When Titans Clash*, p. 26. Bellamy, too, notes that Stalin was desperate to postpone war until 1942 when tanks, guns, and rocket launchers would be ready (*Absolute War*, pp. 116–17). On munitions production, see Overy, *Why the Allies Won*, p. 324. On poor preparation, see Mawdsley, *Thunder in the East*, p. 27, Hill, *The Red Army and the Second World War*, p. 202; Erickson, *The Road to Stalingrad*, p. 66; Glantz and House, *When Titans Clash*, p. 27.

25. M. I. Likhomanov, L. T. Pozina, and E. I. Finogenov, *Partiinoe rukovodstvo evakuatsiei v pervyi period Velikoi Otechestvennoi voiny, 1941–1942* (Leningrad: Izdatel'stvo

Leningradskogo Universiteta, 1985), p. 27; GARF, f. 6822, op. 2, d. 409, ll. 74–100; G. A. Kumanev, "Evakuatsiia naseleniia SSSR. Dostignutie rezul'taty i poteri," in *Liudskie poteri SSSR v period Vtoroi Mirovoi voiny. Sbornik statei* (St. Petersburg: Russko-Baltiiskii Informatsionnyi Tsentr Blits, 1995), p. 145; I. I. Belonosov, "Evakuatsiia naseleniia iz prifrontovoi polosy v 1941–1942," in Iu. A. Poliakov, G. A. Kumanev, N. P. Lipatov, and A. V. Mitrofanova, eds., *Eshelony idut na vostok. Iz istorii perebazirovaniia proizvoditel'nykh sil SSSR v 1941–1942 gg. Sbornik statei i vospominanii* (Moscow: Nauka, 1966), p. 15.

26. Figures for all these categories vary among sources. Poland had few military deaths but massive civilian casualties, losing a greater percentage of its prewar population. For total losses, see E. M. Andreev, L. E. Darskii, and T. L. Khar'kova, "Liudskie poteri SSSR vo Vtoroi Mirovoi voine, Metodika otsenki i rezul'taty"; on civilian losses, M. V. Filimoshin, "Ob itogov ischislenniia sredi mirnogo naseleniia na okkupirovannoi territorii SSSR i RSFSR v gody Velikoi Otechestvennoi voiny"; on military losses, G. F. Krivosheev, "Ob itogakh statisticheskikh issledovanii poter' vooruzhennykh sil SSSR v Velikoi Otechestvennoi voine," all in *Liudskie poteri SSSR v period Vtoroi Mirovoi voiny*, pp. 41–2, 127, 75; Michael Ellman and S. Maksudov, "Soviet Deaths in the Great Patriotic War: A Note," *Europe–Asia Studies*, vol. 46, no. 4 (1994), pp. 671–2 on total deaths, p. 674 on returning POWs, p. 676 on civilian losses. Glantz and House, *When Titans Clash*, p. 292, provide a significantly higher estimation of irrecoverable Red Army losses: more than 11 million and, of these, more than 4.4 million captured or missing in action.

27. "By the Numbers: World Wide Deaths," National WWII Museum, http://www.nationalww2museum.org/learn/education/for-students/ww2-history/ww2-by-the-numbers/world-wide-deaths.html; https://en.wikipedia.org/wiki/World_War_II_casualties.

28. E. P. Thompson, *Beyond the Frontier: The Politics of a Failed Mission, Bulgaria 1944* (Stanford: Stanford University Press, 1997), p. 37.

29. Rodric Braithwaite, *Moscow 1941: A City and Its People* (New York: Alfred A. Knopf, 2006), p. 310.

30. Nina Tumarkin, *The Living and the Dead: The Rise and Fall of the Cult of World War II in Russia* (New York: Basic Books, 1994).

31. See, for example, Johannes due Enstad, *Soviet Russians under Nazi Occupation: Fragile Loyalties in World War II* (Cambridge: Cambridge University Press, 2018); Karel C. Berkhoff, *Harvest of Despair: Life and Death in Ukraine under Nazi Rule* (Cambridge, Mass.: Belknap Press of Harvard University Press, 2004), esp. chs. 1 and 3, and pp. 285–300; Laurie R. Cohen, *Smolensk under the Nazis: Everyday Life in Occupied Russia* (Rochester, N.Y.: University of Rochester Press, 2013); Vladimir Solonari, *A Satellite Empire: Romanian Rule in Southwestern Ukraine, 1941–1944* (Ithaca and London: Cornell University Press, 2019); Burds, "'Turncoats, Traitors, and Provocateurs.'" On the complexity of motivation, see special issue of *Slavic Review*, vol. 75, no. 3 (Fall 2016), including Michael David-Fox, "The People's War: Ordinary People and Regime Strategies in a World of Extremes," pp. 551–9; Seth Bernstein, "Rural Russia on the Edges of Authority: *Bezvlastie* in Wartime Riazan'," November–December 1941," pp. 560–82; Jared McBride, "Peasants into Perpetrators: The OUN-UPA and the Ethnic Cleansing of Volhynia, 1943–1944," pp. 630–54; Amir Weiner, *Making Sense of War: The Second World War and the Fate of the Bolshevik Revolution* (Princeton:

Princeton University Press, 2002); Alexander Statiev, *The Soviet Counterinsurgency in the Western Borderlands* (New York: Cambridge University Press, 2010).

32. https://www.centropa.org/biography/larissa-khusid#During the War.

33. On coercion as the single most important factor, see Oleg Budnitskii, "The Great Patriotic War and Soviet Society: Defeatism, 1941–1942," *Kritika: Explorations in Russian and Eurasian Society*, vol. 15, no. 4 (Fall 2014), p. 791; Karel Berkhoff, *Motherland in Danger: Soviet Propaganda during World War II* (Cambridge, Mass.: Harvard University Press, 2012). On the limited role of coercion, see Roger Reese, *Why Stalin's Soldiers Fought: The Red Army's Military Effectiveness in World War II* (Lawrence: University of Kansas Press, 2011), pp. 13, 25, 27, 173–5, 306; Roger Markwick's excellent review, "Stalinism at War," *Kritika: Explorations in Russian and Eurasian Society*, vol. 3, no. 3 (Summer 2002), p., 510. On support for socialism among workers, see Andrei Dzeniskevich, "The Social and Political Situation in Leningrad during the First Months of the German Invasion: The Psychology of the Workers," in Thurston and Bonwetsch, eds., *The People's War*, p. 79. Richard Bidlack notes that, despite great variation in public opinion, the state was successful in linking war to loyalty to Stalin and the Party, "Propaganda and Public Opinion," in Stone, ed., *The Soviet Union at War*, p. 64.

34. Harrison, "Industry and Economy," p. 26.

Chapter 1

Epigraph: L. I. Pogrebnoi, "O deiatel'nosti Soveta po evakuatsii," in Iu. A. Poliakov, G. A. Kumanev, N. P. Lipatov, and A. V. Mitrofanova, eds., *Eshelony idut na vostok. Iz istorii perebazirovaniia proizvoditel'nykh sil SSSR v 1941–1942 gg. Sbornik statei i vospominanii* (Moscow: Nauka, 1966), p. 205.

1. GARF, f. 6822, op. 1, d. 439, ll. 20–19 (file numbered back to front).

2. G. A. Kumanev, "Voina i evakuatsiia v SSSR, 1941–1942 gody," *Novaia i noveishaia istoriia*, No. 6, 2006, at http://vivovoco.astronet.ru/VV/JOURNAL/NEWHIST/EVACO.HTM.

3. Mark Harrison, *Accounting for War: Soviet Production, Employment, and the Defence Burden, 1940–1945* (Cambridge: Cambridge University Press, 1996), p. 97.

4. Figures are from Kumanev, "Voina i evakuatsiia." Kumanev argues that the number of enterprises evacuated was far higher because many enterprises were evacuated without being officially recorded. M. I. Likhomanov, L. T. Pozina, and E. I. Finogenov, *Partiinoe rukovodstvo evakuatsiei v pervyi period Velikoi Otechestvennoi voiny, 1941–1942* (Leningrad: Izdatel'stvo Leningradskogo Universiteta, 1985), p. 13, cite ten million people evacuated by the end of 1941. On the varying estimates of the number of evacuees, see Chapter 2, n. 3.

5. On estimate of value, see Mark Harrison, "The Second World War," in R. W. Davies, Mark Harrison, and S. G. Wheatcroft, eds., *The Economic Transformation of the Soviet Union, 1913–1945* (Cambridge: Cambridge University Press, 1994), p. 253; Likhomanov, Pozina, and Finogenov, *Partiinoe rukovodstvo evakuatsiei*, p. 27; GARF, f. 6822, op. 2, d. 409, ll. 74–100; I. I. Belonosov, "Evakuatsiia naseleniia iz prifrontovoi polosy v 1941–1942," in Poliakov, *et al.*, eds., *Eshelony idut na vostok*, p. 15. The number of enterprises cited refers to industrial enterprises sent out by rail during the second half of 1941.

6. Likhomanov, Pozina, and Finogenov, *Partiinoe rukovodstvo evakuatsiei*, p. 68.

7. The Western literature includes Sanford R. Lieberman, "Crisis Management in the USSR: The Wartime System of Administration and Control," in Susan Linz, ed., *The Impact of World War II on the Soviet Union* (Totowa, N.J.: Rowman & Allanheld, 1985), pp. 59–76; Mark Harrison, *Soviet Planning in Peace and War 1938–1945* (Cambridge: Cambridge University Press, 1985); Robert Argenbright, "Space of Survival: The Soviet Evacuation of Industry and Population in 1941," in Jeremy Smith, ed., *Beyond the Limits: The Concept of Space and Time in Russian History and Culture* (Helsinki: Suomen Historiallinen Seura, 1999); Rebecca Manley, *To the Tashkent Station: Evacuation and Survival in the Soviet Union at War* (Ithaca: Cornell University Press, 2009); Larry Holmes, *War, Evacuation, and the Exercise of Power: The Center, Periphery, and Kirov's Pedagogical Institute, 1941–1952* (Lanham, Md.: Lexington Books, 2012) and *Stalin's World War II Evacuations: Triumph and Troubles in Kirov* (Lawrence: University Press of Kansas, 2017).

8. Poliakov, *et al.*, eds., *Eshelony idut na vostok*, pp. 7–9.

9. Poliakov, *et al.*, eds., *Eshelony idut na vostok*, p. 8.

10. Poliakov, *et al.*, eds., *Eshelony idut na vostok*, pp. 7–9.

11. John Barber and Mark Harrison, *The Soviet Home Front, 1941–1945: A Social and Economic History of the USSR in World War II* (London and New York: Longman, 1991), p. 132.

12. Kumanev, "Voina i evakuatsiia," citing GARF, f. 8518, op. 27, d. 244; op. 23, d. 224; op. 25, d. 120.

13. Kumanev, "Voina i evakuatsiia," p. 9; Manley, *To the Tashkent Station*, pp. 18–24.

14. Kumanev, "Voina i evakuatsiia," p. 9.

15. GARF, f. 6822, op. 1, d. 502, l. 89.

16. N. F. Dubrovin, "Eshelon za eshelonom," in Poliakov, *et al.*, eds., *Eshelony idut na vostok*, p. 208.

17. G. A. Kumanev, "Evakuatsiia naseleniia SSSR. Dostignutye rezultaty i poteri," in *Liudskie poteri SSSR v period Vtoroi Mirovoi voiny. Sbornik statei* (St. Petersburg: Russko-Baltiiskii Informatsionnyi Tsentr Blits, 1995), p. 142.

18. GARF, f. 6822, op. 1, d. 43, ll. 21–19 (file numbered back to front). Travel expenses would be assumed by the state. Each evacuee would be paid one month's salary in advance and permitted 30 kilograms of baggage.

19. GARF, f. 6822, op. 1, d. 409, ll. 3–4.

20. Postanovlenie TsK VKP (b) i SNK SSSR, "O sozdanii Soveta po evakuatsii," *Izvestiia TsK KPSS*, No. 6 (1990), p. 200; Pogrebnoi, "O deiatel'nosti," p. 202.

21. *Resheniia partii i pravitel'stva po khoziaistvennym voprosam*, vol. III (Moscow: Politizdat, 1968), p. 45.

22. N. A. Voznesensky, *Soviet Economy during the Second World War* (New York: International Publishers, 1949), p. 35.

23. S. N. Kruglov, P. S. Popkov, N. F. Dubrovin, and A. N. Kirpichnikov were also appointed: "O sozdanie Soveta po evakuatsii,'" p. 200.

24. GARF, f. 6822, op. 1, d. 550, contains the protocols of SE meetings from its creation through October 1941.

25. The SE gradually expanded to include about eighty-five officials: Pogrebnoi, "O deiatel'nosti," p. 202; GARF, f. 6822, op. 1, d. 550, l. 1. See also Postanovlenie TsK VKP

(b) i SNK SSSR, June 27, 1941, in "O poriadke vyvoza i razmeshcheniia liudskikh kontingentov i tsennogo imushchestva," *Izvestiia TsK KPSS*, No. 6 (1990), p. 207.

26. Pogrebnoi, "O deiatel'nosti," p. 203.

27. Pogrebnoi, "O deiatel'nosti," pp. 204–5.

28. "O sozdanie Soveta po evakuatsii," p. 200.

29. Dubrovin, "Eshelon za eshelonom," p. 209.

30. GARF, f. 6822, op. 1, d. 550, ll. 1–4.

31. "O poriadke vyvoza i razmeshcheniia liudskikh kontingentov i tsennogo imushchestva," p. 207. The military soviets, appointed by the GKO and organized by army group and "front" (western front, northern front, etc.), were composed of the commander of the front, a member of the front soviet, and the chief of headquarters. In frontline zones, all civil and military authorities were subordinated to the military soviets.

32. "Direktiva SNK SSSR i TsK VKP (b) partiinym i sovetskim organizatsiiam prifrontovykh oblastei," in *Velikaia Otechestvennaia voina. 50 let. Prilozhenie i kalendari dat i sobytii*. Vypusk 1, TASS, 1991, pp. 48–9.

33. Anna Shternshis, "Between Life and Death: Why Some Soviet Jews Decided to Leave and Others to Stay in 1941," *Kritika: Explorations in Russian and Eurasian History*, vol. 15, no. 3 (Summer 2014), pp. 477–504.

34. https://www.centropa.org/biography/raissa-smelaya.

35. Yitzhak Arad, *The Holocaust in the Soviet Union* (Lincoln: University of Nebraska Press, 2010), p. 87.

36. GARF, f. 6822, op. 1, d. 550, ll. 11–12; Postanovlenie Politbiuro TsK VKP (b), "O voprose NKAP," June 27, 1941, *Izvestiia TsK KPSS*, No. 6 (1990), p. 208.

37. GARF, f. 6822, op. 1, d. 409, ll. 4–6.

38. Pogrebnoi, "O deiatel'nosti," p. 206.

39. Dubrovin, "Eshelon za eshelonom," pp. 211–12.

40. GARF, f. 6822, op. 1, d. 64, ll. 48, 67.

41. GARF, f. 6822, op. 1, d. 550, l. 12.

42. GARF, f. 6822, op. 1, d. 409, l. 6.

43. GARF, f. 6822, op. 1, d. 550, l. 12.

44. Dubrovin, "Eshelon za eshelonom," p. 209.

45. Postanovlenie SNK SSSR i TsK VKP (b), "O perevode iz Moskvy Narkomatov i Glavnykh upravlenii," June 29, 1941, *Izvestiia TsK KPSS*, No. 6 (1990), pp. 211–12.

46. GARF, f. 6822, op. 1, d. 409, l. 7.

47. Wendy Z. Goldman, *Inventing the Enemy: Denunciation and Terror in Stalin's Russia* (Cambridge: Cambridge University Press, 2011).

48. "To write" became a synonym for "to denounce." See, for example, RGASPI, f. 17, op. 122, d. 10, ll. 11, 29, 46.

49. RGASPI, f. 17, op. 122, d. 10, l. 8.

50. RGASPI, f. 17, op. 122, d. 10, ll. 25–26.

51. RGASPI, f. 17, op. 122, d. 10, ll. 11–13.

52. RGASPI, f. 17, op. 122, d. 10, ll. 11–13.

53. RGASPI, f. 17, op. 122, d. 10, ll. 11–13.

54. RGASPI, f. 17, op. 122, d. 10, l. 15.

55. RGASPI, f. 17, op. 122, d. 10, ll. 14–15ob.

56. RGASPI, f. 17, op. 122, d. 10, ll. 25–26.

57. RGASPI, f. 17, op. 122, d. 10, l. 30.
58. RGASPI, f. 17, op. 122, d. 18, ll. 6–8.
59. RGASPI, f. 17, op. 122, d. 18, ll. 9–9ob., 22.
60. RGASPI, f. 17, op. 122, d. 10, l. 26.
61. RGASPI, f. 17, op. 122, d. 10, ll. 25–26.
62. RGASPI, f. 17, op. 122, d. 10, l. 28.
63. RGASPI, f. 17, op. 122, d. 10, ll. 64–66.
64. RGASPI, f. 17, op. 122, d. 10, ll. 45–48; 30 hectares is about 74 acres.
65. RGASPI, f. 17, op. 122, d. 10, ll. 49–51.
66. RGASPI, f. 17, op. 122, d. 10, ll. 46–48.
67. RGASPI, f. 17, op. 122, d. 10, ll. 39–40. The prewar boundaries of Kalinin (now Tver') province extended to the Belorussian and Latvian borders.
68. RGASPI, f. 17, op. 122, d. 10, ll. 39–40.
69. RGASPI, f. 17, op. 122, d. 10, l. 28.
70. I. V. Kovalev, *Transport v Velikoi Otechestvennoi voine, 1941–1945* (Moscow: Nauka, 1981), p. 81.
71. GARF, f. 6822, op. 1, d. 409, ll. 4–5, 8, 9, 18, 21, 22.
72. I. V. Kovalev, "Pod ognem vraga," in Poliakov, *et al.*, eds., *Eshelony idut na vostok*, pp. 230–1.
73. GARF, f. 6822, op. 1, d. 550, l. 19.
74. GARF, f. 6822, op. 1, d. 423, ll. 3–5.
75. GARF, f. 6822, op. 1, d. 438, ll. 119, 117; d. 482, l. 11.
76. GARF, f. 6822, op. 1, d. 438, ll. 113–111 (file numbered back to front).
77. GARF, f. 6822, op. 1, d. 550, ll. 24, 27–32; Dubrovin, "Eshelon za eshelonom," p. 207.
78. GARF, f. 6822, op. 1, d. 510, ll. 28, 27–21 (file numbered back to front).
79. John Erickson, *The Road to Stalingrad: Stalin's War with Germany* (New Haven: Yale University Press, 1975), pp. 232–3.
80. GARF, f. 6822, op. 1, d. 550, l. 36; d. 264, ll. 102–101 (file numbered back to front). Barber and Harrison, *The Soviet Home Front*, p. 132, argue that shortages were in large part due to the failure to disperse defense production geographically during industrialization.
81. Likhomanov, Pozina, and Finogenov, *Partiinoe rukovodstvo evakuatsiei*, pp. 118, 124. More than 50 percent of the cattle and sheep (395,300 and 245,000 animals, respectively) and 6 percent of the pigs (15,500) were evacuated in Belorussia.
82. Likhomanov, Pozina, and Finogenov, *Partiinoe rukovodstvo evakuatsiei*, pp. 118, 126.
83. GARF, f. 6822, op. 1, d. 550, l. 19.
84. GARF, f. 6822, op. 1, d. 550, ll. 25–26; d. 92, ll. 1–6, 9, 11–14.
85. GARF, f. 6822, op. 1, d. 550, ll. 34–35, 37.
86. GARF, f. 6822, op. 1, d. 550, ll. 35, 36, 43, 55.
87. GARF, f. 6822, op. 1, d. 550, ll. 50–51.
88. GARF, f. 6822, op. 1, d. 550, l. 55.
89. GARF, f. 6822, op. 1, d. 511, l. 58.
90. Likhomanov, Pozina, and Finogenov, *Partiinoe rukovodstvo evakuatsiei*, pp. 119–20.
91. Likhomanov, Pozina, and Finogenov, *Partiinoe rukovodstvo evakuatsiei*, p. 122.

92. GARF, f. 6822, op. 1, d. 511, l. 58.

93. GARF, f. 6822, op. 1, d. 511, ll. 57–56, 55–53 (file numbered back to front).

94. GARF, f. 6822, op. 1, d. 511, l. 10.

95. GARF, f. 6822, op. 1, d. 550, l. 63; Vladimir Solonari, *A Satellite Empire: Romanian Rule in Southwestern Ukraine, 1941–1944* (Ithaca and London: Cornell University Press, 2019), pp. 16–20.

96. On the experience of a Jewish family trapped in Odessa, see Rubin Udler, *The Cursed Years: Reminiscences of a Holocaust Survivor* (Pittsburgh: Chisinau, 2005).

97. GARF, f. 6822, op. 1, d. 550, l. 63.

98. GARF, f. 6822, op. 1, d. 550, l. 72.

99. GARF, f. 6822, op. 1, d. 64, ll. 74–82.

100. GARF, f. 6822, op. 1, d. 64, ll. 73, 24–37, 21, 8–10.

101. GARF, f. 6822, op. 1, d. 64, ll. 89, 90.

102. GARF, f. 6822, op. 1, d. 64, ll. 8–14.

103. As of December 1, 1941, 8,777,600 animals, including 903,800 horses, 3,502,700 cattle, 989,600 pigs, and 3,381,500 sheep, were evacuated: Likhomanov, Pozina, and Finogenov, *Partiinoe rukovodstvo evakuatsiei*, p. 127.

104. Likhomanov, Pozina, and Finogenov, *Partiinoe rukovodstvo evakuatsiei*, pp. 127–8.

105. GARF, f. 6822, op. 1, d. 511, l. 160.

106. GARF, f. 6822, op. 1, d. 550, l. 21. On Gomel', see Likhomanov, Pozina, and Finogenov, *Partiinoe rukovodstvo evakuatsiei*, pp. 62–3.

107. GARF, f. 6822, op. 1, d. 550, ll. 19–21, 27–33.

108. Likhomanov, Pozina, and Finogenov, *Partiinoe rukovodstvo evakuatsiei*, p. 65.

109. Likhomanov, Pozina, and Finogenov, *Partiinoe rukovodstvo evakuatsiei*, p. 64; GARF, f. 6822, op. 1, d. 409, l. 18; d. 469, l. 3; d. 511, l. 13; d. 550, l. 60.

110. GARF, f. 6822, op. 1, d. 511, l. 17.

111. Kumanev, "Voina i evakuatsiia," p. 13; Dubrovin, "Eshelon za eshelonom," p. 211.

112. GARF, f. 6822, op. 1, d. 511, l. 13; d. 550, l. 61.

113. GARF, f. 6822, op. 1, d. 550, ll. 61–62.

114. GARF, f. 6822, op. 1, d. 511, l. 36.

115. GARF, f. 6822, op. 1, d. 550, ll. 68–71.

116. GARF, f. 6822, op. 1, d. 511, l. 28.

117. GARF, f. 6822, op. 1, d. 550, l. 73.

118. Pogrebnoi, "O deiatel'nosti," p. 205.

119. GARF, f. 6822, op. 1, d. 468, l. 2.

120. Quoted by Likhomanov, Pozina, and Finogenov, *Partiinoe rukovodstvo evakuatsiei*, p. 66, and Kumanev, "Voina i evakuatsiia," p. 14.

121. GARF, f. 6822, op. 1, d. 550, l. 90.

122. Likhomanov, Pozina, and Finogenov, *Partiinoe rukovodstvo evakuatsiei*, p. 66.

123. David Stahel and Jonathan House, *When Titans Clash: How the Red Army Stopped Hitler* (Lawrence: University Press of Kansas, 1995), pp. 76–7; David Stahel, *Kiev 1941: Hitler's Battle for Supremacy in the East* (Cambridge: Cambridge University Press, 2012), pp. 7–8, 173, 348–9, 351.

124. GARF, f. 6822, op. 1, d. 264, ll. 26, 47–6, 50, 54.

125. GARF, f. 6822, op. 1, d. 550, ll. 90, 91.

126. Kumanev, "Voina i evakuatsiia," p. 15.

127. GARF, f. 6822, op. 1, d. 264, ll. 60, 134–133.

128. GARF, f. 6822, op. 1, d. 264, ll. 99–95.

129. GARF, f. 6822, op.1, d. 264, ll. 95–71.

130. GARF, f. 6822, op. 1, d. 550, l. 91.

131. GARF, f. 6822, op. 1, d. 438, ll. 140, 147.

132. The note was written to the military brigade commissar of the Staff of the Main Branch of the Rear: GARF, f. 6822, op. 1, d. 438, l. 154.

133. GARF, f. 6822, op. 1, d. 264, ll. 142–136; RGASPI, f. 17, op. 122, d. 18, ll. 140–142.

134. http://www.history.com/this-day-in-history/germans-overrun-mariupol-in-southern-russia.

135. GARF, f. 6822, op.1, d. 383, ll. 5–6.

136. GARF, f. 6822, op. 1, d. 383, l. 1.

137. Alexander Hill, *The Red Army and the Second World War* (Cambridge: Cambridge University Press, 2017), p. 264.

138. Pogrebnoi, "O deiatel'nosti," p. 206. Pogrebnoi's account was published just after Khrushchev's de-Stalinization campaign, during which towns and provinces named after Stalin were renamed. Stalino became Donetsk.

139. Likhomanov, Pozina, and Finogenov, *Partiinoe rukovodstvo evakuatsiei*, pp. 83–4.

140. On the distinction between refugees and evacuees, see chapter 2, and Manley, *To the Tashkent Station*, pp. 1, 8, 18–21.

141. GARF, f. 6822, op. 1, d. 550, l. 15.

142. GARF, f. 6822, op. 1, d. 409, l. 9.

143. On the subject of nationality and evacuation, see M. N. Potemkina, "Evakuatsiia i natsional'nye otnosheniia v sovetskom tylu v gody Velikoi Otechestvennoi voiny," *Otechestvennaia istoriia*, No. 3 (2002), http://vivovoco.ibmh.msk.su/VV/JOURNAL/RUHIST/EVAC.HTM.

144. Karel Berkhoff, *Motherland in Danger: Propaganda during World War II* (Cambridge, Mass.: Harvard University Press, 2012), pp. 135–65.

145. Vasily Grossman, *A Writer at War: A Soviet Journalist with the Red Army, 1941–1945*, ed. and trans. by Antony Beevor and Luba Vinogradova (New York: Vintage Books, 2007), pp. 259–60.

146. On the murder of the Jews, see Ilya Ehrenburg and Vasily Grossman, *The Complete Black Book of Soviet Jewry* (London: Routledge, 2003); on partisan warfare, see Nechama Tec, *Defiance: The Bielski Partisans* (New York: Oxford University Press, 1993); Anike Walke, *Partisans and Pioneers: An Oral History of Nazi Genocide in Belorussia* (New York: Oxford University Press, 2015); Kenneth Slepyan, *Stalin's Guerrillas: Soviet Partisans in World War II* (Lawrence: University Press of Kansas, 2006). On the burning of villages, see Elim Klimov's powerful film, *Idi i smotri* (*Come and See*).

147. Belonosov, "Evakuatsiia naseleniia," pp. 17–21, 28. The areas around the Volga included Gor'kii, Penza, Kuibyshev, Stalingrad, and Saratov, and the autonomous republics of Tatariia and Chuvashiia. Destinations further east included the provinces of Kirov, Chkalov, Molotov, Sverdlovsk, Cheliabinsk, Omsk, and Novosibirsk, the autonomous republics of Udmurtiia and Bashkiriia, the Altai Territory, and the Central Asian republics of Kazakhstan and Uzbekistan.

148. GARF, f. 6822, op. 1, d. 550, ll. 11–12, ll. 20–21; d. 510, ll. 10–9; d. 43, ll. 49–25.

149. GARF, f. 6822, op. 1, d. 550, ll. 23, 30–31, 37–38, 44.

150. GARF, f. 6822, op. 1, d. 550, ll. 38–39. On experiences of intelligentsia in Tashkent, see Manley, *To the Tashkent Station*, pp. 148–196. On response of the local inhabitants of Kirov, see Holmes, *War, Evacuation, and the Exercise of Power*, 40–58, 88–106.

151. GARF, f. 6822, op. 1, d. 550, ll. 31–32; d. 482, l. 21.

152. GARF, f. 6822, op. 1, d. 510, ll. 20, 18, 16, 28.

153. GARF, f. 6822, op. 1, d. 409, l. 169; d. 550, l. 65; d. 510, ll. 30–29.

154. GARF, f. 6822, op. 1, d. 550, l. 57.

155. GARF, f. 6822, op. 1, d. 510, ll. 33–31.

156. GARF, f. 6822, op. 1, d. 482, l. 16.

157. For the percentage growth in each area, see Belonosov, "Evakuatsiia naseleniia," p. 30, and Chapter 2, table 2.1.

158. Pavel Polian, *Against Their Will: The History and Geography of Forced Migrations in the USSR* (Budapest: Central European University Press, 2004), pp. 122, 329.

159. GARF, f. 6822, op. 1, d. 482, ll. 2, 1.

160. Likhomanov, Pozina, and Finogenov, *Partiinoe rukovodstvo evakuatsiei*, pp. 74–5; Dubrovin, "Eshelon za eshelonom," p. 212. Kovalev was also head of traffic on the railways. See also Rodric Braithwaite, *Moscow 1941: A City and Its People* (New York: Alfred A. Knopf, 2006), pp. 219–34.

161. Dubrovin, "Eshelon za eshelonom," p. 212.

162. Dubrovin, "Eshelon za eshelonom," pp. 212–13.

163. Dubrovin, "Eshelon za eshelonom," p. 213. Kalenchevksaia Square is the old name of Komsomol Square, the site of three of Moscow's major train stations, the Leningrad, Iaroslavl', and Kazan' stations. The Kazan' station was the main terminus for moving people out of the city.

164. NA IRI-RAN, f. 2, r. 5, op. 50, d. 13, ll. 1, 2, 3 (interview conducted in 1947).

165. Mary Leder, *My Life in Stalinist Russia: An American Woman Looks Back* (Bloomington: Indiana University Press, 2001), p. 195.

166. Dubrovin, "Eshelon za eshelonom," p. 214.

167. Belonosov, "Evakuatsiia naseleniia," p. 22.

168. Alexander Werth, *Russia at War, 1941–1945* (New York: Carroll and Graf, 1964), p. 237.

169. Dubrovin, "Eshelon za eshelonom," p. 215; Likhomanov, Pozina, and Finogenov, *Partiinoe rukovodstvo evakuatsiei*, pp. 77, 81.

170. http://ivgoradm.ru/pobeda70/history.htm; excerpted from K. E. Baldin, *Ivanovo-Voznesensk. Iz proshlogo v budushchee* (Ivanovo: Episheva O. V., 2011).

171. RGASPI, f. 17, op. 88, d. 45, ll. 12–14.

172. RGASPI, f. 17, op. 88, d. 45, ll. 14–15.

173. RGASPI, f. 17, op. 88, d. 45, ll. 15–16.

174. RGASPI, f. 17, op. 88, d. 45, ll. 2–4, 16–18; see also ll. 18–19.

175. RGASPI, f. 17, op. 88, d. 45, ll. 18–19.

176. RGASPI, f. 17, op. 88, d. 45, ll. 22–23.

177. RGASPI, f. 17, op. 88, d. 45, ll. 2, 23–34, 4, 22–23.

178. Likhomanov, Pozina, and Finogenov, *Partiinoe rukovodstvo evakuatsiei*, p. 81.

179. GARF, f. 6822, op. 1, d. 409, l. 144.

180. GARF, f. 6822, op. 1, d. 511, ll. 145–132.

181. GARF, f. 6822, op. 1, d. 409, l. 144.

182. GARF, f. 6822, op. 1, d. 438, ll. 7–6, 8, 5–2.

183. See problems in Sumy province in northeastern Ukraine: GARF, f. 6822, op. 1, d. 511, l. 39; and in Dnepropetrovsk, d. 469, l. 29.

184. GARF, f, 6822, op. 1, d. 511, ll. 45–44.

185. GARF, f. 6822, op. 1, d. 438, l. 86.

186. GARF, f. 6822, op. 1, d. 438, ll. 77–76.

187. GARF, f. 6822, op. 1, d. 438, l. 142.

188. Pogrebnoi, "O deiatel'nosti," p. 206.

189. GARF, f. 6822, op. 1, d. 550, l. 68.

190. GARF, f. 6822, op. 1, d. 438, ll. 140–120.

191. GARF, f. 6822, op. 1, d. 511, l. 162.

192. See case of chemical factories in October 1941 in GARF, f. 6822, op. 1, d. 438, ll. 120–110, and d. 511, l. 62, on canning factories.

193. GARF, f. 6822, op. 1, d. 468, ll. 7–5 (file numbered back to front).

194. Likhomanov, Pozina, and Finogenov, *Partiinoe rukovodstvo evakuatsiei*, pp. 81, 82; Dubrovin, "Eshelon za eshelonom," pp. 206–7.

195. Likhomanov, Pozina, and Finogenov, *Partiinoe rukovodstvo evakuatsiei*, p. 84.

196. Likhomanov, Pozina, and Finogenov, *Partiinoe rukovodstvo evakuatsiei*, p. 129.

197. Dubrovin, "Eshelon za eshelonom," pp. 216–18.

198. Dubrovin, "Eshelon za eshelonom," pp. 218–19.

199. Pogrebnoi, "O deiatel'nosti," p. 205.

200. Erickson, *The Road to Stalingrad*, p. 235.

201. GARF, f. 6822, op. 1, d. 510, ll. 20, 18, 16; GARF, f. A-482, op. 47, d. 539, ll. 112–113; APRK (Arkhiva Prezidenta Respublika Kazakhstana), f. 725, op. 4, d. 339, l. 29 (thanks to Natalie Belsky for providing a copy of this latter document).

202. RGASPI, f. 17, op. 22, d. 18, ll. 52–53.

Chapter 2

Epigraph: I. I. Belonosov, "Evakuatsiia naseleniia iz prifrontovoi polosy v 1941–1942," in Iu. A. Poliakov, G. A. Kumanev, N. P. Lipatov, and A. V. Mitrofanova, eds., *Eshelony idut na vostok. Iz istorii perebazirovaniia proizvoditel'nykh sil SSSR v 1941–1942 gg. Sbornik statei i vospominanii* (Moscow: Nauka, 1966), pp. 24–5.

1. https://www.centropa.org/biography/frieda-portnaya. See also the story of Elena Kozhina, *Through the Burning Steppe: A Memoir of Wartime Russia, 1942–1943* (New York: Riverhead Books, 2002).

2. Rebecca Manley, *To the Tashkent Station: Evacuation and Survival in the Soviet Union at War* (Ithaca: Cornell University Press, 2009); Larry Holmes, *War, Evacuation, and the Exercise of Power: The Center, Periphery, and Kirov's Pedagogical Institute, 1941–1952* (Lanham, Md.: Lexington Books, 2012) and *Stalin's World War II Evacuations: Triumph and Troubles in Kirov* (Lawrence: University Press of Kansas, 2017).

3. Marina Nikolaevna Potemkina, "Evakuatsionno-reevakuatsionnye protsessy i evakonaselenie na Urale v 1941–1948 gg.," Doctor of Historical Sciences dissertation, Ekaterinburg, 2004, pp. 108–9; "Bezhentsy i evakuirovannye v gody voiny," at http://moyapobeda.ru/bezhency-i-evakuirovannye-v-gody-vojny.html. Potemkina explains the wide divergence as the result of different methods of calculation. Some historians use data on the numbers of passengers recorded on rail and water transport but miss the large number of refugees who fled on trucks, in horse-drawn carts, or on foot. Others use the records of local evacuation authorities, who logged the number of evacuees resettled in their area. Still others make estimates based on demographic data, comparing actual populations in specific locations with what their populations would have been if prewar trends had continued undisturbed. An unknown number of those who fled did not move east but stayed close to the front and thus were not captured by the registration figures. Some may have been counted more than once.

4. http://www.nnre.ru/istorija/yekonomika_sssr_v_gody_velikoi_otechestvennoi_ voiny_1941_1945_gg/p5.php, citing *Istoriia Velikoi Otechestvennoi voiny Sovetskogo Soiuza. 1941–1945*, vol. II, pp. 548–9; Poliakov, *et al.*, eds., *Eshelony idut na vostok*, p. 26; APRK (Arkhiv Prezidenta Respubliki Kazakhstana), f. 708, op. 5/1, d. 195, l. 63; f. 725, op. 4, d. 339, l. 67. We are grateful to Natalie Belsky for providing us with the data for Kazakhstan.

5. RGAE, f. 4372, op. 45, d. 317, l. 142.

6. GARF, f. 6822, op. 1, d. 482, l. 42.

7. https://www.centropa.org/biography/agnessa-margolina#During%20the%20war.

8. RGAE, f. 4372, op. 45, d. 317, l. 142; Potemkina, "Evakuatsionno-reevakuatsionnye protsessy," Appendices 8 and 9.

9. For data on Sverdlovsk, Cheliabinsk, and Chkalov provinces and Udmurtiia, see Potemkina, "Evakuatsionno-reevakuatsionnye protsessy," Appendix 6. The same was true of Novosibirsk province in Western Siberia: GARF, f. A-327, op. 2, d. 30, l. 185.

10. Potemkina, "Evakuatsionno-reevakuatsionnye protsessy," pp. 123–4.

11. Potemkina, "Evakuatsionno-reevakuatsionnye protsessy," p. 125.

12. GARF, f. A-327, op. 2, d. 39, ll. 3–3ob.

13. Potemkina, "Evakuatsionno-reevakuatsionnye protsessy," p. 125.

14. GARF, f. 6822, op. 1, d. 438, l. 74.

15. http://kbsh.rzd.ru/static/public/ru?STRUCTURE_ID=5139. For examples from other rail junctions, see GARF, f. 6822, op. 1, d. 439, ll. 16, 11–6 (file numbered back to front).

16. GARF, f. 6822, op. 1, d. 511, ll. 10–9 (file numbered back to front).

17. GARF, f. 6822, op. 1, d. 482, ll. 9, 10.

18. https://www.centropa.org/biography/ida-kristina.

19. GARF, f. 6822, op. 1, d. 482, ll. 39–40.

20. GARF, f. 6822, op. 1, d. 510, ll. 49–48 (file numbered back to front).

21. GARF, f. 6822, op. 1, d. 510, ll. 57–53.

22. GARF, f. 6822, op. 1, d. 510, ll. 56–49.

23. GARF, f. A-482, op. 47, d. 1422, l. 3.

24. See, for example, the interviews: https://www.centropa.org/biography/agnessa-margolina; https://www.centropa.org/biography/dora-postrelko; https://www.centropa.org/biography/rakhil-givand-tikhaya; https://www.centropa.org/biography/efim-bezrodniy.

25. NA IRI-RAN, f. 2, r. 5, op. 7, d. 13, ll. 19–21.

26. Potemkina, "Evakuatsionno-reevakuatsionnye protsessy," p. 129, citing L. G. Dvorson, *V gody Velikoi Otechestvennoi voiny 1941–1945 gg. Bessmertnyi podvig naroda* (Perm', 2000), p. 146.

27. Interview with Viktor K., Donald Filtzer, Baltimore, January 8, 1997.

28. GARF, f. A-482, op. 47, d. 685, ll. 147–149, 192.

29. GARF, f. A-482, op. 47, d. 685, ll. 170–172.

30. See chapters by Roberta Manley, Wendy Z. Goldman, and Donald Filtzer in Wendy Z. Goldman and Donald Filtzer, eds., *Hunger and War: Food Provisioning in the Soviet Union During World War II* (Bloomington: Indiana University Press, 2015).

31. NA IRI-RAN, f. 2, r. 5, op. 45, d. 17, l. 4.

32. GARF, f. A-327, op. 2, d. 44, ll. 5–6.

33. RGAE, f. 1562, op. 20, d. 253, ll. 13, 112; d. 500, ll. 12, 106.

34. Donald Filtzer, *The Hazards of Urban Life in Late Stalinist Russia: Health, Hygiene, and Living Standards* (Cambridge: Cambridge University Press, 2010), chs. 1 and 3, and pp. 315–17.

35. GARF, f. A-374, op. 11, d. 28, l. 17; op. 34, d. 1540, ll. 5, 31.

36. Filtzer, *Hazards*, pp. 316–18.

37. GARF, f. 9226, op. 1, d. 221, ll. 67–70. They accumulated important experience during the mass movement of peasants into the cities, the forced deportation of alleged kulaks during collectivization, and the transfer of prisoners to and within the Gulag camps.

38. "Polozhenie o mediko-sanitarnom obsluzhivanii grazhdanskogo naseleniia, evakuiruemogo iz ugrozhaemykh raionov. Utverzhdeno narkomom zdravoookhraneniia Soiuza SSR i soglasovano s zam. Narkoma putei soobshchenii 30/vi/1941 g.," *Sbornik prikazov i instruktsii NKzdrava SSSR*, No. 2, Moscow, 1942, pp. 26–9.

39. *Sbornik prikazov i instruktsii NKZdrava SSSR*, No. 2, Moscow, 1942, pp. 25–6; GARF, f. 9226, op. 1, d. 636, ll. 74–77, 83–84; GARF, f. A-482, op. 47, d. 685, ll. 86, 86ob.

40. NA IRI-RAN, f. 2, r. 5, op. 35, d. 25, ll. 12, 14, 15, 17.

41. On the measles epidemic, see Filtzer, *Hazards*, pp. 277–81, and Ol'ga Nikolaevna Dodonova, "Kor' v SSSR, 1930–1943 god," Candidate of Medical Sciences dissertation, Moscow, 1945. On typhus, see GARF, f. A-482, op. 52s, d. 92, l. 16ob.; d. 131, l. 9; d. 187, ll. 10, 14ob.; RGAE, f. 1562, op. 18, d. 264, ll. 6, 218, 219.

42. RGASPI, f. 17, op. 122, d. 10, l. 37.

43. https://www.centropa.org/biography/semyon-falk.

44. RGASPI, f. 17, op. 122, d. 10, ll. 36–38.

45. RGASPI, f. 17, op. 122, d. 10, ll. 68–70.

46. GARF, f. 6822, op. 1, d. 339, l. 105.

47. GARF, f. A-482, op. 47, d. 685, ll. 1, 1ob., 3ob.

48. GARF, f. A-482, op. 47, d. 685, ll. 8, 8ob.

49. GARF, f. A-482, op. 47, d. 685, ll. 1ob., 2.

50. https://www.centropa.org/biography/evgenia-gendler; https://www.centropa.org/biography/rakhil-givand-tikhaya.

51. GARF, f. A-327, op. 2, d. 18, ll. 112, 112ob.; d. 26, l. 4ob.; d. 3, l. 1; d. 37, l. 143.

52. Marina Vasil'evna Gontsova, "Povsednevnaia zhizn' naseleniia industrial'nogo tsentra v gody Velikoi Otechestvennoi voiny (na materialakh goroda Nizhnii Tagil)," Candidate of Historical Sciences dissertation, Nizhnii Tagil, 2011, pp. 121–123, 127–128.

53. GARF, f. A-482, op. 47, d. 2322, l. 7; d. 3431, ll. 8–11.

54. Gontsova, "Povsednevnaia zhizn'," pp. 114–16, 122–3.

55. Decree of the Soviet of People's Commissars of the USSR, 13 September 1941, "O stroitel'stve zhilykh pomeshchenii dlia evakuirovannogo naseleniia," http://maxpark.com/community/5167/content/1794985.

56. Vera Valer'evna Solov'eva, "Bytovye usloviia personala promyshlennykh predpriiatii Urala v 1941–1945 gg. Gosudarstvennaia politika i strategii adaptatsii," Candidate of Historical Sciences dissertation, Ekaterinburg, 2011, pp. 114–15, citing *Sbornik rukovodiashchikh materialov po kommunal'nomu khoziaistvu (na voennoe vremia)* (Moscow and Leningrad, 1942), pp. 178–9.

57. Gontsova, "Povsednevnaia zhizn'," p. 117.

58. Gonstova, "Povsednevnaia zhizn'," pp. 122–3.

59. GARF, f. 5451, op. 30, d. 9, ll. 68–72.

60. GARF, f. 5451, op. 30, d. 1, ll. 15–17.

61. Solov'eva, "Bytovye usloviia," p. 118; Gontsova, "Povsednevnaia zhizn'," p. 128.

62. GARF, f. 5451, op. 30, d. 1, ll. 15–17.

63. Solov'eva, "Bytovye usloviia," pp. 120–1; Gontsova, "Povsednevnaia zhizn'," pp. 118–19; GARF, f. 5451, op. 43, d. 210, ll. 445, 446ob. (file numbered back to front).

64. GARF, f. 5451, op. 43, d. 199, l. 43.

65. Solov'eva, "Bytovye usloviia," pp. 120–1; Gontsova, "Povsednevnaia zhizn'," pp. 118–19; GARF, f. 5451, op. 43, d. 210, ll. 445, 446ob. Individual house building did take off after the war and became the largest contribution to new housing stock. See Mark B. Smith, *Property of Communists: The Urban Housing Program from Stalin to Khrushchev* (De Kalb: Northern Illinois University Press, 2010).

66. Solov'eva, "Bytovye usloviia," p. 115.

67. GARF, f. 5451, op. 43, d. 210, l. 446; GARF, f. A-482, op. 47, d. 1345, ll. 133, 151.

68. RGASPI, f. M-1, op. 8, d. 64, ll. 113–114.

69. GARF, f. 6822, op. 1, d. 539, ll. 32–33.

70. GARF, f. 6822, op. 1, d. 550, l. 40.

71. GARF, f. 6822, op. 1, d. 550, l. 88.

72. RGASPI, f. 17, op. 22, d. 10, l. 52.

73. Factory No. 77, the Kirov factory, is not to be confused with the Leningrad Kirov Factory—Leningradskii Kirovskii Zavod—from which tank production was split off in 1933.

74. See, for example, GARF, f. 6822, op. 1, d. 469, ll. 18–19.

75. Keith Dexter and Ivan Rodionov, "The Factories, Research and Design Establishments of the Soviet Defence Industry: A Guide. Ver. 20," University of Warwick, Department of Economics, May 2018, https://warwick.ac.uk/vpk/.

76. GARF, f. 6822, op. 1, d. 101, ll. 3–2 (file numbered back to front).

77. GARF, f. 6822, op. 1, d. 469, l. 4. See also l. 36.

78. GARF, f. 6822, op. 1, d. 469, ll. 4–6.

79. GARF, f. 6822, op. 1, d. 469, ll. 24, 30, 34.

80. GARF, f. 6822, op. 1, d. 469, l. 1.

81. GARF, f. 6822, op. 1, d. 469, l. 37.

82. Lennart Samuelson, *Tankograd. The Formation of a Soviet Company Town: Cheliabinsk, 1900s–1950s* (Basingstoke: Palgrave Macmillan, 2011), pp. 221–2.

83. GARF, f. 6822, op. 1, d. 439, ll. 2–1.

84. GARF, f. 6822, op. 1, d. 502, l. 58. See also ll. 50–58 on similar pleas to return to Moscow.

85. RGAE, f. 8875, op. 46, d. 103, ll. 4, 10ob., 11 (December 1943 figures).

86. Solov'eva, "Bytovye usloviia," p. 163.

87. Donald Filtzer, *Soviet Workers and De-Stalinization: The Consolidation of the Modern System of Soviet Production Relations, 1953–1964* (Cambridge: Cambridge University Press, 1992), pp. 26–8, 168–9.

88. G. A. Goncharov, "Stroitel'nye organizatsii ural'skogo regiona v usloviiakh voennogo vremeni (1941–1945 gody)," *Vestnik Cheliabinskogo gosudarstvennogo universiteta*, 2012, no. 11 (265), *Istoriia*, Vypusk 50, pp. 51–5. There were thirty-six OSMCh in the Urals, including thirteen in Sverdlovsk province and twelve in Cheliabinsk province.

89. RGAE, f. 1562, op. 329, d. 570, ll. 11, 13.

90. NA IRI-RAN, f. 2, r. 5, op. 16, d. 4, ll. 9ob., 10, 12ob., 13, 13ob.

91. NA IRI-RAN, f. 2, r. 5, op. 16, d. 2, ll. 2–3, 6–8ob.

92. NA IRI-RAN, f. 2, r. 5, op. 16, d. 5, ll. 1–5, 10, 10ob.

93. The account that follows is based on the oral testimonies of managers and workers of factory No. 22 gathered some time around April 1943: NA IRI-RAN, f. 2, r. 5, op. 7, d. 3, ll. 1–4, 17–19; d. 6, ll. 1–4, 6–9ob.; d. 9, ll. 6–7ob.; d. 11, l. 5ob.

94. NA IRI-RAN, f. 2, r. 5, op. 7, d. 13, l. 24ob.

95. Samuelson, *Tankograd*, pp. 198–9, 202–3.

96. John Erickson, *The Road to Stalingrad: Stalin's War with Germany* (New Haven: Yale University Press, 1975), p. 235.

97. Mark Harrison, *Accounting for War: Soviet Production, Employment, and the Defence Burden, 1940–1945* (Cambridge: Cambridge University Press, 1996), pp. 68–9.

Chapter 3

Epigraph: RGASPI, f. 17, op. 88, d. 122, l. 13.

1. G. A. Kumanev, *Sovetskii tyl v pervyi period Velikoi Otechestvennoi voiny* (Moscow: Nauka, 1988), p. 311.

2. A. V. Liubimov, *Torgovlia i snabzhenie v gody Velikoi Otechestvennoi voiny* (Moscow: Izdatel'stvo Ekonomika, 1968), p. 56.

3. https://www.centropa.org/biography/raisa-roitman.

4. On starvation mortality in the home front industrial regions, see Donald Filtzer, "Starvation Mortality in Soviet Home Front Industrial Regions during World War II,"

in Wendy Z. Goldman, and Donald Filtzer, eds., *Hunger and War: Food Provisioning in the Soviet Union during World War II* (Bloomington: Indiana University Press, 2015), pp. 265–335. Leningrad, which occupies a special place between front and rear, is outside the scope of this chapter. Almost one million people died in the city, which was under siege for 900 days. See Richard Bidlack and Nikita Lomagin, *The Leningrad Blockade, 1941–1944: A New Documentary History from the Soviet Archives* (New Haven: Yale University Press, 2007); David M. Glantz, *The Siege of Leningrad: 900 Days of Terror* (London: Cassell Military Paperbacks, 2001); Harrison Salisbury, *The 900 Days: The Siege of Leningrad* (Cambridge, Mass.: Da Capo Press, 2003); Alexis Peri, *The War Within: Diaries from the Siege of Leningrad* (Cambridge, Mass.: Harvard University Press, 2017); Sergei Yarov, *Leningrad 1941–1942: Morality in a City under Siege* (Cambridge, UK: Polity Press, 2017); Anna Reid, *Leningrad: The Epic Siege of World War II* (New York: Walker Books, 2011).

5. Karen Hagemann and Stephanie Schuler-Springorum, eds., *Home/Front: The Military, War and Gender in Twentieth-Century Germany* (Oxford: Berg, 2002), p. 8.

6. On war and revolution, see Harriet Applewhite and Darline Levy, eds., *Women and Politics in the Age of Democratic Revolution* (Ann Arbor: University of Michigan Press, 1993); Belinda Davis, *Home Fires Burning: Food, Politics, and Everyday Life in World War I Berlin* (Chapel Hill: University of North Carolina Press, 2000); Lars Lih, *Bread and Authority in Russia, 1914–1921* (Berkeley: University of California Press, 1990); Lizzie Collingham, *The Taste of War: World War Two and the Battle for Food* (New York: Penguin Press, 2012).

7. Historians differ sharply about the role of the state. William Moskoff, *The Bread of Affliction: The Food Supply in the USSR during World War II* (Cambridge: Cambridge University Press, 1990), p. 111, argues that the state abandoned provisioning the home front. Other historians assert the opposite. U. G. Cherniavskii, *Voina i prodovol'stvie. Snabzhenie gorodskogo naseleniia v Velikuiu Otechestvennuiu voinu (1941–1945 gg.)* (Moscow: Nauka, 1964), concluded, based on detailed calculations from the archives, that the state remained the single largest food provider to the urban population. See also John Barber and Mark Harrison, *The Soviet Home Front, 1941–1945: A Social and Economic History of the USSR in World War II* (London: Longman, 1991), pp. 77–93; and A. K. Sokolov, "Sotsial'no-trudovye otnosheniia na sovetskikh predpriiatiiakh v gody voiny," in A. N. Sakharov and A. S. Seniavskii, eds., *Narod i voina, 1941–1945 gg.* (Moscow: Institut Rossiiskoi Istorii RAN, 2010). Of the sources cited here, only Cherniavskii used Soviet archives.

8. Elena Osokina, *Our Daily Bread: Socialist Distribution and the Art of Survival in Stalin's Russia, 1927–1941* (Armonk, N.Y.: M. E. Sharpe, 2001); Julie Hessler, *A Social History of Soviet Trade: Trade Policy, Retail Practices, and Consumption, 1917–1953* (Princeton: Princeton University Press, 2004); Amy Randall, *The Soviet Dream World of Retail Trade and Consumption in the 1930s* (Basingstoke: Palgrave Macmillan, 2008).

9. Cherniavskii, *Voina i prodovol'stvie*, p. 67.

10. Oleg Khlevnyuk and R. W. Davies, "The End of Rationing in the Soviet Union, 1934–1935," *Europe–Asia Studies*, vol. 5, no. 4 (1999), pp. 557–609. Meat and fish rationing was eliminated in October 1935, and rationing of manufactured goods in January 1936. See Osokina, *Our Daily Bread*, pp. 140–4.

11. Vera V. Solov'eva, "Bytovye usloviia personala promyshlennykh predpriiatii Urala v 1941–1945 gg. Gosudarstvennaia politika i strategii adaptatsii," Candidate of Historical Sciences dissertation, Ekaterinburg, 2011, pp. 70–1.

12. Osokina, *Our Daily Bread*, pp. 172–7.

13. The Third Five-Year-Plan was to cover January 1938 to December 1942 but was abandoned as a result of the war: Cherniavskii, *Voina i prodovol'stvie*, p. 67; N. A. Voznesensky, *Soviet Economy during the Second World War* (New York: International Publishers, 1949), pp. 77, 35.

14. *Direktivy KPSS i sovetskogo pravitel'stva po khoziaistvennym voprosam, 1929–1945 gody*, vol. II (Moscow: Gosudarstvennoe Izdatel'stvo Politicheskoi Literatury, 1957), pp. 705–6; RGAE, f. 7971, op. 1, d. 895, ll. 39–94; Cherniavskii, *Voina i prodovol'stvie*, pp. 70–2.

15. Liubimov, *Torgovlia i snabzhenie*, p. 51.

16. RGASPI, f. 17, op. 88, d. 31, ll. 29–30.

17. RGAE, f. 7971, op. 1, d. 895, l. 63; Cherniavskii, *Voina i prodovol'stvie*, pp. 82, 95–7; Liubimov, *Torgovlia i snabzhenie*, p. 33.

18. Liubimov, *Torgovlia i snabzhenie*, p. 47.

19. Cherniavskii, *Voina i prodovol'stvie*, p. 178.

20. Every group received a different amount: workers and ITR, for example, received 125 coupons per month, white-collar employees—100, dependants and children—80. See Liubimov, *Torgovlia i snabzhenie*, pp. 41–2.

21. RGAE, f. 7971, op. 1, d. 981, l. 4.

22. Moskoff, *The Bread of Affliction*, pp. 71, 72; P. I. Veshchikov, "Rol' tyla v bespereboinom obespechenii deistvuiushchego fronta prodovol'stviem," in T. M. Bulavkina and M. V. Stegantsev, eds., *Edinstvo fronta i tyla v Velikoi Otechestvennoi voine 1941–1945* (Moscow: Akademiia, 2007), p. 83; GARF, f. 6822, op. 1, d. 64, l. 1; d. 438, l. 13; d. 469, l. 24.

23. Cherniavskii, *Voina i prodovol'stvie*, p. 67. The severity of the cuts far outstripped the decline in the home front population.

24. Cherniavskii, *Voina i prodovol'stvie*, p. 173.

25. A. V. Mitrofanova, *Rabochii klass SSSR nakanune i v gody Velikoi Otechestvennoi voiny, 1938–1945*, vol. III (Moscow: Nauka, 1984), p. 409.

26. Osokina, *Our Daily Bread*, pp. 166–77; on mortality in 1940, see RGAE, f. 1562, op. 33, d. 2638, ll. 82–82ob., available at http://istmat.info/files/uploads/38434/rgae_1562.33.2638_svedeniya_ob_umershih_po_vozrastam_i_polu_1933-1955.pdf; Iurii A. Gor'kov, *Gosudarstvennyi komitet oborony postanovliaet, 1941–1945. Tsifry i dokumenty* (Moscow: Olma Press, 2002) pp. 172–5. The country only recouped its prewar levels of food production between 1947 (potatoes and vegetables) and 1956 (cows).

27. Mark Harrison notes that 1943 marked the lowest point in household consumption; see *Accounting for War: Soviet Production, Employment, and the Defense Burden, 1940–1945* (Cambridge: Cambridge University Press, 1996), pp. 104–7. Liubimov, *Torgovlia i snabzhenie*, p. 54, makes the same argument.

28. Calculating actual consumption and caloric intake is difficult. There are two basic methods. One method uses household budget studies of individual or family

consumption, which record the foods that were consumed on a weekly or monthly basis, to calculate the daily calorie intake of groups, both as snapshots in time and as change over time. Prior to the war, the Central Statistical Administration (TsSU) enrolled hundreds of families in every major town in a sophisticated system of surveys. The TsSU conducted a few indicative surveys in 1942 and 1943, but had to suspend the systematic collection of budget data during the war. Another method, used by Cherniavskii, Gor'kov, and Mitrofanova, calculates the amount of food available through central state stocks and other sources (subsidiary farms, gardens, etc.) and divides these aggregates by the number of people entitled to the stocks. This "top-down" method, however, tells nothing about hierarchies of distribution, corruption, theft, etc. It also imperfectly accounts for gaps between the Commissariat of Trade's planned allocations and what the local trade organizations actually received. Bakery stoppages, adulteration, pilfering, embezzlement, spoilage, and other chronic problems all widened the gap between plan and delivery. Cherniavskii's calculations can be taken as the upper limit of consumption, while still showing clearly the dramatic fall from the prewar years.

29. Helene Sinnreich, "Hunger in the Ghettos," in Wendy Z. Goldman and Joe W. Trotter, Jr., eds., *The Ghetto in Global History: 1500 to the Present* (London: Routledge, 2018), pp. 110-26; Rebecca Manley, "Nutritional Dystrophy: The Science and Semantics of Starvation in World War II," in Goldman and Filtzer, eds., *Hunger and War*, pp. 206-64.

30. Filtzer, "Starvation Mortality," pp. 321-3.

31. On military provisioning, see Brandon Schechter, "The State's Pot and the Soldier's Spoon: Rations (Paëk) in the Red Army," in Goldman and Filtzer, eds., *Hunger and War*, pp. 98-157.

32. Cherniavskii, *Voina i prodovol'stvie*, pp. 74-5; RGAE, f. 7971, op. 1, d. 895, l. 62.

33. RGASPI, f. 17, op. 122, d. 19, l. 121ob. See Irkutsk, for example.

34. Cherniavskii, *Voina i prodovol'stvie*, pp. 74-5; RGAE, f. 7971, op. 1, d. 895, l. 62.

35. GARF, f. 5451, op. 43, d. 199, l. 47.

36. GARF, f. 5451, op. 43, d. 199, l. 82.

37. GARF, f. 5451, op. 43, d. 199, ll. 87-86 (file numbered from back to front). There was also a difference in wages. In 1943 the average monthly wage in aviation was 616 rubles versus 338 in light industry: RGAE, f. 1562, op. 329, d. 960, ll. 57-59.

38. GARF, f. 5451, op. 43, d. 199, l. 68.

39. RGAE, f. 1562, op. 15, d. 1562, ll. 52-53.

40. An order of the Commissariat of Trade, dated July 17, 1943, provided for privileged provisioning of political, trade union, and economic officials: "O snabzhenii rukovodiashchikh rabotnikov partiinykh, komsomol'skikh, sovetskikh, khoziaistvennykh i profsoiuznykh organizatsii," RGASPI, f. 17, op. 122, d. 49, ll. 26-28; RGAE, f. 7971, op. 1, d. 199, ll. 15-3; GARF, f. 7678, op. 8, d. 243, ll. 6, 6ob.; I. A. Danilova, "Reorganizatsiia raboty gosudarstvennoi torgovoi seti v gody Velikoi Otechestvennoi voiny," *Vestnik arkhivista*, available at http://www.vestarchive. ru/component/content/article/56/1773-reorganizaciia-raboty-gosudarstvennoi-torgovoi-seti-v-gody-velikoi-otechestvennoi-voiny-na-ujnom-yr.html.

41. GARF, f. 5451, op. 43, d. 116, ll. 87–86 (file numbered back to front).
42. Rebecca Manley, *To the Tashkent Station: Evacuation and Survival in the Soviet Union at War* (Ithaca: Cornell University Press, 2009); on the plight of the intelligentsia, see pp. 148–95.
43. GARF, f. 5451, op. 43, d. 325a, ll. 115, 114.
44. Soviet statisticians used a modified version of the Atwater scale, which set the caloric needs of an adult male at 1.0, and an adult woman at 0.8: Stephen G. Wheatcroft, "Soviet Statistics of Nutrition and Mortality during Times of Famine, 1917–1922 and 1931–1933," *Cahiers du Monde Russe*, vol. 38, no. 4 (October–December 1997), p. 539.
45. See Peri, *The War Within*, pp. 94–5, on the family as a unit of redistribution.
46. Filtzer, "Starvation Mortality," pp. 286, 302–5.
47. N. A. Aralovets, "Smertnost' gorodskogo naseleniia tylovykh raionov Rossii, 1941–1945 gg.," in *Liudskie poteri SSSR v period Vtoroi Mirovoi voiny. Sbornik statei* (St. Petersburg: Russko-Baltiiskii Informatsionnyi Tsentr BLITs, 1995), p. 157.
48. Liubimov, *Torgovlia i snabzhenie*, p. 35.
49. Liubimov, *Torgovlia i snabzhenie*, pp. 34–40. On milk shortages, see Chapter 8. The concession to prisoner workers applied to prisoners rented out to civilian enterprises by the NKVD, not to those in Gulag camps. It followed an April 1943 complaint from VTsSPS to Liubimov that management at the Gor'kii Motor Vehicle Factory (GAZ) was illegally diverting food from its regular workforce to prisoners: GARF, f. 5451, op. 43, d. 236, ll. 16–17, and d. 522, l. 270.
50. GARF, f. 7676, op. 14, d. 68, l. 64.
51. Alexis Peri, "Queues, Canteens and the Politics of Location in Diaries of the Leningrad Blockade, 1941–1942," in Goldman and Filtzer, eds., *Hunger and War*, pp. 192–5.
52. Cherniavskii, *Voina i prodovol'stvie*, p. 102; RGAE, f. 7971, op. 3, d. 258, ll. 35–36.
53. GARF, f. 5451, op. 43, d. 199, ll. 42–41 (file numbered back to front).
54. Liubimov, *Torgovlia i snabzhenie*, pp. 64–5.
55. http://istmat.info/node/18420, taken from RGAE, f. 1562, op. 41, d. 239 (sheet numbers not specified); Gor'kov, *Gosudarstvennyi komitet oborony postanovliaet*, pp. 481–2.
56. RGASPI, f. 17, op. 122, d. 49, l. 1. On bread stoppages in Gor'kii, see d. 18, l. 93.
57. Liubimov, *Torgovlia i snabzhenie*, p. 66.
58. RGASPI, f. 17, op. 122, d. 19, ll. 109, 110, 112, 2–3; see also d. 80, ll. 1–3, on problems in other cities.
59. RGAE, f. 7971, op. 16, d. 248, l. 68.
60. GARF, f. 5451, op. 43, d. 199, ll. 29–27.
61. GARF, f. 5451, op. 43, d. 199, ll. 101–100.
62. RGASPI, f. 17, op. 122, d. 19, ll. 110, 112; GARF, f. 5451, op. 43, d. 199, ll. 58–58ob., 75.
63. Kumanev, *Sovetskii tyl*, p. 317.
64. Liubimov, *Torgovlia i snabzhenie*, pp. 113, 116–18.
65. RGAE, f. 7971, op. 3, d. 258, ll. 38–39. On shortages of utensils in the 1930s, see Donald Filtzer, *Soviet Workers and Stalinist Industrialization: The Formation of Modern Soviet Production Relations, 1928–1941* (London: Pluto Press, 1986), p. 172;

and Wendy Z. Goldman, *Women at the Gates: Gender and Industry in Stalin's Russia* (New York: Cambridge University Press, 2002), p. 240.

66. GARF, f. 5451, op. 43, d. 199, ll. 12–10, 25, 24.

67. GARF, f. 5451, op. 43, d. 325a, l. 115.

68. GARF, f. 5451, op. 43, d. 199, l. 142.

69. GARF, f. 5451, op. 43, d. 199, ll. 79–78.

70. GARF, f. 5451, op. 43, d. 199, ll. 58–58ob.

71. Liubimov, *Torgovlia i snabzhenie*, p. 114.

72. On problems with provisioning workers mobilized from Central Asia into the armaments factories, see RGASPI, f. 17, op. 122, d. 50, ll. 5–36.

73. RGASPI, f. 17, op. 88, d. 45, ll. 39–40.

74. RGASPI, f. 17, op. 122, d. 19, l. 110.

75. GARF, f. 5451, op. 43, d. 199, ll. 114–112, 115.

76. GARF, f. 5451, op. 43, d. 199, ll. 26, 100.

77. GARF, f. 5451, op. 43, d. 199, l. 85.

78. GARF, f. 5451, op. 43, d. 199, l. 84.

79. GARF, f. 5451, op. 43, d. 236, l. 19.

80. RGASPI, f. 17, op. 122, d. 74, ll. 89–90.

81. RGASPI, f. 17, op. 122, d. 74, l. 89.

82. GARF, f. 7678, op. 7, d. 215, ll. 3, 4; d. 198, l. 33; op. 13, d. 74, l. 81.

83. Liubimov, *Torgovlia i snabzhenie*, p. 123.

84. GARF, f. 5451, op. 43, d. 199, l. 61a.

85. In Russian, Otdel rabochego snabzheniia. The industrial commissariats created Administrations of Workers' Provisioning (GlavURSy) to supervise and distribute food from central state stocks to the factory ORSy. See Liubimov, *Torgovlia i snabzhenie*, pp. 58–60, 62, 63; Mitrofanova, *Rabochii klass SSSR*, p. 413; Cherniavskii, *Voina i prodovol'stvie*, pp. 100–1.

86. GARF, f. 5451, op. 43, d. 199, ll. 61a, 65.

87. RGASPI, f. 17, op. 122, d. 19, l. 112.

88. Liubimov, *Torgovlia i snabzhenie*, pp. 60–1; RGASPI, f. 17, op. 122, d. 19, ll. 123–123ob.

89. *Direktivy KPSS i sovetskogo pravitel'stva po khoziaistvennym voprosam*, p. 723.

90. The Party began attaching land to factories for farming and animal husbandry in 1939 to supplement stocks for retail stores and factory canteens. The farms were placed under the administration of the local trade organizations. On September 7, 1940, the Soviet of People's Commissars and the Central Committee ordered various organizations to establish subsidiary farms on land distributed by the local soviet executive committees for use by factory canteens. See Cherniavskii, *Voina i prodovol'stvie*, pp. 130–2, 134, 145–6; Solov'eva, "Bytovye usloviia," pp. 97–9, 175–6.

91. The industrial commissariats alone received 550 state farms. See Mitrofanova, *Rabochii klass SSSR*, p. 413; Liubimov, *Torgovlia i snabzhenie*, pp. 61–2.

92. Solov'eva, "Bytovye usloviia," pp. 99–101, 178; Larisa Ianovna Lonchinskaia, "Massovoe soznanie naseleniia ural'skikh oblastei v gody Velikoi Otechestvennoi voiny," Candidate of Historical Sciences dissertation, Cheliabinsk, 2002, p. 200.

93. GARF, f. 7678, op. 7, d. 154, l. 24; Solov'eva, "Bytovye usloviia," pp. 100–1.

94. *Direktivy KPSS i sovetskogo pravitel'stva po khoziaistvennym voprosam*, vol. 2, pp. 734–3.

95. Cherniavskii, *Voina i prodovol'stvie*, pp. 141–2.

96. GARF, f. 5451, op. 43, d. 522, ll. 209–208, 248 (file numbered back to front).

97. GARF, f. 5451, op. 43, d. 199, ll. 6–5.

98. Mitrofanova, *Rabochii klass SSSR*, p. 414.

99. Collingham, *The Taste of War*, p. 70. On the potato as more recent supplementary nutrition, see Nancy Ries, "Potato Ontology: Surviving Postsocialism in Russia," *Cultural Anthropology*, vol. 24, no. 2 (May 2009), pp. 181–212.

100. Donald Filtzer and Wendy Z. Goldman, "Introduction: The Politics of Food and War," in Goldman and Filtzer, eds., *Hunger and War*, pp. 18–20. The potato gained even more importance in 1944. For the USSR as a whole, average consumption from factory and personal plots rose to 101 kilograms, enough to provide an extra 231 calories and 4 grams of protein to the daily diet: Cherniavskii, *Voina i prodovol'stvie*, p. 145.

101. Cherniavskii, *Voina i prodovol'stvie*, p. 145.

102. RGAE, f. 7971, op. 5, d. 60, l. 1.

103. Veshchikov, "Rol' tyla," p. 86.

104. Jean Levesque, "A Peasant Ordeal: The Soviet Countryside," in David Stone, ed., *The Soviet Union at War, 1941–1945* (Barnsley, UK: Pen and Sword Books, 2010), p. 193.

105. Levesque, "A Peasant Ordeal," p. 195.

106. RGAE, f. 7971, op. 5, d. 60, l. 5.

107. Cherniavskii, *Voina i prodovol'stvie*, pp. 154–5, 163, 185.

108. GARF, f. 5451, op. 43, d. 132, l. 52.

109. See Aaron Hale-Dorrell, "The Kolkhoz Market and Provisioning the Home Front during the Second World War," presented to the conference on "Stalinism and War," sponsored by the Higher School of the Economy, Moscow, May 2016.

110. RGAE, f. 7971, op. 5, d. 60, l. 43.

111. RGAE, f. 1562, op. 329, d. 1128, ll. 71–73ob., and d. 1127, l. 13; Kristy Ironside, "Stalin's Doctrine of Price Reductions during the Second World War and Postwar Reconstruction," *Slavic Review*, vol. 75, no. 3 (Fall 2016), p. 663; Moskoff, *The Bread of Affliction*, pp. 98–101.

112. GARF, f. 5451, op. 43, d. 199, l. 48.

113. GARF, f. 5451, op. 43, d. 522, l. 269.

114. RGAE, f. 7971, op. 5, d. 60, l. 2.

115. Quote from the secretary of the Palekh district party committee, GARF, f. 5451, op. 43, d. 199, ll. 41, 40.

116. GARF, f. 5451, op. 43, d. 199, ll. 37–36, 33.

117. RGAE, f. 7971, op. 5, d. 60, ll. 1–2ob; op. 1, d. 981, l. 1.

118. RGAE, f. 7971, op. 5, d. 60, ll. 1ob.–3, 38.

119. Crystallized sugar was first extracted from the beet in Germany in the mid-eighteenth century, and commercial manufacture took off in the early nineteenth century after the Haitian revolution made the importation of sugar from sugarcane more difficult.

120. RGAE, f. 7971, op. 1, d. 981, l. 37.

121. RGAE, f. 7971, op. 1, d. 981, l. 46.

122. GARF, f. 8131, op. 20, d. 72, l. 67.

123. RGAE, f. 7971, op. 5, d. 59, l. 16.

124. GARF, f. 5452, op. 22, d. 55, l. 12.

125. GARF, f. 5452, op. 22, d. 31, ll. 95–96.

126. GARF, f. 5452, op. 22, d. 5, ll. 168–172.

127. GARF, f. 5452, op. 22, d. 31, l. 97.

128. *Trud*, June 6, 1943; Liubimov, *Torgovlia i snabzhenie*, pp. 119–20. Dog rose, for example, had multiple medical uses dating back to ancient Greece, deriving its name from the belief that the root could cure the bite of a rabid dog.

129. Solov'eva, "Bytovye usloviia," p. 184.

130. Solov'eva, "Bytovye usloviia," p. 181.

131. S. Radznevskaia, "Kak zaseiat' ogorod," *Rabotnitsa* 9 (May 1942), pp. 14–16.

132. GARF, f. 5452, op. 22, d. 25, ll. 105, 57, 58, 61ob.–65; d. 31, ll. 63–63ob., 68, 93, 94.

133. Manley, "Nutritional Dystrophy," pp. 212–35.

134. http://scisne.net/a-1750.

135. NA IRI-RAN, f. 2, r. 5, op. 35, d. 39, ll. 1–1ob. Yeast production halted in 1944 when the factory switched from starch to clay for sizing.

136. Liubimov, *Torgovlia i snabzhenie*, p. 121.

137. RGASPI, f. 17, op. 122, d. 74, l. 89.

138. GARF, f. 5452, op. 22, d. 12, l. 64ob; d. 31, l. 94.

139. Liubimov, *Torgovlia i snabzhenie*, pp. 120–1.

140. http://resources.chelreglib.ru:6007/el_izdan/kalend2011/yuk.html.

141. Liubimov, *Torgovlia i snabzhenie*, pp. 121–2.

142. Liubimov, *Torgovlia i snabzhenie*, p. 120.

143. http://scisne.net/a-1750 (translation by Wendy Z. Goldman).

144. Alexis Peri, "Queues, Canteens, and the Politics of Location in Diaries of the Leningrad Blockade, 1941–1942," in Goldman and Filtzer, eds., *Hunger and War*, pp. 200–2, provides an example of this phenomenon in Leningrad when Elizaveta Sokolova, the head of the Institute of Party History, managed to have her staff transferred to the highest ration category.

145. GARF, f. 5451, op. 43, d. 522, l. 120.

146. GARF, f. 7971, op. 5, d. 539, ll. 5–9.

147. GARF, f. 5451, op. 43, d. 199, l. 102.

148. GARF, f. 5451, op. 43, d. 199, ll. 102, 46, 49–48.

149. GARF, f. 5451, op. 43, d. 236, ll. 9–11.

150. GARF, f. 5451, op. 43, d. 199, ll. 31–30.

151. RGASPI, f. 17, op. 122, d. 49, ll. 3–3ob., 7.

152. GARF, f. 5451, op. 43, d. 199, ll. 105–104, 23–22; RGASPI, f. 17, op. 122, d. 18, l. 2.

153. The role of Lend-Lease food aid is discussed in Chapter 8.

154. Moskoff, *The Bread of Affliction*, p. 238, writes, "Civilians were fed not because of the system but in spite of it."

155. GARF, f. 5451, op. 43, d. 199, l. 64.
156. RGASPI, f. 17, op. 122, d. 19, l. 125.

Chapter 4

Epigraph: GARF, f. 5451, op. 43, d. 325a, ll. 115–114 (file numbered back to front).

1. RGASPI, f. 17, op. 122, d. 47, ll. 6–9, letter dated March 16, 1943.
2. Vitalii S. Pushkarev, "40-e. Stanovlenie 'chernogo' rynka," *Posev. Obshchestvenno-politicheskii zhurnal*, No. 1 (January 2002), p. 31.
3. RGASPI, f. 17, op. 122, d. 47, l. 7.
4. RGASPI, f. 17, op. 122, d. 47, l. 7.
5. GARF, f. 5451, op. 43, d. 199, l. 54.
6. GARF, f. 5451, op. 43, d. 199, ll. 119ob., 119.
7. GARF, f. 5451, op. 43, d. 199, ll. 119–118 (file numbered back to front).
8. RGASPI, f. 17, op. 122, d. 49, l. 26.
9. GARF, f. 5451, op. 43, d. 199, l. 119ob.
10. GARF, f. 5451, op. 43, d. 325a, l. 146.
11. GARF, f. 5451, op. 43, d. 325a, ll. 98, 146–145. These allocations are during the period July–September 1942. The document gives the amounts for the entire three-month period; we have converted them to daily per capita portions.
12. GARF, f. 5451, op. 43, d. 325a, ll. 116, 115, 146; d. 199, l. 141.
13. GARF, f. 5451, op. 43, d. 325a, l. 145; d. 199, ll. 140–141ob.
14. In the case of the Kirov factory in early 1942, for example, there were roughly four times as many workers as ITR at the factory (Lennart Samuelson, *Tankograd. The Formation of a Company Town: Cheliabinsk, 1900s–1950s* [Basingstoke: Palgrave Macmillan, 2011], pp. 197, 226). Managers, ITR, and workers were all supposed to receive 72 grams of meat and fish each day. Instead, managers received 285 grams, ITR 132, and workers just 61. If each technical specialist had received 72 grams of meat and fish a day instead of 132, these 60 grams would have given each worker an extra 15 grams, which would have taken them slightly over their ration allowance.
15. GARF, f. 5451, op. 43, d. 199, l. 118.
16. RGASPI, f. 17, op. 88, d. 45, l. 41.
17. GARF, f. 5451, op. 43, d. 325a, l. 144, on lists in the Magnitogorsk iron and steel combine.
18. GARF, f. 5451, op. 43, d. 199, l. 140.
19. GARF, f. 5451, op. 43, d. 325a, l. 112.
20. GARF, f. 5451, op. 43, d. 325a, l. 112.
21. GARF, f. 5451, op. 43, d. 199, ll. 72, 71, 59, 70–69, 59ob.
22. RGASPI, f. 17, op. 122, d. 19, l. 90.
23. Marina Vasil'evna Gontsova, "Povsednevnaia zhizn' naseleniia industrial'nogo tsentra v gody Velikoi Otechestvennoi voiny (na materialakh goroda Nizhnii Tagil)," Candidate of Historical Sciences dissertation, Nizhnii Tagil, 2011, pp. 194–5.
24. Gontsova, "Povsednevnaia zhizn'," p. 194.

25. Order (Prikaz) of Narkomtorg SSSR, July 17, 1943, "O snabzhenii rukovodiashchikh rabotnikov partiinykh, komsomol'skikh, sovetskikh, khoziaistvennykh i profsoiuznykh organizatsii," RGASPI, f. 17, op. 122, d. 49, ll. 26–28; RGAE, f. 7971, op. 1, d. 199, ll. 3–15; GARF, f. 7678, op. 8, d. 243, ll. 6, 6ob. Group I, the most privileged group, included the heads of republic, territory, provincial, regional, and urban party, Komsomol, and All-Union trade union organizations, and union central committees and their deputies; secretaries of party district committees and deputy chairs of soviet district executive committees in Moscow and Leningrad; the heads of major economic organizations, first secretaries of party district committees and the chairs of district soviet executive committees. Group II covered personnel working in republic, territory, provincial, regional, and urban party, Komsomol, soviet, and trade union organizations, in trade union central committees, large-scale economic organizations, and personnel of equivalent status, together with secretaries of rural party district committees. Group III included all remaining leading personnel in party, Komsomol, soviet, economic, and trade union organizations.

26. GARF, f. 7678, op. 8, d. 243, ll. 6, 6ob.

27. GARF, f. 7678, op. 8, d. 243, ll. 6, 6ob. Official allocations for bread were in grams per day; other foods are in grams, milliliters (milk), or units (eggs) per month, which we have converted into daily portions. Calorie values are those established by the Central Statistical Administration in 1925, *Trudy TsSU*, vol. XXII, vypusk 1, 1925: *Normal'nyi sostav i pishchevoe znachenie prodovol'stvennykh produktov*: 189 kcal per 100 grams of rye bread; an average of 150 kcal per 100 grams of the various available kinds of meat and fish (including canned goods); 800 kcal per 100 grams of fats; 344 kcal per 100 grams of groats (grains) and pasta products; 389 kcal per 100 grams of sugar and confectionery goods; 56 kcal per single egg; 64 kcal per 100 ml of milk; 217 kcal per 100 grams of dried fruits; 84 kcal per 100 grams of potatoes; and 25 kcal per 100 grams of vegetables.

28. RGAE, f 7971, op. 1, d. 999, ll. 13, 15.

29. GARF, f. 5451, op. 43, d. 522, ll. 6–1 (file numbered back to front).

30. RGAE, f. 7971, op. 16, d. 248, l. 23.

31. RGAE, f. 7971, op. 16, d. 247, ll. 73–73ob.

32. RGAE, f. 7971, op. 16, d. 247, ll. 70–71.

33. Wendy Z. Goldman, *Women at the Gates: Gender and Industry in Stalin's Russia* (New York: Cambridge University Press, 2002), pp. 242–3. Stalin's speech, "New Conditions—New Tasks of Economic Construction," was delivered on June 23, 1931, and published in *Trud* on July 5. On the production communes, see Donald Filtzer, *Soviet Workers and Stalinist Industrialization: The Formation of Modern Soviet Production Relations, 1928–1941* (London: Pluto Press, 1986), pp. 102–6.

34. RGAE, f. 7971, op. 16, d. 295, l. 38. See the example of redistribution of bread stocks to children in Mordoviia.

35. GARF, f. 5451, op. 43, d. 199, ll. 73, 56.

36. GARF, f. 5451, op. 43, d. 199, ll. 79–76.

37. GARF, f. 5451, op. 43, d. 187, l. 131.

38. GARF, f. 5451, op. 43, d. 236, ll. 116–117.

39. RGAE, f. 7971, op. 16, d. 295, l. 25.

40. RGAE, f. 7971, op. 16, d. 247, ll. 12–12ob.

41. RGAE, f. 7971, op. 16, d. 247, ll. 20, 12ob.

42. RGAE, f. 7971, op. 16, d. 246, ll. 13–35.

43. RGAE, f. 7971, op. 16, d. 246, ll. 71–90.

44. RGAE, f. 7971, op. 16, d. 248, ll. 37–43.

45. RGAE, f. 7971, op. 16, d. 247, ll. 22–23, 29.

46. RGAE, f. 7971, op. 16, d. 246, l. 95.

47. RGAE, f. 7971, op. 16, d. 246, ll. 173–174.

48. Pushkarev, "40-e. Stanovlenie 'chernogo' rynka," p. 32.

49. RGAE, f. 7971, op. 16, d. 246, ll. 175–176.

50. RGAE, f. 7971, op. 16, d. 246, ll. 176–177.

51. GARF, f. 8131, op. 20, d. 72, ll. 14–15.

52. RGAE, f. 7971, op. 16, d. 295, l. 78.

53. GARF, f. 5451, op. 43, d. 522, l. 147.

54. RGAE, f. 7971, op. 16, d. 247, l. 11.

55. RGAE, f. 7971, op. 16, d. 246, ll. 180–181.

56. https://iremember.ru/memoirs/grazhdanskie/rakhlina-darya-markovna.   Rakhina wrote her reminiscences in 1990 when she was eighty-five as a letter to her children to be read after her death. She died in 1995.

57. RGAE, f. 7971, op. 16, d. 246, l. 182.

58. GARF, f. 8131, op. 21, d. 300, l. 5.

59. RGAE, f. 7971, op. 16, d. 246, ll. 182–183.

60. RGAE, f. 7971, op. 16, d. 246, ll. 184–186.

61. RGAE, f. 7971, op. 16, d. 295, l. 93.

62. RGAE, f. 7971, op. 16, d. 247, l. 8.

63. Pushkarev, "40-e. Stanovlenie 'chernogo' rynka," p. 32.

64. RGAE, f. 7971, op. 5, d. 58, l. 2.

65. GARF, f. 5452, op. 22, d. 9, l. 12.

66. GARF, f. 5451, op. 43, d. 199, ll. 73–72, 60.

67. GARF, f. 5451, op. 43, d. 199, l. 140.

68. GARF, f. 5451, op. 43, d. 325a, ll. 144, 113.

69. RGAE, f. 7971, op. 16, d. 295, l. 79.

70. RGAE, f. 7971, op. 16, d. 246, ll. 179–180.

71. RGAE, f. 7971, op. 16, d. 248, ll. 72, 74.

72. RGAE, f. 7971, op. 16, d. 246, l. 187; GARF, f. 5451, op. 43, d. 199, l. 10.

73. GARF, f. 8131, op. 21, d. 303, l. 111.

74. RGAE, f. 7971, op. 16, d. 246, ll. 187–191. On theft of cards in Molotov province, see GARF, f. 8131, op. 21, d. 300, l. 7.

75. RGAE, f. 7971, op. 16, d. 246, ll. 187–191.

76. GARF, f. 5451, op. 43, d. 199, l. 10.

77. GARF, f. 5451, op. 43, d. 199, l. 41.

78. GARF, f. 5451, op. 43, d. 325a, l. 148.

79. GARF, f. 8131, op. 20, d. 72, ll. 124–125.

80. RGAE, f. 7971, op. 16, d. 246, l. 193.

81. Julie Hessler, *A Social History of Soviet Trade: Trade Policy, Retail Practices, and Consumption, 1917–1953* (Princeton: Princeton University Press, 2004), pp. 268–70.

82. RGAE, f. 7971, op. 5, d. 60, l. 47.

83. RGAE, f. 7971, op. 5, d. 60, l. 174; Kristy Ironside, "Stalin's Doctrine of Price Reductions during the Second World War and Postwar Reconstruction," *Slavic Review*, vol. 75, no. 3 (Fall 2016), p. 663, citing the massive transfer of money from the cities to countryside, suggests that peasants were still willing to trade for cash.

84. RGAE, f. 7971, op. 5, d. 60, l. 74.

85. RGAE, f. 7971, op. 5, d. 60, l. 1ob.

86. Hessler, *A Social History of Soviet Trade*, p. 272.

87. RGAE, f. 7971, op. 16, d. 246, ll. 177–178.

88. RGAE, f. 7971, op. 16, d. 248, l. 29.

89. RGAE, f. 7971, op. 16, d. 246, ll. 177–178.

90. Pushkarev, "40-e. Stanovlenie 'chernogo' rynka," p. 31.

91. RGAE, f. 7971, op. 5, d. 60, ll. 2ob., 182, 36–37.

92. GARF, f. 5451, op. 30, d. 1, ll. 25–26.

93. RGAE, f. 7971, op. 5, d. 60, l. 44ob.

94. RGASPI, f. 17, op. 122, d. 74, l. 209.

95. GARF, f. 5451, op. 43, d. 325a, l. 144.

96. GARF, f. 5451, op. 43, d. 325a, ll. 113, 108–107, 140.

97. Pushkarev, "40-e. Stanovlenie 'chernogo' rynka," p. 31.

98. GARF, f. 5451, op. 43, d. 325a, l. 113; d. 199, l. 140.

99. RGAE, f. 7971, op. 5, d. 60, ll. 2ob.–3.

100. RGAE, f. 7971, op. 5, d. 60, l. 176.

101. RGAE, f. 7971, op. 16, d. 248, ll. 84, 85; William Moskoff, *The Bread of Affliction: The Food Supply in the USSR during World War II* (Cambridge: Cambridge University Press, 1990), p. 170.

102. The Central Statistical Administration (TsSU), which conducted extensive budget studies in the 1920s and 1930s, was unable to continue this work during the war. It did, however, conduct limited studies during 1942 and 1943. The budget study of young workers in Cheliabinsk was conducted by an investigatory commission sponsored by the Central Committee, not the TsSU, and gathered data on income and expenses, including wages, additional earnings, and the amounts spent on the most common expenditures: food, tobacco, clothing, rent, laundry, baths and haircuts, shoe and clothing repair, entertainment, daily transport, newspapers and books, and organizational dues. It calculated amounts spent on rations, in canteens, and in the market. See GARF, f. 5451, op. 43, d. 325a, ll. 133–104.

103. GARF, f. 5451, op. 43, d. 325a, ll. 133–124.

104. GARF, f. 5451, op. 43, d. 325a, l. 105.

105. GARF, f. 5451, op. 43, d. 325a, l. 104.

106. GARF, f. 5451, op. 43, d. 325a, ll. 105, 129.

107. GARF, f. 5451, op. 43, d. 325a, l. 130.

108. GARF, f. 5451, op. 43, d. 325a, l. 127.

109. G. A. Liubimov, *Torgovlia i snabzhenie v gody Velikoi Otechestvennoi voiny* (Moscow: Izdatel'stvo Ekonomika,1968), p. 67.

110. RGASPI, f. 17, op. 122, d. 50, 1. 4. See, for example, the letter from Kirghiz miners to the Central Committee that launched the investigations in Molotov province, discussed in Chapter 6.

111. For full text of letter, see RGASPI, f. 17, op. 122, d. 47, ll. 6–9.

112. V. Pavlenko and G. Pavlenko, "Vannikov, Boris L'vovich," in *Cheliabinskaia Oblast'. Entsiklopediia*, vol. I (Cheliabinsk: Izdatel'skii Tsentr IuUrGU, 2003), p. 565.

113. RGASPI, f. 17, op. 122, d. 47, l. 14.

114. RGASPI, f. 17, op. 122, d. 47, l. 17.

115. GARF, f. 5451, op. 43, d. 199, l. 122.

116. Liubimov, *Torgovlia i snabzhenie*, pp. 68, 69.

117. RGAE, f. 7971, op. 5, d. 58, ll. 1–2.

118. "Ob usilenii bor'by s raskhishcheniem i razbazarivaniem prodovol'stvennykh i promyshlennykh tovarov (i obrazovanii v sostave NKT GU Gosudarstvennoi torgovoi inspektsii)," in Liubimov, *Torgovlia i snabzhenie*, p. 48.

119. RGAE, f. 7971, op. 16, d. 246, ll. 170–173; d. 248, l. 195; RGAE, f. 7971, op. 16, d. 248, ll. 88–88ob.

120. GARF, f. 8131, op. 37, d. 1436, l. 180; see also RGAE, f. 7971, op. 16, d. 246, ll. 170–173.

121. RGAE, f. 7971, op. 16, d. 248, ll. 258–260.

122. RGAE, f. 7971, op. 16, d. 248, ll. 180–180ob.

123. RGAE, f. 7971, op. 16, d. 295, l. 85.

124. RGAE, f. 7971, op. 16, d. 295, ll. 53–52 (file numbered back to front).

125. RGAE, f. 7971, op. 16, d. 295, l. 50.

126. U. G. Cherniavskii, *Voina i prodovol'stvie. Snabzhenie gorodskogo naseleniia v Velikuiu Otechestvennuiu voinu (1941-1945 gg.)* (Moscow: Nauka, 1964), pp. 111–19; Liubimov, *Torgovlia i snabzhenie*, p. 70.

127. *Postanovlenie XII Plenuma Vsesoiuznogo tsentral'nogo soveta professional'nykh soiuzov* (Molotov: Gorkom VKP(b), 1944), pp. 20–8.

128. GARF, f. 5452, op. 22, d. 55, l. 22ob.

129. GARF, f. 5452, op. 22, d. 9, ll. 22–23.

130. GARF, f. 5451, op. 43, d. 325a, l. 144.

131. GARF, f. 5451, op. 43, d. 199, ll. 28–26.

132. RGASPI, f. 17, op. 122, d. 81, ll. 77–78.

133. V. N. Khaustov, V. P. Naumov, and N. S. Plotnikova, eds., *Lubianka. Stalin i NKVD-NKGB-GUKR "Smersh," 1939–mart 1946* (Moscow: Materik, 2006), pp. 422–3.

134. GARF, f. 5451, op. 43, d. 325a, l. 113.

135. GARF, f. 5451, op. 43, d. 199, l. 102.

136. James Heinzen, *The Art of the Bribe: Corruption under Stalin, 1943-1953* (New Haven and London: Yale University Press, 2016); L. M. Timofeev, "Institutsional'naia korruptsiia sotsialisticheskoi sistemy," in Iurii Afanas'ev, ed., *Sovetskoe obshchestvo. Vozniknovenie, razvitie, istoricheskii final*, vol. II (Moscow: Rossiiskii Gosudarstvennyi Universitet, 1997), pp. 508–44.

137. Pushkarev, "40-e. Stanovlenie 'chernogo' rynka."

138. B. Alexandrov, "The Soviet Currency Reform," *Russian Review*, vol. 8, no. 1 (January 1949), pp. 58, 56–61; V. S. Pushkarev, "Razvitie 'chernogo rynka' v period Velikoi Otechestvennoi voiny i ego vliianie na sostoianie vnutrennogo rynka strany," in T. M. Bulavkina and M. V. Stegantsev, eds., *Edinstvo fronta i tyla v Velikoi Otechestvennoi voine, 1941–1945* (Moscow: Akademiia, 2007), p. 190; Ironside, "Stalin's Doctrine of Price Reductions," pp. 665, 667–71; Donald Filtzer, *Soviet Workers and Late Stalinism: Labour and the Restoration of the Stalinist System after World War II* (Cambridge: Cambridge University Press, 2002), pp. 77–8; Alec Nove, *An Economic History of the Soviet Union* (Harmondsworth: Penguin, 1972), p. 308; Hessler, *A Social History of Soviet Trade*, pp. 288–9.

139. RGASPI, f. 17, op. 122, d. 47, ll. 6–9.

Chapter 5

Epigraph: RGASPI, f. 17, op. 125, d. 108, l. 295.

1. V. N. Zemskov, "Organizatsiia rabochei sily i uzhestochenie trudovoi zakonodatel'stva v gody voiny s fashistskoi germaniei," *Politicheskoe prosveshchenie*, No. 2 (79), 2014, accessed at http://www.politpros.com/journal/read/?ID=3167&journal=160&sphrase_id=12205, p. 4, notes that between 1942 and 1945 the Committee to Enumerate and Distribute the Labor Force mobilized more than 3 million people for permanent jobs, 2 million teenagers for vocational schools, and and 6.7 million people for seasonal work. For permanent work alone, see Table 5.1 for additional sources of mobilization.

2. Thomas Sugrue, *The Origins of the Urban Crisis: Race and Inequality in Postwar Detroit* (Princeton: Princeton University Press, 2005); Emily Yellin, *Our Mothers' War: American Women at Home and at the Front during World War II* (New York: Free Press, 2005); Claudia Koonz, *Mothers in the Fatherland: Women, the Family, and Nazi Politics* (New York: St. Martin's Press, 1988); Nicholas Stargardt, *The German War: A Nation under Arms, 1939–1945* (New York: Basic Books, 2015), pp. 64, 139–40, 295–7.

3. The Russian term "*trudosposobnyi*," usually translated as "able-bodied," literally means "work-capable," that is, anyone able to do some kind of work, which under wartime conditions also included the ill and infirm.

4. Mark Harrison, "Resource Mobilization for World War II: The USA, UK, USSR, and Germany, 1938–1945," *Economic History Review*, vol. 41, no. 2 (1988), pp. 171–92, http://www2.warwick.ac.uk/fac/soc/economics/staff/mharrison/public/ehr88postprint.pdf, p. 19.

5. Mark Harrison, *Accounting for War: Soviet Production, Employment, and the Defence Burden, 1940–1945* (Cambridge: Cambridge University Press, 1996), p. 267.

6. V. B. Tel'pukhovskii, "Geroizm rabochego klassa," in G. N. Sevostianov, ed., *Voina i obshchestvo, 1941–1945*, book I (Moscow: Nauka, 2004), p. 8.

7. Wendy Z. Goldman, *Women at the Gates: Gender and Industry in Stalin's Russia* (New York: Cambridge University Press, 2002), ch. 3 and p. 269 (table 8.5); V. S. Murmantseva, *Sovetskie zhenshchiny v Velikoi Otechestvennoi voine* (Moscow: Mysl', 1974), p. 20.

8. Tel'pukhovskii, "Geroizm," p. 9.

9. GARF, f. 6822, op. 1, d. 511, ll. 159–153 (file numbered back to front).

10. On the early Soviet experience with mass mobilization of labor, see Donald Filtzer, *Soviet Workers and Stalinist Industrialization: The Formation of Modern Soviet Production Relations, 1928–1941* (London: Pluto Press, 1986), chs. 2 and 3. On the labor exchanges, see Goldman, *Women at the Gates*, pp. 111–16, 120–6.

11. The term used in Russian was "*nerabotaiushchii*" or nonworking, not "*bezrabotnyi*" or unemployed. In this case, the more general English term "unemployed" is used as synonymous with nonworking for the sake of readability.

12. Early plans, for example, involved no reliance on the vocational training schools. During the first six months of the war their entire intake of students (307,420) went to two-year training courses for highly skilled trades. These workers would not have been available to industry until late 1943. See GARF, f. 9507, op. 2, d. 425, ll. 2, 3.

13. GARF, f. 9517, op. 1, d. 15, ll. 16–23.

14. Zemskov, "Organizatsiia rabochei sily," p. 2.

15. GARF, f. 5451, op. 43, d. 293b, l. 253; RGAE, f. 1562, op. 329, d. 1151, ll. 7–10; Zemskov, "Organizatsiia rabochei sily," p. 4; A. V. Mitrofanova, *Rabochii klass SSSR nakanune i v gody Velikoi Otechestvennoi voiny, 1938-1945 gg.* (Moscow: Nauka, 1984), p. 354.

16. Edict of the Presidium of the Supreme Soviet of the USSR, June 26, 1940, "O perekhode na vos'michasovoi rabochii den', na semidnevnuiu rabochuiu nedeliu i o zapreshchenii samovol'nogo ukhoda rabochikh i sluzhashchikh s predpriiatii i uchrezhdenii," *Izvestiia*, June 27, 1940.

17. Edict of the Presidium of the Supreme Soviet of the USSR, June 26, 1941, "O rezhime rabochego vremeni rabochikh i sluzhashchikh v voennoe vremia," available at http://www.libussr.ru/doc_ussr/ussr_4322.htm.

18. GARF, f. 9517, op. 1, d. 1, ll. 1, 2, 3, 4, 5, 6, 7, 8, 9, 11, 12, 13, 15.

19. GARF, f. 9517, op. 1, d. 1, ll. 21, 94, 98, 99, 14, 187, 198, 165, 199.

20. GARF, f. 9517, op. 1, d. 1, ll. 2, 3, 4, 139–143, 158, 132.

21. GARF, f. 9517, op. 1, d. 1, ll. 241–243.

22. GARF, f. 9517, op. 1, d. 1, ll. 28, 29, 30, 31, 32, 33, 34, 35, 36, 37, 38, 39, 40.

23. GARF, f. 9517, op. 1, d. 1, ll. 50–57.

24. As quoted from the factory's newspaper in Zemskov, "Organizatsiia rabochei sily," p. 2.

25. RGASPI, f. 17, op. 88, d. 31, l. 15; Murmantseva, *Sovetskie zhenshchiny*, pp. 23–5. By the end of 1942 women were 55 percent of manual workers in industry and 24 percent in construction: RGAE, f. 1562, op. 329, d. 571, l. 5 (industry), and d. 570, l. 4 (construction).

26. GARF, f. 9517, op. l, d. l, ll. 77–79.

27. GARF, f. 9517, op. 1, d. 1, ll. 219–224.

28. Tel'pukhovskii, "Geroizm," p. 35.

29. Edict of the Presidium of the Supreme Soviet of the USSR, December 26, 1941, "Ob otvetstvennosti rabochikh i sluzhashchikh predpriiatii voennoi promyshlennosti za samovol'nyi ukhod s predpriiatii," *Vedomosti Verkhovnogo Soveta SSSR*, No. 2 (161), January 12, 1942, available at http://www.libussr.ru/doc_ussr/ussr_4336.htm. The defense sectors initially included aviation, ammunitions, warship construction, tanks, chemicals, and armaments; the list expanded steadily over the course of the war. See Chapter 7.

30. Edict of the Presidium of the Supreme Soviet of the USSR, February 13, 1942, "O mobilizatsii na period voennogo vremeni trudosposobnogo gorodskogo naseleniia dlia raboty na proizvodstve i stroitel'stve," http://www.libussr.ru/doc_ussr/ussr_4341.htm.

31. GARF, f. 9517, op. 1, d. 1, ll. 65, 83.

32. GARF, f. 9517, op. 1, d. 1, ll. 1, 2, 3.

33. GARF, f. 9517, op. 1, d. 10, ll. 32, 38, 40, 53, 35, 36.

34. GARF, f. 9517, op. 1, d. 10, ll. 5, 20.

35. GARF, f. 9517, op. 1, d. 10, ll. 28, 35–37.

36. GARF, f. 9517, op. 1, d. 10, ll. 22, 21, 65, 49.

37. GARF, f. 9517, op. 1, d. 10, l. 138. See also l. 122.

38. GARF, f. 9517, op. 1, d. 10, ll. 83, 87–93.

39. Murmantseva, *Sovetskie zhenshchiny*, p. 22.

40. GARF, f. 9517, op. 1, d. 14, ll. 1–11.

41. GARF, f. 9517, op. 1, d. 10, l. 47.

42. GARF, f. 9517, op. 1, d. 10, ll. 114–115.

43. GARF, f. 9517, op. 1, d. 10, l. 15.

44. http://www.libussr.ru/doc_ussr/ussr_4352.htm.

45. Mitrofanova, *Rabochii klass SSSR*, pp. 428–32.

46. GARF, f. 9517, op. 1, d. 10, ll. 139–140.

47. GARF, f. 9517, op. 1, d. 10, ll. 140, 146.

48. GARF, f. 9517, op. 1, d. 10, ll. 110–111.

49. RGASPI, f. 17, op. 122, d. 19, ll. 40–58.

50. RGASPI, f. 17, op. 122, d. 19, ll. 40–58.

51. RGASPI, f. 17, op. 122, d. 19, ll. 59–66, 47.

52. GARF, f. 9517, op. 1, d. 10, ll. 6–7.

53. People would retain the right to their former jobs and residences, while those already employed could retain a portion of their permanent salaries: http://militera.lib.ru/docs/da/nko_1941-1942/14.html.

54. http://www.libussr.ru/doc_ussr/ussr_4364.htm. Lowering the age for boys to fifteen now placed the FZO in competition with the RU and ZhU, which took children aged fourteen and fifteen.

55. http://www.libussr.ru/doc_ussr/ussr_4366.htm.

56. RGASPI, f. 17, op. 125, d. 107, ll. 39–41.

57. RGASPI, f. 17, op. 125, d. 107, l. 41.

58. RGASPI, f. 17, op. 125, d. 107, ll. 39–41.

59. RGASPI, f. 17, op. 125, d. 107, l. 41.

60. RGASPI, f. 17, op. 125, d. 107, l. 41.

61. RGASPI, f. 17, op. 125, d. 107, l. 42.

62. RGASPI, f. 17, op. 125, d. 107, ll. 43–44.

63. RGASPI, f. 17, op. 125, d. 107, ll. 34–35.

64. RGASPI, f. 17, op. 125, d. 107, l. 36.

65. RGASPI, f. 17, op. 125, d. 107, l. 36.

66. RGASPI, f. 17, op. 125, d. 107, l. 38. On the systematic protection of runaway Labor Reserve students in rural areas, see Chapter 7.

67. RGASPI, f. 17, op. 125, d. 107, ll. 46–47.

68. GARF, f. 5451, op. 43, d. 325a, ll. 148–147 (file numbered back to front).

69. Alexis Peri, *The War Within: Diaries from the Siege of Leningrad* (Cambridge, Mass.: Harvard University Press, 2017), p. 90, notes the contrary: in besieged Leningrad, people who remained with their families fared *worse* in terms of material and emotional wellbeing than those who cared only for themselves.

70. GARF, f. 5451, op. 43, d. 199, l. 127.

71. GARF, f. 5451, op. 43, d. 199, l. 144.

72. RGASPI, f. 17, op. 125, d. 107, ll. 6–9.

73. GARF, f. 5451, op. 43, d. 325a, l. 143.

74. RGASPI, f. 17, op. 125, d. 107, ll. 6–9.

75. RGASPI, f. 17, op. 125, d. 107, ll. 8–9.

76. RGASPI, f. 17, op. 125, d. 107, ll. 9–13.

77. RGASPI, f. 17, op. 125, d. 107, l. 16.

78. GARF, f. 5451, op. 43, d. 325a, ll. 121, 119, 118; d. 199, ll. 145–144 (file numbered back to front).

79. GARF, f. 5451, op. 43, d. 325a, ll. 122–120, quote from l. 121.

80. RGASPI, f. 17, op. 125, d. 107, ll. 48–52, 54, 45, 56–57.

81. GARF, f. 5451, op. 30, d. 1, ll. 3–5.

82. See "O mnogochislennykh faktakh formal'no-biurokraticheskogo otnosheniia k molodym rabochim i neotlozhennykh merakh po usileniiu raboty komsomol'skikh organizatsii sredi nikh." The text of the decree and discussion around it are in RGASPI, f. M-1, op. 3, d. 289, ll. 60–72.

83. GARF, f. 5451, op. 30, d. 1, ll. 28–35.

84. GARF, f. 5451, op. 43, d. 231, ll. 631, 632 (file numbered back to front).

85. GARF, f. 5451, op. 43, d. 199, ll. 147, 142.

86. RGASPI, f. 17, op. 125, d. 107, ll. 45–48.

87. RGASPI, f. 17, op. 122, d. 18, l. 122.

88. Report from V. G. Nasedkin, Chief of the Gulag, to L. P. Beria, "O rabote GULAGa za gody voiny (1941–1944)," in A. I. Kokurin and N. V. Petrov, eds., *GULAG (Glavnoe upravlenie lagerei) 1917–1960* (Moscow: Mezhdunarodnyi fond "Demokratiia," Izdatel'stvo "Materik," 2000), p. 275 (hereafter referred to as Nasedkin report). Nasedkin claimed that the NKVD directed 975,000 prisoners to the army. In addition, 53,000 Polish and Czechoslovak prisoners were released to fight in Polish and Czechoslovak military units. Another NKVD document, prepared just after Nasedkin's report, noted that these figures did not include prisoners transferred from

prisons (as opposed to camps and colonies) to the Red Army during 1944: Kokurin and Petrov, *GULAG*, p. 428. See also Steven A. Barnes, *Death and Redemption: The Gulag and the Shaping of Soviet Society* (Princeton: Princeton University Press, 2011), pp. 114–15.

89. GARF, f. 6822, op. 1, d. 482, ll. 36–37.

90. RGASPI, f. 17, op. 3, d. 1041, l. 126; GARF, f. 8131, op. 37, d. 1248, ll. 5, 6, 9–9ob., 11, 12, 37, 42, 96–96ob.

91. On the fluid continuum from "free" citizen to prisoner, see Oleg Khlevniuk, "The Gulag and Non-Gulag as One Interrelated Whole," *Kritika: Explorations in Russian and Eurasian History*, vol. 16, no. 3 (Summer 2015), pp. 479–98.

92. V. N. Zemskov, "Smertnost' zakliuchennykh v 1941–1945 gg.," in *Liudskie poteri SSSR v period vtoroi mirovoi voiny. Sbornik statei* (St. Petersburg: Russko-Baltiiskii informatsionnyi tsentr BLITs, 1995), p. 175. These figures are for the camps only; they exclude the labor colonies and special settlements.

93. Edwin Bacon, *The Gulag at War: Stalin's Forced Labor System in the Light of the Archives* (Basingstoke: Macmillan, 1994), pp. 26, 29–30. On peasant special settlers, see Lynne Viola, *The Unknown Gulag: The Lost World of Stalin's Special Settlements* (Oxford: Oxford University Press, 2007).

94. Wilson T. Bell, *Stalin's Gulag at War: Forced Labour, Mass Death, and Soviet Victory in the Second World War* (Toronto: University of Toronto Press, 2019), pp. 55–63.

95. It was longstanding Gulag policy to release prisoners who were close to death so that camps would not have to feed unproductive workers, and their deaths would not compromise camp mortality statistics. According to Golfo Alexopoulos, this policy was temporarily suspended during 1942 and 1943 but resumed again in 1944, although Wilson Bell's work on Siblag suggests application of the suspension was far from clear cut. See Golfo Alexopoulos, *Illness and Inhumanity in Stalin's Gulag* (New Haven: Yale University Press, 2017), pp. 140–7; Wilson T. Bell, "Forced Labor on the Home Front: The Gulag and Total War in Western Siberia, 1940–1945," in Michael David-Fox, ed., *The Soviet Gulag: Evidence, Interpretation, and Comparison* (Pittsburgh: University of Pittsburgh Press, 2016), pp. 123–5. The first historian to highlight this issue was V. A. Isupov, *Demograficheskie katastrofy i krizisy v Rossii v pervoi polovine XX veka. Istoriko-demograficheskie ocherki* (Novosibirsk: Sibirskii khronograf, 2000), p. 164.

96. Figures are from Bacon, *The Gulag at War*, p. 170, and Nasedkin report, p. 277. The figure fluctuated from 196,310 workers in August 1943 to 208,595 in January 1944, and back down to 194,415 in June 1944. As the war drew to an end the NKVD also rented out to the commissariats captured prisoners of war—316,000 in 1944 alone. See Barnes, *Death and Redemption*, p. 127.

97. Nasedkin report, p. 276; Bacon, *The Gulag at War*, pp. 163–6. In industrial construction, for example, there were 134,570 prisoners recorded in October 1942, 75,886 in May 1943, and 108,499 at the end of 1944. Similarly, there were 396,510 prisoners on railway construction in October 1942, after which the number fell sharply to 220,576 in May 1943 and 119,964 at the end of 1944. Similar contractions occurred in the other sectors served by the Gulag.

98. Estimated from Nasedkin report, pp. 289–91, and Harrison, *Accounting for War*, p. 180.

99. Nasedkin report, p. 276.

100. A. V. Zakharchenko, "Lagerno-proizvodstvennyi kompleks v povol'zhe. Zakliuchennye osobstroia NKVD SSSR na stroitel'stve aviatsionnykh zavodov v raione g. Kuibysheva, 1940–1943 gg.," in L. I. Borodkin, S. A. Krasil'nikov, and O. V. Khlevniuk, eds., *Istoriia Stalinizma. Prinuditel'nyi trud v SSSR. Ekonomika, politika, pamiat'. Materialy mezhdunarodnoi konferentsii, Moskva, 28–29 oktiabria 2011 g.* (Moscow: Rosspen, 2013), pp. 221–39; Kuibyshev population data from RGAE, f. 1562, op. 20, d. 484, l. 34.

101. Marina Vasil'evna Gontsova, "Povsednevnaia zhizn' naseleniia industrial'nogo tsentra v gody Velikoi Otechestvennoi voiny (na materialakh goroda Nizhnii Tagil)," Candidate of Historical Sciences dissertation, Nizhnii Tagil, 2011, pp. 145–6; V. M. Kirillov, *Istoriia repressii v Nizhnetagil'skom regione Urala. 1920-e v nachalo 1950-kh gg.*, Part 2 (Nizhnii Tagil: Ural'skii gosudarstvennyi universitet, Nizhnetagil'skii gosudarstvennyi pedagogicheskii institut, 1996), pp. 11–13.

102. Historians did not become aware of the Labor Army until the 1990s when the Russian archives made previously classified documents available. Before this period, no history of the war had made reference to a Labor Army, and the only proof of its existence was in the memory of those mobilized into its ranks. The first references were discovered by two groups of Russian researchers, working simultaneously on different subjects: one on Soviet ethnic Germans who were deported and then mobilized for labor, and the other on labor in the eastern industrial towns. Yet these and other historians do not agree on the definition, purpose, and history of the Labor Army. Some maintain that the Labor Army was synonymous with the ethnic Germans who were mobilized for compulsory labor duty. Others consider this definition too narrow, noting that Uzbeks, Turkmens, Kazakhs, those who were liberated from the occupied territories (including Jews who survived), those repatriated from abroad, and soldiers accused of desertion were also mobilized into its ranks. They argue that the political purpose of the Labor Army was to isolate *all* potential fifth columnists from other citizens. Still others broaden the definition even further to include *any* construction battalion, workers' column, or group under the Special Construction and Erection Units (Osobye stroitel'no-montazhnye chasti, or OSMCh), the construction organization that was deployed on successive sites and projects. For an excellent review of the historiography on the Labor Army, see G. A. Goncharov, "'Trudovaia armiia' perioda Velikoi Otechestvennoi voiny. Rossiiskaia istoriografiia," in L. I. Borodkin, *Ekonomicheskaia istoriia. Obozrenie*, Vypusk 7 (Moscow, 2001), pp. 154–62; Rubin Udler, *The Cursed Years: Reminiscences of a Holocaust Survivor* (Pittsburgh: Chisinau, 2005). After liberation, Udler, a Jewish teenager who survived occupation on a collective farm, was sent to work in the mines with the Labor Army. At the end of the war, he was released and reunited with his family.

103. G. A. Goncharov, "Ispol'zovanie 'Trudovoi armii' na Urale v 1941–1945 gg.," in Borodkin, Krasil'nikov, and Khlevniuk, eds., *Istoriia Stalinizma*, pp. 146–50.

104. GARF, f. 5451, op. 30, d. 1, ll. 23–24ob.
105. Mortality as calculated by number of deaths divided by the average number of prisoners for the year; 1943 calculated from figures supplied in a report from the Gulag's Administration for the Accounting and Distribution of Prisoners (OURZ), cited in V. M. Kirillov, "Fizicheskoe sostoianie kontingentov zakliuchennykh i trudmobilizovannykh nemtsev ITL Bakalstroi/Cheliabmetallurgstroi, pokazateli ikh trudoispol'zovaniia (1942–1946)," in Borodkin, Krasil'nikov, and Khlevniuk, eds., *Istoriia Stalinizma*, p. 128; figures for 1942, pp. 114–15.
106. https://www.centropa.org/biography/isaac-serman#During%20the%20war.
107. A. A. German and A. N. Kurochkin, *Nemtsy SSSR v "Trudovoi armii"* (Moscow: Gotika, 2000), pp. 67, 170. Of the 315,000 enrolled in the Labor Army, 182,000 worked in NKVD camps and 133,000 were contracted out to industrial commissariats.
108. The texts of all the deportation laws are in Vladimir Andreevich Auman and Valentina Georgievna Chebotareva, eds., *Istoriia rossiiskikh nemtsev v dokumentakh (1763–1992 gg.)* (Moscow: Mezhdunarodnyi institut gumanitarnykh programm, 1993), pp. 159–62, 164–8. The order expelling Germans from the military is discussed in German and Kurochkin, *Nemtsy SSSR v "Trudovoi armii,"* pp. 48–9.
109. N. F. Bugai, *Mobilizovat' nemtsev v rabochie kolonny ... I. Stalin. Sbornik dokumentov* (Moscow: Gotika, 1998), pp. 102–5, 251–3.
110. Decrees of January 10, February 14, and October 7, 1942: Auman and Chebotareva, eds., *Istoriia rossiiskikh nemtsev v dokumentakh*, pp. 168–9, 170, 172–3; decree of October 14, 1942: Bugai, *Mobilizovat' nemtsev*, pp. 44–5. On the liquidation of German collective farms in Kazakhstan (Decree of Soviet of People's Commissars, November 19, 1942), see Bugai, *Mobilizovat' nemtsev*, p. 47.
111. German and Kurochkin, eds., *Nemtsy SSSR v "Trudovoi armii,"* pp. 67, 170.
112. Calculated from German and Kurochkin, eds., *Nemtsy SSSR v "Trudovoi armii,"* p. 170, and RGAE, f. 1562, op. 329, d. 1126.
113. German and Kurochkin, eds., *Nemtsy SSSR v "Trudovoi armii,"* p. 114, "Al'bom diagramm o rozhdaemosti i smertnosti naseleniia RSFSR za gody otechestvennoi voiny," prepared by the Scientific-Methodological Bureau of Sanitary Statistics, Narkomzdrav RSFSR in 1945. The Al'bom is in GARF, f. A-482, op. 52s, d. 188, diagram 55.
114. Material on camps compiled from German and Kurochkin, eds., *Nemtsy SSSR v "Trudovoi armii,"* pp. 163–9.
115. Bugai, *Mobilizovat' nemtsev*, pp. 138–9.
116. V. M. Kirillov, "Obshchie zakonomernosti i spetsifika soderzhaniia trudmobilizovannykh rossiiskikh nemtsev v lageriakh prinuditel'nogo truda na Urale," *Vestnik Iuzhno-Ural'skogo gosudarstvennogo universiteta*, seriia "Sotsial'no-gumanitarnye nauki," 2015, vol. 15, no. 1, p. 32.
117. By December 1942, youth under twenty-five and adult women composed 59 percent of the workforce in defense and heavy industry. In the ammunition, machine-building, mining, armaments, food, and dairy industries they constituted 70 percent of the labor force; in textiles and light industry, up to 85 percent. The share of older

workers (above fifty) rose from 9 to 12 percent, and teenagers from 6 to 15 percent. See Tel'pukhovskii, "Geroizm," p. 12.

118. NA IRI-RAN, f. 2, r. 5, op. 50, d. 4, ll. 3–3ob.; d. 17, ll. 1ob., 2.

119. NA IRI-RAN, f. 2, r. 5, op. 45, d. 1, ll. 15–16.

120. Alexander Werth, *Russia at War, 1941–1945* (New York: Carroll and Graf, 1964), pp. 496, 517–18.

Chapter 6

Epigraph: L. S. Gatagova, A. P. Kosheleva, L. A. Rogovaia, and J. Cadiot, eds., *TsK VKP(b) i natsional'nyi vopros, kniga 2, 1933–1945* (Moscow: Rosspen, 2009), pp. 776–8. Thanks to Charles Shaw for drawing this source to our attention.

1. Jean Levesque, "A Peasant Ordeal: The Soviet Countryside," in David Stone, ed., *The Soviet Union at War, 1941–1945* (Barnsley, UK: Pen and Sword Books, 2010), pp. 194–5; R. P. Sosnovskaia, *Geroicheskii trud vo imia pobedy* (Leningrad: Izdatel'stvo Leningradskogo Universiteta, 1973), pp. 122, 119; V. S. Murmantseva, *Sovetskie zhenshchiny v Velikoi Otechestvennoi voine* (Moscow: Mysl', 1974), pp. 26–8, 35.

2. GARF, f. 9517, op. 1, d. 15, ll. 1–4.

3. GARF, f. 9517, op. 1, d. 15, l. 11.

4. See, for example, GARF, f. 9517, op. 1, d. 26, ll. 17–18, 92.

5. GARF, f. 9517, op. 1, d. 15, l. 16.

6. GARF, f. 9517, op. 1, d. 19, ll. 364 a–z, 364 zh, 327–325, 145 (file numbered back to front); d. 32, l. 511.

7. GARF, f. 9517, op. 1, d. 15, l. 14.

8. GARF, f. 9517, op. 1, d. 15, l. 26.

9. GARF, f. 9517, op. 1, d. 15, ll. 29–30.

10. See, for example, RGASPI, f. 17, op. 122, d. 45, l. 1.

11. GARF, f. 9517, op. 1, d. 39, l. 138.

12. GARF, f. 9517, op. 1, d. 4, ll. 93–112.

13. See, for example, GARF, f. 9517, op. 1, d. 26, l. 76.

14. RGASPI, f. 644, op. 1, d. 64, ll. 37–39; Boris Danilovich Shmyrov, "Trudmobilizovannye Sredne-aziatskogo voennogo okruga na stroikakh i promyshlennykh predpriiatiiakh iuzhnogo Urala v gody Velikoi Otechestvennoi voiny," Candidate of Historical Sciences dissertation, Cheliabinsk, 2016, pp. 199–202.

15. RGASPI, f. 17, op. 122, d. 50, l. 5.

16. RGASPI, f. 17, op. 122, d. 50, l. 9.

17. RGASPI, f. 17, op. 122, d. 50, l. 11.

18. RGASPI, f. 17, op. 122, d. 50, ll. 6, 7.

19. RGASPI, f. 17, op. 122, d. 50, ll. 2–4. Thanks to Charles Shaw for providing an additional reference to this document.

20. RGASPI, f. 17, op. 122, d. 50, l. 17.

21. GARF, f. 5451, op. 30, d. 1, ll. 23–24ob. See also Marina Vasil'evna Gontsova, "Povsednevnaia zhizn' naseleniia industrial'nogo tsentra v gody Velikoi

Otechestvennoi voiny (na materialakh goroda Nizhnii Tagil)," Candidate of Historical Sciences dissertation, Nizhnii Tagil, 2011, p. 198.

22. RGASPI, f. 17, op. 122, d. 50, l. 8.

23. RGASPI, f. 17, op. 122, d. 50, ll. 5–5ob.

24. RGASPI, f. 17, op. 122, d. 50, ll. 20–25. Some historians consider these sectors part of the Labor Army although not all of its jobs were filled by deportees.

25. Shmyrov, "Trudmobilizovannye," pp. 44, 66, 76, 93.

26. Vera Valer'evna Solov'eva, "Bytovye usloviia personala promyshlennykh predpriiatii Urala v 1941–1945 gg. Gosudarstvennaia politika i strategii adaptatsii," Candidate of Historical Sciences dissertation, Ekaterinburg, 2011, pp. 247–8.

27. GARF, f. A-482, d. 1430, ll. 20–21.

28. Shmyrov, "Trudmobilizovannye," p. 88.

29. GARF, f. 7678, op. 8, d. 245, ll. 12–13.

30. Shmyrov, "Trudmobilizovannye," pp. 138–40.

31. RGASPI, f. 17, op. 122, d. 50, ll. 13–14.

32. RGASPI, f. 17, op. 122, d. 50, ll. 36–37.

33. GARF, f. 8131, op. 37, d. 1219, ll. 99–103, 105.

34. GARF, f. 8131, op. 37, d. 1440, l. 42.

35. RGASPI, f. 17, op. 122, d. 50, ll. 33–34, 26–32.

36. GARF, f. A-482, op. 47, d. 2219, l. 124.

37. GARF, f. A-482, op. 47, d. 1432, ll. 1, 1ob., 2.

38. RGASPI, f. 17, op. 122, d. 50, l. 6.

39. RGASPI, f. 17, op. 122, d. 50, l. 6.

40. RGASPI, f. 17, op. 122, d. 50, ll. 26–32; Shmyrov, "Trudmobilizovannye," p. 117; GARF, f. A-482, op. 47, d. 1430, ll. 36, 36ob.

41. GARF, f. A-482, op. 52s, d. 80, ll. 202ob., 203.

42. GARF, f. A-482, op. 47, d. 1432, ll. 5–5ob.; RGASPI, f. 17, op. 122, d. 80, ll. 40–42.

43. Shmyrov, "Trudmobilizovannye," p. 142.

44. Decree of the Soviet of People's Commissars SSSR, October 18, 1942, "O poriadke snabzheniia prodovol'stvennymi i promyshlennymi tovarami rabochikh promyshlennykh predpriiatii," in A. R. Dzeniskevich, ed., *Leningrad v osade. Sbornik dokumentov o geroicheskoi oborone Leningrada v gody Velikoi Otechestvennoi voiny, 1941–1944* (St. Petersburg: Liki Rossii, 1995), pp. 244–5.

45. RGASPI, f. 17, op. 122, d. 80, ll. 40–42.

46. RGASPI, f. 17, op. 122, d. 50, ll. 26–32.

47. Solov'eva, "Bytovye usloviia," p. 246.

48. GARF, f. A-482, op. 52s, d. 80, l. 203.

49. Gontsova, "Povsednevnaia zhizn'," pp. 198–9, 201.

50. Solov'eva, "Bytovye usloviia," pp. 245–6, 249.

51. Gatagova, *et al.*, *TsK VKP(b) i natsional'nyi vopros*, pp. 776–8. The original document is from RGASPI, f. 17, op. 117, d. 371, ll. 97–98.

52. Solov'eva, "Bytovye usloviia," pp. 247–8.

53. GARF, f. 9517, op. 1, d. 19, l. 443.

54. GARF, f. 9517, op. 1, d. 19, l. 371.

55. GARF, f. 9517, op. 1, d. 19, ll. 259–227 (file numbered back to front); Murmantseva, *Sovetskie zhenshchiny*, p. 61.

56. Alexander Werth, *Russia at War, 1941–1945* (New York: Carroll and Graf, 1964), p. 685.

57. GARF, f. 9517, op. 1, d. 19, ll. 437–428.

58. GARF, f. 9517, op. 1, d. 19, ll. 321, 319–314.

59. GARF, f. 9517, op. 1, d. 19, l. 336.

60. GARF, f. 9517, op. 1, d. 19, l. 116; d. 26, l. 98.

61. GARF, f. 9517, op. 1, d. 26, l. 93.

62. See Karel C. Berkhoff, *Harvest of Despair: Life and Death in Ukraine under Nazi Rule* (Cambridge, Mass.: Belknap Press of Harvard University Press, 2004), pp. 141–86; Jeffrey W. Jones, *Everyday Life and the "Reconstruction" of Soviet Russia during and after the Great Patriotic War, 1943–1948* (Bloomington: Slavica Publishers, 2008), pp. 42–76; Karl D. Qualls, *From Ruins to Reconstruction: Urban Identity in Soviet Sevastopol after World War II* (Ithaca: Cornell University Press, 2009), pp. 1–23; Anatoly Kuznetsov, *Babi Yar: A Document in the Form of a Novel* (New York: Farrar, Straus, and Giroux, 1970).

63. GARF, f. 9517, op. 1, d. 19, l. 22.

64. GARF, f. 9517, op. 1, d. 19, ll. 86–83.

65. GARF, f. 9517, op. 1, d. 26, l. 136.

66. GARF, f. 9517, op. 1, d. 26, ll. 124, 131.

67. GARF, f. 9517, op. 1, d. 26, l. 175.

68. GARF, f. 9517, op. 1, d. 26, ll. 13, 32–33.

69. GARF, f. 9517, op. 1, d. 19, ll. 311–308, 302–285.

70. GARF, f. 9517, op. 1, d. 26, l. 67.

71. GARF, f. 9517, op. 1, d. 26, l. 236.

72. GARF, f. 9517, op. 1, d. 26, l. 95.

73. GARF, f. 9517, op. 1, d. 26, l. 140.

74. Brandon Schechter, "The State's Pot and the Soldier's Spoon: Rations (*Paëk*) in the Red Army," in Wendy Z. Goldman and Donald Filtzer, eds., *Hunger and War: Food Provisioning in the Soviet Union during World War II* (Bloomington: Indiana University Press, 2015), pp. 132–3.

75. See, for example, GARF, f. 9517, op. 1, d. 26, ll. 116–118.

76. GARF, f. 9517, op. 1, d. 26, l. 69.

77. GARF, f. 9517, op. 1, d. 26, l. 75.

78. GARF, f. 9517, op. 1, d. 26, l. 76.

79. GARF, f. 9517, op. 1, d. 26, l. 79.

80. GARF, f. 9517, op. 1, d. 26, l. 90.

81. GARF, f. 9517, op. 1, d. 26, l. 213.

82. See the ruse employed by the Commissariat of Electric Power Stations: GARF, f. 9517, op. 1, d. 26, l. 221.

83. GARF, f. 9517, op. 1, d. 26, ll. 1–2.

84. GARF, f. 9517, op. 1, d. 26, l. 12.

85. GARF, f. 9517, op. 1, d. 26, ll. 105–115.

86. GARF, f. 9517, op. 1, d. 15, l. 10; d. 26, l. 21.

87. GARF, f. 9517, op. 1, d. 15, ll. 33–35.

88. GARF, f. 9517, op. 1, d. 26, ll. 17–18.

89. GARF, f. 9517, op. 1, d. 26, l. 21; RGASPI, f. 17, op.122, d. 45, l. 33.

90. GARF, f. 9517, op. 1, d. 26, l. 69.

91. GARF, f. 9517, op. 1, d. 26, ll. 86–88.

92. GARF, f. 9517, op. 1, d. 32, ll. 133–145.

93. GARF, f. 9517, op. 1, d. 32, ll. 209, 244–255.

94. GARF, f. 9517, op. 1, d. 26, ll. 183–189.

95. GARF, f. 9517, op. 1, d. 26, l. 77.

96. RGASPI, f. 17, op. 122, d. 74, ll. 125–126.

97. RGASPI, f. 17, op. 122, d. 74, ll. 125–126.

98. RGASPI, f. 17, op. 122, d. 74, l. 128.

99. GARF, f. 9517, op. 1, d. 15, l. 37.

100. GARF, f. 9517, op. 1, d. 15, l. 38.

101. GARF, f. 9517, op. 1, d. 15, ll. 40a–42. Convictions are from GARF, f. 9492, op. 6, d. 14, l. 9 (we are grateful to Peter Solomon for making these data available). The law against refusing mobilization was set by an Edict of the Presidium of the USSR Supreme Soviet, of February 13, 1942.

102. GARF, f. 9517, op. 1, d. 39, ll. 25–28, 80. On Ivanovo and Iaroslavl' provinces, see f. 9517, op. 1, d. 39, ll. 81–83.

103. GARF, f. 9517, op. 1, d. 39, ll. 6–7ob.

104. GARF, f. 9517, op. 1, d. 39, ll. 6–7ob.

105. GARF, f. 9517, op. 1, d. 39, ll. 6–7ob.

106. GARF, f. 9517, op. 1, d. 39, ll. 8–8ob., 9ob.

107. GARF, f. 9517, op. 1, d. 39, l. 7ob.

108. GARF, f. 9517, op. 1, d. 39, l. 8.

109. GARF, f. 9517, op. 1, d. 39, l. 9.

110. GARF, f. 9517, op. 1, d. 39, ll. 11–13.

111. GARF, f. 9517, op. 1, d. 32, ll. 487–506ob.

112. GARF, f. 9517, op. 1, d. 39, ll. 34–36.

113. GARF, f. 9517, op. 1, d. 39, l. 61.

114. GARF, f. 9517, op. 1, d. 37, ll. 12, 6.

115. GARF, f. 9517, op. 1, d. 37, l. 82.

116. See petitions from Marii republic and Kursk provincial soviet, for example: GARF, f. 9517, op. 1, d. 39, ll. 37, 60.

117. GARF, f. 9517, op. 1, d. 39, ll. 138–139.

118. GARF, f. 9517, op. 1, d. 39, l. 140.

119. GARF, f. 9517, op. 1, d. 39, l. 159.

120. GARF, f. 9517, op. 1, d. 39, l. 207.

121. The GKO directed a halt to mobilization in October 1943 (Shmyrov, "Trudmobilizovannye," pp. 73–5, 212). For examples of enterprises sending workers back to Central Asia, see Shmyrov, "Trudmobilizovannye," pp. 71–2; GARF, f. A-482, op. 47, d. 1430, ll. 36–37; GARF, f. A-482, op. 52s, d. 80, l. 203. On the demobilization order of 1944, see Solov'eva, "Bytovye usloviia," pp. 248–9.

122. Gatagova, *et al.*, *TsK VKP(b) i natsional'nyi vopros*, pp. 819–20. The original document is in RGASPI, f. 17, op. 117, d. 415, l. 29.

123. RGASPI, f. 17, op. 122, d. 80, ll. 38–39.

124. RGASPI, f. 17, op. 122, d. 80, ll. 40–44, 47, 48.

125. RGASPI, f. 17, op. 122, d. 80, l. 62.

126. Gatagova, *et al.*, *TsK VKP(b) i natsional'nyi vopros*, p. 966. The original document is in RGASPI, f. 17, op. 121, d. 373, l. 25.

127. On gripping participant accounts of the battle, see Jochen Hellbeck, *Stalingrad: The City That Defeated the Third Reich* (New York: Public Affairs, 2015).

128. GARF, f. 5451, op. 43, d. 521, l. 124.

129. RGASPI, f. 17, op. 122, d. 80, ll. 65–68, 72. On responses from the commissariats and provincial party secretaries, see ll. 70–95. Mikhailov's information was drawn from a report dated August 20, 1944, from F. Grishaenkov, Secretary of the Stalingrad Provincial Committee of the Komsomol: RGASPI, f. M-1, op. 8, d. 203, ll. 163–173.

130. RGASPI, f. 17, op. 122, d. 45, l. 18.

131. GARF, f. 5431, op. 30, d. 9, ll. 66–66ob.

132. RGASPI, f. 17, op. 122, d. 84, ll. 31–33; d. 74, ll. 202–203, 209, 210.

133. RGASPI, f. 17, op. 122, d. 74, ll. 205–208, 202, 210.

134. Decree of the Soviet of People's Commissars of the USSR, June 30, 1944, "O nalozhenii shtrafa za narushenie pravil po okhrane truda i tekhnike bezopasnosti," http://www.libussr.ru/doc_ussr/ussr_4495.htm.

135. RGASPI, f. 17, op. 122, d. 81, l. 82.

136. RGAE, f. 1562, op. 329, d. 1151, ll. 7–10. The authorities were more successful in meeting their plan for seasonal labor—83.4 percent.

137. GARF, f. 9517, op. 1, d. 37, ll. 3–6, 2.

138. RGAE, f. 1562, op. 329, d. 1151, l. 6.

139. V. N. Zemskov, "Organizatsiia rabochei sily i uzhestochenie trudovoi zakonodatel'stva v gody voiny s fashistskoi germaniei," *Politicheskoe prosveshchenie*, No. 2 (79), 2014, accessed at http://www.politpros.com/journal/read/ ?ID=3167&journal=160&sphrase_id=12205, p. 5.

Chapter 7

Epigraphs: GARF, f. 9507, op. 1, d. 51, l. 226; f. 5451, op. 26, d. 316, l. 22ob. Special thanks to Martin Kragh for exchange of research materials. See his "Soviet Labour Law during the Second World War," *War in History*, vol. 18, no. 4 (November 2011), pp. 531–46, and "Stalinist Labour Coercion during World War II: An Economic Approach," *Europe-Asia Studies*, vol. 63, no. 7 (September 2011), pp. 1253–73, the first work published on this topic.

1. GARF, f. 8131, op. 37, d. 1842, l. 1.

2. Donald Filtzer, *Soviet Workers and Stalinist Industrialization: The Formation of Modern Soviet Production Relations, 1928–1941* (London: Pluto Press, 1986), ch. 2 and p. 141.

3. The most severe was the law of December 28, 1938, which expelled leavers from enterprise housing, increased the amount of notice workers had to give before leaving, and tied disability and pension benefits to length of service at a given enterprise. See Filtzer, *Soviet Workers and Stalinist Industrialization*, pp. 233–4, 239–40.

4. GARF, f. 5451, op. 43, d. 293b, ll. 253, 251; RGAE, f. 1562, op. 329, d. 1151, ll. 6, 7–10. The Komitet was more successful in meeting its targets for seasonal workers—80.7 percent in 1943 and 83.4 percent in 1944.

5. Roger Reese, *Why Stalin's Soldiers Fought: The Red Army's Military Effectiveness in World War II* (Lawrence: University of Kansas Press, 2011), pp. 306, 25–7, 151–75, notes that the state's ability to enforce compliance in the army was also limited, and draft evasion and desertion persisted despite strong support for the war effort.

6. GARF, f. 5451, op. 43, d. 293b, l. 205; RGAE, f. 1562, op. 329, d. 1126, ll. 133–134.

7. Mobilization figures are from Table 5.1. Changes in the number of workers are from *Narodnoe khoziaistvo SSSR v Velikoi Otechestvennoi voine 1941–1945 gg. Statisticheskii sbornik* (Moscow: Goskomstat SSSR, Informatsionno-izdatel'skii tsentr, 1990), ch. 21, available at http://istmat.info/node/371. The figures in the tables are for workers and clerical employees together. We have deflated them by the wartime percentage of workers in each of industry, construction, and transport.

8. GARF, f. 5451, op. 43, d. 293a, ll. 3, 3ob.

9. Following the pact, the press dropped all anti-fascist propaganda and, when Germany invaded Poland, blamed Britain and France for launching an imperialist war. Official speeches and articles to this effect appeared almost daily in September 1939 and regularly thereafter. See in particular Molotov's speeches to the USSR Supreme Soviet, October 31, 1939, "O vneshnei politike Sovetskogo Soiuza" (Moscow: Ogiz, 1939), and March 29, 1940, "O vneshnei politike pravitel'stva," *Pravda*, March 30, 1940. Papers regularly published Hitler's speeches without criticism or comment (*Trud*, February 1 and 26, 1940) and defended the German conquest of Denmark and Norway as legitimate defensive operations in response to Anglo-French aggression (*Trud*, April 10 and May 5, 1940). For a sober analysis of the implications of the fall of France, see *Trud*, June 24, 1940.

10. Edict of the Presidium of the Supreme Soviet of the USSR, June 26, 1940, "O perekhode na vos'michasovoi rabochii den', na semidnevnuiu rabochuiu nedeliu i o zapreshchenii samovol'nogo ukhoda rabochikh i sluzhashchikh s predpriiatii i uchrezhdenii," *Izvestiia*, June 27, 1940. A fuller discussion of the prewar labor laws is in Filtzer, *Soviet Workers and Stalinist Industrialization*, pp. 107–15 and ch. 9.

11. GARF, f. 7678, op. 13, d. 37, l. 17.

12. Peter H. Solomon, Jr., *Soviet Criminal Justice under Stalin* (Cambridge: Cambridge University Press, 1996), pp. 298–325.

13. GARF, f. 9492, op. 6, d. 14, l. 11. We are grateful to Peter Solomon for making data in this file available to us. Slightly different figures appear in V. N. Zemskov, "Ukaz ot 26 iiunia 1940 goda ... (eshche odna kruglaia data)," *Raduga*, no. 6, 1990, p. 45.

14. Edict of the Presidium of the USSR Supreme Soviet, December 26, 1941, "Ob otvetstvennosti rabochikh i sluzhashchikh predpriiatii voennoi promyshlennosti za samovol'nyi ukhod s predpriiatii," *Vedomosti Verkhovnogo Soveta SSSR*, No. 2 (161), January 12, 1942.

15. "Spisok otraslei promyshlennosti i predpriiatii, na kotorye rasprostraniaetsia Ukaz Prezidiuma Verkhovnogo Soveta Soiuza SSR ot 26 dekabria 1941 goda." This is a late edition of this document, printed in October 1944. The copy used here is in GARF, f. 8131, op. 37, d. 1843, ll. 46–57.

16. Edicts of the Presidium of the USSR Supreme Soviet, "O vvedenii voennogo polozheniia na vsekh zheleznykh dorogakh," April 15, 1943, and "O vvedenii voennogo polozheniia na morskom i rechnom transporte," May 9, 1943. These laws provided for prosecution under Article 193[7] of the Criminal Code of the RSFSR, which governed military crimes, and the corresponding articles of the criminal codes of the other Soviet republics. Here, too, offenders were tried by military tribunals. See http://www.libussr.ru/doc_ussr/ussr_4418.htm (railways), and http://www.consultant.ru/cons/cgi/online.cgi?req=doc&base=ES U&n=37149#009695205449909161 (water transport). See also Zemskov, "Ukaz ot 26 iiunia 1940 goda," p. 46.

17. After their repeal, job-changing remained illegal, but came under the milder Edict of June 26, 1940. The latter remained in force until Nikita Khrushchev repealed it in April 1956, soon after his Secret Speech, although it was seldom applied after Stalin's death. See Edict of the Presidium of the USSR Supreme Soviet, April 25, 1956, "Ob otmene sudebnoi otvetstvennosti rabochikh i sluzhashchikh za samovol'nyi ukhod s predpriiatii i iz uchrezhdenii i za progul bez uvazhitel'noi prichiny," *Vedomosti Verkhovnogo Soveta SSSR*, 1956, no. 10, art. 203.

18. In 1945 industry, construction, transport, and services employed 27,263,000 people: Mark Harrison, *Accounting for War: Soviet Production, Employment, and the Defence Burden, 1940–1945* (Cambridge: Cambridge University Press, 1996), p. 272.

19. Decree of Soviet of People's Commissars of the USSR, October 18, 1942, "O poriadke snabzheniia prodovol'stvennymi i promyshlennymi tovarami rabochikh promyshlennykh predpriiatii," in A. R. Dzeniskevich, ed., *Leningrad v osade. Sbornik dokumentov o geroicheskoi oborone Leningrada v gody Velikoi Otechestvennoi voiny, 1941–1944* (St. Petersburg: Liki Rossii, 1995), pp. 244–5.

20. It is impossible to make a more precise calculation here because we do not know how many workers were employed in all the enterprises subject to the December 1941 Edict. Sectors and individual factories were constantly being added to the list, and not all those convicted were workers. In 1944 the 26 defense and defense-related commissariats tracked by the TsSU employed around 5.4 million workers. If we take this as the denominator, 1 out of every 7.7 workers was convicted of labor "desertion." However, figures from the aviation industry in 1943 showed that its factories employed nearly 60 percent more workers than Gosplan officially recorded. These workers were not idle: they worked on construction, growing food, in small workshops, in provisioning, and other jobs outside factories' plans. They received wages and rations, but neither Gosplan nor the Aviation Commissariat had any idea what they did. If this was typical of industry as a whole, it would imply that "only" 1 out of every 13.3 workers was convicted

of labor desertion. This is still a daunting statistic. See RGAE, f. 1562, op. 329, d. 960, ll. 101–102.

21. GARF, f. 9492, op. 6, d. 14, l. 10.

22. The figures for 1943 and 1944 are from GARF, f. 8131, op. 37, d. 1844, l. 110. The document only gives figures through November 1944, broken down by quarter. To arrive at an annual figure of 801,355, we extrapolated a figure for December from the October–November total of 86,580. We should make one qualification here, however. An unknown number of workers "deserted" more than once, that is, they fled from one enterprise, took up a job somewhere else, perhaps even under an assumed name, and then fled again. Therefore, if there were 1,334,246 "desertions" during 1943–1944, the number of actual "deserters" was somewhat lower, although there is no way to determine by how much.

23. GARF, f. 8131, op. 37, d. 1842, ll. 1–2.

24. There is good reason to suspect that the "capture rate" fell well below 40 percent from mid-1944 onward. Had it remained stable, when the war ended in 1945 Gulag camps should have held around 384,000 labor deserters (40 percent of 960,897 convictions; see Table 7.1). The historian V. N. Zemskov notes that the July 1945 amnesty of Gulag prisoners, declared in honor of victory over Nazi Germany, freed 221,719 people sentenced under the anti-quitting laws for defense workers. Sentences for labor desertion were long, and any labor deserter sent to the Gulag at any time during the war was likely still to be serving their sentence in July 1945. Thus the number freed can be seen as a proxy for those convicted who were actually caught and imprisoned. Even allowing for prisoners who may have died or been given early release and thus were no longer in the camps at the time of the amnesty, this still leaves a very large discrepancy between those receiving clemency and the number of prisoners implied by the Procuracy. See V. N. Zemskov, "Organizatsiia rabochei sily i uzhestochenie trudovoi zakonodatel'stva v gody voiny s fashistskoi germaniei," *Politicheskoe prosveshchenie*, No. 2 (79), 2014, p. 9, accessed at http://www.politpros.com/journal/read/?ID=3167&journal=160&sphrase_id=12205.

25. It is in the nature of Soviet statistics that we have to work with figures drawn from a range of different reports that do not necessarily cover the exact same time frame. This is the case here. Our data for total convictions cover the full twenty-four months of 1943 and 1944; our figures for referred cases of alleged labor "desertion" cover only twenty-three months, from January 1943 through November 1944. Here our figures for the number of cases accepted and rejected cover the twenty-six months from January 1, 1942 to March 1, 1944.

26. GARF, f. 8131, op. 37, d. 1842, ll. 1–2.

27. GARF, f. 8131, op. 37, d. 1436, ll. 1, 2.

28. Solomon, *Soviet Criminal Justice under Stalin*, pp. 298–325. See also Filtzer, *Soviet Workers and Stalinist Industrialization*, pp. 236–52.

29. GARF, f. 8131, op. 37, d. 1440, ll. 5–7.

30. RGASPI, f. M-1, op. 8, d. 157, l. 85.

31. RGASPI, f. M-1, op. 8, d. 155, ll. 21, 137.

32. GARF, f. 8131, op. 37, d. 1620, ll. 20–22ob.

33. GARF, f. 8131, op. 37, d. 1219, ll. 9, 9ob.

34. GARF, f. 8131, op. 37, d. 1219, ll. 10–10ob.; d. 1436, l. 251.

35. Roughly 70 percent of the intake into the Labor Reserve schools during 1942–1944 was from the countryside: GARF, f. 9507, op. 2, d. 418, l. 1.

36. Olga Kucherenko, *Soviet Street Children and the Second World War: Welfare and Social Control under Stalin* (London: Bloomsbury, 2016), pp. 100–1.

37. GARF, f. 8131, op. 37, d. 1482, l. 269.

38. GARF, f. 9507, op. 1, d. 218, ll. 1–2; op. 2, d. 418, l. 1.

39. GARF, f. 9507, op. 1, d. 51, l. 219.

40. GARF, f. 8131, op. 37, d. 1481, ll. 1, 1ob.

41. S. S. Vilenskii, A. I. Kokurin, G. V. Atmashkina, and Iu. I. Novichenko, *Deti GULAGa. 1918–1956* (Moscow: Mezhdunarodnyi fond "Demokratiia," 2002), pp. 392–3; Kucherenko, *Soviet Street Children and the Second World War*, p. 102. On the origin of the juvenile corrective labor colonies, see Wendy Z. Goldman, *Women, the State, and Revolution: Soviet Family Policy and Social Life, 1917–1936* (New York: Cambridge University Press, 1993), pp. 304–27.

42. RGASPI, f. 17, op. 126, d. 39, l. 46. We are grateful to Catriona Kelly for providing us with these figures.

43. GARF, f. 8131, op. 37, d. 1481, ll. 20ob., 40, 70.

44. GARF, f. 8131, op. 37, d. 1481, ll. 71, 129.

45. GARF, f. 8131, op. 37, d. 1481, ll. 2, 129ob.

46. R. P. Sosnovskaia, *Geroicheskii trud vo imia pobedy* (Leningrad: Izdatel'stvo Leningradskogo Universiteta, 1973), pp. 126, 109–11.

47. GARF, f. 9507, op. 1, d. 218, ll. 1–2; op. 2, d. 418, l. 1. In 1944 "net" flight from the schools, that is, those who ran away illegally less the number apprehended and brought back to the schools was just 8.6 percent in the FZO, 5.3 percent in RU and ZhU, and 6.9 percent for all schools taken together. See GARF, f. 9507, op. 2, d. 446, l. 2.

48. Edict of the Presidium of the USSR Supreme Soviet, December 28, 1940, "Ob otvetstvennosti uchashchikhsia remeslennykh, zheleznodorozhnykh uchilishch i shkol FZO za narushenie distsipliny i za samovol'nyi ukhod iz uchilishcha (shkoly)," *Vedomosti Verkhovnogo Soveta SSSR*, No. 1 (116), January 5, 1941. The law was repealed in July 1951, when absenteeism was also decriminalized.

49. GARF, f. 9492, op. 6, d. 14, ll. 10, 16.

50. GARF, f. 8131, op. 37, d. 1481, ll. 41–41ob.

51. GARF, f. 9507, op. 1, d. 53, l. 20.

52. GARF, f. 9507, op. 1, d. 51, l. 226.

53. GARF, f. 5451, op. 43, d. 234a, l. 29.

54. GARF, f. 8131, op. 37, d. 1481, ll. 42, 42ob.

55. V. F. Zima, *Golod v SSSR 1946–1947 godov. Proiskhozhdenie i posledstviia* (Moscow: Institut Rossiiskoi Istorii RAN, 1996), p. 15.

56. RGASPI, f. 17, op. 125, d. 107, ll. 36–39.

57. This section is drawn from GARF, f. 8131, op. 37, d. 1219, ll. 143–159. The main documents are a handwritten letter from Litovskikh to P. Kudriavtsev, Deputy

Procurator of the USSR, dated November 23, 1943, ll. 143–145; a lengthy report from Litovskikh, dated 5 December 1943, addressed to Moskatov, head of the GUTR, with a copy to Kudriavtsev, ll. 149–155; an explanatory letter from Orlov, Dzerzhinskii district procurator, to Kudriavtsev, dated November 25, 1943, ll. 147–148; and various telegrams from Kudriavtsev, mainly to Orlov, scattered through the collection.

58. GARF, f. 5451, op. 26, d. 316, l. 22ob.

59. GARF, f. 8131, op. 37, d. 1844, ll. 108, 110.

60. In December 1942, the last date for which we have found comprehensive figures for the social composition of the workforce, workers and apprentices under the age of eighteen were 15.3 percent of production personnel in industry and construction: RGAE, f. 1562, op. 329, d. 570, l. 4; d. 571, l. 5. During January–June 1943 teenagers younger than eighteen were 30.5 percent of all those convicted of labor "desertion," and 28.1 percent of convictions during July–December. If anything, their importance declined further during the first half of 1944, when they made up 26.6 percent of convictions. In this same period, workers aged between eighteen and twenty-five were a further 38 percent. Only by combining the two categories could the authorities show that the overwhelming majority (64.6 percent) of labor deserters were "young." See GARF, f. 8131, op. 37, d. 1842, ll. 1, 148.

61. Iron and steel: RGAE, f. 8875, op. 46, d. 103, ll. 3, 16. See also the cases of the electrical industry (GARF, f. 8131, op. 37, d. 1844, l. 247) and the footwear industry (GARF, f. 5451, op. 26, d. 316, l. 47).

62. Ammunition industry: GARF, f. 7678, op. 13, d. 1842, ll. 201–204; armaments industry: GARF, f. 5451, op. 43, d. 293b, l. 92. Factories Nos. 63 (Nizhnii Tagil), 50 (Penza), and 259 (Zlatoust): GARF, f. 7678, op. 13, d. 83, ll. 42–43, 48–50; factory No. 557 (Moscow): GARF, f. 7678, op. 13, d. 1842, l. 201; factory No. 8, Sverdlovsk: GARF, f. 7678, op. 8, d. 415, ll. 17, 17ob.

63. GARF, f. 8131, op. 37, d. 1841, ll. 171, 186.

64. GARF, f. 8131, op. 37, d. 1841, l. 205 (labor desertion); GARF, f. A-482, op. 47, d. 2225, l. 182 (starvation).

65. GARF, f. 8131, op. 37, d. 1841, ll. 219–223.

66. GARF, f. A-482, op. 47, d. 2313, l. 147.

67. GARF, f. 8131, op. 37, d. 1844, ll. 22–23, 26, 46.

68. GARF, f. 8131, op. 37, d. 1837, ll. 200, 206.

69. RGAE, f. 8875, op. 46, d. 118, ll. 4, 6; GARF, f. 8131, op. 37, d. 1841, ll. 273, 291. For reasons that are hard to understand, labor desertion in the Stalinugol' trust around the city of Stalino (now Donetsk) was much lower than the rest of the Donbass—it was even marginally below the coal industry average, with just under one out of every five workers deserting. This was in sharp contrast to the postwar period. During January–September 1947, the famine year when labor desertion reached a postwar peak, Stalinugol' had the highest number of deserters of all the USSR's major coal combines: GARF, f. 8131, op. 37, d. 4041, l. 103.

70. Between 1946 and 1957 Rybinsk was renamed Shcherbakov.

71. GARF, f. 8131, op. 37, d. 1842, ll. 116–117; GARF, f. 5451, op. 43, d. 293b, ll. 220, 219.

72. Full text available at http://man-with-dogs.livejournal.com/559676.html.

73. GARF, f. 8131, op. 37, d. 1842, ll. 134–137.

74. GARF, f. 8131, op. 37, d. 1842, l. 231. See also Oleg V. Khlevniuk, "Deserters from the Labor Front: The Limits of Coercion in the Soviet War Economy," *Kritika: Explorations in Russian and Eurasian History*, vol. 20, no. 3 (Summer 2019), pp. 498–9.

75. GARF, f. 8131, op. 37, d. 1842, l. 116ob.

76. GARF, f. 8131, op. 37, d. 1842, l. 135.

77. GARF, f. 8131, op. 37, d. 1844, l. 112.

78. Between July and November 1944 the authorities in these regions apprehended 25,578 at-large convicted deserters, more than offset by the failure to locate 39,358 deserters newly convicted during this time. The figures show that in absentia trials were still taking place, despite being banned by the June decree. See GARF, f. 8131, op. 37, d. 1844, ll. 123, 124, 129; d. 1845, l. 30.

79. GARF, f. 8131, op. 37, d. 1842, ll. 71, 80–81. In Ukraine there were also quite practical reasons why it was necessary to curb the search for deserters. Procuracies could not draw up case documents because they had too few staff and paper was in desperately short supply (ll. 80–81, 87).

80. GARF, f. 8131, op. 37, d. 1842, ll. 95–96.

81. GARF, f. 8131, op. 37, d. 1841, l. 101. Counterexamples of show trials are on ll. 37, 45, 61.

82. The example here is from the Kamyshin mine administration, part of the coalfields in Stalingrad province, where two managers received three and four years "deprivation of freedom" respectively: GARF, f. 8131, op. 37, d. 1842, ll. 193–193ob.

83. GARF, f. 8131, op. 37, d. 1837, l. 292. The list of provinces over which deserters from Magnitogorsk were scattered was actually much longer than this. We have cited only the most important ones here.

84. GARF, f. 8131, op. 37, d. 1837, ll. 45–46, 102, 199, 211.

85. Edict of Presidium of the USSR Supreme Soviet, 30 December 1944, "Ob amnistii litsam samovol'no ushedshim s predpriiatii voennoi promyshlennosti i dobrovol'no vozvrativshimsia na eti predpriiatiia," in *Sbornik zakonov SSSR i ukazov Prezidiuma Verkhovnogo Soveta SSSR, 1938–1975*, vol. III (Moscow: Izvestiia Sovetov Deputatov Trudiashchikhsia SSSR, 1975), pp. 406–7.

86. Edict of the Presidium of the USSR Supreme Soviet, 7 July 1945, "Ob amnistii v sviazi s pobedoi nad gitlerovskoi Germaniei," in *Sbornik zakonov SSSR i ukazov Prezidiuma Verkhovnogo Soveta SSSR, 1938–1975*, vol. III, pp. 407–8. The amnesty applied to: anyone serving a sentence of three years or less; all those convicted under the Edict of December 26, 1941, irrespective of length of sentence; military personnel convicted under Article 28 of the RSFSR Criminal Code whose sentences had been temporarily suspended; and those convicted of violating a range of military regulations. People not in these categories serving sentences longer than three years were to have the time remaining on their sentences cut by half. Significantly, excluded from the amnesty were political prisoners, and anyone convicted of theft of socialist property under the law of August 7, 1932, "banditry," counterfeiting, or premeditated murder or assault.

Also excluded were those with repeated convictions for embezzlement, theft, robbery, or "hooliganism."

87. On postwar application of the labor desertion law, see Donald Filtzer, *Soviet Workers and Late Stalinism: Labour and the Restoration of the Stalinist System after World War II* (Cambridge: Cambridge University Press, 2002), ch. 5.

88. See n. 24 in this chapter.

89. GARF, f. 8131, op. 37, d. 1844, l. 110.

Chapter 8

Epigraph: RGASPI, f. M-1, op. 8, d. 236, l. 59.

1. Elena Skrjabina, *Siege and Survival: The Odyssey of a Leningrader* (Carbondale: Southern Illinois University Press, 1971), p. 96.

2. Typhus ravaged the armies of the eastern front during World War I and, together with an even worse epidemic during the Civil War, cost several million lives in Russia alone. Case fatality rates were high. See Paul Weindling, *Epidemics and Genocide in Eastern Europe, 1890–1945* (Oxford: Oxford University Press, 2000), p. 433; Hans Zinsser, *Rats, Lice and History* (New Brunswick: Transaction Publishers, 2008), p. 299.

3. On the measles epidemic, see Donald Filtzer, *The Hazards of Urban Life in Late Stalinist Russia: Health, Hygiene, and Living Standards, 1943–1953* (Cambridge: Cambridge University Press, 2010), pp. 277–81; and Ol'ga Nikolaevna Dodonova, "Kor' v SSSR, 1930–1943 god," Candidate of Medical Sciences dissertation, Moscow, 1945.

4. Mary M. Leder, *My Life in Stalinist Russia: An American Woman Looks Back* (Bloomington: Indiana University Press, 2001), p. 220.

5. RGAE, f. 1562, op. 33, d. 2638, ll. 82–83ob., available at http://istmat.info/files/uploads/38434/rgae_1562.33.2638_svedeniya_ob_umershih_po_vozrastam_i_polu_1933-1955.pdf.

6. GARF, f. 8009, op. 14, d. 241, ll. 89, 96, 99, 100, 129.

7. Infant mortality in the RSFSR in 1940 was 40 percent higher than infant mortality in England, France, and the Netherlands in 1901–1905: Filtzer, *Hazards*, p. 258. In 1939, urban areas of the USSR had 181 tuberculosis deaths per 100,000 population (causes of death in rural areas were not recorded), more than four times the rate in the United States (urban and rural). The US figure is not as straightforward as it seems. Among the white population there were 37.2 tuberculosis deaths per 100,000, but among the nonwhite population it was 191.9. Soviet mortality figures are derived from RGAE, f. 1562, op. 33, d. 2638, ll. 73, 82–84ob., 93–94ob., available at http://istmat.info/files/uploads/38434/rgae_1562.33.2638_svedeniya_ob_umershih_po_vozrastam_i_polu_1933-1955.pdf; and *Chislennost' naseleniia SSSR na 17 ianvaria 1939 g.* (Moscow: Gosplanizdat, 1941), p. 6, accessed at http://istmat.info/node/46314. United States data are from Forrest E. Linder and Robert D. Grove, *Vital Statistics Rates in the United States, 1900–1940* (Washington, D.C.: United States Government Printing Office, 1947), pp. 64, 238–42, 315, 550, 573, 936, and *Vital Statistics of the United States 1940, Part I: Natality and Mortality Data for the*

United States Tabulated by Place of Occurrence with Supplemental Tables for Hawaii, Puerto Rico, and the Virgin Islands (Washington, D.C.: United States Government Printing Office, 1941), pp. 21, 178. See also "Tuberculosis Mortality and Mortality Rate, England and Wales, 1913–2013," Public Health England publication, no date, no longer available online. On sanitary reform in North American and Western Europe, see Filtzer, *Hazards*, pp. 7–10.

8. On food shortages, see Elena Osokina, *Our Daily Bread: Socialist Distribution and the Art of Survival in Stalin's Russia, 1927–1941* (Armonk, N.Y.: M. E. Sharpe, 2001), pp. 166–77. On mortality, see RGAE, f. 1562, op. 33, d. 2638, ll. 82–82ob., available at http://istmat.info/files/uploads/38434/rgae_1562.33.2638_svedeniya_ob_umershih_po_vozrastam_i_polu_1933-1955.pdf.

9. GARF, f. A-482, op. 52s, d. 45, ll. 220, 221; op. 47, d. 448, ll. 42, 43; op. 47, d. 685, ll. 100, 101. On the closure of the tuberculosis network, see M. N. Preobrazhenskaia, "Bor'ba s tuberkulezom," prepared for the Scientific-Methodological Bureau of Sanitary Statistics, People's Commissariat of Health of the USSR and RSFSR, GARF, f. 8009, op. 6, d. 1875, ll. 6, 6ob., 7. On malaria, see RGAE, f. 1562, op. 18, d. 264, ll. 20, 21; d. 330, ll. 79–80, 82; GARF, f. A-482, op. 47, d. 2204, l. 37. On the number of civilian doctors, see GARF, f. 8009, op. 14, d. 241, ll. 86, 96; GARF, f. A-482, op. 47, d. 2030, l. 95. On the contraction of resources, see GARF, f. A-482, op. 47, d. 515, ll. 241, 243; d. 2032, ll. 49, 49ob.

10. RGAE, f. 1562, op. 20, d. 500, gives demographic data for all major towns and cities during 1941–1944. Here we cite, in order of mention, ll. 18, 80, 42, 25, 26.

11. GARF, f. A-374, op. 34, d. 1540, ll. 1, 29; RGAE, f. 1562, op. 20, d. 500, ll. 25, 26, 42, 61, 64, 98.

12. Filtzer, *Hazards*, pp. 277–8; Dodonova, "Kor' v SSSR," pp. 79–81, 86–7, 110.

13. Dodonova, "Kor' v SSSR," pp. 112–16; Filtzer, *Hazards*, pp. 279–81. The true number of deaths during the epidemic will never be known. Officially there were 86,600 deaths in urban areas during 1941 and 1942, but probably two-thirds of these were concentrated during July 1941–June 1942, when the number of cases and case fatality rates were at their highest. Dodonova ("Kor' v SSSR," p. 130) insisted that this was an underestimate, since during the second half of 1941 there was widespread underreporting and misdiagnosis. Since roughly half of all cases were in the countryside (GARF, f. A-482, op. 52s, d. 54, l. 105), where causes of death were not recorded and where medical services were especially poor, it seems safe to assume that at least the same number of deaths occurred in rural areas as in the towns.

14. GARF, f. A-374, op. 11, d. 28, ll. 11, 12. These are data for urban areas of the RSFSR in 1940.

15. Iu. F. Dombrovskaia, "Pnevmonii u distrofikov i rakhitikov," in *Trudy plenumov Soveta lechebno-profilakticheskoi pomoshchi detiam Ministerstva zdravookhraneniia SSSR i Ministerstva zdravookhraneniia RSFSR* (Moscow: Medgiz, 1948), p. 36.

16. A. I. Perevoshchikova, "Gipotrofii v iasliakh goroda Izhevska i bor'ba s nimi," Candidate of Medical Sciences dissertation, Izhevsk State Medical Institute, 1944, pp. 52–3.

17. GARF, f. A-482, op. 47, d. 440, l. 41.
18. GARF, f. A-482, op. 47, d. 539, ll. 6ob., 7 (Cheliabinsk province); GARF, f. 5451, op. 43, d. 234, l. 19 (Gor'kii province).
19. GARF, f. 8009, op. 21, d. 44, ll. 1–2ob., 3, 37.
20. GARF, f. A-482, op. 47, d. 1247, l. 19.
21. Shipyard workers in Arkhangel'sk adopted the practice when their dependants lost their rations of nonbread foodstuffs in September 1942, as did workers in Sverdlovsk province in mid-1944. See GARF, f. 5451, op. 43, d. 132b, l. 17 (Arkhangel'sk); GARF, f. A-482, op. 52s, d. 82, l. 310 (Sverdlovsk province); RGAE, f. 1884, op. 31, d. 7199, ll. 20–21 (Perm' railway).
22. Filtzer, *Hazards*, p. 235; David Ransel, *Village Mothers: Three Generations of Change in Russia and Tataria* (Bloomington: Indiana University Press, 2005), pp. 35–6.
23. Leder, *My Life in Stalinist Russia*, p. 220.
24. GARF, f. A-482, op. 47, d. 529, ll. 70–92.
25. On "malted milk," see GARF, f. 8009, op. 21, d. 44, ll. 18ob., 35, 36ob. The Central Scientific Pediatric Research Institute of the Commissariat of Public Health of the USSR worked out detailed instructions on how to make "yeast milk" in October 1943, and it became available shortly thereafter: GARF, f. A-482, op. 47, d. 2136, ll. 170–172.
26. GARF, f. A-482, op. 47, d. 1263, ll. 123–125.
27. GARF, f. A-482, op. 47, d. 515, l. 115ob.
28. GARF, f. A-482, op. 47, d. 44, ll. 18–18ob. For similar accounts in other towns, see ll. 35–36ob.
29. GARF, f. A-482, op. 47, d. 1300, l. 62.
30. GARF, f. A-482, op. 47, d. 1250, l. 25ob.
31. GARF, f. 5451, op. 43, d. 210, l. 447.
32. GARF, f. 5451, op. 43, d. 234, ll. 47, 46; d. 192, ll. 65–46, 87, 83 (both files numbered back to front).
33. Perevoshchikova, "Gipotrofii," pp. 40–79, 87, 103, 109–45.
34. GARF, f. A-482, op. 47, d. 2063, ll. 32ob.–21ob. (file numbered back to front).
35. A. A. Dormidontov, "Osnovnye napravleniia po bor'be s rakhitom v usloviiakh severnogo Urala," *Pediatriia*, no. 3, 1945, pp. 38–41; M. I. Dement'ev, "K voprosu o rakhite v voennoe vremia," *Pediatriia*, no. 3, 1945, pp. 47–8; S. O. Dulitskii, "Rakhit voennogo vremeni," *Pediatriia*, no. 3, 1945, pp. 41–7. The lack of vitamin C in the diet was serious enough, but scurvy during the war, which in extreme cases could be fatal, was mainly a disease of older children and adults: GARF, f. 5451, op. 43, d. 236, ll. 9, 10, 11.
36. GARF, f. A-374, op. 11, d. 222, ll. 2–2ob., 3–3ob. These figures are for urban areas of the RSFSR and exclude Bashkiriia, Orel province, and Stavropol' Territory.
37. GARF, f. A-482, op. 47, d. 573, ll. 2ob., 3, 10, 19, 20, 52.
38. GARF, f. A-482, op. 47, d. 1983, l. 174.
39. Christopher Burton, "Medical Welfare during Late Stalinism: A Study of Doctors and the Soviet Health System, 1945–1953," Ph.D. dissertation, University of Chicago, 2000, pp. 33–8, 264–9.

40. GARF, f. 5451, op. 43, d. 228, l. 163; Mark Harrison, *Accounting for War: Soviet Production, Employment, and the Defence Burden, 1940–1945* (Cambridge: Cambridge University Press, 1996), p. 272.

41. Donald Filtzer, *Soviet Workers and Stalinist Industrialization: The Formation of Modern Soviet Production Relations, 1928–1941* (London: Pluto Press, 1986), pp. 100, 193, 303–4 n. 66.

42. RGAE, f. 8848, op. 15, d. 2361, ll. 33, 34, 34ob.

43. GARF, f. 9226, op. 1, d. 693, ll. 151, 179, 180.

44. *Sbornik ofitsial'nykh materialov po sanprosvetrabote. Spravochnik sanprosvetrabotnika* (Moscow, 1944), pp. 91–102; L. P. Zabolotskaia and I. S. Sokolov, "Sanitarnoe prosveshchenie v gody Velikoi Otechestvennoi voiny (po materialam 1 Ob"edinennogo plenuma Sovetov po sanitarnomu prosveshcheniiu Narkomzdrava SSSR i Narkomzdrava RSFSR, iiul' 1944 g.)," in *Sanitarnoe prosveshchenie. Sbornik posviashchennyi voprosam sanitarnogo prosveshcheniia v gody Velikoi Otechestvennoi voiny* (Moscow, 1948), p. 44.

45. GARF, f. 5451, op. 43, d. 189, l. 52 (October 1942); RGAE, f. 1562, op. 329, d. 1125, l. 30 (June 1941). The data are from large-scale surveys carried out in the months in question. We have extrapolated annual rates from the monthly figures.

46. RGAE, f. 1562, op. 18, d. 265, ll. 3–6, 8–9; d. 278, ll. 14–18; d. 301, ll. 2, 4–6, 9–11, 15.

47. Edict of the Presidium of the USSR Supreme Soviet, June 26, 1941, "O rezhime rabochego vremeni rabochikh i sluzhashchikh v voennoe vremia," available at http://www.libussr.ru/doc_ussr/ussr_4322.htm.

48. GARF, f. 7678, op. 15, d. 31, l. 1.

49. RGAE, f. 1562, op. 18, d. 265, ll. 3–6, 8–9; d. 278, ll. 14–18; d. 301, ll. 2, 4–6, 9–11, 15.

50. GARF, f. A-482, op. 47, d. 2204, l. 37 (GAZ); d. 2202, l. 16 (Stankozavod). See also GARF, f. A-482, op. 52s, d. 80, l. 90 (Kuibyshev defense factories); op. 47, d. 515, l. 21ob. (factory No. 19 in Molotov). There were, of course, exceptions. At the large iron and steel combine at Magnitogorsk, part of an industry where serious skin infections were the rule, days lost to skin infections were a fifth of the industry average in 1943 and less than one-tenth in 1944: GARF, f. A-482, op. 47, d. 2210, l. 52.

51. GARF, f. A-482, op. 52s, d. 43, ll. 262ob.–263; d. 45, l. 110.

52. References are too numerous to list in their entirety. For indicative examples, see GARF, f. A-482, op. 47, d. 1351, ll. 145, 163; d. 617, l. 140.

53. GARF, f. A-482, op. 47, d. 1346, l. 63.

54. GARF, f. A-482, op. 52s, d. 43, l. 262ob.; d. 81, ll. 181ob., 182, 183.

55. Catherine J. Field, Ian R. Johnson, and Patricia D. Schley, "Nutrients and Their Role in Host Resistance to Infection," *Journal of Leukocyte Biology*, vol. 71 (January 2002), pp. 25–6; Ananda S. Prasad, "Zinc Deficiency Has Been Known of for 40 Years But Ignored by Global Health Organizations," *British Medical Journal*, vol. 326, 22 February 2003, pp. 409–10, available at http://www.ncbi.nlm.nih.gov/pmc/articles/PMC1125304/.

56. RGAE, f. 1562, op. 18, d. 265, ll. 2, 3, 5, 6, 8–10; d. 278, ll. 14–15ob., 16ob., 17, 18; d. 301, ll. 2, 4, 6, 7, 9, 11, 15.

57. For the Kuzbass, accidents per worker are from GARF, f. 5451, op. 27, d. 22, l. 38; fatalities are from GARF, f. 7416, op. 4, d. 14, l. 11. For basic chemicals: GARF, f. 5451, op. 27, d. 21, l. 156; Gor'kii Motor Vehicle Factory: GARF, f. A-482, op. 47, d. 617, l. 143 (the GAZ figures are for January–April 1942 compared to January–April 1941).

58. GARF, f. A-482, op. 52s, d. 82, ll. 78, 78ob.; op. 47, d. 1221, l. 11. The shortage of light bulbs proved a long-term problem, extending well into the postwar period. See Donald Filtzer, *Soviet Workers and Late Stalinism: Labour and the Restoration of the Stalinist System after World War II* (Cambridge: Cambridge University Press, 2002), p. 211.

59. RGASPI, f. 17, op. 88, d. 351, ll. 27–28.

60. GARF, f. 8131, op. 37, d. 1219, ll. 124, 125.

61. GARF, f. A-482, op. 47, d. 1351, ll. 19, 22–24.

62. GARF, f. A-482, op. 52s, d. 79, ll. 209ob., 210.

63. GARF, f. 9226, op. 1, d. 693, l. 180.

64. GARF, f. 9226, op. 1, d. 693, l. 230.

65. *Sbornik ofitsial'nykh materialov* (1944), p. 96.

66. For an example of especially serious exposure to both lead and asbestos dust, see factory No. 575 in Sverdlovsk province: GARF, f. 9226, op. 1, d. 693, ll. 224–225.

67. GARF, f. A-482, op. 52s, d. 44, ll. 22, 74, 75, 77, 79.

68. GARF, f. A-482, op. 52s, d. 43, ll. 114ob.–115ob.

69. The discussion here and in the next paragraph is based on Donald Filtzer, "Factory Medicine in the Soviet Defense Industry during World War II," in Susan Grant, ed., *Soviet Healthcare from an International Perspective: Comparing Professions, Practice and Gender, 1880–1960* (London: Palgrave Macmillan, 2017), pp. 80–91. The campaign was modeled on a similar initiative launched in December 1938: Filtzer, *Soviet Workers and Stalinist Industrialization*, p. 239.

70. GARF, f. A-482, op. 52s, d. 44, ll. 23ob.–24.

71. GARF, f. 5451, op. 43, d. 210, l. 450; GARF, f. A-482, op. 47, d. 515, l. 100, and d. 620, ll. 235, 237, 241; *Meditsinskii rabotnik*, July 3, 1942.

72. RGAE, f. 1562, op. 329, d. 1125, l. 30.

73. GARF, f. A-482, op. 47, d. 2025, l. 43; d. 2218, ll. 225–226.

74. Wendy Z. Goldman, *Women at the Gates: Gender and Industry in Stalin's Russia* (New York: Cambridge University Press, 2002), pp. 194–202; Filtzer, *Soviet Workers and Stalinist Industrialization*, p. 64.

75. RGAE, f. 1562, op. 329, d. 571, ll. 5, 7–10, 12, 15–17, 20, 22, 25, 28, 29, 31, 32, 54. Specifically, women were 39 percent of workers in iron and steel; 43 percent in nonferrous metals; 41 percent in shipbuilding; 29 percent in tanks; 38 percent in aviation; and 25 percent in coalmining.

76. RGAE, f. 1562, op. 329, d. 572, ll. 3, 4, 136. This pattern of female employment did not fundamentally change after the war but persisted until the end of the Soviet Union. See Donald Filtzer, *Soviet Workers and De-Stalinization: The Consolidation of the Modern System of Soviet Production Relations, 1953–1964* (Cambridge: Cambridge University Press, 1992), ch. 7, and *Soviet Workers and the Collapse of Perestroika: The*

Soviet Labour Process and Gorbachev's Reforms, 1985–1991 (Cambridge: Cambridge University Press, 1994), pp. 163–80.

77. GARF, f. 7678, op. 7, d. 133, ll. 9–11; GARF, f. 8009, op. 6, d. 1920, l. 57.

78. On derogation of women who were at the front, see Svetlana Alexievich, *The Unwomanly Face of War: An Oral History of Women in World War II* (New York: Random House, 2018), p. 219. On the 1944 law, see Mie Nakachi, "Population, Politics, and Reproduction: Late Stalinism and Its Legacy," in Juliane Fürst, ed., *Late Stalinist Russia: Society between Reconstruction and Reinvention* (London: Routledge, 2006, pp. 23–45. The text of the law itself can be found at https://www.lawmix.ru/docs_cccp/3096; original source, *Vedomosti Verkhovnogo Soveta SSSR*, 1944, No. 37. On the so-called bachelor tax, see Kristy Ironside, "Between Fiscal, Ideological, and Social Dilemmas: The Soviet 'Bachelor Tax' and Post-War Tax Reform, 1941–1962," *Europe–Asia Studies*, vol. 69, no. 6 (August 2017), pp. 855–78.

79. GARF, f. A-482, op. 47, d. 2203, ll. 17–27; op. 52s, d. 125, ll. 17–17ob.; GARF, f. 8009, op. 6, d. 1920, l. 57; GARF, f. 7678, op. 15, d. 74, ll. 5ob., 6, 7ob. On Magnitogorsk, see GARF, f. A-482, op. 47, d. 2210, ll. 14, 15.

80. Filtzer, *Hazards*, pp. 13–17, 391 n. 92.

81. GARF, f. 8009, op. 14, d. 241, l. 86; Burton, "Medical Welfare," p. 65.

82. RGAE, f. 1562, op. 33, d. 2638, ll. 83–83ob., 93–4, available at http://istmat.info/files/uploads/38434/rgae_1562.33.2638_svedeniya_ob_umershih_po_vozrastam_i_polu_1933-1955.pdf.

83. V. A. Isupov, *Demograficheskie katastrofy i krizisy v Rossii v pervoi polovine XX veka. Istoriko-demograficheskie ocherki* (Novosibirsk: Sibirskii khronograf, 2000), p. 161.

84. Population figures are from RGAE, f. 1562, op. 20, d. 484, ll. 32–38. Deaths are from Donald Filtzer, "Starvation Mortality in Soviet Home Front Industrial Regions during World War II," in Wendy Z. Goldman and Donald Filtzer, eds., *Hunger and War: Food Provisioning in the Soviet Union during World War II* (Bloomington: Indiana University Press, 2015), pp. 286–96 and Appendix B (pp. 336–8).

85. Gillian Cronjé, "Tuberculosis and Mortality Decline in England and Wales, 1851–1910," in Robert Woods and John Woodward, eds., *Urban Disease and Mortality in Nineteenth-Century England* (London: Batsford Academic and Educational, 1984), pp. 81–2.

86. I. A. Shaklein, "O likvidatsii sanitarnikh posledstvii otechestvennoi voiny v oblasti tuberkuleza," in *Materialy nauchnoi sessii Sverdlovskogo oblastnogo Nauchno-issledovatel'skogo tuberkuleznogo instituta po voprosam epidemiologii i kliniki tuberkuleza i organizatsii bor'by s nim* (Sverdlovsk: Sverdlovskii Oblastnoi Nauchno-Issledovatel'skii Tuberkuleznyi Institut, 1948), p. 4.

87. GARF, f. 8009, op. 6, d. 1875, ll. 6–7.

88. Ancel Keys, Josef Brožek, Austin Henschel, Olaf Mickelsen, Henry Longstreet Taylor, et al., *The Biology of Human Starvation* (Minneapolis: University of Minnesota Press, 1950), pp. 1017–21; Myron Winick, ed., *Hunger Disease: Studies by the Jewish Physicians in the Warsaw Ghetto*, trans. from Polish by Martha Osnos (New York: John Wiley & Sons, 1979), pp. 21–2; Josef Brožek, Samuel Wells, and Ancel Keys, "Medical Aspects of Semistarvation in Leningrad (Siege 1941–1942), *American Review of*

Soviet Medicine, vol. 4, no. 1 (October 1946), p. 81. For a detailed discussion of the pioneering work of Leningrad doctors in studying the etiology and treatment of starvation, see Rebecca Manley, "Nutritional Dystrophy: The Science and Semantics of Starvation in World War II," in Goldman and Filtzer, eds., *Hunger and War*, pp. 206–64.

89. J. P. Cegielski and D. N. McMurray, "The Relationship between Malnutrition and Tuberculosis: Evidence from Studies in Humans and Experimental Animals," *International Journal of Tuberculosis and Lung Disease*, vol. 8, no. 3 (2004), pp. 287–8.

90. Despite an official order that local statistical offices were to conceal starvation deaths on cause-of-death returns, a careful examination of these returns shows that it is possible to make accurate assessments of how many people died of starvation, at least in urban areas (causes of death in rural areas were not recorded). For the methodology used, see Filtzer, "Starvation Mortality," pp. 272–7.

91. RGAE, f. 1562, op. 33, d. 2638, ll. 93–94ob., available at http://istmat.info/files/uploads/38434/rgae_1562.33.2638_svedeniya_ob_umershih_po_vozrastam_i_polu_1933-1955.pdf.

92. Filtzer, "Starvation Mortality," p. 298.

93. GARF, f. A-374, op. 11, d. 222, l. 2ob. The data are for the urban RSFSR and exclude Bashkiriia, Orel province, and Stavropol' Territory.

94. GARF, f. 8131, op. 37, d. 1436, ll. 48, 48ob.

95. GARF, f. 7678, op. 13, d. 57, l. 26.

96. Filtzer, "Starvation Mortality," pp. 318–20.

97. GARF, f. A-482, op. 52s, d. 82, l. 130.

98. GARF, f. A-482, op. 52s, d. 82, l. 130.

99. GARF, f. 7678, op. 15, d. 54, l. 26.

100. GARF, f. 5451, op. 43, d. 301, ll. 15, 41–42, 42ob., 49.

101. Filtzer, "Starvation Mortality," pp. 318–20.

102. GARF, f. A-482, op. 47, d. 2030, l. 73ob.

103. GARF, f. 5451, op. 43, d. 187, l. 131; d. 236, ll. 116, 117; GARF, f. 7678, op. 7, d. 215, ll. 3, 4, and op. 8, d. 243, l. 67.

104. GARF, f. 7678, op. 13, d. 57, l. 19ob.

105. "In these circumstances, paraphrasing M. Weber, workers were confronted by the question, not how much they needed to work in order to earn more, but whether the bonuses would compensate for the energy expended on this work, given the widespread starvation and emaciation of Urals workers": Larisa Ianovna Lonchinskaia, "Massovoe soznanie naseleniia ural'skikh oblastei v gody Velikoi Otechestvennoi voiny," Candidate of Historical Sciences dissertation, Cheliabinsk, 2002, p. 217.

106. GARF, f. 5451, op. 43, d. 188, l. 219.

107. GARF, f. 7678, op. 13, d. 41, ll. 13, 15ob., 16, 126.

108. Vera Valer'evna Solov'eva, "Bytovye usloviia personala promyshlennykh predpriiatii Urala v 1941–1945 gg. Gosudarstvennaia politika i strategii adaptatsii," Candidate of Historical Sciences dissertation, Ekaterinburg, 2011, p. 146. For a detailed account of wartime deductions, see two articles by Kristy Ironside, "Rubles for Victory: The Social Dynamics of State Fundraising on the Soviet Home Front,"

Kritika: Explorations in Russian and Eurasian History, vol. 15, no. 4 (Fall 2014), pp. 799–828, and "Between Fiscal, Ideological, and Social Dilemmas."

109. GARF, f. 7678, op. 13, d. 41, ll. 70, 74.
110. Lonchinskaia, "Massovoe soznanie," p. 171.
111. For wages, see RGAE, f. 1562, op. 329, d. 960, ll. 57–58 (both with ob.), 59; for women workers, see RGAE, f. 1562, op. 329, d. 571, l. 28.
112. GARF, f. 5451, op. 43, d. 236, ll. 85, 85ob., 97.
113. Manley, "Nutritional Dystrophy," pp. 216–35.
114. Manley, "Nutritional Dystrophy," pp. 230–3, 245–7, 249–51; M. I. Slonim, "Alimentarnaia distrofiia v usloviiakh voennogo vremeni," in M. I. Slonim, *Izbrannye raboty* (Tashkent: Izdatel'stvo AN UzSSR, 1949), pp. 35–45.
115. Filtzer, "Starvation Mortality," pp. 321–3.
116. Ashraf Khodzhaev, "Funktsiia zheludki pri alimentarnoi distrofii," Candidate of Medical Sciences dissertation, Tashkent, 1946, pp. 50–8; RGAE, f. 1562, op. 33, d. 2638, ll. 92ob., 94ob., available at http://istmat.info/files/uploads/38434/rgae_1562.33.2638_svedeniya_ob_umershih_po_vozrastam_i_polu_1933-1955.pdf.
117. Filtzer, "Starvation Mortality," pp. 324–9, 333–5.
118. Richard Overy, *Why the Allies Won* (New York and London: W. W. Norton and Co., 1995), pp. 4–5, 19, 182–4; Mark Harrison, "Industry and Economy," in David Stone, ed., *The Soviet Union at War, 1941–1945* (Barnsley, UK: Pen and Sword, 2010), p. 26.
119. Filtzer, *Hazards*, pp. 315–20.

Chapter 9

Epigraph: Quoted in A. S. Seniavskii and E. S. Seniavskaia, "Ideologiia voiny i psikhologiia naroda," in A. N. Sakharov and A. S. Seniavskii, eds., *Narod i voina. Ocherki istorii Velikoi Otechestvennoi voiny 1941–1945 gg.* (Moscow: Institut Rossiiskoi Istorii RAN, 2010), p. 148.

1. See http://www.dictionary.com/browse/propaganda; https://en.wikipedia.org/wiki/Propaganda#Etymology. "Propaganda" is commonly defined as "information, ideas, or rumors deliberately spread widely to help or harm a person, group, movement, institution, or nation." Derived from the Latin, *propagare*, meaning to spread or disseminate, it had its origin in a body created by the Catholic Church in 1622, Congregatio de Propaganda Fide (Congregation for Propagating the Faith). With the rise of literacy and mass media in the twentieth century, the word took on a pejorative connotation.

2. Quotes respectively from Richard Overy, *Why the Allies Won* (New York and London: W. W. Norton and Co., 1995), p. 22, and Oleg Budnitskii, "The Great Patriotic War and Soviet Society: Defeatism, 1941–1942," *Kritika: Explorations in Russian and Eurasian History*, vol. 15, no. 4 (Fall 2014), p. 781. On support, see also Gennadi Bordiugov, "The Popular Mood in the Unoccupied Soviet Union: Continuity and Change during the War," and Mikhail Gorinov, "Muscovites' Moods 22 June 1941 to May 1942," in Robert W. Thurston and Bernd

Bonwetsch, eds., *The People's War: Responses to World War II in the Soviet Union* (Urbana: University of Illinois Press, 2000), pp. 54–70, 108–36.

3. Jean Levesque, "A Peasant Ordeal: The Soviet Countryside," in David Stone, ed., *The Soviet Union at War, 1941–1945* (Barnsley, UK: Pen and Sword Books, 2010), pp. 182–214. On peasant responses to occupation, see Johannes Due Enstad, *Soviet Russians under Nazi Occupation: Fragile Loyalties in World War II* (Cambridge: Cambridge University Press, 2018); Karel C. Berkhoff, *Harvest of Despair: Life and Death in Ukraine under Nazi Rule* (Cambridge, Mass.: Belknap Press of Harvard University, 2004), esp. chs. 1 and 3, and pp. 285–300; Laurie R. Cohen, *Smolensk under the Nazis: Everyday Life in Occupied Russia* (Rochester, N.Y.: University of Rochester Press, 2013). On motivations, see special issue of *Slavic Review*, vol. 75, no. 3 (Fall 2016), including Michael David-Fox, "The People's War: Ordinary People and Regime Strategies in a World of Extremes," pp. 551–9; Seth Bernstein, "Rural Russia on the Edges of Authority: *Bezvlastie* in Wartime Riazan', November–December 1941," pp. 560–82; Jared McBride, "Peasants into Perpetrators: The OUN-UPA and the Ethnic Cleansing of Volhynia, 1943–1944," pp. 630–54; Amir Weiner, *Making Sense of War: The Second World War and the Fate of the Bolshevik Revolution* (Princeton: Princeton University Press, 2001); Alexander Statiev, *The Soviet Counterinsurgency in the Western Borderlands* (New York: Cambridge University Press, 2010).

4. Quote from Seniavskii and Seniavskaia, "Ideologiia voiny i psikhologiia naroda," p. 148. David Brandenburger, *National Bolshevism: Stalinist Mass Culture and the Formation of Modern Russian National Identity, 1931–1956* (Cambridge, Mass.: Harvard University Press, 2002) and *Propaganda State in Crisis: Soviet Ideology, Indoctrination, and Terror under Stalin, 1927–1941* (New Haven: Yale University Press, 2012), argues that the state turned to Russian heroes in creating a common Soviet identity because the Terror had destroyed the Party's ability to tell a coherent story about its past. On a more inclusive Soviet patriotism, see Jonathan Brunstedt, "Building a Pan-Soviet Past: The Soviet War Cult and the Turn Away from Ethnic Particularism," *Soviet and Post-Soviet Review*, vol. 38 (2011), pp. 149–71, and Jeremy Smith, "Non-Russian Nationalities," in Stone, ed., *The Soviet Union at War*, pp. 215–37. See also Serhy Yekelchyk, "Stalinist Patriotism as Imperial Discourse: Reconciling the Ukrainian and Russian 'Heroic Pasts,' 1939–1945," *Kritika: Explorations in Russian and Eurasian History*, vol. 3, no. 1 (Winter 2002), pp. 51–80, on non-Russian martial traditions in the republics.

5. See, for example, Andrei Dzeniskevich, "The Social and Political Situation in Leningrad during the First Months of the German Invasion: The Psychology of the Workers," in Thurston and Bonwetsch, eds., *The People's War*, pp. 71–83; Roger D. Markwick and Euridice Charon Cardona, *Soviet Women on the Front Line in the Second World War* (New York: Palgrave Macmillan, 2012), pp. 1–6.

6. On wartime propaganda as effective, see Richard Bidlack, "Propaganda and Public Opinion," in Stone, ed., *The Soviet Union at War*, pp. 65–6; N. D. Kozlov, *Obshchestvennoe soznanie v gody Velikoi Otechestvennoi voiny* (St. Petersburg: Leningradskii Oblastnoi Institut Usovershenstvovaniia Uchitelei, 1995); V. F. Zima, *Mentalitet narodov Rossii v voine 1941–1945 godov* (Moscow: Institut Rossiiskoi Istorii RAN, 2000). Richard Stites, "Russia's Holy War," and Jeffrey Brooks, "*Pravda* Goes to War," in Richard Stites, ed., *Culture and Entertainment in Wartime Russia* (Bloomington: Indiana University Press,

1995), pp. 1–8, 9–27, argue that propaganda drew effectively on "deep wells of national pride and emotional themes." See also Lisa Kirschenbaum, "'Our City, Our Hearths, Our Families': Local Loyalties and Private Life in Soviet World War II Propaganda," *Slavic Review*, vol. 59, no. 4 (Winter 2000), pp. 825–47. Karel Berkhoff, *Motherland in Danger: Soviet Propaganda during World War II* (Cambridge, Mass.: Harvard University Press, 2012), pp. 29–67, 85–97, 115, 191–2, 276–7, and Richard Brody, "Ideology and Political Mobilization: The Soviet Home Front during World War II," *Carl Beck Papers in Russian and East European Studies*, no. 1104, October 1994, argue that dogmatism, shortages of transport, fuel, electricity, paper, and personnel, and inadequate radio links reduced the efficacy of propaganda.

7. R. P. Sosnovskaia, *Geroicheskii trud vo imia pobedy* (Leningrad: Izdatel'stvo Leningradskogo Universiteta, 1973), p. 113.

8. Vasily Grossman, *A Writer at War: A Soviet Journalist with the Red Army, 1941–1945*, ed. and trans. by Antony Beevor and Luba Vinogradova (New York: Vintage Books, 2007), pp. 259–61; John Garrard and Carol Garrard, *The Bones of Berdichev: The Life and Fate of Vasily Grossman* (New York: Free Press, 1996); David Shneer, *Through Soviet Jewish Eyes: Photography, War, and the Holocaust* (New Brunswick, N.J.: Rutgers University Press, 2012).

9. G. A. Kumanev, *Sovetskii tyl v pervyi period Velikoi Otechestvennoi voiny* (Moscow: Nauka, 1988), p. 56.

10. https://www.centropa.org/biography/jacob-mikhailov.

11. Kumanev, *Sovetskii tyl*, p. 67.

12. Seniavskii and Seniavskaia, "Ideologiia voiny i psikhologiia naroda," p. 134.

13. For radio and printed texts, see https://ru.wikipedia.org/wiki/Выступление_В._М._Молотова_по_радио_22_июня_1941_года.

14. RGASPI, f. 17, op. 122, d. 14, ll. 17–18.

15. *Pravda*, June 23, 1941.

16. RGASPI, f. 17, op. 122, d. 17, l. 15. See also stirring descriptions in Anna Krylova, *Soviet Women in Combat: A History of Violence on the Eastern Front* (New York: Cambridge University Press, 2011); and Markwick and Cardona, *Soviet Women on the Front Line in the Second World War*, pp. 32–55.

17. RGASPI, f. 17, op. 122, d. 14, ll. 17–18.

18. https://www.ibiblio.org/pha/timeline/410703awp.html.

19. https://www.centropa.org/biography/jacob-mikhailov.

20. Quote from James von Geldern, "Radio Moscow: The Voice from the Center," in Stites, ed., *Culture and Entertainment*, p. 47. See also Berkhoff, *Motherland in Danger*, pp. 36–7; Brody, "Ideology and Political Mobilization," pp. 8–9.

21. RGASPI, f. 17, op. 88, d. 31, ll. 31, 36.

22. RGASPI, f. 17, op. 88, d. 31, ll. 31–32, 36–37.

23. RGASPI, f. 17, op. 88, d. 31, ll. 32–35.

24. RGASPI, f. 17, op. 88, d. 31, ll. 32–33, 35.

25. RGASPI, f. 17, op. 88, d. 31, ll. 32–34.

26. Gorinov, "Muscovites' Moods 22 June 1941 to May 1942," p. 118.

27. RGASPI, f. 17, op. 88, d. 45, ll. 42–43. See Chapter 1 on the Ivanovo riots.

28. RGASPI, f. 17, op. 88, d. 45, ll. 37–42.

29. RGASPI, f. 17, op. 88, d. 45, ll. 37, 46–47.

30. RGASPI, f. 17, op. 88, d. 45, ll. 43–46.

31. RGASPI, f. 17, op. 88, d. 45, ll. 48–50.

32. RGASPI, f. 17, op. 122, d. 19, ll. 81–86, 79–81, 87–89.

33. Red Army chorus: https://www.youtube.com/watch?v=MAvgDhI01_A. On wartime music, see Suzanne Ament, *Sing to Victory! Song in Soviet Society during World War II* (Brookline, Mass.: Academic Studies Press, 2019).

34. RGASPI, f. 17, op. 88, d. 31, ll. 15–20; d. 113, ll. 2–8.

35. RGASPI, f. 17, op. 88, d. 122, ll. 1–3.

36. http://olga-berggolc.gatchina3000.ru/091.htm; Ol'ga Fedorovna Berggol'ts, *Stikhi i poemy* (Leningrad: Sovetskii pisatel', 1979), written May 1942 (translation: Wendy Z. Goldman).

37. For translation, see http://www.sovlit.net/war/nameofkirov.html.

38. In English translation and in Russian: https://ruverses.com/konstantin-simonov/wait-for-me-i-will-return/4727/.

39. Olga Berggolts, *Daytime Stars: A Poet's Memoir of the Revolution, the Siege of Leningrad, and the Thaw* (Madison: University of Wisconsin Press, 2018).

40. Russian text in http://olga-berggolc.gatchina3000.ru/068.htm, written June 1941; also in Berggol'ts, *Stikhi i poemy* (translation by Wendy Z. Goldman).

41. Alexander Werth, *Russia at War, 1941–1945* (New York: Carroll and Graf, 1964), pp. 189–97, quotes on pp. 189, 194; John Erickson, *The Road to Stalingrad: Stalin's War with Germany* (New Haven: Yale University Press, 1975), pp. 249–96.

42. Werth, *Russia at War*, p. 253.

43. RGASPI, f. 17, op. 122, d. 20, ll. 1–10.

44. https://www.marxists.org/reference/archive/stalin/works/1941/11/06.htm; Joseph Stalin, *The Great Patriotic War of the Soviet Union* (New York: Greenwood Press, 1969). In 1943 Stalin dissolved the Communist International in order to placate the Soviet Union's allies. A new, patriotic song replaced the "Internationale" as the national anthem.

45. RGASPI, f. 17, op. 125, d. 104, ll. 35–36.

46. Alexander Statiev, "'La Garde meurt, mais ne se rend pas!': Once Again on the 28 Panfilov Heroes," *Kritika: Explorations in Russian and Eurasian History*, vol. 13, no. 4 (Fall 2012), pp. 769–98; Berkhoff, *Motherland in Danger*, pp. 62–4. In the case of the Panfilov men, an investigation by the military prosecutor of the USSR in 1948 concluded that a journalist had invented most of the details. In 2015, the director of the State Archive of the Russian Federation, Sergei Mironenko, publicly stated the story to be a myth, and posted the earlier investigation's report online: http://statearchive.ru/607. Mironenko was fired from his position soon thereafter.

47. Werth, *Russia at War*, p. 255.

48. Berkhoff, *Motherland in Danger*, pp. 117, 116–33, 136–7. On the Soviet response to the Holocaust, see the chapter titled "A Bestial Plan for Physical Extermination," pp. 134–166, and footnote, pp. 330–3. Berkhoff argues that there was no "conspiracy of silence," as some historians charge. See also Kiril Feferman, *Soviet Jewish*

Stepchild: The Holocaust in the Soviet Mindset, 1941–1964 (Saarbrücken: VDM Verlag, 2009). The two-page spread in *Trud*, May 8, 1945, however, which carried the Soviet Extraordinary Commission's report on Auschwitz, did not mention that any of the victims were Jews. It noted, "Through shootings, starvation, poisoning, and the most monstrous tortures, in Auschwitz the Germans exterminated more than four million citizens of the Soviet Union, Poland, France, Belgium, Holland, Czechoslovakia, Yugoslavia, Romania, Hungary, and other countries."

49. *Krasnaia zvezda*, April 28, 1942. Molotov's note can also be found at https://mywebs. su/blog/history/22923/.

50. RGASPI, f. 17, op. 88, d. 122, l. 8; f. 17, op. 125, d. 104, ll. 7–17.

51. https://history.wikireading.ru/150569; see also http://www.hrono.ru/dokum/194_dok/19420501stal.php.

52. Werth, *Russia at War*, pp. 410–20; Berkhoff, *Motherland in Danger*, pp. 170–4.

53. On the influence of war correspondents, see Louise McReynolds, "Dateline Stalingrad: Newspaper Correspondents at the Front," in Stites, ed., *Culture and Entertainment*, pp. 28–43.

54. Mikhail Sholokhov, "Nauka nenavisti," *Pravda*, June 22, 1942, and republished one day later in *Krasnaia zvezda*.

55. Werth, *Russia at War*, p. 411. Roger Reese, *Why Stalin's Soldiers Fought: The Red Army's Military Effectiveness in World War II* (Lawrence: University of Kansas Press, 2011), p. 179, notes that Red Army soldiers saw so much suffering that such articles did more "to validate their hate than induce it."

56. For original version, see http://byker80.livejournal.com/6792.html.

57. For a live reading in Russian with English subtitles, see https://www.liveleak.com/view?i=6a0_1366841683#O2kkzO4YDJo1Lqro.99.

58. Il'ia Erenburg (Ilya Ehrenburg), "Ubei," *Krasnaia zvezda*, July 24, 1942. See also http://vivovoco.astronet.ru/VV/PAPERS/HISTORY/ERENBURG/KILLHIM.HTM.

59. McReynolds, "Dateline Stalingrad," p. 41.

60. Aleksandr F. Shkliaruk, *Nasha pobeda. Plakaty Velikoi Otechestvennoi voiny, 1941–1945 godov* (Moscow: Kontakt-Kul'tura, 2010), pp. 6–7, 10, 76, 100–1. See also Seniavskii and Seniavskaia, "Ideologiia voiny i psikhologiia naroda," p. 181.

61. RGASPI, f. 17, op. 125, d. 82, ll. 7–10.

62. RGASPI, f. 17, op. 88, d. 113, l. 31.

63. RGASPI, f. 17, op. 125, d. 82, l. 13. On the Rzhev salient and losses, see G. F. Krivosheev, ed., *Rossiia i SSSR v voinakh XX veka. Poteri vooruzhennykh sil. Statisticheskoe issledovanie* (Moscow: Olma-Press, 2001), p. 277; https://ru.wikipedia.org/wiki/Ржевская_битва.

64. Khrushchev, later noting that Stalin had rejected the military suggestions to retreat from Khar'kov in 1942, said, "And what was the result of this? The worst we had expected. The Germans surrounded our Army concentrations and as a result [of the Khar'kov counterattack] we lost hundreds of thousands of our soldiers. This is Stalin's military 'genius.' This is what it cost us." See https://www.marxists.org/archive/khrushchev/1956/02/24.htm.

65. RGASPI, f. 17, op. 88, d. 113, l. 31.

66. RGASPI, f. 17, op. 125, d. 82, ll. 13–14.

67. RGASPI, f. 17, op. 88, d. 113, l. 31; d. 119, l. 5; f. 17, op. 125, d. 82, l. 14.

68. RGASPI, f. 17, op. 88, d. 113, l. 31ob. (emphasis added).

69. RGASPI, f. 17, op. 88, d. 113, ll. 7–8, 31ob., 32–33.

70. RGASPI, f. 17, op. 125, d. 82, ll. 16–17.

71. https://www.marxists.org/russkij/stalin/t15/t15_23.htm. Alexander Hill, *The Red Army and the Second World War* (Cambridge: Cambridge University Press, 2017), p. 354, calls the speech "an unusually open admission of the situation."

72. Werth, *Russia at War*, pp. 387–410, 412 (emphasis in original).

73. Chuikov quoted in Werth, *Russia at War*, p. 453.

74. Bordiugov, "The Popular Mood in the Unoccupied Soviet Union," p. 63.

75. RGASPI, f. 17, op. 125, d. 82, ll. 19–21.

76. RGASPI, f. 17, op. 125, d. 82, ll. 22–26, 30–37.

77. RGASPI, f. 17, op. 125, d. 104, ll. 154–155, 157.

78. RGASPI, f. 17, op. 88, d. 122, ll. 5–7ob.

79. RGASPI, f. 17, op. 122, d. 19, l. 74.

80. https://www.centropa.org/biography/galina-barskaya.

81. V. S. Murmantseva, *Sovetskie zhenshchiny v Velikoi Otechestvennoi voine* (Moscow: Mysl', 1974), pp. 50–3; RGASPI, f. 17, op. 122, d. 18, ll. 52–63.

82. Sosnovskaia, *Geroicheskii trud*, pp. 127–8.

83. Von Geldern, "Radio Moscow," p. 51 and passim. Berkhoff, *Motherland in Danger*, pp. 90–7, considers the radio programs less effective due to military censorship.

84. RGASPI, f. 17, op. 122, 18, ll. 123–135.

85. RGASPI, f. 17, op. 125, d. 104, ll. 34–39.

86. http://srgvs.ru/arhangelsk-v-gody-vov-1941-1945-g; RGASPI, f. 17, op. 125, d. 104, l. 204.

87. RGASPI, f. 17, op. 125, d. 104, l. 204; op. 88, d.113, ll. 28, 28ob., 29ob.

88. RGASPI, f. 17, op. 88, d. 122, ll. 15–15ob.

89. RGASPI, f. 17, op. 122, d. 18, ll. 104–108.

90. N. F. Bugai, "Deportatsiia narodov," in G. N. Sevost'ianov, ed., *Voina i obshchestvo, 1941–1945*, Book 2 (Moscow: Institut Rossiiskoi Istorii, 2004), pp. 306–30; Jeremy Smith, "Non-Russian Nationalities," pp. 230, 234.

91. http://www.hrono.ru/dokum/194_dok/19410825beri.php. Over the course of the war, more than one million Soviet Germans were sent into exile. See Chapter 5.

92. RGASPI, f. 17, op. 122, d. 10, ll. 72–77.

93. Joshua Rubenstein and Vladimir Naumov, eds., *Stalin's Secret Pogrom: The Postwar Inquisition of the Jewish Anti-Fascist Committee* (New Haven: Yale University Press, 2001); Konstantin Azadovskii and Boris Egorov, "From Anti-Westernism to Anti-Semitism," *Journal of Cold War Studies*, vol. 4, no. 1 (Winter 2002), pp. 66–80; Shimon Redlich, *War, Holocaust, and Stalinism: A Documented History of the Jewish Anti-Fascist Committee* (New York: Routledge, 2016); G. Kostyrchenko, *V plenu u krasnogo faraona. Politicheskie presledovaniia evreev v SSSR v poslednee stalinskoe desiatiletie* (Moscow: Mezhdunarodnoe otnoshenie, 1994).

94. RGASPI, f. 17, op. 125, d. 84, ll. 5–7.

95. Aleksandrov named Oistrakh, Gilel's, Flier, Fikhtengol'ts, Ginzburg, and Pantofil'-Nechetskaia in particular. See RGASPI, f. 17, op. 125, d. 123, ll. 21–24, reprinted http://www.alexanderyakovlev.org/fond/issues-doc/68347.

96. RGASPI, f. 17, op. 122, d. 18, ll. 93–97.

97. RGASPI, f. 17, op. 88, d. 119, ll. 1–2, 4.

98. RGASPI, f. 17, op. 122, d. 112, ll. 1–15. See also ll. 16–19, 21–25, and 27–35, on letters sent to the Odessa soviet.

99. Marina Vasil'evna Gontsova, "Povsednevnaia zhizn' naseleniia industrial'nogo tsentra v gody Velikoi Otechestvennoi voiny (na materialakh goroda Nizhnii Tagil)," Candidate of Historical Sciences dissertation, Nizhnii Tagil, 2011, pp. 194, 195.

100. "Zabota o bytovykh nuzhdakh naseleniia," *Pravda*, January 5, 1942; also reproduced in *Trud*, January 6, 1942.

101. RGASPI, f. 17, op. 88, d. 119, ll. 2–4. On difficulties of soldiers' wives, see Roger Markwick and Beate Fieseler, "The Rear Area in the Great Patriotic War: Red Army Men's Wives and Families Struggle for Survival in Yaroslavl," *Bylye gody*, vol. 28 (2), January 2013.

102. Sosnovskaia, *Geroicheskii trud*, p. 123; Seniavskii and Seniavskaia, "Ideologiia voiny i psikhologiia naroda," pp. 187–8; Brandon Schechter, *The Stuff of Soldiers: A History of the Red Army through Objects* (Ithaca: Cornell University Press, 2019), pp. 114–16.

103. https://www.centropa.org/biography/yakov-voloshyn.

104. Konstantin Simonov, "Lager' unichtozheniia," *Krasnaia zvezda*, August 10, 1944, https://0gnev.livejournal.com/789530.html.

105. Quoted by Oleg Budnitskii, "The Intelligentsia Meets the Enemy: Educated Soviet Officers in Defeated Germany, 1945," *Kritika: Explorations in Russian and Eurasian History*, vol. 10, no. 3 (Summer 2009), p. 629.

106. There are no reliable statistics for how many women were raped and how many soldiers participated. The topic was for many years surrounded by silence both in the Soviet Union and in East and West Germany. Rape continued to be a serious problem throughout the Soviet occupation zone until 1947 when the soldiers were finally confined to their bases, and subject to strong disciplinary measures. See Norman Naimark, *The Russians in Germany: A History of the Soviet Zone of Occupation* (Cambridge, Mass.: Harvard University Press, 1997), pp. 69–140; Atina Grossmann, "A Question of Silence: The Rape of German Women by Occupation Soldiers," *October,* vol. 72 (Spring 1995), pp. 42–63); Catherine Merridale, *Ivan's War: The Red Army, 1939–1945* (London: Faber & Faber, 2005), pp. 268–71, 275–7, 299–300; Schechter, *The Stuff of Soldiers*, pp. 233–7; and Anonymous, *A Woman in Berlin* (London: Virago, 2005), a diary of a German woman about her personal experience.

107. Editorial on February 9, 1945, quoted by Werth, *Russia at War*, p. 967.

108. Il'ia Erenburg (Ilya Ehrenburg), "Kvatit!," *Krasnaia zvezda*, April 11, 1945.

109. G. Aleksandrov, "Tovarishch Erenburg uproshchaet," *Pravda*, April 14, 1945, p. 2. Berkhoff, *Motherland in Danger* (pp. 189–93), notes that Aleksandrov sought to make an example of Ehrenburg, in part to undercut Hitler's equation of Bolshevism and Jewishness.

110. See Jochen Hellbeck, *Stalingrad: The City That Defeated the Third Reich* (New York: Public Affairs, 2015), pp. 28–9, on fighting for Mamaev Kurgan, the heights overlooking Stalingrad.

111. Gontsova, "Povsednevnaia zhizn'," p. 195.

Chapter 10

Epigraphs: GARF, f. 5452, op. 22, d. 25, ll. 190, 88.

1. Alexander Werth, *Russia at War, 1941–1945* (New York: Carroll and Graf, 1964), p. 767.

2. A. T. Tvardovskii, *Stikhotvoreniia i poemy v dvukh tomakh* (Moscow: Khudozhestvennaia Literatura, 1951). See http://militera.lib.ru/poetry/russian/tvardovsky/21.html (translation by Wendy Z. Goldman).

3. GARF, f. 9226, op. 1, d. 838, ll. 35–41, 49–50, 107–109.

4. GARF, f. 5452, op. 22, d. 25, l. 9.

5. Alexander Statiev, *The Soviet Counterinsurgency in the Western Borderlands* (New York: Cambridge University Press, 2010), pp. 56–8, 67–79. On German occupation, see Alexander Dallin, *German Rule in Russia, 1941–1945* (New York: St. Martin's Press, 1957); Ilya Ehrenburg and Vasily Grossman, eds., *The Complete Black Book of Soviet Jewry* (London: Routledge, 2003); Wendy Lower, *Nazi Empire-Building and the Holocaust in Ukraine* (Chapel Hill: University of North Carolina Press, 2005); Johannes Due Enstad, *Soviet Russians under Nazi Occupation: Fragile Loyalties in World War II* (Cambridge: Cambridge University Press, 2018); Karel C. Berkhoff, *Harvest of Despair: Life and Death in Ukraine under Nazi Rule* (Cambridge, Mass.: Belknap Press of Harvard University Press, 2004); Laurie R. Cohen, *Smolensk under the Nazis: Everyday Life in Occupied Russia* (Rochester, N.Y.: University of Rochester Press, 2013); Yitzhak Arad, *The Holocaust in the Soviet Union* (Lincoln: University of Nebraska Press, 2013).

6. On reconstruction, see Jeffrey W. Jones, *Everyday Life and the "Reconstruction" of Soviet Russia during and after the Great Patriotic War, 1943–1948* (Bloomington: Slavica Publishers, 2008), pp. 42–76; Karl D. Qualls, *From Ruins to Reconstruction: Urban Identity in Soviet Sevastopol after World War II* (Ithaca: Cornell University Press, 2009), pp. 13–23; and Martin J. Blackwell, *Kyiv as Regime City: The Return of Soviet Power after Nazi Occupation* (Rochester, N.Y.: University of Rochester Press, 2016), ch. 1.

7. Amir Weiner, *Making Sense of War: The Second World War and the Fate of the Bolshevik Revolution* (Princeton: Princeton University Press, 2001), p. 91.

8. RGASPI, f. 17, op. 122, d. 56, ll. 38–39, 42–43. Those who died also included those killed at the front. Jeffrey Burds, "'Turncoats, Traitors, and Provocateurs': Communist Collaborators, the German Occupation, and Stalin's NKVD, 1941–1943," *East European Politics and Societies: and Cultures*, vol. 32, no. 3 (August 2018), pp. 606–38, contends that losses were mainly due to expulsions for collaboration rather than murder by Germans.

9. RGASPI, f. 17, op. 122, d. 56, l. 43.

10. RGASPI, f. 17, op. 122, d. 56, ll. 20–27, 77; Jones, *Everyday Life*, p. 167.

11. Burds, "'Turncoats, Traitors, and Provocateurs,'" p. 621.

12. Weiner, *Making Sense of War*, pp. 108–10.

13. RGASPI, f. 17, op. 122, d. 56, l. 77.

14. RGASPI, f. 17, op. 88, d. 351, l. 1; Blackwell, *Kyiv as Regime City*, pp. 87–92. For an excellent discussion of party verification procedures, see Weiner, *Making Sense of War*, pp. 83–126.

15. RGASPI, f. 17, op. 122, d. 56, ll. 31–37.

16. Weiner also makes the point about suspicion toward those who survived a group arrest: *Making Sense of War*, p. 111.

17. https://www.centropa.org/biography/basya-chaika.

18. Jones, *Everyday Life*, pp. 160–6.

19. "O sem'iakh lits, sotrudnichavshikh s Germanskimi vlastiami" and "O sozdanii fil'tratsionnykh punktov," in V. N. Khaustov, V. P. Naumov, and N. S. Plotnikova, eds., *Lubianka. Stalin i NKVD-NKGB-GUKR "Smersh," 1939–mart 1946* (Moscow: Materik, 2006), p. 324.

20. http://srgvs.ru/rostov-na-donu-v-gody-vov.

21. "Shifrotelegramma B. A. Dvinskogo I. V. Stalinu o vyselenii semei izmennikov rodiny iz Rostovskoi oblasti," in Khaustov, *et al.*, *Lubianka*, p. 348.

22. "Spetssoobshchenie L. P. Berii I. V. Stalinu o repressiiakh v otnoshenii chlenov semei izmennikov rodiny," in Khaustov, *et al.*, *Lubianka*, pp. 349–50.

23. Postanovlenie GKO, "O chlenakh semei izmennikov rodiny," in Khaustov, *et al.*, *Lubianka*, pp. 350–1.

24. "Zapiska B. N. Merkulova I. V. Stalinu, napravlennaia chlenam i kandidatam Politbiuro TsK VKP (b) o likvidatsii shpionov, diversantov, i nemetskikh posobnikov v osvobozhdennykh raionakh" and Postanovlenie TsK VKP (b) "Ob organizatsii Narodnogo komissariata gosudarstvennoi bezopastnosti," in Khaustov, *et al.*, *Lubianka*, pp. 361–71, 371–2.

25. https://ru.wikisource.org/wiki/ Указ_Президиума_ВС_СССР_19.04.1943_№_39.

26. Cohen, *Smolensk under the Nazis*, pp. 257–9. A short film of the trial and the hanging in Krasnodar was made in 1943: https://www.youtube.com/watch?v=dhWVzEqHBLc.

27. "Spetssoobshchenie L. P. Berii I. V. Stalinu i V. M. Molotovu ob 'ochistke' osvobozhdennykh ot protivnika territorii," in Khaustov, *et al.*, *Lubianka*, pp. 406–8.

28. "Spetssoobshchenie L. P. Berii I. V. Stalinu, V. M. Molotovu, G. M. Malenkovu o rabote operativno-chekistskikh grupp po 'ochistke' Krymskoi ASSR ot 'antisovetskogo' elementa," in Khaustov, *et al.*, *Lubianka*, pp. 423–5.

29. "Spetssoobshchenie L. P. Berii I. V. Stalinu, V. M. Molotovu, G. M. Malenkovu o rabote proverochno-filtratsionnykh punktov po priemy Sovetskikh grazhdan," in Khaustov, *et al.*, *Lubianka*, p. 485.

30. Statiev, *The Soviet Counterinsurgency*, pp. 172–3.

31. RGASPI, f. 17, op. 122, d. 55, ll. 24–25.

32. Blackwell, *Kyiv as Regime City*, pp. 34–7.

33. https://www.centropa.org/biography/yelizaveta-dubinskaya#During%20the%20war.

34. Blackwell, *Kyiv as Regime City*, pp. 108–13, 158–86.

35. https://www.centropa.org/biography/naomi-deich#During%20the%20war.

36. Weiner, *Making Sense of War*, pp. 89–90; Nechama Tec, *Defiance: The Bielski Partisans* (New York: Oxford University Press, 1993), p. 99; Kenneth Slepyan, *Stalin's Guerrillas: Soviet Partisans in World War II* (Lawrence: University of Kansas Press, 2006), pp. 219–20. See also testimony of a Jewish partisan in a Soviet brigade in the film *Partisans of Vilna* (1986, dir. Joshua Waletzky).

37. RGASPI, f. 17, op. 122, d. 20, ll. 17–20.

38. *O vypolnenii postanovleniia SNK SSSR i TsK VKP (b) ot 21 avgusta 1943 goda "O neotlozhnykh merakh po vosstanovleniiu khoziaistva v raionakh, osvobozhdennykh ot nemetskoi okkupatsii." Otchet Komiteta pri Sovnarkome po vosstanovleniiu khoziaistva v raionakh, osvobozhdennykh ot nemetskoi okkupatsii* (Moscow: OGIZ Gosudarstvennoe Izdatel'stvo Politicheskoi Literatury, 1944); U. G. Cherniavskii, *Voina i prodovol'stvie. Snabzhenie gorodskogo naseleniia v Velikuiu Otechestvennuiu voinu (1941–1945 gg.)* (Moscow: Nauka, 1964), pp. 109, 96.

39. Wendy Z. Goldman, "Not by Bread Alone: Food, Workers, and the State," in Wendy Z. Goldman and Donald Filtzer, eds., *Hunger and War: Food Provisioning in the Soviet Union during World War II* (Bloomington: Indiana University Press, 2015), p. 67; Iurii Gor'kov, *Gosudarstvennyi komitet oborony postanovliaet, 1941–1945. Tsifry i dokumenty* (Moscow: Olma-Press, 2002), pp. 481–2.

40. Blackwell, *Kyiv as Regime City*, pp. 110–11.

41. GARF, f. 5452, op. 22, d. 5, ll. 34–36.

42. GARF, f. 5452, op. 22, d. 25, ll. 9–9ob.

43. Dmitrii D'iakov, "Pryzhok v bezdnu. Kak Voronezh vystupil vo Vtoruiu Mirovuiu voinu," *Voronezhskii Kur'er*, No. 16 (January 2010), p. 4, http://nashahistory.ru/materials/voronezh-v-gody-velikoy-otechestvennoy-voyny.

44. GARF, f. 5452, op. 22, d. 25, l. 88.

45. GARF, f. 5452, op. 22, d. 25, l. 190.

46. GARF, f. 5452, op. 22, d. 25, ll. 83–84.

47. GARF, f. 9517, op. 1, d. 50, l. 98.

48. Weiner, *Making Sense of War*, p. 71.

49. GARF, f. 9517, op. 1, d. 50, ll. 100, 19–17, 36, 76–74, 98, 63, 66 (file numbered back to front).

50. GARF, f. 9517, op. 1, d. 50, ll. 35, 16, 36, 75.

51. GARF, f. 9517, op. 1, d. 50, ll. 35, 74, 36, 6, 85, 84.

52. GARF, f. 7971, op. 16, d. 295, l. 24.

53. RGASPI, f. 17, op. 88, d. 351, ll. 32–38.

54. GARF, f. 9517, op. 1, d. 50, l. 4.

55. GARF, f. 9517, op. 1, d. 50, ll. 5, 4.

56. GARF, f. 9517, op. 1, d. 50, ll. 31, 34, 77, 20.

57. GARF, f. 9517, op. 1, d. 50, ll. 37, 25, 24, 3.

58. RGASPI, f. 17, op. 88, d. 351, ll. 27–28, 32–37. See also report on Kuban in GARF, f. 9517, op. 1, d. 50, ll. 78, 81, 139; Blackwell, *Kyiv as Regime City*, pp. 49, 47.

59. GARF, f. 9517, op. 1, d. 50, ll. 36–35, 81, 275, 73, 37, 31.

60. GARF, f. 9517, op. 1, d. 50, ll. 2–1, 275.

61. GARF, f. 9517, op. 1, d. 50, ll. 1, 43–42, 20.

62. GARF, f. 9517, op. 1, d. 50, ll. 34, 30, 47, 278, 268.

63. GARF, f. 9517, op. 1, d. 50, ll. 24, 22, 12, 42, 8.

64. GARF, f. 9517, op. 1, d. 50, l. 96.

65. "Spetssoobshchenie L. P. Berii I. V. Stalinu, V. M. Molotovu, G. M. Malenkovu, o provedenii chekistsko-voiskovykh operatsii po likvidatsii vooruzhennykh formirovanii OUN," "Spetssoobshchenie L. P. Berii I. V. Stalinu s prilozheniem donesenii NKVD Ukrainskoi SSR o rezul'tatakh operatsii po likvidatsii vooruzhennykh formirovanii OUN," in Khaustov, et al., Lubianka, pp. 447, 473; Grzegorz Rossolinski-Liebe, Stepan Bandera: The Life and Afterlife of a Ukrainian Nationalist: Fascism, Genocide, and Cult (Stuttgart: Ibidem Verlag, 2014); Statiev, The Soviet Counterinsurgency, pp. 123–32, quotes on pp. 46, 131; Per A. Rudling, "The OUN, the UPA, and the Holocaust: A Study in the Manufacturing of Historical Myths," Carl Beck Papers in Russian and East European Studies, No. 2107, 2011.

66. GARF, f. 9517, op. 1, d. 50, ll. 96, 41–40.

67. GARF, f. 9517, op. 1, d. 50, ll. 45, 49, 48, 100.

68. GARF, f. 9517, op. 1, d. 50, l. 46.

69. RGASPI, f. 17, op. 88, d. 351, ll. 91, 39–41, 50.

70. Statiev, The Soviet Counterinsurgency, p. 130; GARF, f. 9517, op. 1, d. 50, ll. 15, 24, 72, 70, 71, 21.

71. Jones, Everyday Life, pp. 46, 56–8; Qualls, From Ruins to Reconstruction, pp. 1–2, 15–22.

72. RGASPI, f. 17, op. 122, d. 45, l. 64.

73. Tvardovskii, Stikhotvoreniia i poemy. See http://militera.lib.ru/poetry/russian/tvardovsky/21.html.

74. GARF, f. 9517, op. 1, d. 33, ll. 54, 71–72, 151.

75. GARF, f. 9517, op. 1, d. 32, ll. 39, 43–47.

76. GARF, f. 9517, op. 1, d. 32, ll. 524–525.

77. RGAE, f. 1562, op. 329, d. 1151, l. 6.

78. GARF, f. 9517, op. 1, d. 32, ll. 67–68.

79. GARF, f. 9517, op. 1, d. 32, l. 523.

80. GARF, f. 9517, op. 1, d. 32, ll. 312–329, 331–349.

81. GARF, f. 9517, op. 1, d. 33, ll. 96, 98, 99, 100–140, 162, 164, 165.

82. GARF, f. 9517, op. 1, d. 33, ll. 151–154, 331–333, 349.

83. GARF, f. 9517, op. 1, d. 33, ll. 177–328; d. 39, l. 91. In Georgia, of the 3,460 people mobilized, almost half were sent to the mines.

84. Nicolas Werth, "Mass Crimes under Stalin (1930-1953)," in "Online Encyclopedia of Mass Violence," at https://www.sciencespo.fr/mass-violence-war-massacre-resistance/en/document/mass-crimes-under-stalin-1930-1953.html (from N. Bugai, Deportatsiia narodov Kryma [Moscow: INSAN, 1997], pp. 45–64).

85. GARF, f. 9517, op. 1, d. 39, ll. 116–117.

86. GARF, f. 9517, op. 1, d. 39, l. 184.

87. GARF, f. 9517, op. 1, d. 39, l. 185.

88. GARF, f. 9517, op. 1, d. 50, ll. 107, 69, 91, 290–285. Mobilization into vocational schools did continue after the war. See Donald Filtzer, Soviet Workers and Late

Stalinism: Labour and the Restoration of the Stalinist System after World War II (Cambridge: Cambridge University Press, 2002), pp. 34–9.

89. https://www.centropa.org/biography/yelizaveta-dubinskaya#During%20the%20 war.

90. Weiner, *Making Sense of War*, p. 91.

91. "Podpisanie akta bezogovorochnoi kapituliatsii Germanskikh vooruzhennikh sil," *Pravda*, May 9, 1945, p. 1; "Strana prazdnuet velikuiu pobedu," *Pravda*, May 11, 1945, p. 3; Werth, *Russia at War*, pp. 968–9.

92. https://www.centropa.org/biography/sophia-abidor#During%20the%20war.

Conclusion

1. We are grateful to Dr. Aleksei Kilichenkov, historian of military technology at Russian State University for the Humanities, for this information.

2. https://www.centropa.org/biography/arkadiy-redko.

3. See Tables 7.1 and 7.2.

4. In Russian, translation by Wendy Z. Goldman:

Я с вами равный среди равных,
Я камнем стал, но я живу!
И вы принявшие Москву
В наследство от сограждан ратных,
Вы, подарившие века мне,
Вы — все, кто будет после нас,
Не забывайте ни на час,
Что я смотрю на вас из камня.

Bibliography

Archives

Archive holdings for the People's Commissariats are catalogued under their postwar title of Ministries.

GARF (Gosudarstvennyi arkhiv Rossiiskoi federatsii—State Archive of the Russian Federation)

Main Reading Room

f. 5451 All-Union Soviet of Trade Unions (Vsesoiuznyi sovet professional'nikh profsoiuzov)

f. 5452 Central Committees of the Unions of Workers in State Trade, Public Catering, and Consumer Cooperatives (Tsentral'nye komitety profsoiuzov rabotnikov gosudarstvennoi torgovli, obshchestvennogo pitaniia i potrebitel'skoi kooperatsii)

f. 6822 Soviet for Evacuation under the USSR Soviet of People's Commissars (Sovet po evakuatsii pri SNK SSSR)

f. 7416 Central Committees of the Unions of Workers in the Coal Industry (Tsentral'nye komitety profsoiuzov rabochikh ugol'noi promyshlennosti)

f. 7676 Opis' 14 Central Committee of the Union of Workers in the Automotive and Tractor Industry (Tsentral'nyi komitet profsoiuza rabochikh avtomobil'noi i traktornoi promyshlennosti)

f. 7678 Central Committees of the Unions of Workers in Aviation and Defense Industry (Tsentral'nye komitety profsoiuzov rabochikh aviatsionnoi i oboronnoi promyshlennostei)

f. 8009 Ministry of Public Health of the USSR (Ministerstvo zdravookhraneniia SSSR)

f. 8114 Jewish Anti-Fascist Committee (Evreiskii antifashistskii komitet)

f. 8131 Procuracy of the USSR (Prokuratura SSSR)

f. 9226 State Sanitary Inspectorate of the USSR Commissariat of Public Health (Gosudarstvennaia sanitarnaia inspektsiia Komissariata zdravookhraneniia SSSR)

f. 9507 Ministry of Labour Reserves of the USSR (Ministerstvo trudovykh rezervov SSSR)

f. 9517 Committee to Enumerate and Distribute the Labor Force under the USSR Soviet of People's Commissars (Komitet po uchetu i raspredeleniiu rabochei sily pri SNK SSSR)

Reading Room 2

f. A-327 Chief Administration of Resettlement under the Council of Ministers of the RSFSR and Its Predecessors (Glavnoe pereselencheskoe upravlenie pri SM RSFSR i ego predshestvenniki)

f. A-374 Statistical Administration of the RSFSR (Statisticheskoe upravlenie RSFSR)

f. A-482 Ministry of Public Health of the RSFSR (Narodnyi komissariat zdravookhraneniia RSFSR)

RGAE (Rossiiskii gosudarstvennyi arkhiv ekonomiki—Russian State Archive of the Economy)

f. 1562 Central Statistical Administration of the USSR (Tsentral'noe statisticheskoe upravlenie SSSR)

f. 4372 State Planning Commission of the USSR (Gosudarstvennyi planovyi komitet SSSR)

f. 7971 Ministry of Trade of the USSR (Ministerstvo torgovlia SSSR)

f. 8848 Ministry of the Electrotechnical Industry of the USSR (Ministerstvo elektrotekhnicheskoi promyshlennosti SSSR)

f. 8875 Ministry of the Iron and Steel Industry of the USSR (Ministerstvo chernoi metallurgii SSSR)

RGASPI (Rossiiskii gosudarstvennyi arkhiv sotsial'no-politicheskoi istorii—Russian State Archive of Socio-Political History)

f. 17, op. 88 Information Sector of the Organizational-Instructional Department of the Central Committee of the Communist Party (Sektor informatsii organizatsionno-instruktorskogo otdela TsK VKP(b))

f. 17, op. 122 Organizational-Instructional Department of the Central Committee of the Communist Party (Organizatsionno-instruktorskii otdel TsK VKP(b))

f. 17, op. 125 Propaganda and Agitation Administration of the Central Committee of the Communist Party (Upravlenie propaganda i agitatsii TsK VKP(b))

f. 644 State Committee for Defense of the USSR (Gosudarstvennyi komitet oborony SSSR)

f. M-1 Central Committee of the All-Union Leninist Communist Union of Youth (Vsesoiuznyi Leninskii kommunisticheskii soiuz molodezhi—Komsomol)

NA IRI-RAN (Nauchnyi arkhiv Institut Rossiiskoi istorii Rossiiskaia akademiia nauk—Scientific Archive of the Institute of Russian History of the Russian Academy of Sciences)

f. 2, razdel 5 The Rear—The War Economy (Tyl—Voennaia ekonomika)

RGAKFD Russian State Archive of Cinema and Photography Documents (Rossiiskii gosudarstvennyi arkhiv kinofotodokumentov)

Books, Articles, and Dissertations

Aleksandrov, B., "The Soviet Currency Reform," *Russian Review*, vol. 8, no. 1 (January 1949), pp. 56–61.

Aleksandrov, G., "Tovarishch Erenburg uproshchaet," *Pravda*, April 14, 1945, p. 2.

Alexievich, Svetlana, *The Unwomanly Face of War: An Oral History of Women in World War II* (New York: Random House, 2018).

Alexopoulos, Golfo, *Illness and Inhumanity in Stalin's Gulag* (New Haven: Yale University Press, 2017).

Amar, Tarik Cyril, *The Paradox of Ukrainian Lviv: A Borderland City between Stalinists, Nazis, and Nationalists* (Ithaca, N.Y.: Cornell University Press, 2015).

Ament, Suzanne, *Sing to Victory! Song in Soviet Society during World War II* (Brookline, Mass.: Academic Studies Press, 2019).

Andreev, E. M., I. E. Darskii, and T. L. Khar'kova, "Liudskie poteri SSSR vo Vtoroi Mirovoi voine. Metodika otsenki i rezul'taty," in *Liudskie poteri SSSR v period Vtoroi Mirovoi voiny*, pp. 36–42.

Anonymous, *A Woman in Berlin* (London: Virago, 2005).

Applewhite, Harriet, and Darline Levy, eds., *Women and Politics in the Age of Democratic Revolution* (Ann Arbor: University of Michigan Press, 1993).

Arad, Yitzhak, *The Holocaust in the Soviet Union* (Lincoln: University of Nebraska Press, 2010).

Aralovets, N. A., "Smertnost' gorodskogo naseleniia tylovykh raionov Rossii, 1941–1945 gg.," in *Liudskie poteri SSSR v period Vtoroi Mirovoi voiny*, pp. 154–9.

Argenbright, Roger, "Space of Survival: The Soviet Evacuation of Industry and Population in 1941," in Jeremy Smith, ed., *Beyond the Limits: The Concept of Space in Russian History and Culture* (Helsinki: Suomen Historiallinen Seura, 1999), pp. 207–39.

Auman, Vladimir Andreevich, and Valentina Georgievna Chebotareva, eds., *Istoriia rossiiskikh nemtsev v dokumentakh (1763–1992 gg.)* (Moscow: Mezhdunarodnyi institut gumanitarnykh programm, 1993).

Azadovskii, Konstantin, and Boris Egorov, "From Anti-Westernism to Anti-Semitism," *Journal of Cold War Studies*, vol. 4, no. 1 (Winter 2002), pp. 66–80.

Bacon, Edwin, *The Gulag at War: Stalin's Forced Labor System in the Light of the Archives* (Basingstoke: Macmillan, 1994).

Baldin, K. E., *Ivanovo-Voznesensk. Iz proshlogo v budushchee* (Ivanovo: Episheva O.V., 2011).

Baranov, V. P., N. M. Moskalenko, A. V. Timchenko, and E. P. Chelyshev, *Velikaia Otechestvennaia voina, 1941–1945* (Moscow: Ministerstvo Oborony Rossiiskoi Federatsii, 2012).

Barber, John, and Mark Harrison, *The Soviet Home Front, 1941–1945: A Social and Economic History of the USSR in World War II* (London: Longman, 1991).

Barnes, Steven A., *Death and Redemption: The Gulag and the Shaping of Soviet Society* (Princeton: Princeton University Press, 2011).

Bell, Wilson T., "Forced Labor on the Home Front: The Gulag and Total War in Western Siberia, 1940–1945," in Michael David-Fox, ed., *The Soviet Gulag: Evidence, Interpretation, and Comparison* (Pittsburgh: University of Pittsburgh Press, 2016), pp. 114–35.

Bell, Wilson T., *Stalin's Gulag at War: Forced Labour, Mass Death, and Soviet Victory in the Second World War* (Toronto: University of Toronto Press, 2019).

Bellamy, Chris, *Absolute War: Soviet Russia in the Second World War* (New York: Alfred Knopf, 2007).

Belonosov, I. I., "Evakuatsiia naseleniia iz prifrontovoi polosy v 1941–1942," in Poliakov, et al., eds., *Eshelony idut na vostok*, pp. 15–30.

Berggolts, Olga, *Daytime Stars: A Poet's Memoir of the Revolution, the Siege of Leningrad, and the Thaw* (Madison: University of Wisconsin Press, 2018).

Berggol'ts, Ol'ga, *Stikhi i poemy* (Leningrad: Sovetskii pisatel', 1979).

Berkhoff, Karel C., *Harvest of Despair: Life and Death in Ukraine under Nazi Rule* (Cambridge, Mass.: Belknap Press of Harvard University Press, 2004).

Berkhoff, Karel, *Motherland in Danger: Soviet Propaganda during World War II* (Cambridge, Mass.: Harvard University Press, 2012).

Bernstein, Seth, "Rural Russia on the Edges of Authority: *Bezvlastie* in Wartime Riazan', November–December 1941," *Slavic Review*, vol. 75, no. 3 (Fall 2016), pp. 560–82.

Bidlack, Richard, "The Political Mood in Leningrad during the First Year of the Soviet– German War," *Russian Review*, 59 (January, 2000), pp. 96–113.

Bidlack, Richard, "Propaganda and Public Opinion," in Stone, ed., *The Soviet Union at War*, pp. 45–68.

Bidlack, Richard, "Survival Strategies in Leningrad during the First Year of the Soviet– German War," in Thurston and Bonwetsch, eds., *The People's War*, pp. 84–107.

Bidlack, Richard, and Nikita Lomagin, *The Leningrad Blockade, 1941–1944: A New Documentary History from the Soviet Archives* (New Haven: Yale University Press, 2007).

Blackwell, Martin J., *Kyiv as Regime City: The Return of Soviet Power after Nazi Occupation* (Rochester, N.Y.: University of Rochester Press, 2016).

Bordiugov, Gennadi, "The Popular Mood in the Unoccupied Soviet Union: Continuity and Change during the War," in Thurston and Bonwetsch, eds., *The People's War*, pp. 54–70.

Borodkin, L. I., S. A. Krasil'nikov, and O. V. Khlevniuk, eds., *Istoriia Stalinizma. Prinuditel'nyi trud v SSSR. Ekonomika, politika, pamiat'. Materialy mezhdunarodnoi konferentsii, Moskva, 28–29 oktiabria 2011 g.* (Moscow: Rosspen, 2013).

Braithwaite, Rodric, *Moscow 1941: A City and Its People* (New York: Alfred A. Knopf, 2006).

Brandenburger, David, *National Bolshevism: Stalinist Mass Culture and the Formation of Modern Russian National Identity, 1931–1956* (Cambridge, Mass.: Harvard University Press, 2002).

Brandenburger, David, *Propaganda State in Crisis: Soviet Ideology, Indoctrination, and Terror under Stalin, 1927–1941* (New Haven: Yale University Press, 2012).

Brody, Richard, "Ideology and Political Mobilization: The Soviet Home Front during World War II," *Carl Beck Papers in Russian and East European Studies*, no. 1104, October 1994.

Brooks, Jeffrey, "*Pravda* Goes to War," in Stites, ed., *Culture and Entertainment in Wartime Russia*, pp. 9–27.

Browning, Christopher R., *The Origins of the Final Solution: The Evolution of Nazi Jewish Policy, September 1939–March 1942* (Lincoln: University of Nebraska Press, 2004).

Brožek, Josef, Samuel Wells, and Ancel Keys, "Medical Aspects of Semistarvation in Leningrad (Siege 1941–1942), *American Review of Soviet Medicine*, vol. 4, no. 1 (October 1946), pp. 70–86.

Brunstedt, Jonathan, "Building a Pan-Soviet Past: The Soviet War Cult and the Turn Away from Ethnic Particularism," *Soviet and Post-Soviet Review*, vol. 38 (2011), pp. 149–71.

Budnitskii, Oleg, "The Great Patriotic War and Soviet Society: Defeatism, 1941–1942," *Kritika: Explorations in Russian and Eurasian History*, vol. 15, no. 4 (Fall 2014), pp. 767–97.

Budnitskii, Oleg, "The Intelligentsia Meets the Enemy: Educated Soviet Officers in Defeated Germany, 1945," *Kritika: Explorations in Russian and Eurasian History*, vol. 10, no. 3 (Summer 2009), pp. 629–82.

Bugai, N. F., "Deportatsiia narodov," in G. N. Sevost'ianov, ed., *Voina i obshchestvo, 1941– 1945*, book 2 (Moscow: Institut Rossiiskoi Istorii, 2004), pp. 306–30.

Bugai, N. F., *Mobilizovat' nemtsev v rabochie kolonny ... I. Stalin. Sbornik dokumentov* (Moscow: Gotika, 1998).

Burds, Jeffrey, "'Turncoats, Traitors, and Provocateurs': Communist Collaborators, the German Occupation, and Stalin's NKVD, 1941-1943," *East European Politics and Societies: and Cultures*, vol. 32, no. 3 (August 2018), pp. 606-38.

Burton, Christopher, "Medical Welfare during Late Stalinism: A Study of Doctors and the Soviet Health System, 1945-1953," Ph.D. dissertation, University of Chicago, 2000.

Cegielski, J. P., and D. N. McMurray, "The Relationship between Malnutrition and Tuberculosis: Evidence from Studies in Humans and Experimental Animals," *International Journal of Tuberculosis and Lung Disease*, vol. 8, no. 3 (2004), pp. 286-98.

Cherniavskii, U. G., *Voina i prodovol'stvie. Snabzhenie gorodskogo naseleniia v Velikuiu Otechestvennuiu voinu (1941-1945 gg.)* (Moscow: Nauka, 1964).

Chislennost' naseleniia SSSR na 17 ianvaria 1939 g. (Moscow: Gosplanizdat, 1941).

Cohen, Laurie R., *Smolensk under the Nazis: Everyday Life in Occupied Russia* (Rochester, N.Y.: University of Rochester Press, 2013).

Collingham, Lizzie, *The Taste of War: World War Two and the Battle for Food* (New York: Penguin Press, 2012).

Conroy, Mary Schaeffer, *Medicines for the Soviet Masses during World War II* (Lanham, Md.: University Press of America, 2008).

Cronjé, Gillina, "Tuberculosis and Mortality Decline in England and Wales, 1851-1910," in Robert Woods and John Woodward, eds., *Urban Disease and Mortality in Nineteenth-Century England* (London: Batsford Academic and Educational, 1984), pp. 79-101.

Dallin, Alexander, *German Rule in Russia, 1941-1945* (New York: St. Martin's Press, 1957).

Danishevskii, I. M., ed., *Kuznitsa pobedy. Podvig tyla v gody Velikoi Otechestvennoi voiny* (Moscow: Izdatel'stvo Politicheskoi Literatury, 1974).

David, Michael Z., "Vaccination against Tuberculosis with BCG – a Study of Innovation in Soviet Public Health, 1925-1941," in Frances L. Bernstein, Christopher Burton, and Dan Healey, eds., *Soviet Medicine: Culture, Practice, and Science* (Dekalb: Northern Illinois University Press, 2010), pp. 132-54.

David-Fox, Michael, "The People's War: Ordinary People and Regime Strategies in a World of Extremes," *Slavic Review*, vol. 75, no. 3 (Fall 2016), pp. 551-9.

Davies, R. W., Mark Harrison, and S. G. Wheatcroft, eds., *The Economic Transformation of the Soviet Union, 1913-1945* (Cambridge: Cambridge University Press, 1994).

Davis, Belinda, *Home Fires Burning: Food, Politics, and Everyday Life in World War I Berlin* (Chapel Hill: University of North Carolina Press, 2000).

Dean, Martin, "Editor's Introduction," in Martin Dean, ed., *Encyclopedia of Camps and Ghettos, 1933-1945, Ghettos in German-Occupied Eastern Europe*, Vol. II, part A (Bloomington: Indiana University Press, 2012), pp. xliii–xlviii.

Dement'ev, M. I., "K voprosu o rakhite v voennoe vremia," *Pediatriia*, no. 3, 1945, pp. 47-8.

Dexter, Keith, and Ivan Rodionov, "The Factories, Research and Design Establishments of the Soviet Defence Industry: A Guide. Ver. 20," University of Warwick, Department of Economics. May 2018, https://warwick.ac.uk/vpk/.

Direktivy KPSS i sovetskogo pravitel'stva po khoziaistvennym voprosam, 1929-1945 gody, vol. II (Moscow: Gosudarstvennoe Izdatel'stvo Politicheskoi Literatury, 1957).

Dodonova, Ol'ga Nikolaevna, "Kor' v SSSR, 1930-1943 god," Candidate of Medical Sciences dissertation, Moscow, 1945.

Dombrovskaia, Iu. F., "Pnevmonii u distrofikov i rakhitikov," in *Trudy plenumov Soveta lechebno-profilakticheskoi pomoshchi detiam Ministerstva zdravookhraneniia SSSR i Ministerstva zdravookhraneniia RSFSR* (Moscow: Medgiz, 1948).

Dormidontov, A. A., "Osnovnye napravleniia po bor'be s rakhitom v usloviiakh severnogo Urala," *Pediatriia*, no. 3, 1945, pp. 38–41.

Dubrovin, N. F. "Eshelon za eshelonom," in Poliakov, *et al.*, eds., *Eshelony idut na vostok*, pp. 208–19.

Dulitskii, S. O., "Rakhit voennogo vremeni," *Pediatriia*, no. 3, 1945, pp. 41–7.

Dzeniskevich, A. R., ed., *Leningrad v osade. Sbornik dokumentov o geroicheskoi oborone Leningrada v gody Velikoi Otechestvennoi voiny, 1941–1944* (St. Petersburg: Liki Rossii, 1995).

Dzeniskevich, Andrei, "The Social and Political Situation in Leningrad during the First Months of the German Invasion: The Psychology of the Workers," in Thurston and Bonwetsch, eds., *The People's War*, pp. 71–83.

Ehrenburg, Ilya, and Vasily Grossman, *The Complete Black Book of Soviet Jewry* (London: Routledge, 2003).

Ellman, Michael, and S. Maksudov, "Soviet Deaths in the Great Patriotic War: A Note," *Europe–Asia Studies*, vol. 46, no. 4 (1994), pp. 671–80.

Enstad, Johannes Due, *Soviet Russians under Nazi Occupation: Fragile Loyalties in World War II* (Cambridge: Cambridge University Press, 2018).

Erenburg, Il'ia [Ilya Ehrenburg], "Kvatit!," *Krasnaia zvezda*, April 11, 1945.

Erickson, John, *The Road to Stalingrad: Stalin's War with Germany* (New Haven: Yale University Press, 1975).

Feferman, Kiril, *Soviet Jewish Stepchild: The Holocaust in the Soviet Mindset, 1941–1964* (Saarbrücken: VDM Verlag, 2009).

Fest, Joachim, *Hitler* (New York: Mariner Books, 2002).

Field, Catherine J., Ian R. Johnson, and Patricia D. Schley, "Nutrients and Their Role in Host Resistance to Infection," *Journal of Leukocyte Biology*, vol. 71 (January 2002), pp. 16–32.

Field, Mark G., *Doctor and Patient in Soviet Russia* (Cambridge, Mass.: Harvard University Press, 1957).

Filimoshin, M. V., "Ob itogov ischislenniia sredi mirnogo naseleniia na okkupirovannoi territorii SSSR i RSFSR v gody Velikoi Otechestvennoi voiny," in *Liudskie poteri SSSR v period Vtoroi Mirovoi voiny*, pp. 124–31.

Filtzer, Donald, "Factory Medicine in the Soviet Defense Industry during World War II," in Susan Grant, ed., *Soviet Healthcare from an International Perspective: Comparing Professions, Practice and Gender, 1880–1960* (London: Palgrave Macmillan, 2017), pp. 77–95.

Filtzer, Donald, *The Hazards of Urban Life in Late Stalinist Russia: Health, Hygiene, and Living Standards* (Cambridge: Cambridge University Press, 2010).

Filtzer, Donald, *Soviet Workers and De-Stalinization: The Consolidation of the Modern System of Soviet Production Relations, 1953–1964* (Cambridge: Cambridge University Press, 1992).

Filtzer, Donald, *Soviet Workers and Late Stalinism: Labour and the Restoration of the Stalinist System after World War II* (Cambridge: Cambridge University Press, 2002).

Filtzer, Donald, *Soviet Workers and Stalinist Industrialization: The Formation of Modern Soviet Production Relations, 1928–1941* (London: Pluto Press, 1986).

Filtzer, Donald, *Soviet Workers and the Collapse of Perestroika: The Soviet Labour Process and Gorbachev's Reforms, 1985-1991* (Cambridge: Cambridge University Press, 1994).

Filtzer, Donald, "Starvation Mortality in Soviet Home Front Industrial Regions during World War II," in Goldman and Filtzer, eds., *Hunger and War*, pp. 265-335.

Filtzer, Donald, and Wendy Z. Goldman, "Introduction: The Politics of Food and War," in Goldman and Filtzer, eds., *Hunger and War*, pp. 1-43.

Garrard, John, and Carol Garrard, *The Bones of Berdichev: The Life and Fate of Vasily Grossman* (New York: Free Press, 1996).

Gatagova, L. S., A. P. Kosheleva, L. A. Rogovaia, and J. Cadiot, eds., *TsK VKP(b) i natsional'nyi vopros, kniga 2, 1933-1945* (Moscow: Rosspen, 2009).

German, A. A., and A. N. Kurochkin, *Nemtsy SSSR v "Trudovoi armii"*, (Moscow: Gotika, 2000).

Glantz, David M., *The Siege of Leningrad: 900 Days of Terror* (London: Cassell Military Paperbacks, 2001).

Glantz, David M., and Jonathan House, *When Titans Clash: How the Red Army Stopped Hitler* (Lawrence: University Press of Kansas, 1995).

Goldman, Wendy Z. *Inventing the Enemy: Denunciation and Terror in Stalin's Russia* (Cambridge: Cambridge University Press, 2011).

Goldman, Wendy Z., "Not by Bread Alone: Food, Workers, and the State," in Goldman and Filtzer, eds., *Hunger and War*, pp. 44-97.

Goldman, Wendy Z., *Terror and Democracy in the Age of Stalin: The Social Dynamics of Repression* (New York: Cambridge University Press, 2007).

Goldman, Wendy Z., *Women at the Gates: Gender and Industry in Stalin's Russia* (New York: Cambridge University Press, 2002).

Goldman, Wendy Z., *Women, the State, and Revolution: Soviet Family Policy and Social Life, 1917-1936* (New York: Cambridge University Press, 1993).

Goldman, Wendy Z., and Donald Filtzer, eds., *Hunger and War: Food Provisioning in the Soviet Union during World War II* (Bloomington: Indiana University Press, 2015).

Goncharov, G. A., "Ispol'zovanie 'Trudovoi armii' na Urale v 1941-1945 gg.," in Borodkin, Krasil'nikov, and Khlevniuk, eds., *Istoriia Stalinizma*, pp. 132-54.

Goncharov, G. A., "Stroitel'nye organizatsii ural'skogo regiona v usloviiakh voennogo vremeni (1941-1945 gody)," *Vestnik Cheliabinskogo gosudarstvennogo universiteta*, 2012, no. 11 (265), *Istoriia*. Vypusk 50, pp. 51-5.

Goncharov, G. A., "'Trudovaia armiia' perioda Velikoi Otechestvennoi voiny. Rossiiskaia istoriografiia," in L. I. Borodkin, *Ekonomicheskaia istoriia. Obozrenie*, Vypusk 7 (Moscow, 2001), pp. 154-62.

Gontsova, Marina Vasil'evna, "Povsednevnaia zhizn' naseleniia industrial'nogo tsentra v gody Velikoi Otechestvennoi voiny (na materialakh goroda Nizhnii Tagil)," Candidate of Historical Sciences dissertation, Nizhnii Tagil, 2011.

Gorinov, Mikhail M., "Muscovites' Moods, 22 June 1941 to May 1942" in Thurston and Bonwetsch, eds., *The People's War*, pp. 108-36.

Gor'kov, Iurii A., *Gosudarstvennyi komitet oborony postanovliaet, 1941-1945. Tsifry i dokumenty* (Moscow: Olma Press, 2002).

Gregory, Paul R., *The Political Economy of Stalinism: Evidence from the Soviet Secret Archives* (Cambridge: Cambridge University Press, 2004).

Grinchar, N. N., "Voprosy bor'by s tuberkulezom - v poriadok dnia," *Biulleten' Moskovskogo oblastnogo otdela zdravookhraneniia*, no. 9-10, 1943, pp. 13-18.

Grossman, Atina, "A Question of Silence: The Rape of German Women by Occupation Soldiers," *October*, vol. 72 (Spring 1995), pp. 42–63.

Grossman, Vasily, *A Writer at War: A Soviet Journalist with the Red Army, 1941–1945*, ed. and trans. by Antony Beevor and Luba Vinogradova (New York: Vintage Books, 2007).

Hagemann, Karen, and Stephanie Schuler-Springorum, eds., *Home/Front: The Military, War and Gender in Twentieth-Century Germany* (Oxford: Berg, 2002).

Hagenloh, Paul, *Stalin's Police: Public Order and Mass Repression in the USSR, 1926–1941* (Baltimore: Johns Hopkins University Press, 2009).

Harrison, Mark, *Accounting for War: Soviet Production, Employment, and the Defence Burden, 1940–1945* (Cambridge: Cambridge University Press, 1996).

Harrison, Mark, "Industrial Mobilisation for World War II: A German Comparison," in Mark Harrison and John Barber, eds., *The Soviet Defence Industry Complex from Stalin to Khrushchev* (Basingstoke and London: Macmillan Press, 2000), pp. 99–117.

Harrison, Mark, "Industry and Economy," in Stone, ed., *The Soviet Union at War*, pp. 15–44.

Harrison, Mark, "Resource Mobilization for World War II: The USA, UK, USSR, and Germany, 1938–1945," *Economic History Review*, vol. 41, no. 2 (1988), pp. 171–92, http://www2.warwick.ac.uk/fac/soc/economics/staff/mharrison/public/ehr88postprint.pdf.

Harrison, Mark, *Soviet Planning in Peace and War 1938–1945* (Cambridge: Cambridge University Press, 1985).

Harrison, Mark, "The USSR and Total War: Why Didn't the Soviet Economy Collapse in 1942?" in Roger Chickering, Stig Forster, and Bernd Greiner, eds., *A World at Total War: Global Conflict and the Politics of Destruction, 1937–1945* (Cambridge: Cambridge University Press, 2010), pp. 137–56.

Heinzen, James, *The Art of the Bribe: Corruption under Stalin, 1943–1953* (New Haven and London: Yale University Press, 2016).

Hellbeck, Jochen, *Stalingrad: The City That Defeated the Third Reich* (New York: Public Affairs, 2015).

Hessler, Julie, *A Social History of Soviet Trade: Trade Policy, Retail Practices, and Consumption, 1917–1953* (Princeton: Princeton University Press, 2004).

Hill, Alexander, *The Red Army and the Second World War* (Cambridge: Cambridge University Press, 2017).

Holmes, Larry, *Stalin's World War II Evacuations: Triumph and Troubles in Kirov* (Lawrence: University Press of Kansas, 2017).

Holmes, Larry, *War, Evacuation, and the Exercise of Power: The Center, Periphery, and Kirov's Pedagogical Institute, 1941–1952* (Lanham, Md.: Lexington Books, 2012).

Ironside, Kristy, "Between Fiscal, Ideological, and Social Dilemmas: The Soviet 'Bachelor Tax' and Post-War Tax Reform, 1941–1962," *Europe–Asia Studies*, vol. 69, no. 6 (August 2017), pp. 855–78.

Ironside, Kristy, "Rubles for Victory: The Social Dynamics of State Fundraising on the Soviet Home Front," *Kritika: Explorations in Russian and Eurasian History*, vol. 15, no. 4 (Fall 2014), pp. 799–828.

Ironside, Kristy, "Stalin's Doctrine of Price Reductions during the Second World War and Postwar Reconstruction," *Slavic Review*, vol. 75, no. 3 (Fall 2016), pp. 655–77.

Istoriia Velikoi Otechestvennoi voiny, tom 10, *Gosudarstvo, obshchestvo i voina* (Moscow: Kuchkovo pole, 2014).

Isupov, V. A., *Demograficheskie katastrofy i krizisy v Rossii v pervoi polovine XX veka. Istoriko-demograficheskie ocherki* (Novosibirsk: Sibirskii khronograf, 2000).

Jones, Jeffrey W., *Everyday Life and the "Reconstruction" of Soviet Russia during and after the Great Patriotic War, 1943-1948* (Bloomington: Slavica Publishers, 2008).

Kay, Alex J., *Exploitation, Resettlement, Mass Murder: Political and Economic Planning for German Occupation Policy in the Soviet Union, 1940-1941* (New York: Berghahn Books, 2006).

Kay, Alex J., "Germany's Staatssekretare, Mass Starvation and the Meeting of 2 May 1941," *Journal of Contemporary History*, vol. 41, no. 4 (2006), pp. 685-700.

Kay, Alex J., "The Purpose of the Russian Campaign Is the Decimation of the Slavic Population by Thirty Million: The Radicalization of German Food Policy in Early 1941," in Kay, Rutherford, and Stahel, eds., *Nazi Policy on the Eastern Front, 1941*, pp. 101-29.

Kay, Alex J., Jeff Rutherford, and David Stahel, eds., *Nazi Policy on the Eastern Front, 1941: Total War, Genocide, and Radicalization* (Rochester, N.Y.: University of Rochester Press, 2012).

Keys, Ancel, Josef Brožek, Austin Henschel, Olaf Mickelsen, Henry Longstreet Taylor, et al., *The Biology of Human Starvation* (Minneapolis: University of Minnesota Press, 1950).

Khaustov, V. N., "Organy gosudarstvennoi bezopastnosti v tylu i na fronte," in G. N. Sevost'ianov, ed., *Voina i obshchestvo, 1941-1945*, book 2 (Moscow: Institut Rossiiskoi Istorii, 2004), pp. 359-74.

Khaustov, V. N., V. P. Naumov, and N. S. Plotnikova, eds., *Lubianka. Stalin i NKVD-NKGB-GUKR "Smersh," 1939-mart 1946* (Moscow: Materik, 2006).

Khlevniuk, Oleg V., "Deserters from the Labor Front: The Limits of Coercion in the Soviet War Economy," *Kritika: Explorations in Eurasian History*, vol. 20, no. 3 (Summer 2019), pp. 481-504.

Khlevniuk, Oleg, "The Gulag and Non-Gulag as One Interrelated Whole," *Kritika: Explorations in Russian and Eurasian History*, vol. 16, no. 3 (Summer 2015), pp. 479-98.

Khlevnyuk, Oleg, and R. W. Davies, "The End of Rationing in the Soviet Union, 1934-1935," *Europe-Asia Studies*, vol. 5, no. 4 (1999), pp. 557-609.

Khodzhaev, Ashraf, "Funktsiia zheludki pri alimentarnoi distrofii," Candidate of Medical Sciences dissertation, Tashkent, 1946.

Kirillov, V. M. "Fizicheskoe sostoianie kontingentov zakliuchennykh i trudmobilizovannykh nemtsev ITL Bakalstroi/Cheliabmetallurgstroi, pokazateli ikh trudoispol'zovaniia (1942-1946)", in Borodkin, Krasil'nikov, and Khlevniuk, eds., *Istoriia Stalinizma*, pp. 109-31.

Kirillov, V. M., *Istoriia repressii v Nizhnetagil'skom regione Urala. 1920-e v nachalo 1950-kh gg.*, Part 2 (Nizhnii Tagil: Ural'skii gosudarstvennyi universitet, Nizhnetagil'skii gosudarstvennyi pedagogicheskii institut, 1996).

Kirillov, V. M., "Obshchie zakonomernosti i spetsifika soderzhaniia trudmobilizovannykh rossiiskikh nemtsev v lageriakh prinuditel'nogo truda na Urale," *Vestnik Iuzhno-Ural'skogo gosudarstvennogo universiteta*, seriia "Sotsial'no-gumanitarnye nauki," 2015, vol. 15, no. 1, pp. 30-4.

Kirschenbaum, Lisa, "'Our City, Our Hearths, Our Families': Local Loyalties and Private Life in Soviet World War II Propaganda," *Slavic Review*, vol. 59, no. 4 (Winter 2000), pp. 825-47.

Kokurin, A. I., and N. V. Petrov, eds., *GULAG (Glavnoe upravlenie lagerei) 1917–1960* (Moscow: Mezhdunarodnyi fond "Demokratiia," Izdatel'stvo "Materik," 2000).

Koonz, Claudia, *Mothers in the Fatherland: Women, the Family, and Nazi Politics* (New York: St. Martin's Press, 1988).

Kostyrchenko, G., *V plenu u krasnogo faraona. Politicheskie presledovaniia evreev v SSSR v poslednee stalinskoe desiatiletnie* (Moscow: Mezhdunarodnoe otnoshenie, 1994).

Kovalev, I. V., "Pod ognem vraga," in Poliakov, *et al.*, eds., *Eshelony idut na vostok*, pp. 230–2.

Kovalev, I. V., *Transport v Velikoi Otechestvennoi voine, 1941–1945* (Moscow: Nauka, 1981).

Kozhina, Elena, *Through the Burning Steppe: A Memoir of Wartime Russia, 1942–1943* (New York: Riverhead Books, 2002).

Kozlov, N. D., *Obshchestvennoe soznanie v gody Velikoi Otechestvennoi voiny* (St. Petersburg: Leningradskii Oblastnoi Institut Usovershenstvovaniia Uchitelei, 1995).

Kragh, Martin, "Soviet Labour Law during the Second World War," *War in History*, vol. 18, no. 4 (November 2011), pp. 531–46.

Kragh, Martin, "Stalinist Labour Coercion during World War II: An Economic Approach," *Europe–Asia Studies*, vol. 63, no. 7 (September 2011), pp. 1253–73.

Kravchenko, G. S., *Ekonomika SSSR v gody Velikoi Otechestvennoi Voiny, 1941–1945* (Moscow: Izdatel'stvo "Ekonomika," 1970).

Krivosheev, G. F., "Ob itogakh statisticheskikh issledovanii poter' vooruzhennykh sil SSSR v Velikoi Otechestvennoi voine," in *Liudskie poteri SSSR v period Vtoroi Mirovoi voiny*, pp. 71–81.

Krivosheev, G. F., ed., *Rossiia i SSSR v voinakh XX veka. Poteri vooruzhennykh sil. Statisticheskoe issledovanie* (Moscow: Olma-Press, 2001).

Krylova, Anna, *Soviet Women in Combat: A History of Violence on the Eastern Front* (New York: Cambridge University Press, 2011).

Kucherenko, Olga, *Soviet Street Children and the Second World War: Welfare and Social Control under Stalin* (London: Bloomsbury, 2016).

Kudelko, S. M., S. I. Posokhov, and E. V. G'iakova, eds., *Gorod i voina. Khar'kov v gody Velikoi Otechestvennoi voiny* (St. Petersburg: Aleteiia, 2012).

Kumanev, G. A., "Evakuatsiia naseleniia SSSR. Dostignutie rezultaty i poteri," in *Liudskie poteri SSSR v period Vtoroi Mirovoi voiny*, pp. 137–46.

Kumanev, G. A., *Sovetskii tyl v pervyi period Velikoi Otechestvennoi voiny* (Moscow: Nauka, 1988).

Kumanev, G. A., "Voina i evakuatsiia v SSSR, 1941–1942 gody," *Novaia i noveishaia istoriia*, No. 6, 2006, at http://vivovoco.astronet.ru/VV/JOURNAL/NEWHIST/EVACO.HTM.

Kuznetsov, Anatoly, *Babi Yar: A Document in the Form of a Novel* (New York: Farrar, Straus, and Giroux, 1970).

Leder, Mary, *My Life in Stalinist Russia: An American Woman Looks Back* (Bloomington: Indiana University Press, 2001).

Levesque, Jean, "A Peasant Ordeal: The Soviet Countryside," in Stone, ed., *The Soviet Union at War*, pp. 182–214.

Levitin, F. I., "Bor'ba s tuberkulezom v SSSR v period otechestvennoi voiny," *Sovetskoe zdravookhranenie*, No. 12, 1943, pp. 9–15.

Lieberman, Sanford R., "Crisis Management in the USSR: The Wartime System of Administration and Control," in Susan Linz, ed., *The Impact of World War II on the Soviet Union* (Totowa, N.J.: Rowman & Allanheld, 1985), pp. 59–76.

Lih, Lars, *Bread and Authority in Russia, 1914–1921* (Berkeley: University of California Press, 1990).

Likhomanov, M. I., L. T. Pozina, and E. I. Finogenov, *Partiinoe rukovodstvo evakuatsiei v pervyi period Velikoi Otechestvennoi voiny, 1941–1942* (Leningrad: Izdatel'stvo Leningradskogo Universiteta, 1985).

Linder, Forrest E., and Robert D. Grove, *Vital Statistics Rates in the United States, 1900–1940* (Washington, D.C.: United States Government Printing Office, 1947).

Liubimov, G. A., *Torgovlia i snabzhenie v gody Velikoi Otechestvennoi voiny* (Moscow: Izdatel'stvo Ekonomika, 1968).

Liudskie poteri SSSR v period Vtoroi Mirovoi voiny. Sbornik statei (St. Petersburg: Russko-Baltiiskii Informatsionnyi Tsentr BLITs, 1995).

Lonchinskaia, Larisa Ianovna, "Massovoe soznanie naseleniia ural'skikh oblastei v gody Velikoi Otechestvennoi voiny," Candidate of Historical Sciences dissertation, Cheliabinsk, 2002.

Lower, Wendy, *Nazi Empire-Building and the Holocaust in Ukraine* (Chapel Hill: University of North Carolina Press, 2005).

Manley, Rebecca, "Nutritional Dystrophy: The Science and Semantics of Starvation in World War II," in Goldman and Filtzer, eds., *Hunger and War*, pp. 206–64.

Manley, Rebecca, *To the Tashkent Station: Evacuation and Survival in the Soviet Union at War* (Ithaca: Cornell University Press, 2009).

Markwick, Roger, "Stalinism at War," *Kritika: Explorations in Russian and Eurasian History*, vol. 3, no. 3 (Summer 2002), pp. 509–20.

Markwick, Roger D., and Euridice Charon Cardona, *Soviet Women on the Front Line in the Second World War* (New York: Palgrave Macmillan, 2012).

Markwick, Roger, and Beate Fieseler, "The Rear Area in the Great Patriotic War: Red Army Men's Wives and Families Struggle for Survival in Yaroslavl," *Bylye gody*, vol. 28 (2), January 2013.

Mawdsley, Evan, *Thunder in the East: The Nazi–Soviet War 1941–1945* (London: Bloomsbury, 2016).

McBride, Jared, "Peasants into Perpetrators: The OUN-UPA and the Ethnic Cleansing of Volhynia, 1943–1944," *Slavic Review*, vol. 75, no. 3 (Fall 2016), pp. 630–54.

McLoughlin, Barry, and Kevin McDermott, eds., *Stalin's Terror: High Politics and Mass Repression in the Soviet Union* (Basingstoke: Palgrave, 2003).

McReynolds, Louise, "Dateline Stalingrad: Newspaper Correspondents at the Front," in Stites, ed., *Culture and Entertainment in Wartime Russia*, pp. 28–43.

Merridale, Catherine, *Ivan's War: The Red Army, 1939–1945* (London: Faber & Faber, 2005).

Michman, Dan, *The Emergence of German Ghettos during the Holocaust* (New York: Cambridge University Press, 2011).

Mitrofanova, A. V., *Rabochii klass SSSR nakanune i v gody Velikoi Otechestvennoi voiny, 1938–1945 gg.* (Moscow: Nauka, 1984).

Molotov, V. M., "O vneshnei politike Sovetskogo Soiuza," report to the USSR Supreme Soviet, October 31, 1939 (Moscow: Ogiz, 1939).

Moskoff, William, *The Bread of Affliction: The Food Supply in the USSR during World War II* (Cambridge: Cambridge University Press, 1990).

Murmantseva, V. S., *Sovetskie zhenshchiny v Velikoi Otechestvennoi voine* (Moscow: Mysl', 1974).

Murphy, David, *What Stalin Knew: The Enigma of Barbarossa* (New Haven: Yale University Press, 2005).

Naimark, Norman, *The Russians in Germany: A History of the Soviet Zone of Occupation* (Cambridge, Mass.: Harvard University Press, 1997).

Nakachi, Mie, "Population, Politics, and Reproduction: Late Stalinism and Its Legacy," in Juliane Fürst, ed., *Late Stalinist Russia: Society between Reconstruction and Reinvention* (London: Routledge, 2006), pp. 23–45.

Narodnoe khoziaistvo SSSR v Velikoi Otechestvennoi voine 1941–1945 gg. Statisticheskii sbornik (Moscow: Goskomstat SSSR, Informatsionno-izdatel'skii tsentr, 1990).

Narodnoe khoziaistvo SSSR za 60 let. Iubileinyi statisticheskii sbornik (Moscow: Statistika, 1977).

Nove, Alec, *An Economic History of the Soviet Union* (Harmondsworth: Penguin, 1972).

O vypolnenii postanovleniia SNK SSSR i TsK VKP (b) ot 21 avgusta 1943 goda "O neotlozhnykh merakh po vosstanovleniiu khoziaistva v raionakh, osvobozhdennykh ot nemetskoi okkupatsii." Otchet Komiteta pri Sovnarkome po vosstanovleniiu khoziaistva v raionakh, osvobozhdennykh ot nemetskoi okkupatsii (Moscow: OGIZ Gosudarstvennoe Izdatel'stvo Politicheskoi Literatury, 1944).

Oifebakh, M. I., and M. A. Klebanov, *Tuberkulez*, 2nd edition (Moscow: Medgiz, 1943).

Osokina, Elena, *Our Daily Bread: Socialist Distribution and the Art of Survival in Stalin's Russia, 1927–1941* (Armonk, N.Y.: M. E. Sharpe, 2001).

Overy, Richard, *Why the Allies Won* (New York and London: W. W. Norton and Co., 1995).

Pavlenko, V., and G. Pavlenko, "Vannikov, Boris L'vovich," in *Cheliabinskaia oblast'. Entsiklopediia*, vol. I (Cheliabinsk: Izdatel'stvo Tsentr IuUrGU, 2003), p. 565.

Perevoshchikova, A. I., "Gipotrofii v iasliakh goroda Izhevska i bor'ba s nimi," Candidate of Medical Sciences dissertation, Izhevsk State Medical Institute, 1944.

Peri, Alexis, "Queues, Canteens and the Politics of Location in Diaries of the Leningrad Blockade, 1941–1942," in Goldman and Filtzer, eds., *Hunger and War*, pp. 158–205.

Peri, Alexis, *The War Within: Diaries from the Siege of Leningrad* (Cambridge, Mass.: Harvard University Press, 2017).

Pogrebnoi, L. I., "O deiatel'nosti Soveta po evakuatsii," in Poliakov, *et al.*, eds., *Eshelony idut na vostok*, pp. 201–7.

Poliakov, Iu. A., G. A. Kumanev, N. P. Lipatov, and A. V. Mitrofanova, eds., *Eshelony idut na vostok. Iz istorii perebazirovaniia proizvoditel'nykh sil SSSR v 1941–1942 gg. Sbornik statei i vospominanii* (Moscow: Nauka, 1966).

Polian, Pavel, *Against Their Will: The History and Geography of Forced Migrations in the USSR* (Budapest: Central European University Press, 2004).

"Polozhenie o mediko-sanitarnom obsluzhivanii grazhdanskogo naseleniia, evakuiruemogo iz ugrozhaemykh raionov. Utverzhdeno narkomom zdravookhraneniia Soiuza SSR i soglasovano s zam. Narkoma putei soobshchenii 30/vi/1941 g.," *Sbornik prikazov i instruktsii NKZdrava SSSR*, no. 2, Moscow, 1942, pp. 26–9.

Postanovlenie XII Plenuma Vsesoiuznogo tsentral'nogo soveta professional'nykh soiuzov (Molotov: Gorkom VKP(b), 1944).

Potemkina, M. N., "Evakuatsiia i natsional'nye otnosheniia v sovetskom tylu v gody Velikoi Otechestvennoi voiny," *Otechestvennaia istoriia*, No. 3 (2002), http://vivovoco. ibmh.msk.su/VV/JOURNAL/RUHIST/EVAC.HTM.

Potemkina, Marina Nikolaevna, "Evakuatsionno-reevakuatsionnye protsessy i evakonaselenie na Urale v 1941–1948 gg." Doctor of Historical Sciences dissertation, Ekaterinburg, 2004.

Prasad, Ananda S., "Zinc Deficiency Has Been Known of for 40 Years But Ignored by Global Health Organizations," *British Medical Journal*, vol. 326 (22 February 2003), pp. 409–10, available at http://www.ncbi.nlm.nih.gov/pmc/articles/PMC1125304/.

Pushkarev, Vitalii S., "40-e. Stanovlenie 'chernogo' rynka," *Posev. Obshchestvenno-politicheskii zhurnal*, No. 1 (January 2002), pp. 29–35.

Pushkarev, V. S., "Razvitie 'chernogo rynka' v period Velikoi Otechestvennoi voiny i ego vliianie na sostoianie vnutrennogo rynka strany," in T. M. Bulavkina, M. V. Stegantsev, eds., *Edinstvo fronta i tyla v Velikoi Otechestvennoi voine, 1941–1945* (Moscow: Akademiia, 2007), pp. 187–93.

Qualls, Karl, D., *From Ruins to Reconstruction: Urban Identity in Soviet Sevastopol after World War II* (Ithaca: Cornell University Press, 2009).

Randall, Amy, *The Soviet Dream World of Retail Trade and Consumption in the 1930s* (Basingstoke: Palgrave Macmillan, 2008).

Ransel, David, *Village Mothers: Three Generations of Change in Russia and Tataria* (Bloomington: Indiana University Press, 2005).

Redlich, Shimon, *War, Holocaust, and Stalinism: A Documented History of the Jewish Anti-Fascist Committee* (New York: Routledge, 2016).

Reese, Roger R., "The Red Army and the Great Purges," in J. Arch Getty and Roberta Manning, eds., *Stalinist Terror: New Perspectives* (Cambridge: Cambridge University Press, 1993), pp. 198–214.

Reese, Roger R., *Why Stalin's Soldiers Fought: The Red Army's Military Effectiveness in World War II* (Lawrence: University Press of Kansas, 2011).

Reid, Anna, *Leningrad: The Epic Siege of World War II* (New York: Walker Books, 2011).

Resheniia partii i pravitel'stva po khoziaistvennym voprosam, vol. III (Moscow: Politizdat, 1968).

Ries, Nancy, "Potato Ontology: Surviving Postsocialism in Russia," *Cultural Anthropology*, vol. 24, no. 2 (May 2009), pp. 181–212.

Romanov, R. E., "Sovetskoe gosudarstvo i rabochie v gody Velikoi Otechestvennoi voiny. Sotsial'no-trudovye otnosheniia v sfere zaniatosti," in V. I. Shishkin, ed., *Vlast' i obshchestvo v Sibiri v XX veke. Sbornik nauchnikh statei*, vypusk 6 (Novosibirsk: Parallel, Institute of History of the Siberian Division of the Russian Academy of Sciences, 2015), pp. 209–26.

Römer, Felix, "The Wehrmacht in the War of Ideologies: The Army and Hitler's Criminal Orders on the Eastern Front," in Kay, Rutherford, and Stahel, eds., *Nazi Policy on the Eastern Front, 1941*, pp. 73–100.

Rossolinski-Liebe, Grzegorz, *Stepan Bandera: The Life and Afterlife of a Ukrainian Nationalist: Fascism, Genocide, and Cult* (Stuttgart: Ibidem Verlag, 2014).

Rozental', A. S., "Khronicheskie rasstroistva pitaniia i pishchevareniia (gipotrofiia-atrofiia) v rannem detskom vozraste," Doctor of Medical Sciences dissertation, Moscow, 1943.

Rubenstein, Joshua, and Vladimir Naumov, eds., *Stalin's Secret Pogrom: The Postwar Inquisition of the Jewish Anti-Fascist Committee* (New Haven: Yale University Press, 2001).

Rudling, Per A., "The OUN, the UPA, and the Holocaust: A Study in the Manufacturing of Historical Myths," *Carl Beck Papers in Russian and East European Studies*, no. 2107, 2011.

Sakharov, A. N., and A. S. Seniavskii, eds., *Narod i voina. Ocherki istorii Velikoi Otechestvennoi voiny, 1941–1945 gg.* (Moscow: Institut Rossiiskoi Istorii RAN, 2010).

Salisbury, Harrison, *The 900 Days: The Siege of Leningrad* (Cambridge, Mass.: Da Capo Press, 2003).

Samuelson, Lennart, *Tankograd. The Formation of a Soviet Company Town: Cheliabinsk, 1900s–1950s* (Basingstoke: Palgrave Macmillan, 2011).

Sbornik ofitsial'nykh materialov po sanprosvetrabote. Spravochnik sanprosvetrabotnika (Moscow, 1944).

Sbornik zakonov SSSR i ukazov Prezidiuma Verkhovnogo Soveta SSSR, 1938–1975, vol. III (Moscow: Izvestiia Sovetov Deputatov Trudiashchikhsia SSSR, 1975).

Schechter, Brandon, "The State's Pot and the Soldier's Spoon: Rations (*Paëk*) in the Red Army," in Goldman and Filtzer, eds., *Hunger and War*, pp. 98–157.

Schechter, Brandon, *The Stuff of Soldiers: A History of the Red Army in World War II through Objects* (Ithaca: Cornell University Press, 2019).

Seniavskii, A. S., and E. S. Seniavskaia, "Ideologiia voiny i psikhologiia naroda," in Sakharov and Seniavskii, eds., *Narod i voina*, pp. 122–235.

Shaklein, I. A., "O likvidatsii sanitarnikh posledstvii otechestvennoi voiny v oblasti tuberkuleza," in *Materialy nauchnoi sessii Sverdlovskogo oblastnogo Nauchno-issledovatel'skogo tuberkulezngo instituta po voprosam epidemiologii i kliniki tuberkuleza i organizatsii bor'by s nim* (Sverdlovsk: Sverdlovskii Oblastnoi Nauchno-Issledovatel'skii Tuberkuleznyi Institut, 1948), pp. 3–9.

Shearer, David, *Policing Stalin's Socialism: Repression and Social Order in the Soviet Union, 1924–1953* (New Haven: Yale University Press, 2009).

Shkliaruk, Aleksandr F., *Nasha pobeda. Plakaty Velikoi Otechestvennoi voiny, 1941–1945 godov* (Moscow: Kontakt-Kul'tura, 2010).

Shmyrov, Boris Danilovich, "Trudmobilizovannye Sredne-aziatskogo voennogo okruga na stroikakh i promyshlennykh predpriiatiiakh iuzhnogo Urala v gody Velikoi Otechestvennoi voiny," Candidate of Historical Sciences dissertation, Cheliabinsk, 2016.

Shneer, David, *Through Soviet Jewish Eyes: Photography, War, and the Holocaust* (New Brunswick, N.J.: Rutgers University Press, 2012).

Shternshis, Anna, "Between Life and Death: Why Some Soviet Jews Decided to Leave and Others to Stay in 1941," *Kritika: Explorations in Russian and Eurasian History*, vol. 15, no. 3 (Summer 2014), pp. 477–504.

Siegelbaum, Lewis, and Leslie Moch, *Broad Is My Native Land: Repertoires and Regimes of Migrations in Russia's Twentieth Century* (Ithaca: Cornell University Press, 2014).

Sinnreich, Helene, "Hunger in the Ghettos," in Wendy Z. Goldman and Joe W. Trotter, Jr., eds., *The Ghetto in Global History, 1500 to the Present* (London: Routledge, 2018), pp. 110–26.

Skrjabina, Elena, *Siege and Survival: The Odyssey of a Leningrader* (Carbondale: Southern Illinois University Press, 1971).

Slepyan, Kenneth, *Stalin's Guerrillas: Soviet Partisans in World War II* (Lawrence: University Press of Kansas, 2006).

Slonim, M. I., "Alimentarnaia distrofiia v usloviiakh voennogo vremeni," in M. I. Slonim, *Izbrannye raboty* (Tashkent: Izdatel'stvo AN UzSSR, 1949), pp. 35–45.

Smith, Jeremy, "Non-Russian Nationalities," in Stone, ed., *The Soviet Union at War*, pp. 161–78.

Smith, Mark B., *Property of Communists: The Urban Housing Program from Stalin to Khrushchev* (De Kalb: Northern Illinois University Press, 2010).

Sokolov, A. K., "Sotsial'no-trudovye otnosheniia na sovetskikh predpriiatiiakh v gody voiny," in Sakharov and Seniavskii, eds., *Narod i voina*, pp. 93–8.

Solomon, Peter H. Jr., *Soviet Criminal Justice under Stalin* (Cambridge: Cambridge University Press, 1996).

Solonari, Vladimir, *A Satellite Empire: Romanian Rule in Southwestern Ukraine, 1941–1944* (Ithaca and London: Cornell University Press, 2019).

Solov'eva, Vera Valer'evna, "Bytovye usloviia personala promyshlennykh predpriiatii Urala v 1941–1945 gg. Gosudarstvennaia politika i strategii adaptatsii," Candidate of Historical Sciences dissertation, Ekaterinburg, 2011.

Sosnovskaia, R. P., *Geroicheskii trud vo imia pobedy* (Leningrad: Izdatel'stvo Leningradskogo Universiteta, 1973).

Stahel, David, *Kiev 1941: Hitler's Battle for Supremacy in the East* (Cambridge: Cambridge University Press, 2012).

Stahel, David, *Operation Barbarossa and Germany's Defeat in the East* (New York and Cambridge: Cambridge University Press, 2009).

Stahel, David, and Jonathan House, *When Titans Clash: How the Red Army Stopped Hitler* (Lawrence: University Press of Kansas, 1995).

Stalin, Joseph, *The Great Patriotic War of the Soviet Union* (New York: Greenwood Press, 1969).

Stargardt, Nicholas, *The German War: A Nation under Arms, 1939–1945* (New York: Basic Books, 2015).

Statiev, Alexander, "'La Garde meurt, mais ne se rend pas!': Once Again on the 28 Panfilov Heroes," *Kritika: Explorations in Russian and Eurasian History*, vol. 13, no. 4 (Fall 2012), pp. 769–98.

Statiev, Alexander, *The Soviet Counterinsurgency in the Western Borderlands* (New York: Cambridge University Press, 2010).

Stites, Richard, ed., *Culture and Entertainment in Wartime Russia* (Bloomington: Indiana University Press, 1995).

Stites, Richard, "Russia's Holy War," in Stites, ed., *Culture and Entertainment in Wartime Russia*, pp. 1–8.

Stone, David, ed., *The Soviet Union at War, 1941–1945* (Barnsley, UK: Pen and Sword Books, 2010).

Sugrue, Thomas, *The Origins of the Urban Crisis: Race and Inequality in Postwar Detroit* (Princeton: Princeton University Press, 2010).

Tec, Nechama, *Defiance: The Bielski Partisans* (New York: Oxford University Press, 1993).

Tel'pukhovskii, V. B., "Geroizm rabochego klassa," in G. N. Sevostianov, ed., *Voina i obshchestvo, 1941–1945*, book I (Moscow: Nauka, 2004), pp. 6–25.

Tel'pukhovskii, V. B., "Izmeneniia v sostave promyshlennykh rabochikh SSSR v period Velikoi Otechestvennoi voiny," *Voprosy istorii*, No. 6 (1960), pp. 27–42.

Thompson, E. P., *Beyond the Frontier: The Politics of a Failed Mission, Bulgaria 1944* (Stanford: Stanford University Press, 1997).

Thurston, Robert W., and Bernd Bonwetsch, eds., *The People's War: Responses to World War II in the Soviet Union* (Urbana: University of Illinois Press, 2000).

Timofeev, L. M., "Institutsional'naia korruptsiia sotsialisticheskoi sistemy," in Iurii Afanas'ev, ed., *Sovetskoe obshchestvo. Vozniknovenie, razvitie, istoricheskii final*, vol. II (Moscow: Rossiiskii Gosudarstvennyi Universitet, 1997), pp. 508–44.

Tooze, Adam, *The Wages of Destruction: The Making and Breaking of the Nazi Economy* (New York: Viking Penguin, 2006).

Tsepkalova, A. A., "Gulag na stroitel'stve promyshlennykh ob"ektov. Rol' kontingentov Glavpromstroia," in Borodkin, Krasil'nikov, and Khlevniuk, eds., *Istoriia Stalinizma*, pp. 88–107.

Tumarkin, Nina, *The Living and the Dead: The Rise and Fall of the Cult of World War II in Russia* (New York: Basic Books, 1994).

Tvardovskii, A. T., *Stikhotvoreniia i poemy v dvukh tomakh* (Moscow: Khudozhestvennaia Literatura, 1951).

Udler, Rubin, *The Cursed Years: Reminiscences of a Holocaust Survivor* (Pittsburgh: Rubin Udler, 2005).

Vatlin, A. Iu., *Terror raionnogo masshtaba. "Massovye operatsii" NKVD v Kuntsevskom raione Moskovskoi oblasti, 1937–8 gg.* (Moscow: Rosspen, 2004).

Velikaia Otechestvennaia voina. 50 let. Prilozhenie i kalendari dat i sobytii. Vypusk 1, TASS, 1991.

Veshchikov, P. I., "Rol' tyla v bespereboinom obespechenii deistvuiushchego fronta prodovol'stviem," in T. M. Bulavkina and M. V. Stegantsev, eds., *Edinstvo fronta i tyla v Velikoi Otechestvennoi voine 1941–1945* (Moscow: Akademiia, 2007), pp. 81–7.

Vilenskii, S. S., A. I. Kokurin, G. V. Atmashkina, and Iu. I. Novichenko, *Deti GULAGa. 1918–1956* (Moscow: Mezhdunarodnyi fond "Demokratiia," 2002).

Viola, Lynne, *The Unknown Gulag: The Lost World of Stalin's Special Settlements* (Oxford: Oxford University Press, 2007).

Vital Statistics of the United States 1940, Part I: Natality and Mortality Data for the United States Tabulated by Place of Occurrence with Supplemental Tables for Hawaii, Puerto Rico, and the Virgin Islands (Washington, D.C.: United States Government Printing Office, 1941).

von Geldern, James, "Radio Moscow: The Voice from the Center," in Stites, ed., *Culture and Entertainment in Wartime Russia*, pp. 44–61.

Voznesenskii, N. A., *Voennaia ekonomika SSSR v period Otechestvennoi voiny* (Moscow: Gospolitizdat, 1948).

Voznesensky, N. A., *Soviet Economy during the Second World War* (New York: International Publishers, 1949).

Walke, Anike, *Partisans and Pioneers: An Oral History of Nazi Genocide in Belorussia* (New York: Oxford University Press, 2015).

Weindling, Paul, *Epidemics and Genocide in Eastern Europe, 1890–1945* (Oxford: Oxford University Press, 2000).

Weiner, Amir, *Making Sense of War: The Second World War and the Fate of the Bolshevik Revolution* (Princeton: Princeton University Press, 2001).

Werth, Alexander, *Russia at War, 1941–1945* (New York: Carroll and Graf, 1964).

Wheatcroft, Stephen G., "Soviet Statistics of Nutrition and Mortality during Times of Famine, 1917–1922 and 1931–1933," *Cahiers du Monde Russe*, vol. 38, no. 4 (October–December 1997), pp. 525–57.

Winick, Myron, ed., *Hunger Disease: Studies by the Jewish Physicians in the Warsaw Ghetto*, trans. from Polish by Martha Osnos (New York: John Wiley & Sons, 1979).

Yarov, Sergei, *Leningrad 1941–1942: Morality in a City under Siege* (Cambridge, UK: Polity Press, 2017).

Yekelchyk, Serhy, "Stalinist Patriotism as Imperial Discourse: Reconciling the Ukrainian and Russian 'Heroic Pasts,' 1939–1945," *Kritika: Explorations in Russian and Eurasian History*, vol. 3, no. 1 (Winter 2002), pp. 51–80.

Yellin, Emily, *Our Mothers' War: American Women at Home and at the Front during World War II* (New York: Free Press, 2005).

Zabolotskaia, L. P., and I. S. Sokolov, "Sanitarnoe prosveshchenie v gody Velikoi Otechestvennoi voiny (po materialam 1 Ob"edinennogo plenuma Sovetov po sanitarnomu prosveshcheniiu Narkomzdrava SSSR i Narkomzdrava RSFSR, iiul' 1944 g.)," in *Sanitarnoe prosveshchenie. Sbornik posviashchennyi voprosam sanitarnogo prosveshcheniia v gody Velikoi Otechestvennoi voiny* (Moscow, 1948), pp. 36–57.

Zakharchenko, A. V., "Lagerno-proizvodstvennyi kompleks v povol'zhe. Zakliuchennye osobstroia NKVD SSSR na stroitel'stve aviatsionnykh zavodov v raione g. Kuibysheva, 1940–1943 gg.," in Borodkin, Krasil'nikov, and Khlevniuk, eds., *Istoriia Stalinizma*, pp. 221–39.

Zemskov, V. N., "Organizatsiia rabochei sily i uzhestochenie trudovogo zakonodatel'stva v gody voiny s fashistskoi Germaniei," *Politicheskoe prosveshchenie*, No. 2 (79), 2014, accessed at http://www.politpros.com/journal/read/?ID=3167&journal=160&sphrase_id=12205.

Zemskov, V. N., "Smertnost' zakliuchennykh v 1941–1945 gg," in *Liudskie poteri SSSR v period Vtoroi Mirovoi voiny*, pp. 174–7.

Zemskov, V. N., *Spetsposelentsy v SSSR, 1930–1960* (Moscow: Nauka, 2003).

Zemskov, V. N., "Ukaz ot 26 iiunia 1940 goda ... (eshche odna kruglaia data)," *Raduga*, no. 6, 1990, pp. 43–8.

Zima, V. F., *Golod v SSSR 1946–1947 godov. Proiskhozhdenie i posledstviia* (Moscow: Institut Rossiiskoi Istorii RAN, 1996).

Zima, V. F., *Mentalitet narodov Rossii v voine 1941–1945 godov* (Moscow: Institut Rossiiskoi Istorii RAN, 2000).

Zinsser, Hans, *Rats, Lice and History* (New Brunswick: Transaction Publishers, 2008).

Zubkova, Elena, *Pribaltika i Kreml', 1940–1953* (Moscow: Rosspen, 2008).

Index